Electrical Power Generation Conventional and Renewable

Dr. Tanmoy Deb

ELECTRICAL POWER GENERATION

Conventional and Renewable

[For B.Tech, M.Tech, AMIE (India), GATE and UPSC (Engineering Services)]

DR. TANMOY DEB

Ph.D.(EE.JMI), M.Tech (PSD), M.Tech (CI), B.E. (NIT Gold Medalist), M.Phil (Management), M.B.A., DMM, DMM, DBA.

FIE, FIETE, FIIPE, FISLE, FIOV, MISTE, MBES, MSESI, MIWWA, MTSI, AMIIIE

KHANNA BOOK PUBLISHING CO. (P) LTD.

Publisher of Engineering and Computer Books

4C/4344, Ansari Road, Darya Ganj, New Delhi-110002

Phone : 011-23244447-48 **Mobile:** +91-9910909320

E-mail : contact@khannabooks.com

Website : www.khannabooks.com

Price: ₹ 495.00

Electrical Power Generation—
Conventional and Renewable

by **Dr. Tanmoy Deb**

ISBN: 978-93-86173-37-9

First Edition: 2017
Second Edition: 2024

To view complete list of books, please scan the QR Code:

Published by:
Khanna Book Publishing Co. (P) Ltd.
CIN: U22110DL1998PTC095547

Visit us at: www.khannabooks.com
Write us at: contact@khannabooks.com

Printed in India by: SPS Printers

Dedicated to

My wife Mrs. Putul Deb
and
My son Mr. Aniket Deb

About the Author

Dr. Tanmoy Deb graduated in Electrical Engineering from NIT Surat with distinction and Gold Medal. He did M.Tech (Power System & Drives), M.Tech (Control and Instrumentation), MBA, MPhil (Management). He was awarded Ph.D in Electrical Engineering by Jamia Millia Islamia (Central University). He has authored three books and 51 research publications. He is member of 12 professional societies and was honorary secretary (Delhi Chapter) of Indian Institution of Industrial Engineers (2006-08). He has 30 years of Experience in teaching and industry.

PREFACE

Subject of electrical power generation is very close to my heart as I had the opportunity to work in operation, maintenance and projects related to thermal power plant, gas turbine power plant and diesel power plant. Moreover, I had the opportunity to visit nuclear power plant, hydro electric power plant, solar photovoltaic plant, wind and biomass based power plants. In addition to this, I was trained in combined cycle power plant operation at National Power Training Institute (NPTI), Badarpur, New Delhi. Later on, in my teaching career, I had taught subjects of power station practice and renewable energy sources for many semesters. I had combined my practical experience of power plant operation with theoretical background to deliver lectures to B.Tech and M.Tech students.

Locating a good book which combined both conventional and renewable power generation to a desirable depth was indeed a challenging task. This is my humble attempt to fill this gap so that student community is benefitted from my rich industrial and teaching experience of three decades. This book covers syllabus of subjects viz Power Station Practice, Renewable Energy Resources, Energy Management and Technology, Electrical Power Generation, Non-conventional Energy Sources, Power Plant Engineering etc. of all major universities and institutes in India. Students of Institution of Engineers (I) (for AMIE-section B) and Indian Institution of Industrial Engineers (I) (for Grad IIIE-section B) will find this book very useful.

The complete material of this book has been 'class tested' including solved and unsolved numerical problems which are adopted from various universities/competitive examinations. The balanced coverage of all major topics and subtopics are dealt to a reasonable depth. The language of the book has been kept simple.

My journey of quest for knowledge was continually blessed by my father late Sh. Bibhuti Bhushan Deb and my mother late Smt. Maya Deb who had been my pillars of strength. I wish to thank my wife Mrs. Putul Deb who not only actively encouraged in my work but also kept me free from other household responsibilities.

I shall be failing in my duty if I do not acknowledge the active support of my brother Dr. Tapomoy Deb (Vice President – J.K. Lakshi Cements) and my uncle Sh. Ajit Ranjan Deb (Ex Branch Manager – East India Pharmaceutical Works).

Every care has been taken to remove errors, misprints etc. but despite all sincere efforts some errors might have crept in. Author will be highly grateful if such errors/misprints are brought to the notice. All criticisms are welcome for improvement of this book.

Author

CONTENTS

Contents

Chapter

INTRODUCTION TO POWER GENERATION

Learning Objectives

After reading this chapter, reader will be able to

- Understand the sources of power generation, classification of energy sources and need for renewable energy sources.
- Explore various generation technologies used in non-renewable and renewable sector.
- Understand Indian power generation sector including coal, oil, gas and nuclear sector.
- Understand structure of deregulated electricity markets, load forecasting techniques and distributed generation.

"Is it a fact or have I dreamt it–that by means of electricity, the world of matter has become a great nerve, vibrating thousands of miles in a breathless point of time".

—Nathaniel Hawthorn

1.1. INTRODUCTION

Energy is a gift of nature to mankind. It is a vital input that sustains and improves life on earth. In fact, consumption of energy is an indicator of economic progress of a nation.

Abundant energy is available on our earth. However, all available energy can not be directly used without using some conversion technique to useful form. Energy from sun is directly used for variety of household applications, such as drying, heating, evaporation etc. Biomass energy can be used directly for cooking purpose. However, some form of energy can not be used directly, such as wind energy, nuclear energy etc. Hence, all available forms of energy are converted into electrical energy, as it can be easily transmitted, stored and utilized in various forms.

The field of electrical power generation is vast and employs variety of complex technologies. The horizon of this technology is expanding everyday.

In this chapter, the reader will be acquainted with various methods of generation of power and their control. The subject encompasses almost all available methods of power generation related to conventional and non-conventional fields. Some sources of power generation are commercially viable today while others are not. However, with rapid change in technological development, non-viable technologies may become viable in not so distant future.

1.2. SOURCES OF ENERGY

The various sources of energy on earth are sun, wind, water, fossil fuels, heat of earth (geothermal), ocean thermal, tidal and wave, nuclear fuels and biomass.

Sun is the main source of energy on earth. The energy is harnessed either directly or by conversion into electricity (solar photovoltaic cells) or into steam (solar thermal). India is fortunate to receive abundant amount of solar energy throughout the year. This prompted Govt. of India to install large number of solar power plants consisting of PV cells.

Wind flows due to terrestrial temperature difference. This energy is harnessed using wind turbines which convert motion of wind turbine into electrical energy. India occupies 5th place in world in terms of installed capacity in wind energy sector.

Energy of falling water is utilized to drive a hydro-turbine. The mechanical motion of this turbine is converted into electrical energy. About 15% of total installed capacity is from hydro sources.

Fossil fuels are mainly coal, petroleum oil and natural gas. India has large reserve of coal but small reserve of oil and gas. About 60% of total installed capacity in India is from coal. While gas and oil form comparatively much smaller capacity in total installed generation capacity.

Geothermal energy is the heat energy of earth which comes out either in the form of volcanic erruption or in the form of hot steam from the earth. India has very little scope of this energy in Gulf of Cambay in Gujarat.

Ocean holds a large reservoir of energy in the form of tidal, wave and ocean thermal energy. In India, this energy has so far not been harnessed though potential for tidal energy exists in Gulf of Kutchh in Gujarat and Sunderbans in West Bengal.

India produces power through nuclear energy. But the total contribution of nuclear power is 2% of total installed capacity.

Biomass is abundantly available in rural areas and is used for cooking, lighting and power generation. Although the installed capacity of biomass fed power plants is small but there is a thrust by Government of India and is expected to grow in near future. This may provide source for rural electrification.

1.3. CLASSIFICATION OF ENERGY SOURCES

All forms of energy are classified as per following—

(*i*) **Primary and secondary energy sources**—Primary sources of energy are found in nature, such as coal, oil, gas etc. While secondary source of energy are converted form of primary energy, such as steam, electricity, hot water etc.

(*ii*) **Renewable and non-renewable sources of energy**—Renewable sources of energy are those which never get exhausted, such as energy from sun, wind, hydro power etc. While non-renewable sources of energy are those which are depleted due to use. e.g., coal, oil, gas etc.

(*iii*) **Commercial and non-commercial energy**—Commercial energy is available in the market for a price e.g. coal, oil, gas, electricity. While non-commercial energy is not available in the market for a price e.g. agricultural waste, cattle dung, solar energy for drying, animal power for transport etc.

1.4. IMPORTANCE OF ELECTRICAL ENERGY

Among all forms of energy, electrical energy is most widely used due to ease of transmission, control and flexibility. It is superior to other forms of energy, such as chemical, heat, light, mechanical, sound etc. It is cleanest form of energy, as it does not produce smoke, dust or poisonous gases. It can be easily converted to other forms of energy, such as heat, light, mechanical or chemical. Although a greater part of energy consumption is non-electrical (transport and industrial), however, there is a rising trend towards higher electrical energy consumption. The power generation capacity in India too has risen from 1362 MW at the time of independence to 2,84,303.39 MW (as of December 31, 2015). With greater thrust on power generation sector, more and more large power plants are coming up (Ultra Mega Power Plants of capacity 4000 MW and above). With improvement in standard of living, power consumption is rising at a higher rate causing an annual shortfall of 8%. This has necessitated to open up power sector to private sector participation in generation, transmission and distribution. With the result, there is flurry of activities going on in generation sector with private players contributing a sizable chunk of installed capacity. Even the unit sizes of alternators have increased from 120 MW, 210 MW, 500 MW to 660 MW and 800 MW.

75% of population in India has access to electricity compared to 99.5% in China. Hence, a huge gap exists between demand and supply. This gap is being narrowed down by rapid expansion in generation, transmission and distribution capacity.

1.5. INDIAN POWER GENERATION SCENARIO

India ranks sixth in the total energy consumption in the world. The total installed capacity has increased from 1362 MW in 1947 to 2,84,303.39 MW till 31.12.2015. The average energy shortage is 8% and peak energy shortage is 13%. The annual per capita consumption is 733 kWh which is one of the lowest in the world (USA-12, 815 kWh, Japan-6,788 kWh, Russia-8,188 kWh). The primary energy mix consists of thermal (60.8%). hydro (15.0%), oil (0.36%), gas (8.6%), nuclear (2.1%) and renewable sources (13.1%). The breakup is shown in figure 1.1. Power generation capacity based on ownerships is shown in figure 1.2.

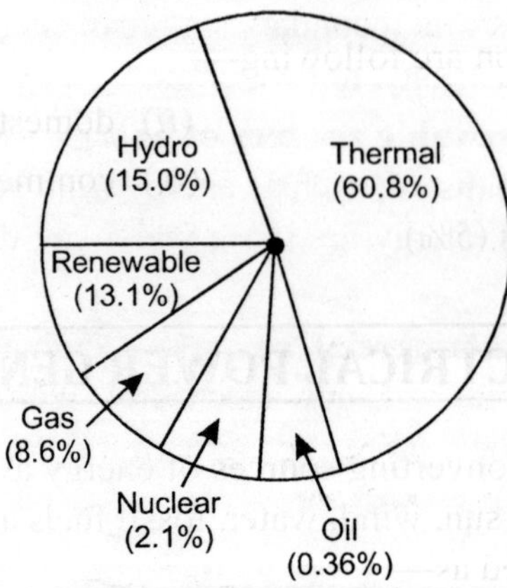

Figure. 1.1. Primary energy mix (Dec. 2015)

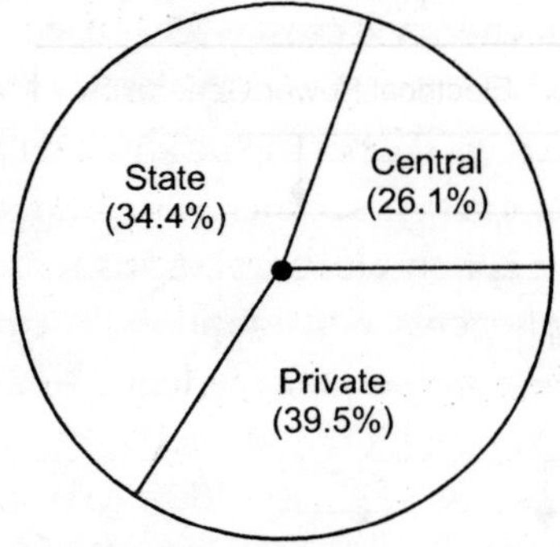

Figure. 1.2. Power generation capacity based on ownership (Dec. 2015)

Total installed capacity—(grid interactive) of renewable energy is 37,415.53 MW (31.12.2015). The breakup is shown in figure 1.3.

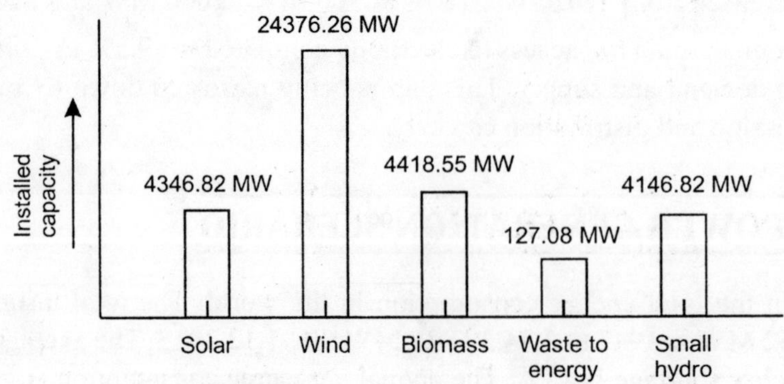

Figure 1.3. Renewable energy mix

In renewable energy generation, the highest installed capacity is in wind power generation followed by biomass and small hydro. The potential for wind power is 1,02,772 MW, small hydro is 19,749 MW, biomass is 17,538 MW and bagasse based is 5,000 MW.

Sectorwise energy consumption are following—

(*i*) industry (44%), (*ii*) domestic (22%),
(*iii*) agriculture (18%), (*iv*) commercial (9%),
(*v*) railways (2%) and others (5%).

1.6. OVERVIEW OF ELECTRICAL POWER GENERATION

Electrical energy is produced by converting sources of energy available in nature. Various sources of energy available in nature are—sun, wind, water, fossil fuels and nuclear fuels. Electrical power generation can be broadly classified as—

(*a*) conventional or non-renewable power generation and

(*b*) non-conventional or renewable power generation.

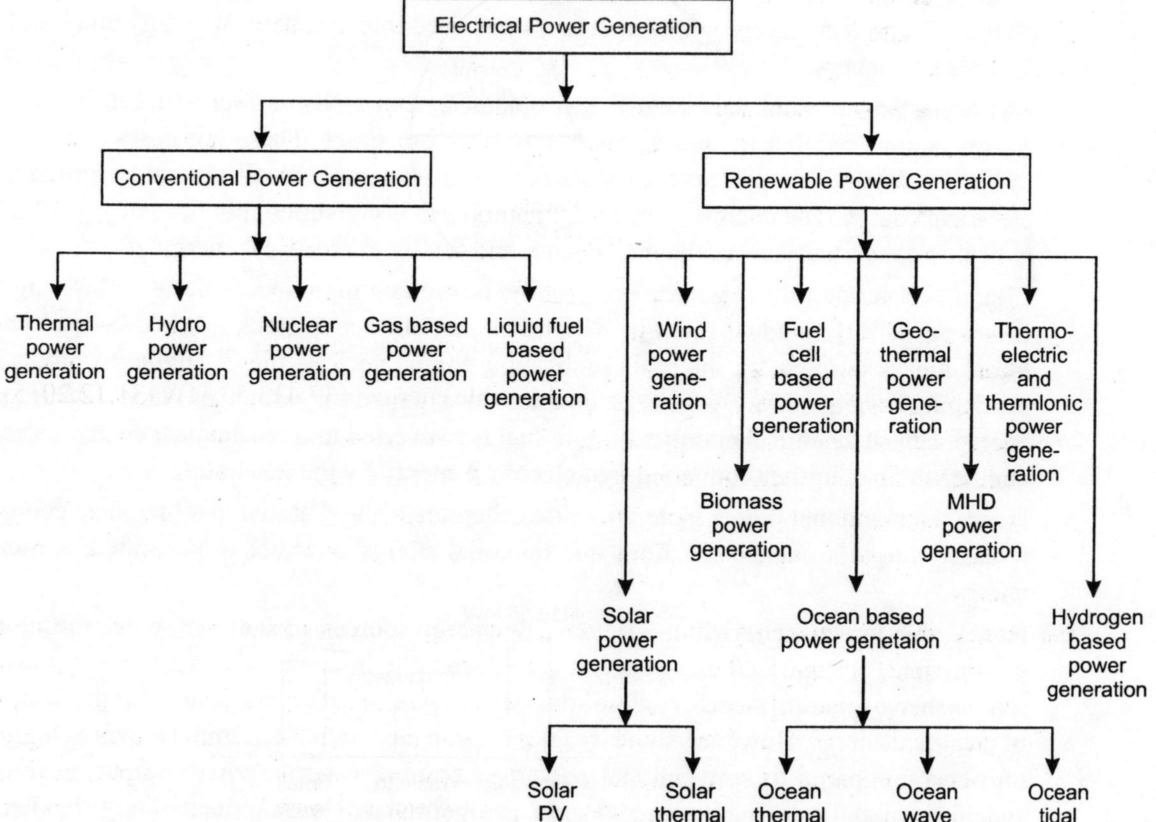

Figure. 1.4. Classification of electrical power generation

(*i*) **Conventional power generation**—Conventional power generation uses energy resources which are finite in quantity and get depleted due to consumption. Examples are coal, oil natural gas, uranium, thorium etc. Hence, due to depletion of these naturally available resources, such type of power generation is not sustainable in the long run.

Thermal power generation uses heat energy produced by burning of coal to raise steam in a boiler. This high temperature and high pressure steam is used to run a steam turbine. This steam turbine is coupled to an electric generator which produces electric power. In this process, heat energy of coal is converted into mechanical energy by the steam turbine. This mechanical energy is converted into electrical energy by the generator.

Hydro power generation is based on principle of gravity. Water falling from a height hits blades of hydro turbine causing it to rotate. This turbine is coupled to a generator which inturn produces electrical energy. The potential energy of water is converted into kinetic energy which drives the turbine. The mechanical energy of turbine is converted into electrical energy by the generator. Strictly speaking, hydropower generation is renewable in nature.

Nuclear power generation is based on nuclear fission reaction in a nuclear reactor. This nuclear reaction generates heat which is used to raise steam in a boiler. The high temperature and high pressure steam is used to drive a steam turbine. This turbine coupled to a generator produces electrical energy. Hence, chemical energy of nuclear fuel is converted into heat energy which inturn is converted into mechanical energy and finally to electrical energy.

Gas based power plant uses natural gas obtained from wells as fuel which is burnt in a combustion chamber of gas turbine to produce hot gases. These hot gases cause gas turbine to rotate. The gas turbine is coupled to a generator which ultimately produces electrical energy. The chemical energy of natural gas is converted into heat energy which is further converted into mechanical energy and finally to electrical energy.

Liquid fuel based power generation uses fuels such as high speed diesel (HSD), light diesel oil (LDO), residual fuel oil (RFO), low sulphur heavy stock oil (LSHS) etc. The liquid fuel is burnt in an internal combustion engine such as diesel engine to produce mechanical energy. This engine is coupled to a generator which produces electrical energy. Hence, chemical energy of liquid fuel is converted into mechanical energy by the engine which is further converted into electrical energy by the generator.

Hence, conventional power generation uses chemical energy stored in a fuel, heat energy released due to a nuclear reactions and potential energy of water to generate electrical energy.

(ii) **Renewable power generation**—Renewable energy sources such as sun, wind, biomass, geo-thermal, ocean based energy etc. are inexhaustible in nature which are continuously replenished by nature. Hence, such sources of energy are sustainable source for generation of electrical energy. However, some issues are associated with these sources such as higher unit cost compared to conventional power generation, variable power output, location specific availability of these sources (wind, geothermal etc), requirement of huge land etc.

Due to fast depletion of fossil fuels, dependance on renewable sources is increasing. There is greater thrust to generate power through these resources due to almost zero environmental impact.

Solar power generation uses energy from sun to produce electricity in two ways. In first route i.e., solar photovoltaic or solar PV, the sun rays falling on PV cells produce electricity directly. In second route i.e., solar thermal, the heat energy of Sun rays is used to generate steam and thereafter electricity is produced by a steam turbine.

Wind power generation uses velocity of wind to rotate a wind turbine. The wind turbine inturn rotates generator which produces electrical energy.

Biomass power plant uses biomass residue left by plants, animals etc. to produce gas which can be burnt to generate heat which in turn can be used to produce electrical energy. In some applications, biomass can be burnt directly to produce heat which can be used to generate electricity.

Ocean based power generation uses thermal energy of water at different depths due to temperature gradient, energy of ocean waves and energy of tides (during high tides) is used to produce power.

Fuel cells produce power by chemical reaction. Geo-thermal power generation utilizes heat energy trapped inside earth to generate electrical power.

MHD or Magneto Hydro Dynamics is a direct conversion process of producing power. When stream of charged gas is passed through a magnetic field, an electric field is produced at right angles to magnetic field. This electric field is used to produce electricity.

Thermo-electric power generation uses principles of Seeback effect. When two dissimilar metals are joined together and one junctions is kept at a higher temperature than other, an electric current flows.

Thermionic emission based power generation uses emission of electrons from certain metals to produce flow of current by directly or indirectly heating the metal.

Hydrogen based power generation is mainly in a fuel cell to generate power. The other applications of hydrogen are in transportation sector and as fuel.

Hence, total power generation is always a good mix of conventional and renewable energy generation as both the sources have their relative merits and demerits. However, due to fast depletion of available fossil fuel resources, there is a compelling need to increase the share of renewable energy sources in the overall generation basket.

1.7. GROWTH OF POWER SECTOR IN INDIA

Thomas Alva Edision established first electrical power station at Pear, New York in 1881. This power plant had six steam engine driven generators supplying power at 110V d.c to 59 consumers in a radius of 1.5 km. With the development of poly phase generators and transformers, a.c. distribution system was put in place in great Washington, USA in 1886. The first single phase a.c. transmission line was laid between Willamette falls and Portland, USA operating at 4kV, single phase. In 1893, the first three phase system came into operation at 2.3 kV in southern California, USA.

The first power station in India was Sidrapong micro-hydel plant (130 kW) near Darjeeling at the end of 19th century. Sivasamudram hydro power plant was installed with a capacity of 4.5 MW in 1902. By the end of 1939, installed capacity had increased to 1200 MW. At the time of independence, the installed capacity rose to 1362 MW which eventually reached, 2,84,303.39 MW (as on Dec, 2015). Of the total installed capacity, 60.8% is thermal, 15.0% hydro, 8.6% gas based, 2.1% nuclear, 0.36% oil based and 13.1% renewable.

India is endowed with large deposits of coal and hydro potential. However, oil and gas reserves are scarce. Availability of energy resources in India is shown in table 1.1.

Table no. 1.1. Energy resources availability in India

Source	*Cost of power plant (Rs Crore/MW)*	*Emission (CO_2 eq. Ton per MWh)*	*Reserve*	*Longivity*
Coal	4–5	1.1	1,05,820 million MT	70 years
Oil	2.5	0.62	1200 million MT	10 years
Gas	3.5	0.47	1.5 TCM	20 years
Nuclear	8–13	Zero	70,000 ton of Uranium 200 ton of Plutonium	40 years with Uranium

The transmission sector also grew with generation. The transmission voltage increased from 33 kV to present 765 kV level. The next voltage level is 1200 kV. The status of transmission sector is given in table no-1.2.

Table no. 1.2. Development of transmission sector (2015)

Sr. No.	*Transmission Voltage*	*Circuit km*
1.	765 kV AC	19,602
2.	400 kV AC	1,38,170
3.	220 kV AC	1,51,218
4.	$\pm$ 500 kV HVDC	9,432

1.8. ORGANISATION OF POWER SECTOR IN INDIA

A power network is a complex interconnected system spread over large geographic area consisting of power generation plants, transmission and distribution networks. Management of power system in India is mostly state owned. Central, state and few private players generate, transmit and distribute power. Each state has a generation, transmission and distribution company. Entire country is divided into five regions—northern, western, southern, eastern and northeastern. In addition to govt. organisations, few private sector utilities also manage distribution in cities like Delhi, Kolkata, Ahmedabad, Surat, Mumbai etc. Due to enactment of Electricity Act, 2003, generation, transmission and distribution is thrown open to private players. The power is generated at 11 kV to 33 kV and transmitted at 132 kV, 220 kV, 400 kV and 765 kV. All regional grids are interconnected through Extra High Voltage (EHV) links and High Voltage Direct Current (HVDC) links thereby facilitating inter-regional power transfer.

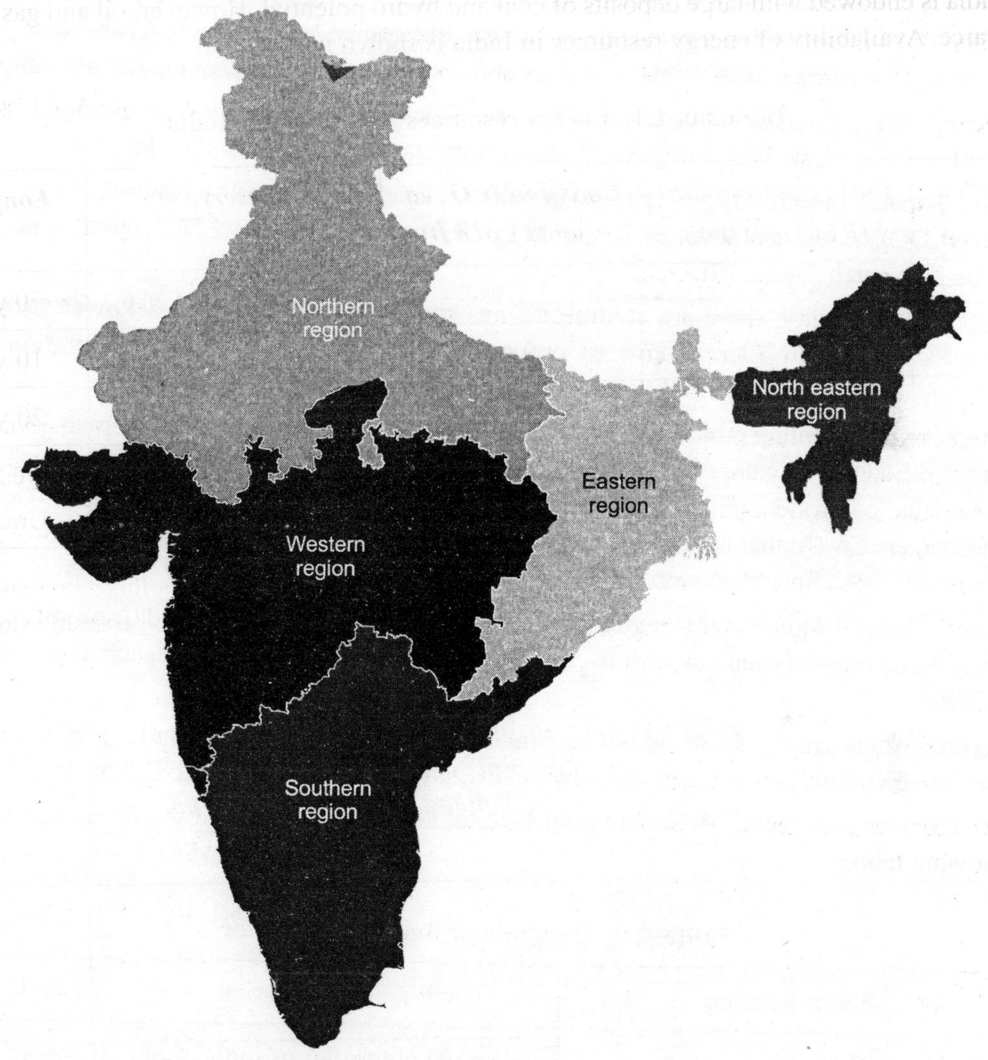

Figure. 1.5. Regional electricity grids

1. **Northern region**—J&K, Punjab, Haryana, Delhi, U.P., Uttarakhand, H.P., Rajasthan.
2. **Western region**—Maharashtra, Gujarat, M.P., Chhattisgarh, Goa, Daman, Diu, Dadra and Nagar Haveli.
3. **Southern region**—Tamil Nadu, Kerala, Andhra Pradesh, Telangana, Karnataka, Puducherry.
4. **Eastern region**—West Bengal, Odisha, Bihar, Jharkhand, Sikkim.
5. **North Eastern region**—Assam, Meghalaya, Nagaland, Tripura, Arunachal Pradesh, Mizoram, Manipur.

The policy making related to power sector is vested with central and state govt. Planning of generation and transmission is carried out by Central Electricity Authority (CEA) and state planning department. CEA carries out feasibility studies and advises central govt. on power planning issues.

The regulatory mechanism consists of Central Electricity Regulatory Commission (CERC) at the apex level with State Electricity Regulatory Commission (SERC) at state level.

Load dispatch (control of power flow) at national level is managed by National Load Dispatch Centre (NLDC), at regional level by Regional Load Dispatch Centre (RLDC) and at state level by State Load Dispatch Centre (SLDC).

In generation sector, there are central utilities such as National Thermal Power Corporation (NTPC), National Hydro Electric Power Corporation (NHPC), Nuclear Power corporation of India (NPCIL) etc. controlled by central govt.

There are joint venture power companies such as North Eastern Electric Power Co. (NEEPCO), Tehri Hydro Electric Development Corporation (THDC), Damodar Valley Corporation (DVC) etc. There are state controlled generation companies such as APGENCO (Andhra Pradesh Generation Co.), Mahagen Co (Maharashtra Generating Co.) etc. There are Independent Power Producers (IPP) such as GVK, Spectrum etc.

Central transmission sector is regulated by central govt through Power Grid Corporation of India (PGCIL). State transmission network is controlled by respective state govts. such as APTRNSCO, KPTCL etc.

Trading of electricity is carried out by Power Trading Corporation of India (PTC) across state borders while within the state, it is done by NTPC, NHPC, Tata Power and Reliance.

Structure of coal sector, Petroleum and Natural Gas sector and nuclear power sector is given in following tables.

Table–1.3. Structure of Indian Coal Sector

(*i*)	Policy Making	→	Central and state govt.
(*ii*)	Planning	→	Coal controller of India, Govt. of India.
(*iii*)	Regulation	→	Coal Controller of India, Govt. of India.
(*v*)	Mining Companies	→	(*a*) Coal India and its subsidiaries.
			(*b*) Neyveli Lignite Corporation.
			(*c*) Singreni Collieries Ltd.
			(*d*) Private coal blocks for captive mining.
(*v*)	Mining equipment	→	Bharat Earth Moving Equipments Ltd.

Table 1.4. Structure of Petroleum and Natural Gas sector

(*i*)	Policy-making	Ministry of Petroleum and Natural Gas, GOI.	
(*ii*)	Planning	(*a*) Ministry of Petroleum and Natural Gas, GOI.	
		(*b*) Planning Commission.	
		(*c*) Petroleum Planning and Analysis Cell.	
(*iii*)	Regulation	(*a*) Directorate of Hydrocarbon (upstream).	
		(*b*) Petroleum and Natural Gas Regulatory Board.	
(*iv*)	Exploration and Production	**Public Sector**	**Private**
		(*a*) ONGC	(*a*) Cairn
		(*b*) OIL	(*b*) Essar
		(*c*) OVL	
		(*d*) GSPC	
(*v*)	Refineries	(*a*) CPCL	(*a*) RPL
		(*b*) BRPL	(*b*) Essar
		(*c*) NRL	
		(*d*) MRPL	
(*vi*)	Marketing Co.	(*a*) GAIL	
		(*b*) IGL	
		(*c*) MGL	

Table–1.5. Structure of Nuclear sector in India

(*i*)	Policy-making	Department of Atomic Energy, GOI.
(*ii*)	Planning	Department of Atomic Energy, GOI.
(*iii*)	Regulation	(*a*) Atomic Energy Regulatory Board.
		(*b*) Atomic Energy Commission.
(*iv*)	Power Generation Company	(*a*) Nuclear Power Corporation of India.
(*v*)	Input Suppliers	(*a*) Heavy Water Board.
		(*b*) Nuclear Fuel Complex.
		(*c*) Indian Rare Earths Ltd.
		(*d*) Uranium Corporation of India.
(*vi*)	Financial Institution	Board of Research in Nuclear Sciences.

1.9. DEREGULATION OF POWER SECTOR

Deregulation refers to removal of government control over power utility. It encompasses unbundling of hitherto vertically integrated power utility into separate generation, transmission and distribution companies as distinct business entity. The purpose of deregulation is to involve private sector so that competition is introduced leading to improvement in service, competitive price of electricity, infusion of capital necessary for infrastructure upgradation etc. Ultimately, consumer gets benefitted due to lower cost of electricity delivered.

Chile was the first country in the world which started the deregulation of its power sector way back in 1982. Success of this business model was followed by UK in 1990; Argentina, Sweden and Norway in 1992; Bolivia and Columbia in 1993; Australia in 1994; New Zealand in 1996; Panama, Costa Rica, Honduras, Guatemala and El Salvador in 1997 and so on. In India, Odisha was the first state which unbundled its electricity board in 1996. This was followed by other states, such as Haryana (1998), Andhra Pradesh and Karnataka (1999), Delhi and Rajasthan (2002) and so on.

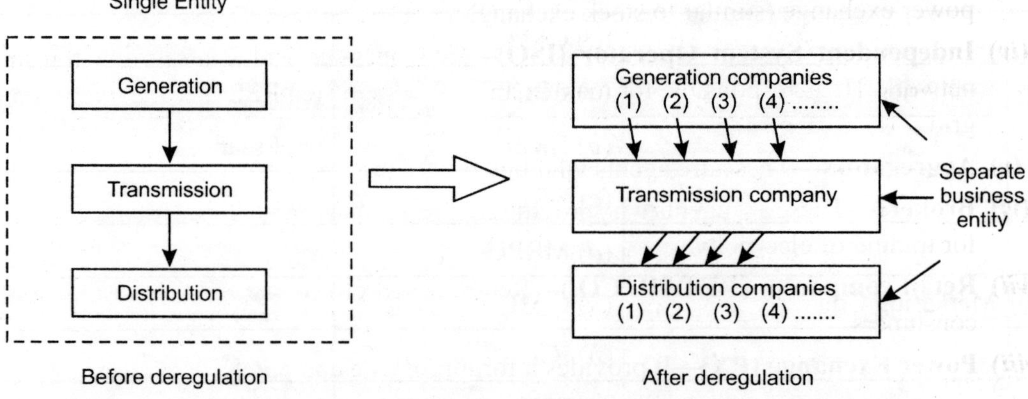

Figure. 1.6. Structure of electricity sector before and after deregulation

The Electricity Laws (Amendment) Act, 1991 allowed participation of private sector in operation and maintenance of power generation companies. A regulatory body was established through the enactment of Electricity Regulatory Commission Act, 1998. Thereafter, Electricity Act, 2003 ushered in deregulation of electricity sector in India.

1.9.1. Aims of Deregulation

Following are the aims of deregulation in electricity sector–

(*i*) allow participation of private sector so as to improve operational efficiency, infuse fresh capital necessary for infrastructure upgradation, introduce competition, infuse new technology in operation and maintenance etc.

(*ii*) rationalize the price of electricity.

(*iii*) give choice of supplies of electricity to consumer.

(*iv*) allow government to invest scarce financial resources to other priority sectors.

(*v*) free the govt. from running the business of electricity generation, transmission and distribution which was weighed down by political and economic reasons.

In short, purpose of deregulation is to allow a business entity to run as a profitable enterprise with the ultimate aim of customer satisfaction.

1.9.2. Structure of Deregulated Electricity Market

A deregulated electricity market is a place with large number of players operating with complex rules. The description of various market participants are given below–

(*i*) **Generating companies or GENCOs**—These are power producing companies which generate power and sell to other entities.

(*ii*) **Transmission companies or TRANSCOs**—Transco carry power from GENCOs through transmission network and deliver to distribution companies or DISCOs. Transco builds, owns and operates transmission system in a specified area.

(*iii*) **Distribution companies or DISCOs**—DISCOs distribute electricity through distribution network to consumers. They buy electricity from GENCOs or from spot market called power exchange (similar to stock exchange).

(*iv*) **Independent System Operator (ISO)**—ISO operates and controls the transmission network. He is responsible for maintenance of system stability, security and reliability of grid.

(*v*) **Aggregators**—These are agents who buy power for group of customers.

(*vi*) **Brokers**—These are agents who provide energy ancillary services and work as middleman for trading of electricity.

(*vii*) **Retail companies (RETAIL CO.)**—Retailers sell electricity and services to individual consumers.

(*viii*) **Power Exchange (PX)**—It provides a forum for sale and purchase of electricity.

1.10. GREENHOUSE EFFECT AND GLOBAL WARMING

Greenhouse effect is a natural process in which sun's energy heats up the earth's atmosphere. Out of total energy received from sun, about 30% of it is reflected back to space by cloud, ice, snow, sand or other reflecting surfaces. The rest of the energy is absorbed by earth's atmosphere and reradiated. Certain gases called greenhouse gases such as methane, nitrous oxide, carbon dioxide, water vapours, ozone and chlorofluoro carbons (CFC) absorb and retain heat thereby raising the temperature of atmosphere. This makes earth habitable otherwise it could have been as lifeless and cold as Mars or Moon.

However, due to anthropogenic (manmade) activities, level of green house gases is rising resulting in trapping of more heat in the earth's atmosphere (greenhouse gases act as a blanket and prevent escape of this heat back to space). This is increasing the average temperature of earth's atmosphere over the years. Generation of greenhouse gases result from industrialization, burning of fossil fuels (oil, coal and gas) and deforestation. Deforestation alone increases accumulation of carbon dioxide in the atmosphere by 6% to 17%.

This unchecked rise in global warming (due to retention of heat in atmosphere) will lead to significant changes in climate, rise in sea level, extreme weather condition, acidification of oceans and seas etc. So, to mitigate the effects of global warming, concentration of greenhouse gases in earth's atmospheres need to be reduced on warfooting basis. As the conventional power plants (based on coal, oil or gas) release carbon dioxide and other harmful gases, it is imperative to develop alternative technologies for power generation so as to preserve the environment.

1.11. IMPACT OF CONVENTIONAL POWER PLANTS ON ENVIRONMENT

Power produced from fossil fuels, such as coal, oil and gas causes environmental pollution, such as air pollution, water pollution, soil pollution, noise pollution, harmful radiations apart from global warming.

Following tables 1.6. and 1.7 give an indication of greenhouse gas emission from conventional sources of power generation.

Table 1.6. Carbon dioxide Emission

Sr. No	*Power source*	*Emission* CO_2 *Equi. Ton/MWh*
1.	Thermal	1.1
2.	Oil based	0.62
3.	Gas based	0.47
4.	Hydro	nil
5.	Nuclear	nil

Table 1.7. Green House Gas (GHG) Emission

Sr. No	**Sector**	**GHG Emission (% age)**
1.	Electricity	38
2.	Transport	7
3.	Residential	7
4.	Agriculture	18
5.	Cement	7
6.	Iron & steel	6
7.	Other Manufacturing	9

Above tables show that power generation is a major source of pollution. Out of all sources of conventional power generation, thermal power generation contributes maximum CO_2 emission followed by oil based and gas based power generation.

Thermal power plant emits number of harmful gaseous substances such as sulphur oxides (SO_x), nitrogen oxides (No_x), carbon dioxide, carbon mono-oxide, particulate matter etc.

In addition, discharge of water at higher temperature from cooling towers affects aquatic life. Water discharged from thermal power plant contains chemicals such as biocides, corrosion inhibitors, scale cleaning chemicals, boiler dosing chemicals etc. which cause water and soil pollution.

Oil based power plants emit harmful gases such as sulphur oxides, nitrogen oxides, carbon dioxide, carbon mono-oxide, etc.

Nuclear power plant though do not generate pollution but pose threat of radiation leakage. The radiation hazard emanates from abnormal plant operation and improper nuclear waste disposal. The gaseous discharge contains iodine and tritium in vapour form. Liquid effluents contain fission and activation products. So, strictly speaking, nuclear plants are not free from pollution.

On the other hand, hydro power plants though do not produce effluents but cause submergence of large tract of land and displacement of large population. So, it creates a social and economic impact on society rather than pollution.

Hence, all types of conventional power generation produce pollution. However, with latest pollution abatement technologies, impact has been minimized though not eliminated. Nevertheless, it is the price one has to pay till other forms of generation having least or no pollution are available.

1.12. ENERGY SECURITY

India has 17% of world's population and 0.4% of oil reserve, 0.4% of gas reserve and 6% of coal reserves. Energy usage has direct impact on a country's GDP (Gross Domestic Product). Hence, availability of energy resources is absolutely essential for a rapidly growing and resource starved Indian economy. Therefore, energy security for a fast developing country like India is of paramount importance. India's dependence on imported fossil fuels is given in table 1.6.

Table 1.6. India's dependence on imported fossil fuels (current & projected)

Year	*Coal*	*Oil*	*Gas*	*Overall*
2012	18%	77%	23%	31%
2047	62%	88%	49%	60%

As indicated in table No. 1.6, the future dependance on imported fossil fuel is bound to increase manifold. This grim situation brings energy security into picture.

International Energy Agency (IEA) defines energy security as "the uninterrupted availability of energy sources at an affordable price". It is the ability of energy system of a country to maintain a balance between supply and demand in the event of unexpected changes in energy supply. Energy insecurity may result from volatility of crude prices, insufficient investment in domestic energy infrastructure, international conflicts (e.g. Iraq war), sanctions on oil producing countries (e.g., on Iran etc). In order to safeguard energy supply system from such unforeseen circumstances, it is imperative to improve energy security by following measures—

(*i*) **by improving energy efficiency**–It means efficiency of utilization of energy resource. For example, improvement of energy efficiency through energy labelling of appliances, energy efficient buildings, smart grid mission, energy audit of industries etc.

(*ii*) **by maximization of domestic production**–Domestic production is not exposed to international risks. Hence, encouragement for investment in domestic energy infrastructure is required by the government.

(*iii*) **by development of reliable network**–Development of reliable energy channel is needed so that energy is available, when needed. For example, investment in overseas energy infrastructure project (mines, oil fields), long term price agreement of energy sources with supplier countries etc.

(*iv*) **by reducing dependance on scarce fossil fuels**–Energy security can be improved by developing alternate source of energy generation. For example, shift from fossil fuel based power generation to renewable energy sources, use of hydrogen as transport fuel, use of fuel cell as transport fuel etc.

(*v*) **by building energy source reserve**–Fossil fuels can be stored for a short duration by building storage facilities. Energy can be purchased and stocked when crude prices are low. This can also be used as a hedge against inflation or price surge.

Hence, for sustainable economic development of a country, sound energy security measures are needed. Power generation in the energy chain plays a very vital role in this direction.

1.13. LOAD FORECASTING TECHNIQUES

Load forecasting is to estimate the expected load in future. It is done for short term, medium term and long term. Short term is from one hour to a week, medium term is from one month to one year and long term is one year and more. Short term load forecast is needed for power plant to determine loading schedule of generators. Medium term load forecast is needed for operation and maintenance planning. Long term scheduling helps for planning of generator addition, transmission & distribution line addition and upgradation etc.

Various factors affecting load forecast are following—

(*i*) time factor (such as hour of day, day or night, week/day/weekend, time of year-season).

(*ii*) weather condition (temperature and humidity).

(*iii*) class of consumers (industrial, commercial, domestic and agriculture).

(*iv*) specific events (festivals, sports events, marriages etc.).

(*v*) strata of society of population.

(*vi*) price of electricity charged to consumer.

Various techniques of load forecasting are following.

(*i*) **Multiple regression technique**—In this technique, a statistical relationship is established amongst variables, such as weather condition, total load, type of day etc. Historical data is used in weighted least square estimation method.

(*ii*) **Exponential smoothing**—In this technique, a mathematical model is developed using historical data and future load is predicted.

(*iii*) **Stochastic time series**—This technique also forms a mathematical model based on historical data and uses time series method to predict load.

(*iv*) **Adaptive load forecasting**—This technique uses regression analysis based on Kalman filter theory. An online software is used which modifies automatically based on changing load conditions.

(*v*) **Curve fitting**—This technique forms a curve by joining data points. A software package develops a forecasting polynomial curve based on criterion of minimum quadratic error using peaks of load.

(*vi*) **Soft computing based load forecasting techniques**—Soft computing based techniques, such as fuzzy logic, neural network, genetic algorithm etc. are used for load forecasting. These techniques do not use any mathematical model.

(*vii*) **ARMAX Model**—This technique involves use of evolutionary programming to determine ARMAX model parameters of load demand.

1.14. RECENT TRENDS IN POWER GENERATION TECHNOLOGIES

The conventional sources of power generation being fossil fuel based, generate pollution. Hence, thrust is towards use of non-conventional sources of power, such as solar, wind, biomass etc. However, the cost of generated power from these sources is high compared to conventional sources. Also, conversion efficiency is poor and supply is erratic as it is dependent on vagaries of nature.

There is use of clean coal technology in thermal power generation, such as fluidised bed combustion boilers, super critical boilers, coal bed methane etc. Since, India has large reserves of coal, hence thermal power is going to remain a dominant source of power in foreseable future. In hydro-sector, mini and micro hydel power plants are given preference due to lower cost, lower gestation period and least effect on population around the project site. In nuclear and gas based projects, major bottleneck is the scarcity of fuel.

According to planning commission, the projected power generation mix (assuming 8% economic growth) in the year 2020 would be 2,25,000 MW of thermal, 50,000 MW of hydro, 25000 MW of gas and diesel, 7,280 MW of nuclear, 25,000 MW of wind, 6,000 MW of solar, 4,000 MW of biomass & others and 45,000 MW of captive power (total—3,87,280 MW).

Apart from generation, there is bottleneck in transmission infrastructure. To facilitate inter-regional power transfer, a number of EHVAC and HVDC links have been made. There is a proposal to raise the transmission voltage to 1200 kV. Also, FACTS (Flexible AC Transmission System) devices are being installed in transmission system to enhance power flow.

With the deregulation of electricity sector, it is expected that capital infusion necessary for infrastructure development will be available from private sector players resulting in a balanced development of India's energy sector.

1.15. DISTRIBUTED GENERATION

It is defined as on site power generation on a small scale. The power generation source is located close to the load centre and generation capacity is small (less than 10 MW). Examples are—rooftop solar power generation, small wind turbines, natural gas fired micro-turbines, small reciprocating engines etc. This type of generation is also known as decentralized generation. Advantages of such type of generation are following—

(*i*) no need to lay transmission and distribution lines.

(*ii*) no transmission losses.

(*iii*) higher reliability.

(*iv*) acts as a backup power.

(*v*) low cost of generation.

(*vi*) better power quality.

Both conventional and non-conventional energy sources are used for distributed generation. In conventional power generation, micro-turbines (upto 300 kW), reciprocating engines (upto 10 MW), fuel cells (upto 20MW) are used. While in non-conventional power generation, solar (upto 1 MW), wind turbine (upto 1 MW) and biomass (upto 5 MW) are used. This type of system may be isolated or grid connected.

Sometimes, hybrid power generation is also used, such as diesel power generation with solar photovoltaic. During daytime, solar power is used while during night, diesel generators are used (e.g. in Sundarbans in West Bengal and in Laddakh). Normally, such systems are adopted where the location is far away from the grid.

This mode of power generation is ideal for remote areas where availability of grid is not there or cost of laying transmission and distribution lines is very high (e.g. in hilly area). It is expected that in future, there will be micro grids employing distributed power generation which will be located around the load clusters.

CHAPTER SUMMARY

India's power generation sector leapfrogged from generation of 1362 MW in 1947 to more than 2,84,303 MW, (2015). There is average energy shortage of 8% and peak energy shortage of 13%. The share of private sector in power generation is about 31.5%. The transmission network has increased from voltage level of 132 kV to 765 kV AC. The high voltage DC transmission voltage level of 800 kV is being used today. However, this pace of development could not match the galloping demand resulting in shortfall in average and peak demand.

Due to depleting fossil fuel reserves, there is a greater thrust on development of renewable energy sources. Solar PV, wind and biomass generation have risen rapidly over the last two decades. But thermal power generation still remains the main source of energy.

The power sector is organised in five regional electricity grids viz northern grid, western grid, southern grid, eastern grid and northeastern grids. These grids are interlinked with EHVAC and HVDC links enabling transfer of power between two regional grids. The national grid formed due to interconnection of regional grids is controlled by national load dispatch centre at Delhi (operated by Power Grid Corporation of India).

Indian coal sector is controlled by central govt. at policy-making, planning and regulatory level. Mining is carried out by govt. companies as well as by private companies.

Petroleum and natural gas sector is controlled by central govt. at planning, policy-making and regulatory stage. While exploration is carried out by govt. as well as private companies. Retail sales of petroleum products is still controlled by govt. companies.

The nuclear power generation sector in India is totally controlled by central govt. including planning, policy-making, regulation and power generation.

With deregulation of electricity sector, there is private participation in generation and distribution. This will help to narrow down gap between demand and supply.

REVIEW QUESTIONS

Q. 1. What are the various sources of energy available on planet earth?

Q. 2. Discuss classification of energy sources.

Q. 3. Write a brief note on Indian generation sector.

Q. 4. Write a brief note on growth of Indian transmission voltage level after independence.

Q. 5. Discuss the status of renewable energy sector development in the past one decade.

Q. 6. Justify the importance of electrical energy.

Q. 7. Differentiate between non-renewable and renewable energy generation.

Q. 8. Discuss the reasons for slow growth of renewable energy generation in India.

Q. 9. Why nuclear power generation constitutes only 2% of total installed capacity compared to renewable energy generation which is 13% of total installed capacity?

Q. 10. Comment "Hydrogen is fuel for the future."

Q. 11. Give a brief details of organisation of Indian power sector.

Q. 12. Discuss contribution of Power Grid Corporation of India towards development of national grid.

Q. 13. Discuss structure of Indian petroleum and natural gas sector.

Q. 14. What is the meaning of deregulation of power sector? What is the need and impact of deregulation in Indian power sector?

Q. 15. Discuss the structure of deregulated electricity market.

Q. 16. What is market power? How does it impact sale of electricity in a market?

Q. 17. Write a brief note on pollution caused by coal based power generation.

Q. 18. What are the latest coal based power generation technologies?

Q. 19. Write a brief note on latest trends in power generation technologies.

Q. 20. Development of wind power generation is faster than other renewable energy sources. Comment.

Multiple Choice Questions

1. Which renewable energy has highest installed capacity?
(*a*) solar (*b*) wind
(*c*) biomass (*d*) geothermal
(*e*) ocean wave

2. Secondary source of energy is
(*a*) coal (*b*) oil
(*c*) natural gas (*d*) electricity

3. Following is not a renewable energy source.
(*a*) wind (*b*) biomass
(*c*) solar (*d*) natural gas

4. Which is not commercial energy
(*a*) coal (*b*) natural gas
(*c*) agriculture waste (*d*) electricity

5. Which of the following is secondary source of energy
(*a*) oil (*b*) coal
(*c*) gas (*d*) hot water

6. Identify renewable energy source
(*a*) coal (*b*) hydro
(*c*) nuclear (*d*) oil

7. Ocean thermal energy resource uses energy of
(*a*) ocean (*b*) wind
(*c*) sun (*d*) waves

8. The number of electricity grids in the country are—
(*a*) three (*b*) four
(*c*) five (*d*) six

9. ONGC is a
(*a*) gas generation company (*b*) gas distribution company
(*c*) petroleum distribution company (*d*) none of these

10. GAIL is a
(*a*) gas generation company (*b*) gas distribution company
(*c*) petroleum exploration company (*d*) none of these

SHORT ANSWER TYPE QUESTIONS

Q. 1. Where is national load dispatch centre situated?

Q. 2. Write three advantages of renewable energy sources over non-renewable energy sources.

Q. 3. Name five biomass sources used for power generation.

Q. 4. Why small hydro is preferred over large hydro?

Q. 5. What is the function of Atomic Energy Regulatory Board?

Q. 6. Name private organisations involved in oil exploration.

Q. 7. State five advantages of deregulation of electricity sector.

Q. 8. Which electricity law paved the way for deregulation of electricity sector in India?

Q. 9. What is the role of (*a*) power exchange (*b*) retail companies and (*c*) aggregators.

Q. 10. Write four detrimental impact of coal based power generation on environment.

Answer to MCQ

1. (*b*) **2.** (*d*) **3.** (*d*) **4.** (*c*) **5.** (*d*)

6. (*b*) **7.** (*c*) **8.** (*c*) **9.** (*a*) **10.** (*b*)

Chapter

ECONOMIC OPERATION OF POWER PLANTS

Learning Objectives

After reading this chapter, reader will be able to

- Understand basic terms used in power generation.
- Understand classification of cost, meaning and methods of calculation of depreciation and meaning and types of tariff.
- Grasp basics of power factor and methods of improvement.
- Understand factors governing selection of unit rating of a power plant and sharing of load between base load and peak load plants.

"If you can't explain it simply, you don't understand it well enough" — Albert Einstein

2.1. INTRODUCTION

Capital cost of any engineering project decides the feasibility of project. The operation of power plant is no different case. Aim of any power generating station is to produce power at lowest unit cost. This will enable the delivery of this power to consumers at a reasonable rate. However, determination of cost of power generation is complex because cost depends upon several factors, such as infrastructure cost, cost of fuel, depreciation, governmental regulations etc. and these factors vary with time. Hence, it is difficult to take into account all these factors realistically yet produce power and deliver to consumers at a reasonable rate. More so, because electricity like water is a basic necessity of life and unlike water can not be stored.

In this chapter, various factors affecting cost of generation are explained. Concept of depreciation, tariff and economic load dispatch are explained. The factors affecting size and rating of generators are explained with brief writeup on load forecasting. This will enable the reader to understand the economics of power generation.

2.2. TERMS ASSOCIATED WITH POWER GENERATION

Before concept of economic operation is studied, it is necessary to be familiar with terms used in power generation.

(*i*) **Base Load**—It is a fixed load which remains on the power plant almost the whole day.

(*ii*) **Peak Load**—The demand over and above base load is peak load. It is sudden increase in load which stays for a short duration.

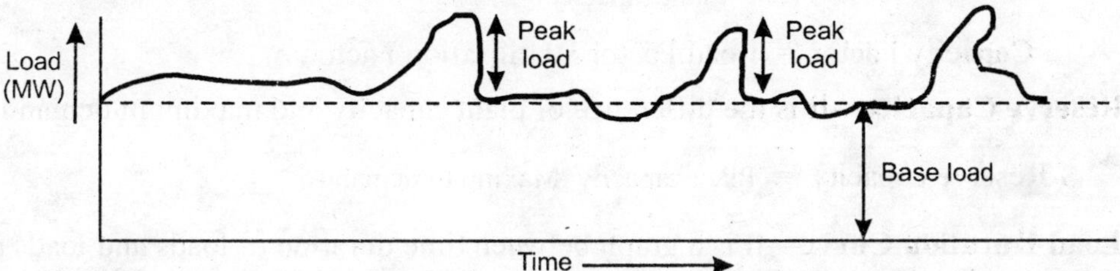

Figure 2.1. Base & Peak load.

(*iii*) **Hot Reserve**—It is a generating capacity in operation but not in service. As the demand rises, the unit is started and synchronised with the bus bar.

(*iv*) **Spinning Reserve**—It is a generating capacity connected to bus and already running but not loaded. To meet sudden demand, the unit is immediately loaded.

(*v*) **Connected Load**—It is aggregate of continuous rating of all loads connected to the supply system.

(*vi*) **Maximum Demand**—It is the maximum load demand on a generating station in a given period.

(*vii*) **Average Demand**—It is the average of load demand on a generating station in a given period.

(*viii*) **Demand Factor**—It is the ratio of maximum demand on a generating station to the average demand.

$$\text{Demand Factor} = \frac{\text{Maximum demand}}{\text{Average demand}}$$

(*ix*) **Load Factor**—It is the ratio of average demand to maximum demand in a given period.

$$\text{Load Factor} = \frac{\text{Average demand}}{\text{Maximum demand}}$$

(*x*) **Diversity Factor**—It is the ratio of sum of individual maximum demand to the maximum demand on the power station.

$$\text{Diversity Factor} = \frac{\text{Sum of individual max imum demand}}{\text{Maximum demand on power station}}$$

It is always more than unity.

(*xi*) **Utilisation Factor or Plant Use Factor**—It is the ratio of units generated to the product of plant capacity and the number of hours for which the plant was in use.

$$\text{U.F} = \frac{\text{Station output in kWh}}{\text{Plant capacity X hours of use}}$$

(*xii*) **Capacity Factor**—It is the ratio of actual energy produced to the maximum energy that could have been produced.

$$\text{C.F} = \frac{\text{Actual energy produced}}{\text{Maximum energy that could have been produced}}$$

$$= \frac{\text{Average demand}}{\text{Plant capacity}}$$

Capacity Factor = Load Factor x Utilisation Factor.

(*xiii*) **Reserve Capacity**—It is the difference of plant capacity and maximum demand.

Reserve capacity = Plant capacity–Maximum demand

(*xiv*) **Load Duration Curve**—It is a graph between time duration of loads and loads arranged in descending order of magnitude.

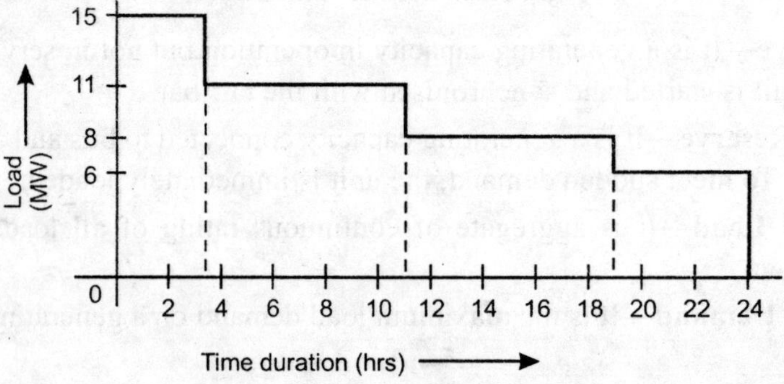

Figure 2.2. Load duration curve

(*xv*) **Load Curve**—It shows variation of load on a power plant from time to time. If the variation is plotted on hourly basis, it is called daily load curve. Similarly, It could be monthly or annual load curve. The area under the curve shows total units generated in a day or a month or a year. The area of the curve divided by number of hours represents average demand on power station.

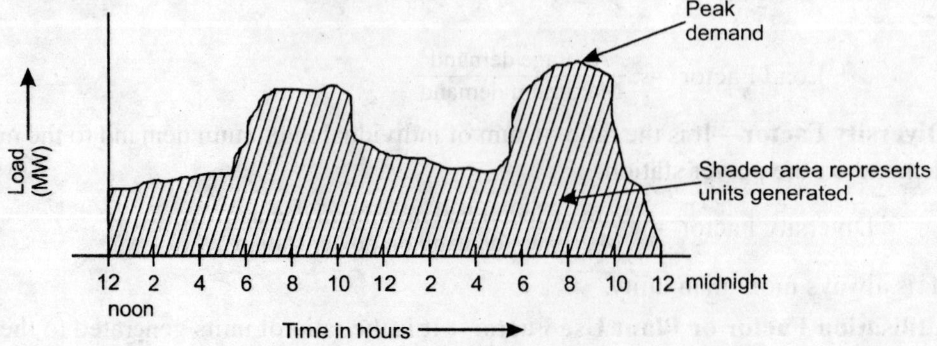

Figure 2.3. Daily load curve

(*xvi*) **Dump Power**—It is power available in excess of load requirement. It happens in case of hydro power plant when surplus water is available.

(*xvii*) **Co-incidence Factor**—It is ratio of maximum demand on power station to sum of individual maximum demand. It is reciprocal of diversity factor.

$$\text{Co-incidence Factor} = \frac{\text{Maximum demand on power station}}{\text{Sum of individual maximum demand}}$$

It is less than unity.

(*xviii*) **Heat Rate**—It is the amount of heat input required to generate one unit of electricity (cal/kWh).

Example 2.1

A thermal power plant has a connected load of 50 MW and a maximum demand of 30 MW. Total 61.5×10^6 units are generated in a year. Calculate (i) demand factor (ii) load factor.

Solution:

(*i*) $\text{Demand Factor} = \frac{\text{Maximum demand}}{\text{Connected load}} = \frac{30}{50} = 0.6$ Ans.

(*ii*) $\text{Load Factor} = \frac{\text{Average demand}}{\text{Maximum demand}}$

$$\text{Average demand} = \frac{\text{Units generated/year}}{\text{hours in a year}} = \frac{61.5 \times 10^6}{8760} = 7020 \text{ kW}$$

$$\text{L.F} = \frac{7020}{30 \times 10^3} = 0.234 \text{ Ans.}$$

Example 2.2

A captive power plant feeds four load clusters having peak loads of 500 kW, 1000 kW, 2000 kW and 4000 KW. The diversity factor of load at plant is 1.5 and annual load factor is 60% Calculate maximum demand on station and annual energy supplied.

Solution:

$$\text{Maximum Demand} = \frac{\text{Sum of individual max imum demand}}{\text{`Diversity factor}}$$

$$\text{M.D.} = \frac{500 + 1000 + 2000 + 4000}{1.5} = \frac{7500}{1.5} = 5000 \text{ kW Ans.}$$

$$\text{Load Factor} = \frac{\text{No.of units generated / year}}{\text{Maximum demand} \times 8760}$$

$$\text{No. of units generated} = \text{L.F} \times \text{Maximum demand} \times 8760$$

$$= 0.6 \times 5000 \times 8760$$

$$= 262.8 \times 10^5 \text{ kWh} \quad \textbf{Ans.}$$

Example 2.3

A hydro power plant supplies power to following category of consumers—

Domestic consumer = 50 kW, commercial consumer = 200 kW

Industrial consumer = 1000 kW, Agricultural consumer = 750 kW

If maximum demand on plant is 1500 kW and units generated per year is 20×10^5, find

(*i*) diversity factor and (*ii*) annual load factor.

Solution:

$$(i)\ \text{Diversity Factor} = \frac{50 + 200 + 1000 + 750}{1500} = 1.33\ \textbf{Ans.}$$

$$(ii)\ \text{Load factor} = \frac{\text{Average demand}}{\text{Maximum demand}}$$

$$\text{Average demand} = \frac{\text{Units generated/year}}{\text{hours in year}} = \frac{20 \times 10^5}{8760} = 228.3\ \text{kW}$$

$$\text{L.F.} = \frac{228.3}{1500} = 0.1522 \text{ or } 15.22\%\ \textbf{Ans.}$$

Example 2.4

A power plant has following daily load cycle—

Time (hours)	0–6	6–10	10–12	12–16	16–20	20–24
Load (MW)	20	40	50	45	70	50

Draw load curve and find

(*i*) maximum demand (*ii*) units generated per day

(*iii*) average load (*iv*) load factor.

Solution:

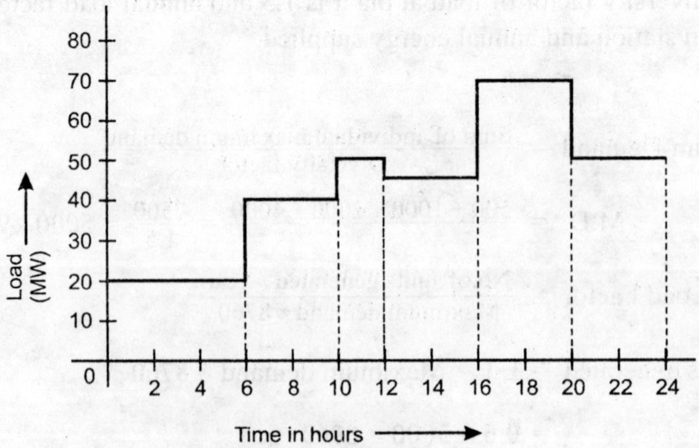

Figure 2.4. Load curve

(*i*) From daily load curve, it is observed that maximum demand is 70 MW.

∴ Maximum Demand = 70 MW **Ans.**

(*ii*) Units generated/day = Area of load curve

$$= [20 \times 6 + 40 \times 4 + 50 \times 2 + 45 \times 4 + 70 \times 4 + 50 \times 4] \times 10^3 \text{ kWH}$$

$$= 1040 \times 10^3 \text{ kWh } \textbf{Ans.}$$

(*iii*) $\text{Average demand} = \dfrac{\text{Units generated/day}}{24 \text{ hours}} = \dfrac{1.04 \times 10^6}{24} = 43.3 \times 10^3 \text{ kW } \textbf{Ans.}$

(*iv*) $\text{Load factor} = \dfrac{\text{Average demand}}{\text{Maximum demand}} = \dfrac{43.3 \times 10^3}{70 \times 10^3} = 0.619 \text{ or } 61.9\% \textbf{ Ans.}$

Example 2.5

A thermal power plant has three units of 10 MW, 7 MW and 5 MW respectively. The annual load duration curve can be considered as a straight line from 3 MW to 15 MW. Calculate

(*i*) Installed Capacity.

(*ii*) Plant factor.

(*iii*) Units generated/year.

(*iv*) Load factor and.

(*v*) Utilisation factor.

Solution:

(*i*) Installed capacity of power plant = Sum of rating of all units

$$= 10 + 7 + 15$$

$$= \textbf{22 MW Ans.}$$

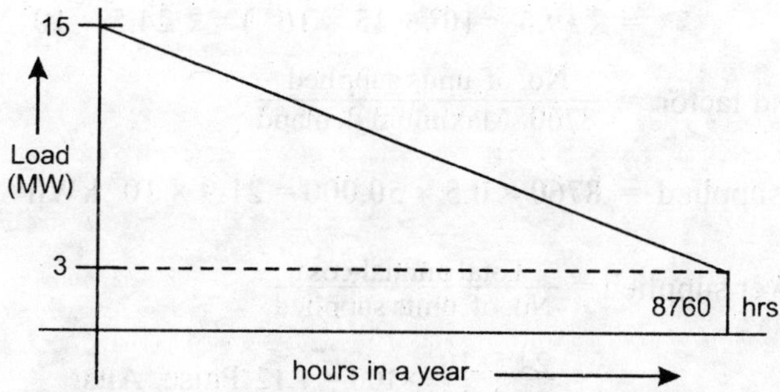

Figure 2.5. Load Curve

(*ii*) $\text{Plant factor} = \dfrac{\text{Average demand}}{\text{Plant capacity}}$

$$\text{Average demand} = \frac{1}{2}[15 + 3] = 9 \text{ MW}$$

$$\therefore \quad \text{Plant factor} = \frac{9}{22} = 0.409 \text{ or } \textbf{40.9\% Ans.}$$

(iii) Units generated/year = Area under the load curve

$$= \frac{1}{2}[15 + 3] \times 8760 = \textbf{78840} \times \textbf{10}^3 \textbf{ kWh Ans.}$$

(*iv*) Load factor = $\frac{9000}{15000}$ = 0.6 or **60% Ans.**

(*v*) Utilisation factor = $\frac{\text{Maximum demand}}{\text{Plant capacity}} = \frac{15}{22}$ = 0.68 or **68% Ans.**

Example 2.6.

Calculate cost /kWh of power supplied by a power plant with a maximum demand of 50 MW. Other details are given below-

(*i*) Capital cost of power plant = ₹ 95×10^5

(*ii*) Cost of fuel and oil/year = ₹ 9×10^5

(*iii*) Salaries, wages and taxes = ₹ 6×10^5

Annual load factor is 50%. The rate of interest and depreciation is 10%.

Solution:

$$\begin{aligned}\text{Annual fixed charges} &= \text{10\% of capital cost}\\ &= \text{10\% of } 95 \times 10^5\\ &= ₹\ 9.5 \times 10^5\end{aligned}$$

$$\begin{aligned}\text{Total running charges} &= \text{cost of fuel \& oil + salaries, wages \& taxes.}\\ &= ₹\ (9 \times 10^5 + 6 \times 10^5) = ₹\ 15 \times 10^5\end{aligned}$$

$$\begin{aligned}\text{Total annual cost} &= \text{Fixed charges + Running charges}\\ &= ₹\ (9.5 \times 10^5 + 15 \times 10^5) = ₹\ 24.5 \times 10^5\end{aligned}$$

$$\text{Annual load factor} = \frac{\text{No. of units supplied}}{8760 \times \text{Maximum demand}}$$

$$\therefore \quad \text{No. of units supplied} = 8760 \times 0.5 \times 50{,}000 = 21.9 \times 10^7 \text{ kWh}$$

$$\text{Cost per unit of power supplied} = \frac{\text{Total annual cost}}{\text{No. of units supplied}}$$

$$= \frac{24.5 \times 10^5}{21.9 \times 10^7} \times 100 = 1.12 \text{ Paise. } \textbf{Ans.}$$

Example. 2.7

Calculate thermal efficiency of a coal based power plant from following data. Also, calculate coal consumption/ year.

Load factor = 40%, Boiler efficiency= 85%, Turbine efficiency = 90%

Maximum demand = 20 MW, Coal consumption = 0.876 kg/unit.

Price of coal = ₹ 29.53/tonne

Solution:

$$\begin{aligned}\text{Thermal efficiency} &= \text{Boiler efficiency} \times \text{Turbine efficiency}\\ &= 0.85 \times 0.90 = 0.765 \textbf{ Ans.}\end{aligned}$$

$$\text{Load factor} = \frac{\text{No.of units generated/year}}{8760\times\text{Maximum demand}}$$

$\therefore$ No. of units generated/year = $20000\times0.4\times8760 = 7008\times10^4$ kWh.

$$\text{Coal consumption/year} = \frac{7008\times10^4\times0.876\times29.53}{1000}$$

$$= ₹\ 1,811,450\ \textbf{Ans.}$$

2.3. CLASSIFICATION OF COST OF GENERATION

The cost of power generation can be categorised into three classes-

(*i*) Fixed cost.

(*ii*) Semi fixed cost and

(*iii*) Variable cost.

(*i*) **Fixed cost**—This type of cost does not depend upon the maximum demand on the generating station and units produced. This type of cost is present even if power plant is not running. For example, salaries of high officials, interest paid on capital, investment on plant & machinery etc.

(*ii*) **Semi fixed cost**—This type of cost depends upon maximum demand but is independent of units generated. For example, depreciation of capital cost of plant and machinery, civil work, transmission & distribution network, taxes and insurance, salaries of clerical staff, compensation given to workers etc.

(iii) Variable cost—This type of cost is proportional to number of units generated. For example, fuel cost, repair & maintenance cost, wages of operational staff, cost of spares and consumables etc.

The total annual cost of generation is represented by following expression-

$$\text{Total cost} = \text{A} + \text{B kW} + \text{C kWh} \qquad ...(2.1)$$

Where A,B and C are constants. First term represents fixed cost, second term represents semi fixed cost and last term represents variable cost.

2.4. DEPRECIATION

It is the reduction in value of an asset (machinery,building etc.) due to wear and tear and obsolescence. Once a physical asset is built, the deterioration of the asset starts from the very first day. The rate of this wear and tear is dependent upon operating environment, operation and maintenance practices, loading on the equipment etc. The depreciation of asset could be due to physical wear and tear or functional obsolescence or technological obsolescence. Functional obsolescence refers to inability of equipment to deliver required output of acceptable quantity and quality. Technological obsolescence refers to change in technology due to introduction of new type of raw material, requirement of improved quality etc. Hence, asset need to be replaced due to physical obsolescence, functional obsolescence & technological obsolescence.

Every asset has a useful economic life. For example, coach of a passenger train has a useful life of 20 years while that of oil tanker has 25 years of life. A thermal power plant has an economic life of 25 years, a nuclear power plant has 25 years while a hydro-electric power plant may last 80 years.

The economical useful life means a period during which the cost of operation and maintenance is such that it is economical to run the asset. After the expiry of useful life, the asset may still function but the operation and maintenance cost may be so high as it is better to replace it with a new equipment. However, the replacement of an existing asset requires money. So, to plan for future replacement of a newly purchased asset, a fixed amount is kept aside every year so that at the end of useful economic life of that asset, it may be replaced with a new one. But, it is difficult to decide the amount of money to be kept aside every year. Accordingly, there are several methods of determination of depreciation of an asset.

The various methods of determination of depreciation are:

(*i*) Straight line method.

(*ii*) Diminishing value method and

(*iii*) Sinking fund method.

(*i*) **Straight line method**—In this method, a fixed amount is set aside as depreciation every year based upon useful economic life of asset and total depreciation.

$$\text{Accordingly, Annual depreciation} = \frac{\text{Total depreciation}}{\text{Useful economic life}}$$

$$= \frac{\text{Initial cost–salvage value}}{\text{Useful economic life}} = \frac{P - S}{n} \quad \text{...(2.2)}$$

Where, salvage value refers to scrap value of the asset.

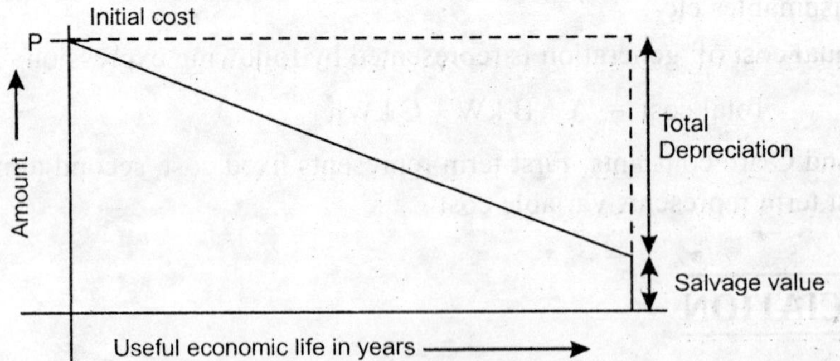

Figure 2.6. Straight line method

Although, it is a very simple method but it suffers from following drawbacks-

(*a*) Assumption of constant depreciation is wrong. Because, asset does not deteriorate at a constant rate throughout its economic life. Rather, depreciation is slower in the initial years and gradually increases with the time.

(*b*) This method does not consider the interest earned on the amount set aside every year. Because, the amount set aside is kept in a bank which earns interest on the capital.

(*ii*) **Diminishing value method**–In this method, a depreciation charge is applied to purchase cost and then it is applied to diminishing value. The diminishing rate depends upon useful economic life of asset. Accordingly, depreciation charges are high during initial years and low during late years.

Let P = Capital cost of asset.

S = Salvage value of asset after useful economic life.

n = Useful economic life of asset.

x = Annual unit depreciation.

∴ Value of asset after one year $= P - Px$ ...(2.3)

$$= P(1 - x)$$

Value of asset after two years = Diminished value – Annual depreciation

$$= [(P - Px) - (P - Px)x]$$

$$= P(1 - x)^2 \quad \text{...(2.4)}$$

Value of asset after n years $= P(1 - x)^n$

Or salvage, $S = P(1 - x)^n$ ...(2.5)

or $(1 - x)^n = \frac{S}{p} = (1 - x) = \left(\frac{S}{P}\right)^{1/n}$, Annual depreciation, $x = 1 - \left(\frac{S}{P}\right)^{1/n}$

Deposit to be made at the end of first year $= xP$

$$= P\left[1 - \left(\frac{S}{P}\right)^{1/n}\right] \quad \text{...(2.6)}$$

Deposit to be made at the end of second year $= x(1 - x)P$

$$= P\left(\frac{S}{P}\right)^{\frac{1}{n}}\left[1 - \left(\frac{S}{P}\right)^{\frac{1}{n}}\right] \text{ and so on.}$$

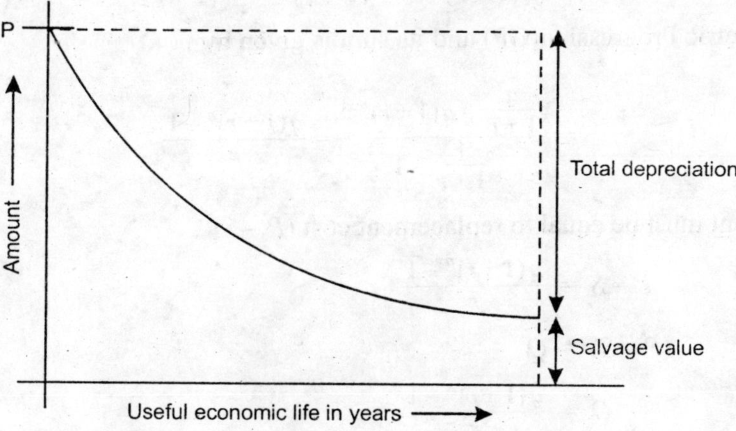

Figure 2.7. Diminishing Value method

This is a better method compared to straight line method. However, this method suffers from following drawbacks.

(*a*) Depreciation charges are heavy during initial years & low in late years.

(*b*) The interest earned on the amount set aside is not taken into consideration.

(iii) **Sinking fund method**—In this method, a fixed depreciation charge is made every year and the amount is invested so that it earns compound interest annually.

The fixed depreciation charge is decided such that cost of replacement of asset is equal to sum of total annual instalment and interest accumulated.

Let

P = Capital cost of asset.

S = Salvage value of asset after useful economic life.

n = Useful economic life of asset.

r = Annual rate of interest.

Annual deposit q will earn interest rq in first year such that this amount is worth $(q + rq)$ or $q(1 + r)$ at the end of first year.

Similarly, it will be $q(1 + r)^2$ at the end of two year.

At the end of n years, it becomes $q(1 + r)^n$

Amount q deposited at the end of first year in $(n - 1)$ years becomes

$$= q(1 + r)^{n-1} \quad \text{...(2.6)}$$

Amount q deposited at the end of second year in $(n - 2)$ years becomes $= q(1 + r)^{n-2}$ ...(2.7)

Similarly, amount q deposit at end of $(n - 1)$ year becomes

$$= q(1 + r)^{n-(n-1)}$$

$$= q(1 + r) \quad \text{...(2.8)}$$

Hence, after n year the total sinking fund will be—

$$= q[(1 + r)^{n-1} + (1 + r)^{n-2} + (1 + r)^{n-3} + ... + (1 + r)] \quad \text{...(2.9)}$$

This is a Geometric Progression(GP) and its sum is given by

$$= \frac{\frac{q}{1+r} - q(1+r)^{n-1}}{\frac{1}{1+r} - 1} = \frac{q(1+r)^n - 1}{r} \quad \text{...(2.10)}$$

This total amount must be equal to replacement cost $(P - S)$

$$\therefore \quad P - S = \frac{q(1+r)^n - 1}{r} \quad \text{...(2.11)}$$

Let $\quad (P - S) = Q$

$$\therefore \quad Q = \frac{q(1+r)^n - 1}{r}$$

Annual deposit

$$q = \frac{Qr}{(1+r)^n - 1} \quad \text{... (2.12)}$$

Example 2.8.

A gas fired furnace costs ₹ 50,000 and has a salvage value of ₹ 2,000. The useful economic life may be taken as 20 years. Find the depreciated value of the furnace at the end of 10 years. Estimate the value by

(*i*) Straight line method.

(*ii*) Diminishing value method.

(*iii*) Sinking fund method at 8% annual compound interest.

Solution:

Given,

Capital cost of furnace, (P) = ₹ 50,000

Salvage value (S) = ₹ 2000

Useful economic life of furnace(n) = 20 years

(*i*) By straight line method—

Annual deposit to be made—

$$q = \frac{P-S}{n} = \frac{50{,}000-2000}{20} = ₹\ 2400$$

Depreciated value at end of 10 years—

$$= P - 10q = 50{,}000 - 10 \times 2400 = ₹\ 26{,}000$$ **Ans.**

(*ii*) By Diminishing value method—

$$\text{Annual depreciation, } x = 1-\left(\frac{S}{P}\right)^{\frac{1}{n}} \Rightarrow 1-\left[\frac{2{,}000}{50{,}000}\right]^{\frac{1}{20}}$$

$$x = 1-\left[\frac{1}{25}\right]^{\frac{1}{20}} \Rightarrow 0.8513$$

$$\text{Value of furnace after 10 years} = P(1-x)^{10}$$

$$= 50{,}000(1-0.8513)^{10}$$

$$= 50{,}000(0.1487)^{10}$$

$$= 5\times 10^{4} \times 5.28578 \times 10^{-9}$$

$$= ₹\ 2.6429\times 10^{-4}$$ **Ans.**

(*iii*) By Sinking fund method—

Rate of interest (r) = 8%

Cost of replacement $(Q) = P - S$

$$= 50{,}000 - 2000 = ₹\ 48{,}000$$

$$\text{Annual deposit in Sinking fund, } q = \frac{Qr}{(1+r)^{n}-1} = \frac{48{,}000\times 0.08}{(1+0.08)^{20}-1}$$

$$= \frac{3840}{4.661-1} = \frac{3840}{3.661} = ₹\ 1048.8937$$

Total amount collected at the end of 10 years—

$$= \frac{q(1+r)^n - 1}{r} = \frac{1048.8937(1+0.08)^{10} - 1}{0.08}$$

$$= ₹\ 15194.864$$

Depreciated value of plant at the end of 10 years

$$= 50{,}000 - 15194.864$$

$$= ₹\ 34805.136$$ **Ans.**

Example 2.9

Erection cost of a thermal power plant is ₹ 2×10^8. If the life of plant is 25 years, salvage value is 15% and rate of interest is 8%, Calculate annual depreciation by

(*a*) Straight line method.

(*b*) Sinking fund method.

Solution:

(*a*) Straight line method

$$= \frac{2\times10^8(1-0.15)}{25} = ₹\ 6.8 \times 10^6 \text{ per year}$$ **Ans.**

(*b*) Sinking fund method

$$= 2\times10^8(1-0.15)\left[\frac{0.08}{(1.08)^{25}-1}\right]$$

$$= ₹\ 232 \times 10^6 \text{ per year}$$ **Ans.**

Example 2.10

A 1000 kVA distribution transformer costs ₹ 20,000. At the end of 20 years of useful life, the salvage value is ₹ 1000. Calculate depreciated value of transformer at the end of 10 years by

(*i*) Straight line method.

(*ii*) Sinking fund method with 8% annual rate of interest.

Solution:

Capital cost of transformer (P) = ₹ 20,000

Salvage value (S) = ₹ 1000

Useful life (n) = 20 years

(*i*) Straight line method

$$\text{Annual deposit, } q = \frac{P-S}{n} = \frac{20{,}000-1000}{20} = ₹\ 950$$

Depreciated value of plant at end of 10 years

$$= P - q \times 10 = 20{,}000 - 950 \times 10 = ₹\ 10{,}500$$ **Ans.**

(ii) Sinking fund method

$$\text{Annual deposit } (q) = (P-S)\left[\frac{r}{(1+r)^n - 1}\right]$$

$$= \frac{(20{,}000 - 1000) \times 0.08}{(1.08)^{20} - 1} = ₹\,415.20$$

Total deposit collected at the end of 10 years

$$= \frac{q(1+r)^{10} - 1}{r} = \frac{415.20 \times (1.08)^{10} - 1}{0.08}$$

$$= ₹\,6{,}015$$

Depreciated value of plant at the end of 10 years

$$= 20{,}000 - 6{,}015 = ₹\,13{,}985$$ **Ans.**

Example 2.11

The capital cost of an economiser is ₹ 12,000 with a life of 16 years. The economiser is purchased on annual instalment of ₹ 425 at 5% rate of interest. Fund the salvage value of economiser after 16 years using sinking fund method.

Solution:

Capital cost of economiser (P) = ₹ 12,000

Useful life (n) = 16 years

Annual rate of interest (r) = 5%

Annual deposit in sinking fund (q) = ₹ 425

$$\text{Amount calculated at the end of 16 years } (s) = \frac{q(1+r)^{16} - 1}{r}$$

$$= \frac{425(1+0.05)^{16} - 1}{0.05} = ₹\,10{,}054$$

Salvage value at the end of 16 years(s)=

$$= 12{,}000 - 10{,}054 = ₹\,2{,}946$$ **Ans.**

2.5. TARIFF

It is the rate at which electrical energy is supplied to consumers. These are rules devised to supply electricity to different classes of consumers.

Tariff takes into account cost of power generation, ability of consumers to pay and services rendered. Accordingly, there are different types of tariff suitable for different class of consumers viz domestic consumer, commercial consumer, industrial consumer(small&bulk), agricultural consumer and municipal corporations.

2.5.1. Objectives of Tariff

The main objective of tariff is to distribute equally the cost of power generation and cost of supply to different classes of consumers. Hence, tariff must include following—

(*i*) Recovery of cost of investment in generation, transmission and distribution.

(*ii*) Recovery of cost of operation and maintenance of power plant, transmission and distribution network.

(*iii*) Recovery of cost of electricity generated.

(*iv*) Recovery of cost of metering system, billing and collection of dues.

(*v*) A good return on the investment.

2.5.2. Desirable Characteristics of Tariff

A well designed tariff must contain following elements—

(*i*) Good return on the investment.

(*ii*) It should be as simple as possible and easy to understand.

(*iii*) It should be fair to different classes of consumers so that they are satisfied.

(iv) It should be attractive so that consumers are encouraged to use more electricity.

2.5.3. Types of Tariff

Various types of tariff commonly used are listed below—

(*i*) **Flat Demand Tariff**—This is one of the oldest type of tariff. In this case, demand of each consumer was fixed based on number of lamps in a household and consumer was charged based on total load in kW and a fixed rate per kW. Hence, electricity bill = load in kW × ₹/kW of electricity rate.

This is a simple method which does not require metering, billing and accounting cost. However, this method treats all types of consumers in same way. Since, a fixed rate is paid irrespective of usage, hence consumer tends to keep all their appliances switched on. This method is useful for street lights, traffic light and road signages where consumption is fixed and can be predicted.

(*ii*) **Simple Tariff**—This type of tariff is based on number of units consumed. The bill is equal to number of units consumed×cost/unit of electricity.

$$\text{Cost/unit} = \frac{\text{Anuual fixed and operating cos t}}{\text{Units consumed per year}}$$

This method suffers from drawback. These is no distinction between different classes of consumers. Due to fixed rate, a consumer tends to keep his appliances connected to mains.

(*iii*) **Flat Rate Tariff**—This type of tariff uses different rate for lighting load and power load. Billing is done through separate meters as lighting load and power load rates are different. Total bill = Lighting units consumed × rate/unit + power units consumed ×rate/unit.

(*iv*) **Block Rate Tariff**—First block of energy is charged at a higher rate and succeeding blocks of energy are charged at progressively reduced rate. So, the consumers are encouraged to use more electricity.

For example—

(*a*) First 100 units are charged at 5 ₹/unit

(*b*) Next 200 units are charged at 4.50 ₹/unit

(*c*) Next 300 units are charged at 4 ₹/unit

(*d*) Units exceeding 600 are charged at 3 ₹/unit

(*v*) **Two Part Tariff**—It consists of two components-a fixed charge and a running charge. The fixed charge is proportional to the maximum demand and running charge is proportional to the number of units consumed.

Total electricity bill = A × maximum demand of consumer + B × number of units consumed

where, A = charge/maximum demand in ₹/kW

B = charge/unit in ₹/kWh.

(*vi*) **Maximum Demand Tariff**—It consists of two components–a fixed charge based on maximum demand actually measured and a running charge.

Total electricity bill = A × maximum demand actually measured + B × number of units consumed.

where, A = charge/maximum demand in ₹/kW actually measured

B = charge/unit in ₹/kWh.

(*vii*) **Power Factor Tariff**—This type of tariff encourages consumers to have higher power factor and penalizes for low power factor.

It consists of two components–a fixed charge based on maximum demand measured in kVA and a running charge.

Total electricity bill = A × maximum demand actually measured in kVA + B × number of units consumed.

where, A = charge/maximum demand in ₹/kVA

B = charge/unit in ₹/kWh.

There is a modified version of this tariff charged to industrial consumers. An average power factor of 0.9 is assumed as reference and a penalty for fall in power factor for each 0.01 unit below the reference power factor is levied. Similarly, a bonus is also given for increase in power factor for each 0.01 unit above the reference power factor.

(*viii*) **Three Part Tariff**—This type of tariff is composed of three components–a fixed charge, a semi fixed charge and a variable charge. Fixed charge recovers cost of supplying electricity to consumer, semi fixed charge is proportional to the maximum demand in kW or kVA and variable charge is proportional to the units consumed.

Total electricity bill = $A + B$ × kW + C × kWh.

where, A = a fixed charge

B = a semi fixed charge in ₹/kW or kVA maximum demand

C = a variable charge in ₹/kWh.

(*ix*) **Off Peak Hour Tariff**—To shift the load from peak hours to off peak hours, this type of tariff charges reduced rate during off peak hours (10 pm to 6 am) and higher rate during peak hours (6 pm to 10 pm). Load may also be restricted to lighting load only. This type of tariff is used for commercial and industrial consumers.

Example 2.12

An industrial consumer has a maximum demand of 50 kW at 0.85 p.f lagging and annual load factor of 60%. Two tariff choices are available to the consumer.

(*i*) ₹ 200 per kVA of MD + ₹ 0.03 per kWh and

(*ii*) ₹ 50 per kVA of MD + ₹ 0.07 per kWh. Determine most economical tariff.

Solution:

$$\text{kW} = \text{kVA} \cos\phi, \qquad \text{kVA} = \frac{\text{kW}}{\cos\phi} = \frac{50}{0.85} = 58.82$$

$$\text{Average power} = \text{Maximum demand} \times \text{load factor}$$

$$= 50 \times 0.6 = 30 \text{ kW}$$

$$\text{Energy consumed/year} = 30 \times 8760 = 2{,}62{,}800 \text{ kWh}$$

Tariff (*i*) Maximum demand charges = ₹ 200/kVA maximum load demand

$$= 200 \times 58.82 = ₹\ 11{,}764$$

$$\text{Energy charges} = 0.03 \times 2{,}62{,}800 = ₹\ 7{,}884$$

$$\therefore \quad \text{Annual charges} = 11{,}764 + 7{,}884 = ₹\ 19{,}648$$

Tariff (*ii*) Maximum demand charges = ₹ 50/kVA = 50 ×58.82

$$= ₹\ 2{,}941$$

$$\text{Energy charges} = 0.07 \times 2{,}62{,}800 = ₹\ 18{,}396$$

$$\therefore \quad \text{Annual charges} = 2{,}941 + 18{,}396 = ₹\ 21{,}337$$

Comparing two tariff, tariff (*i*) is economical.

Example 2.13

A tyre manufacturing unit consumes 40 lakh units/year with a maximum demand of 1 MW at 0.8 p.f. lagging. The maximum demand charges are ₹ 5/kVA, maximum demand and energy charges are ₹ 0.35/kWh. Calculate the annual energy charges. Also, Calculate the reduction in the bill if maximum demand is reduced to 900 kW at 0.9 p.f. lagging.

Solution:

$$\text{Maximum kVA demand} = \frac{1000}{0.8} = 1250$$

$$\text{Annual maximum demand charges} = ₹\ 5 \times 1250 \times 60$$

$$= ₹\ 75{,}000$$

$$\text{Annual energy charges} = ₹\ 0.35 \times 40 \times 10^5 = ₹\ 14 \times 10^5$$

$$\text{Load factor} = \frac{40 \times 10^5}{1000 \times 8760} = 0.4566 \text{ or } 45.66\%$$ **Ans.**

At same load factor, units consumed annually

$$= 8760 \times 900 \times 0.4566 = 3.6 \times 10^6$$

$$\text{Maximum kVA demand} = \frac{900}{0.9} = 1000$$

$$\text{MD charge for 1000 kVA} = ₹\ 60 \times 1000 = ₹\ 60 \times 10^3$$

$$\text{Energy charges} = ₹\ 3.6 \times 10^6 \times 0.35 = ₹\ 1260 \times 10^3$$

$$\text{Annual saving} = 1475 \times 10^3 - 1260 \times 10^3 = ₹\ 155 \times 10^3$$ **Ans.**

Example 2.14

Determine the average unit cost for consuming 500 kWh under block rate tariff.

First 50 units = 4 ₹/unit

Next 50 units = 3.60 ₹/unit

Next 50 unit = 3.00 ₹/unit

Next 50 unit = 2.50 ₹/unit

Remaining units = 2.00 ₹/unit

Solution:

(*a*) Cost of energy for first 50 units = 50 × 4 ₹/unit = ₹ 200

(*b*) Cost of energy for next 50 units = 50 × 3.60 ₹/unit = ₹ 180

(*c*) Cost of energy for next 50 units = 50 × 3.00 ₹/unit = ₹ 150

(*d*) Cost of energy for next 50 units = 50 × 2.50 ₹/unit = ₹ 125

(*e*) Remaining units = 300 × 2 ₹/unit = ₹ 600

$$\text{Total energy cost} = 200 + 180 + 150 + 125 + 600 = ₹\ 1255$$

$$\text{Average unit cost} = \frac{1255}{500 \text{ units}} = 2.51\ ₹/\text{unit}$$ **Ans.**

Example 2.15

Determine the number of units so consumed that two part tariff is equal to flat rate tariff.

(*i*) two part tariff = 1500 ₹/kW maximum demand + 2.00 ₹/unit

(*ii*) flat rate tariff = 3 ₹/ unit

Given: Maximum demand = 15 kW.

Solution:

Assume x units to be consumed so that both tariff are equal

$$\therefore \quad 1500 \times 15 + 2 \times x = 3 \times x$$

$$x = 1500 \times 15 = 22{,}500 \text{ units}$$ **Ans.**

Example 2.16

A commercial consumer has a constant load of 250 kW at 0.8 p.f. lag. The load duration is 10 hours per day for 300 days per year. Calculate energy bill under following tariff schemes—

(*i*) ₹ 1.20 per kWh + ₹ 1200 per kVA per year

(*ii*) ₹ 1.20 per kWh + ₹ 1200 per year + 25 paise per kvarh.

Solution:

$$\text{Given, Maximum demand} = 250 \text{ kW}$$

$$\text{Annual consumption} = \text{constant load} \times \text{hours per day} \times \text{days per annum}$$

$$= 250 \times 10 \times 300 = 7{,}50{,}000 \text{ kWh}$$

$$\text{kVA Maximum demand} = \frac{\text{kW}}{\text{P.f.}} = \frac{250}{0.8} = 312.5$$

$$\text{kvarh per year} = \text{kWh} \times \tan(\cos^{-1} 0.8)$$

$$= 75{,}0000 \times \tan(\cos^{-1} 0.8)$$

$$= 5{,}62{,}500$$

(*i*) Energy bill under tariff scheme (*i*)

$$= 1.20 \times 7{,}50{,}000 + 1200 \times 312.5$$

$$= ₹\ 12.75 \times 10^5$$ **Ans.**

(*ii*) Energy bill under tariff schemes (*ii*)

$$= 1.20 \times 7{,}50{,}000 + 1200 \times 250 + 0.25 \times 5{,}62{,}500$$

$$= 9 \times 10^5 + 3 \times 10^5 + 1.40625 \times 10^5$$

$$= 13.40 \times 10^5$$ **Ans.**

2.6. ECONOMICS OF POWER FACTOR IMPROVEMENT

Power factor is defined as ratio of real power to apparent power.

$$\text{power factor} = \frac{\text{Real power}}{\text{Apparent power}} = \frac{\text{kW}}{\text{kVA}}$$

$$(\text{kVA})^2 = (\text{kW})^2 + (\text{kvar})^2 \qquad \text{...(2.14)}$$

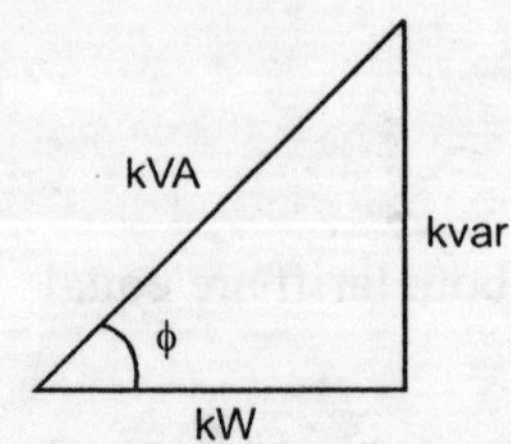

Figure 2.8. Power triangle

In ac circuits, power factor comes into picture due to phase difference between circuit current and applied voltage. If the current lags behind the applied voltage, the power factor is lagging. If current and voltage both are in phase with each other, the power factor is unity. If current leads the applied voltage, power factor is leading.

2.6.1. Sources of Low Power Factor

Low power factor results due to absorption of reactive power by various equipments. Following equipments contribute to low power factor—

(*i*) All induction motors and transformers operate at low lagging power factor.

(*ii*) All induction, arc and resistance furnaces operate at low lagging power factor.

(*iii*) All discharge lamps, such as high pressure mercury vapour lamp, high pressure sodium vapour lamp, low pressure sodium vapour lamp, neon lamp, fluorescent lamp, arc lamp etc. operate at low lagging power factor.

(*iv*) Arc welding and resistance welding equipments operate at low lagging power factor.

(*v*) All thyristor controlled devices operate at low lagging power factor (also generate harmonics).

2.6.2. Disadvantages of Low Power Factor

Power supplied to a 3 phase system is given by-

$$P = \sqrt{3}\, V_L I_L \cos\phi. \qquad ...(2.15)$$

where,

V_L = line voltage

I_L = line current

If a given amount of power is to be supplied at a given voltage then

$$I_L \cos\phi = \text{constant}$$

or

$$\cos\phi \propto \frac{1}{I_L} \qquad ...(2.16)$$

i.e. power factor ($\cos\phi$) is inversely proportional to the line current. Hence, lower the power factor, higher is the current drawn from supply. Hence, a higher value of current causes—

(*i*) more *IR* or voltage drop in supply line.

(*ii*) more I^2R losses in transmission lines, bus bars, switchgears, generators, motors and transformers leading to higher losses and higher temperature rise.

(*iii*) for same power to be delivered at rated voltage, conductor size need to be increased resulting in higher cost, size and weight of equipment.

(*iv*) poor power factor increases the electricity bill due to low power factor penalty for industrial consumers.

(*v*) higher I^2R losses cause reduction in overload carrying capacity of machines and also affects life of insulation.

Hence, low power factor leads to several disadvantages.

2.6.3. Methods of Power Factor Improvement

Various methods of power factor improvement are given below—

(*i*) **Reducing the amount of reactive power drawn from line**—This is done by avoiding operation of induction motors and transformers at no-load or reduced load. By correcting available supply voltage.

(*ii*) **Using static capacitors**

Capacitors are connected in parallel across the load to increase the power factor. Capacitor draws a leading current from the supply which tends to neutralize the lagging component of current drawn by the load. In a three phase system, capacitors are either connected in star or in delta.

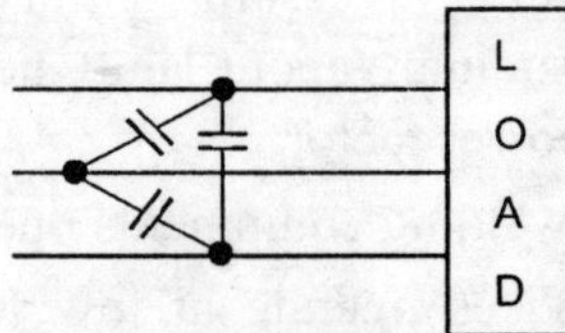

Figure 2.9. Delta connected capacitors

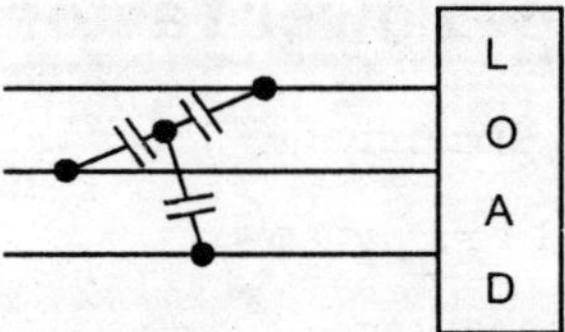

Figure 2.10. Star connected capacitors

The value of capacitor to be connected can be calculated.

The active component of current remains constant.

Hence, $$I_a = I\cos\phi_1 \quad ...(2.17)$$

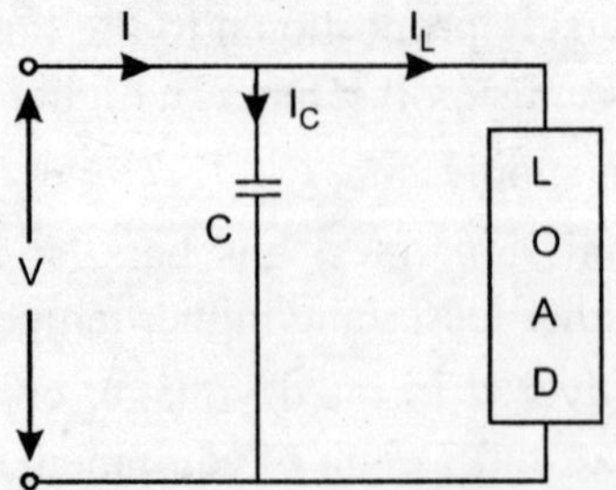

Figure 2.11. Calculation of value of capacitance across load

Now, quadrature component of load current without capacitor

$$= I_a \tan\phi_1 \quad ...(2.18)$$

Quadrature component of load current with capacitor

$$= I_a \tan \phi_2 \quad \text{...(2.19)}$$

Current drawn by capacitor

$$I_c = I_a (\tan \phi_1 - \tan \phi_2) \quad \text{...(2.20)}$$

Applied voltage $V = I_c X_c = I_c \dfrac{1}{2\pi fc}$ ...(2.21)

Hence, capacitance required

$$C = \frac{I_c}{2\pi fV} \quad \text{...(2.22)}$$

***(iii)* Using Synchronous Condenser**

It is a synchronous motor running at leading excitation thereby drawing leading VARs (volt ampere reactive power) which neutralises lagging VARs in the line. Hence, power factor of the system is improved.

***(iv)* Phase Advancers**

It is an induction motor equipped with a.c. excitor that supplies exciting current to rotor at slip frequency. Excitor and motor are mounted on same shaft. Purpose of this excitor is to supply excitation current to machine so that angle between line voltage and excitation current is small or power factor is high.

2.6.4. Most Economical Power Factor

An economical power factor is one which provides maximum annual savings.

Let P = kW demand of consumer

$\cos \phi_1$ = initial power factor

$\cos \phi_2$ = desired power factor

Q = reactive power

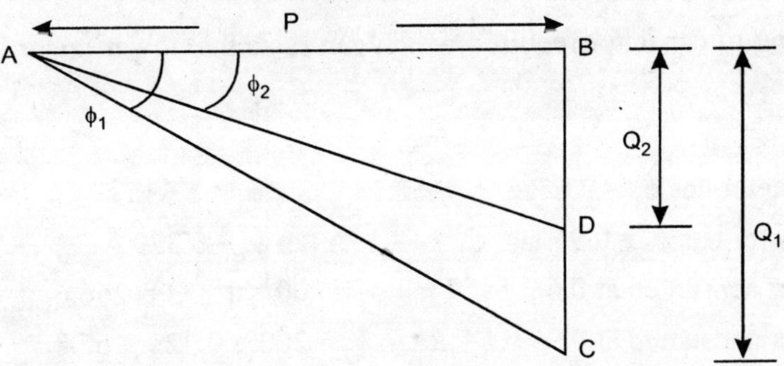

Figure 2.12. Power factor improvement

Initial reactive power demand $BC = P \tan \phi_1$ ...(2.23)

Initial kVA demand $AC = \dfrac{P}{\cos \phi_1}$ ...(2.24)

If power factor is raised to $\cos \phi_2$, new kVA demand

$$AD = \frac{P}{\cos \phi_2} \quad (2.24)$$

$$\text{Saving in kVA demand} = AD - AC$$

$$= \frac{P}{\cos \phi_1} - \frac{P}{\cos \phi_2} \quad ...(2.25)$$

Let ₹ x be the annual cost per kVA maximum demand.

$$\therefore \text{ Annual saving in maximum demand} = x\left[\frac{P}{\cos \phi_1} - \frac{P}{\cos \phi_2}\right] \quad ...(2.26)$$

kvar neutralised by p.f. correction equipment $= BD = BC - CD = P \tan \phi_1 - P \tan\phi_2$ ...(2.27)

Let ₹ y be annual cost of power factor correction equipment per kvar.

∴ Annual charges towards power factor correction equipment

$$= y(P \tan \phi_1 - P \tan \phi_2) \quad ...(2.28)$$

$$\therefore \text{ Annual saving} \quad S = x\left[\frac{P}{\cos \phi_1} - \frac{P}{\cos \phi_2}\right] - y(P \tan \phi_1 - P \tan \phi_2) \quad ...(2.29)$$

For, maximum saving differentiating annual saving S w.r. to ϕ_2

$$\therefore \quad \frac{dS}{d\phi_2} = -x P \sec \phi_2 \tan \phi_2 + y P \sec^2 \phi_2 = 0$$

or $$-x \tan \phi_2 = y \sec \phi_2$$

or $$\sin \phi_2 = \frac{y}{x} \quad ...(2.30)$$

$$\therefore \quad \sin\phi_2 = \frac{y}{x} = \frac{\text{Annual cost of power factor correction eqmt/kvar}}{\text{Annual tariff per kVA maximum demand}}$$

$$\therefore \text{ Most economical power factor } \cos \phi_2 = \sqrt{1-(\sin \phi_2)^2} = \sqrt{1-\left(\frac{y}{x}\right)^2} \quad ...(2.31)$$

Example 2.16.

Determine the rating of capacitor required which can raise the power factor of 200 kW load from 0.6 lag to 0.95 lag.

Solution:

Initial power factor $\cos \phi_1 = 0.6$ lag, $\phi_1 = 53.13°$, $\tan \phi_1 = 1.333$

Final power factor $\cos \phi_2 = 0.95$ lag, $\phi_2 = 18.19°$, $\tan \phi_2 = 0.329$

Reactive power consumed at 0.6 p.f $= P \tan \phi_1 = 200 \times 1.333 = 266.6$

Reactive power consumed at 0.95 p.f $= P \tan \phi_2 = 200 \times 0.329 = 65.8$

Net reactive kVAr supplied by capacitor = 266.6 – 65.8 = 200.8 kvar

Example 2.17.

A 200 kW load with a p.f of 0.8 lag is operating in parallel with a synchronous motor consuming 50kW. The excitation of the motor is so adjusted that overall p.f. is 0.9 lag. Calculate the p.f of synchronous motor.

Solution:

load, $P_1 = 200$ kW, $\cos\phi_1 = 0.8$ lag

Synchronous motor load, $P_2 = 50$ kW, $\cos\phi_2 = ?$

Overall p.f., $\cos\phi = 0.9$ lag.

Reactive power drawn by load $Q_1 = P_1 \tan\phi_1 = 200 \times 0.75 = 150$ kvar.

Overall reactive power $Q = (P_1 + P_2)\tan\phi$

$= (200 + 50) \times 0.4843 = 121.1$ kvar

Reactive power supplied by synchronous motor $Q = 121.1 - 150$

$= 28.9$ kvar

Apparent power of synchronous motor, $S = \sqrt{Q^2 + P_2^2}$

$= \sqrt{(121.1)^2 + (50)^2}$

$= 57.7$ kVA

Power factor at which synchronous motor is working ($\cos\phi$)

$= \frac{P_2}{S} = \frac{50}{57.7} = 0.866$ lead **Ans.**

Example 2.18.

A tyre manufacturing plant has an average demand of 100 kW and an annual load factor of 0.6. The existing power factor is 0.75 lag. The electricity is supplied at a tariff of ₹ 100/kVA maximum demand per year plus ₹ 0.05 per kWh. It is decided to use capacitors for p.f. correction at ₹ 60/kvar. Calculate the p.f at which maximum saving will take place. Also, Calculate the saving.

Solution:

Maximum demand charges, x = ₹ 100/kVA/year

Cost of Capacitors, y = ₹ 60/kvar/year

Most economical p.f. $= \sqrt{1-\left(\frac{y}{x}\right)^2} = \sqrt{1-\left(\frac{60}{100}\right)^2} = 0.8$ lag.

Maximum kW demand $= \frac{100}{0.6} = 166.67$ kW

Maximum kVA demand at 0.75 P.f $= \frac{100}{0.75} = 133.33$ kVA

Maximum kVA demand at 0.8 p.f $= \frac{100}{0.8} = 125$ kVA

Annual saving = (133.33 – 125) × 100 = ₹ 833 **Ans.**

Example 2.19

Determine the rating of a capacitor required to increase power factor of an induction motor to 0.85 lag from 0.65 lag running at a load of 4 kW, 50 Hz and 230V.

Solution:

Given, $\cos\phi_1 = 0.65, \cos\phi_2 = 0.85, P = 4$ kW

Reactive power of motor at inital p.f. = $P \tan\phi_1$

$$Q_1 = 4 \times \tan(\cos^{-1} 0.65) = 4.676 \text{ kvar}$$

Reactive power of motor at final p.f. = $P \tan\phi_2$

$$Q_2 = 4 \times \tan(\cos^{-1} 0.85) = 2.479 \text{ kvar}$$

∴ Reactive power supplied by capacitor $Q_c = 4.676 - 2.479$

Power drawn from mains = $VI_c = V \cdot \frac{V}{X_c} = V \cdot \frac{V}{\frac{1}{2\pi fc}}$

$$Q_c = 2\pi fcV^2$$

$$\therefore \quad Q_c = 2\pi fcV^2 = 2197$$

$$C = \frac{2197}{2\pi \times 50 \times (230)^2} = 132.2\mu\text{f}$$ **Ans.**

Example 2.20

A power plant supplies to (*i*) a heater load of 200kW, (*ii*) An induction motor of 200 hp, 0.7 p.f. lag and 80% efficiency (*iii*) a synchronous motor of 100 hp, 90% efficiency. How much should be the p.f. of synchronous motor so that overall p.f. is unity.

Solution:

(*i*) Heater load, $P_1 = 200$ kW, $\cos\phi_1 = 1$

(*ii*) Induction motor, $P_2 = \frac{200 \times 735.5}{0.8} = 183.875$ kW

$$\cos\phi_2 = 0.7, \tan\phi_2 = 1.0202$$

Reactive power, $Q_2 = P_2 \tan\phi_2 = 183.875 \times 1.0202$

$$= 187.59 \text{ kvar}$$

(*iii*) Synchronous motor, $P_3 = \frac{100 \times 735.5}{0.9} = 81.72$ kW

Total active power $P = P_1 + P_2 + P_3 = 200 + 183.875 + 81.72$

$$P = 465.59 \text{ kW}$$

Overall power factor required is unity and hence overall reactive power is zero.

$$\therefore \quad 0 = Q_1 + Q_2 + Q_3$$

Reactive power of Synchronous motor

$$Q_3 = 0 - Q_1 - Q_2$$

$$= 0 - 0 - 187.59 = -187.59 \text{ kvar}$$

Apparent power of synchronous motor

$$S = \sqrt{P_3^2 + Q_3^2}$$

$$= \sqrt{(81.72)^2 + (187.59)^2}$$

$$S = 204.62 \text{ kVA}$$

Power factor of synchronous motor $\cos\phi_3 = \frac{P_3}{S_3} = \frac{81.72}{204.62} = 0.3994$ lead **Ans.**

Example 2.21

A power plant supplies power to consumers at a tariff of ₹ 100 kVA maximum demand + ₹ 0.05 per kWh. A consumer wishes to increase the power factor with the help of phase advancing unit costing ₹ 45 per kvar. The interest and depreciation may be taken as 10% Determine most economical power factor of consumer.

Solution:

Annual cost per kvar of phase advancing unit $= \frac{45}{10} =$ ₹ 4.50

For most economical power factor,

$$\sin\phi = \frac{y}{x}$$

where, x = annual tariff/kvar

y = annual cost of phase advancing unit/kvar

$$\therefore \quad \text{Sin}\,\phi = \frac{y}{x} = \frac{4.5}{100} = 0.045$$

Or $\phi = \sin^{-1}(0.045) = 2°35'$

∴ Most economical power factor, cos ϕ,

$$= \cos 2°35'$$

$$= 0.999 \text{ lag}$$ **Ans.**

Example 2.22

Determine tine most economical power factor when tariff is ₹ 90 per kVA maximum demand plus a flat rate per kwh. Cost of phase advancing unit is ₹ 70/kVA. Assume depreciation and interest rate at 10%.

Solution:

Annual cost of phase advancing unit $(y) = 70 \times \frac{10}{100}$

= ₹ 7/kVA

Annual tariff per kAV (x) = ₹ 90/kVA

$$\therefore \quad \text{Most economical p.f.} = \sqrt{1-\left(\frac{y}{x}\right)^2} = \sqrt{1-\left(\frac{7}{90}\right)^2}$$

$$= 0.996 \text{ lag}$$ **Ans.**

2.7. DETERMINATION OF UNIT SIZE AND RATING OF GENERATORS

Following are the factors which need to be considered for selecting unit size and rating of generators in a power station—

(*i*) The combined capacity of all generators must be able to meet the peak demand of the station.

(*ii*) The number and sizes of units should be so selected that they approximately fit the annual load curve of the station.

(*iii*) The size of the unit selected should be such that it should work at near full load.

(*iv*) To meet future load requirement, the plant capacity should be 15-20% more than expected maximum demand.

(*v*) Additional units as reserve capacity should be maintained so as to take care of breakdown or scheduled maintenance.

(*vi*) Unit with equal capacity and same make be selected so that spare parts can be interchanged and maintenance is easier. This will reduce spare parts inventory.

2.8. LOAD SHARING BETWEEN BASE LOAD AND PEAK LOAD PLANTS

Base load plants run continuously near or at full capacity. These plants supply power at low running cost and high capital cost. While peak load plants are run for few hours in a year and work at low load. These plants supply power at high running cost and low capital cost. Peak load plants should be able to start quickly and able to follow load variations. Example of base load plants are nuclear power plant, hydro plant and thermal plant. While peak load plants are gas turbine power plant, diesel power plant etc.

It is desired to have economic operational mix of base load and peak load power plant.

Let operating cost of base load plant = ₹$(a_1\text{kW} + b_1\text{kWh})$

Operating cost of peak load plant = ₹$(a_2\text{kW} + b_2\text{kWh})$

P = Maximum demand on power plant.

x = Total number of units generated.

P_1 = Maximum demand on base load plant.

x_1 = No. of units generated by base load plant.

$P_2 = P - P_1$ = Maximum demand on peak load plant.

$x_2 = x - x_1$ = No. of units generated by peak load plant.

Total annual cost of operation of power plant

$$C = a_1P_1 + a_2(P - P_1) + b_1x_1 + b_2(x - x_1) \quad ...(2.33)$$

$$= P_1(a_1 - a_2) + a_2P + x_1(b_1 - b_2) + b_2x \quad ...(2.34)$$

For minimum cost $\dfrac{dC}{dP_1} = 0$

$$0 = \frac{dC}{dP_1} = (a_1 - a_2) + \frac{dx_1}{dP_1}(b_1 - b_2) \qquad (2.35)$$

or

$$\frac{dx_1}{dP_1} = \frac{(a_1 - a_2)}{(b_2 - b_1)} \qquad (2.36)$$

For economical load sharing, peak load power plant need to operate for $\frac{(a_1 - a_2)}{(b_2 - b_1)}$ hours/year.

Example 2.23

Two power stations A and B have following annual tariff—

$$\text{Station } A = ₹\ 75{,}000 + ₹\ 80 \text{ kW} + ₹\ 0.02 \text{ kWh}$$

$$\text{Station } B = ₹\ 50{,}000 + ₹\ 50 \text{ kW} + ₹\ 0.03 \text{ kWh}$$

Calculate installed capacity of each station. Also, calculate hours per year of peak load station so as to give minimum generated cost per unit.

Solution:

From tariff, it is seen that station A has lower running cost. Hence, station A should be used as base load station and station B as peak load station.

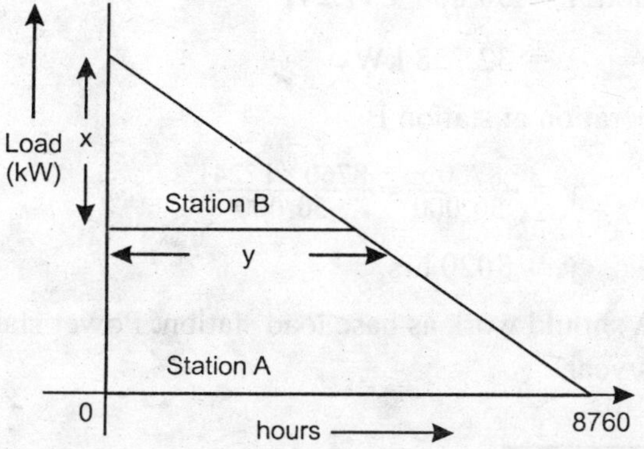

Figure 2.13. Load Sharing

Assume $\qquad x$ = installed capacity of station B in kW

$\qquad y$ = hours of operation of station B

$\therefore$ Installed capacity of station $A = (50000 - x)$

Units generated/ year at station B

$$= \text{Area under the curve}$$

$$= \frac{1}{2}xy$$

$$= \frac{1}{2} \times x \times \frac{8760\,x}{50000}$$

$$= 0.0876\,x^2$$

Units generated/year at station $A = \frac{1}{2} \times 50000 \times 8760 - 0.0876\,x^2$

$$= 219 \times 10^6 - 0.0876\,x^2$$

Annual cost of station $B = 50000 + 50x + 0.03 \times 0.0876\,x^2$

Annual cost of station $A = 70000 + 80\,(50000 - x) + 0.02(219 \times 10^6 - 0.0876\,x^2)$

$$= 8.455 \times 10^6 - 80x - 0.00175\,x^2$$

∴ Annual cost of station A & B

$$C = (50000 + 50\,x + 0.00262\,x^2) + (8.455 \times 10^6 - 80x - 0.00175x^2)$$

$$C = 85{,}05{,}000 - 30x + 0.0087\,x^2$$

For minimum operating cost, $\frac{dC}{dx} = 0$

$$\therefore \quad \frac{dC}{dx} = 0 - 30 + 2 \times 0.0087\,x = 0$$

$$x = 17{,}241 \text{ kW}$$

∴ Capacity of station B = 17,241 kW **Ans.**

Capacity of station A = 50,000 – 17,241

= 32,758 kW **Ans.**

Number of hours of operation at station B

$$y = \frac{8760\,x}{50{,}000} = \frac{8760 \times 17241}{50{,}000}$$

y = 3020 hrs. **Ans.**

Hence, power station A should work as base load station. Power station B should work as peak load station for 3020 hours/year.

2.9. LOAD FORECASTING

It is the process of estimation of future load demand on a power station. The installed capacity of new power station is decided based on this forecast. It is done for short term and long term.

Short term forecast is used for day to day operation of power plant. It requires atleast a day in advance so as to schedule the generation i.e. depending upon load expected, a generation schedule is prepared which tells us which generator will have how much load. It is derived from daily/ weekly trends, weather fluctuations, social events (festival season, marriage season) etc. A statistical method is used for forecasting.

Long term forecasting is used to plan for expansion of generating capacity. Historical data provides a basis for growth trend when extrapolated. It essentially involves curve fitting technique. Once the type of curve is known, forecast can be made at desired future points. The curves could be straight line, parabola, exponential, gompertz or a combination.

Another forecast method uses co-relation technique which tries to relate population, employment, industrial licenses, weather data etc. to forecast load.

2.10. COST OF SETTING UP OF A POWER PLANT

Type of power plant to be constructed depends upon cost of fuel to be used, availability of fuel, cost of maintenance, labour cost etc. Thereafter, plant location is decided. Choice of location of plant is decided by availability of load, geological condition of soil, availability of water, availability of fuel, distance from load centre, availability of transportation facility, availability of skilled manpower etc.

The cost of power plant depends upon two parameters viz capital or initial cost and operation or running cost. Capital cost consists of following heads-

(*i*) Cost of land.

(*ii*) Cost of construction(building, foundation for machinery, roads etc.).

(*iii*) Cost of machinery (turbine, generator, boiler,engine, heat exchanger, cooling tower, chimney and other auxiliaries).

(*iv*) Errection and commissioning cost of plant and machinery.

(*v*) Overhead charges.

(*vi*) Interest paid on borrowed capital.

The operation or running cost consists of following heads-

(*i*) Fuel cost (including transportation).

(*ii*) Labour cost.

(*iii*) Maintenance cost.

(*iv*) Taxes and duties.

(*v*) Depreciation cost.

(*vi*) Salaries of operational staff.

Hence, cost of power plant is sum of capital cost and operation cost.

CHAPTER SUMMARY

Cost of power generation consists of fixed cost, semi fixed cost and variable or running cost. Tariff is decided by factoring these three types of cost.

Depreciation is the gradual loss of net worth of an asset over a period of time due to several factors, such as wear & tear, technical obsolescence, functional obsolescence etc. There are three main methods of determination of depreciation of plant and machinery viz straight line method, diminishing value method and sinking fund method.

plan is to obtain fair return on investment keeping social welfare in mind as it is basic necessity. Different types of tariff plans are devised for different category of consumers viz agricultural, domestic, commercial and industrial. Low tariff of agricultural and domestic consumers is cross-subsidised by commercial and industrial consumers.

Power factor correction is one of the major objectives of economic operation of power system. Power factor improvement is carried out using static capacitors and synchronous condensers. However, static capacitors are preferred due to low capital cost and zero maintenance cost.

Economic operation of power plants is greatly influenced by fuel cost. So, power plants are so loaded that base load plant shares the maximum stable load while the short time peak load is shared by peak load plants.

FORMULAE.

1. Annual depreciation by

(*a*) straight line method $= \dfrac{[\text{Capital cost} - \text{salvage value}]}{\text{useful economic life}}$

(*b*) diminishing value method $= 1 - \left(\dfrac{\text{Salvage value}}{\text{Capital cost}}\right)^{\frac{1}{\text{useful life}}}$

(*c*) by sinking fund method $= \dfrac{[(\text{Captial cost} - \text{Salvage}) \times \text{rate of interest}]}{[(1 + \text{rate of interest})^{\text{useful life}} - 1]}$

2. Most economical power factor $= \sqrt{1 - \left(\dfrac{\text{annual cost of p.f. correction eqmt per kvar}}{\text{annual tariff per kVA maximum demand}}\right)}$

REVIEW QUESTIONS

Q. 1. Classify cost of power generation.

Q. 2. What is depreciation?. What are the methods of calculation of depreciation?

Q. 3. Define tariff. What are the objectives of tariff?.

Q. 4. Discuss desirable characteristics of tariff.

Q. 5. Explain different types of tariff with suitable example.

Q. 6. Define power factor. What are the disadvantages of low power factor?.

Q. 7. Discuss various sources of low power factor and methods of power factor improvement.

Q. 8. With a suitable phaser diagram show how low power factor is improved using static capacitors.

Q. 9. Derive the expression for most economical power factor.

Q. 10. How the unit sizes and ratings of generators are decided in a power station?.

Q. 11. How the load be shared between a base load and a peak load power plant so that cost of operation is minimum?

Q. 12. Write a brief note on distributed power generation.

Q. 13. What are the advantages and disadvantages of distributed power generation?

Q. 14. Explain the term load forecasting.

Q. 15. Discuss various types of costs involved in setting up of a power plant.

Numerical Questions

Q. 1. The connected load of a power plant is 60 MW and maximum demand is 40 MW. A total of 74×10^6 units are produced in a year. Determine (*i*) demand factor (*ii*) load factor.

[Ans: (*i*) 0.66, (*ii*) 0.211]

Q. 2. A thermal power plant supplies four different loads having peak demand of 650 kW, 800 kW, 1100 kW and 3200 kW. The diversity factor of load at plant is 1.2 and annual load factor is 50%. Determine (*i*) maximum demand on station, (*ii*) annual energy supplied.

[Ans: (*i*) 4791.67 kW, (*ii*) 209.875×10^5 kWh]

Q. 3. A power plant has four units of sizes 25 MW, 7MW,10 MW and 5 MW.

The annual load duration curve can be assumed to be a straight line from 4 MW to 20 MW. Calculate (*i*) installed capacity (*ii*) plant factor (*iii*) annual units generated (*iv*) load factor and (*v*) utilisation factor.

[Ans: (*i*) 47 MW, (*ii*) 25.5%, (*iii*) 105.12×10^3 kWh, (*iv*) 48%, (*v*) 42.55%]

Q. 4. Determine the thermal efficiency of a coal fired power plant,

Given: load factor = 40%, boiler efficiency = 82%, turbine efficiency = 88%, maximum demand = 25 MW, coal consumption = 0.912 kg/unit, price of coal = ₹ 35/tonne.

[Ans: 72.16%, ₹ 27,96,192]

Also calculate cost of annual coal consumption.

Q. 5. A 1500 kVA distribution transformer costs ₹ 56,000. At the end of 25 years of useful life, the salvage value is ₹ 5000. Calculate depreciated value of transformer at the end of 12.5 years by

(*i*) straight line depreciation method.

(*ii*) sinking fund method with 9% annual rate of interest.

[Ans: (*i*) ₹ 30,500, (*ii*) ₹ 43044.39]

Q. 6. Capital cost of an air pre heater is ₹ 25000 with a life span of 15 years. It is purchased on annual instalment of ₹ 900 at 6% rate of interest. Calculate salvage value of air pre-heater after 15 year using sinking fund method.

[Ans: ₹ 4051.627]

Q. 7. Calculate the number of units so consumed that two part tariff is equal to flat rate tariff.

(*i*) two part tariff = 2100 ₹/kW maximum demand + 3.50 ₹/unit.

(*ii*) flat rate tariff = ₹ 4.30/unit.

Given: maximum demand = 20 kW

[Ans: 52500 units]

Q. 8. An industrial consumer has a maximum demand of 72 kW at 0.90 power factor lagging and an annual load factor of 70%. Two different tariff are available. (*i*) ₹ 220 per kVA of MD + ₹ 0.03 kWh and (*ii*) ₹ 50 per kVA of MD + ₹ 0.07 per kWh. Determine most economical tariff.

[Ans: Tariff (*i*) is economical (*i*) ₹ 30,845, (*ii*) ₹ 34,905]

Q. 9. A picture tube manufacturing plant has an average demand of 200 kW and an annual load factor of 0.7. The existing power factor is 0.8 lag. The electricity is supplied at a tariff of ₹ 250 per kVA maximum demand per year plus ₹ 6 per kWh. It is decided to use p.f. correction capacitors at ₹ 80/kvar. Find p.f. at which maximum saving will take place and actual saving. **[Ans:** (*i*) 0.82, (*ii*) ₹ 357.143]

Q. 10. Calculate the most economical power factor when tariff is 80 ₹/kVA maximum demand+ a flat rate per kWh. Cost of static capacitor unit is ₹ 60 per kVA. Depreciation and interest rate may be assumed to be 11%. **[Ans:** 0.996 lag]

SHORT ANSWER TYPE QUESTIONS

Q. 1. Differentiate between hot reserve and spinning reserve.

Q. 2. Define

(*i*) connected load (*ii*) demand factor

(*iii*) load factor (*iv*) diversity factor.

Q. 3. What is the difference between load curve and load duration curve.

Q. 4. Differentiate between semi fixed cost and fixed cost.

Q. 5. Write three desirable characteristics of a tariff plan.

Q. 6. Why leading power factor is not desirable?.

Q. 7. State three desirable characteristic of distributed power generation.

Q. 8. State three advantages of using static capacitors over synchronous condenser for power factor correction.

Multiple Choice Questions

Q. 1. If the operating cost of a power plant is low then it is

(*a*) peak load plant (*b*) base load plant

(*c*) both (*a*) & (*b*) (*d*) none of these.

Q. 2. If the maximum demand is high then load factor.

(*a*) remains same (*b*) increases

(*c*) decreases.

Q. 3. Diversity factor is

(*a*) equal to unity

(*b*) less than unity

(*c*) more than unity.

Q. 4. Interest paid on capital is considered as

(*a*) running cost (*b*) semi fixed cost

(*c*) fixed cost (*d*) none of these.

Q. 5. Which method does not consider interest earned on capital?

(*a*) straight line method (*b*) diminishing value method

(*c*) sinking fund method

Q. 6. Power factor can be improved by

(*a*) reducing active power (*b*) reducing reactive power

(*c*) both (*a*) & (*b*)

Q. 7. A capacitor

(*a*) supplies reactive power (*b*) absorbs reactive power

(*c*) does both

Answer to MCQ

1. (*b*)	**2.** (*c*)	**3.** (*c*)	**4.** (*c*)	**5.** (*a*)
6. (*b*)	**7.** (*a*)			

THERMAL POWER GENERATION

Learning Objectives

After reading this chapter, reader will be able to

- Understand operation of boiler, steam turbine and alternator.
- Understand process of electricity generation from coal.
- Understand details of fuel circuit, water circuit, flue gas circuit and ash circuit.
- Update on latest technologies viz super critical boilers, fluidised bed circulating boilers, integrated gasification combined cycle and coal bed methane.

" The only source of knowledge is experience"
— Albert Einstein

3.1. INTRODUCTION

In India, 60% of the total power generation is from thermal or steam power plants. This is due to the fact that India has large reserves of coal & lignite. Also, among all fossil fuel find sources of power generation, cost/unit of thermal power plant is lowest. Hence, it will remain a dominant source of power generation in future too.

A thermal power plant converts chemical energy of coal into electrical energy. Coal is burnt in a boiler to raise steam at high pressure and temperature. This high pressure and temperature steam causes steam turbine to rotate. An alternator or electrical generator is coupled to the turbine. The turbine drives the alternator causing it to produce electrical power.

Steam turbine is used to produce power in central utilities. It is also used in captive power plants in industry such as chemical, cement, fertiliser, refinery, petrochemical, paper mills, sugar mills, textiles mills, breweries etc. The steam turbine used in central utilities is of condensing type i.e. the steam enters turbine in gaseous form but leaves in liquid form. In captive power plant, non-condensing type of steam turbines are used. In this case, the steam leaves turbine in gaseous form at reduced temperature and pressure. This exhaust steam is used for process heating. Non-Condensing steam turbine is also called back pressure turbine.

3.2. ADVANTAGES AND DISADVANTAGES OF THERMAL POWER PLANT

Thermal power plant has following advantages & disadvantages—

Advantages—

(*i*) fuel cost of thermal power plant is relatively low.

(*ii*) cost of generated power is lesser than gas and diesel based generation.

(*iii*) low capital cost compared to hydro & nuclear power plants.

(*iv*) it can be installed near load centre as coal can be transported by train and road.

(*v*) less space required compared to hydro power plant.

(*vi*) can respond to changing load.

(*vii*) part of steam generated can be used for process in textile, paper, sugar , fertiliser plants etc.

(*viii*) can work under overload continuously.

(*ix*) heat production system is simple as compared to other systems.

Disadvantages—

(*i*) high pollution releasing soot, smoke and greenhouse gases.

(*ii*) requires long time to start (60 – 600 minutes).

(*iii*) requires large amount of water.

(*iv*) requires large space compared to diesel & gas based plants.

(*v*) it requires long time for construction (42 – 48 months).

(*vi*) auxiliary power consumption is quite high (8 – 10%) compared to gas & diesel based power plants.

(*vii*) low efficiency (24 – 30%).

(*ix*) poor part load efficiency.

(*x*) more manpower required compared hydro, diesel & gas based plants.

(*xi*) handling of coal and disposal of ash is quite difficult.

3.3. CHOICE OF SITE FOR THERMAL POWER PLANT

Following factors are considered for choice of a site for thermal power plant—

(*i*) **Close to load centre**—Power plants should be closer to the load centre to minimize the transmission & distribution losses & cost of laying lines.

(*ii*) **Availability of water**—Since the plant requires large amount of water, such plants should be located near river or canal.

(*iii*) **Requirement of land**—Large amount of land is required to house power plant, staff colony, ash disposal area etc. Hence, sufficient land should be available at reasonable price with provision for future expansion. The soil should have good bearing capacity to allow the installation of heavy plant & machinery.

(*iv*) **Availability of coal**—Plant should be located near to coal mine so that cost of transportation of coal is minimum.

(*v*) **Availability of transportation facility**—Plant should be located near rail, road or rivers or sea so as to allow easy transportation of coal, machinery & other materials.

(*vi*) **Sufficient area for ash disposal**—A thermal power plant generates large amount of ash. Hence, sufficient land must be available for its disposal.

(*vii*) **Away from populated area**—Due to generation of fumes, gases, noise and flyash etc., the plant should be located away from the populated area.

3.4. INPUT-OUTPUT, HEAT RATE AND INCREMENTAL COST CURVES

Input-output curve is a graph between power output in MW and fuel input in kcal/hour. It is actually a non-linear graph but for simplicity it is shown as linear in fig. 3.1.

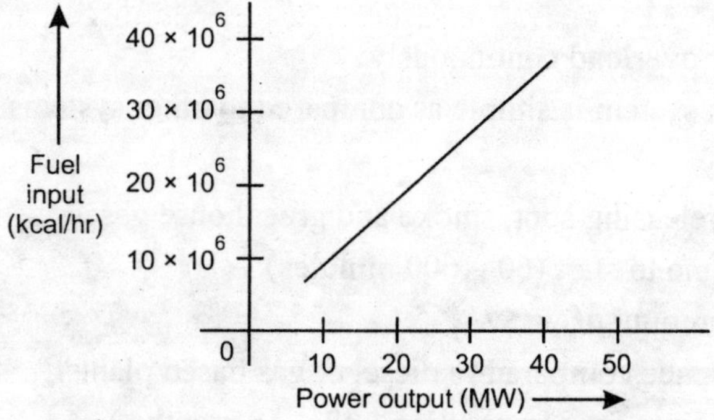

Figure 3.1. Input-Output Curve of thermal power plant

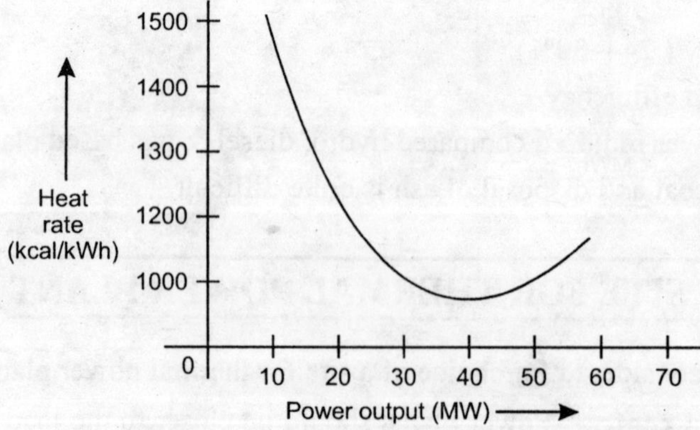

Figure 3.2. Heat rate curve of thermal power plant

(*a*) Heat rate is defined as the ratio of input heat energy to the corresponding output.

$$\therefore \qquad \text{Heat rate} = \frac{\text{Input heat energy}}{\text{Output}}$$

It is the input heat energy required to produce required output. So, for example, to produce 80 MW, how much heat input will be required?

(*b*) Reciprocal of heat rate is called efficiency (overall).

$$\text{Thermal efficiency} = \frac{\text{Mechanical energy produced by turbine}}{\text{Heat energy produced by consumption of coal}}$$

$$\text{Overall efficiency} = \frac{\text{Electrical energy output}}{\text{Heat energy input}}$$

$$= \text{Efficiency of boiler} \times \text{efficiency of turbine} \times \text{efficiency of generator}$$

$$\eta_{overall} = \eta_{boiler} \times \eta_{turbine} \times \eta_{generator}$$

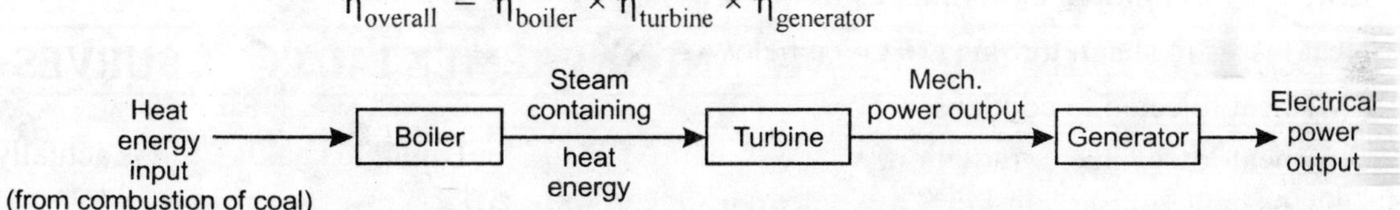

Figure 3.3. Overall efficiency of thermal power plant

Thermal power plant has low efficiency due to heat losses at condenser and stack (chimney).

$$\text{Incremental fuel cost} = \frac{\Delta\, input}{\Delta output}$$

Fuel cost consists of cost of fuel and cost of various consumable, such as lubricants, water, water treatment chemicals, wages etc.

However, it is difficult to calculate the incremental cost of these consumables and so only fuel cost is considered. Incremental fuel cost curve is shown in fig. 3.4

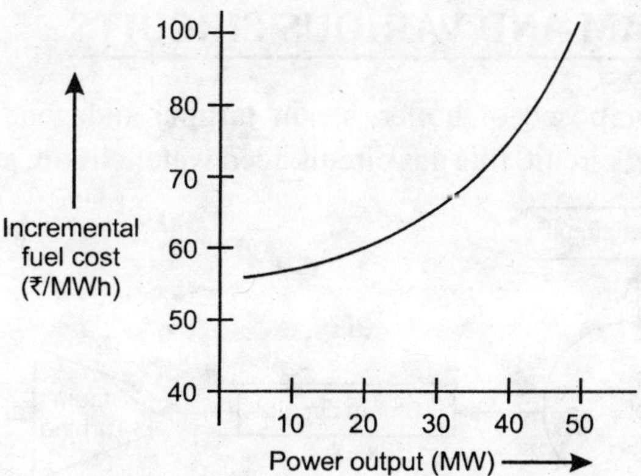

Figure 3.4. Incremental fuel cost curve

Incremental fuel cost helps to decide which generator to load first. The generator having least incremental fuel cost is loaded first.

3.5. LOSSES IN A THERMAL POWER PLANT

A thermal power plant is composed of three vital components viz boiler, steam turbine and generator.

The various losses taking place in a boiler are given below—

(*a*) flue gas losses (heat carried away by gases escaping through chimney).

(*b*) heat loss due to ash and unburnt carbon.

(*c*) heat loss from boiler due to radiation & leakages.

(*d*) heat loss due to moisture in fuel.

(*e*) unknown losses.

Efficiency of modern boiler ranges from 76-84%.

Heat losses in steam turbine are given below—

(*a*) heat rejected to condenser.

(*b*) heat losses due to radiation.

(*c*) friction losses.

Heat losses in electrical generator are described below—

(*a*) copper or I^2R losses in stator and rotor.

(*b*) iron losses in stator.

(*c*) friction and windage loss.

(*d*) stray loss.

Efficiency of generator ranges from 86 - 92%. The overall thermal power plant efficiency is about 28%. This is due to large heat loss in condenser.

3.6. BLOCK DIAGRAM AND VARIOUS CIRCUITS

Thermal power plant is composed of boiler, steam turbine and generator. The boiler has coal handing circuit, ash handling circuit, flue gas circuit, feed water circuit, steam circuit and air circuit.

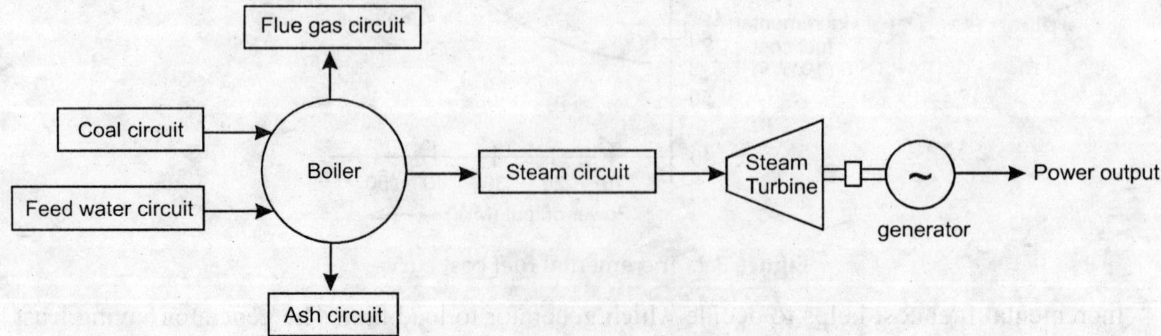

Figure 3.5. Block diagram of thermal power plant

(*i*) **Coal circuit**—It comprises coal unloading system (wagon tipplers), coal storage, coal crushers, coal feeders and pulverised mill. This is shown in following flow chart.

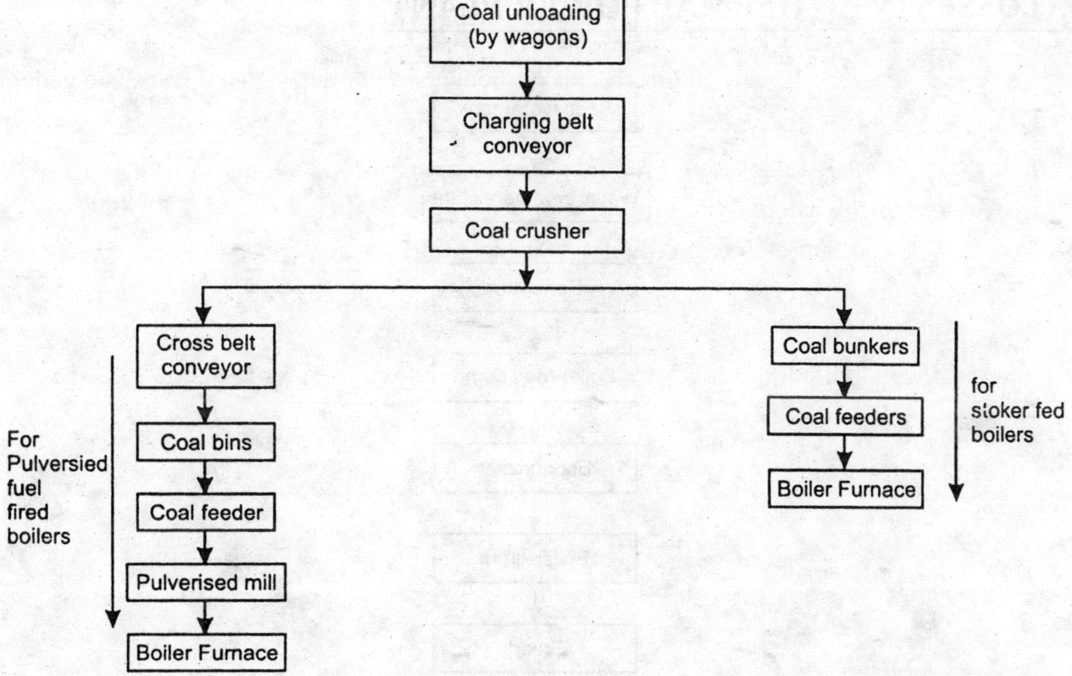

Figure 3.6. Coal Circuit

Coal circuit provides either pulverised coal (powdered coal) or coal briquets for supply to boiler furnace. The coal is carried in wagons and is unloaded by wagon tipplers in a yard. This is then transported to coal crusher by charging belt conveyor. Coal crusher breaks the large chunks of coal into smaller sizes. One part of this crushed coal is supplied to the stoker fed boiler (boiler using coal briquettes or smaller size of crushed coal) & the rest goes to the pulverised mill for conversion into powdered form. This pulverised coal is fed to the pulverised coal fired boiler (modern boiler use pulverised coal for better combustion).

(*ii*) **Feed water circuit**—Feed water circuit comprises water storage tank, water treatment plant, de-aerator, boiler feed pump, economiser and boiler drum.

This is depicted in flow chart in fig 3.7.

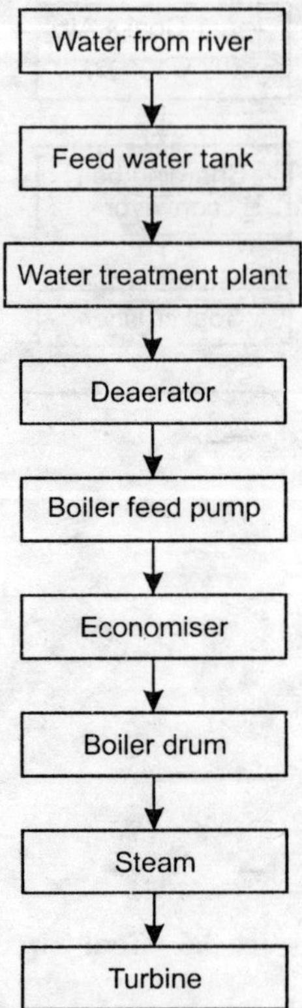

Figure 3.7. Feed water circuit

Feed water circuit provides the treated water (demineralised water) to boiler for converting it into steam. Modern high pressure boilers require extremely good quality of water. Water is drawn from river and is pumped into feed water tank. This is then pumped to water treatment plant where it is filtered (comprising cation and anion units). This demineralised water which is free from all impurities is fed to deaerator to remove the dissolved gases in water. Thereafter, it is fed to economiser using boiler feed pump. From economiser, water goes to boiler drum to be converted into steam.

Finally, steam is fed to the steam turbine to produce mechanical power output.

(*iii*) **Flue gas circuit**—Flue gas circuit carries the heat (produced by combustion of coal) to boiler tubes. The tubes contain water (in water tube boiler) which receive heat from flue gas (flue gases are hot gases produced after combustion of fuel). This is shown in fig 3.8.

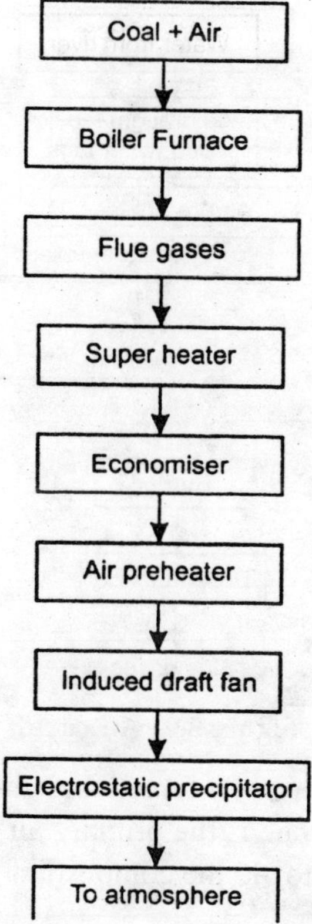

Figure 3.8. Flue gas circuit

Pulverised coal & air is fed to boiler furnace for combustion. Hot gases produced after combustion are led to super heater (it super heats the saturated steam). The flue gases are then fed to economiser (used to heat feed water) and air preheater (used to heat air supplied for combustion). The flue gases are then sucked into stack by an induced draught fan. The gases then rise through the stack & pass through electrostatic precipitator (to arrest fly ash particles in flue gases) before being released to atmosphere.

(*iv*) **Air circuit**—Air circuit provides air required for combustion of coal. This is shown in fig. 3.9.

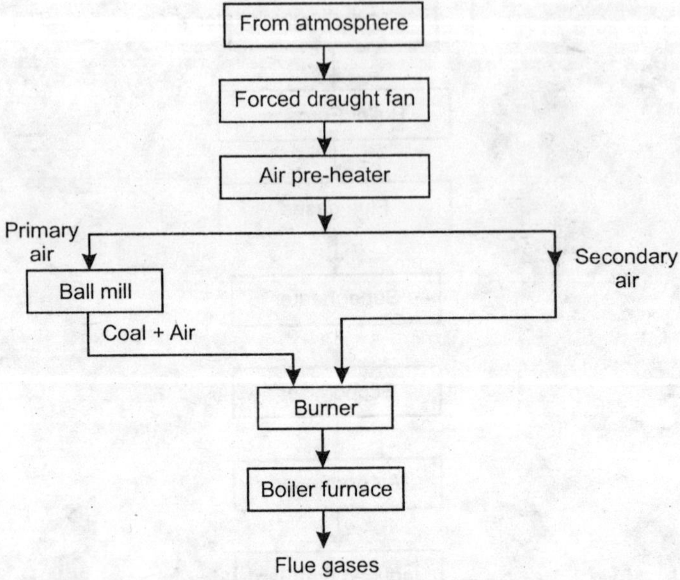

Figure 3.9. Air circuit

Air is sucked from atmosphere by a forced draught fan. It is led to air pre-heater. This air is divided into two circuits–one is the primary air which is used to carry pulverised fuel to burner. The other is used to aid the combustion process. Finally, it emerges as flue gas from the boiler furnace.

(*v*) Ash circuit—Ash circuit carries away the ash produced after combustion of coal in the furnace. This is called " bottom ash ". This is shown in fig 3.10.

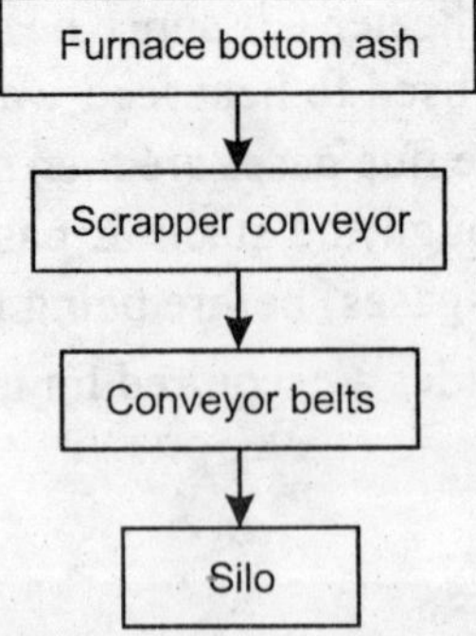

Figure 3.10. Ash circuit

The furnace bottom ash is released by the scrapper conveyor & loaded onto conveyer belts. This is then conveyed to silo for removal by trucks (for land reclamation, manufacturing of fly ash bricks etc.).

(*vi*) Fly ash circuit—Fly ash circuit removes ash collected from flue gases (these are fine ash particles suspended in flue gases). This is shown in fig 3.11.

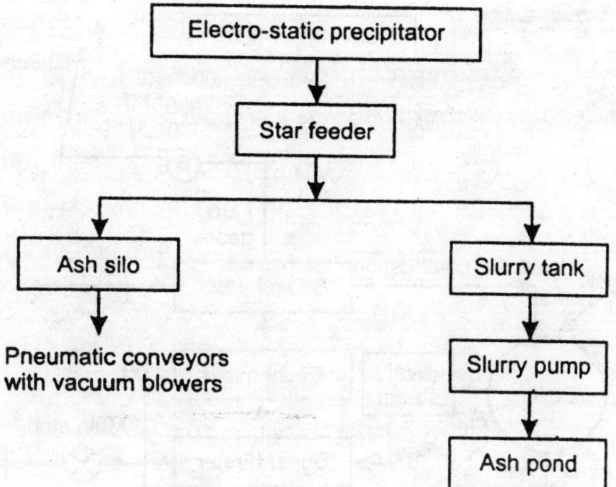

Figure 3.11. Fly ash circuit

Fly ash is collected from the bottom part of the electrostatic precipitator. It is partly fed to ash silo for pneumatic conveying & partly to slurry pumped to ash pond. From silos & ash pond, it is transported to disposal site (for fly ash brick manufacturing).

Layout of thermal plant—Layout of a thermal power plant comprises of various parts viz boiler house, turbine and generator house, coal handling yard, water treatment plant, ash disposal plant and switch yard.

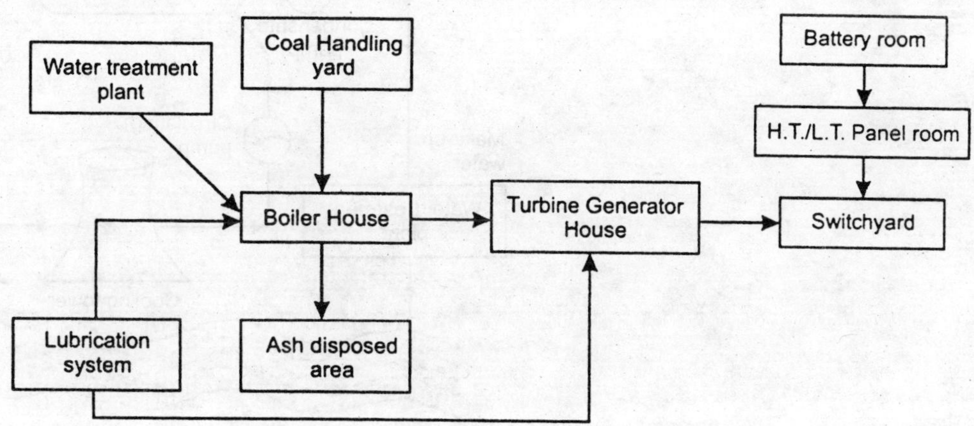

Figure 3.12. Layout of thermal power plant

3.7. SCHEMATIC ARRANGEMENT OF THERMAL POWER PLANT

Schematic arrangement of thermal power plant is shown below—

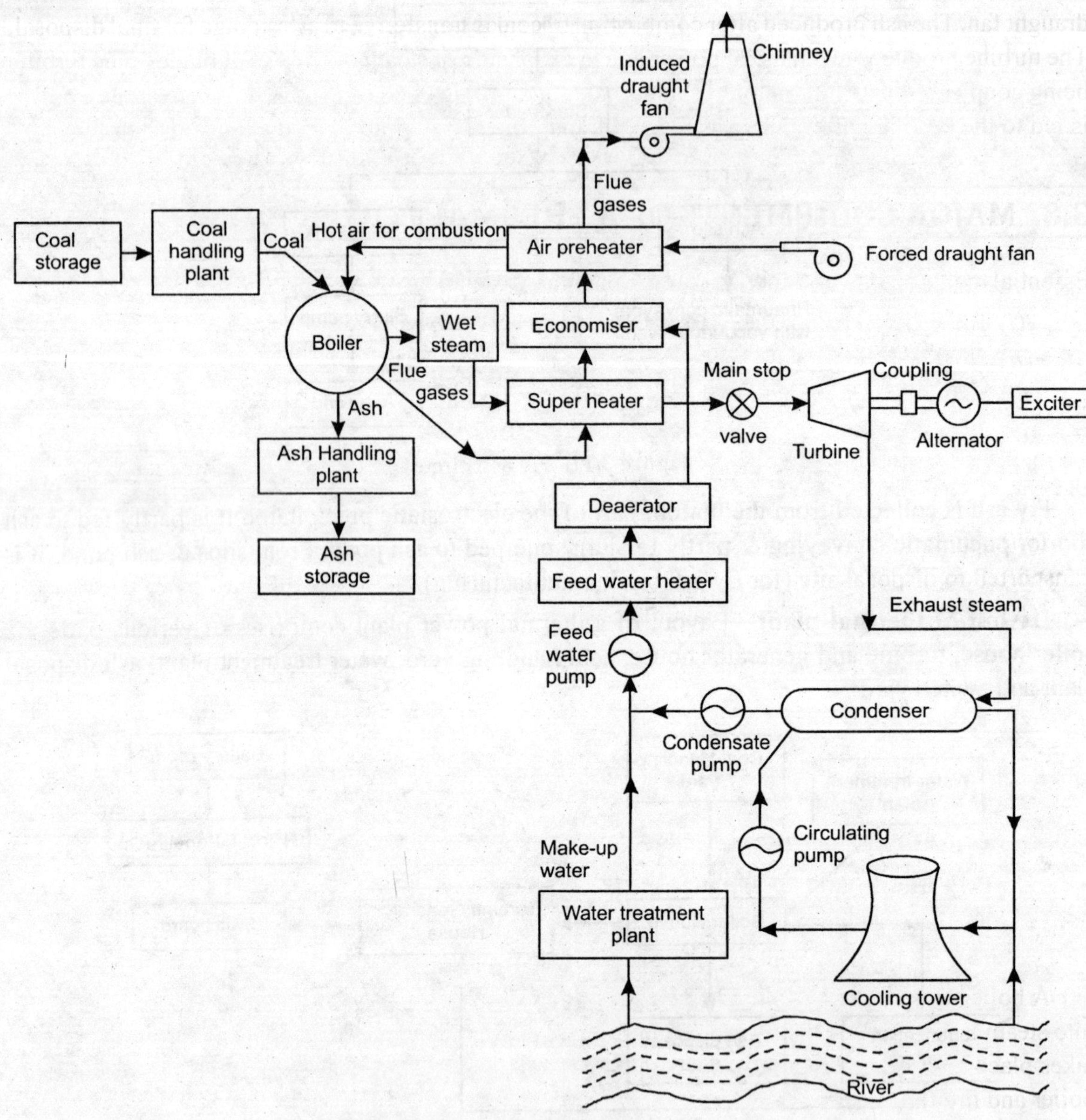

Figure 3.13. Single line diagram of thermal power plant

Boiler is the heart of thermal power plant. Coal is crushed in ball mills and pulverised to feed the furnace. Water treatment plant feeds water to deaerater, economiser & boiler drum. Combustion of coal produces flue gases. These gases flow over superheater (converts wet steam to superheated steam), economiser, air-preheater and released to atmosphere through chimney. The wet steam from steam drum is superheated in a super- heater and is led to steam turbine. After expansion of the superheated steam, the exhaust steam is fed to condenser where it is converted into liquid form. This liquefied form of steam is pumped back into boiler through feed water pump via economiser.

The air for combustion is preheated in air pre-heater and fed to boiler furnace through forced draught fan. The ash produced after combustion of coal is transferred to ash storage for final disposal. The turbine produces mechanical power due to expansion of steam over rows of blades. The turbine being coupled with an alternator, turbine rotates and produces electric power. The generated power is fed to the bus bar. After that, it is fed to a transformer to step-up & feed a transmission line.

3.8. MAJOR EQUIPMENTS OF A THERMAL POWER PLANT

Essential components of a thermal power plant are listed below—

(*i*) Boiler.
(*ii*) Coal handling plant.
(*iii*) Ash handling plant.
(*iv*) Water treatment plant.
(*v*) Cooling towers.
(*vi*) Steam turbine.
(*vii*) Alternator.
(*viii*) Power plant instrumentation.
(*ix*) Electrical control and protection equipment.
(*x*) Power plant auxiliaries.
(*xi*) Station transformer.

(*i*) **Boiler**–Boiler comprises of following elements—

(*a*) water & steam drum
(*b*) furnace
(*c*) super heater
(*d*) economiser
(*e*) air preheater
(*f*) de-aerator
(*g*) electrostatic precipitator
(*h*) induced & forced draught fans.
(*i*) feed water & condensate pumps
(*j*) chimney or stack
(*k*) condenser

A boiler is a closed vessel that converts water into steam. The heat required to convert water into steam is provided in the furnace by burning coal. The heat transfer from furnace to boiler tubes takes place through conduction, convection and radiation. Boilers are of two types viz.-water tube boiler and fire tube boiler.

A water tube boiler consists of water drum, steam drum and tubes connecting them. Since water circulates in the tubes, hence such a construction is called water tube boiler. The tubes can be horizontal or vertical and accordingly the boiler is called horizontal or vertical tube boiler. The water circulation in boiler may be natural or forced. Water tube boilers have high evaporation capacity, high working pressure and quick raising of steam.

A fire tube boiler consists of tubes through which hot flue gases flow. The tubes are surrounded by water. It is compact, occupies less space and has low initial cost. This type of boiler is used for small capacity & low pressure steam.

The choice of boiler is governed by the output steam required per hour, its temperature, pressure, space required, load factor, initial cost, maintenance cost, labour cost and fuel cost.

With super critical technology, pressure & temperature are as high as 350 atmosphere & 600 °C respectively. The efficiency is about 90%.

(*a*) **Water and steam drum**—A water and fire tube boiler is shown in figure as 3.14 and 3.15 respectively.

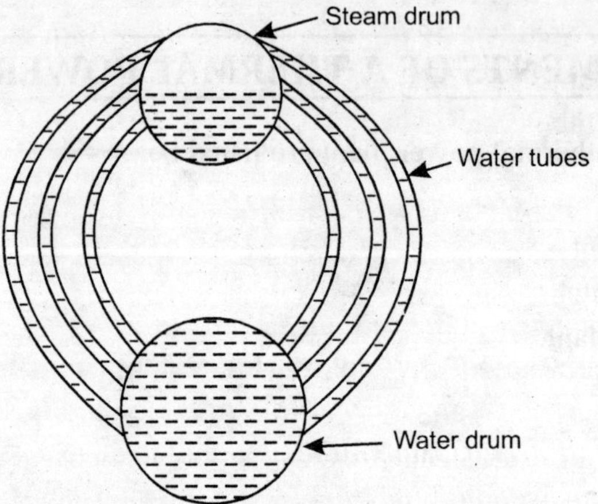

Figure 3.14. Water tube boiler

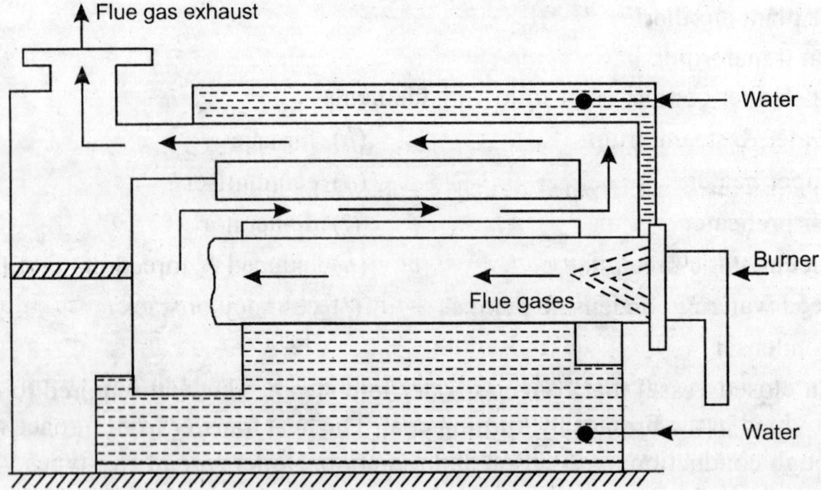

Figure 3.15. Fire tube boiler

In a water tube boiler, water circulates through the tubes and hot gas or flue gases produced after combustion of fuel pass over these tubes. The heat of the flue gases is transferred to the water circulating through tubes. The water rises through the tubes and reaches the steam drum. So, a convection current is set up between water drum and steam drum. This flow can be natural or forced. In forced system, pump is used to increase the flow rate thereby improving the heat transfer rate. Forced circulation helps to reduce the size and weight of the boiler, reduces scaling problem, ensures uniform heating & better temperature control leading to higher boiler efficiency.

So, as the temperature of water rises, it gets converted into steam. The steam being lighter than water rises & gets collected in the steam drum. The steam so accumulated in the steam drum is known as the wet steam. This wet steam is superheated in a superheater to remove water particles before being fed to the steam turbine.

On the other hand, a fire tube or smoke tube boiler is opposite to water tube boiler. The flue gases flow through tubes & are surrounded by water. Depending upon the number of times the flue gases traverse the length of the boiler, it is called 2 pass, 3 pass or 4 pass boiler. Higher the number of flue gas passes, greater the heat transfer. Usually, small capacity boiler (upto 15 T/hr) are fire tube boilers. There are no steam drum or water drum as in water tube boiler.

(*b*) **Furnace**—Boiler furnace is a place where combustion of fuel takes place. The furnace walls are made of refractory bricks (heat resisting bricks). The wall of furnace may or may not be water cooled. At one end, a burner is located. Burner causes fuel to burn using fuel & air & thus, generates hot gases or flue gases.

In a thermal power plant, either coal briquettes are used (in small capacity boiler) or pulverised coal is used.

Small coal pieces called briquettes are fed into furnace grate (a wire mesh travelling chain). The combustion of coal takes place over the grate & ash is discharged into other side.

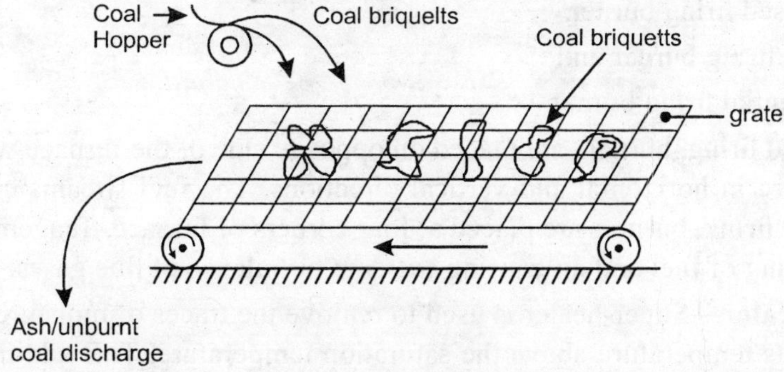

Figure 3.16. Stoker

Pulverised coal fired system uses burner to burn finely powdered coal. Initially, diesel or other auxiliary fuel is used to light up the burner. Once a steady temperature is maintained, pulverised coal is fed into the burner & auxiliary fuel supply is stopped. The pulverised coal then burns & generates flue gases. The ash generated after combustion gets collected at the furnace bottom & fine ash particles are carried away by the flue gases. Also, poor quality coal (more ash content) can be easily burnt by this method. All large capacity boilers use pulverised coal. The pulverisation of coal takes place in coal mills where coal is ground into fine particles and then pneumatically conveyed to burner for combustion.

Now, the advantages of pulverised fuel firing are following—

(*i*) rapid and better combustion.

(*ii*) coal with high ash content can be burnt.

(*iii*) smaller quantity of excess air is required for combustion due to increase in surface area of coal.

(*iv*) higher boiler efficiency.

(*v*) no clinker formation (small coal particles after burning fuse together forming a bigger lump called clinker). This chokes the furnace grate.

(*vi*) easier ash handling.

(*vii*) easy to meet load fluctuations.

(*viii*) easier boiler firing.

However, the disadvantages of the pulverised fuel firing are given below—

(*i*) coal mill & auxiliary systems are required which are expensive.

(*ii*) lot of fly ash is generated.

(*iii*) risk of explosion due to powdered coal.

(*iv*) coal mill consumes energy & are maintenance intensive.

(*v*) electrostatic precipitator is required to arrest the flyash.

Pulverised coal is burnt in coal burners. The pulverised coal is conveyed to burner through primary air and secondary air is fed separately below the burner. A good burner should be able to produce a stable flame causing complete combustion of fuel. The coal burners are of three types viz.

(1) opposed firing burner.

(2) cross firing burner and

(3) tangential firing burner.

In opposed firing, burners are placed on opposite side of the furnace wall. In cross firing, burners fire in horizontal and vertical directions. The fuel streams cross each other. In tangential firing, burners are placed at four corners of furnace. Tangential firing results in good mixing of fuel and air causing extreme turbulence of flue gases.

(*c*) **Super–heater**—Super-heater is used to remove the traces of moisture from the steam & increase its temperature above the saturation temperature. This addition of extra energy provides more heat energy to turbine & hence, higher power generation may be achieved. Superheated steam causes less erosion & corrosion of turbine blades and allows steam to be carried over longer distances without much heat loss. Also, quantity of steam required for a given output is reduced thereby reducing turbine size. It consists of tubes made of carbon steel, upto 950°F steam temperature. Carbon molebdnum steel (upto 1050°F steam temperature). The super-heater tubes are heated by flue gases during their passage from furnace to the stack. A super-heater is of three types—

(*i*) convection (*ii*) radiant and

(*iii*) combination of the two.

Convection super-heater receives the heat entirely through convection from flue gases. The temperature of superheat increases with increase in steam output. This is due to the fact that the flue gases flow over the super-heater tubes and steam flow within tubes that increases the rate of heat transfer and mean temperature difference. In radiant, temperature of superheat falls with the increase in steam output. This is due to the fact that with increase in steam output, the furnace temperature rises at a slower pace compared to steam output lending to fall in steam temperature.

Third type of super-heater uses the characteristics of both these types. In addition to super- heaters, re-heaters are also employed in the boiler. The purpose is to re-heat the partly expanded steam from turbine. This ensures that steam does not condense till the last stage of turbine. This improves the thermal efficiency & prevents erosion & corrosion of blades of last stage.

(*d*) **Economiser**—Economiser is a device that is used to recover heat from the flue gases before leaving the water tubes, super-heater tubes and re- heater tubes. This increases the boiler efficiency by 10 – 12% by reducing fuel consumption by 5 – 15%. Also, it reduces thermal stresses in boiler joints due to higher temperature of feed water. However, the extra cost of installation, maintenance & cleaning is justified by fuel saving, high pressure & temperature conditions.

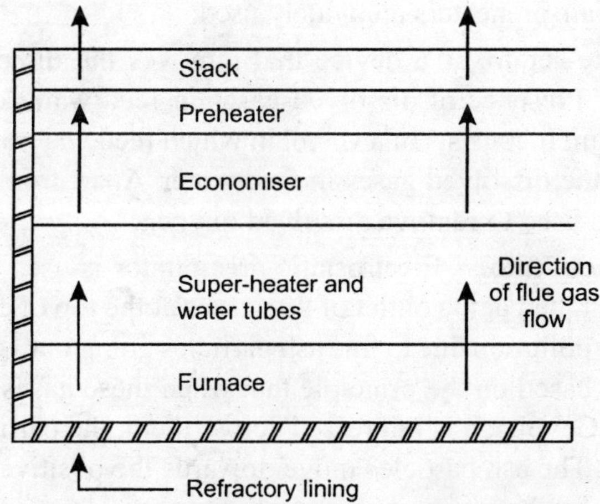

Figure 3.17. Location of economiser in boiler

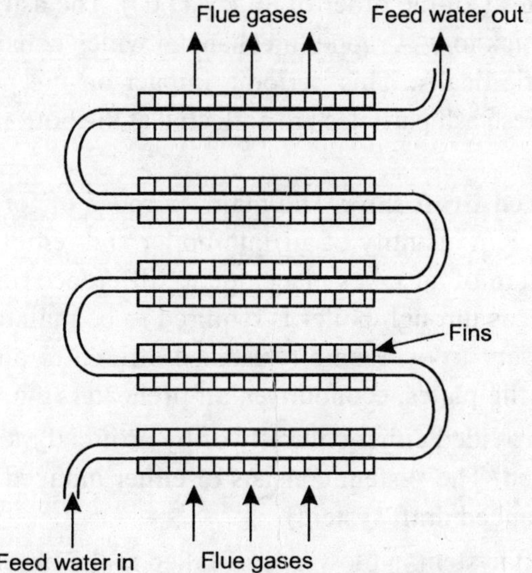

Figure 3.18. Finned tube economiser

Economiser increases the temperature of feed water before being fed into boiler. It consists of finned tube bundle over which flue gases flow. The purpose of the finned tubes is to increase the surface area of tubes for higher heat transfer. The inlet temperature of feed water is about 84°C and outlet temperature is upto 275°C.

(*e*) **Air-preheater**—Air preheater is used to recover the heat from flue gases after leaving economiser. It is used to preheat air for combustion. This increases the combustion rate, lowers stack temperature & hence, increases the overall efficiency.

Air pre-heaters are of two types—(*i*) recuperative and (*ii*) regenerative type. Recuperative type pre-heaters are of plate type or tubular type construction. This type of air pre-heater occupies more space & rate of heat transfer is considered as slow. While regenerative type are compact, occupy less space and have large heat transfer surface. Therefore, recuperative type air-preheaters are widely used.

(*f*) **De-aerator**—A de-aerator is a device that removes the dissolved gases especially O_2 from feed water. Presence of dissolved gases in feed water causes corrosion of water tubes & water drum. It consists of a vessel in which feed water is heated by a low pressure steam to liberate the dissolved gases in feed water. Apart from de-aerator, certain boiler chemicals are also used to remove dissolved oxygen.

(*g*) **Electrostatic precipitator**—Electrostatic precipitator is used to arrest the flyash in the flue gases. It is installed at the outlet of flue gases at the top of chimney. The purpose of it is to minimize the pollution due to fine ash particles going out with the exhaust gases from the chimney. It is based on the principle that when these gases are passed through a pair of plates and a D.C. voltage is impressed across them, the particles have affinity towards the positive plate. The ash particles move towards the positive plates (get lodged into it which is removed by the rapper motor mechanism).

It consists of a wire mesh installed at the top of the chimney. A high voltage D.C. supply is given to the plates (of the order of 30 kV D.C.). The ash particles are attracted to the positive plates & stick to it. A rapper mechanism which consists of a rapper motor, strikes the wire mesh periodically. This periodic impact on the positive plate causes the ash particles to fall. These ash particles are collected at the bottom of the chimney & disposed off.

(*h*) **Forced and induced draft fan**—The main purpose of forced and induced draft fan is to supply the sufficient quantity of air into boiler and remove the exhaust gases through stack. The circulation of air takes place due to difference of pressure and is called draft. The flow of air or gas through boiler is required to be maintained by providing the draft. The draft is necessary to overcome resistance offered to air and gas flow by fuel bed, ducts, dampers, baffle plates, economiser, air preheaters etc.

The draft can be provided either naturally or by artificial means. In large boiler, artificial means are employed. The system consists of either induced draft fan or forced draft fan or both (called balanced draft system).

In the induced draft system, a blower is installed at the base of the stack and it sucks the flue gases out of the boiler. This causes a pressure drop inside the stacks & makes entry of the fresh air into boiler. In forced draft system, a blower forces air through furnace, economiser, air preheater & stack. But the induced or forced draft fans alone are not sufficient to maintain necessary draft in the boiler. So, both the induced & forced draft fans are used (called balanced draft).

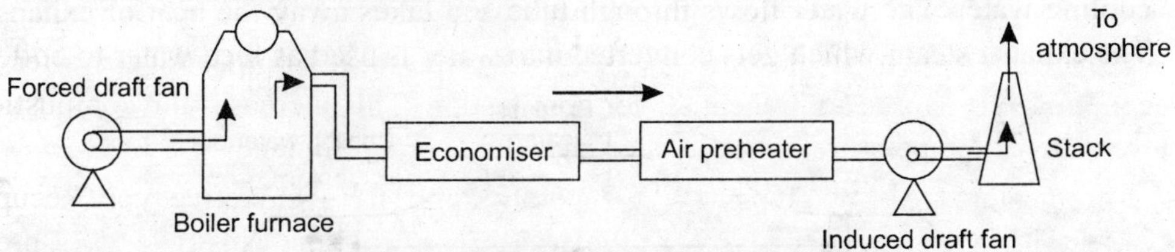

Figure 3.19. Balanced draft system

(*i*) **Feed water and condensate pumps**—Boiler requires water which is converted into steam. The steam after expansion in steam turbine is condensed in a condenser. The condensed water is again fed into boiler. However, due to the loss of water on account of leakages, blow down etc, certain amount of water is required to be fed into boiler. This is called make-up water and is 1 – 4% of the total water requirement.

The water obtained from river, lake or borewell is properly treated to remove impurities etc. This treated water is fed to the boiler using feed water pump.

While condensate pump removes the condensate from the condenser and feeds low pressure heater and de-aerator.

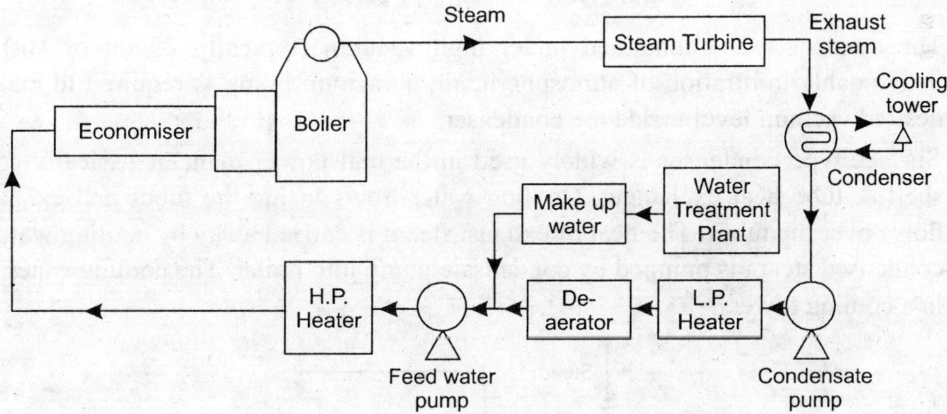

Figure 3.20. Water flow circuit

(*j*) **Stack**—Stack is used to exhaust the flue gases into atmosphere. The stack may be of masonry construction or of fabricated steel structure. The height of stack is decided based on the flow rate of exhaust gases, temperature of gases etc. A higher height of stack allows the pollutants to be dispersed over large area & protects the ecosystem from high temperature of exhaust gases.

(*k*) **Condenser**—Steam after expansion over steam turbine blades is condensed into condenser. The condenser is maintained below atmospheric pressure so as to allow the steam to expand to very low pressure. This increases the thermal efficiency of boiler. The condensed exhaust steam is again fed into boiler. This reduces fresh intake of water from the water treatment plant.

Condensers are of two types (*i*) jet type and (*ii*) surface type. In jet type condenser, exhaust steam mixes with cooling water and condensate can not be recovered as feed water to boiler. In surface type condenser, there is no direct contact between exhaust steam and cooling water. The water flows through tube and takes away the heat of exhaust steam. The exhaust steam which gets converted into water is used as feed water to boiler.

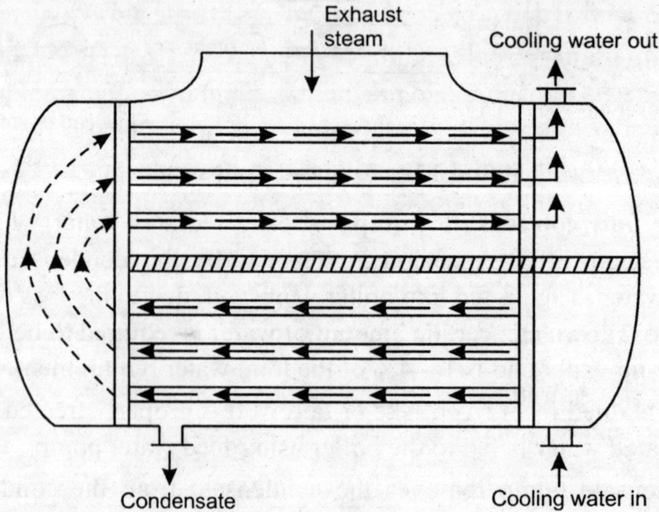

Figure 3.21. Surface type condenser

The condenser is maintained under high vacuum (typically 25mm of Hg). Due to unavoidable infiltration of atmospheric air, a vacuum pump is required to maintain the desired vacuum level inside the condenser.

Surface type condenser is widely used in thermal power plant. It basically consists of shell & tube heat exchanger. Cooling water flows inside the tubes and exhaust steam flows over the tubes. The heat of exhaust steam is carried away by cooling water and the condensed steam is pumped by condensate pump into boiler. The cooling water is cooled in a cooling tower.

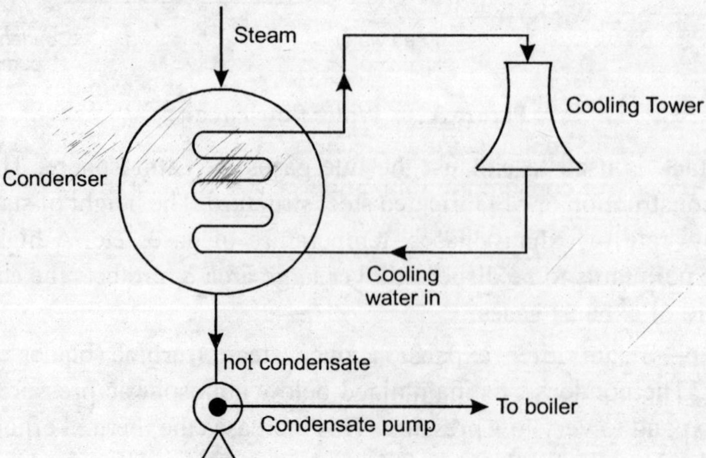

Figure 3.22. Condenser Circuit

So, a boiler comprises of (*a*) water & steam drum (*b*) furnace (*c*) super heater (*d*) economiser (*e*) air pre-heater (*f*) de-aerator (*g*) electrostatic precipitator (*h*) induced and forced draft fans (*i*) feed water and condensate pumps (*j*) stack and (*k*) condenser.

Thermal power plant apart from boiler consists of coal handling plant, ash handling plant, water treatment plant, cooling towers, steam turbine, alternator, power plant instrumentation and electrical control and protection equipments. These are explained below in detail.

(*ii*) Coal handling plant—Coal handling plant feeds coal to the boiler furnace for combustion. coal from mines is transported to the thermal plant by rail, road or by river. Usually, large capacity plants are located near coal mines and are called pit-head plant. This results in considerable saving in transportation cost. To have an idea of quantity of coal required daily, 2000 ton of coal is required for a 200MW plant. Plant located near load centres employ rail transportation mode. The coal received from mines is stored in coal handling yard. Unloading of coal is done by wagon tipplers, rotary car dumpers, cranes & buckets etc. This coal is stored in outdoor storage yard and then transferred to covered storage such as bins, bunkers, silos etc.

Coal storage is required to ensure continuous supply of coal. The coal from the covered storage yard is taken to coal crusher. The coal passes through magnetic separators and screens to coal crusher where coal is crushed into the coal briquettes of 25-30 mm size. This size of coal is suitable for stoker fired boiler where it is fed to the boiler grate for combustion. For pulverised fuel firing, coal briquettes are taken to pulverising mill which crushes the coal briquettes into fine powder form. This pulverised coal is conveyed by hot air to coal burner for firing.

Advantages of using the pulverised coal are given below—

(*i*) low grade coal having high ash content can be easily burnt.
(*ii*) boiler can be started quickly.
(*iii*) rate of combustion can be controlled easily.
(*iv*) less excess air is required for combustion.
(*v*) no chance of clinker formation.
(*vi*) pre-heated air can be used.

Disadvantage are given below—

(*i*) requires investment in coal preparation plant.
(*ii*) presence of fine coal dust may cause explosion.
(*iii*) auxiliary power consumption increases.
(*iv*) requires good deal of maintenance.
(*v*) plant requires electrostatic precipitator to arrest fine ash particles in exhaust gases.

Pulverising mill consists of coal mill. It is of the three types viz ball mill, contact mill and impact mill.

(*a*) Ball mill—It consists of a steel cylinder filled with steel balls. The cylinder is rotated slowly while the coal is fed into it. The balls pulverise the coal by crushing. Hot air is used to convey this pulverised coal to classifiers. Classifiers return over size particles to the mill for grinding. From classifiers, this pulverised coal is carried by hot air to burner.

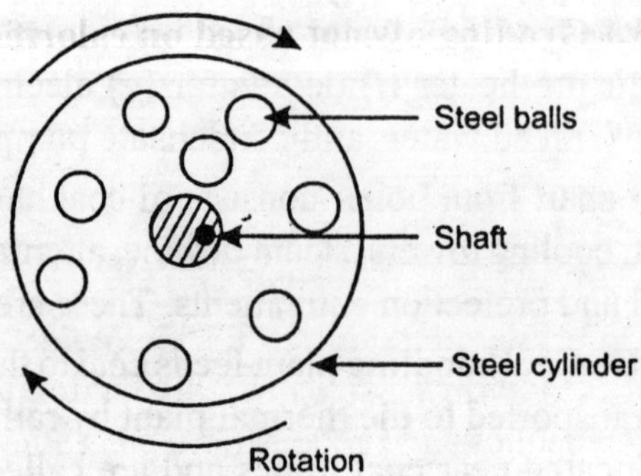

Figure 3.23. Ball mill

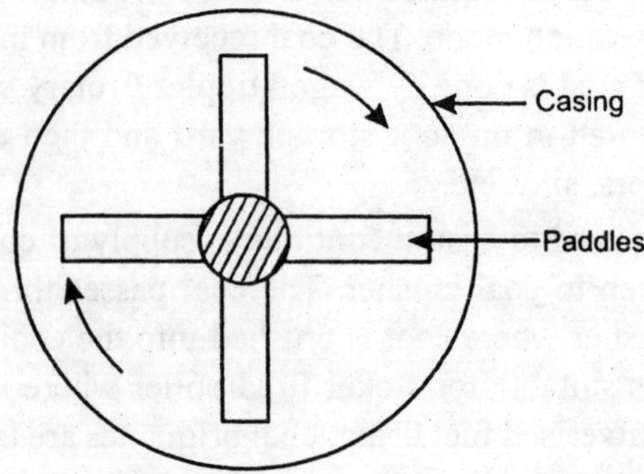

Figure 3.24. Impact mill

(*b*) **Contact mill**—It consists of a stationary and a power driven rolling elements which move against each other. Coal is made to pass through these rollers till the required size of fineness is obtained. The bigger particles are returned for grinding. The fine particles are conveyed by hot air to the burner. It requires less space & is quieter in operation but requires high capital cost.

(*c*) **Impact mill**—In this mill, coal is crushed to powder by hammering action of paddles. While large size particles are crushed again and fine particles are conveyed by air to burner. This type of mill is low cost and simple in operation but requires more maintenance & consumers more energy.

(*ii - a*) **Coal**—Fuel used in thermal power plant is coal. Coal was formed by decomposition of vegetation buried deep under the earth millions of years ago. The vegetation under high pressure & temperature inside the earth got converted into coal. With aging process, coal became harder, oxygen & moisture content decreases while carbon content decreases. Accordingly, coal is classified into three major types viz. Anthracite, bituminous & lignite coal. Anthracite is the oldest coal and is composed of carbon, little volatile matter & almost no moisture content (where volatile matter means those constituents which vaporise when coal is heated). The Indian coal is graded according to the calorific value as per following table 3.1

Table 3.1 Grading of coal based on calorific value

Grade	*Calorific Value ranges (kcal/kg)*
A	**> 6200**
B	5600 – 6200
C	4940 – 5600
D	4200 – 4940
E	3360 – 4200
F	2400 – 3360
G	1300 – 2400

Usually, grade D, E & F are available in India.

A typical gross calorific value of various coals is given in table 3.2.

Table 3.2 Calorific value of various coals

Type of coal	*GCV (kcal/kg)*
Indian coal	4000
Indonesian coal	5500
South African coal	6000

A typical ultimate analysis of coal is given in table 3.3:

Table 3.3 Ultimate analysis of coal

Parameter	*Indian Coal (%)*	*Indonesian Coal (%)*
Moisture	5.98	9.43
Mineral matter	38.63	13.99
Carbon	41.11	58.96
Hydrogen	2.76	4.16
Nitrogen	1.22	1.02
Sulphur	0.41	0.56
Oxygen	9.89	11.88

Table 3.4 gives sizes of coal for various types of firing.

Table 3.4 Size of coal for various types of firing

S.No.	*Types of firing*	*Size (mm)*
1.	Hand firing	
	(*a*) Natural draft	25–75
	(*b*) Forced draft	25–40
2.	Stoker firing	
	(*a*) Chain grate	
	(*i*) Natural draft	25–40
	(*ii*) Forced draft	15–25
	(*b*) Spreader stoker	15–25
3.	Pulverised fuel firing	75% below 75 micron
4.	Fluidized bed boiler	< 10 mm

(*iii*) Ash handling plant

Indian coal contains high amount of ash (ash as high as 40%). Such quality of coal upon burning produce large amount of ash.

A typical 2000 MW plant produces 500 tons of ash per day. The disposal of such huge quantity of ash requires elaborate arrangement. Ash is removed from furnace called "bottom ash" and flyash collected from electrostatic precipitator. Ash is so removed that either it may be taken for land filling or dumping in a abandoned mine or for making the flyash bricks.

Handling and disposal of flyash poses several problems, such as abrasive nature of ash and dusty nature creates difficulty in handling, produces corrosive acid when mixed with water, tendency to form clinkers (lumps) etc. Due to these operational difficulties, an elaborate arrangement need to be designed to tackle all these issues.

The ash (both furnace bottom and flyash) handling systems are of following types—

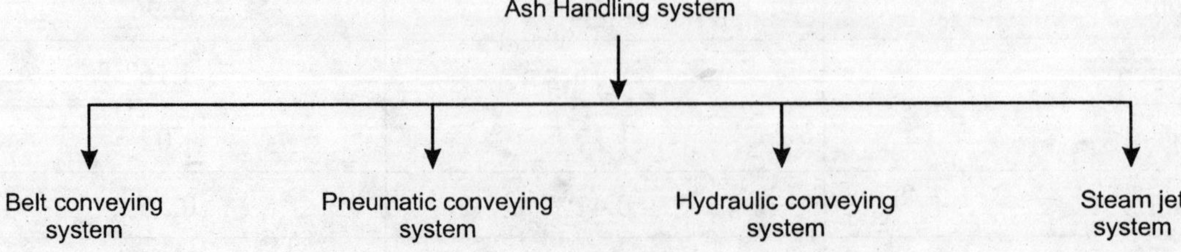

Figure 3.25. Types of ash handling system

(*a*) **Belt Conveying System**

Ash is conveyed through belt conveyor to the dumping site. The hot ash falls through a water seal over the conveyor to reduce the temperature of hot ash. The ash is continuously carried and dumped over the designated site. The typical carrying capacity per hour is 3 tonnes at a speed of 0.3 m/minute. Such systems are cheap and simple and are suitable for small size power plants.

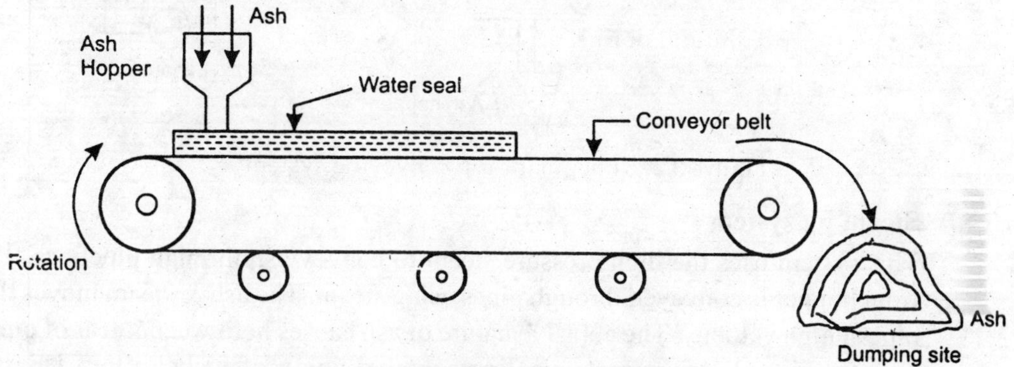

Figure 3.26. Belt conveying system

(*b*) **Hydraulic conveying system**

In this system, ash is carried by water stream in a closed channel and is disposed off at the desired site. The system is of two types viz-high pressure system and low pressure system. In high pressure system, water nozzles at top and side sprinkle water and cool hot ash. The ash and water is made to flow to a sump where water and ash are separated. Ash is disposed off at desired site and water is re-circulated.

This method is clean and dustless but expensive to instal and maintain.

In low pressure system, ash falls over a trough, carrying water. Water carries the ash to the sump. The ash and water are separated by screens. Ash is removed through carrier unit and led to dumping place. The water is re-circulated

(*c*) **Pneumatic conveying system**

This method uses compressed air to transport ash over long distances. The ash from boiler passes through silo. Then, it is conveyed through pipe. As the air is sucked in, it carries ash alongwith it & and is discharged at ash hoppers. The compressed air is filtered and then exhausted to the atmosphere.

This system can carry ash over long distances and is clean system. However, it causes excessive wear and tear in pipelines due to its abrasive nature and requires considerable maintenance periodically.

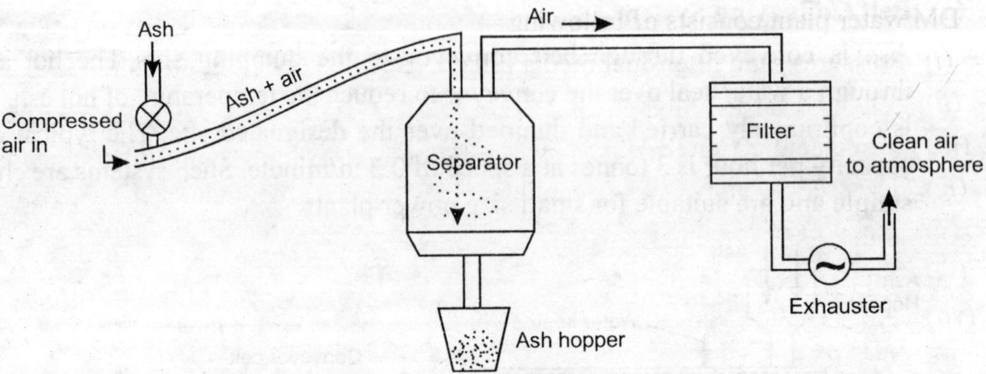

Figure 3.27. Pneumatic ash conveying system

(*d*) Steam jet system

This system uses the high pressure steam to convey ash through pipelines. The ash from hopper is conveyed through pipes using steam. The ash & steam moves through pipe at high velocity. The abrasive nature of ash causes high wear & tear of pipelines. To minimize abrasive wear, pipeline contains lining of nickel alloy. This system occupies small space and is used where there is space crunch and path of ash travel is not straight. Such systems are suitable for the small and medium size plants.

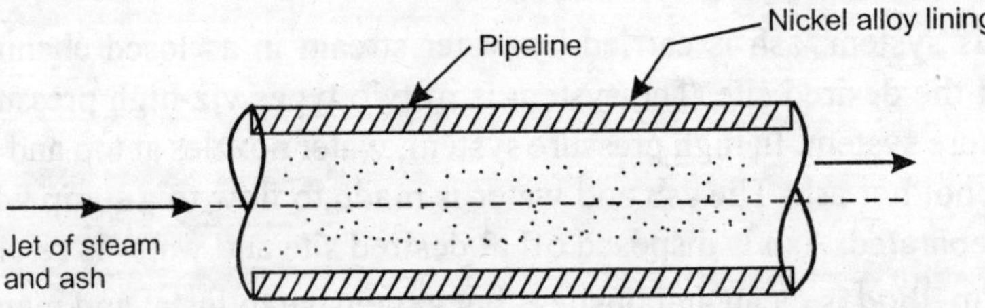

Figure 3.28. Pipeline carrying ash and steam

(*iv*) Water treatment plant—A thermal power plant requires huge amount of water everyday for boiler and cooling tower. The quality of water required for boiler and cooling tower are different. Raw water available from rivers, streams, lakes or borewells can not be used directly due to the presence of impurities in it. Hence, it is necessary to condition or purify water before it can be used in the plant. A water treatment plant provides right quality of water round the clock. Usually, two types of water are required in thermal power plant viz (*a*) demineralised water (*b*) soft water. Raw water if used directly in a boiler may cause scale formation in tubes which may lead to tube failure ultimately.

De-mineralised water (DM water) is the purest form of water having no impurities and is produced by ion exchange. While soft water is produced by removing hardness due to chlorides, sulphates & bicarbonates of calcium & magnesium. DM water is used in high pressure boilers for raising steam and soft water is used in cooling tower for cooling exhaust steam in condenser.

(*a*) DM water plant

Raw water obtained from rivers, lakes, borewells etc. are first sent to the pre-treatment plant where suspended impurities etc. are removed. The raw water is then fed to DM water plant.

DM water plant consists of following—

(*i*) Pressures sand filter/dual media filter.

(*ii*) activated carbon filter.

(*iii*) strong acid cation (SAC).

(*iv*) degasser tower

(*v*) strong base anion (SBA).

(*vi*) mixed bed filters.

(*vii*) DM water storage tank.

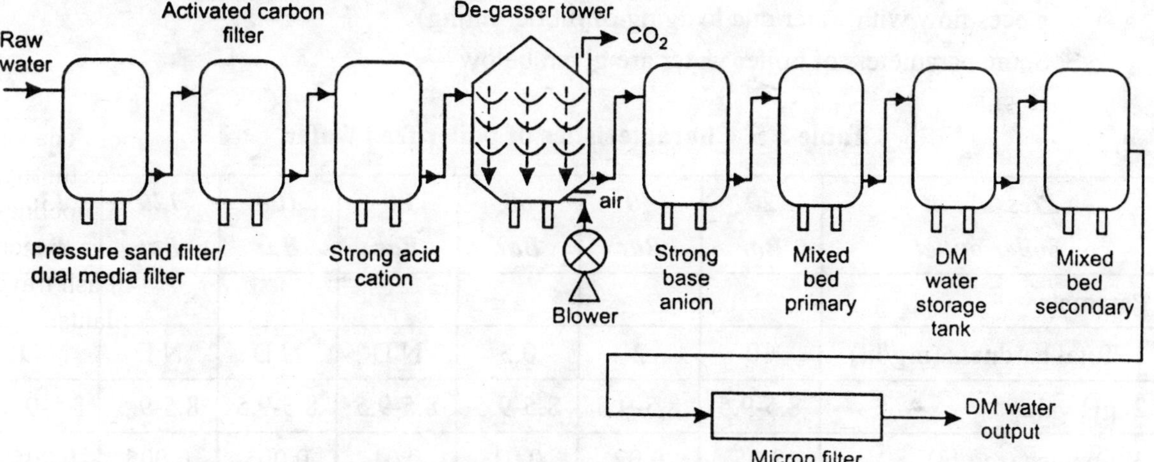

Figure 3.29. DM water plant flow diagram

(*i*) **Pressure sand filter/Dual media filter**—It consists of two different sizes of sand lying one above the other. Water is made to fall over the sand bed. Water percolates through sand bed leaving behind suspended impurities in it. After certain hours of usage, the sand bed gets clogged with impurities. A jet of water is passed through the bed from bottom in the sand bed. Thereafter, the filter becomes ready for next cycle of usage.

(*ii*) **Activated Carbon Filter**—Water obtained from pressure sand filter is free from suspended impurities. It is now fed to activated carbon filter. The vessel contains activated carbon which is used to remove odour and colour from the water. The activated carbon gets exhausted after certain time & is replaced with fresh activated carbon.

(*iii*) **Strong Acid Cation (SAC)**—This vessel contains ion-exchange resin which exchanges cations present in water such as Ca^{++}, Mg^{++}, etc. So, water after passing through resin (a chemical compound which traps cations in its structure), water is free from any cation. This makes water acidic (pH below 7).

(*iv*) **De-gasser Tower (DGT)**—Water from SAC is taken into degasser tower. Water flows over from top to bottom over a packed bed (helps to split water into more streams thereby increasing surface area). An air blower blows air into the packed bed tower from bottom to top. This helps to release carbon dioxide in the water. This inturn reduces load on the next vessel i.e. strong base anion (SBA).

(*v*) **Strong Base Anion (SBA)**—This vessel contains ion-exchange resin which exchanges anions present in the water such as Cl^-, SO_4, CO_3^- etc. So, any anions present in water are trapped by the resin & water coming on of it is pure H_2O (pH is 6.5 to 6.8).

(*vi*) **Storage Tank**—This tank stores DM water for further use. To prevent dissolution of carbon dioxide present in air, PVC balls are kept over the surface of water (this is only in case of ultrapare DM water).

(*vii*) **Mixed Bed**—As and when DM water is required, the water from storage tank passes through a mixed bed and then through a micron filter which removes fine resin partiles, fine rubber pieces etc. (vessels- SAC & mixed bed are rubber lined & the fine rubber pieces flow with water due to aging of rubber lining).

Some parameters of boiler water are given below—

Table 3.5 Characteristics of boiler feed water

Pressure at Boiler outlet	***20 Bar***	***40 Bar***	***60 Bar***	***80 Bar***	***100 Bar***	***120 Bar***	***130 Bar***
Parameter							
1. Total hardness (mg/lit)	10	2	0.5	N D	N D	N D	N D
2. pH value	8.5-9.5	8.5-9.5	8.5-9.5	8.5-9.5	8.5-9.5	8.5-9.5	8.5-9.5
3. Oxygen (mg/lit)	0.05	0.02	0.01	0.01	0.005	0.005	0.005
4. Fe + Cu + N: (mg/lit)	—	—	0.02	0.02	0.01	0.01	0.01

Note- ND - Not Detectable

Table 3.6 Characteristics of water inside boiler

Pressure at boiler outlet (bar)	***20***	***40***	***60***	***80***	***100***	***120***	***130***
Sodium phosphate as Na_3 Po_4 (mg/lit)	50–100	30–70	20–50	10-40	5–20	3–10	—
Caustic Alkalinity (Max) (mg/lit)	300	150	60	30	10	5	2
Total Alkalinity (Max) (mg/lit)	700	500	300	200	100	40	10
Silica as Sio_2, (Max) (mg/lit)	0.4 of Caustic Alkalinity	—	20	10	#	#	#
Sodium Sulphite as Na_2 So_3 (mg/lit)	30-50	20-40	15-30	10-20	#	#	#
Hydrazine as $N_2 H_4$ (mg/lit)	0.1-1.0	0.1–0.5	0.05–0.3	0.05–0.1	#	#	#

Dissolved solids (Max) (mg/lit)	3000	2000	1200	700	350	100	15
Chloride as Cl, (Max) (mg/lit)	—	—	—	—	10	5	1
Suspended Solids, (Max) (mg/lit)	200	50	—	—	—	—	—

Note—depends on circumstances

1. Cooling Tower and spray ponds—

(a) Cooling Tower—Water is required to condense steam in condenser.

A typical 2000 MW plant require 1500 × 10^6 gallons /day of cooling water.

A cooling tower is a concrete or steel hyperbolic structure which consists of a reservoir at the bottom to the store water. The hot water from the condenser is allowed to fall from top of cooling tower. This falling water comes in contact with air & losses heat. To prevent escape of water along with air, eliminators are installed at the top of the cooling tower. The system loses water due to evaporation & drift. So, make up water is required to cover up water losses. The cooling tower can be as high as 150 m.

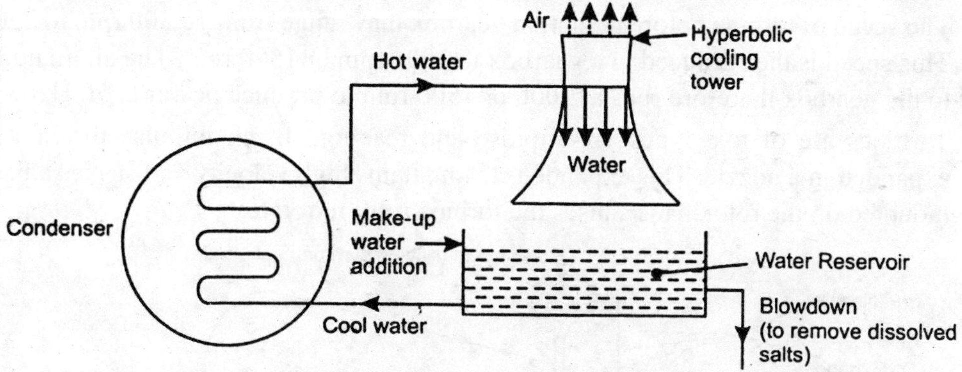

Figure 3.30. Cooling Tower

About 48-52 % of heat input is rejected in the cooling tower.

Usually, hyperbolic cooling towers are used in the thermal power plants. In other applications, packed bed cooling tower with mechanical draught is used.

Hyperbolic cooling towers are natural draught system. The reserve purges water (called blow down) & fresh water is added to maintain required salt concentration in water.

Spray pond is also used to reject heat into atmosphere. It insists of a water reservoir in which hot water is sprayed through nozzles. The water is cooled by evaporation and convection when it comes in contact with air. Disadvantage of this system is that large reservoir is required and lot of water is carried away by air when wind velocity is high.

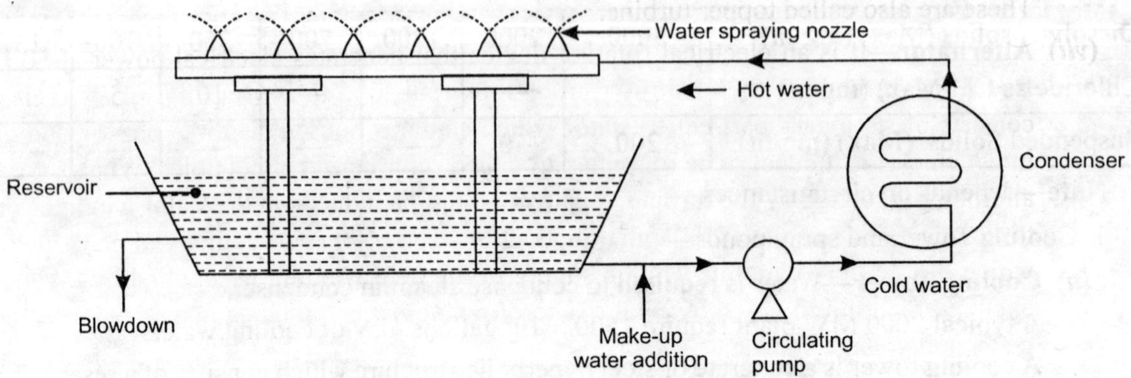

Figure 3.31. Spray Pond

(vi) **Steam Turbine**—It converts heat energy of steam into kinetic energy and is used to drive alternator to produce power. It is based on the principle that steam escaping from a nozzle attains high velocity. This velocity is dependent upon initial and final heat content of steam. The difference of initial and final heat content gets converted into kinetic energy. The speed of turbine before reduction gearbox may range from 10,000 rpm to 25000 rpm. This speed is then reduced in a gearbox to 3000 rpm or 1500 rpm. The alternator coupled to the gearbox therefore runs at 3000 or 1500 rpm to produce power at 50 Hz.

Turbines are of two types viz-impulse and reaction. In an impulse turbine, steam is expanded in a nozzle. This expanded steam attains high velocity and strikes a fixed blade mounted on the rotor. This causes the turbine rotor to rotate.

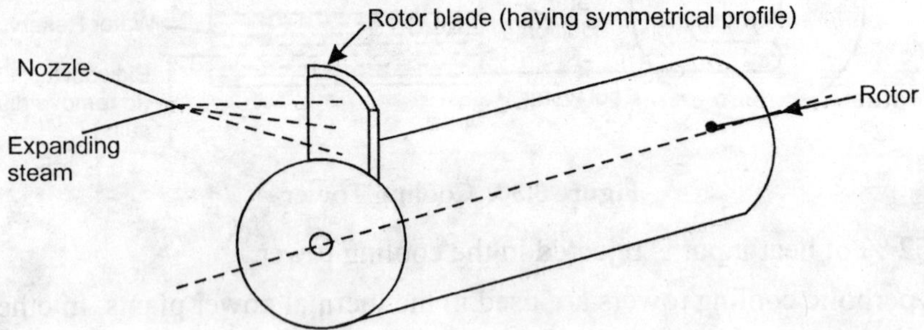

Figure 3.32. Nozzle and rotor blade

In a reaction turbine, partial expansion of steam takes place in nozzle and remaining expansion takes place on rotor blades. The velocity of steam increases as it expands over rotor blades. There is difference of pressure on two sides of rotor blade.

In actual practice, steam turbine is a combination of reaction & impulse type.

In thermal power plant, two types of turbines are used viz. condensing type and back-pressure type. Condensing type turbines are used in thermal power plant. While back-pressure turbines are used in captive power plants in industry.

In condensing type, the steam after leaving turbines is condensed in a condenser. This causes reduction in thermal efficiency. While in back-pressure type, steam leaves the turbine at a lower pressure. This low pressure steam is used in process for heating purpose.

These are also called topper turbine.

(*vii*) **Alternator**—It is an electrical rotating device that generates electrical power at 50 Hz frequency. It rotates either at 1500 rpm or 3000 rpm so as to produce power at 50 Hz. It consists of stationary part called stator which contains houses the three phase windings in which emf is induced. The rotating part called rotor has d.c. field poles. When rotor of alternator is rotated by the turbine, it causes emf to be induced in the stator windings due to Faraday's law of electro-magnetic induction. The rotor is of cylindrical construction which has dc field winding. The dc supply to the field winding is supplied by the main exciter which inturn is fed by pilot exciter. An automatic voltage regulator (AVR) keeps generated voltage constant.

The number of field poles on the rotor are 2 or 4. To reduce peripheral velocity, the diameter of rotor is kept small and its length is increased. Due to high mechanical stresses at high speed, rotor is made of chromium-nickel steel or chromium-nickel molybdenum steel. The rotor has rectangular slots with tapered teeth which houses field winding in the shape of rectangular strips. The strips are held in place by steel or bronze wedges.

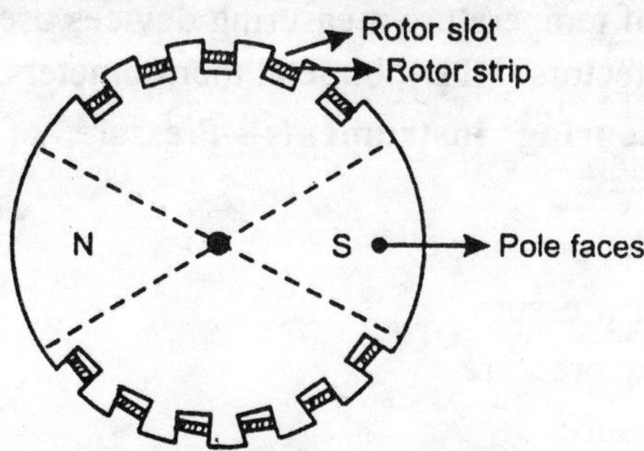

Figure 3.33. Rotor pole

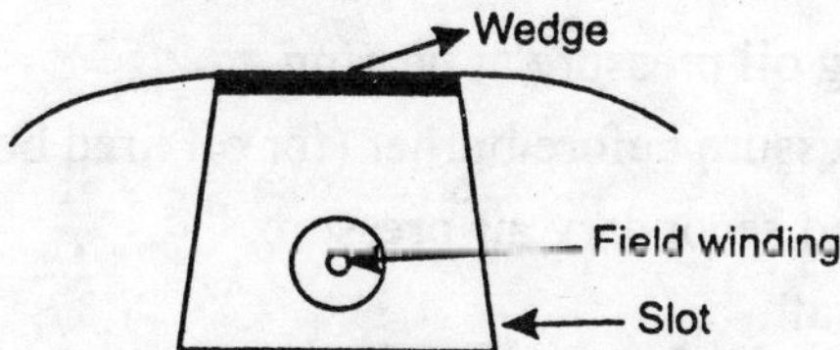

Figure 3.34. Tapered rotor slot

The cylindrical rotor construction has its advantage viz. robust construction & noise free operation, good dynamic balancing, high operating speed, less windage loss and sinusoidal flux distribution around periphery. The rated voltage is 11–25 kV and power factor is 0.85 lagging. Main Exciter has voltage of 125–250 V DC. Upto 50 MW, alternators are air-cooled and above this are hydrogen cooled. The alternators are available in the sizes of 10 MW to 1500 MW (lower sizes are used for captive power generation in industry).

(*viii*) **Power plant Instrumentation & control**

Instruments are needed to measure and indicate deviation of a variable from set point. Automatic control corrects the deviation and restores the stable operating state. To indicate deviations, annunciators are used. Annunciators are panels that indicate deviation of a parameter by a flashing light and hooter sound so as to draw attention of boiler operator. The instruments are used for measurement of various parameters such as temperature, pressure, level, flow, pH etc. Electrical measuring instruments are ammeters, voltmeters, wattmeters, powerfactor meters, kVAr meters, frequency meters, synchroscope etc. Both, indicating and recording type instruments are used.

(*a*) **Temperature measuring instruments**—The temperature of following variables are meausred.

1. Steam temperature at output and at superheaters.
2. Temperature of metal body of turbine casing, super-heaters and reheaters.
3. Air pre-heater inlet and outlet temperature of air.
4. Turbine bearing oil temperature.
5. Flue gas temperature at different zones.
6. Generator winding, bearing and core temperature.
7. Flame temperature inside furnace.

Various types of temperature measuring devices used are thermocouples, resistance temperature detectors (RTD), bimetal thermometers, pyrometers etc.

(*b*) **Pressure measuring instruments**—Pressure of the following variables are measured—

1. Steam outlet pressure.
2. Feed water pressure.
3. Condensate pressure.
4. Drum pressure.
5. Deaerator pressure.
6. Vacuum in condenser.
7. Lubricating oil pressure at bearing.
8. Fuel oil pressure before burner (for oil fired boilers).
9. Primary and secondary air pressure.
10. Furnace draft.

Pressure measuring instruments used are bourden gauge, diaphragm gauge, liquid manometer etc.

(*c*) **Level measuring instruments**—Level at following points are measured—

1. Boiler drum water level.
2. Condensate level in condensate tank.
3. Water level in deaerator.
4. Feed water tank level.
5. Lubricating oil level in tank.

(*d*) **Flow measurement**—Flow is measured at following points—

1. Feed water flow.
2. Steam flow.

3. Fuel flow.
4. Condensate flow.
5. Air flow after forced draft fan.

Flow is measured using orifice and sensors.

(e) **Measurement of other parameters**—Various other parameters measured are given as follows.

Parameter	Location
1. pH of water.	In feed water
2. Conductivity of water	
3. Dissolved oxygen in boiler water.	
4. Percentage oxygen.	In flue gas
5. Carbon dioxide	
6. Carbon monoxide	
7. Hydrogen pressure	In Alternator
8. Hydrogen purity	
9. Vibration of alternator	
10. Turbine shaft eccentricity	In Turbine
11. Vibration at turbine bearing.	
12. Turbine casing expansion	
13. Current	In Alternator
14. Voltage	
15. Power factor	
16. Frequency	
17. Power	

(ix) **Electrical Control and protection equipment**—Various types of control and protection equipment & used are given below—

For alternator protection:

1. Over voltage relay.
2. Under voltage relay.
3. Over current relay.
4. Earth fault relay.
5. Field failure relay.
6. Rotor earthfault relay.
7. Differential protection.
8. Antimotoring relay.
9. Negative phase sequence relay.
10. Synchronising relay.

For Turbine protection:

11. Low condenser vacuum trip.
12. Low lub. oil pressure trip.
13. Overspeed trip.
14. Fire protection trip.
15. Thrust bearing trip.
16. High vibration trip

for Control system:

17. Data acquisition system.
18. Hydrogen purity system.
19. Electro-mechanical controllers.
20. PID controllers.

(*x*) **Power plant auxiliaries**—These are equipment that assist major equipments such as boiler, turbine etc. to function.

1. **Boiler auxiliaries**—These are following—
   - — Forced draft fan—It feeds air into boiler.
   - — Induced draft fan—it sucks air into stack.
   - — Boiler feed pump—It feeds water into boiler drum.
   - — Air pre-heater—It pre-heats combustion air.
   - — Secondary air fan—It feeds air for combustion.
   - — Soot blower—It blows away soot from boiler tube surface.
   - — Pulverising mill—It converts coal into fine powder.
   - — exhausters.
2. **Coal and ash auxiliaries**—These are following—

— Stackers—It stacks raw coal at unloading place.

— Elevators—It transfers coal.

— Wagon tipplers—It unloads coal from railway wagons by tilting wagon.

— Conveyors—It conveys coal to coal mill.

— Cranes—It is used for lifting of heavy equipments.

— Hoists—It is used for lifting of equipments.

3. **Turbine and alternator auxiliaries**—These are following—

— Feed water pump—It feeds water to deaerator.

— Condensate pump—It feeds water from condensate tank to CP heater.

— Vacuum pump—It maintains vacuum inside condenser.

— Ventilating fans.

— Oil pumps—These are used for lubricating purpose.

— Governor control—It controls steam input to turbine.

— Main exciter—It feeds dc supply to field of alternator.

— Pilot excitor—It generates supply for main excitor.

— Turning gear motor—It is used to slowly rotate turbine shaft when steam turbine is at rest. This is done to prevent sagging of turbine shaft due to its heavy weight.

4. **Miscellaneous auxiliaries**—These are following—

— Water pump for fire protection.

— Air compressor for pneumatically operated instruments.

— Rapper motor for electrostatic precipitator (for flyash removal).

(*xi*) **Auxiliary supply transformers**—Auxiliary supply is required to feed power station auxiliaries for both essential and nonessential equipments. Essential auxiliaries are those without which power plant cannot work e.g. feed water pump, condensate pump, forced draft fan, induced draft fan, circulating pump, lighting, primary air fan, pulverised fuel feeder etc. Station auxiliaries consume 8–10% of generated power. Auxiliaries are supplied from two transformers viz. station transformer receiving supply from grid and unit transformer receiving supply from main generator. All essential auxiliaries are supplied from unit transformers and non-essential auxiliaries from station transformer.

3.9. HEAT BALANCE

Heat balance is the record of all heat losses taking place in a power plant. Various heat losses are given below—

(*i*) heat carried by flue gases	—	4.5 %
(*ii*) moisture in fuel	—	4.5 %
(*iii*) combustible in ash	—	0.25 %
(*iv*) combustible in dust	—	0.25 %
(*v*) radiation and unaccounted losses	—	90.45 %

The overall thermal efficiency of power plant is very low about 30%. This is due to the large amount of heat rejected in the condenser.

3.10. FLUIDISED BED COMBUSTION BOILER

Fluidisation is a process of mixing air and fuel which remains in a suspended state in air stream. Fuel is suspended in air by blowing a jet of air through it. This process provides more chemical reaction leading to better heat transfer. This process is suitable to burn fuels that are difficult to ignite or have high ash content e.g. high ash coal, coal mine waste, petroleum coke, anthracite, biomass, agricultural waste etc. The combustion temperature range is 840° to 950°C. In this temperature range, nitrogen oxide formation is lower and there is no tendency to form clinker (large size lumps).

It consists of enclosed space filled with sand and other inert material which rests on a perforated base. When air is passed upward through the bed, the individual particles are suspended in air stream. The bed is then in fluidised state. With further increase in air velocity, bubble formation takes place leading to turbulent mixing of air and fuel.

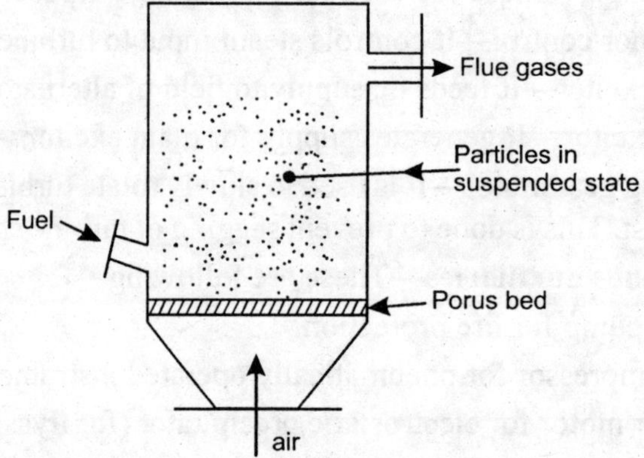

Figure 3.35. Fluidised bed combustion boiler

In order to reduce high temperature, moist air is introduced so that temperature remains within desired temperature band.

Advantages of FBC are following—

(*i*) high boiler efficiency (typically 84%).

(*ii*) reduced boiler size.

(*iii*) ability to burn variety of fuels: ash content as high as 62% and calorific value as low as 2500 kcal/kg can be used.

(*iv*) low SO_x and NO_x emission.

(*v*) low corrosion and erosion on account of low operating temperature.

(*vi*) no clinker formation (formation of hard chunk due to fusing of silica at higher temperature).

(*vii*) fast response to fluctuating load.

(*viii*) less excess air required.

(*ix*) no soot blowing is required.

(*x*) high reliability and reduced maintenance.

There are three types of fluidised bed combustion boilers—

1. Atmospheric fluidised bed combustion boiler (AFBC).
2. Pressurised fluidised bed combustion boiler (PFBC).
3. Circulating fluidised bed combustion boiler (CFBC).

1. **Atmospheric fluidised bed combustion boiler (AFBC)**—The boiler operates under atmospheric pressure. It uses limestone to capture sulphur released by the combustion of coal. The jet of air suspends mixture of absorbent and burning coal during combustion. Due to the suspension in air, particles turn red hot and flow like fluid.
2. **Pressurised fluidised bed combustion boiler (PFBC)**—It is similar to the AFBC except system operates at an elevated pressure to produce high pressure gas stream to drive gas turbine.
3. **Circulating fluidised bed combustion boiler (CFBC)**—In this type, an arrangement is made to circulate a part of fluidised stream back into boiler.

The capacity of these boilers range from 0.5 T/hr to 100 T/hr.

3.11. SUPER CRITICAL AND ULTRA SUPER CRITICAL BOILERS FOR STEAM GENERATION

Super critical boiler is technologically advanced compared to the pulverised fuel fired boiler. Due to higher temperature and pressure, efficiency is high upto 44% with lower emission level.

Super critical refers to a state of matter where there is no clear distinction between liquid and gaseous phase. For water, it happens at 374.15°C and a pressure of 220.6 bar (225.56 kg/cm^2). So, water when enters a super critical boiler, it ceases to be liquid and gets converted directly into steam. Usually, these boilers operate at a pressure of 250 kg/cm^2 and at a temperature of 540°C. This increase in pressure and temperature increases the cycle efficiency by about 3–4% and decreases fuel consumption by 8–10% with consequent reduction in emission.

For attaining higher efficiency, ultra super critical boilers are used which operate at a pressure of 270 bar and temperature of 580–620°C. It has an efficiency of 42–45% (*i.e.* large subcritical boilers operate at 170 bar and 540°C with an efficiency of 37–42%).

The process of attaining super critical state can be explained as—suppose water is being heated at atmospheric pressure, the temperature at which water converts to steam is 100°C. If heat is further added, temperature does not increase but more steam is produced at 100°C. At atmospheric pressure, latent heat of vaporisation is 2256 kJ/kg.

If water is heated at higher pressure say 100 bar, boiling happens at 311°C and latent heat of vaporisation is 1318 kJ/kg. If pressure of water is increased further to 200 bar, the boiling happens at 366°C and latent heat of vaporisation is 584 kJ/kg. So, it can be observed that with the increase in pressure of water, there is increase in boiling point and decrease in latent heat of vaporisation. With further increase in pressure and temperature, a point is reached where latent heat of vaporization is zero i.e. no boiling takes place and water directly gets converted into steam. The pressure and temperature at which this happens is known as critical pressure and critical temperature. For steam conditions are called super critical boilers. Purpose of using super critical technology is to increase efficiency by about 4%.

Higher operating pressure and temperature requires special type of materials. This is given in the table 3.7.

Table 3.7: Material of construction for super critical boiler

Sr. No.	*Part of boiler*	*Material of construction*
1.	Economiser	Carbon steel
2.	Pressure vessel	Low alloy ferritic steel
3.	Tubes	Austenitic steel
4.	Water walls	Low alloy ferritic steel
5.	Main steam pipe	Medium alloy steel

Major difference between conventional sub critical boiler and super critical boiler are given in table 3.8.

Table 3.8: Comparision of Subcritical & Supercritical boiler

Sr. No.	*Subcritical boiler*	*Supercritical boiler*
1.	System has constant evaporation end point.	System has variable evaporation end point.
2.	It is a drum type boiler in which water steam mixture go to superheater.	It is a drumless boiler. Evaporation takes place in a single pass.

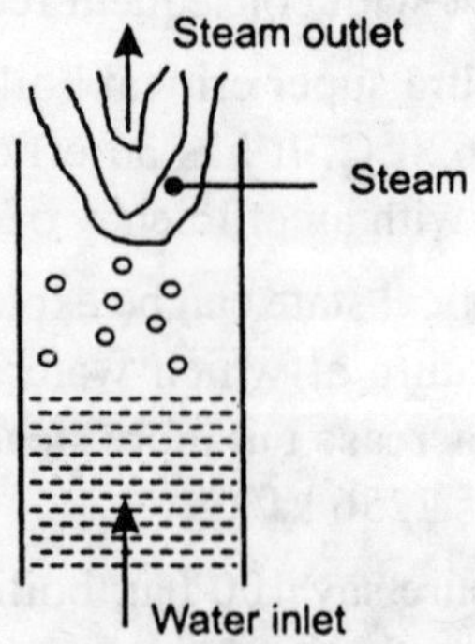

Figure 3.36. Single pass super critical boiler

Advantages of super critical boiler are following—

(*i*) high efficiency of 42–44%.

(*ii*) 4% saving in fuel.

(*iii*) quick start and shut down.

(*iv*) quick response to continuously varying load.

(*v*) can operate under low load.

(*vi*) steam temperature can be maintained over side range of pressure.

(*vii*) different quality of coal can be used.

(*viii*) has reduced carbon dioxide emission (2–3% less)

Disadvantages of super critical boilers are following—

(*i*) high capital cost.

(*ii*) higher temperature and pressure requires superior grade material.

(*iii*) high operation and maintenance cost.

(*iv*) complicate to operate.

(*v*) less flexible operation.

(*vi*) high feed pump energy consumption.

Following table gives comparison of various parameters of subcritical, super critical and ultra super critical boilers—

Table 3.9: Comparison of subcritical, super critical and ultra super critical boilers

Sr. No.	*Type of technology*	*Unit size (MW)*	*Steam pressure (bar)*	*Steam temperature (°C)*	*Reheat temperature (°C)*
1.	Subcritical	500	170	537	537
2.	Super critical	660/800	247–280	565	593
3.	Ultra super critical	1000	295	600	600

3.12. INTEGRATED GASIFICATION COMBINED CYCLE (IGCC)

It is a combination of two technologies viz. gasification that converts coal into synthesis gas and combined cycle operation where both steam turbine (Rankine cycle) and gas turbine (Brayton cycle) are used.

Coal gasification is an incomplete combustion of coal that produces synthesis gas which is a mixture of carbon mono oxide and hydrogen gas. Atleast 98 % of sulphur contaminants are removed as slag (byproduct of gasification). Efficiency of IGCC can reach upto 46%.

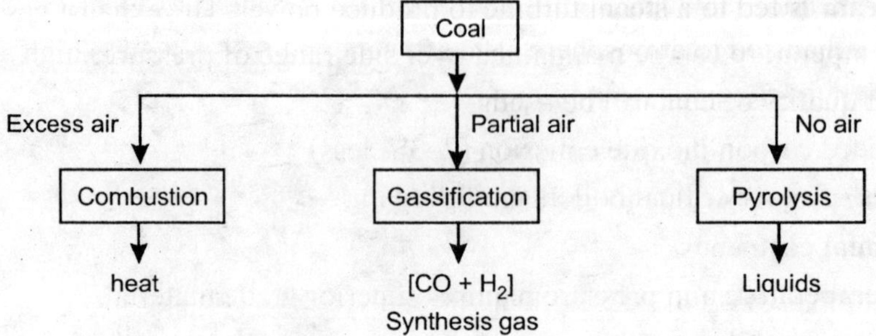

Figure 3.37. Combustion of coal

Process flow chart of IGCC is given below—

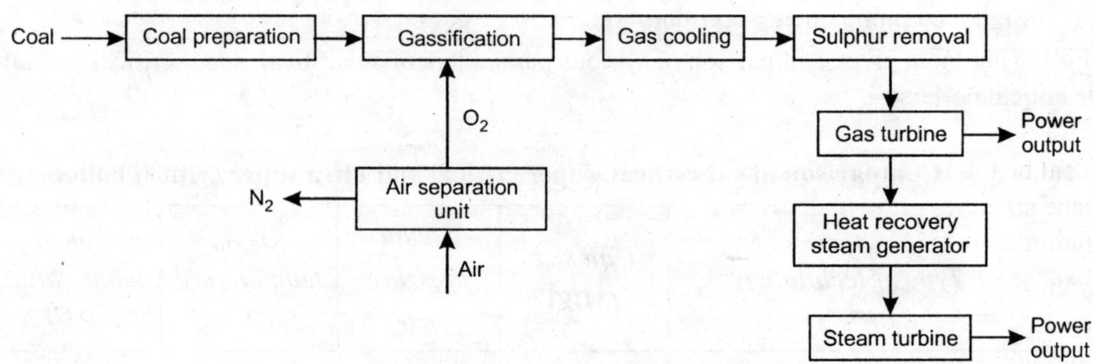

Figure 3.38. Block diagram of IGCC

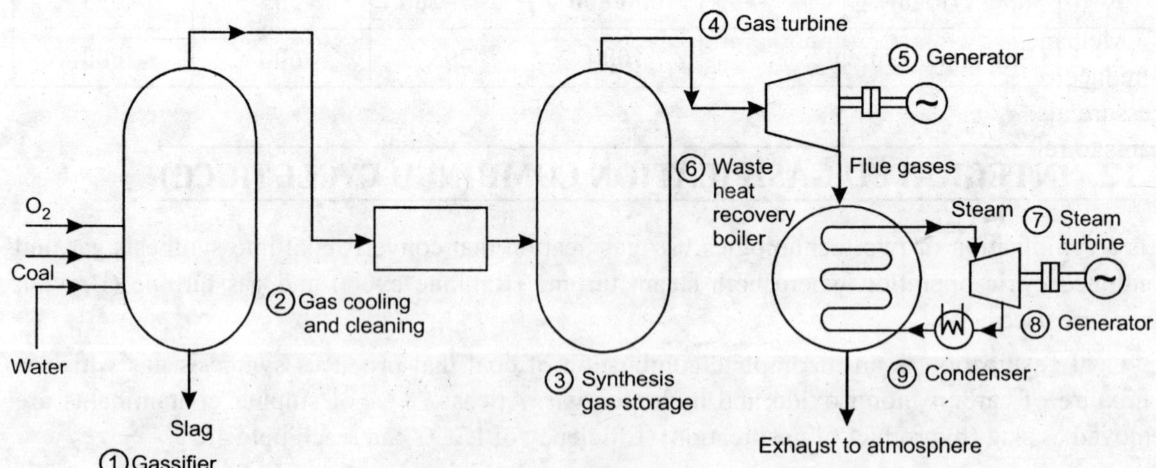

Figure 3.39. Schematic of IGCC

In this system, coal is fed to a gasifier in which oxygen and steam is used to convert it to synthesis gas (mixture of carbon mono oxide and hydrogen gas). This gas is then cooled and cleaned to remove particulate matter and other emissions. This cleaned gas is then burnt in a gas turbine to produce power. The exhaust of gas turbine is led to a waste heat recovery boiler where steam is produced. This steam is fed to a steam turbine to produce power. The exhaust gas from waste heat recovery boiler is exhausted to atmosphere. The efficiency of this system is high–about 46%.

Advantages of IGCC system are following—

(*i*) this system can handle any carbonaceous matter.
(*ii*) emission is very low due to gas clean up
(*iii*) high system efficiency.
(*iv*) substantial reduction in water consumption.
(*v*) pure hydrogen can be produced, if required.
(*vi*) synthesis gas can be used for other purposes.

3.13. NEW SOURCE OF METHANE—COAL BED METHANE (CBM)

Methane is a clean burning fuel and is an alternate source of energy. India has 6.7% of recoverable coal reserves of the world while USA has 28.6%, Russia 18.5%, China 13.5% and Australia 9.0%. The coal bed in the earth can store methane due its moderate intrinsic porosity. Coal bed can store methane six times more than sandstone under same pressure. Amongst all types of coal, anthracite and bituminous coal have higher ability to store methane.

Methane is produced in anthracite and bituminous coal by thermal maturation of their organic compounds. In lignite and sub-bituminuous coal, microbial activity produces methane. The methane thus produced is adsorbed in the coal. Small amount of methane are also found in voids created by coal shrinkage. The application of heat, pressure and biological process causes shrinkage when organic rich peat is transformed.

Methane is extracted from underground coal bed by dewatering the formation layer. This helps to reduce reservoir pressure and hence, allows the gas to flow into well bore. This lowering of pressure also releases methane adsorbed on coal face. Horizontal bore holes are drilled into coal seams to release methane.

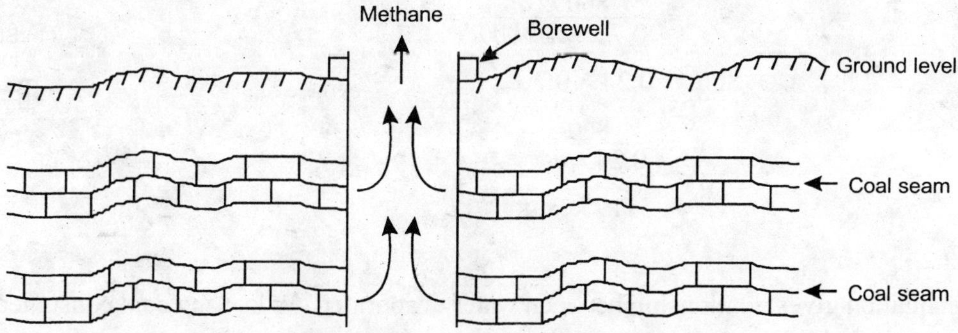

Figure 3.40. Extraction of coal bed methane

Advantages of coal bed methane are following—

(*i*) provides clean burning fuel.
(*ii*) reduces chances of fire or explosion in coal mines.

(*iii*) reduces methane vented to atmosphere from coal mines which causes global warming.

(*iv*) provides an opportunity to utilize coal reserve that is too deep or difficult to mine.

(*v*) drilling of well for methane is safer compared to oil or natural gas as there is extremely low risk of spill or blowout.

Although composition of methane obtained from a well is dependent upon geographical location, but a typical composition of coal bed methane is given below—

(*i*) Methane — 96.2 %

(*ii*) Ethane — 0.01%

(*iii*) Carbon dioxide — 0.1%

(*iv*) Nitrogen — 3.4%

(*v*) Hydrogen — 0.01%

(*vi*) Helium — 0.26%

(*vii*) Higher hydrocarbons — 0.71%

Solved Examples

Example 2.1

A thermal power plant has overall efficiency of 24% and 0.70 kg of coal is required per kWh of energy produced. Find out calorific value of coal.

Solution:

Let us assume x be the calorific value of coal in kcal/kg.

$\therefore$ Heat generated by 0.70 kg of coal = $0.7x$ kcal

Since 1 kWh = 860 kcal

$$\therefore \quad \text{Efficiency } \eta = \frac{\textit{Electrical energy output}}{\textit{Heat energy input}}$$

$$= \frac{860 \; kcal}{0.7 \; x \; kcal/kWh} = 0.24$$

or

$$860 = 0.24 \times 0.7\,x$$

$$x = \frac{860}{0.24 \times 0.7}$$

$$= 5119 \text{ kcal/kg}$$

Ans.

Example 2.2.

Following equation gives relationship between water evaporated (W kg) and coal consumed (C kg) and energy generated (kWh) in 8 hour in a thermal power plant.

$$W = 12000 + 8 \times \text{kWh}$$

$$C = 5200 + 3.1 \times \text{kWh}$$

Calculate

(*i*) the quantity of coal required per hour so as to run the plant at no load.

(*ii*) the limiting value of water evaporated per kg of coal consumed as the station output increases.

Solution:

(*i*) At no load, no electricity is produced.

$\therefore$ kWh = 0 at no load

$$\therefore \quad C = 5200 + 3.1 \times \text{kWh}$$

$$\Rightarrow \quad C = 5200 + 3.1 \times 0$$

or $C = 5200/8\text{-hr}$

$$\text{or} \quad \text{coal consumed/hr} = \frac{5200}{8}$$

$$= 650 \text{ kg} \qquad \textbf{Ans.}$$

(*ii*) $\text{Water evaporated/kg of coal} = \frac{W}{C} = \frac{12000 + 8 \times \text{kWh}}{5200 + 3.1 \times \text{kWh}}$

With increase in plant kWh to infinity, ratio of $\frac{W}{C} = \frac{8}{3.1}$ or 2.58. Hence, limiting value of water evaporated/kg of coal is **2.58. Ans.**

Example 2.3.

A thermal power plant spends ₹ 35 × 10^5 year on coal purchases. The cost of coal is ₹ 410 per ton having a calorific value of 4800 kcal/kg. Find the average load on power plant if thermal efficiency is 28% and electrical efficiency is 88%.

Solution:

$$\text{overall efficiency } \eta_o = \text{thermal efficiency } (\eta_t) \times \text{electrical efficiency } (\eta_e)$$

$$= 0.28 \times 0.88$$

$$= 0.246$$

$$\text{Amount of coal consumed/year} = \frac{35 \times 10^5}{410} \text{ tons}$$

$$= 8750 \text{ tons or } 8750 \times 10^3 \text{ kg}$$

Total heat produced after combustion of coal

$$= \text{coal consumption/year} \times \text{calorific value of coal}$$

$$= 8750 \times 10^3 \text{ kg} \times 4800 \text{ kcal/kg}$$

$$= 42 \times 10^9 \text{ kcal}$$

$$\eta_o = \frac{\textit{Heat output}}{\textit{Heat of combustion}}$$

$$0.246 = \frac{\textit{Heat output}}{42 \times 10^9}$$

$$\text{or} \quad \text{Heat output} = 0.246 \times 42 \times 10^9$$

$$= 10.332 \times 10^9 \text{ kcal}$$

since 1 kWh = 860 kcal

$$\therefore \quad \text{Units generated/year} = \frac{10.332 \times 10^9}{860} \text{ kWh}$$

$$= 12013953.48 \text{ kWh}$$

$$\text{Average load on plant} = \frac{\textit{Units generated/year}}{\textit{hours in a year}}$$

$$= \frac{12013953.48}{8760}$$

$$= 1371.46 \text{ kW}$$ **Ans.**

Example 2.4.

Generate an approximate heat balance sheet for a thermal power plant consuming 0.65 kg of coal per kWh output. Assume, calorific value of coal as 5500 kcal/kg, boiler efficiency 80% and electrical efficiency 82%.

Solution:

$$\text{Total heat input} = 0.65 \text{ kg/kWh} \times 5500 \text{ kcal/kg}$$

$$= 3575 \text{ kcal/kWh}$$

Since 1 kwh = 860 kcal

∴ Equivalent electrical energy for this heat input

$$= \frac{3575}{860} = 4.16 \text{ kWh}$$

$$\text{Losses in boiler} = 4.16 \times 0.18 \qquad \text{(boiler efficiency = 82\%)}$$

$$= 0.7488 \text{ kWh}$$

$$\therefore \quad \text{Heat input to steam} = 4.16 - 0.7488$$

$$= 3.4112 \text{ kWh}$$

With electrical efficiency as 82%, the alternator input $= \dfrac{1}{0.82} = 1.22$ kWh

$$\therefore \quad \text{Alternator loss} = 1.22 - 1 = 0.22 \text{ kWh}$$

$$\text{Loss in turbine} = 3.4112 - 1.22 = 2.1912 \text{ kWh.}$$

Heat balance sheet

Loss (*i*) boiler loss	=	0.7488 kWh
(*ii*) turbine loss	=	2.1912 kWh
(*iii*) alternator loss	=	0.22 kWh
Total loss		3.16 kWh

output = 1 kWh

Input = output + losses = 1 kWh + 3.16 kWh = 4.16 kWh **Ans.**

CHAPTER SUMMARY

A thermal power plant converts chemical energy of coal into electrical energy. Coal is used in fine powdered form called pulverised coal which increases the surface area for combustion. This pulverised coal is burnt in a boiler to generate hot flue gases which carry the heat to raise steam in water tubes. The steam so raised is superheated in a superheater before being fed to steam turbine. The flue gases after passing through superheater, heats water in an economiser before it is fed to boiler. The flue gases then heat up air supplied for combustion in a boiler through air preheater. After heating air, the flue gases are exhausted to atmosphere through an induced draft fan. Water required to raise steam is taken from a nearby river which is filtered and demineralised and fed to boiler drum. Water for cooling of condenser is also drawn from a river which is then filtered and softened to remove hardness due to calcium and magnesium salts. The ash produced after combustion of coal is collected at the bottom of furnace and is called furnace bottom ash. It is carried to ash pond for further disposal. A part of ash escapes through flue gases to chimney which is arrested through an electrostatic precipitator.

The coal is transported to power plant through railway wagons which is initially stored in coal storage yard. Thereafter, this coal is sent to coal crushers. The coal from coal crusher is led to ball mill to convert this coal into powdered form which is then conveyed to the boiler burner for combustion.

The latest technology is to use super critical boiler which results in increase in 3–4% efficiency of boiler.

REVIEW QUESTIONS

Q. 1. State advantages and disadvantages of a thermal power plant.

Q. 2. What are the factors which govern the selection of site for a thermal power plant?

Q. 3. What are various types of losses that take place in a thermal power plant?

Q. 4. Identify the equipments in which maximum energy loss takes place in a thermal power plant.

Q. 5. Draw a block diagram of a thermal power plant and explain the operation.

Q. 6. Discuss the advantages of using pulverised fuel firing over use of coal briquetts.

Q. 7. Describe the function of electrostatic precipitator in a thermal power plant. Does it reduce gaseous pollutants?

Q. 8. Discuss the purpose of using superheated steam in a steam turbine.

Q. 9. What is the purpose of using economiser and air preheater?

Q. 10. Why deaerator is used in a boiler?

Q. 11. Write a brief note on (*i*) ball mill (*ii*) contact mill and (*iii*) impact mill.

Q. 12. What quality of water is used in water drum of boiler, in condenser and cooling tower?

Q. 13. Write a brief note on power plant instrumentation.

Q. 14. What are various protective relays used for protection of alternator?

Q. 15. What are power station auxiliaries? What is the typical power consumption of power station auxiliaries in a thermal power plant?

Q. 16. Give a heat balance sheet of a thermal power plant.

Q. 17. Write a brief note on fluidised bed combustion boiler.

Q. 18. Discuss the differences amongst sub critical, super critical and ultra super critical boilers.

Q. 19. Write a brief note on Integrated Gassification Combined Cycle (IGCC) power plant.

Q. 20. What is coal bed methane? How it can be used as a clean source of energy for power generation?

Q. 21. Discuss the advantages of using coal bed methane for power generation.

Numerical Questions

Q. 1. A thermal power plant having overall efficiency of 30% consumes 0.72 kg of coal per unit. Determine the calorific value of coal used. **[Ans:** 3981.5 kcal/kg]

Q. 2. Efficiencies of boiler, turbine and generator are 85%, 80% and 90% respectively. Calculate overall efficiency. **[Ans:** 61.2%]

Q. 3. Water evaporated (kg) and coal consumed (kg) in a thermal power plant is given by following expression for 8 hours—

water consumed, $W = 12400 + 7.8 \times \text{kWh}$

Coal consumed, $C = 5400 + 3.3 \times \text{kWh}$

Determine—

(*i*) quantity of coal required per hour so as to run the plant at no load.

(*ii*) limiting value of water evaporated per kg of coal consumed as the station output increase. **[Ans:** (*i*) 675 kg (*ii*) 2.634]

Q. 4. Annual cost of purchase of coal is ₹ 42×10^5. The declared calorific value of coal is 4400 kcal/kg and cost per ton is ₹ 620. The plant has thermal efficiency of 26% and electrical efficiency of 85%. Determine the average load on the power plant. **[Ans:** 874.38 kW]

SHORT ANSWER TYPE QUESTIONS

Q. 1. Why pulverised fuel firing is preferred over coal briquette firing?

Q. 2. How flyash from chimney is collected?

Q. 3. Why diameter of steam drum is smaller than water drum?

Q. 4. Why finned tubes are used in water tube boilers?

Q. 5. What is the function of forced draft and induced draft fan?

Q. 6. Why deaerator is used?

Q. 7. Why the height of chimney of a thermal power plant is kept high?

Q. 8. Why are the uses of furnace bottom ash?

Multiple Choice Questions

Q. 1. Maximum energy loss takes place in

(*a*) chimney (*b*) condenser
(*c*) alternator (*d*) steam turbine

Q. 2. Electrostatic precipitator removes

(*a*) sulphur dioxide (*b*) nitrogen dioxide
(*c*) both (*a*) and (*b*) (*d*) flyash

Q. 3. Deaerator is used to remove

(*a*) dissolved salts (*b*) dissolved gasses
(*c*) water hardness (*d*) both (*a*) and (*c*)

Q. 4. Overall efficiency of a typical thermal power plant is

(*a*) 18–24% (*b*) 24–33%
(*c*) 33–42% (*d*) 42–46%

Q. 5. Demineralised water is used in

(*a*) water drum (*b*) cooling tower
(*c*) both (*a*) and (*b*) (*d*) none of these.

Q. 6. Typical auxiliary energy consumption of a thermal power plant is in the range of

(*a*) 5–6% (*b*) 6–8%
(*c*) 8–10% (*d*) 10–12%
(*e*) 12–14%

Q. 7. A thermal power plant converts

(*a*) mechanical energy to electrical energy (*b*) heat energy to mechanical energy
(*c*) chemical energy to electrical energy (*d*) heat energy to electrical energy

Q. 8. A steam turbine converts

(*a*) heat energy to mechanical energy (*b*) mechanical energy to electrical energy
(*c*) chemical energy to mechanical energy (*d*) mechanical energy to heat energy

Q. 9. Speed of alternator in a thermal power plant is

(*a*) 3000 rpm (*b*) 1500 rpm
(*c*) both (*a*) and (*b*) (*d*) 1000 rpm

Q. 10. Alternator used in a thermal power plant is

(*a*) salient pole type (*b*) cylindrical rotor type
(*c*) either (*a*) or (*b*) (*d*) none of these

Answer to MCQ

1. (*b*) **2.** (*d*) **3.** (*b*) **4.** (*b*) **5.** (*a*)
6. (*c*) **7.** (*c*) **8.** (*a*) **9.** (*c*) **10.** (*b*)

Chapter

Hydro Electric Power Generation

Learning Objectives

After reading this chapter, reader will be able to

- Understand various components and their functions in a hydro power plant.
- Appreciate classification, types and applications of hydro turbines.
- Understand characteristic parameters of hydro turbines.
- Understand type of generators and power plant auxiliaries.

" A good scientist is a person with original idea. A good engineer is a person who makes a design that works with as few original ideas as possible. There are no prima donnas in engineering" — Freeman Dyson

4.1 INTRODUCTION

Some 5000 years ago, man utilised the energy of the falling water by water wheel for irrigation purpose. In 2nd century B.C., water mills were used to grind corn. Hydro-electric power plant produces electricity by utilising the energy of the falling water. A dam is constructed across a river or a lake and pressure of the water is utilised to run a hydro-turbine. The hydro-turbine coupled to a generator produces electric power. The dam stores water which contains potential energy and when water flows to hydro-turbine, it is converted into kinetic energy. Turbine converts this kinetic energy into mechanical energy. Generator coupled to the turbine, converts this mechanical energy into electrical energy.

India has a hydro power potential of 84,044 MW at 60% load factor. The installed capacity of hydro power in India is 42623.42 MW (Dec 31, 2015). This is 15% of the total electricity produced in India (284 GW). Hydro potential-basinwise is given in table 4.1.

Table 4.1 Hydro potential in India

River basin	*Potential at 60% load factor (MW)*
Indus	33,832
Ganga	20,711
Central India	4,152
River of western India	9,430
River of southern India	14,511
Brahmaputra	66,065
Total	1,48,701

Table 4.2 Regionwise distribution of hydro-electric power plant installed capacity (Dec 31, 2015)

Northern	–	18,246.77 MW (42.8%)
Western	–	7,447.50 MW (17.5%)
Southern	–	11,478.03 MW (26.9)%
Eastern	–	4,209.12 MW (9.97)
North-eastern	–	1,242.00 MW (2.9%)
Total	–	12,623.42 MW (100%)

Some of the world's largest dams are given in table 4.3 and major hydro-electric plant in India is given in Table 4.4.

Table 4.3 World's largest dams

Sr. No.	*Name*	*Country*	*Installed Capacity (MW)*
1.	Three Gorges	China	22,500
2.	Itaipu	Brazil/Paraguay	14,000
3.	Xiluodu	China	13,860
4.	Guri	Venezuela	10,235
5.	Tucurui	Brazil	8,970
6.	Grand coulee	USA	6,809
7.	Xiangjiba	China	6,448

8.	Longtan	China	6,426
9.	Sayano-shushenskaya	Russia	6,400
10.	Krasnoyarsk	Russia	6,000

Table 4.4 Major hydro-electric plants in India

Sr. No.	*Name*	*State*	*Installed Capacity (MW)*
1.	Tehri hydro	Uttrakhand	2400
2.	Koyna hydro	Maharashtra	1960
3.	Srisailam	Andhra Pradesh	1670
4.	Nathpa Jhakri	Himanchal Pradesh	1500
5.	Sardar Sarovar	Gujarat	1450
6.	Bhakra Nangal	Himanchal Pradesh	1325
7.	Indira Sagar	Madhya Pradesh	1000
8.	Nagarjuna Sagar	Andhra Pradesh	816
9.	Idduki Dam	Kerala	780
10.	Hirakud	Orrisa	307.5

Benefits of hydro-electric power plants are manifold such as electricity generation, flood control, irrigation etc. It is also a non-polluting method of electricity production.

4.2 ADVANTAGES AND DISADVANTAGES OF HYDRO-ELECTRIC PLANTS

Hydro-electric power plant offers many advantages compared to other methods of power generation. The advantages are given below–

(*i*) hydro plant does not require any fuel.

(*ii*) there is no environmental pollution.

(*iii*) hydro plants have very long life (about 50-70 years).

(*iv*) operation and maintenance cost is very low.

(*v*) efficiency of hydro plant is very high and does not reduce with age (about 80%).

(*vi*) it requires lesser number of operating personnel.

(*vii*) cost of land required is low due to its location in remote area.

(*viii*) hydro projects are multi purpose such as irrigation, flood control, navigation, water supply etc.

(*ix*) unit cost of electricity is very low.

(*x*) there is afforestation in surrounding area.

(*xi*) quick start and stop is possible.

(*xii*) there are no standby losses.

Following are the disadvantages—

(*i*) high cost of civil construction.

(*ii*) requires long time to complete.

(*iii*) hydro plant submerges large area. This requires resettlement of large population.

(*iv*) due to remote location, long transmission lines are required to feed power to load centres.

(*v*) generation of power is dependent upon rain.

(*vi*) building of large dams alters water table of region.

(*vii*) siltation (deposition of mud carried by flow of water) reduces water flow, damages turbine due to abrasive action of silt and makes flood control difficult.

(*viii*) building large dams causes serious geological damage e.g. triggering of earthquakes.

(*ix*) difficulty in project implementation due to remoteness.

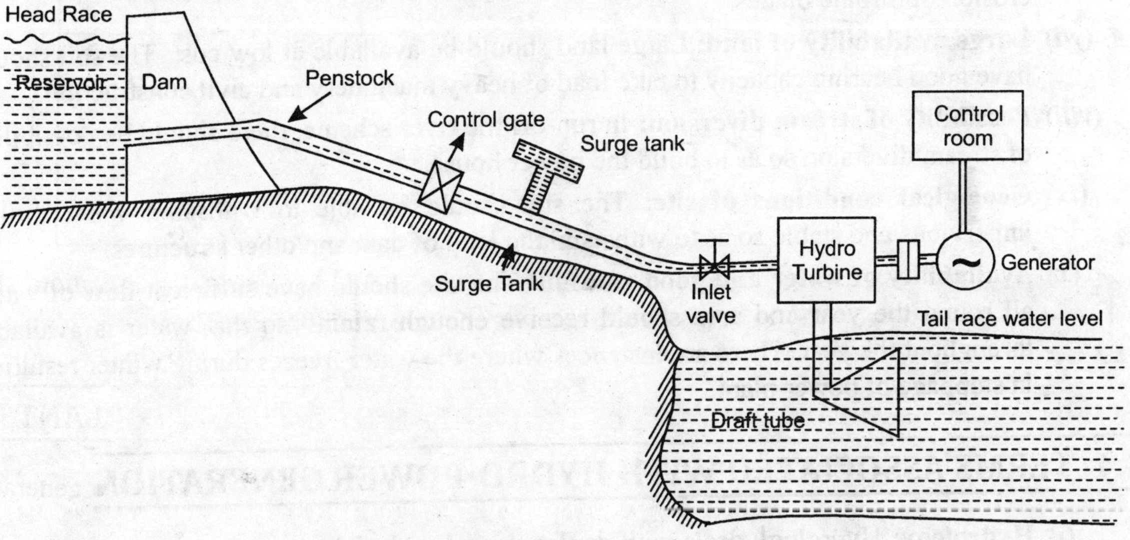

Fig. 4.1 Hydro-electric power plant

4.3 SELECTION OF SITE FOR HYDRO-ELECTRIC POWER PLANT

A hydro-electric power plant should be constructed in a place which has large catchment area, very good rainfall, good subsoil suitable for heavy construction, steep gradient etc. Following are the factors to be considered for selection of site for a hydro-electric power plant–

(*i*) **Large quantity of water at high head:** The electricity produced depends upon flow rate of water and head (height at which water is falling). So, the site should have large quantity of water at very high head. The water should be available all through the year.

(*ii*) **Large water storage:** Due to fluctuation of flow of water, large water storage capacity is required to take care of low flow during lean period. Water storage requires topographical and geological investigations for constructing natural foundation.

(*iii*) **Distance from load centre:** The plant should be located near to the load centre. This reduces the cost of laying transmission line and transmission losses.

(*iv*) **Access to site:** Hydro-electric power plant requires huge civil construction and for this purpose large amount of cement, steel, other building materials and heavy machinery is required to be transported. For this purpose, a rail head and/or road is constructed. The selected site should allow easy construction of rail head or road for transportation of construction material and heavy machinery.

(*v*) **Water pollution:** Water available at site must be free from pollution. The pollution is created by industries upstream which discharge effluents without treatment. This polluted water causes excessive corrosion of metal parts of hydro turbine, penstock etc.

(*vi*) **Siltation:** Siltation is the deposition of mud due to soil erosion. The site selected must be free from siltation. Siltation takes place in region having low or no vegetation and where violent storms takes place. Siltation reduces storage capacity of reservoir and causes erosion of turbine blades.

(*vii*) **Large availability of land:** Large land should be available at low cost. The soil should have good bearing capacity to take load of heavy machinery and civil construction.

(*viii*) **Possibility of stream diversion:** In run-off the river scheme, there should be possibility of stream diversion so as to build the power house.

(*ix*) **Geological conditions of site:** The site should be able to withstand water thrust, impervious and stable so as to withstand the load of dam and other structures.

(*x*) **Availability of water and good rainfall:** The site should have sufficient flow of water all round the year and area should receive enough rainfall so that water is available throughout the year. There are instances where the water freezes during winter resulting in stoppage of power plant.

4.4 TERMS ASSOCIATED WITH HYDRO-POWER GENERATION

(*i*) **Hydrology:** Hydrology deals with depletion and replenishment of water resources over and under the surface. It includes all water that falls on the surface of earth i.e. rainfall and snow. It aims at transportation of water from one place to another and from one form to another.

The knowledge of this science helps to design, plan or construct dams, bridges, irrigation structures, highways, flood control etc.

(*ii*) **Hydrological cycle:** Most of the water resources viz rivers, oceans, lakes, ponds, and underground resources receive water from rainfall and snow. Rain results from evaporation from rivers, lakes, oceans etc. That is precipitated back as rainfall, snow, dew, frost, hail etc. So, this process of evaporation and precipitation is known hydrological cycle.

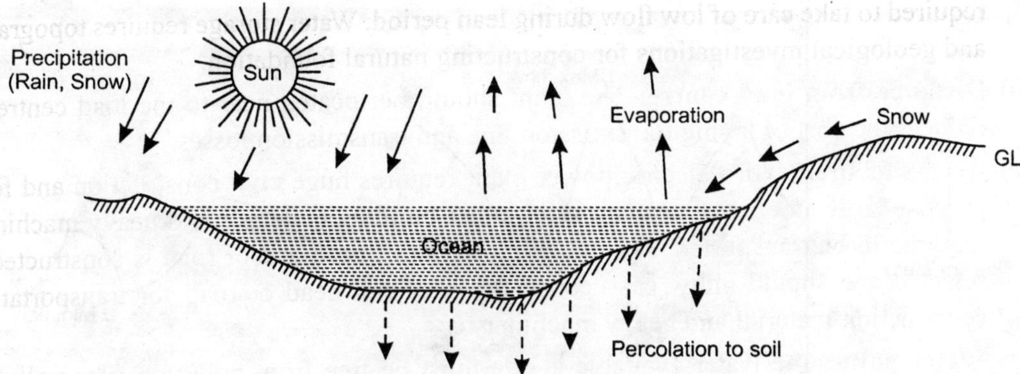

Fig. 4.2 Hydrological cycle

(*iii*) **Precipitation:** Precipitation or rainfall is the total condensation of moisture that reaches the earth's surface in any form. It includes forms of precipitation viz rain, snow, sleet, dew, hail, frost etc.

(*iv*) **Evaporation**: It is the transfer of water from liquid to vapour phase. It represents portion of rainfall that does not reach the point of use. Evaporation results from land and water surfaces and vegetation.

(*v*) **Transpiration:** It is process of water released to atmosphere by plants.

(*vi*) **Run-off:** It is the part of precipitation that is available as streamflow.

So, Run-off = total precipitation – total evaporation

A major part of rain water evaporates, another percolates into soil and form underground storage and some part is taken up by vegetation. The rest flows on the ground surface to form streams. This is known as run-off. This is required for hydro-power generation.

Run-off is affected by rainfall pattern, geology of area, shape and size of catchment area, topography and nature of soil in catchment area, amount of vegetation and weather condition in catchment area.

(*vii*) **Stream flow:** It is the quantity of water flowing in a stream. For the development of hydro-electric plant (HEP), it is necessary to estimate quantity of water flowing and its variation over a long period of time. Streamflow measurements are done to estimate minimum and maximum flow. Minimum flow gives the amount of primary path available throughout the year. The maximum flow gives an estimation of flood level which helps in design of spill-way. The estimated average flow gives the capacity of hydro plant.

(*viii*) **Hydrograph:** It is the graphical representation between discharge with time. Flow or discharge is taken on vertical axis (ordinate) and time on horizontal axis (abscissa). It indicates hydro power available from the stream at different times of day or year. It provides information, such as maximum and minimum flow during the period, average flow during the period and discharge at any time. Area under the curve gives total volume of discharge upto a given time. It is similar to a load curve.

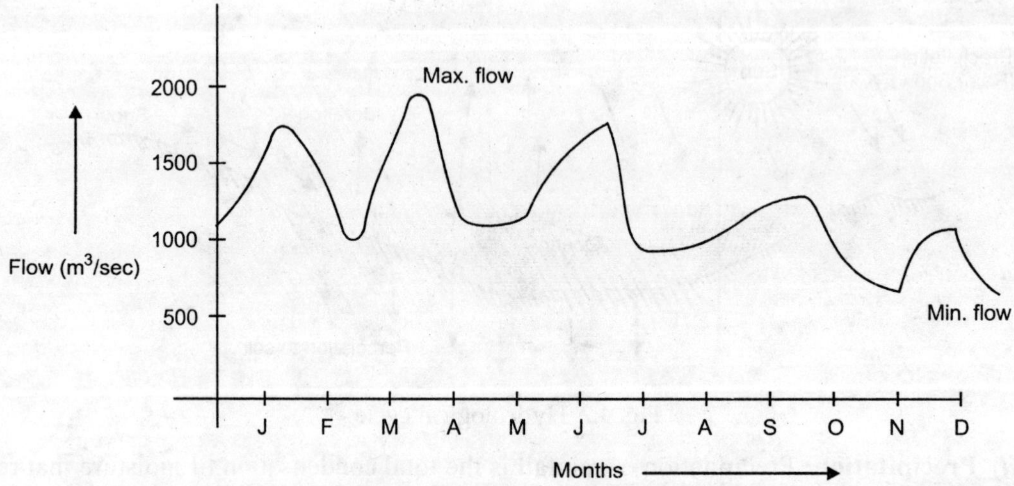

Fig. 4.3 Hydrograph of a river

Hydrograph of stream of river depends upon characteristics of catchment and precipitation over the catchment area.

(*ix*) **Flow duration curve:** It is a graph of flow available during a period against percentage of time. The time may be daily, monthly or yearly.

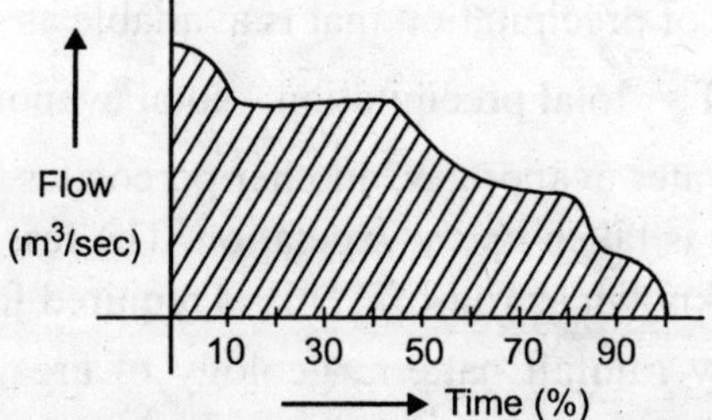

Fig. 4.4 Flow duration curve

The area under the curve represents total quantity of run-off during the period. The curve is used for determination of minimum and maximum flow conditions. The maximum capacity of plant is decided on the basis of minimum flow. This may also be used for flood control.

(*x*) **Mass curve:** It indicates total volume of run-off in cubic meters upto a certain time. The abscissa (*x*-axis) may be day, month or year. Ordinate (*y*-axis) is taken as cubic meter per second for one day or one month. The slope of curve at any point shows rate of flow at that time. Mass curves are used to estimate capacity of storage reservoir.

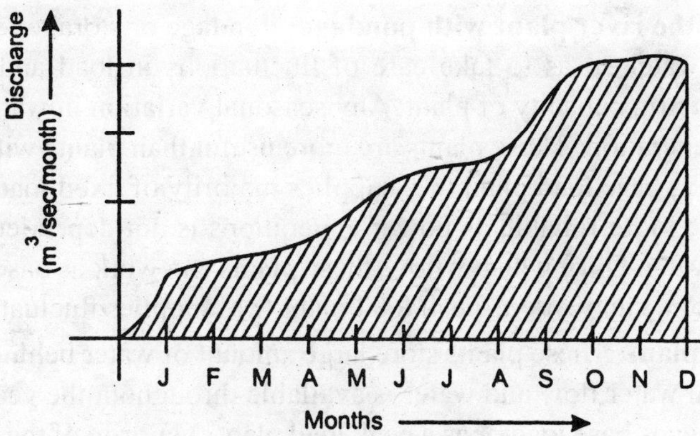

Fig. 4.5 Mass curve

(*xi*) **Storage:** Due to non-uniform flow of water, flow is sometimes in excess or may be deficient. So, for its regulation, artificial storage is needed. This storage helps to provide more water during deficient flow time. This increases firm capacity of power plant. The amount of storage can be acertained from hydrograph. If a horizontal line giving the average flow demand is drawn, the portion of the curve above this line will indicate the amount of water that should be stored in the reservoir during lean period. However, hydrograph varies from year to year hence mass curve will give better idea of storage capacity.

(*xii*) **Pondage:** If the power plant is away from storage reservoir, a small pond is required to meet hourly variations in load demand. The capacity of pond should be able to meet hourly changes for 24 hours.

4.5 CLASSIFICATION OF HYDRO-ELECTRIC POWER PLANTS

Hydro-electric power plants can be classified according to following–

(*i*) **According to availability of water–**

(*a*) run-off the river plant without pondage.

(*b*) run-off the river plant with pondage.

(*c*) storage plant.

(*d*) pumped storage plant.

(a) Run-off the river plant without pondage: In this scheme, water is taken directly from the river and after providing power, it flows downstream. So, there is no pondage or storage of water. Plants can work only if water is available all the time. There is no control over flow of water. During lean period, plant generation is low. But during high flow. Water is wasted water is mainly used for irrigation, navigation and power generation is incidental. At the time of flood, the water level may rise to excessive high level leading to inoperative power plant. So, these plants are used to produce electricity whenever water is available. These plants can be built at low cost.

(*b*) **Run-off the river plant with pondage:** Pondage or storage refers to ability of plant to store water so as to take care of fluctuations in load and water flow. Pondage increases firm capacity of plant. Any seasonal variation in water flow does not affect power generation. These plants are more useful than plants without pondage and can function as base load plant (*i.e.* supplies majority of fixed load continuously). These plants are more reliable as power generations is not dependent upon availability of flow of water. During heavy flow, these plants can work as base load plant and during lean season, can work as peak load plant (*i.e.* supplies fluctuating, or variable load.)

(*c*) **Storage plant:** These plants store large amount of water behind dam, so it is possible to control water flow and water is available throughout the year. These plants can be used either as base load or as a peak load plant. Majority of the plants are storage type (e.g. Bhakhra, Hirakud, Nathpa Jhakri etc.).

(*d*) **Pumped storage plant:** These plants operate as normal hydro-electric power plant during peak time. The water flows from pond to turbine thereby generating power. However, during off-peak time, water at tail pond is used to pump back to head pond so that during peak time, this water can be used for power generation.

So,during generation, the system works as turbine and generator while during off-peak period, system works as pump and motor.

These plants can recover almost 70% of water for reuse. These plants are operated in combination with steam plants as it results in decreased cost of steam plant due to higher load factor. These plants are widely used all over the world and have following advantages—

1. higher peak load capacity of plant at relatively lower cost.
2. improved load factor.
3. high operating efficiency.
4. plant becomes independent of water flow conditions.
5. the unit can operate in voltage regulation mode like a synchronous condenser and improve voltage and power factor.

(*ii*) **According to head–**

(*a*) low head plant.

(*b*) medium head plant.

(*c*) high head plant.

(*a*) **Low head plant:** In this case, a small dam is built across the river to provide necessary head. Usually, head upto 30 m can be classified as low head plant. The classification based on head is little fuzzy as it depends upon choice of turbine, civil engineering work etc.

The power plant is located near the dam therefore no surge tank is required. Due to low head, large quantity of water is required. The pipes carrying water have large diameter and small length. The structure required is expensive. The generators are of low speed and large diameter. The turbines employed are Francis or Kaplan or Propellor type.

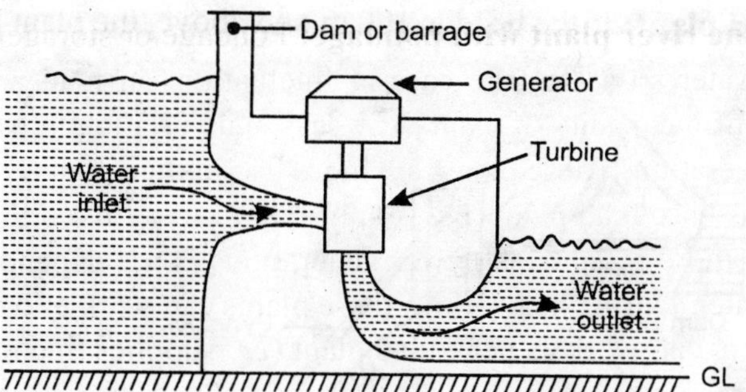

Fig. 4.6 Low head plant

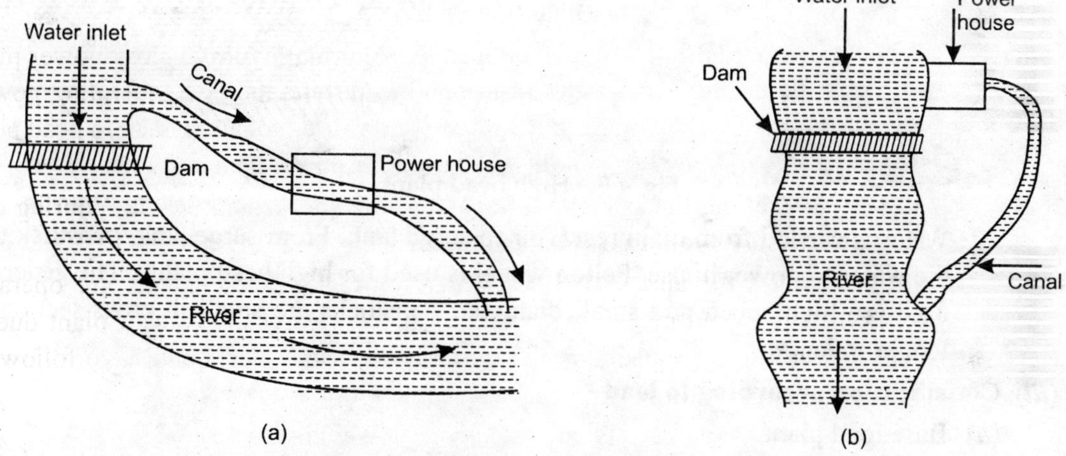

Fig. 4.7 Different locations of power house

(*b*) **Medium head plant:** When operating head of water lies between 30–100m, the plant is classified as medium head plant. The forebay is provided at the beginning of this plant. Water is carried from main reservoir to forebay in open channel and from forebay to turbine through penstock. The forebay works as surge tank. Francis, Propellor or Kaplan turbines are used.

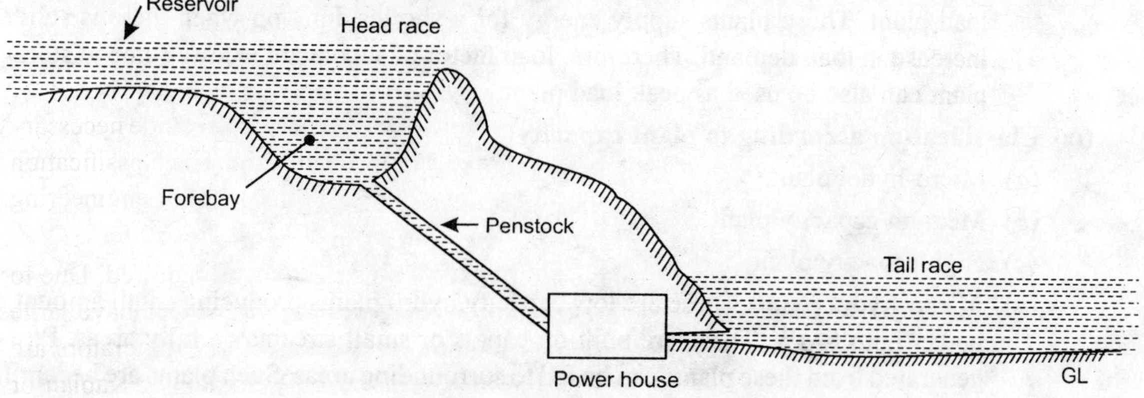

Fig. 4.8 Medium head plant

(c) **High head plant:** If the head is 100 m and above, the plant is classified as high head plant.

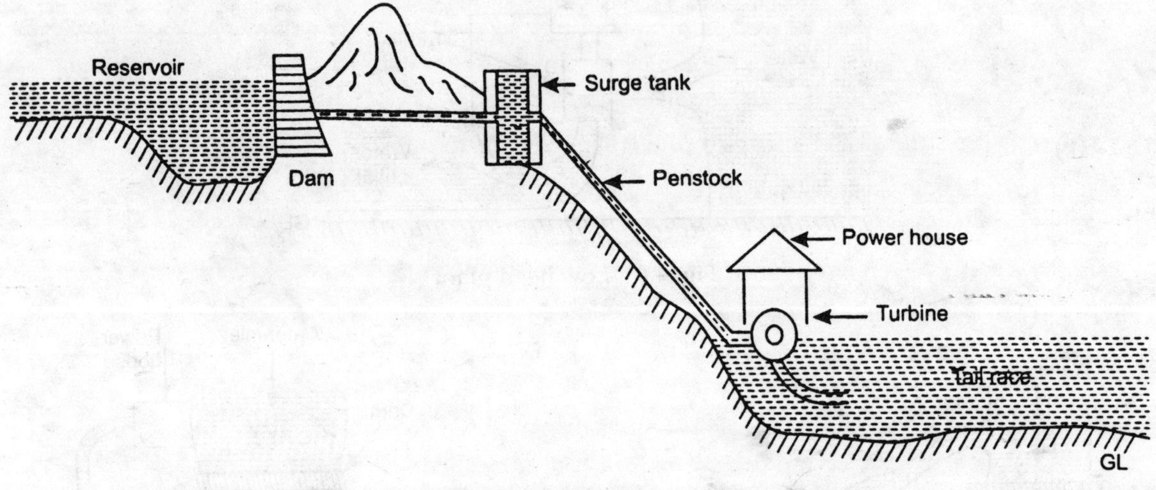

Fig. 4.9 High head plant

Water is carried from main reservoir to surge tank. From surge tank, penstock carry the water to power house. Pelton wheel is used for high head plants. The generators used are high speed and small diameter. Penstocks are small in cross-section and longer in length.

(*iii*) Classification according to load–

(*a*) Base load plant.

(*b*) Peak load plant.

(*a*) Base load plant: Base load plants operate on the base portion of load curve. These plants have large capacity and run continuously on practically constant load. Load factor of such plant is therefore high. Run-off the river plant with pondage and storage plants are used as base load plants.

(*b*) Peak load plant: These plants supply load corresponding to peak portion of load curve. Run-off the river plant with pondage and storage plants can work as peak load plant. These plants supply energy for a shorter duration when there is sudden increase in load demand. Therefore, load factor of such plant is low. Pumped storage plant can also be used as peak load plant.

(*iv*) Classification according to plant capacity:

(*a*) Micro-hydel plant.

(*b*) Medium capacity plant.

(*c*) High capacity plant.

(*a*) Micro-hydel plant: These are low capacity hydro plants producing small amount of power upto 5MW. These are built on canals or small streams on hilly areas. Power generated from these plants can be fed to surrounding areas. Such plants are becoming popular due to problems associated with large dams.

(*b*) **Medium capacity plant:** These plants produce power ranging from 25–100 MW. These plants require dams or barrages to be built on river to produce power.

(*c*) **High capacity plant:** The power capacity of these plants are more than 100 MW. These are very large power plants with huge storage capacity such as Nathpa Jhakri–1500 MW, Bhakra–Nangal–1325 MW, Three Gorges dam 22,500 MW (China), Itaipu dam 14,000 MW (Brazil/Paraguay) etc.

(*v*) **Classification according to place of power house.**

(*a*) Surface power plant

(*b*) Underground power plant

(*a*) **Surface power plant:** In these, power plants are built over the surface.

(*b*) **Underground power plant:** Power plants are built below the surface. Such a plant is built based on technical and economical reasons. Such power plants have advantages such as greater security during war time, low maintenance cost, short length of penstock, small surge tank, easier tail race design, less land required, no risk of landslide, avalanche or forest fire and easier temperature control inside plant. However, such plant have higher cost of construction, extra lighting required, special ventilation and air conditioning need, additional cost of location of transformers and switchgears etc.

Depending upon the topography and character of rock, there are two types of layout for underground power plants. In first case, power plant is located near the intake and has long tail race. This layout has advantage of lower cost of intake structure and quicker turbine control. In second case, plant is located at the end of long pressure tunnel and has short tail-race.

Koyna dam in Maharastra is an example of underground power plant.

4.6 COMPONENTS OF HYDRO-ELECTRIC POWER PLANT

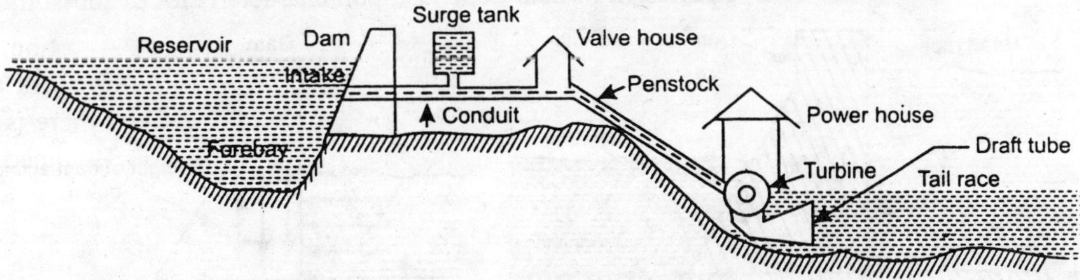

Fig. 4.10 Hydro-electric plant

Various components of hydro-electric power plant are listed below:

(*i*) **Storage reservoir:** The flow of water in a river varies. The flow is very high during rainy season and very low during summer. So, it is necessary to store water during heavy flow and supply the same during lean flow season. The storage of water helps to take care of fluctuations in load. During high demand, more water can be supplied while during low load flow can be curtailed. The capacity of storage reservoir is decided by run-off during high and lean seasons.

Storage can be two types– natural and artificial. Natural reservoir is a lake in high mountains. Artificial reservoir is created by constructing a dam. A low head plant requires large storage.

(*ii*) **Dam:** A dam is a barrier built across a water course (e.g. river, canal etc.) to hold back or control water flow or divert water. A barrage is a structure built across a water course so as to regulate flow of water. It has movable gates which can be raised or lowered to release desired amount of water. Purpose of a dam is manifold i.e. for flood control, irrigation purpose, power generation, navigation and recreation.

In case of hydro power generation, purpose of dam is to increase the head of available water and create artificial storage. It may be used to divert the flow of water so that it can be used for power generation. In any hydro-electric power project, dam constitutes major part of capital cost. Capital cost of dam is dependent upon different, subsoil conditions and hazards such as earthquakes etc. Dams are classified according to following–

(*a*) According to structural design–

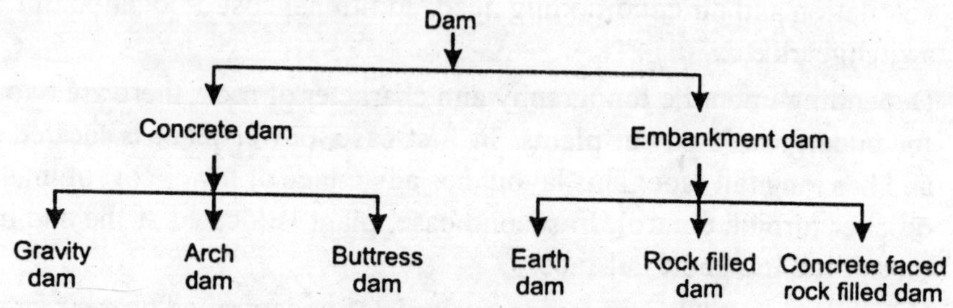

Fig. 4.11 Types of dam

1. **Gravity dam:** This type of dam is built with concrete. The stability of this dam depends upon its weight. Large volume of concrete is used for the construction of this dam. The height of dam depends upon characteristics of sub-soil.

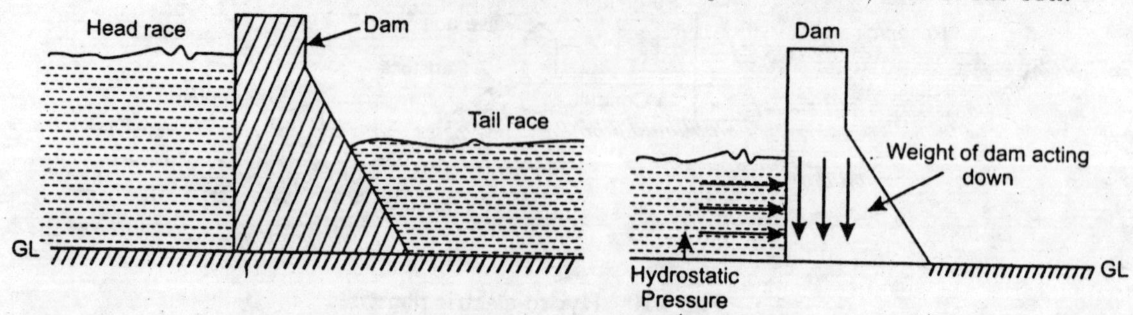

Fig. 4.12 Gravity dam

The dam resists water pressure (hydrostatic pressure) by its weight. It requires strong rocky foundation.

2. **Arch dam:** It's cross-section is that of a arch (curved) and is built on narrow river valleys. It is made of thin RCC (reinforced cement concrete) section and

are higher than gravity dam. The load transmitted on the dam depends upon radius of curvature. The water exerts hydrostatic pressure horizontally to the abuttments. The concave side of dam faces down stream side. The shape of dam helps to retain large part of water.

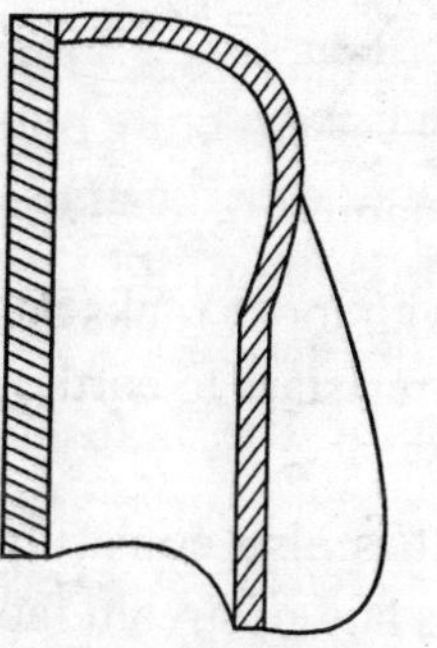

Fig. 4.13 Arch dam

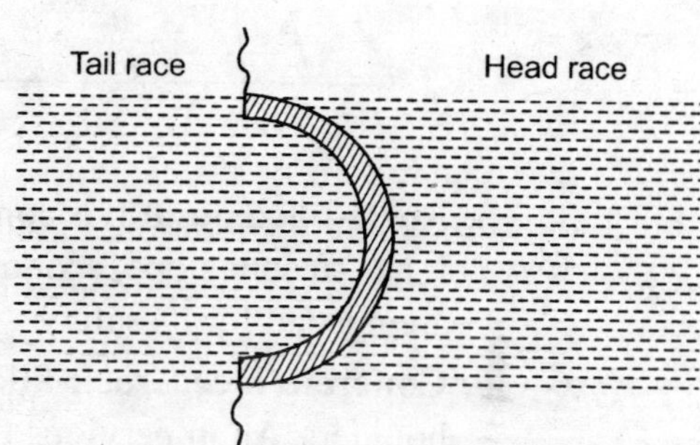

Fig. 4.14 Top view of Arch dam

3. **Buttress dam:** It is a solid gravity dam but uses less concrete and masonry. It has continuous inclined RCC slab upstream supported by a buttress or vertical pier like walls. The inclined upstream face creates a large downward force due to water. This force provides stability to dam. Such a dam is suitable for earthquake prone zone.

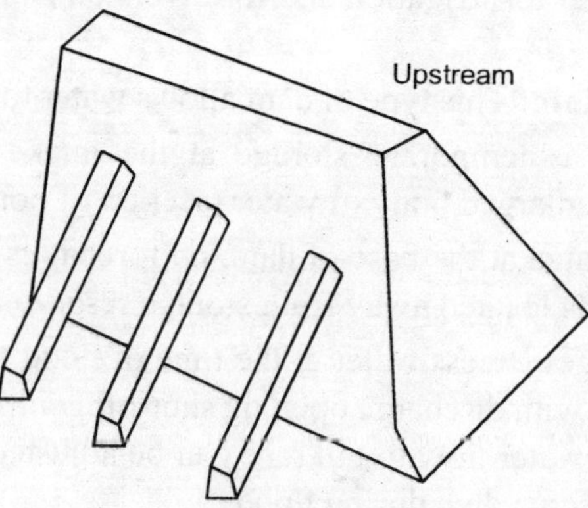

Fig. 4.15 Buttress dam

4. **Earth dam:** This type of dam has large base compared to its height. The dam is constructed by laying compacted soil or soil rock mix to form embankment–trapezoidal in shape across the river. The upstream face of earth dam is protected from erosion by surface layer of flat rock. This type of dam is cheaper than gravity dam. However, this type of dam is subject to erosion, has more seepage of water and is not suitable for spillways. This type of dam is further classified as–homogenous earth dam (uses same type of soil throughout), zoned type earth dam (it has impervious core zone surrounded by relatively pervious zone) and diaphragm type earth dam (an impervious wall of thickness less than 10 m replaces impervious zone).

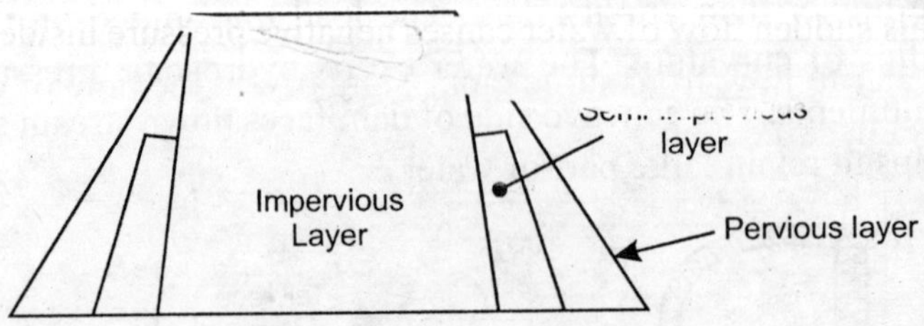

Fig. 4.16 Earth dam

5. **Rock–filled dam:** It is constructed with loose rocks and boulders instead of soil. It has steeper slope, economical and resistant to earthquake. Adequate spillways are needed for its safety.
6. **Concrete faced rock-filled dam:** It is also constructed with loose rocks and boulders, An impervious RCC slab is laid upstream face to reduce seepage. This RCC slab provides water tightness.

(*b*) Classification according to function of dam–

1. **Storage dam:** It is constructed to impound water in periods of surplus supply for use in period of deficiency. Water stored in reservoir is used for irrigation, power generation, water supply, flood control etc.
2. **Diversion dam:** It is constructed over river to divert water into canals, ditches etc. It is used for irrigation and for diversion from a stream to a distant storage reservoir.
3. **Overflow dam:** This type of dam allows water to be discharged over their crest.

(*iii*) Forebay: It serves as temporary storage at the intake to take care of hourly load fluctuations. It is an enlarged body of water (section of pond or canal).

If power plant is located at the base of dam, no forebay is required. However, forebay is required when plant is located away from storage reservoir.

(*iv*) Spillway: It discharges excess water at the time of flood to downstream side. It consists of concrete structure with discharge opening shut-off controlled by gates. So, by adjusting the position of gate, water flow to tail race can be adjusted. This prevents damage to the dam and acts as a safety valve during flood.

(*v*) Intake: Function of intake is to provide passage to flow of water to conduit or penstock. The intake structure is provided with trash racks, screens and booms to prevent entry of debris and ice into turbine.

Intakes with large storage–reservoir is called high pressure intake. With small storage reservoir, it is called low pressure reservoir. This small reservoir takes care of daily or weekly load variations.

(*vi*) Surge tank: Water flow in a pipeline if stopped suddenly results in water wave travelling in opposite direction. This is called water hammer. It puts extra pressure on the pipeline or penstock. In case of severe water hammer, penstock may burst. To prevent this rejected flow due to valve closure, a small reservoir is provided to receive this rejected flow and prevent water hammer pressure. This reservoir is called surge tank. It is located near the power house.

At the time of increase in load, governor opens to allow more flow of water through penstock. This sudden flow of water causes negative pressure inside penstock. This causes additional water to flow from surge tank. Similarly, at the time of decrease in load, there is rise in level in surge tank.

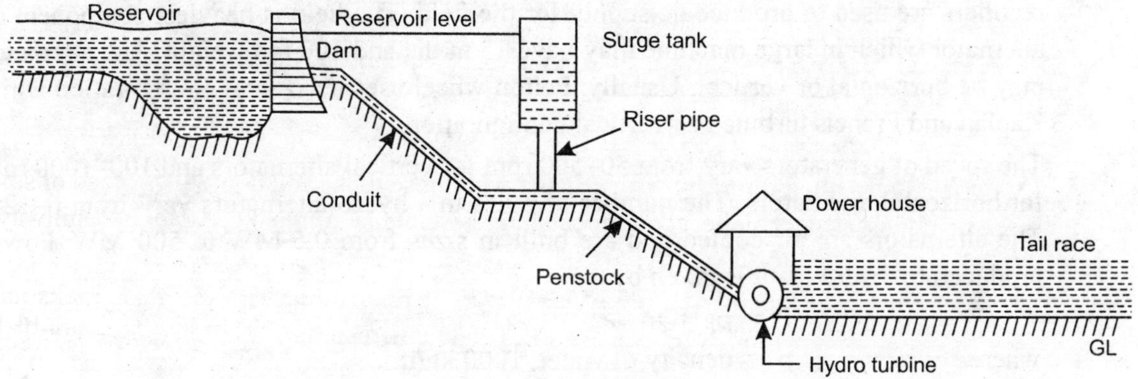

Fig. 4.17 Surge tank

(vii) Penstock: It is a closed conduit which connects forebay or surge tank to casing of turbine. It consists of steel or reinforced cement concrete. Each turbine in a power house has separate penstock or may have branch units to supply two or more units. In long penstocks, care is taken to protect it against water hammer. It may be above the surface or buried below earth surface.

(viii) Trash racks: These are long flat bars spaced vertically which allows restricted flow of water. The spacing between bars vary from 25 mm to 200 mm. The purpose of trash rack is to prevent entry of floating material to turbine. If allowed to enter, these material may the choke the pipe or may enter turbine and result in damage to turbine blades.

(ix) Draft tube: It is an air tight tube attached to runner outlet of turbine. It discharges water from turbine to tail race. Draft tube helps to increase the operating head by an amount equal to height of runner outlet above the tail race. This creates negative pressure head at runner exit. Also, it converts a large proportion of velocity energy rejected from runner into useful pressure head.

(x) Tail race: Water after passing through turbine is discharged to tail race which may lead to same stream or another one. Tail race provides unhindered passage of discharged water to the stream.

(xi) Hydro-turbine: It converts kinetic energy of water into mechanical energy. This mechanical energy is converted into electrical energy by generator. These are built in sizes upto 10^6 HP and speed ranging from 100 rpm to 1000 rpm. Axis of turbine may be horizontal or vertical. Turbine are classified as impulse turbine or reaction turbine. Pelton wheel is an impulse turbine and is suitable for high head and low discharge. Francis and Propellor turbine are reaction turbines. Francis turbine is suitable for medium head and medium discharge. Propellor turbine is suitable for low head and high discharge. Kaplan turbine is a special type of propellor turbine with adjustable blades.

(xii) Hydro-electric generator: Hydro-electric generator is a three phase synchronous alternator. It consists of two main parts–stator and rotor. The stator or stationary part has three phase windings which are housed in slots of laminated steel structure. The rotor houses dc magnetic field. The field poles are salient pole type. DC supply is fed to the field by pilot excitor which are dc compound generators. Recently, static rotating rectifiers are used to produce dc supply for the field. The field is heaviest component of alternator which in large machine may have 15 m dia and 100 ton weight. The alternator may be horizontal or vertical. Usually, Pelton wheel uses horizontal configuration while Kaplan and Francis turbine use vertical configuration.

The speed of generators vary from 50–500 rpm for vertical alternators and 100–1000 rpm for horizontal alternators. The number of poles in a hydro-alternators vary from 6–120. The alternators are air cooled and are built in sizes from 0.5 MW to 500 MW. Power produced by hydro plant is given by

$$P = \rho g H Q \eta \qquad ...(4.1)$$

where ρ = density of water, 1000 kg/m^3

H = water head, m

Q = water discharge, m^3/s

η = efficiency of turbine, generator and gearbox.

g = acceleration due to gravity, 9.81 m/s^2

4.7 HYDRO TURBINES

A hydro-turbine converts energy of falling water into mechanical energy. This mechanical energy is converted into electrical energy by the alternator. Efficiency of hydro-turbine is very high (exceeding 90% at full load). hydro-turbines can be classified according to following–

(*a*) Classification according to flow path–

- **Axial flow turbine:** Flow path of water is parallel to the shaft. Kaplan turbine is an axial flow turbine.
- **Radial flow turbine:** Flow path of water is along the radius or perpendicular to the axis of rotation.
- **Mixed flow turbine:** Water inlet path is radial and outlet is axial. Francis turbine is a mixed flow turbine.
- **Tangential flow turbine:** Flow path of water is in tangential direction. Pelton wheel is a tangential flow turbine.

(*b*) Classification according to action of water on moving blades–

- **Impulse turbine:** In this turbine, water pressure is converted into kinetic energy before entering the runner. The kinetic energy is in the form of high speed jet that strikes the bucket mounted on the periphery of the runner. This impact of jet causes the runner to rotate e.g. Pelton wheel, Turgo, Crossflow turbines.
- **Reaction turbine:** If at inlet of turbine, water possess both kinetic and pressure energy then turbine is known as reaction turbine.

  Turbine casing with runner are fully immersed in water e.g., Francis, Kaplan and Propellor turbines.

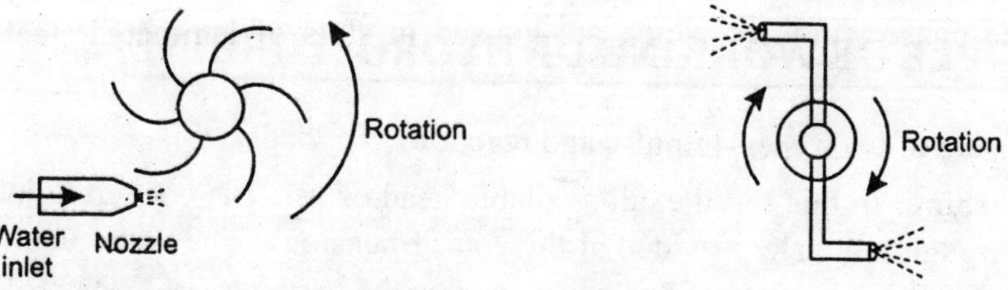

Fig. 4.18 Impulse turbine

Fig. 4.19 Reaction turbine

(c) Classification according to head at inlet of turbine–

- **High head turbine:** Turbine operating with a head of 50 m and more e.g. Pelton wheel.
- **Medium head turbine:** Turbine operating between 50 m and 10 m head is a medium head turbine.
- **Low head turbine:** Turbine operating below 10 m is a low head turbine.

Table 4.5 Classification of hydro-turbine

Turbine	High head > 50 m	Medium head 50 m – 10 m	Low head < 10 m
Impulse	Pelton, Turgo, Multi-jet Pelton	Pelton, Turgo Cross flow	Cross flow
Reaction		Francis	Propellor, Kaplan

(d) Classification according to specific speed: These are of three types–high specific speed, medium specific speed and low specific speed.

- **Specific speed:** It is defined as speed at which a turbine would run when developing 1 meter horse power under a head of 1 metre. It can also be explained as–speed of a turbine identical in shape, geometrical dimension, blade angle, gate opening etc. with the actual turbine but of a size it will develop unit power when working under a unit head.

  It is used for comparing different types of turbines as every turbine has different specific speed.

  Specific speed, $N_s = \dfrac{N\sqrt{P}}{H^{5/4}}$

  N = actual speed of turbine (rpm).

  P = output in metric (hp).

  H = effective head (in metre).

  Performance of turbine can be predicted from specific speed.

4.8 PRINCIPLE OF WORKING OF HYDRO–TURBINE

Hydro–turbines are of two types–impulse and reaction.

Impulse turbine: In this turbine, all available head of water is converted into kinetic energy by passing it through a nozzle provided at the end of penstock. The water coming out of nozzle form a jet. This jet strikes a series of buckets placed on the periphery of a wheel. This causes wheel to rotate. Water is in contact with the bucket at a time and subsequently it flows to the tail race at atmospheric pressure. The turbine casing prevents splashing of water.

Pelton wheel is an impulse turbine.

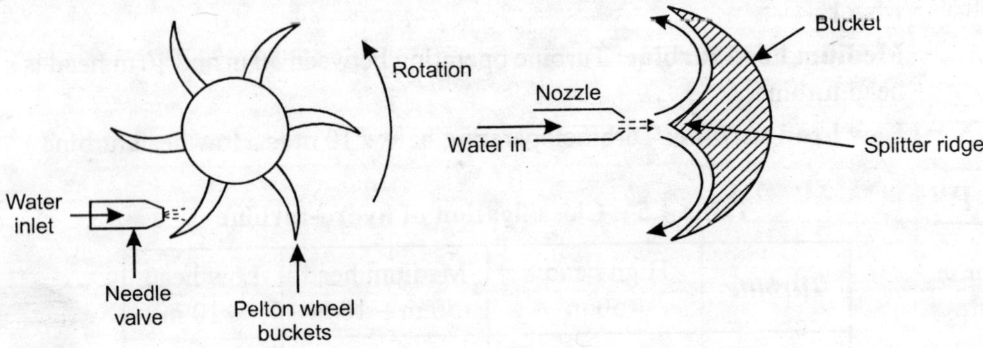

Fig. 4.20 Impulse turbine

Reaction turbine: In this turbine, only a part of available head is converted into kinetic energy at the entrance to the runner. The remaining part of head remains in the form of pressure head. The pressure at the inlet to the turbine is higher than at the outlet. The pressure varies throughout the passage through the turbine. Since, water is under pressure, the entire flow from head race to tail race takes place in a closed conduit. Runner of turbine remains submerged in water throughout the operation of turbine. Hence, turbine casing is required to keep the system under pressure. Kaplan, Francis and Propeller turbines are reaction turbines.

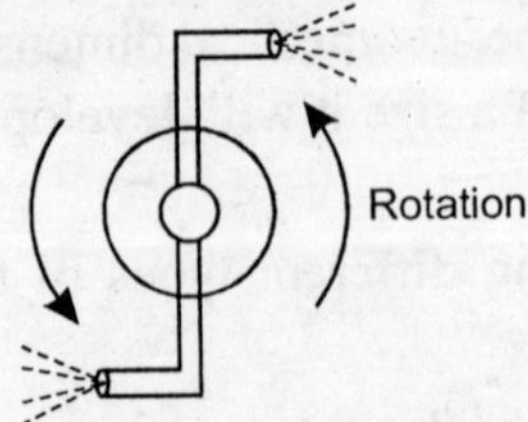

Fig. 4.21 Reaction turbine

Table 4.6 Comparison between impulse and reaction turbine

	Impulse Turbine		*Reaction Turbine*
1.	All potential energy is converted into kinetic energy by nozzle before entering turbine runner.	1.	Only a part of potential energy is converted into kinetic energy before entering turbine runner.
2.	Flow regulation is possible without loss.	2.	Flow regulation is possible with loss.
3.	Unit is installed above tail race.	3.	Unit is kept submerged in water at tail race.
4.	Blades are only in action when they are in front of nozzle.	4.	Blades are in action at all time.
5.	Turbine casing is at atmospheric pressure.	5.	Turbine casing at a pressure higher than atmospheric pressure.

4.9 PELTON WHEEL

It is an impulse turbine suitable for high head and low discharge (head > 200 m). Main parts of pelton wheel are given below–

(*i*) Nozzle and flow regulating equipment.
(*ii*) runner and buckets.
(*iii*) casing.
(*iv*) braking jet.
(*v*) deflector plate

(*i*) **Nozzle:** The available head of water is converted into kinetic energy by the nozzle. Amount of water striking the bucket of runner is controlled by governor providing a spear in the nozzle. The spear is a conical needle operated either by a handwheel or automatically. When spear is pushed forward, amount of water flow is reduced. This reduces the power generated. The movement of spear is controlled by governor.

(*ii*) **Runner and buckets:** The rotating part of turbine on which buckets are mounted is called runner. Elliptical shaped buckets are mounted on the periphery of the runner. Each bucket is double hemi-spherical cup. Each bucket is divided into two symmetrical parts by a dividing wall called splitter. The jet of water strikes the splitter. The splitter divides the jet into two equal parts and comes out at the outer edge of the bucket.

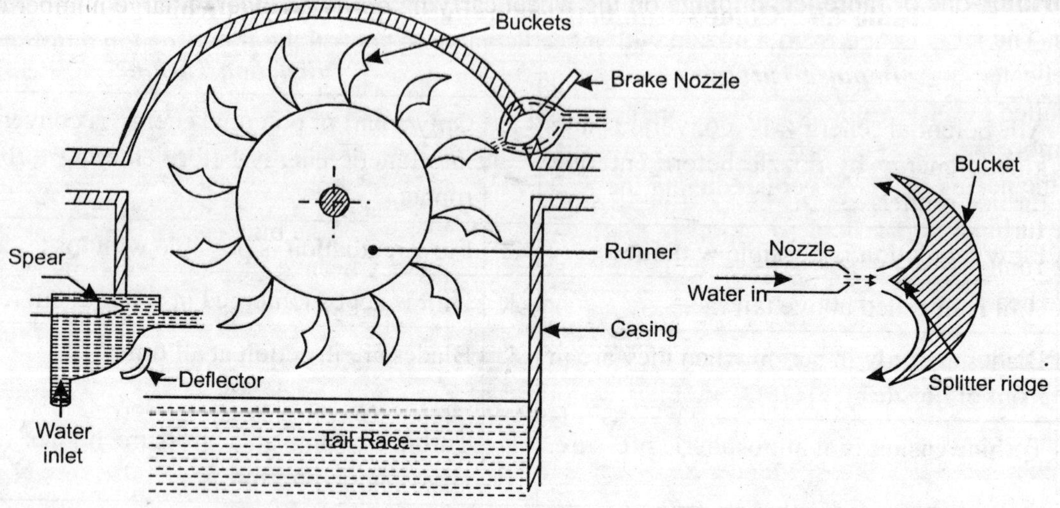

Fig. 4.22 Pelton wheel

Fig. 4.23 Bucket

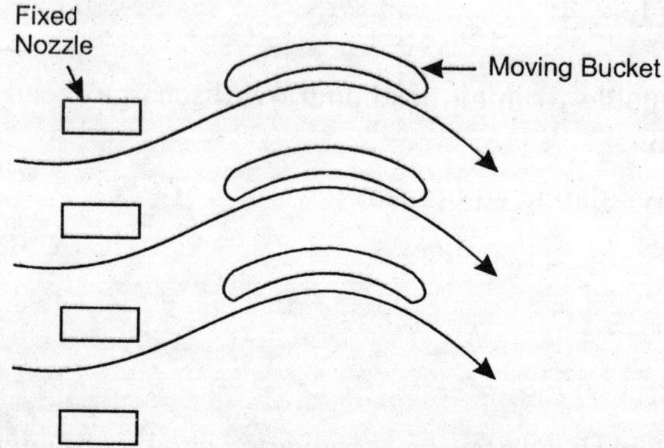

Fig. 4.24 Movement of water through nozzle and bucket

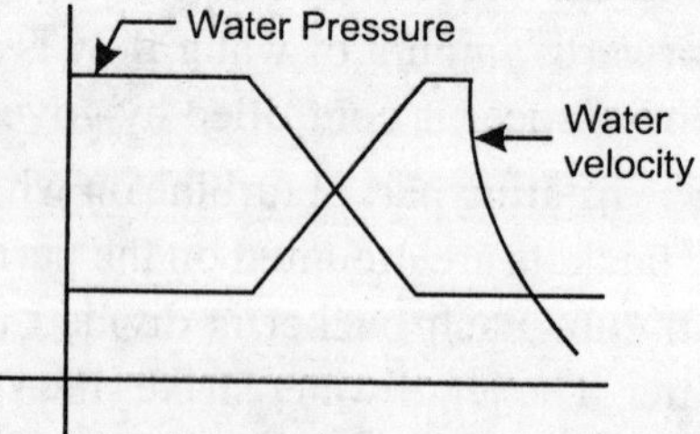

Fig. 4.25 Water pressure and velocity diagram

(iii) **Casing:** It is an outer covering that prevents splashing of water and guides the water to tail race. It operates at atmospheric pressure. It is used to cover the moving part for safety reason.

(iv) **Braking jet:** It is used to stop the turbine. A jet of water issuing out of nozzle strikes the buckets in oposite direction to stop it.

(v) **Deflector plate:** To stop a turbine, jet is deflected by a deflector plate so that it does not impinge on the bucket. This stops the turbine.

Working–one or more jets impinge on the wheel carrying on its periphery a large number of buckets. The jet is issued from a nozzle with a needle valve to control the flow. To stop a turbine, jet is deflected by a plate so that it does not impinge on the bucket. The movement of needle valve is controlled by a governor. When load on the turbine increases, governor pushes the needle outside so that more water can enter the nozzle. Similarly, as the load on generator decreases, the governor pushes the needle inside thereby reducing the water flow out of the nozzle.

The turbine rotor is made of stainless steel, cast steel or bronze. The buckets are bolted or cast onto the runner. The buckets are made of stainless steel, cast steel, bronze, cast iron etc. depending upon the head at the inlet of turbine. Casing is made of cast iron or fabricated steel plates.

4.10 FRANCIS TURBINE

It is a radial flow reaction turbine suitable for medium head and medium discharge (head 2.5 m to 450 m). This type of turbine develops power partly due to velocity of water and partly due to difference of pressure acting on front and back of runner buckets.

Parts of turbine are following—

(*i*) Runner, (*ii*) Guide mechanism, (*iii*) Casing, (*iv*) Draft tube

(*i*) Runner: Runner consists of blades fixed on it. Water glides over the blades with constant velocity and exerts maximum pressure at the top and minimum at the bottom. The water flows radially inward and changes to a downward direction while passing through the runner. As water passes over rotating blades of the runner, both pressure and velocity of water are reduced causing a reaction force to drive the turbine.

(*ii*) Guide mechanism: It consists of an outer ring of stationary guide blades fixed to the casing of turbine and an inner ring consisting of rotating blades forming runner. The water glides over these blades causing velocity and pressure of water to change.

(*iii*) Casing: The casing contains fixed guide blades and keeps pressure inside higher than the atmosphere.

(*iv*) Draft tube: It helps to increase the effective head by an amount equal to difference of runner outlet level and tail race level. The pressure inside draft tube is negative.

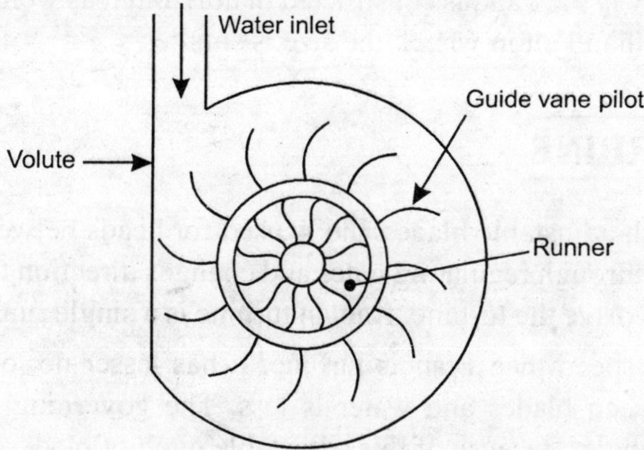

Fig. 4.26 Francis turbine

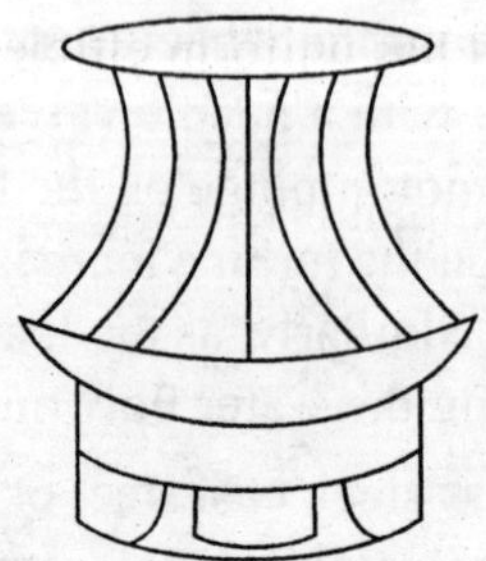

Fig. 4.27 Francis turbine runner

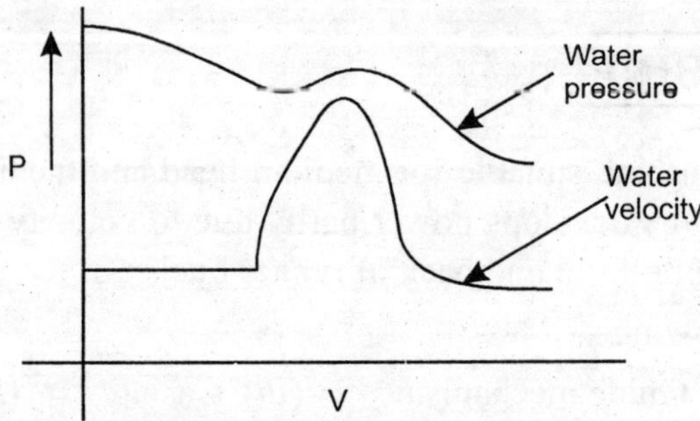

Fig. 4.28 Water pressure and velocity diagram

Working—Water passes over fixed blades (fixed to the casing) with varying pressure. The pressure is maximum at the top and minimum at the bottom. Water then passes over rotating blades of runner where both pressure and velocity decreases causing a reaction force to drive the turbine. Water is then discharged to tail race through a closed tube of increasing cross-section. This tube is called draft tube. This tube increases effective head as the water leaving the runner still posses kinetic energy and this energy is reduced as the water flows through draft tube creating a negative pressure. This increases effective head and efficiency of turbine.

The quantity of water entering the turbine can be controlled by turning the guide blades simultaneously in one direction. This is controlled automatically by governor. In all reaction turbines, cavitation is a serious issue.

The full load efficiency is 92% and is constructed in horizontal as well as in vertical forms. Due to higher operating speed than Pelton wheel, the size is smaller.

4.11 KAPLAN TURBINE

It is a reaction turbine with adjustable blades and is used for heads between 1.5 m to 70 m. Water enters the turbine radially through regulating gates and changes direction to axial flow in the runner causing a reaction force to drive the turbine. Kaplan turbine is a single runner, vertical type turbine.

It has higher specific speed than Francis turbine. It has lesser no. of runner blades (3 to 6). Due to this, friction between blades and water is less. The governing mechanism adjusts both blade opening and blade angle. Because of this adjustable pitch of blades, the turbine is capable of operating over a wide range of heads. It has uniform efficiency at all loads. However, cavitation is a serious problem in this turbine.

Due to its ability to operate as a pump, it is suitable for pumped storage plants.

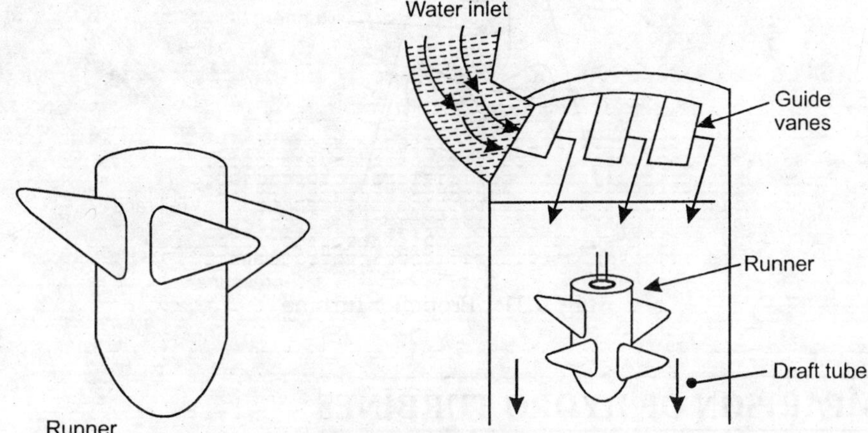

Fig. 4.29 Kaplan turbine runner

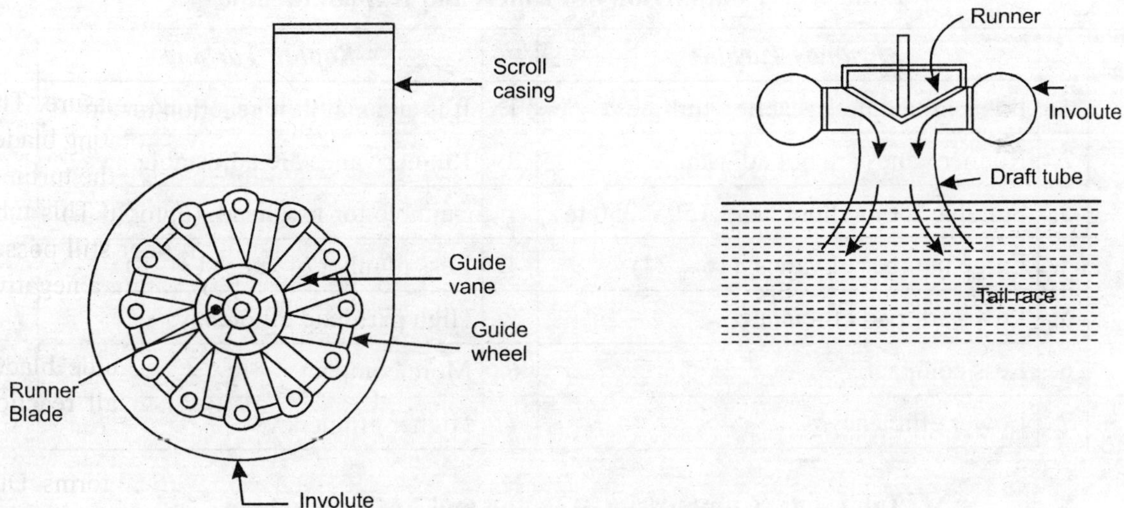

Fig. 4.30 Kaplan turbine

4.12 PROPELLOR TURBINE

It is an axial flow reaction turbine. It has fixed runner blades. The blades may be 3 or 6 in which water contacts all of the blades constantly. It has simple construction but has poor part load efficiency. The efficiency at full load is 92% while at half load, it is 65%.

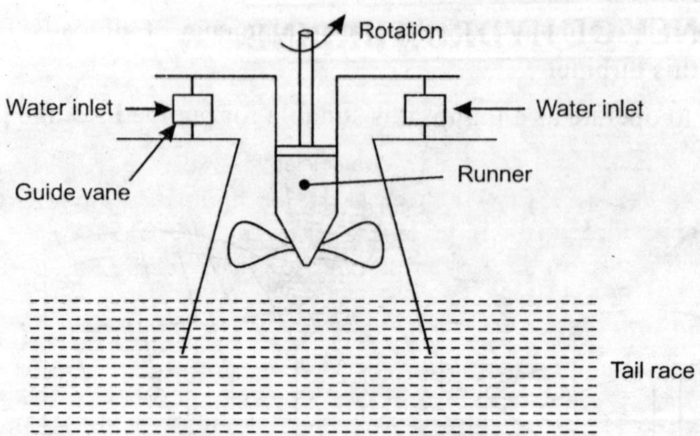

Fig. 4.31 Propellor turbine

4.13 COMPARISON OF HYDRO TURBINES

Table 4.7 Comparison of Francis and Kaplan turbine

	Francis Turbine		*Kaplan Turbine*
1.	It is a mixed flow reaction turbine.	1.	It is an axial flow reaction turbine.
2.	Runner vanes are not adjustable.	2.	Runner vanes are adjustable.
3.	Suitable for medium head. (50 – 250 m)	3.	Suitable for low head. (upto 30 m)
4.	Large number of vanes. (16 – 24)	4.	Less number of vanes (3 – 8)
5.	Low part load efficiency.	5.	High part load efficiency.
6.	Less compact.	6.	More compact.
7.	Lower efficiency.	7.	Higher efficiency.

Table 4.8 Comparison of Pelton and Francis turbine

	Pelton Turbine		*Francis Turbine*
1.	No danger of cavitation.	1.	There is danger of cavitation.
2.	Water hammer is less problematic.	2.	Water hammer is more pronounced.
3.	Variation of operating head cannot be controlled easily.	3.	Variation of operating head can be controlled easily.
4.	Mechanical efficiency decreases faster with wear.	4.	Mechanical efficiency does not fall rapidly with wear.
5.	Size of runner and generator is large.	5.	Size of runner and generator is small.

4.14 EFFICIENCY OF HYDRO TURBINE

Efficiency of hydro turbine are of following types–

(*i*) **Hydraulic efficiency** (η_h): It is defined as ratio of power developed by the runner of a turbine to the power supplied by the water at the inlet of the turbine.

$$\eta_h = \frac{\text{Power developed by runner}}{\text{Power supplied at inlet}}$$

(*ii*) **Mechanical efficiency** (η_m): It is the ratio of power available at the shaft of the turbine to the power developed by the runner.

$$\eta_m = \frac{\text{Power available at the shaft of turbine}}{\text{Power developed by the runner}}$$

(*iii*) **Volumetric efficiency** (η_υ): It is the ratio of volume of water actually striking the runner to the volume of water supplied to the turbine.

$$\eta_\upsilon = \frac{\text{Volume of water actually striking the runner}}{\text{Volume of water supplied to the runner}}$$

(*iv*) **Overall efficiency** (η_o): It is the ratio of power available at the shaft of turbine to the power supplied at the inlet of the turbine.

$$\eta_o = \frac{\text{Power available at the shaft of turbine}}{\text{Power supplied at inlet of turbine}}$$

4.15 CHARACTERISTICS OF HYDRO TURBINE

(*i*) **Head:** Reaction turbines are used for heads upto 500 m. For heads more than 500 m, Pelton wheel is used.

(*ii*) **Efficiency at various loads:** Part load efficiency of Kaplan and Pelton wheel is higher. Whereas part load efficiency of Francis and Propellor turbine is poor.

Variation of efficiency with load for Pelton, Francis and Kaplan turbine is depicted in fig. 4.32.

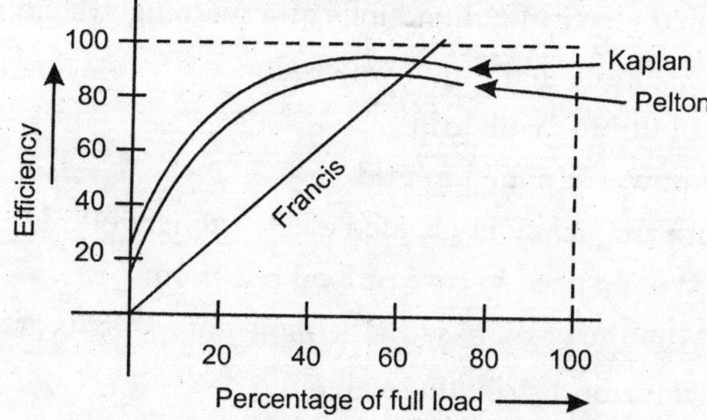

Fig. 4.32 Efficiency of different turbines

(*ii*) **Specific speed:** It is the speed at which a turbine would run when developing 1 metric hp under a head of 1 m. It is given by

$$\text{Specific speed,} \quad N_s = \frac{N\sqrt{P}}{H^{5/4}}$$

where, N = actual speed of turbine (rpm)

P = rated power (hp).

H = head (m).

Table 4.9 Specific speed for various types of turbines

Type of runner	*Specific speed (N_s)*
Pelton	12–30
Turgo	20–70
Crossflow	20–80
Francis	80–400
Propellor and Kaplan	340–1000

(*iv*) **Runaway speed:** It is the maximum speed at which a turbine would run under worst conditions with all gates open. The worst condition could be when entire load is thrown off and turbine governor fails to act. The turbine must be able to withstand this speed. It could be 2–3 times normal speed.

(*v*) **Turbine setting:** Pelton wheel is set at a level higher than highest tail race level. While Francis turbine runner is placed at a level near or below the lowest tail race level.

4.16 GOVERNING OF HYDRO–TURBINE

All hydro–turbines are directly coupled to the alternator which produces power at constant frequency. For constant frequency, the speed of turbine need to be constant at all times. This is achieved by flow of water entering the turbine. Flow of water is regulated by adjusting needle valve in case of impulse turbine and guide vanes in case of reaction turbine. The operation of speed regulation of turbine is called governing. Functions of governing system are following–

(*i*) control of turbine start up and shutdown sequence.

(*ii*) synchronisation of turbine with grid.

(*iii*) control of active power supplied to grid.

(*iv*) control of network frequency in isolated electrical network.

(*v*) protection against overspeed in case of load rejection.

Governors used are hydraulic or oil based. The main components are following–

(*i*) relay or control valve or distributing valve.

(*ii*) servo motor or relay cylinder.

(*iii*) actuator.

(*iv*) oil pump.

(*v*) oil sump or storage.

(*vi*) oil supply pipes.

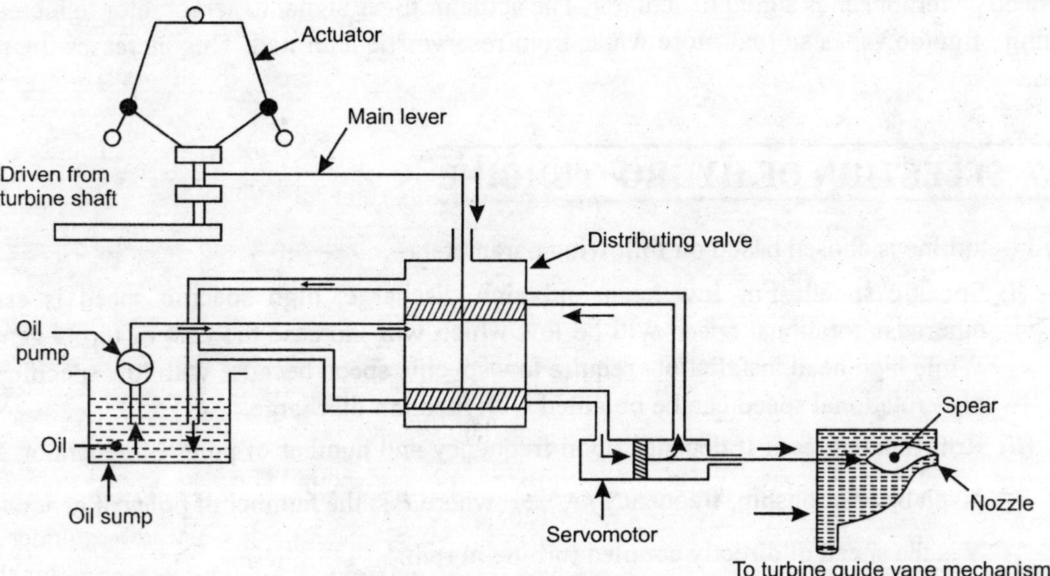

Fig. 4.33 Oil pressure governor

The working of oil pressure governor can be explained. If speed of the turbine falls, the sleeve on the actuator shaft descends and causes the main lever to raise the pistons of distributing valve. As a result, oil under pressure goes to one end of oil cylinder and causes the piston to move to one side. This movement is transmitted to controlling device to open the nozzle of impulse turbine or guide vanes of reaction turbine. If the load is constant, main lever and levers in distributing valve remain in normal position.

In electronic governor system, movement is actuated by servomotor.

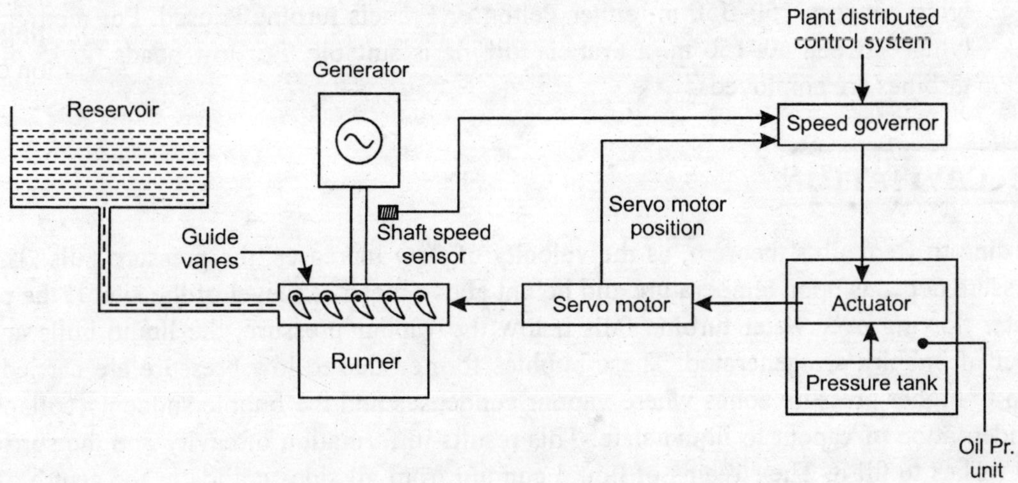

Fig. 4.34 Electronic turbine speed governor

The system consists of speed governor, servomotor, actuator, speed sensor and pressure tank. Upon increase in load on generator, the speed falls this is sensed by shaft speed sensor and conveyed to speed governor. The position of servomotor is sensed by speed governor with decrease in speed, the speed governor sends signal to actuator. The actuator gives signal to servomotor to increase the opening of guide vanes so that more water from reservoir is admitted. This increases the turbine speed.

4.17 SELECTION OF HYDRO–TURBINE

A hydro–turbine is chosen based on following parameters–

(*i*) **Specific speed:** For low head and high discharge, high specific speed is essential otherwise rotational speed will be low which will increase the cost of turbo–generator. While high head installation require low specific speed because with low specific speed, high rotational speed can be obtained with medium discharge.

(*ii*) **Rotational speed:** It depends upon frequency and number of poles of generator. This is given by relationship, frequency $f = \frac{PN}{120}$ where P is the number of poles of generator and N is the speed of directly coupled turbine in rpm.

(*iii*) **Efficiency:** The turbine should be chosen with highest efficiency for various operating conditions. So, full load as well as part load efficiency should be high.

(*iv*) **Cavitation:** Reaction turbines at tail race level is affected by cavitation. The turbine selected must operate without cavitation. This requires critical value of cavitation factor to be taken into design consideration.

(*v*) **Vertical or horizontal turbine shaft:** Vertical shaft turbine works well with large sized reaction turbine. While horizontal shaft arrangement is employed for large size impulse turbine.

(*vi*) **Head:** For very high heads (350 m and above), Pelton wheel is used, For medium heads, lying between 150–350 m, either Pelton or Francis turbine is used. For medium heads lying between 60–150 m, a Francis turbine is suitable. For low heads (2–15 m), Bulb turbines are employed.

4.18 CAVITATION

According to Bernauli's theorem, as the velocity of flow increases, the pressure falls. This drop in pressure depends upon temperature and height above mean sea level of the site. If the pressure of water flowing over water turbine falls below the vapour pressure, the liquid boils and large number of bubbles are generated. These bubbles formed due to low pressure are carried by the stream to higher pressure zones where vapour condenses and the bubble suddenly collapses due to condensation of vapour to liquid state. This results in formation of cavity and the surrounding liquid rushes to fill it. The streams of liquid coming from all sides collide at the centre of cavity generating very high local pressure. This causes pitting or metal erosion on the metallic surface of runner blades or draft tube. This results in failure of runner blades due to fatigue or corrosion.

Cavitation can be avoided by following methods–

(*i*) by selecting a material which can resist cavitation.

(*ii*) by polishing the surfaces or coating cast steel runner and blades with stainless steel.

(*iii*) by selecting a runner of proper specific speed for a given head.

(*iv*) by proper design, so that pressure of water does not fall below vapour pressure.

(*v*) by keeping the runner submerged.

4.19 PLANT LAYOUT

Layout of hydro-electric plant is affected by following factors–

(*i*) nature of project.

(*ii*) available head.

(*iii*) size and number of units proposed.

(*iv*) vertical or horizontal shaft of hydro turbine.

For low head plant, the width of dam is small and hence space available for turbine and generator is limited. With reaction turbine and single vertical runner, the arrangement with machines in a line parallel to the length of turbine house is preferred. The spacing between the units is decided by the width of the scroll casing or size of generator. Horizontal machines of reaction type are best located at right angles to length of turbine. A repair bay is provided at one end of turbine house with sufficient space for dismantling and re–erection.

The arrangement is decided not only by size of turbine and generator but also by operation and maintenance requirement.

4.20 HYDRO PLANT AUXILIARIES

The various auxiliaries used in hydro plant consume 1 to 3% of power generated. The auxiliaries are–governor, lubricating oil pumps, air compressors, high pressure oil pump for generator rotor jacking system, cooling water pumps, dewatering and drainage pumps, gate hoists, valves, battery charging units, ventilation system, water pumps for bearing cooling, compressed air for generator brakes and fire fighting system.

4.21 COST BREAK-UP AND COMPONENT LIFE OF HYDRO POWER PLANT

In a hydro-electric project, civil construction constitutes a large part of project cost and takes long time to complete. A cost break up of major components of a hydro plant is given below–

(*i*) Dam, intake, reservoir. ——— 35% of total project cost.

(*ii*) Turbine and generator. ——— 20% of total project cost.

(*iii*) Land, building and foundation. ——— 30–35% of total project cost.

(*iv*) Switchyard. ——— 5% of total project cost.

The average life of various components of hydro-plant is given below–

(*i*) Dam
  (*a*) Earth, concrete. 150 years
  (*b*) Rock filled dam. 60 years
(*ii*) Reservoir 70–80 years
(*iii*) Penstock
  (*a*) Steel 40–50 years
  (*b*) concrete 25–50 years
(*iv*) Canals, tunnels 50–80 years
(*v*) Generator 25 years
(*vi*) Transformer 50 years
(*vii*) Building 40–50 years
(*viii*) Turbine 5 years
(*ix*) Pumps 25 years

4.22 COMPARISON OF HYDRO AND THERMAL POWER PLANTS

A comparison of hydro and thermal power plants is given below–

Table 4.10 Comparison of hydro and thermal plant

Sr. No.	*Parameter*	*Hydro plant*	*Thermal plant*
1.	Land	very large area required	comparatively less area required
2.	Civil construction cost	very high	medium
3.	Running cost	nil	high
4.	Life of plant	very long (100 years)	long (70 years)
5.	Pollution	nil	very high
6.	Cost of electricity	low	high
7.	Time required for start up	low	high
8.	Overall efficiency	very high (85%)	low (33–36%)
9.	Maintenance cost	low	high
10.	Manpower required	less	more
11.	Construction time required	very high	medium
12.	Simplicity of operation	very simple	complicated

SOLVED EXAMPLES

Ex 4.1. A hydro power plant receives water from a reservoir of capacity 4×10^5 cubic meter at a head of 100 m. Calculate energy available in kWh. Assume overall efficiency as 80%. One cubic metre of water weights 1000 kg.

Solution:

$$\text{Weight of water} = \text{Density} \times \text{volume}$$
$$= 1000 \times 4 \times 10^5 = 4 \times 10^8 \text{ kgm}$$
$$= 9.81 \times 4 \times 10^8 \text{ Newton}$$

$$\text{Energy available} = \text{W.H. } \eta_{overall}$$
$$= \frac{(9.81 \times 4 \times 10^8) \cdot (100) \cdot 0.80}{3600 \times 1000}$$
$$= \mathbf{0.872 \times 10^5 \ kWh} \quad \textbf{Ans.}$$

Ex 4.2. A river has a discharge of 400 litres/sec at a head of 80 m. Is it possible to use single jet Pelton wheel running at 700 rpm. Suggest alternative. Assume, machine efficiency of 87%.

Solution:

$$\text{HP} = \frac{\eta WQH}{75} = \frac{0.87 \times 1 \times 400 \times 80}{75} = 371.2$$

$$\text{Specific speed, } N_S = \frac{N\sqrt{HP}}{H^{5/4}} = \frac{700 \times \sqrt{371.2}}{(80)^{5/4}} = 56.36$$

Since, the specific speed of Pelton wheel varies between 10 and 20, hence Pelton wheel with single jet cannot be used.

Alternative is to use double jet Pelton wheel.

Ex 4.3. Discharge available from a river is 50,000 litres/sec at a head of 12.5 m. Suggest, if two turbines of speed 100 rpm and above and specific speed 400 rpm and below can be used. Determine diameter and type of runner. Assumed, turbine efficiency as 90% and speed ratio (C_u) as 0.87.

Solution:

$$\text{The power available} = \frac{\eta WQH}{75}$$
$$= \frac{0.90 \times 1 \times 50{,}000 \times 12.5}{75} = 7500 \text{ HP}$$

With two turbines, output of each will be 3750 HP.

Specific speed of turbine for a speed of 100 rpm

$$N_s = \frac{N\sqrt{P}}{H^{5/4}} = \frac{100\sqrt{3750}}{(12.5)^{5/4}}$$
$$= \frac{100 \times 61.24}{23.51} = 260 \text{ rpm}$$

We find that for a turbine speed of 100 rpm, specific speed is less than 400 rpm. Francis turbine will be suitable for this case with a speed of 150 rpm.

$$U = C_u \sqrt{2gH} = \frac{\pi DN}{60}$$

$$D = \frac{60 \times C_u \sqrt{2gH}}{\pi N} = \frac{60 \times 0.87 \times \sqrt{2 \times 9.81 \times 12.5}}{\pi \times 150}$$

$$D = \frac{60 \times 0.87 \times 15.66}{\pi \times 150} = \mathbf{1.736\ m} \quad \textbf{Ans.}$$

Ex 4.4. A hydro-electric power plant has a reservoir area of 60 km^2 with a head of 70m. Find the rate at which water level will fall when station is generating 20,000 kW. Assume, overall efficiency of plant as 70%.

Solution:

Area of reservoir = 60 km^2 = 60 × 10^6 m^2

Head H = 70 m

Density of water, w = 1000 kg/m^3

Power generated, P = 20,000 kW

Average power generated P = w Q H × 9.81 × 10^{-3} η kW

$$\text{Discharge required per sec, } Q = \frac{P}{w \times H \times 9.81 \times 10^{-3} \times \eta}$$

$$= \frac{20{,}000}{10^3 \times 70 \times 9.81 \times 10^{-3} \times 0.70}$$

$$= 41.61 \text{ m}^3$$

$$\text{Rate of fall of water level in reservoir} = \frac{Q}{A} = \frac{41.61}{60 \times 10^6} \text{ m/sec}$$

$$= \frac{41.61}{60 \times 10^6} \times 3600 \times 1000 \text{ mm/hr}$$

$$= \mathbf{2.4966\ mm/hr} \quad \textbf{Ans.}$$

Ex 4.5. A hydro-electric power plant operates with a head of 70 m and catchment area of 100 km^2. The average annual rainfall is 400 cm with 20% evaporation loss. Find the average power generated if generator efficiency is 85% and turbine efficiency is 90%.

Solution:

Quantity of water available, Q = catchment area × average annual rainfall × (1 – evaporation loss)

$$Q = 100 \times 10^6 \times \frac{400}{100} (1 - 0.20) = 320 \times 10^6 \text{ m}^3$$

Overall power plant efficiency = Turbine efficiency × generator efficiency

= 0.90 × 0.85 = 0.765

$$\text{Energy available} = \frac{w \times Q \times H \times 9.81 \times \eta}{60 \times 60 \times 1000}$$

$$= \frac{1000 \times 320 \times 10^6 \times 70 \times 9.81 \times 6.765}{60 \times 60 \times 1000}$$

$$= \frac{320 \times 10^6 \times 70 \times 9.81 \times 0.765}{3600}$$

$$= 46.6956 \times 10^6 \text{ kWh}$$

$$\text{Average power, P} = \frac{46.6956 \times 10^6}{8760 \text{ (hours in a year)}} = \mathbf{5330.547\ kW} \quad \textbf{Ans.}$$

Ex 4.6. A hydro-electric power plant has a load factor of 25% as peak load plant. Capacity of generator, head and overall plant efficiency are 15 MW, 40 m and 0.85 respectively. Calculate minimum flow of water so as to operate plant as base load plant.

Solution:

Total units generated at 25% load factor, when operating as peak load plant

$$= 15 \times 10^3 \times 0.25 \text{ kWh}$$

for one week, this becomes $= 15 \times 10^3 \times 0.25 \times 168$ kWh

Let Q be the minimum flow of water required to operate the plant as base load.

Power developed, $P = 9.81 \times Q \times H \times \eta = 9.81 \times Q \times 40 \times 0.85$

$$P = 333.54 \times Q \text{ kW}$$

Total units generated per week

$$= 333.54 \times Q \times 168 \text{ kWh}$$

Now, $333.54 \times Q \times 168 = 15 \times 10^3 \times 0.25 \times 168$

$$Q = \frac{15 \times 10^3 \times 0.25}{333.54} = \mathbf{11.24\ m^3/sec} \quad \textbf{Ans.}$$

Ex 4.7. The run-off data of a river is given below–

Table 4.11 Run-off data

Month	*Average discharge (million m^3/month)*	*Month*	*Average discharge (million m^3/month)*
January	100	July	150
February	50	August	200
March	40	September	220
April	40	October	120
May	0	November	120
June	100	December	80

(*a*) Draw the hydrograph and find average flow, (*b*) draw flow duration curve (*c*) find power available at average flow at a head of 70 m and overall efficiency of 80%. Assume, 30 days in each month.

Solution:

$$\text{Average discharge} = \frac{10^6 \times [100 + 50 + 40 + 40 + 0 + 100 + 150 + 200 + 220 + 120 + 100 + 80]}{12}$$

$$= 100 \times 10^6 \text{ m}^3\text{/month}$$

For flow duration curve following information is necessary–

Table 4.12 Flow duration curve data

Discharge (million m³/month)	*No. of months when flow is available*	*Percentage of time*
220	1	8.33
200	2	16.65
150	3	25.0
120	4	33.3
100	7	58.3
80	8	66.6
50	9	75.0
40	11	91.67
0	12	100

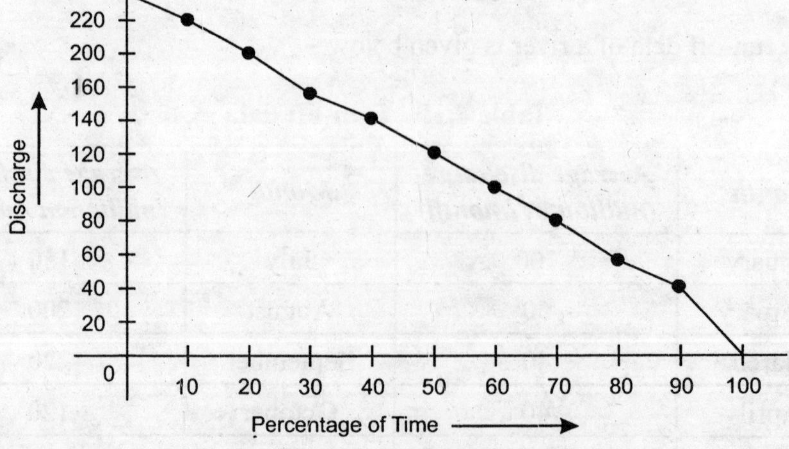

Fig. 4.35 Flow duration curve

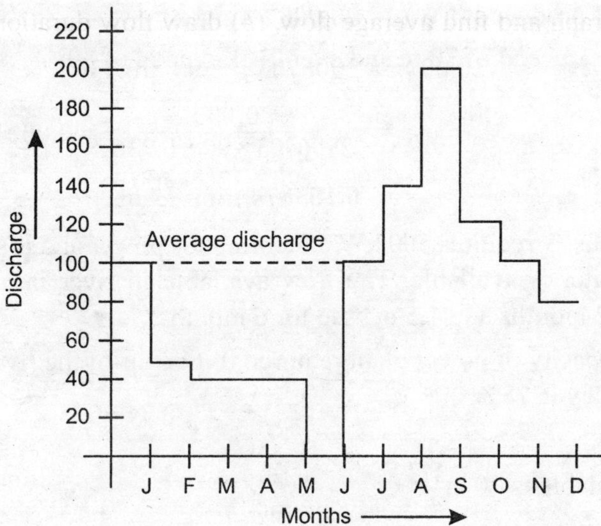

Fig. 4.36 Hydrograph

Ex 4.8. A hydro plant has reservoir capacity of 3.2 km^2 with a capacity of 10^8 m^3. The net head available is 90m. The efficiency of penstock, turbine and generator are 94%, 88% and 89% respectively. Calculate (*a*) total energy that can be generated (*b*) fall in reservoir level if a load of 20 MW is supplied for 3 hours.

Solution:

$$\text{Weight of water in reservoir} = \text{volume of water} \times \text{weight of 1 m}^3 \text{ of water}$$

$$= 10^8 \times 1000 \text{ kg} = 10^{11} \times 9.81 \text{ N}$$

$$\text{Overall efficiency} = 0.94 \times 0.88 \times 0.89$$

$$\eta_0 = 0.736$$

$$\text{Total electrical energy that can be generated} = \text{w} \times \text{H} \times \eta_0$$

$$= (10^{11} \times 9.81) \times (90) \times (0.736) \text{ watt sec.}$$

$$= \frac{10^{11} \times 9.81 \times 90 \times 0.736}{1000 \times 3600} \text{ kWh}$$

$$= 180.504 \times 10^5 \text{ kWh}$$

(*b*) Let fall in level of reservoir in 3 hours be '*p*' meters

$$\text{Average discharge/sec} = \frac{\text{Area of reservoir} \times p}{3 \times 3600} = \frac{3.2 \times 10^6 \times p}{3 \times 3600}$$

$$= 296.3\, p \text{ m}^3$$

$$\text{Weight of water available/sec, w} = 296.3\, p \times 1000 \times 9.81$$

$$= (2906703)\, p \text{ N}$$

$$\text{Average power generated} = \text{w H } \eta_0$$

$$= (2906703)\, p \times 90 \times 0.736$$

$$\text{Power produced (kW)} = 20{,}000 \quad \text{(given)}$$

$$20{,}000 = 2906703\, p \times 90 \times 0.736$$

$$p = \frac{20{,}000}{2906703 \times 90 \times 0.736} = 0.000103874 \text{ m}$$

$$= \mathbf{0.103874 \text{ mm}} \quad \textbf{Ans.}$$

Ex 4.9. A textile industry requires 500 kW of continuous power and is situated near a waterfall where 25 m head of water is available. The flow available in river in a year is 10 m^3/sec for 4 months, 6 m^3/sec, for 2 months and 1.5 m^3/sec for 6 months.

Calculate standby capacity of power plant required if it is run-of the river type without storage. The overall plant efficiency is 78%.

Solution:

When discharge available is 10 m^3/sec

$$\text{Power developed} = w \times H \times \eta_0$$

$$= (10 \times 1000 \times 9.81) \times 25 \times 0.78 \text{ W}$$

$$= 1912.95 \text{ kW}$$

When discharge available is 6m^3/sec.

$$\text{Power available} = w \times H \times \eta_0$$

$$= (6 \times 1000 \times 9.81) \times 25 \times 0.78$$

$$= 1147.77 \text{ kW}$$

When discharge available is 1.5m^3/sec

$$\text{Power available} = w \times H \times \eta_0$$

$$= (1.5 \times 1000 \times 9.81) \times 25 \times 0.78$$

$$= 286.94 \text{ kW}$$

Hence, it is found that when discharge is 10 m^3/sec and 6 m^3/sec more than 500 kW power is available (which is needed by the industry). But, if flow is 1.5 m^3/sec, power available is only 286.94 kW.

This falls short from 500 kW by = 500 – 286.94

= 213.06 kW

So, 213.06 kW standby power is required.

Ex 4.10. A run off the river plant with storage has an installed capacity of 10 MW at a water head of 20 m. The load factor is 40% and overall efficiency is 0.80.

(*a*) Calculate required discharge in m^3/sec.

(*b*) Calculate load factor if discharge is 20 m^3/sec

Solution:

(*a*) Let us calculate units generated per week.

$= \text{Max. demand} \times \text{Load factor} \times \text{hours in a week}$

$= (10 \times 10^3) \times (0.4) \times (24 \times 7) = 67.4 \times 10^3 \text{ kWh}$

Weight of water available/sec $= Q \times 9.81 \times 1000 = 9810\ Q$ Newton

Where Q is the required discharge in m^3/sec.

$$\text{Power produced} = w \times H \times \eta_0$$

$$= (9810\ Q) \times (20) \times (0.80)$$

$$= 156.96\ Q \text{ kWh}$$

$$\text{Units generated week} = (156.96\ Q) \times 168 \text{ kWh}$$

$$\text{Now, } (156.96\ Q \times 168) \text{ kWh} = 67.2 \times 10^3 \text{ kWh}$$

or $$Q = \frac{67.2 \times 10^3}{26369} = \mathbf{25.48\ m^3/sec}$$ **Ans.**

Power developed with a discharge of 20 m^3/sec.

$$= 156.96 \times 20$$

$$= 3139.2 \text{ kW}$$

$$\text{Units generated on that day} = 3139.2 \times 24 = 75341 \text{ kWh}$$

$$\text{L.F.} = \frac{75341}{1.4 \times 24} \times 100 = \mathbf{31.4\%}$$ **Ans.**

Ex 4.11. A hydro-electric power plant has a mean head of 205 m and has a catchment area of 1000 km^2. The average annual rainfall is 125 cm. 20% of this rainfall cannot be used for power generation and there is a head loss of 5 m. The load factor is 75% and turbine generator efficiencies are 90% and 95% respectively. Calculate rating of power plant.

Solution:

Head, $H = 205$ m, Net head $= 205 - 5 = 200$ m

Catchment area $= 1000\ km^2$, Average annual rainfall $= 0.125$ m

L.F. $= 0.75$, $\eta_g = 95\%$,

$\eta_T = 90\%$, 80% of rainfall available for power generation.

Quantity of water available during the year

$$= (1000 \times 10^6) \times 1.25 \times 0.8$$

$$= 10^9 \text{ m}^3$$

$$\text{Quantity of water available/sec} = \frac{10^9}{8760 \times 3600} = 31.7 \text{ m}^3/\text{sec}$$

$$\text{Average power produced} = w\,Q\,H\,\eta_T\,\eta_g \text{ kW}$$

$$= 9.81 \times 31.7 \times 200 \times 0.9 \times 0.95$$

$$= 53177 \text{ MW}$$

$= 53.2$ MW (approx.)

Overall capacity of power plant with a load factor of 75%.

$$= \frac{53.2}{0.75} = 70.9 \text{ MW} \quad \textbf{Ans.}$$

Ex 4.12. Daily load curve data for a certain location is given below–

Table 4.13 Daily load curve data

1.	12 midnight – 5 am	100 MW	5.	1 pm – 5 pm	250 MW
2.	5 am – 8 am	120 MW	6.	5 pm – 9 pm	350 MW
3.	8 am – 12 noon	250 MW	7.	9pm – 12 midnight	150 MW
4.	12 noon – 1 pm	100 MW			

A run-off the river plant with pondage and a steam power plant is proposed to meet above load demand. Run-off data shows a flow of 50 m^3/sec. with a head of 90 m. With hydro plant efficiency of 90% and transmission loss of 5%, calculate the capacity of hydro and steam plant.

Solution:

$$Q = 50 \text{ m}^3/\text{s}, \quad H = 90 \text{ m}, \quad \eta_{hydro} = 90\%, \quad \text{Transmission losses} = 5\%$$

Combined capacity of hydro and steam plant

$$= 5 \times 100 + 3 \times 120 + 4 \times 250 + 1 \times 100 + 4 \times 250 + 4 \times 350 + 3 \times 150$$

$$= 500 + 360 + 1000 + 100 + 1000 + 1400 + 450$$

$$= 4810 \text{ MWh}$$

Average output of hydro plant;

$$P = w\,Q\,H \times \eta_{hydro} \times 10^{-3} \text{ MW}$$

$$= 9.81 \times 50 \times 90 \times 0.9 \times 10^{-3} = 40 \text{ MW}$$

With a transmission loss of 5%,total generation required

$$= 4810 \times 1.05 = 5050 \text{ MWh}$$

$$\text{Hydro plant capacity} = 40 \text{ MW} \times 24 = 960 \text{ MWh}$$

∴ Energy supplied by steam plant

$$= 5050 - 960 = 4090 \text{ MWh}$$

$$\text{Steam plant rating} = \frac{4090}{24}\,\frac{\text{MWh}}{\text{h}} = 170 \text{ MW}$$

Hence, capacity of hydro plant is 40 MW and steam plant is 170 MW. **Ans.**

Ex 4.13. Run-off data of a river at a particular site is given below.

Table 4.14 Run-off data

Month	*Mean discharge* ($\times 10^6$ m^3)	*Month*	*Mean discharge* ($\times 10^6$ m^3)
January	40	July	75
February	25	August	100
March	20	September	110
April	10	October	60
May	0	November	50
June	50	December	40

(*i*) Sketch hydrograph and find mean flow.

(*ii*) Sketch flow duration curve.

(*iii*) Calculate the capacity of proposed power plant at this site if head available is 80 m and overall efficiency of generation is 85%. Assume 30 days in a month.

Solution:

(*i*) Hydrograph is plotted below–

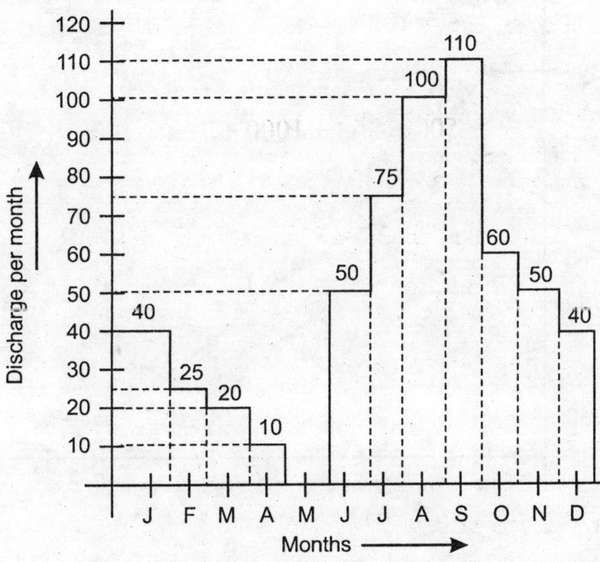

Fig. 4.37 Hydrograph

$$\text{Mean discharge} = \frac{40 + 25 + 20 + 10 + 0 + 50 + 75 + 100 + 110 + 60 + 50 + 40}{12}$$

$$= \frac{580}{12} = 48.3 \times 10^6 \text{ m}^3/\text{month}$$

(*ii*) Flow duration curve– To plot this curve, flow and its duration is also required.

Table 4.15 Flow duration data

Discharge per month	*Total no. of months during which flow is available*	*Percentage time*
0	12	100
10	11	91.7
20	10	83.3
25	9	75
40	8	66.7
50	6	50
60	4	33.3
75	3	25
100	2	16.7
110	1	8.3

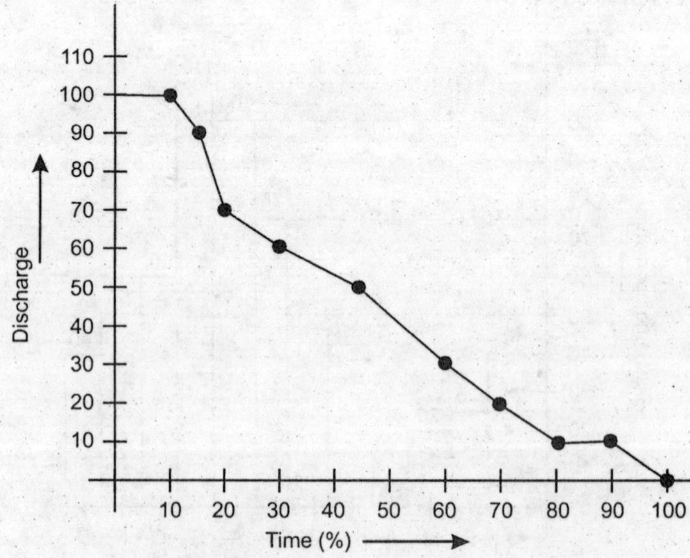

Fig. 4.38 Flow duration curve

CHAPTER SUMMARY

Hydro power is a renewable source of energy which is dependent on amount of precipitation on land surfaces. About 16% of total installed capacity is hydro based. The potential energy of falling water is utilized to run a hydro-turbine for generation of power. This plant has longest gestation period with civil construction forming the largest cost of the total project.

Three types of hydro turbines are used viz Pelton wheel, Francis turbine and Kaplan turbine. For high head and low discharge, Pelton wheel and turgo turbine is used. For medium head and medium discharge, Francis, Turgo and crossflow turbines are used while for low head and large discharge, Kaplan, Propeller and crossflow turbines are used. Hydro plants are of two types-run off the river type and pumped storage type. Pumped storage type hydro plant is used as peak load plant and as a energy storage system. Salient pole alternators are used for power generation. The speed of a hydro alternator is less than 750 rpm as it has large number of poles. Due to low speed, the size of hydro alternator is very large.

Manpower required is much less compared to a thermal power plant and so is the start up time. However, hydro turbines are affected by silt formation especially during rainy season and has to be stopped till silt level reaches an acceptable limit. The power generation is affected during flooding as well as during peak summer when the water level in the reservoir goes very low.

FORMULAE

1. Energy available, $E = 9.81\ \eta_{\text{overall}} \cdot w \cdot H$

   where, w = weight of water, H = head of water (m)

2. Power available, $P = \dfrac{\eta_{\text{overall}}\ w.H\ Q}{75}$

   where Q = discharge (m^3/s)

3. Specific speed, $N_s = \dfrac{N\sqrt{P}}{H^{5/4}}$

   where, P = power output (hp), N = actual speed (rpm)

   H = head (m)

REVIEW QUESTIONS

Q. 1. What are the advantages and disadvantages of a hydro power plant?

Q. 2. Discuss the factors affecting choice of location for a hydro power plant.

Q. 3. Write a brief note on hydro power development in India.

Q. 4. Explain the construction and working of a hydro power plant with a neat sketch.

Q. 5. Differentiate between run off the river plant and pumped storage plant.

Q. 6. What is a micro hydel power plant?

Q. 7. Explain the function of (*i*) surge tank (*ii*) forebay (*iii*) draft tube (*iv*) trash racks.

Q. 8. Discuss different types of dams used for the hydro electric power plant.

Q. 9. Why spillways are provided in a hydro electric power plant?

Q. 10. Write a brief note on types of turbines used in a hydro electric power plant.

Q. 11. Explain w.r. to hydro turbine (*i*) specific speed (*ii*) runner (*iii*) guide mechanism.

Q. 12. Discuss various efficiencies of a hydro turbine.

Q. 13. Discuss characteristics of hydro turbine.

Q. 14. Write a brief on governing of hydro turbine.

Q. 15. What are the factures which govern the selection of hydro turbine.

Q. 16. What is cavitation in hydro turbine? Why should it be avoided?

Q. 17. Write a brief note on hydro power plant auxiliaries.

Q. 18. Compare hydro and thermal power plants.

NUMERICAL QUESTIONS

Q. 1. Reservoir capacity of a hydro power plant is 3.6×10^5 m^3 at a head of 110 m. Overall efficiency of plant is 82%. Density of water is 1000 kg/m^3. Calculate the energy available in kWh. [**Ans.** 88486.2 kWh]

Q. 2. A hydro electric power plant receives 40,000 litres/s at a head of 15.2 m. Efficiency of turbine may be taken as 88% and speed ratio (c_u) as 0.85. Calculate diameter of runner. [**Ans.** 1.87 m]

Q. 3. Reservoir of a hydro electric power plant has a storage capacity of 50 square km with a head of 62 m. The overall efficiency of plant is 80%. Calculate the rate at which the level of water fall will when plant generates 25 MW. [**Ans.** 3.6972 mm/h]

Q. 4. Catchment area of a hydro power plant is 80 sq. km with a head of 82 m. The average annual rainfall is 352 cm with 15% evaporation loss. The efficiency of turbine and generator is 90% and 88% respectively. Determine the average power generated. [**Ans.** 4835.62 kW]

Q. 5. A hydro power plant is being operated as a peak load plant with a load factor of 20%. The plant has a capacity of 20 MW and a head of 32m. The overall plant efficiency may be assumed as 82%. Determine the minimum flow of water required to operate the plant as base load plant for one week. [**Ans.** 15.54 m^3/s]

SHORT ANSWERS TYPES QUESTIONS

Q. 1. What is the average life of a hydro electric power plant?

Q. 2. Why draft tube is needed at tail race of a hydro plant?

Q. 3. What is hydrological cycle?

Q. 4. Explain hydrograph.

Q. 5. Why spillway is provided in a dam?

Q. 6. What is the difference between a storage dam and diversion dam?

Q. 7. Name two impulse type hydro turbine?

Q. 8. What is specific speed of a hydro turbine?

Multiple Choice Questions

Q. 1. The range of high head hydro power plant is

(*a*) 10–50 m (*b*) more than 50 m
(*c*) more than 100 m (*d*) more than 150 m

Q. 2. Francis turbine is

(*a*) impulse turbine (*b*) reaction turbine
(*c*) mixed type turbine

Q. 3. Which of the following is not an impulse turbine?

(*a*) Pelton (*b*) Turgo
(*c*) Cross flow (*d*) Propeller

Q. 4. Turbine casing is at a higher than atmospheric pressure in

(*a*) impulse turbine (*b*) reaction turbine
(*c*) both (*a*) and (*b*) (*d*) none of these

Q. 5. Deflector plate is used to

(*a*) stop a turbine (*b*) to increase speed
(*c*) to prevent water splashing (*d*) none of these

Q. 6. Francis turbine is

(*a*) axial flow turbine (*b*) radial flow turbine
(*c*) mixed flow turbine (*d*) none of these

Q. 7. Kaplan turbine is

(*a*) axial flow turbine (*b*) radial flow turbine
(*c*) mixed flow turbine (*d*) none of these

Q. 8. Pelton wheel is suitable for

(*a*) low head low discharge (*b*) high head low discharge
(*c*) high head high discharge (*d*) low head high discharge

Answer to MCQ

1. (*b*) **2.** (*a*) **3.** (*d*) **4.** (*b*) **5.** (*a*) **6.** (*b*)
7. (*a*) **8.** (*b*)

Chapter

NUCLEAR POWER GENERATION

Learning Objectives

After reading this chapter, reader will be able to

- Understand components, construction and function of a nuclear power plant.
- Understand types of reactors and their operating principles.
- Understand process of electrical power generation in a nuclear power plant.
- Grasp the basics of radiation hazards, their measurement and protection including impact on human beings.

"A little more persistance, a little more effort and what seemed hopeless failure may turn to glorious success" — Elbert Hubbard

5.1. INTRODUCTION

With rising energy demand and fast depletion of fossil fuels, there is urgent need to diversify sources of energy. Nuclear energy offers an alternative to fossil fuel based power generation. However, the technology of manufacture of nuclear reactor, preparation of nuclear fuel, operation and maintenance of nuclear power plant is complex and requires expertise which very few countries possess. In addition, there is shortage of nuclear fuel in India. Hence, the total contribution of nuclear energy in the installed capacity is barely 2%.

India started nuclear power generation immediately after independence and has gained sufficient expertise in operation and maintenance of nuclear powers plants. So, this can become a dominant source of electrical energy in future. India has nuclear power plants located in six states. A detail is provided in table 5.1.

Table 5.1: Operational nuclear power plants in India (as on Dec. 31, 2015)

Sr. No	*Location*	*Type of reactor*	*no. of units (MW)*	*Total capacity (MW)*
1.	Tarapur (Maharashtra)	BWR	2 × 160 2 × 540	1400
2.	Kalpakkam (Tamil Nadu)	PHWR	2 × 220	440
3.	Rawatbhata (Rajasthan)	PHWR	1 × 100 1 × 200 4 × 220	1180
4.	Narora (U.P.)	PHWR	2 × 200	440
5.	Kakrapar (Gujarat)	PHWR	2 × 220	440
6.	Kaiga (Karnataka)	PHWR	4 × 220	880
7.	Kudankulam (Tamil Nadu)	VVER 1000	1 × 1000	1000
				Total 5780

Projects under construction are—Kudankulam (1 × 1000 MW), Rawatbhata (2 × 700 MW) and Kakrapar (2 × 700 MW).

France generates 75% of its total power from nuclear power plants. Similarly, other countries where nuclear energy is the dominant source of power are — Lithuania (73 %), Belgium (57%) Bulgaria (47 %), Sweden (46.8 %), Hungary (38.3 %) etc .

The tardy progress of nuclear power plants in India is due to shortage of nuclear fuel. For this purpose, India has signed agreement with USA for supply of nuclear fuel. The estimated availability of Uranium in India is 78000 tons and Thorium is 3,63,000 tons.

5.2. NUCLEAR FUELS

The nuclear fuels used in atomic reactors are Uranium and Thorium. The physical properties of Uranium and Thorium are given below—

(*i*) **Uranium**—It is found in nature. The uranium deposits are in Great Bear Lake in Canada, Katanger in Belgium Congo, Czech republic and USA. In India, Uranium is found in Jaduguda in Jharkhand and Thorium is available in Kerala.

The natural Uranium U_{92}^{238} contains 0.7 % of fissionable isotope U_{92}^{235}. It is highly reactive in atmosphere hence it is purified in vacuum or in inert atmosphere. The physical properties of Uranium are listed below—

(*a*) Density — 19.13 gm/cm^3

(*b*) Melting point — 1133 °C

(*c*) Boiling point — 3900°C

(*d*) Electrical resistivity — 2 to 4×10^4 micro – ohm cm
(*e*) Thermal conductivity — 0.062 cal/cm-sec-°C at 75°c
— 0.078 cal/cm-sec-°C at 400°C
(*f*) Thermal expansion — 25 to 125 × 10^{-6} per °C
(*g*) Allotropic transformation — Alpha to Beta at 663°C and Beta to Gamma at 764°C.

Uranium oxide (UO_2) appears as black powder and is converted into fuel pellets by cold pressing and sintering at high temperature. Another fuel is uranium carbide (UC) but is used much less. It has higher density and thermal conductivity than uranium oxide. However, it reacts with water and hence is not suitable for water cooled reactor .

(*ii*) **Plutonium**—Plutonium oxide (Pu O_2) is used as reactor fuel. The melting point is 2400°C. Plutonium oxide is mixed with uranium oxide to form mixed oxide fuel (MOX) for fast reactors. Mox has properties similar to uranium oxide.

(*iii*) **Thorium**—It is of relatively lower strength and has poor resistance to corrosion. Due to high cost, it is not a popular fuel. (Th_{90}^{233}) when bombarded with neutron, produces isotope Th_{90}^{233} which can be used in nuclear reactor. Monazite sand contains thorium as ThO_2 with small amount of uranium oxide U_2O_8.

The physical properties of Thorium are listed below—

(*a*) Density = 11.71 gm/cm^3
(*b*) Melting point—1690°C
(*c*) Boiling point—3000°C
(*d*) Electrical resistivity = 18 × 10^{-6} Ω cm at 20°C
(*e*) Thermal conductivity—0.09 cal/sec – cm – °C at 800°C

5.3. NUCLEAR PHYSICS

Energy generated from nuclear reaction is of two types viz fission reaction and fusion reaction. Fission reaction takes place when a neutron hits a nucleus of an atom. The nucleus breaksup and a huge amount of energy is released. While in fission reaction, two nucleui of atoms join together and form a large nucleus with the help of external energy input.

Natural uranium U_{92}^{235} is a readily fissionable material. If a neutron hits its nucleus, it is split and an enormous energy is released. The nucleus also ejects neutrons which further hit other uranium nuclei and the process goes on. This is known as chain reaction.

If the reaction is somehow controlled, then this energy can be utilised to generate power. Fissionable materials are uranium–235, uranium–233 and plutonium–239

Isotopes of Uranium, thorium and radium are unstable and disintegrate spontaneously through electromagnetic radiations. This discharge of energy through electromagnetic radiation is called radioactivity. Three types of particles viz. α, β and γ rays are emitted in the radiation. Exposure to β radiation leads to skin burns and may cause cancer. Exposure to Gamma rays may cause blood related diseases and genetic mutation. To protect from harmful effects of radiation, shielding with metal (for β particle radiation) and thick layer of lead or concrete (for Gamma rays) is provided.

5.4. FISSILE AND FERTILE MATERIALS

The materials which undergo nuclear fission readily are known as fissile materials such as U-235, U-233 and Pu-239 which occur in nature.

Fertile materials are those which are not fissionable but can be converted to a fissionable form. For example, U-238 and Th-232 are not fissionable material but can be converted to Pu -239 and U-233 respectively which are fissionable.

The following chemical reaction shows convertion of Thorium–232 (fertile material) to Uranium–233 (fissile materials)

$$\text{Fertile material} \rightarrow Th_{90}^{232} + n_0^1 \longrightarrow Th_{90}^{233} + V \quad \text{...(5.1)}$$

$$Th_{90}^{233} + e_1^0 \longrightarrow Pa_{90}^{233} \quad \text{...(5.2)}$$

$$Pa_{90}^{233} + e_1^0 \rightarrow U_{92}^{233} \longleftarrow \text{fissile material} \quad \text{...(5.3)}$$

When radioactive fuel such as U_{92}^{233} is bombarded by neutrons under controlled condition, fission reaction takes place and huge energy is released .

$$U_{92}^{235} + n_0^1 \rightarrow U_{92}^{236} \rightarrow Ba_{56}^{137} + Kr_{36}^{97} + 2n_0^1 + \text{Energy} \quad \text{...(5.4)}$$

This is the reaction which takes place in nuclear reactor. To regulate the rate of reaction, control rods made of boron are used. A moderator which is Deuterium Oxide or heavy water (D_2O) is used to slow down fast moving electrons produced by splitting of nucleus.

India is bestowed with large amount of Thorium which is found in Kerala. Thorium is a fissile material. Main fuel U_{92}^{235} is scarcely available in India which prevents large scale power generation through nuclear reactors .

5.5. ADVANTAGES AND DISADVANTAGES OF NUCLEAR POWER GENERATION

Following are the advantages and disadvantages of nuclear power generation—

(*i*) amount of fuel required is very small and hence there are no problems of transportation, storage and handling of fuel.

(*ii*) a nuclear power station requires lesser area compared to a conventional powers plant of same capacity.

(*iii*) use of nuclear energy helps to conserve fossile fuels such as coal, oil and gas which are depleting very fast.

(*iv*) operation of a nuclear power plant is free from pollution.

(*v*) the operating cost of nuclear power plant is low and hence is used as base load plant.

(*vi*) this type of plant can be used to produce fissile material.

Disadvantages—

(*i*) The plant has very high capital cost.

(*ii*) It can not respond to fast changing loads.

(*iii*) Operation and maintenance of plant requires high expertise.

(*iv*) There are chances of radioactive leakage during abnormal operation.

(*v*) Very high quantity of cooling water is required.

(*vi*) Any major accident can severely affect men, animal and environment (like chernobyle in Ukrain).

(*vii*) Disposal of nuclear waste is a big problem.

5.6. SELECTION OF SITE FOR NUCLEAR POWER PLANT

Following factors affect the site selection for nuclear power plant—

(*i*) **Availability of water**—Site should be selected near a river, pond or sea as large quantity of water is required for cooling.

(*ii*) **Distance from habitated area**—Due to possibility of radiation leakage, nuclear power plants are situated away from the populated area.

(*iii*) **Transport facility**—Transport facility is required during construction stage. Rail and road–transport facility should be available.

(*iv*) **Nearness to load centre**—The power plant should be as close to load centre as radiation safety consideration will allow. This reduces transmission cost & losses.

(*v*) **Facility for nuclear waste disposal**—Nuclear waste being radioactive in nature, it usually disposed off away from human habitation. Normally, waste is encased and buried in the seabed or kept underground.

5.7. NUCLEAR MATERIALS

Following are various nuclear materials used in a nuclear power plant—

(*i*) **Nuclear fuels**—Fuels mainly used are natural Uranium (U-235), enriched uranium (2 to 5% U-235), plutonium and uranium (U-233).

(*ii*) **Coolant**—Coolant is a medium that transfers heat from reactor core to the heat exchanger or boiler. Various types of coolant used are water, heavy water (D_2O), liquid sodium or helium.

(*iii*) **Moderating material**—Moderating material slows down neutrons until its kinetic energy reaches average kinetic energy of surrounding particles. Materials used are water, heavy water, Lithium, Beryllium, Graphite and mixture of Lead and Bismuth.

(*iv*) **Cladding material**—Cladding material prevent mixing of fuel and coolant. These are Beryllium, Steel, Zirconium, Magnesium etc.

(*v*) **Control rod materials**—Control rods are used in reactors to control the rate of reaction. These are Boron, Cadmium, Hafnium etc.

(*vi*) **Shielding material**—Shielding is used to confine thermal neutrons and secondary radiation inside the reactor. Concrete is cheapest and widely used material.

5.8. NUCLEAR REACTOR

Nuclear reactor is a vessel where nuclear fission reaction takes place. The heat generated due to the fission reaction is removed by coolant.

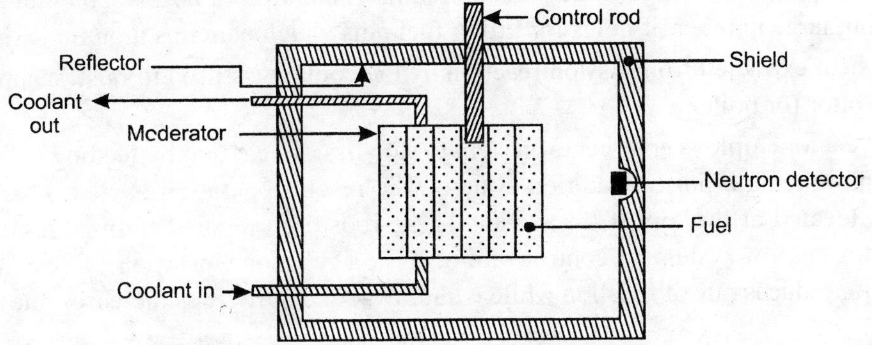

Figure 5.1. Construction of nuclear reactor

Various parts of nuclear reactor are described below—

(*i*) **Reactor core**—It houses the fuel rods where fission reaction takes place. It consists of double walled concrete construction with the annular space being kept at vacuum through a filtration and pump back system to ensure zero radiation leak in the worst case scenario of an accident.

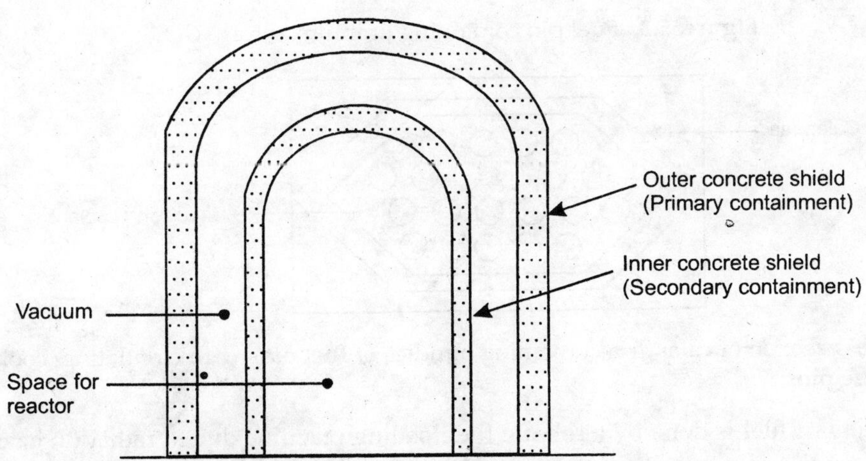

Figure 5.2. Construction of reactor building

The heat removal from the moderator and reactor auxiliary system is done by an independent closed loop cooling water system. The heat from this cooling water, in turn, is removed by tertiary closed loop cooling system using induced draft cooling towers which dissipate heat to surrounding. There is a leak detection system that detects incipient radiation leak.

The reactor is a horizontal cylindrical vessel made of stainless steel 304 L with horizontal coolant channels (made of Zirconium–Niobium alloy) containing fuel bundles. Coolant is circulated around fuel bundles. This coolant transfers heat to a secondary coolant.

A fuel pin containing uranium oxide surrounded by Zirconium cladding is placed inside a fuel bundle. The fuel bundles are housed in a calendria (a horizontal cylindrical vessel having large number of holes for fitting fuel pins which contains uranium oxide.)

The heat extracted from fission reaction by the coolants is used to raise steam in a steam generator (or boiler).

The reactor employs emergency system to stop fission reaction by feeding a chemical and by introducing a poison addition system. The reactor operation is controlled by control rods located at the top of the vessel. These rods are operated through a computerised reactor control system to control rate of fission reaction. Insertion of control rods into reactor reduces rate of reaction while withdrawal of control rods increases rate of reaction.

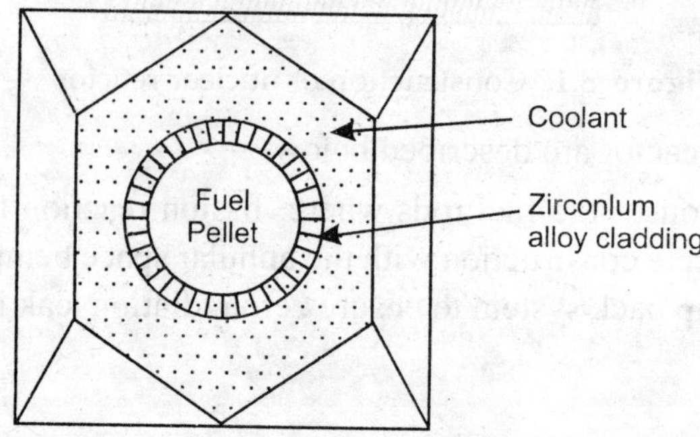

Figure. 5.3. Fuel pin containing uranium oxide (UO_2)

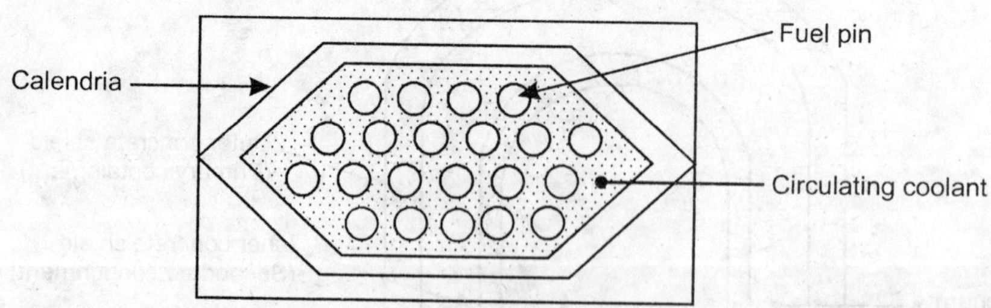

Figure. 5.4. Cross-section of calendria containing bundles of fuel pins with circulating coolant around these pins.

Loading of fuel is done by a robotic fuel loading machine due to radiation hazard.

(ii) **Fuel**—Fuel used are U^{235}, U^{233} and Pu^{239}. U^{235} occurs in nature while U^{233} and Pu^{239} are formed in the reactor. Fuel is housed in rods called fuel pin for easy insertion and removal from the calendria.

Uranium ore is mined in Jaduguda, Bhatin, Narwa Pahad and Turandih (all in Jharkhand state).

(*iii*) **Moderator**—Purpose of moderator is to slow down fast moving neutrons to slow speed (called thermal neutrons) so that fission reaction can take place with natural uranium as fuel. Heavy water, Graphite or Beryllium are used as moderator.

Heavy water or deutarium oxide (D_2O) is made from light water or H_2O. 30 litres of light water is used to produce one litre of heavy water. Following table 5.2 gives comparison of heavy water and light water characteristic parameters.

Table 5.2: Comparison of properties of heavy water and light water

Sr. No	*Parameter*	*Heavy water (D_2O)*	*Light water (H_2O)*
1.	Molecular weight	20.028	18.015
2.	Specific gravity at 25°C	1.1044	0.997
3.	Freezing point	–328°C	0°C
4.	Boiling point	101.42°C	100°C
5.	Refractive index	1.328	1.333

In India, there are six heavy water plants located at Baroda, (Gujarat), Thal (Maharashta), RawatBhata (Rajasthan), Hazira (Gujarat), Tuticorin (Tamil Nadu) and Manuguru (Andhra Pradesh).

(*iv*) **Control rods**—Control rods are used to control rate of nuclear fission reaction so that chain reaction is maintained at steady state. These rods are also used to shutdown the reactor during emergency. These are basically neutron absorbing material such as Boron, Cadmium, Hafnium etc.

(*v*) **Coolant**—A coolant is a medium that carries away heat produced due to fission reaction to a steam generator to raise steam. The coolant used are liquid metal (sodium, NaK), gas (Helium, Carbon dioxide, Hydrogen, air) or heavy water (D_2O).

(*vi*) **Reflector**—Reflector covers inside surface of reactor to prevent escape of neutrons from the core. It helps to bounce the escaping neutrons back to the core. This sustains the chain reaction.

(*vii*) **Shielding**—It provides protection against alpha, beta and gamma rays and neutrons produced due to the chain reaction. It is a radiation shield that absorbs harmful radiation.

(*viii*) **Containment**—It is a structure around the reactor core that protects the surroundings from the radiation leak due to a malfunction in a reactor. It is composed of thick concrete and steel structure.

5.9. CLASSIFICATION OF NUCLEAR REACTORS

(*i*) Classification based on type of reaction—

(*a*) **Thermal reactors**—These reactors use slowed or thermal neutrons. Fast moving neutrons are slowed down by moderator material. Majority of reactors are of this type.

(*b*) **Fast neutron reactor**—These reactors use fast neutrons for fission reaction with more highly enriched fissile material (enrichment 20% or more)

(*ii*) **Classification based on type of moderator material—**

(*a*) **Graphite moderated reactors**—These reactor use graphite as moderator.

(*b*) **Water moderated reactors—**

1. **Light water moderated reactors**—These reactors use ordinary water to cool and moderate reactor.
2. **Heavy water moderated reactors**—These reactors use heavy water.

(*c*) **Light element moderated reactors**—These reactors use Beryllium or Lithium as moderator.

(*d*) **Organically moderated reactors**—These reactors use biphenyl and terphenyl as coolant and moderator.

(*iii*) **Classification based on coolant type—**

(*a*) **Water cooled reactors**—These are of two types viz. pressurised water reactor (PWR) and boiling water reactor (BWR).

(*b*) **Liquid metal cooled reactor**—These reactors use liquid metal coolant such as sodium, NaK, lead, lead-bismuth eutectic.

(*c*) **Gas cooled reactors**—These reactors are cooled by an inert gas such as helium.

(*d*) **Molton salt reactor**—These reactors are cooled by mixture of molten salts such as mixture of lithium flouride and beryllium fluoride.

(*iv*) **Classification based on reactor design—**

(*a*) **Generation—I** Reactors developed in 1950–1960s.

(*b*) **Generation—II** Reactors developed upto 1990s. About 85% of reactors are of this type.

(*c*) **Generation—III** Reactors are of latest design developed during operating period of generations–II design and are improved version of generation–II.

(*d*) **Generation—IV** Reactors are on drawing board stage and are not expected to be operational before 2020.

(*v*) **Classification based on use—**

(*a*) used for power generation.

(*b*) used for marine propulsion (e.g. nuclear powered submarine)

(*c*) used for transmutation of elements (creation of radioactive isotopes, production of nuclear weapon etc.).

(*d*) used for research and training.

5.9.1. Pressurised Water Reactor (PWR)

This is a most common type of reactor used for power generation as well as for naval propulsion. This reactor uses ordinary water as moderator and coolant. The cooling system consists of primary circuit and secondary circuit. Primary circuit flows through the core of the reactor at high pressure while secondary circuit is used to generate steam.

This type of reactor uses enriched uranium oxide fuel encased in zirconium alloy cladding. Water is used as coolant and moderator. The water is pressurised to about 150 atmosphere to prevent boiling. The water in reactor reaches a temperature of 325°C. Primary coolant flows from reactor core to heat exchanger and back to the core with the help of a pump. The secondary cooling circuit operates at a lower pressure and water boils in the heat exchanger. Steam thus formed is used to drive steam turbine. After expansion of steam over turbine blades, the exhaust steam is cooled in a condenser and fed back to the heat exchanger.

The primary circuit contains a pressuriser in the form of a pressure vessel with a heating coil at the bottom and water spray arrangement at the top. When primary circuit pressure decreases, heating coils get on and generates steam by boiling water thereby increasing steam pressure in the primary circuit. However, if the pressure becomes high, cold water is sprayed in the pressuriser. The steam is condensed and hence pressure is reduced.

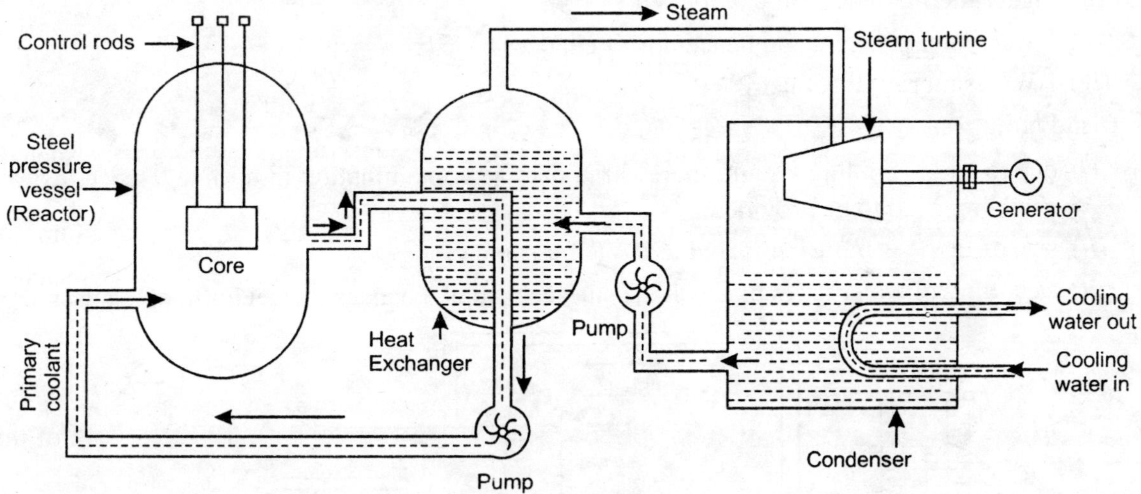

Figure. 5.5. Pressurised Water Reactor (PWR)

Advantages of PWR—

(*i*) compact design.

(*ii*) high power density.

(*iii*) low cost of coolant and moderator.

(*iv*) good response to increase in load demand.

(*v*) reactor cools down if water starts bubbling.

Disadvantages—

(*i*) generation of low temperature (250°C) steam.

(*ii*) due to high pressure, chances of leakage of coolant.

(*iii*) expensive cladding material is required to prevent corrosion.

(*iv*) can not be used to breed new fuel.

(*v*) high auxiliary power consumption.

5.9.2. Boiling Water Reactor (BWR)

This type of reactor uses single circuit with water at pressure of 75 atmosphere and temperature of 285°C. It uses enriched uranium oxide as fuel. Ordinary water is used as coolant and moderator. A BWR can follow load variation better than PWR. Feed water enters the reactor at the bottom and gets evaporated into steam due to heat of fission reaction. This steam leaves reactor at the top and enters turbine. After expansion inside turbine, steam is condensed and fed back to heat exchanger. Since the water around the reactor core is contaminated with traces of radio nuclides, hence radiological protection is provided to turbine.

Advantages of BWR—

(*i*) due to single water circuit, size of pressure vessel is small.

(*ii*) higher thermal efficiency than PWR (33%).

(*iii*) lower water pressure and hence, lower chances of leakage.

(*iv*) BWR is more stable than PWR.

Disadvantages—

(*i*) due to single cooling circuit, there is radioactive contamination in turbine. Hence, extra shielding need to be provided.

(*ii*) size of BWR is more compared to PWR for same rating.

(*iii*) as boiling of water takes place on the surface of fuel, chances of fuel burnout is possible.

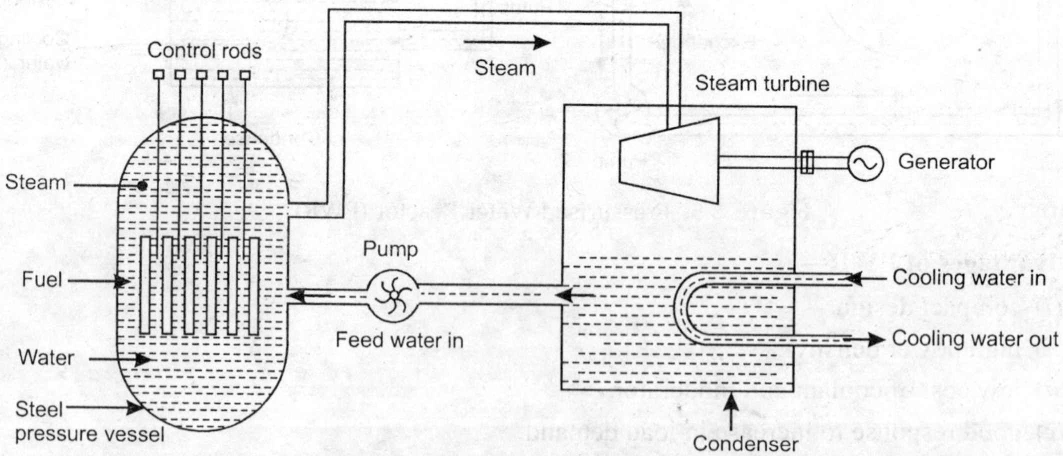

Figure. 5.6. Boiling Water Reactor (BWR)

5.9.3. Heavy Water Cooled and Moderated (CANDU) Reactor

This is pressurised heavy water reactor (PHWR) developed in canada as CANDU type reactor. CANDU stands for Canadian Deuterium Uranium. This reactor uses natural uranium and heavy water as moderator. It has primary and secondary cooling water circuit carrying heavy water. Control rods are not required as control is achieved by varying moderator level in the reactor. The moderator is housed in a large tank called calendria which contains several hundred pressure tubes which contains fuel.

Advantages—

(*i*) it does not require enriched uranium.

(*ii*) reactor control is simple due to absence of control rods.

(*iii*) low fuel consumption.

(*iv*) can be refuelled while operating.

Disadvantages—

(*i*) neutron absorption in deuterium leads to production of tritium, a radioactive material.

(*ii*) use of costly heavy water (D_2O).

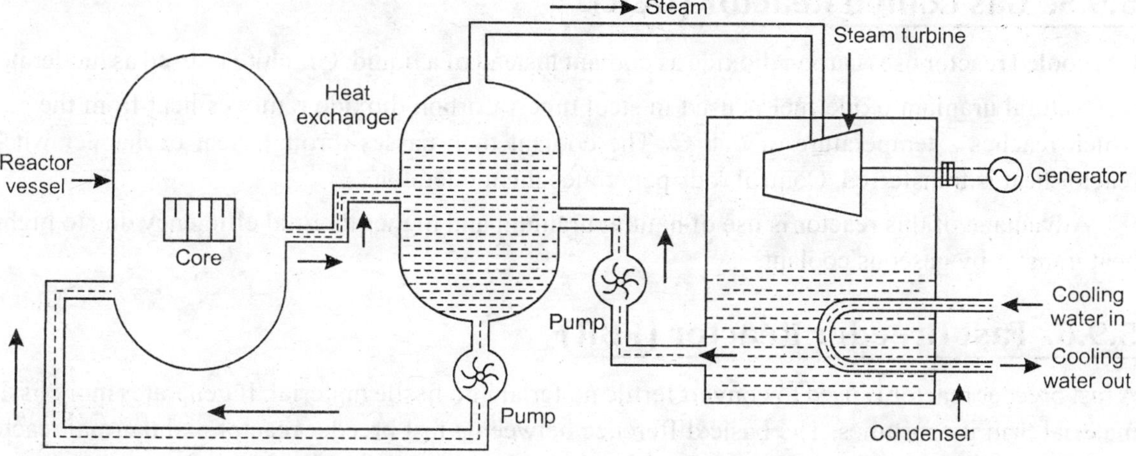

Figure. 5.7. CANDU type reactor (PHWR)

5.9.4. Liquid Metal Cooled Reactor (Sodium Graphite Reactor)

This type of reactor provides advantage of high temperature as in PWR reactor but with lesser pressure. Liquid sodium is used as heat transferring medium. The heat is transferred from reactor core to the heat exchanger where steam is raised. Due to difficulty in handling of sodium, two heat transfer circuits are used. Primary circuit uses liquid sodium while secondary circuit uses NaK (sodium potassium). Due to violent reaction of sodium with air, this circuit is air tight.

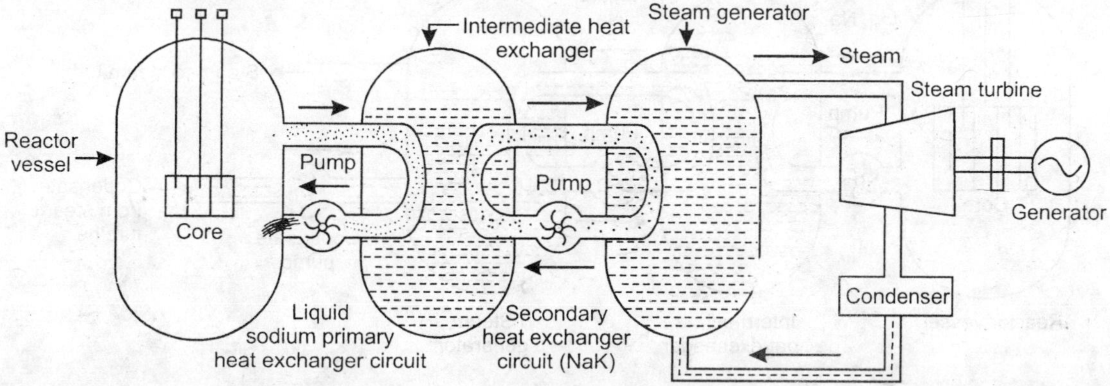

Figure. 5.8. Liquid metal cooled reactor

Advantages—

(*i*) reduced pressure in primary heat transfer circuit.
(*ii*) steam production at high temperature and pressure.
(*iii*) reduced containment required due to low coolant pressure.

Disadvantages—

(*i*) use of enriched fuel.
(*ii*) complex core design.
(*iii*) risk of sodium leakage.
(*iv*) higher cost due to intermediate heat exchanger.

5.9.5. Gas Cooled Reactor (GCR)

Gas cooled reactor uses carbon dioxide as coolant instead of a liquid. Graphite is used as moderator.

Natural uranium oxide fuel is used in steel tubes. Carbon dioxide removes heat from the core which reaches a temperature of 650°C. The coolant then passes through heat exchanger where reactor heat is transferred. Control rods penetrates the moderator.

Advantage of this reactor is use of natural uranium and higher thermal efficiency due to higher heat transfer by gaseous coolant.

5.9.6. Fast Breeder Reactor (FBR)

A fast breeder reactor is used to convert fertile material into fissile material. It generates more fissile material than it consumes. The basic difference between a fast breeder reactor and thermal reactor is that latter is used to produce heat from fissile nuclear material while former is used to convert fertile to fissile material.

The core of reactor consisting of steel tubes contains fissile material. This fissile material is surrounded by a blanket of uranium. There are two cooling circuit-primary and secondary. In both circuits, liquid sodium/potassium is used as a coolant. Reactor core and primary heat exchanger are separated by a neutron shield made of graphite. The core of the reactor contains enriched uranium (more than 10%). The reactor produces Pu^{239} and U^{233}.

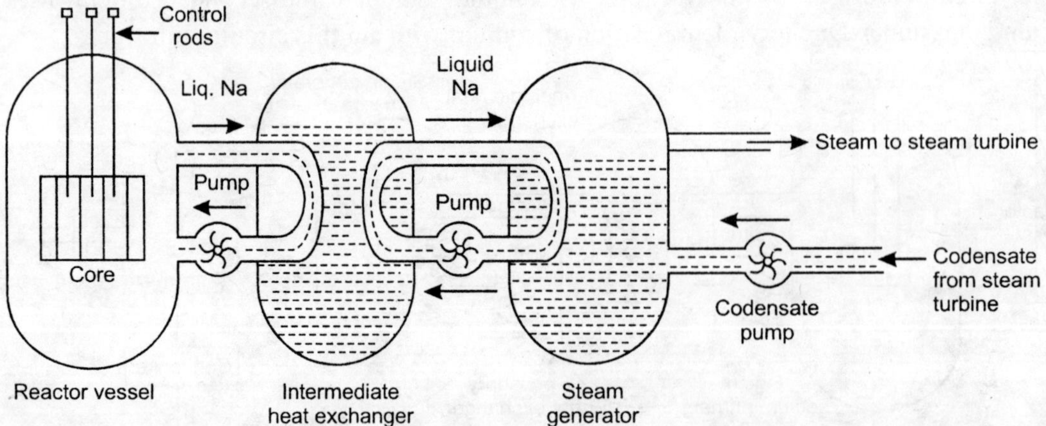

Figure. 5.9. Fast Breeder Reactor (FBR)

5.9.7. RBMK Reactor (Reaktor Bolshoy Moschnosti Kanalniy)

This reactor is used to produce power and plutonium. It uses water as coolant and graphite as moderator. The fuel used is un-enriched uranium. However, due to safety issues, only few operating reactors are left in erstwhile Soviet Union.

5.9.8. Molten Salt Reactor (MSR)

This reactor uses fuels dissolved in fluoride salt. The rector possesses high efficiency and high power density. It does not have high pressure and incorporates many safety features.

5.9.9. Aqueous Homogeneous Rector (AHR)

It contains nuclear salts dissolved in water. It is mixed with a coolant and neutron moderator.

5.10. NUCLEAR POWER PLANT

A nuclear power plant is similar to thermal power plant except the heat produced in a nuclear power plant is due to a chemical reaction in a reactor. Except reactor, other major components, such as steam turbine and generator are similar. A major portion of a nuclear power plant is occupied by special facilities, such as fuel element fabrication area, fuel element preparation area, radioactive storage area, waste disposal apparatus area, storage area for fuel, coolant and moderator storage area etc.

A nuclear power plant consists of following major components—

(*i*) Reactor. (*ii*) Steam generator. (*iii*) Steam turbine.
(*iv*) Condenser. (*v*) Cooling tower. (*vi*) Generator.
(*vii*) Refuelling pool (*viii*) Spent fuel pool (*ix*) Nuclear safety systems

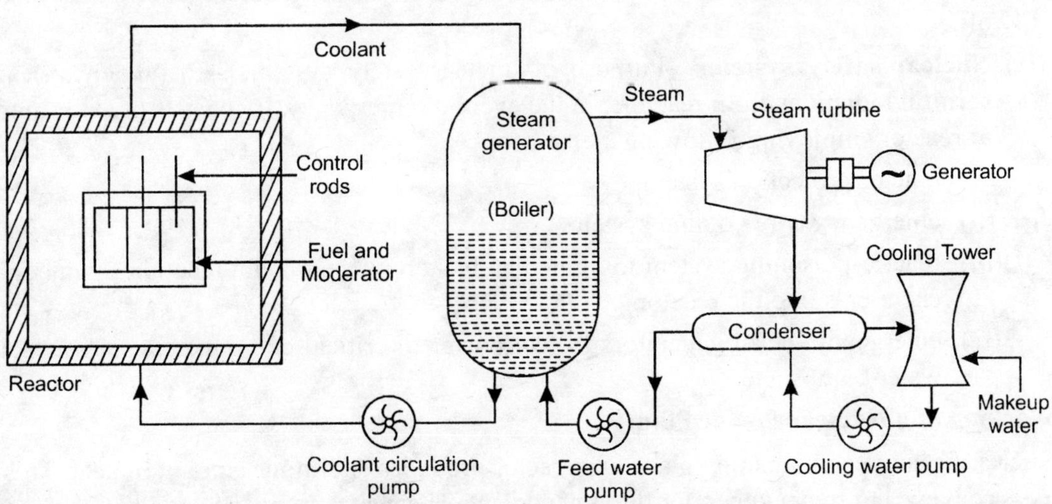

Figure. 5.10. Schematic of a nuclear power plant

(*i*) **Reactor**—Fission reaction takes place in a reactor. It is a source of heat generation which is used to produce steam. The heat generated in a reactor is carried away by coolant to a steam generator. Various types of coolant used are water (H_2O), heavy water (D_2O), liquid sodium, or helium. Life of reactor is about 30 operating years.

(*ii*) **Steam generator**—It is a boiler where water is converted into steam by the heat carried by coolant from reactor. The steam raised is superheated in a superheater for feeding to steam turbine.

(*iii*) **Steam turbine**—Steam turbine converts heat energy of superheated steam into mechanical energy. It consists of rows of blades on turbine rotor and stator part through which steam expands transferring thermal energy.

(*iv*) **Condenser**—It is a heat exchanger in which the exhaust steam after expansion in steam turbine loses its heat and condenses into water. The heat of exhaust is carried away by cooling water. The cooling water releases this heat to atmosphere through cooling tower. The heat transfer from exhaust steam to cooling water is through indirect contact. Cooling water flows through tubes while exhaust steam flows over these tubes (it is a shell and tube heat exchanger).

(*v*) **Cooling tower**—Water carrying heat of exhaust steam from condenser gets cooled here. The hot cooling water carrying heat of exhaust steam is sprayed at a height which percolates through fills which break water into fine droplets thereby increasing the cooling surface area. A part of this water gets evaporated. The water lost due to evaporation and drift (water droplets carried away by air) is compensated by feeding makeup water.

(*vi*) **Generator**—It is a cylindrical rotor, 2 pole, 3000 rpm, three phase synchronous generator which is mechanically coupled to the steam turbine. The rotating steam turbine causes generator to rotate thereby producing electricity.

(*vii*) **Refueling pool**—This is an area where refuelling or loading of fresh fuel into reactor is done.

(*viii*) **Spent fuel pool**—The spent fuel from reactor is stored here before it is suitably disposed off.

(*ix*) **Nuclear safety systems**—Purpose of nuclear safety system is to prevent release of harmful radiations from reactors, in the event of emergency. It consists of safe shutdown of reactor employing following elements—

- (*i*) reactor protection system.
- (*ii*) emergency core cooling system.
- (*iii*) reactor poisoning system to immediately stop nuclear chain reaction by injection of chemicals into the reactor.
- (*iv*) emergency diesel generators to feel power to critical components, such as cooling water pumps, etc.

Working of a Nuclear Power Plant

Nuclear fission reaction taking place in a reactor produces enormous amount of heat. This heat energy is conveyed to steam generator through coolant. The heat contained in coolant causes water in steam generator to get converted into steam. This steam is supplied to a steam turbine. This high temperature and high pressure steam expands over series of blades of steam turbine producing rotation. Hence, thermal energy of steam is converted into electrical energy by the generator coupled to the steam turbine.

5.11. REFUELLING AND LIFE OF A NUCLEAR REACTOR

Like every power plant, a nuclear power plant also needs to be refuelled periodically. However, due to low fuel consumption, refuelling period is longer compared to other conventional power plants. A thermal power plant, gas turbined based plant or diesel power plant need fuel continuously so as to produce electricity. But a nuclear power plant does not require continuous refuelling rather it is done at an interval of 1-2 years. Also, refuelling process is quite cumbersome and elaborate as it requires shutdown of reactor so that pressure vessel could be opened. Usually, entire fuel is not replaced rather 25 to 33% fuel is loaded. Only RBMK and CANDU type reactors can be refuelled in running condition.

The fuel is kept in the form of pellets which are housed in Zirconium alloy tubes. These are then called fuel rods. Zirconium metal is chosen due to its corrosion resistant property and ability to pass neutrons. A number of fuel rods are bundled together to form a fuel assembly. The entire fuel assembly is loaded into the reactor core.

The operating life of a nuclear reactor is 30 to 40 years. However, this can be extended upto 60 years. After completion of useful economic life, a reactor need to be decommissioned and spent fuel left need to be disposed off safely.

5.12. NUCLEAR WASTE DISPOSAL

After a fuel is consumed, what is left in a reactor is nuclear waste. As a fuel, it is composed of mostly uranium (or thorium), oxygen and steel. After nuclear reaction, many uranium atoms are split into various isotopes of transition metals. This waste or spent fuel is highly radioactive so much so that exposure of few seconds will cause death due to acute radiation sickness within few days.

Initially, spent fuel is kept under water for few years till radiation levels have reduced. This is then kept in a storage cask made of concrete placed underground. To protect against accidents, spent fuel is mixed with neutron eating atoms, such as boron.

India has a policy to reprocess waste to fuel next generation reactors. However, this produces highly radioactive waste, such as plutonium–239. India has three spent fuel reprocessing plants at Tarapur (Maharashtra), Trombay (Maharashtra) and Kalpakkam (Tamil Nadu). USA has highest inventory of spent fuel lying with them followed by Canada, Japan, France, Russia and South Korea.

For disposal purpose, radioactive waste is seggregated into three categories—low radioactivity material, medium radioactivity material and high radioactivity material. Low radioactivity material is stored without high level of shielding. Medium radioactivity material is stored for about 5 years to allow decay of radioactivity. High radioactivity material is stored under water for years to allow radioactivity to decay to an acceptable level.

Safe method of nuclear waste disposal is still a matter of exploration and debate. No permanent foolproof method is available to dispose off nuclear waste safely.

5.13. SUMMARY OF VARIOUS TYPES OF NUCLEAR REACTORS

Following table 5.3 gives summary of nuclear reactors, coolant used, moderator used and fuel used.

Table 5.3: Summary of various types of nuclear reactors

Sr. No.	*Type of reactor*	*Fuel used*	*Moderator*	*Coolant*
1.	Boiling Water Reactor (BWR)	Enriched Uranium dioxide	Water	Water
2.	Pressurised Water Reactor (PWR)	Enriched Uranium dioxide	Water	Water
3.	Pressurised Heavy Water Reactor (PHWR)	Natural Uranium dioxide	Heavy water	Heavy water
4.	Fast Breeder Reactor (FBR)	Uranium oxide and Plutonium oxide	None	Liquid Sodium
5.	Gas cooled Reactor (GCR)	Natural Uranium	Graphite	Carbon dioxide
6.	Advanced Gas Cooled Reactor (AGCR)	Enriched Uranium oxide	Graphite	Carbon dioxide
7.	High Temperature Gas Cooled Reactor (HTGCR)	Enriched Uranium oxide	Graphite	Helium
8.	Graphite Moderated Boiling Water Reactor (RBMK)	Enriched Uranium dioxide	Graphite	Water

5.14. RADIATION MEASUREMENT AND PROTECTION

Radiation is energy emitted in the form of high energy particles. Emitted radiation is of two forms viz. as waves having energy but no mass, such as electromagnetic radiation (Sunrays, *x*-rays, cosmic radiation etc.). Another form of radiation is emitted as particles having energy and mass, such as alpha particles, beta particles, neutrons etc.

Radiation can be of two types viz ionizing and non-ionizing radiation. A non-ionizing radiation transfer energy into a body through which it passes but unable to break molecular bonds due to insufficient energy. Examples of non- ionizing radiation are heat, visible light, microwaves, radio waves etc. While ionizing radiation transfer energy into a body through which it passes and carries sufficient energy to break molecular bonds. Examples are alpha particles, beta particles, gamma rays, neutrons, *x*-rays etc. All nuclear radiations are ionizing radiations and hence, are biologically harmful.

Although, a small amount of radiation is always present in the surroundings due to natural ambient radiation, soil, buildings, food, drinking water, medicines etc. These are background radiations and are of very low intensity. For example, a person travelling on a short flight is exposed to 5 μ Sv (micro sievert-unit of absorbed radiation) and on a long intercontinental flight, it is 30 μ Sv. X-ray scanner in airport security can expose a person to 5 μ Sv. Usually, a background radiation of 2.4 m Sv/years is experienced by everyone. However, the level of these radiations are very low and do not produce any long term effect on human body.

Persons working in the vicinity of a nuclear power plants may get exposed to high level of harmful radiation in case of abnormal/accidental event. Alpha, beta, gamma rays and neutrons are harmful ionizing radiations which emanate from nuclear reactors and nuclear fuels.

(*i*) **Alpha particles**—These particles have very limited ability to penetrate objects and are usually blocked by paper, few inches of air, human skin etc. So, external exposure to alpha particles is safe but can be dangerous if inhaled or swallowed.

(*ii*) **Beta particles**—These can penetrate objects to a greater depth than alpha particles. These can be blocked by thin sheet of plastic or metal, few feet of air, block of wood etc.

(*iii*) **Gamma and *x*-rays**—These rays possess high energy level and can penetrate objects to a greater depth than alpha and beta particles. These rays can be blocked by few inches of lead, several feet of concrete etc.

(*iv*) **Neutrons**—Neutrons can penetrate objects to still greater depth than gamma and *x*-rays. These can travel very long distances in air and can be blocked by a very thick layer of concrete or water.

5.14.1. Radiation Measurement

Radiation is measured in four different units depending upon the parameter to be measured—

(*i*) **Measurement of radioactivity**—The amount of ionizing radiation emitted by a material is measured in terms of number of atoms decay in a given time (radioactivity). Its unit is 'Becqueral (Bq)' and 'Curie (Ci)'.

(*ii*) **Measurement of radiation exposure**—The amount of radiation travelling through air is measured in 'Roentgen (R)' and 'Coulomb per kg (C/kg)'.

(*iii*) **Measurement of absorbed dose**—The amount of radiation absorbed by a body is measured in 'Radiation Absorbed Dose (rad) and 'Gray (Gy)'.

(*iv*) **Measurement of dose equivalent**—The amount of radiation absorbed and its medical effect on body is measured in 'Roentgen Equivalent Man (rem)' and 'Sievert (Sv)'. Beta and gamma radiations have equal dose equivalent radiation but alpha and neutron radiations have high dose equivalent radiation. Hence, these radiations are more harmful to human. A radiation exposure of 5 m Gy and more can cause cancer.

When radiation dose is small, cells/tissues are damaged but these cells repair themselves. In rare cases, a small dose may result in genetic mutation. However, if the radiation dose is higher, there is damage to DNA resulting in cell death.

Equivalence of units of radiation measurement is given bellow—

(*i*) 1 Gray (Gy) = 1 J/kg,

(*ii*) Roentgen (R) = 1 radiation absorbed dose (rad) = 1 roentgen equivalent man (rem).

(*iii*) 1 Gray = 100 rad.

(*iv*) 1 Sievert = 100 rem

(*v*) 1 Bequerel = 2.7×10^{-11} Curie

Radioactive decay is given by following expression.

$$\text{Radioactive decay, } A = A_0 e^{-\lambda t} \qquad \text{...(5.5)}$$

where, A = present amount of radioactivity.

A_0 = original amount of radioactivity.

λ = decay constant = $0.693/t_{0.5}$.

t = amount of time elapsed from A_0 to A

Different units of radiation can be co-related by an example. Consider a person is sitting under a mango tree. Suppose, number of mangoes are falling from the tree. This is equivalent to radioactivity (number of disintegration per second) in Becquerel. The number of falling mangoes hitting the person sitting under the tree is equivalent to absorbed dose in gray. The effect of mangoes hitting the person's body (based on size and weight of mangoes) is equivalent to dose equivalent in sievert.

5.14.2. Biological Effects of Ionizing Radiation

Levels of radiation is measured using various instruments, such as Geiger counter, liquid scintillation counter etc. The impact of radiation on a human body is due to either direct action or indirect action. In direct action, ionizing radiation is absorbed by the body. Structure of macromolecules in body becomes abnormal resulting in biological changes. In indirect action, ionizing radiation in a medium generates free radicals which cause damage to cells. An irrepairable damage to DNA causes cell death. Extensive levels of cell death can lead to organ failure and death of a person. An improperly repaired DNA may result in development of cancer. However, degree of sensitivity of tissues to radiation depends upon the type of tissue. Radiation sensitive tissues in a human body are breast tissue, bone marrow cells, mucus lining of small intestine, immune response cells, all stem cells etc. While radiation resistant tissues are heart tissue, large arteries and veins, mature blood cells, muscle cells, neurons of nervous system etc. Following table gives effect of acute radiation exposure to human body.

Table 5.4: Effects of acute radiation exposure to human

Sr. No.	*Radiation dose (R)*	*Effect on human body*
1.	10^4 (Single dose over whole body)	Death within hours
2.	500–1200 (Single dose, whole body)	Death within days
3.	250–500 (Single dose, whole body)	Death within several weeks

4.	50–350 (Single dose, whole body)	Vomiting, diarrhoea, skin reddening, loss of hair, blisters.
5.	100 (Single dose, whole body)	Reduced white cell count.
6.	400–500 (Local low level *x*-ray)	Temporary hair loss.
7.	600–900 (Local exposure to eye)	Cataract.

However, persons working in nuclear power plants are never exposed to such high levels of radiation (except in case of accidents, such as Chernobyle in Ukraine or Fukushima in Japan). The safe level of radiation exposure to persons working in such area are given in following table.

Table 5.5: Occupational radiation exposure limit

Sr. No.	*Part of Human Body*	*Yearly Radiation Limit (Adult) mrem*	*Yearly Radiation Limit (minor < 18 years) mrem*
1.	Whole body	5000	500
2.	Lens of eye	15000	1500
3.	Hands, forearm, elbow, lower legs, feet	50,000	5000
4.	Single organ	50,000	5000

5.14.3. Protection Against Ionizing Radiation

There are three primary means of protection against ionizing radiation viz.—

(*i*) **Time**—Minimization of duration of exposure. Lesser the duration of exposure, lesser is the damage to the human body.

(*ii*) **Distance**—Maximization of distance from the radioactive source. Greater the distance from the radioactive source, lesser the damage caused.

(*iii*) **Shielding**—Introduction of shield or barrier against source of radiation. This means using protective wear, such as gloves, coats, eye protection etc.

However, such high levels of radiation exposure seldom occurs. Natural Radioactivity of some objects is given in following table 5.6.

Table 5.6: Radioactivity of some objects

Sr No	*Object*	*Level of radiation*
1.	Adult human	4500 Bq
2.	1 kg of coffee	1000 Bq

3.	Air in 100 m^2	upto 30,000 Bq
4.	1 kg of coal ash	2000 Bq
5.	Radioisotope for medical diagnosis	70 million Bq
6.	1 kg Uranium	25 million Bq

From above table, it is clear that radioactivity is always present in our surrounding. Gravity of exposure depends upon intensity, duration and distance from source of radiation. However, use of protective measures ensure safety in the event of an accident.

5.15. STATUS OF NUCLEAR POWER GENERATION IN INDIA

Following table 5.7 gives status of nuclear power generation in India.

Table 5.7: Status of Nuclear Power Generation in India

Sr. No.	*Plant*	*Type*	*Capacity (MWe)*	*Date of Commercial operation*
1.	Tarapur Atomic Power Station, Unit–1, Maharashtra	BWR	160	October 28, 1969
2.	Tarapur Atomic Power Station, Unit–2, Maharashtra	BWR	160	October 28, 1969
3.	Tarapur Atomic Power Station, Unit–3, Maharashtra	PHWR	540	August 18, 2006
4.	Tarapur Atomic Power Station, Unit–4, Maharashtra	PHWR	540	September 12, 2005
5.	Rajasthan Atomic Power Station, Unit–1, Rajasthan	PHWR	100	December 16, 1973
6.	Rajasthan Atomic Power Station, Unit–2, Rajasthan	PHWR	200	April 1, 1981
7.	Rajasthan Atomic Power Station, Unit–3, Rajasthan	PHWR	220	June 1, 2000
8.	Rajasthan Atomic Power Station, Unit–4, Rajasthan	PHWR	220	December 23, 2000
9.	Rajasthan Atomic Power Station, Unit–5, Rajasthan	PHWR	220	February 4, 2010
10.	Rajasthan Atomic Power Station, Unit–6, Rajasthan	PHWR	220	March 31, 2010

11.	Madras Atomic Power Station, Unit–1, Tamil Nadu	PHWR	220	January 27, 1984
12.	Madras Atomic Power Station, Unit–2, Tamil Nadu	PHWR	220	March 21, 1986
13.	Kaiga Generating Station, Unit–1, Karnataka	PHWR	220	November 16, 2000
14.	Kaiga Generating Station, Unit–2, Karnataka	PHWR	220	March 16, 2000
15.	Kaiga Generating Station, Unit–3, Karnataka	PHWR	220	May 6, 2007
16.	Kaiga Generating Station, Unit–4, Karnataka	PHWR	220	January 20, 2011
17.	Kudankulam Atomic Power Project, Unit–1, Tamil Nadu	PWR	1000	December 31, 2014
18.	Narora Atomic Power Station, Unit–1, U.P.	PHWR	220	January 1, 1991
19.	Narora Atomic Power Station, Unit-2, U.P.	PHWR	220	July 1, 1992
20.	Kakrapar Atomic Power Station, Unit–1, Gujarat	PHWR	220	May 6, 1993
21.	Kakrapar Atomic Power Station, Unit–2, Gujarat	PHWR	220	September 1, 1995

Table 5.8: Status of Projects Under Construction

S. No.	*Project*	*Capacity (MWe)*	*Expected Commercial Operation*
1.	Kudankulam Atomic Power Project, Unit–2	1 × 1000	Dec., 2015 (first criticality)
2.	Rajasthan Atomic Power Plant, Unit–7, 8	2 × 700	Unit 7–June, 2016 Unit 8–Dec., 2016
3.	Kakrapar Atomic Power Project, Unit–3 and 4	2 × 700	Unit-3–Under review Unit-4–Under review

CHAPTER SUMMARY

Nuclear Power Plant uses nuclear fuel, such as uranium–235 to produce heat due to chemical reaction. This heat is used to generate steam in a steam generator. The steam from steam generator is used to run a steam turbine to produce electricity. Except for the method of heat generation, rest of the plant components are similar to a thermal power plant. However, all equipment are designed to withstand a certain level of radiation without material failure.

The chemical reaction or chain reaction takes place inside a concrete and steel vessel called reactor. The inside of the vessel is lined with shielding and reflecting material. The rate of reaction is controlled by control rods. A coolant is used to remove heat generated due to fission reaction. This primary coolant transfers heat to steam generator where water is converted into steam. An alternator is coupled to steam turbine which is of cylindrical rotor construction.

A good number of reactor designs are available which use different cooling and moderator materials. Most of the reactors used in India are PHWR type (only Tarapur uses BWR). PHWR uses natural uranium as fuel and heavy water as coolant and moderator. While BWR uses enriched uranium as fuel and water as coolant and moderator.

Disposal of spent nuclear fuel is an issue. It is encased in ceramic and concrete material and placed in seabeds. There is persistent danger of ionizing radiations in nuclear power plant during an abnormal operation. However, protective measures are built in the reactor control system to shut it down and contain the radiation leakage. Emergency evacuation procedures are also in place.

REVIEW QUESTIONS

Q. 1. Discuss briefly status of nuclear power generation in India.

Q. 2. Write a brief note on nuclear fuels.

Q. 3. Differentiate between fissile and fertile materials.

Q. 4. Explain nuclear chain reaction.

Q. 5. What are the advantages and disadvantages of nuclear power generation?

Q. 6. How site for nuclear power plant is selected?

Q. 7. Write short notes on—

(*i*) moderating materials. (*ii*) cladding material

(*iii*) control rod materials.

Q. 8. What are shielding materials? What is the purpose of these materials?

Q. 9. Explain with a neat sketch, construction of nuclear reactor.

Q. 10. What are different types of rectors? Explain in detail BWR reactor.

Q. 11. Compare PWR and BWR reactors.

Q. 12. Discuss types of coolants used in a nuclear power plant.

Q. 13. Differentiate between fast breeder reactor and thermal reactor.

Q. 14. Draw a neat sketch and explain the working of PWR.

Q. 15. Draw a neat sketch and explain the working of PHWR.

Q. 16. Write a brief note on Gas Cooled Reactor.

Q. 17. Describe in detail construction and working of nuclear power plant.

Q. 18. Write a short note on refuelling and life of a nuclear reactor.

Q. 19. How spent fuel from nuclear power plant is disposed off?

Q. 20. What is nuclear radiation? How nuclear radiation is measured?

Q. 21. Explain different units of radiation measurement.

Q. 22. Explain biological effects of nuclear radiation on human beings.

Q. 23. What are various means of protection against nuclear radiation?

Q. 24. Discuss limits of radiation exposure to personnel working in a nuclear powers plant.

SHORT ANSWER TYPE QUESTIONS

Q. 1. What are different types of ionizing radiation which emanate from radioactive materials?

Q. 2. Which nuclear fuel is used by nuclear power plant for power generation?

Q. 3. What are different types of moderating materials used?

Q. 4. List three materials used for control rod fabrication?

Q. 5. What are various shielding materials used?

Q. 6. What is the primary function of coolant in a reactor?

Q. 7. What are thermal neutrons?

Q. 8. What is half life of a radioactive material?

Q. 9. Differentiate between ionizing and non-ionizing radiation.

Q. 10. Which type of radiation travel a longer distance in a medium?

Multiple Choice Questions

Q. 1. Which nuclear fuel is used for power generation.

(*a*) Plutonium (*b*) Thorium
(*c*) Uranium-235 (*d*) Uranium-238.

Q. 2. Which is a fissile material.

(*a*) Uranium-235 (*b*) Uranium-233
(*c*) Plutonium-239 (*d*) All of these

Q. 3. Which is a fertile material

(*a*) Thorium-232 (*b*) Uranium-338
(*c*) Uranium-235 (*d*) both(*a*)and(*b*)

Q. 4. Which of the following materials is used as cladding material

(*a*) Berryllium (*b*) Zirconium
(*c*) Magnesium (*d*) Stainless steel
(*e*) All of these.

Q. 5. Which of the following is not a material used for control rod.

(*a*) Boron (*b*) Cadmium
(*c*) Hafnium (*d*) Zirconium

Q. 6. Calendria is meant to

(*a*) produce steam (*b*) hold fuel pins
(*c*) control rate of reaction (*d*) absorb excess neutrons

Q. 7. Heavy water is used as

(*a*) coolant (*b*) moderator

(*c*) shielding material (*d*) both (*a*)&(*b*).

Q. 8. Purpose of reflector is to

(*a*) reflect heat radiations back into reactor.

(*b*) stop escape of neutrons.

(*c*) act as radiation shield.

(*d*) all of these.

Q. 9. Purpose of control rod is to

(*a*) control rate of nuclear reaction. (*b*) shutdown a reactor.

(*c*) prevent radiation leakage. (*d*) all of these.

Q. 10. Nuclear power plant works as

(*a*) base load plant. (*b*) peak load plant.

(*c*) both (*a*) & (*b*). (*d*) none of these.

Answer to MCQ

1. (*c*)	**2.** (*d*)	**3.** (*d*)	**4.** (*e*)	**5.** (*d*)
6. (*b*)	**7.** (*d*)	**8.** (*b*)	**9.** (*a*)	**10.** (*a*)

Chapter

GAS TURBINE BASED POWER GENERATION

Learning Objectives

After reading this chapter, reader will be able to

- Understand various components and working of an open cycle and closed cycle gas turbine power plant.
- Understand operation of co-generation, combined cycle and tri-generation.
- Gain knowledge of various types of liquids and gaseous fuels used in gas turbine.
- Update on newly developed source of natural gas called shale gas.

"The science of today is the technology of tomorrow." — Edward Teller

6.1. INTRODUCTION

A gas turbine power plant uses natural gas as fuel. Combustion of this gas produces flue gases at high temperature and pressure which is expanded in gas turbine to produce power. These power plants are used as peak load station. There are several advantages of these power plants, such as fast start up (less than 5 minutes), compact and modular design, low installation time, less space requirement and easier and faster maintenance. These turbines are available in small capacity as compared to steam turbines.

Gas turbines are used for power generation, aircraft propulsion, marine propulsion etc. Apart from natural gas as fuel, gas turbine can also use Naptha and high speed diesel as secondary and tertiary fuels. However, unlike in engines, the quality of fuel required is very high. For this purpose, natural gas used is desulphurised or sweetened with very low vanadium content. These turbines use sophisticated controls systems using softwares (depending upon make of turbine). Due to high level of automation employed, these can run unattended. All offshore petroleum drilling rigs use gas turbine for driving compressors.

Due to scarcity of natural gas, the existing gas turbine plants are running at reduced capacity (because natural gas is used as feedstock for fertilises plants and first priority is given to them).

6.2. ADVANTAGES AND DISADVANTAGES OF GAS TURBINE PLANT

Following are the advantages and disadvantages of gas turbine based power plants—

Advantages—

(*i*) a gas turbine plant can be started quickly.

(*ii*) it has high reliability.

(*iii*) it has clean exhaust gases.

(*iv*) it requires very low quantity of cooling water.

(*v*) it has no standby losses.

(*vi*) space required is very less.

(*vii*) number of operating and maintenance staff required is less.

(*viii*) it requires less installation time.

(*ix*) auxiliary consumption is very low.

(*x*) part load efficiency is high.

(*xi*) turbine can be operated with multiple fuels in the absence of natural gas. e.g. high speed diesel, and naptha.

Disadvantages—

(*i*) it can not use heavy residual petroleum as fuel (e.g. RFO).

(*ii*) low efficiency.

(*iii*) high maintenance cost.

(*iv*) it requires external power supply to start the compressor.

(*v*) high specific fuel consumption.

(*vi*) smaller unit sizes.

(*vii*) efficiency is affected by higher ambient temperature.

(*viii*) requires high quality fuel .

6.3. LOCATION AND SITE SELECTION

Following factors need to be considered for selection of site for a gas turbine plant—

***(i)* Availability of fuel**—Fuel should be available at reasonable price.

***(ii)* Distance from load centre**—The plant should be as near the load centre as possible to reduce transmission cost and losses.

***(iii)* Availability of transport facilities**—Transport facilities should be available.

***(iv)* Availability of land**—Land should be available at a cheaper price.

***(v)* Low atmospheric pollution**—The site should have low atmospheric pollution as life of air suction filters are affected by it.

6.4. CLASSIFICATION OF GAS TURBINE POWER PLANTS

Gas turbine power plants are classified according to the following criteria—

1. According to application—

(*i*) Mobile application—

(*a*) aircraft propulsion.

(*b*) marine propulsion.

(*ii*) Stationary application—

(*a*) power generation.

(*b*) source of motive power (to drive pumps, compressors etc.).

2. According to cycle used—

(*i*) open cycle (*ii*) closed cycle

3. According to arrangement—

(*i*) single shaft (*ii*) multi-shaft

(*iii*) intercooled (*iv*) regenerative

(*v*) combination

4. According to fuel used—

(*i*) Liquid fuel (Naptha and high speed diesel).

(*ii*) Gaseous fuel (Natural gas).

6.5. GAS TURBINE FUELS

Gas turbine uses gaseous as well as liquid fuels. The primary fuel used is natural gas while secondary fuel can be high speed diesel and tertiary fuel can be naptha.

A brief characteristics of fuels used in gas turbine is described below—

(*i*) Gaseous fuel used in gas turbine is natural gas obtained from oil wells.

The advantages of gaseous fuels are following—

(*a*) better combustion due to good mixing of air and fuel.

(*b*) clean and eco-friendly.

(*c*) higher efficiency of operation.

(*d*) easy transportation of fuel through pipelines.

(*e*) no trace heating required during winter.

The disadvantages are following—

(*a*) difficult to store natural gas.

(*b*) fire and explosion hazard.

(*c*) chances of gas leakage.

Natural gas contains 80% methane and rest higher hydrocarbons, hydrogen sulphide, carbon dioxide etc. The calorific value is about 55000 kJ/kg. Although composition of gases vary from well to well. A typical composition of natural gas is given in table 6.1.

Table 6.1: Composition of natural gas

Sr. No.	*Constituents*	*% by weight*
(*i*)	Methane	70–90
(*ii*)	Ethane Propane Butane	0–20
(*iii*)	Carbon dioxide	0–8
(*iv*)	Oxygen	0–0.2
(*v*)	Nitrogen	0–5
(*vi*)	Hydrogen Sulphide	0–5
(*vii*)	Rare gases (Ar, He, Ne, Xe)	trace

Table 6.2: Parameters of natural gas

Sr. No.	*Parameter*	*Value*
(*i*)	Density	0.717 kg/m^3
(*ii*)	Flash point	–188°C
(*iii*)	Auto ignition temperature	537°C
(*iv*)	Maximum burning temperature	2148°C

Natural gas can be cooled to liquid state to enable transportation through ships. This is known as LNG or liquefied natural gas.

(*ii*) **Liquid fuels**—In the absence of natural gas, high speed diesel and naptha are used as alternate liquid fuels.

(*a*) **High Speed Diesel (HSD)**—It is used as a secondary fuel in gas turbine. Since, it is an expensive fuel, hence it is used for emergency power generation. The characteristics of high speed diesel are given in table 6.3.

Table 6.3: Characteristics of HSD

Sr. No.	*Parameter*	*Value*
(*i*)	Density (at 15°C)	0.78–0.80 gm/ml
(*ii*)	Pour point	+ 6°C max
(*iii*)	Flash point	32°C
(*iv*)	Kinematic viscosity (at 38°C)	2.0–7.5 cst
(*v*)	Gross calorific value	10,500 kcal/kg
(*vi*)	water content by volume	0.2% max.

(*b*) **Naptha**—Naptha is used as a feedstock in fertilizer plant and as tertiary fuel in gas turbine. It is a clean fuel with low emission and good turbine efficiency. However, it is highly inflammable and is imported. It requires careful handling and storage to avoid contamination with sodium, potassium, lithium, calcium and vanadium. Characteristics of naptha are described in table 6.4.

Table 6.4: Characteristics of Naptha

Sr. No.	*Parameter*	*Valve*
(*i*)	Density (at 15°C)	0.66–0.75 gm/ml
(*ii*)	Flash point	23°C
(*iii*)	Kinematic viscosity (at 38°C)	0.5–0.7 cst
(*iv*)	Gross calorific Value	10,200 kcal/kg
(*v*)	Water content by volume	0.5 % max.
(*vi*)	Sulphur content by mass	0.2 % max

6.6. LAYOUT OF GAS TURBINE POWER PLANT

An efficient layout of a power plant reduces capital expenditure and improves operational efficiency. A gas turbine power plant is very compact requiring very less space. Smaller capacity gas turbine are skid mounted and hence, are easy to install and operate. A typical layout of gas turbine power plant is given in Fig. 6.1.

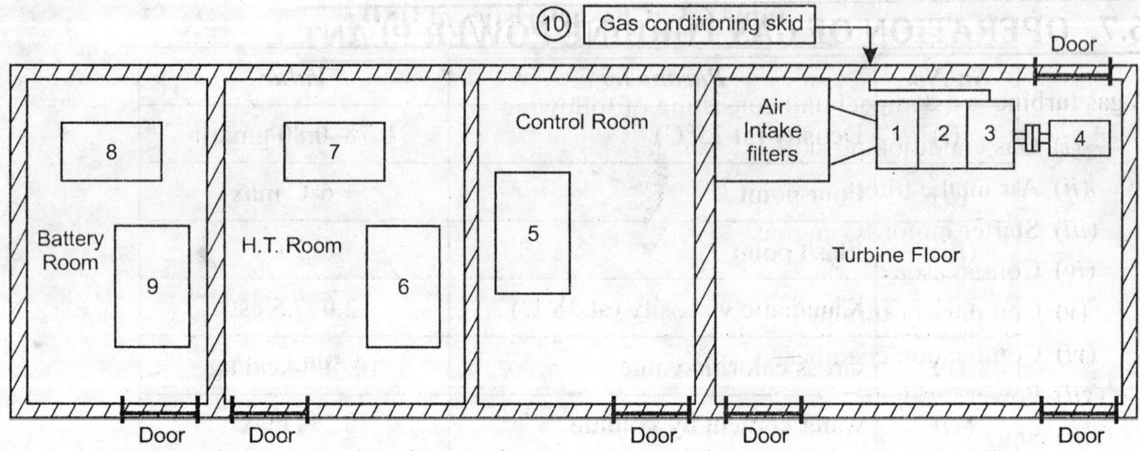

Figure 6.1. Layout of gas turbine power plant

1— Starting motor/diesel engine,
2— Compressor,
3— Power turbine & Compressor turbine
4— Synchronous Generator,
5— Turbine control panel,
6— Turbine auxiliary panel
7— High tension breaker panel,
8— Battery charger panel,
9— Battery bank
10— Gas conditioning skid

Layout of gas turbine power plant consists of following—

(*i*) **Turbine floor**—Turbine floor houses gas turbine, generator and starting motor (for small capacity turbine/diesel engine for large capacity turbine). It has air intake filters placed at the roof of turbine floor that provides filtered air to the compressor. The exhaust gases from power turbine are led to a stack. Gas conditioning skid supplies purified gas at desired pressure to gas turbine.

(*ii*) **Control room**—It houses turbine control panels. Gas turbines are automatic controlled devices with a video display unit (VDU) which shows all operational parameters. In case of any abnormality in any section of turbine, an audio-visual warning appears on the VDU so that operator can take required action. In case of an emergency, turbine automatically shuts down with corresponding display and audio warning on VDU. Due to automatic control, these units are safe to operate and may not require presence of an operator.

(*iii*) **H.T. Room**—High tension room houses an auxiliary control panel which feeds power to turbine axillaries, such as lubricating oil cooler, starter motor etc. A high tension panel houses generator circuit breaker and outgoing circuit breakers to feed power to load.

(*iv*) **Battery room**—Battery room houses battery charger panel and battery bank to supply reliable power for turbine protection and control.

6.7. OPERATION OF GAS TURBINE POWER PLANT

A gas turbine is a compact unit consisting of following—

(*i*) Gas conditioning skid.
(*ii*) Air intake filters.
(*iii*) Starter motor/IC engine.
(*iv*) Compressor.
(*v*) Compressor turbine.
(*vi*) Combustion chamber.
(*vii*) Power turbine.
(*viii*) Stack.
(*ix*) Synchronous generator.
(*x*) Turbine controls.
(*xi*) Auxiliary panels.

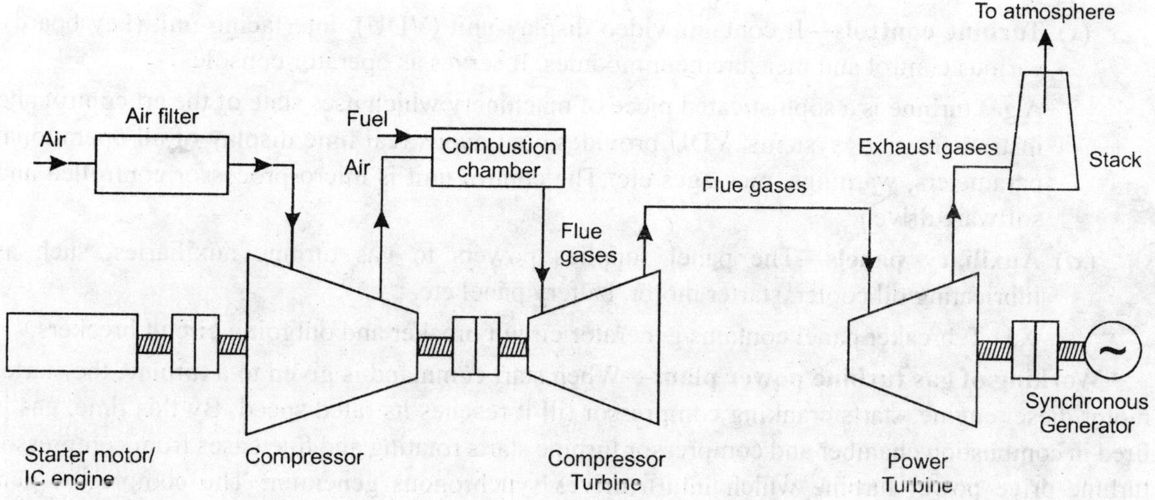

Figure 6.2. Gas turbine power plant

(*i*) **Gas conditioning skid**—Gas turbine requires very good quality fuel. So, natural gas is first filtered, to remove particles and moisture/droplets. Then, this gas at required pressure and temperature is fed to the turbine.

In case of liquid fuel, the fuel need to be filtered/centrifuged to provide an acceptable level of purity before it is fed to the turbine.

(*ii*) **Air intake filters**—It sucks in air from the atmosphere and provides filtered air to the compressor. This air is used for combustion, cooling and air sealing purposes.

(*iii*) **Starter motor/IC engine**—A gas turbine is not self starting and needs cranking. This initial start is provided by an electric motor (for small capacity turbines) or by a diesel engine (for large capacity turbines). Once compressor reaches near rated speed, the turbine starts working and starting mechanism is automatically disengaged.

(iv) **Compressor**—Purpose of compressor is to provide compressed air for combustion, cooling and air sealing purposes. About 1/3rd of power output of gas turbine is used to drive the compressor.

(v) **Compressor turbine**—It is used to drive the compressor after turbine starts producing power and starter motor/IC engine is disengaged. The flue gases from combustion chamber is used to run the compressor turbine.

(vi) **Combustion Chamber**—Combustion chamber or combustor burns fuel to produce flue gases. It houses a number of nozzles which injects air and fuel for combustion. The temperature of each nozzle is measured and monitored.

(vii) **Power turbine**—Power turbine contains rows of coated blades where flue gases at a temperature of about 1200°C expand. This expansion of flue gases provide mechanical motion which is transmitted to the generator to produce electricity.

(viii) **Stack**—It has a layer of stainless steel inside the stack to withstand high flue gas temperature of about 525° – 560°C.

(ix) **Generator**—It is a three phase cylindrical rotor alternator which runs at 1500 or 3000 rpm to produce power.

(x) **Turbine controls**—It contains video display unit (VDU), interfacing unit (key board), various control and measurement modules. It serves as operator console.

A gas turbine is a sophisticated piece of machinery which uses state of the art control and instrumentation systems. VDU provides continuous real time display of all operational parameters, warnings, messages etc. The control unit is micro-processor controlled and software driven.

(xi) **Auxiliary panels**—The panel supplies powers to gas turbine auxiliaries, such as lubricating oil cooler, starter motor, battery panel etc.

A H.T. breaker panel contains generator circuit breaker and outgoing circuit breakers.

Working of gas turbine power plant—When start command is given to a turbine, the starter motor/diesel engine, starts cranking compressor till it reaches its rated speed. By this time, gas is fired in combustion chamber and compressor turbine starts rotating and flue gases from compressor turbine drive power turbine which inturn drives synchronous generator. The compressor gets disengaged from starter motor once the speed reaches the rated value.

Once the turbine starts rotating, the coupled generator produces power. The load can be transferred to turbine by closing generator circuit breaker.

A gas turbine can be quickly started in about 5 minutes and can be loaded immediately.

6.8. OPEN AND CLOSED CYCLE GAS TURBINE POWER PLANT

A gas turbine power plant is operated either in open cycle or in closed cycle mode. Closed cycle operation yields better efficiency than open cycle operation.

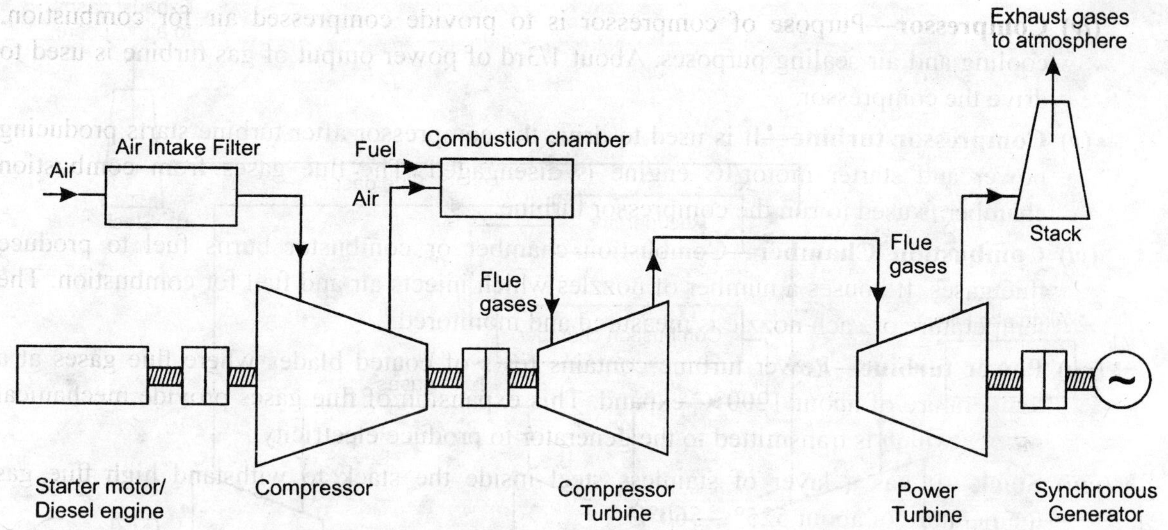

Figure 6.3. Open cycle gas turbine power plant

Open cycle gas turbine power plant consists of following components—

(*i*) Starter motor/Diesel engine.

(*ii*) Air intake filter.

(*iii*) Compressor.

(*iv*) Combustion chamber or combustor.

(*v*) Compressor turbine.

(*vi*) Power turbine.

(*vii*) Synchronous generator.

Air from atmosphere is sucked through air intake filter by the compressor. The air is compressed by the compressor by passing it through layers of fixed and moving blades. This compressed air is fed to combustion chamber with fuel. After combustion (air fuel ratio is about 70:1), the flue gases are expanded over a series of blades in a compressor turbine. After expansion of flue gases in compressor turbine, the flue gases are allowed to expand in a power turbine. The power turbine is coupled to a generator thereby causing it to rotate and produce power.

Function of compressor turbine is to rotate compressor after the starter motor/Diesel engine is disengaged. The starting mechanism gets disengaged after cranking the compressor to rated speed and starting of combustion in combustion chamber.

After expansion of flue gases in power turbine, the gases escape to atmosphere through a stack.

The efficiency of open cycle is about 30%. A large chunk of heat energy is carried away by flue gases escaping to atmosphere through the stack. In order to improve thermal efficiency of cycle, following configuration are also used in open cycle operation.

(*a*) **Use of Recuperator**—Recuperator uses the heat energy of exhaust gases after expansion in power turbine to heat compressed air before being fed to combustion chamber. This increases cycle efficiency by 5–6%.

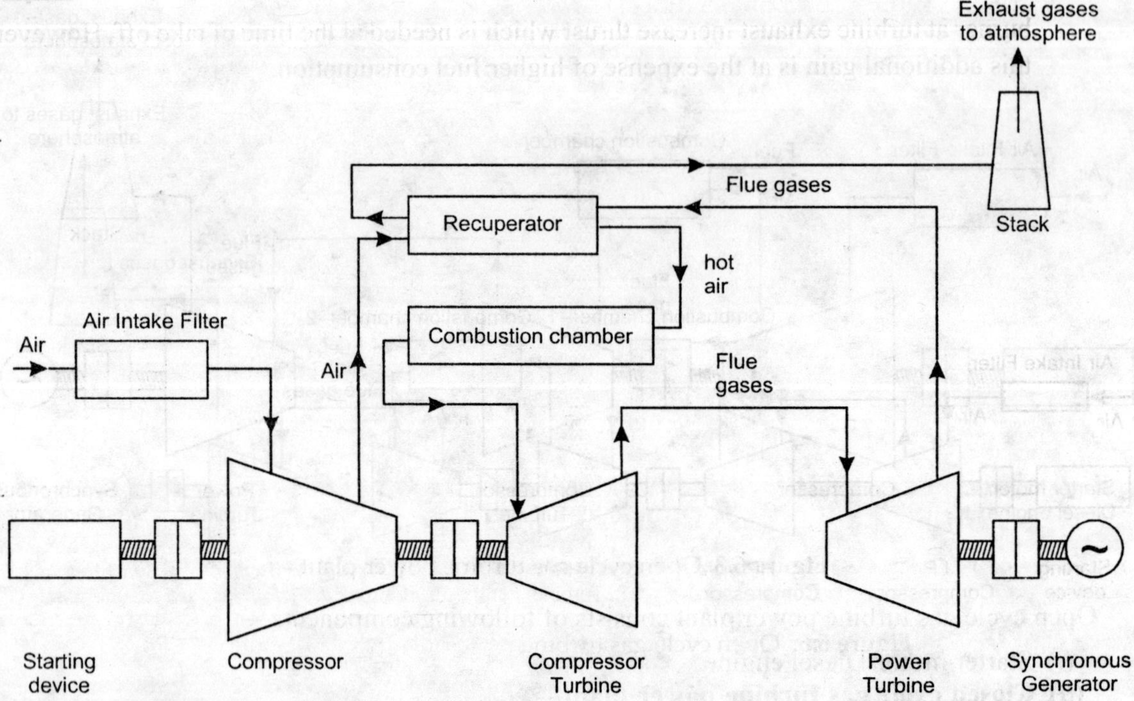

Figure 6.4. Open cycle gas turbine power plant using recuperator

(*b*) **Use of Intercooler**—Intercooler cools the hot compressed gas after low pressure (LP) compressor. Cooling reduces the volume of compressed air and less energy is required to compress it further by high pressure (HP) compressor. This increases the output of turbine.

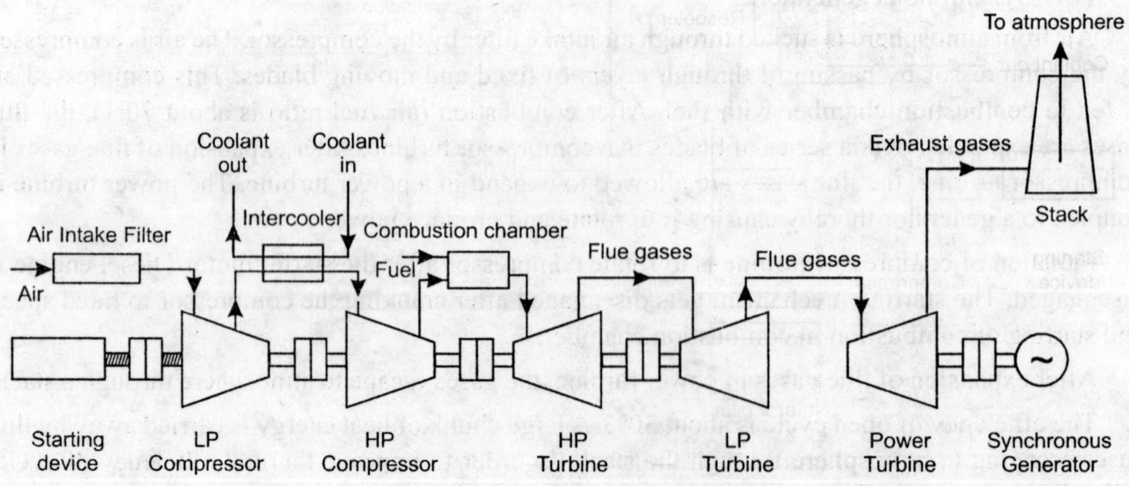

Figure 6.5. Open cycle gas turbine power plant using intercooler

(*c*) **Use of reheater**—In this configuration, after expansion of flue gases in HP turbine, these are reheated in another combustion chamber. This extra addition of heat increases the cycle efficiency by 1–3%. This scheme is used in jet aircraft engines. Addition of an after burner at turbine exhaust increase thrust which is needed at the time of take off. However, this additional gain is at the expense of higher fuel consumption.

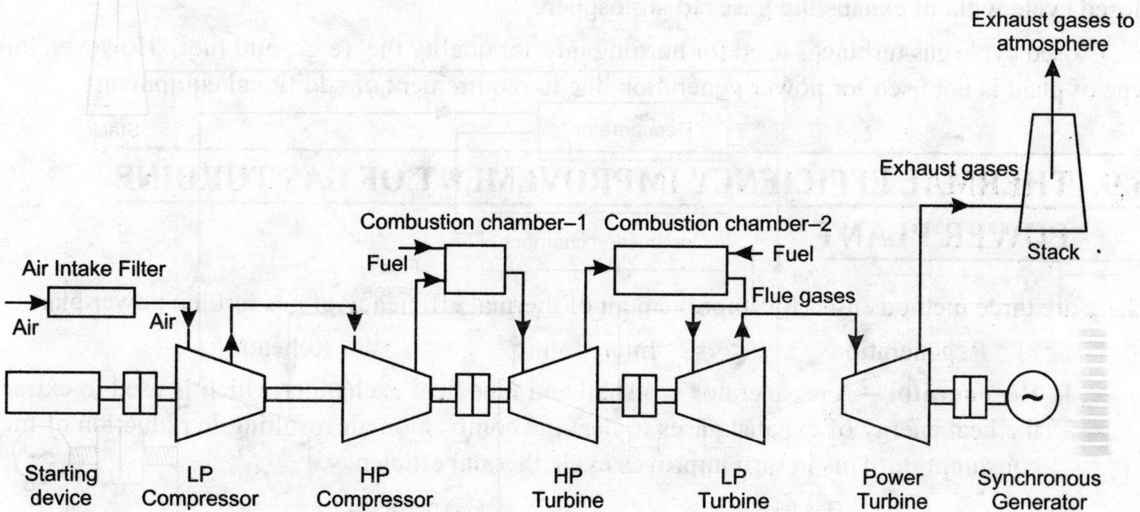

Figure 6.6. Open cycle gas turbine power plat using reheater

(ii) **Closed cycle gas turbine power plant**—The exhaust gas of an open cycle gas turbine is at a temperature of about 525°–560°C and hence contains sufficient heat energy. By utilizing this heat energy, the cycle efficiency can be further increased.

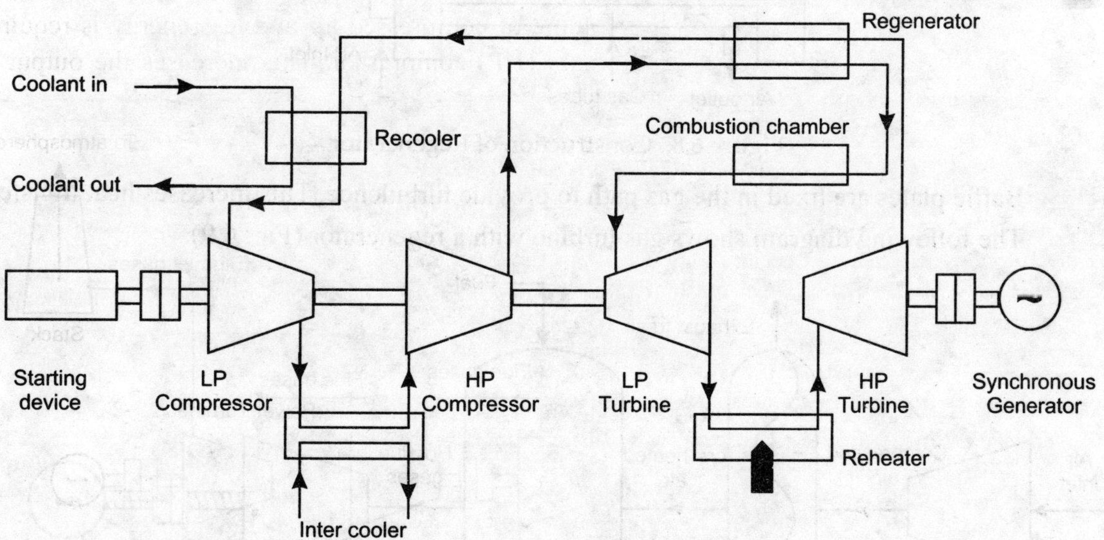

Figure 6.7. Closed cycle gas turbine power plant

In closed cycle system, the working medium is heated externally and circulated through compressor, regenerator and recooler. Heat of compression is removed by intercooler which after HP compressor is heated in regenerator before being fed to combustion chamber. The hot flue gases from combustion chamber expand in a LP turbine. After expansion, the gases are further heated in a reheater and fed to HP turbine. After expansion in HP turbine, the gases pass through regenerator.

The heat of exhaust gases from HP turbine is used to heat up air being fed to combustion chamber. The outlet from regenerator is fed to recooler before feeding to LP compressor. This completes a closed cycle without exhausting gases to atmosphere.

Closed cycle gas turbine is used for burning inferior quality fuel (e.g. solid fuel). However, this type of plant is not used for power generation due to requirement of additional equipments.

6.9. THERMAL EFFICIENCY IMPROVEMENT OF GAS TURBINE POWER PLANT

There are three methods used for improvement of thermal efficiency of gas turbine power plant—

1. Regeneration 2. Intercooling 3. Reheating

1. **Regenerator**—A regenerator is a shell and tube heat exchanger which is used to extract the heat energy of exhaust gases to heat the combustion air resulting in reduction of fuel consumption. This in turn improves cycle thermal efficiency.

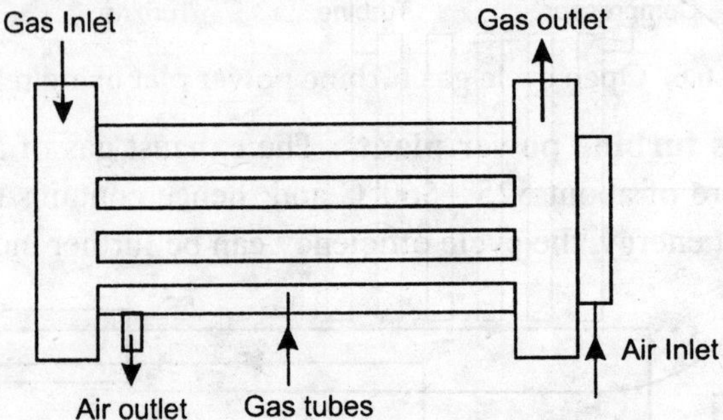

Figure 6.8. Construction of Regenerator

Baffle plates are fixed in the gas path to provide turbulence. This increases heat transfer. The following diagram shows gas turbine with a regenerator (Fig. 6.9).

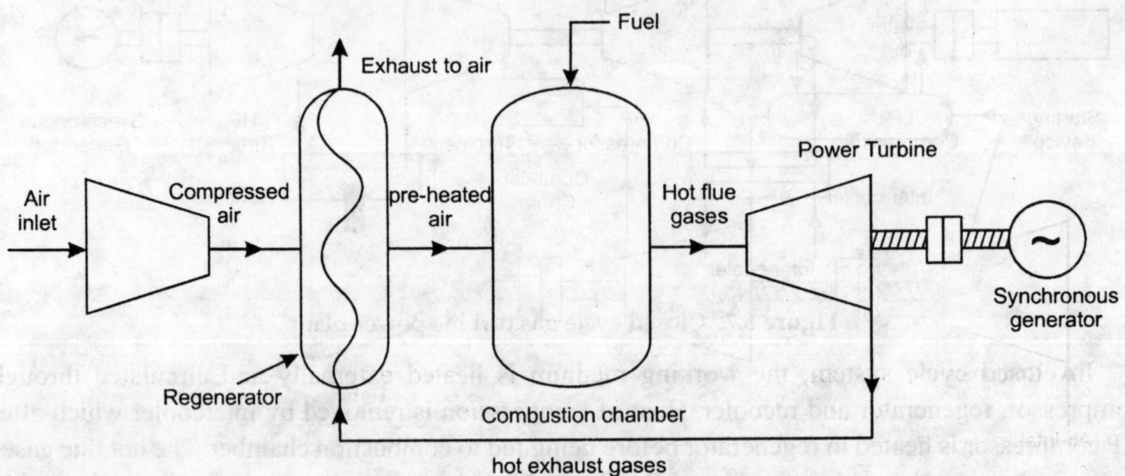

Figure 6.9. Gas turbine with regenerator

The compressed air from compressor is passed through regenerator where it picks up heat of exhaust gases in the regenerator. This preheated air is fed to combustion chamber. The flue gas produced from combustion chamber is expanded in powers turbine to produce electricity.

2. **Intercooler**—Purpose of intercooler is to cool the compressed air from compressor. Cooling of compressed air reduces volume which in turns reduces the power required to compress the air. The cooling of compressed air is done in one or more than one stages depending upon the saving in the work done and extra cost of intercooler.

   Intercooling improves efficiency and air rate. This reduces size of turbine and compressor. Intercooler consists of crossflow shell and tube heat exchanger, cooling water flows through tubes while compressed air flows over the tubes. The heat of compressed air is taken up by cooling water.

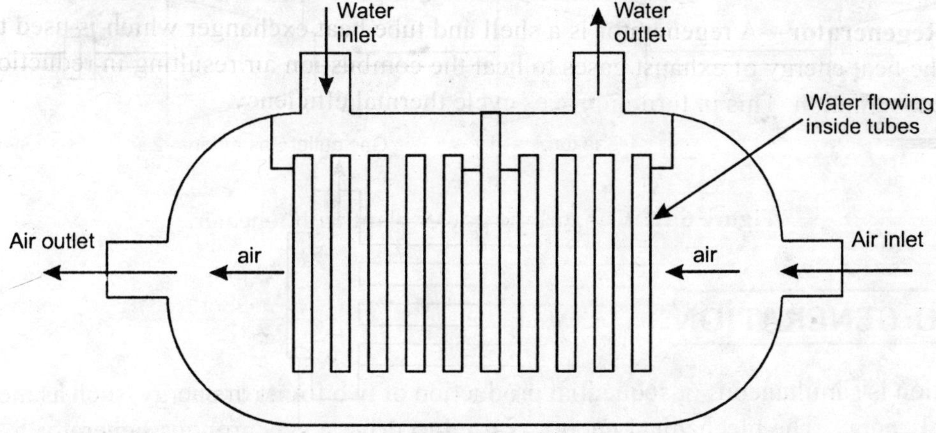

Figure 6.10. Construction of intercooler

Following figure 6.11 shows intercooler connected between two compression stages.

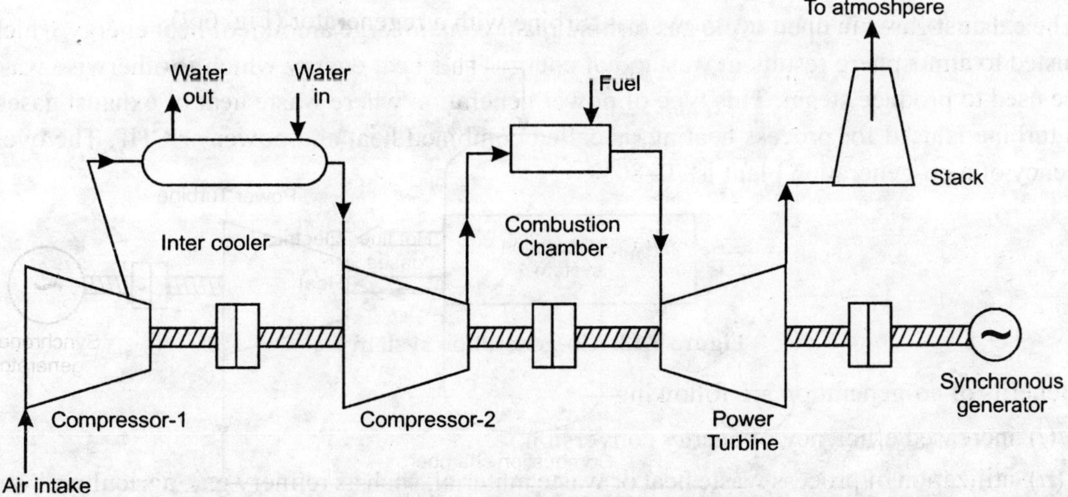

Figure 6.11. Gas turbine power plant with intercooler

3. **Reheater**—Reheating helps to improve power output. Additional combustion chambers are used to feed heat to the flue gases which have partially expanded over the power turbine. This generates additional power output thereby improving the thermal efficiency of the cycle. Just as intercooler is used to reduce compression power required, reheating is used to inject additional heat to the partially expanded gases to get additional work done.

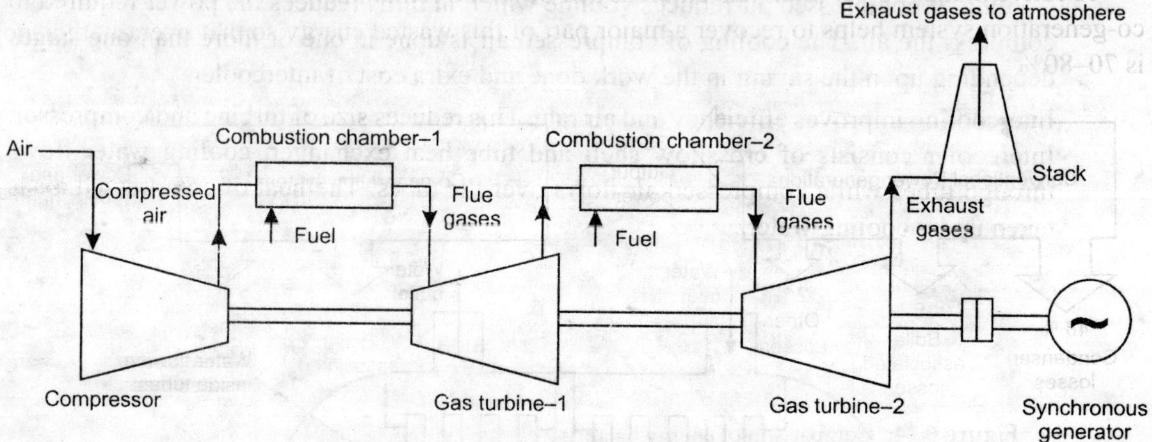

Figure 6.12. Gas turbine power plant with reheater.

6.10. CO-GENERATION

Co-generation is simultaneous or sequential production of two forms of energy, such as mechanical and thermal energy. The mechanical energy is used to drive a synchronous generator to produce electricity. The thermal energy is used for generating steam in a boiler or heat recovery steam generator (HRSG) for use in process heating. Hence, co-generation is simultaneous production of electricity and heat using a single fuel.

The exhaust gases in open cycle gas turbine plant contain large amount of heat energy which if exhausted to atmosphere results in wastage of energy. This heat energy which is otherwise wasted can be used to produce steam. This type of power generation where waste heat of exhaust gases of a gas turbine is used for process heating, is called combined heat and power or CHP. The overall efficiency of a co-generation plant is 70–80%.

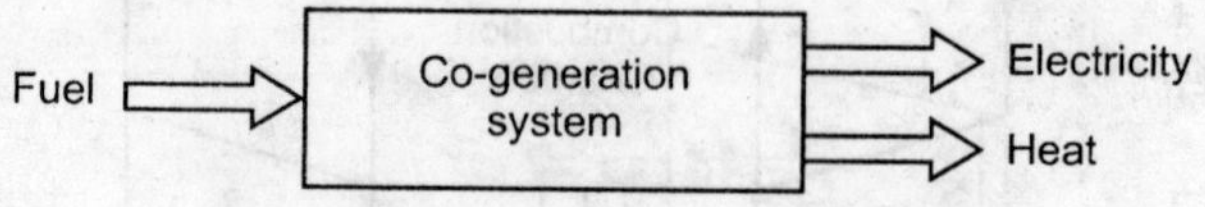

Figure 6.13. Co-generation system

Benefits of co-generation are following—

(*i*) increased efficiency of energy conversion.

(*ii*) utilization of process waste heat or waste material, such as refinery gas, agricultural waste etc.

(*iii*) conservation of fossil fuel.

(*iv*) lower emission to environment .

(*v*) lower energy cost.

(*vi*) improved energy security.

A conventional power plant has efficiency of 35% and remaining 65% of energy is wasted. A co-generation system helps to recover a major part of this wasted energy so that overall efficiency is 70–80%

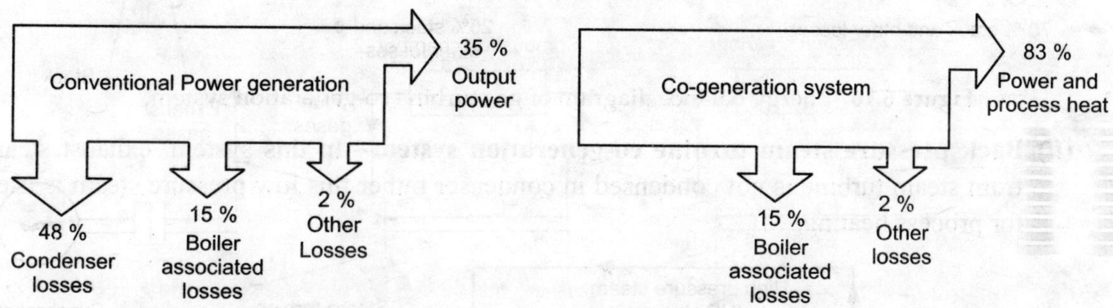

Figure 6.14. Comparison of energy balance in a conventional and co-generation system

There are two types of co-generation systems viz. topping cycle and bottoming cycle. Generally topping cycle is used where fuel is first used to generate electricity or mechanical energy and a portion of waste heat is then used to provide useful thermal energy.

In bottoming cycle, first useful heat is produced for manufacturing process by burning fuel and part of this heat is recovered to produce electricity. This cycle is used in process industries such as glass, steel etc. which use very high temperature furnaces.

Various configurations of co-generation system is described below—

(*i*) **open cycle gas turbine co-generation system**—In this system, exhaust gases from gas turbine are not directly released to atmosphere through stack rather these gases are passed through a waste heat recovery generator (WHRG). It generates steam from heat energy of exhaust gases. The temperature of exhaust gases after gas turbine is 450°–600°C. The steam so generated is used for process heating in industries.

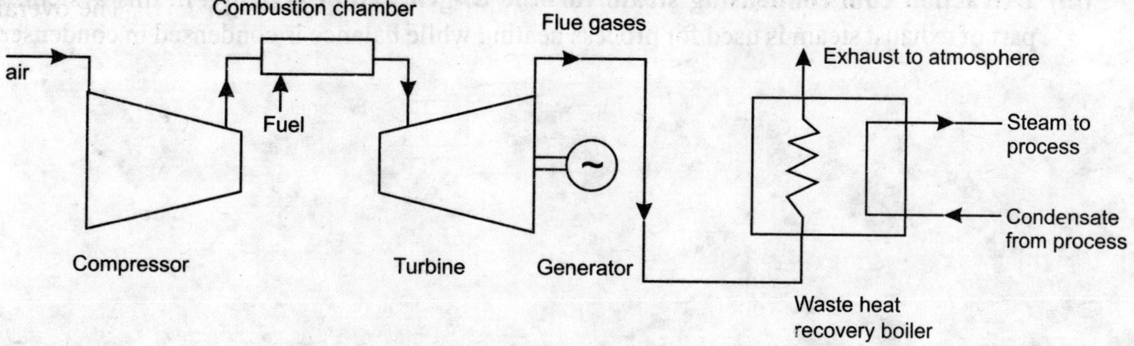

Figure 6.15. Open cycle gas turbine co-generation system

In this system, out of total energy input, 25% is available as power while 50% is available for process heat. The energy balance diagram is given in figure 6.16.

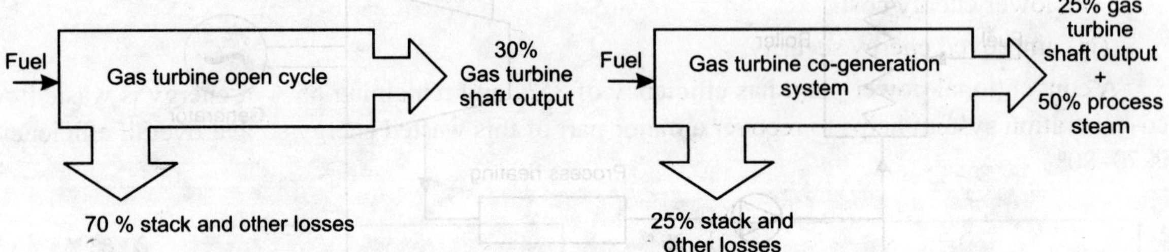

Figure 6.16. Energy balance diagram of gas turbine co-generation system.

(ii) **Back pressure steam turbine co-generation system**—In this system, exhaust steam from steam turbine is not condensed in condenser rather this low pressure steam is used for process heating.

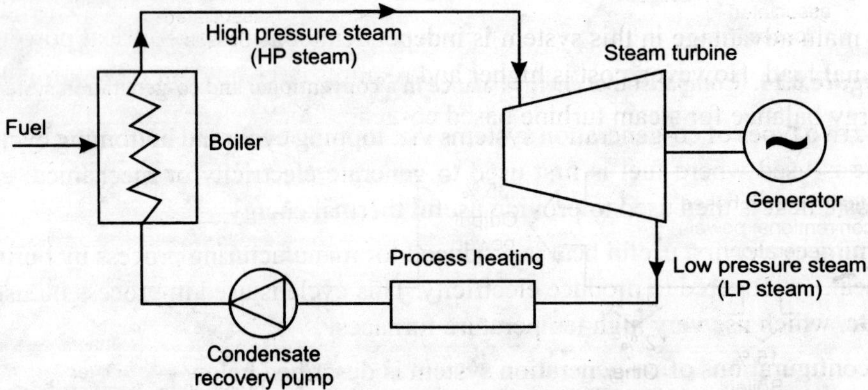

Figure 6.17. Back pressure steam turbine co-generation system

This system has advantages such as low cost, lesser water requirement (absence of condenser), high efficiency. However, electrical load and output can not be matched all the time. Size of steam turbine become larger.

(iii) **Extraction cum condensing steam turbine co-generation system**—In this system, a part of exhaust steam is used for process heating while balance is condensed in condenser.

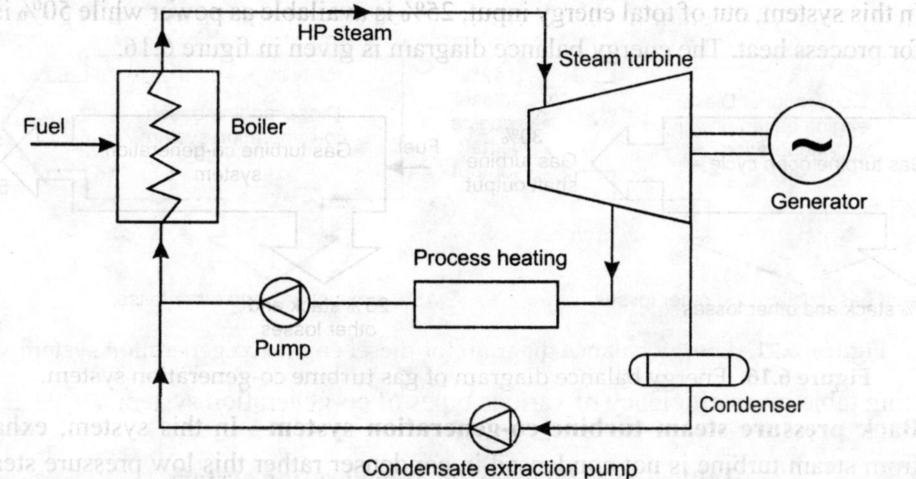

Figure 6.18. Extraction-cum condensing steam turbine co- generation system

The main advantage in this system is independent control of electrical power output and thermal load. However, cost is higher and requires large amount of water in condenser. Energy balance for steam turbine based co-generation system is described in figure 6.19.

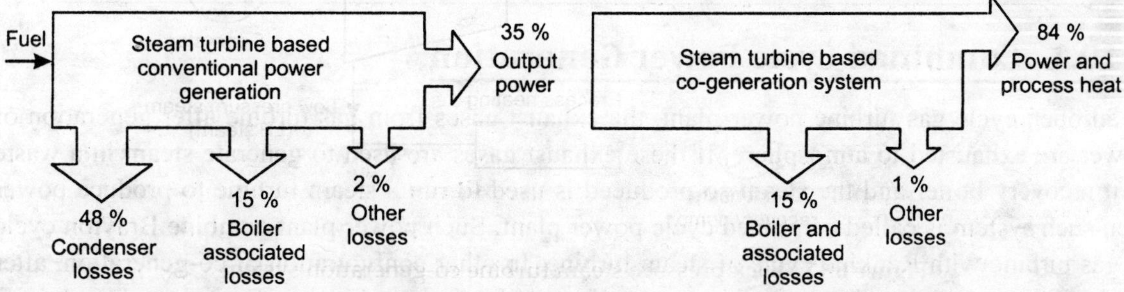

Figure. 6.19. Energy balance diagram for extraction-cum condensing steam turbine co-generation system.

(*iii*) Diesel engine based co-generation system—In this system, exhaust gases from a diesel engine is used to generate steam in a waste heat recovery boiler (WHRB). This steam is used for process heating.

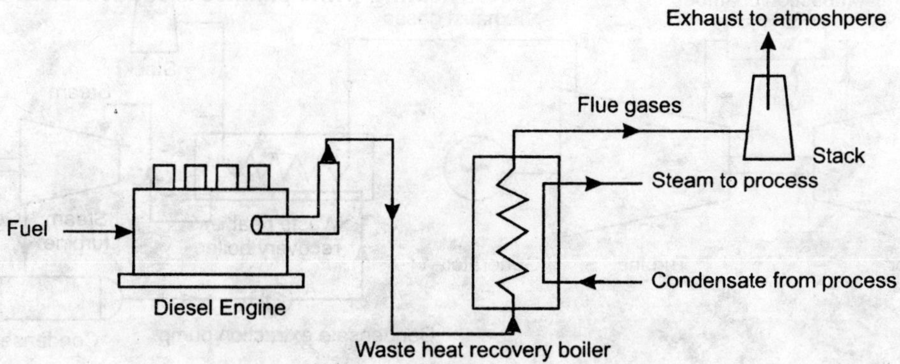

Figure. 6.20. Diesel engine based co-generation system

The energy balance diagram for diesel engine based co- generation system is given in fig, 6.21

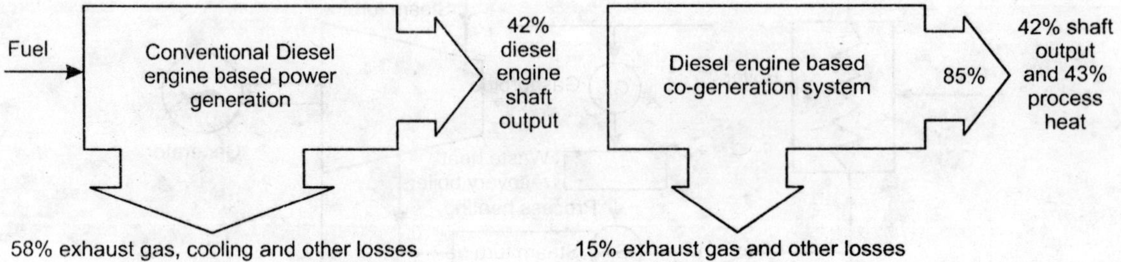

Figure. 6.21. Energy balance diagram for diesel engine co-generation system

Following table gives efficiency of various types of co-generation system.

Table 6.5: Efficiency of co-generation system

Sr No	*Type of Co-generation System*	*Overall Efficiency (%)*
1.	Gas turbine co-generation system	70–85
2.	Extraction-cum condensing steam turbine co-generation system	60–80
3.	Diesel engine based co-generation system	75–85

6.10.1. Combined Cycle Power Generation

In an open cycle gas turbine power plant, the exhaust gases from gas turbine after generation of power are exhausted to atmosphere. If these exhaust gases are used to generate steam in a waste heat recovery boiler and the steam so produced is used to run a steam turbine to produce power then such system is called combined cycle power plant. Such power plant combine Brayton cycle of gas turbine with Rankine cycle of steam turbine. In other configuration of co-generation, after producing power, waste heat of exhaust gases is used for process heating. But in combined cycle operation, after power generation by gas turbine, exhaust gases are used to produce power through a steam turbine.

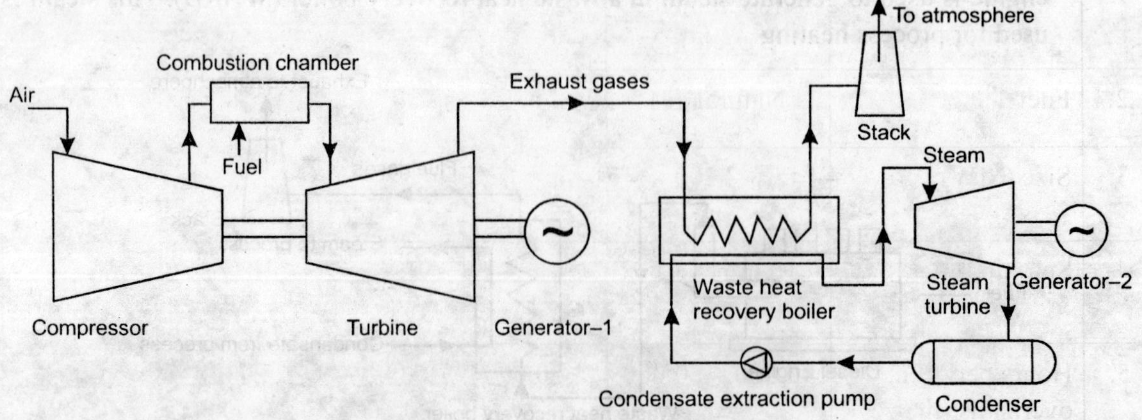

Figure. 6.22. Combined cycle power plant

If efficiency of gas turbine is taken as 33% and steam turbine as 36% then combined cycle efficiency is 57%.

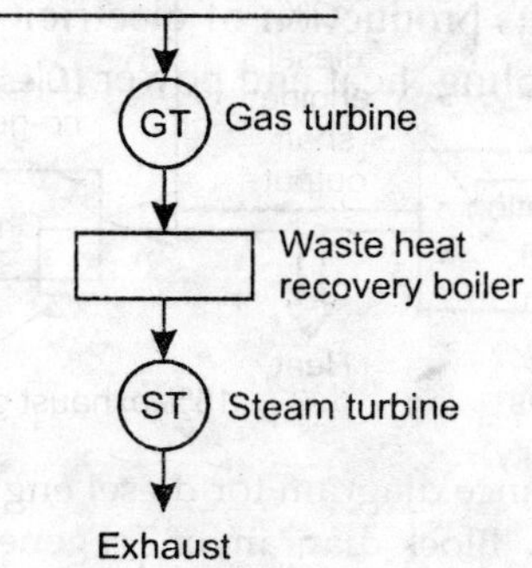

Figure. 6.23. Efficiency of combined cycle power plant

Combined cycle efficiency, η_{CC}

$$= \eta_{GT} + \eta_{ST} - \eta_{GT}\,\eta_{ST}, \quad \text{where } \eta_{GT} = \text{Gas turbine efficiency}$$

$$= 0.33 + 0.36 - 0.33 \times 0.36 \qquad \eta_{ST} = \text{Steam turbine efficiency}$$

$$= 0.5712$$

$$\eta_{CC} = 57.12\ \%$$

A summary of co- generation systems is given in table 6.6

Table 6.6: Comparison of various types of co-generation systems

Sr. No.	*Parameter*	*Gas turbine*	*Steam turbine*	*Diesel engine*	*Gas engine*	*Micro turbine*
1.	Electric efficiency (LHV)	25 – 40% (open cycle) 40 – 60% (combined cycle)	30 – 42%	30 – 50%	25 – 45%	20 – 30%
2.	Fuel	Natural gas	All types	Diesel	Natural gas	Natural gas
3.	Size (MW)	3 – 200	Any size	0.05 – 5	0.05 – 5	0.025 – 0.25
4.	Start up time	10 min – 1 hr	1 hr – 1 day	10 sec	10 sec	60 sec
5.	Hours between overhauls (hr)	30,000 – 50,000	> 50,000	15,000 – 20,000	15,000 – 20,0000	5,000 – 40,000

6.11. TRI GENERATION

Tri generation refers to simultaneous production of electricity, heat and cooling using single fuel. This is also known as combined cooling, heat and power (CCHP).

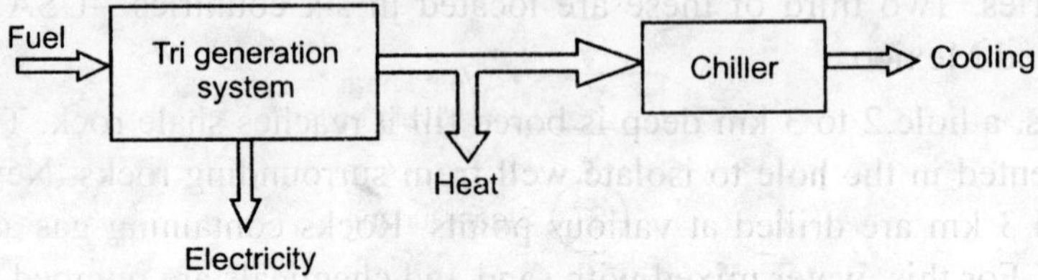

Figure. 6.24. Block diagram of Tri generation system

In this system, exhaust gases from gas turbine is used to raise steam in a waste heat recovery boiler. This steam is used partly to produce chilled water through a vapour absorption chiller and remaining is used for process heating. The overall system efficiency is of the order of 86% to 93%.

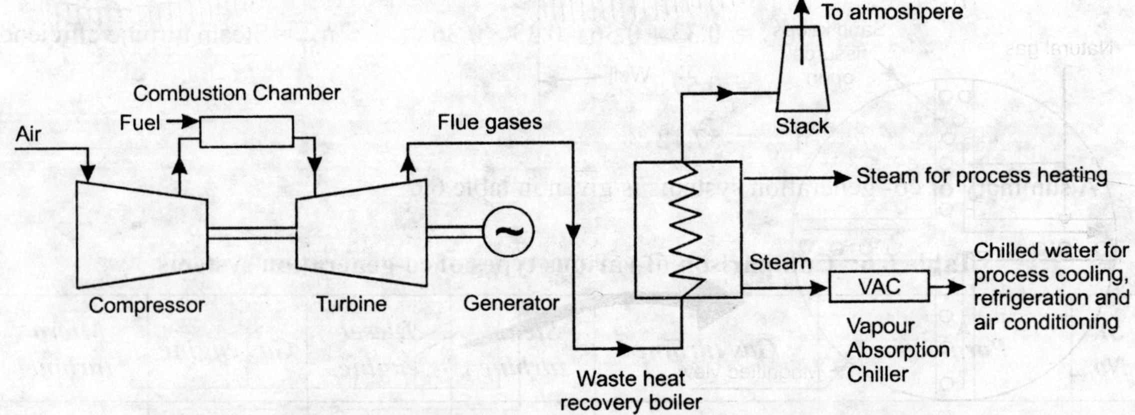

Figure. 6.25. Process flow diagram of tri generation system

Benefits of tri generation are following—

(*i*) low operating cost and life cycle cost.

(*ii*) cheap energy.

(*iii*) no moving parts in vapour absorption chiller and hence, low maintenance.

(*iv*) noiseless chiller operation.

(*v*) chiller uses water as refrigerant hence, no depletion of ozone layer.

(*vi*) higher efficiency.

(*vii*) increased energy security and reliability.

(*viii*) reduced carbon footprint.

6.12. EMERGING SOURCE OF NATURAL GAS – SHALE GAS

Shale gas is a natural gas entrapped in a commonly occurring rock called shale. Shale rocks have low permeability so flow of gas through these rocks is more difficult than through a conventional gas reservoir. Shale gas sources are scattered and require drilling of many holes over a short period. It is obtained through horizontal drilling and hydraulic fracturing.

According to an estimate, 7795 trillion cubic feet of technically recoverable shale gas resources exist in 41 countries. Two third of these are located in six countries—USA, China, Argentina, Algeria, Canada and Mexico.

In this process, a hole 2 to 3 km deep is bored till it reaches shale rock. Then, steel tubes are inserted and cemented in the hole to isolate well from surrounding rocks. Next, horizontal holes ranging from 1 to 3 km are drilled at various points. Rocks containing gas are fractured to free the entrapped gas. For this, water mixed with sand and chemicals are pumped into ground at high pressure to produce cracks in underground rocks. The sand holds the crack open thereby allowing the gas to flow into the well.

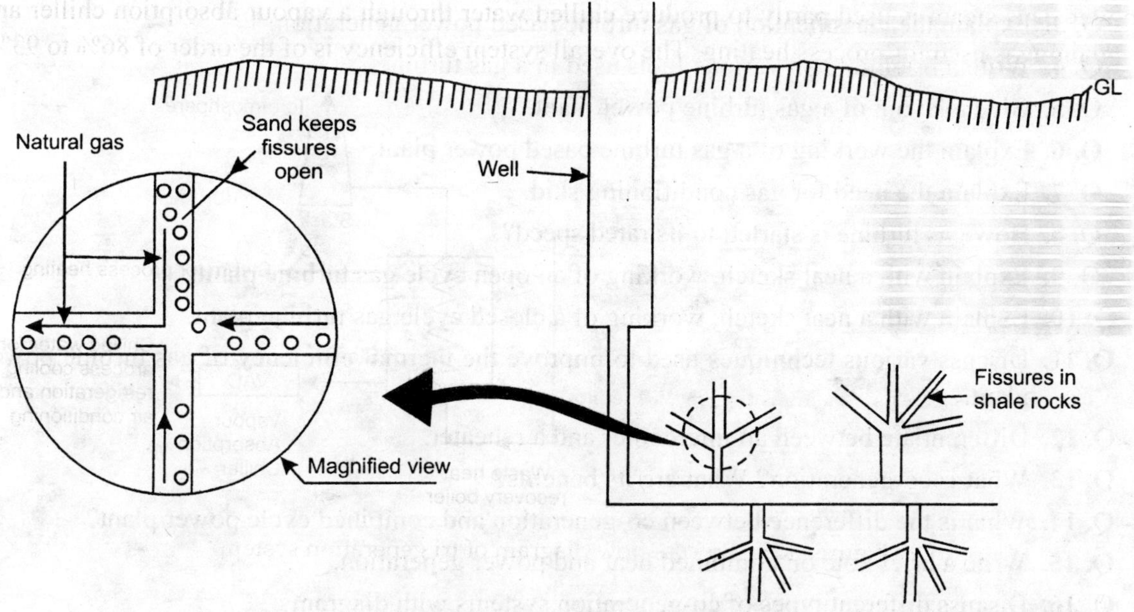

Figure. 6.26. Shale gas drilling

CHAPTER SUMMARY

A gas turbine based power generation is used as peak load station due to its ability to quickly start and stop. This type of generation is preferred where sufficient quantity of natural gas is available. Smaller capacity turbine sets are available in skid mounted condition. The plant can use both gases and liquid fuels, such as natural gas, high speed diesel and naptha. The fuel is burnt in a combustion chamber or combustor to generate flue gases. These gases are expanded over series of static and moving blades in a gas turbine thereby producing mechanical motion. The mechanical motion is converted into electrical energy by a synchronous generator. Unlike other plants, gas turbine requires high purity fuels. The specific fuel consumption is high compared to IC engine. The maximum open cycle efficiency that can be achieved is 30%. Co-generation and combined cycle operation leads to higher cycle efficiency. Co-generation mode is preferred where both heat and electrical energy is required. Combined cycle operation is used for generation of electrical energy only. A new method called tri generation is used to generate electrical power, steam and hot /chilled water for process cooling or air conditioning.

The plant is very neat and clean and employs fewer operating personnel compared to a thermal power plant and uses highly sophisticated computer controlled system. The plant can be quickly started in less than five minutes. However, maintenance of these turbines is expensive and requires skilled manpower.

REVIEW QUESTIONS

Q. 1. Discuss relative merits and demerits of gas turbine based power generation.

Q. 2. Discuss the factors affecting selection of site for gas turbine.

Q. 3. Explain the classification of gas turbine based power generation.

Q. 4. Write a brief note on various fuels used in a gas turbine.

Q. 5. Give a layout of a gas turbine power plant.

Q. 6. Explain the working of a gas turbine based power plant.

Q. 7. Explain the need for gas conditioning skid.

Q. 8. How gas turbine is started to its rated speed?

Q. 9. Explain with a neat sketch, working of an open cycle gas turbine plant.

Q. 10. Explain with a neat sketch, working of a closed cycle gas turbine plant.

Q. 11. Discuss various techniques used to improve the thermal efficiency of gas turbine power plant.

Q. 12. Differentiate between an intercooler and a reheater.

Q. 13. What is co-generation? What are its benefits?

Q. 14. What is the difference between co-generation and combined cycle power plant?

Q. 15. Write a brief note on combined heat and power generation.

Q. 16. Discuss different types of co-generation systems with diagrams.

Q. 17. What is tri- generation? Differentiate between tri-generation and co-generation.

Q. 18. Write a detailed note on shale gas.

SHORT ANSWERS TYPES QUESTIONS

Q. 1. Write three advantage of gas turbine based power generation over thermal power generation.

Q. 2. State three applications of gas turbine other than power generation.

Q. 3. Mention five advantages of gaseous fuels over liquid fuels.

Q. 4. Mention two alternate fuel which are used in gas turbine.

Q. 5. What is the function of compressor turbine in gas turbine power plant?

Q. 6. State three benefits of co-generation.

Q. 7. Compare co-generation and tri-generation.

Q. 8. How shale gas is extracted?

Multiple Choice Questions

Q. 1. With increase in ambient temperature, efficiency of gas turbine

(*a*) increases (*b*) decreases

(*c*) remains same (*d*) depends on relative humidity.

Q. 2. Standby losses in a gas turbine are

(*a*) low (*b*) high

(*c*) depends on ambient temperature.

Q. 3. Major constituent of natural gas is

(*a*) nitrogen (*b*) oxygen

(*c*) methane (*d*) ethane and butane

Q. 4. A gas conditioning skid is used to

(*a*) regulate temperature of gas (*b*) regulate pressure of gas

(*c*) filter gas (*d*) all of these.

Q. 5. Alternator used in a gas turbine is

(*a*) salient pole type (*b*) cylindrical rotor type

(*c*) permanent magnet type (*d*) all of these.

Q. 6. A co-generation plant produces

(*a*) mechanical and thermal energy (*b*) mechanical and electrical energy

(*c*) thermal and electrical energy (*d*) none of these

Q. 7. A combined cycle plant produces

(*a*) mechanical and thermal energy (*b*) thermal and electrical energy

(*c*) mechanical and electrical energy (*d*) none of these

Q. 8. A gas turbine and steam turbine plant works on

(*a*) brayton and rankine cycle (*b*) rankine and brayton cycle

(*c*) brayton and otto cycle (*d*) otto and diesel cycle.

Q. 9. Cycle efficiency of gas turbine can be increased by

(*a*) lowering inlet temperature of air (*b*) using high calorific value fuel

(*c*) both (*a*) and (*b*) (*d*) none of these.

Answer to MCQ

1. (*b*)	**2.** (*a*)	**3.** (*c*)	**4.** (*d*)	**5.** (*b*)
6. (*c*)	**7.** (*b*)	**8.** (*a*)	**9.** (*c*)	

Chapter

DIESEL BASED POWER GENERATION

Learning Objectives

After reading this chapter, reader will be able to

- Understand construction and working of diesel power plant.
- Understand characteristics of variety of liquid fuels used in diesel engine.
- Understand characteristics and applications of slow and high speed diesel engines.
- Learn sizing and selection of DG sets for power generation application.
- Grasp the difference in different types of conventional power generation.

"Technology feeds on itself. Technology makes more technology possible." — Alvin Toffler

7.1. INTRODUCTION

A diesel power plant employs diesel engine (a compression ignition engine) as prime mover to produce electricity. The diesel engine converts energy of liquid fuels into mechanical power output. The mechanical output is converted to electrical energy by the generator coupled to the engine. The capacity of diesel power plant ranges from few kW to 50 MW. These power plants are used as emergency backup in industries, hospitals, hotels, malls, hostels, airports etc. due to high cost of diesel fuel. However, in some industries these engines are run continuously using low cost liquid fuels, such as residual fuel oil, furnace oil, low sulphur heavy stock oil etc.

Being a reciprocating engine, it requires more maintenance than steam or gas turbines.

7.2. ADVANTAGES AND DISADVANTAGES OF DIESEL POWER PLANT

Advantages-

(*i*) it has low installation cost.

(*ii*) it has short period of installation.
(*iii*) it has high efficiency (43–45%).
(*iv*) can use variety of fuels.
(*v*) minimum quantity of cooling water is required.
(*vi*) it has short startup time and hence, is ideal for peak load.
(*vii*) the plant can be located anywhere (even on rooftop).
(*viii*) plant design and layout is simple.
(*ix*) it has low capital cost/kW amongst other power plants.
(*x*) it requires less operating staff compared to thermal and nuclear power plants.
(*xi*) it has good part load efficiency.
(*xii*) it has no standsby losses.
(*xiii*) it requires less space for fuel storage.

Disadvantages-

(*i*) high cost per unit due to high cost of diesel fuel.
(*ii*) high maintenance cost.
(*iii*) engine size is a limitation.
(*iv*) low life of engine (about 10 years).
(*v*) low overload bearing capacity.

7.3. SELECTION OF SITE FOR DIESEL POWER PLANT

Following are the factors that need to be considered for selection of site for a diesel power plant—

(*i*) **Access to site**—The site selected should be easily accessible through road and rail.
(*ii*) **Availability of cooling water**—Cooling water must be available in sufficient quantity.
(*iii*) **Nearness to load centre**—It should be as close to load centre as possible.
(*iv*) **Nearness to source of fuel supply**—The site should be so selected that ample quantity of fuel is available.
(*v*) **Condition of soil**—The condition of soil should be such that heavy foundation can be constructed.
(*vi*) **Distance from populated area**—The site should be away from populated area due to noise and pollution.

7.4. CLASSIFICATION OF DIESEL ENGINES

Diesel engines are classified according to -

1. Mobility—

(*i*) **Stationary Diesel Engines**—These engines are used for power generation.
(*ii*) **Marine Diesel Engines**—These engines are used in ships for propulsion.

2. Speed of Operation—

(*i*) **Low speed engine**—Engine speed less than 300 rpm are classified as low speed engine. These engines find application as marine engine. These engines can use variety of liquid fuels due to longer time available for combustion.

(*ii*) **Medium speed engine**—Engine speed between 300–1000 rpm find application for power generation.

(*iii*) **High speed engine**—Engine speed of 1000 rpm and above come under this category. These engines use high speed diesel (HSD) or light diesel oil (LDO) as fuel. These are used as emergency power generators.

3. Frame of Engines—

(*i*) **Horizontal engines**—These are small capacity engines used for providing motive power.

(*ii*) **Vertical engines**—These are large capacity multi cylinder engines used for power generation.

4. Number of Cylinders—

(*i*) **Single/two to four cylinders**—These are used for very small capacity pumps.

(*ii*) **Six to eight cylinders**—These are commonly used for power generation.

5. Type of Aspiration—

(*i*) **Naturally aspirated engines**—These engines draw air from atmosphere due to downward movement of piston in the cylinders. No artificial methods are employed to increase suction air volume. Such engines are used for small capacity generator sets.

(*ii*) **Turbo charged engines**—These engines employ turbo-charger which increases suction air volume into the cylinder. Such engines are suitable for high capacity generator sets.

7.5. COMPARISON OF HIGH SPEED AND LOW SPEED ENGINES

Table 7.1 Comparison of low and high speed engines

Sr No	*Parameter*	*Low speed engine*	*High speed engine*
1.	Wear and tear of engine components	low	high
2.	Life of engine	more	less
3.	Sturdiness of engine	more	less
4.	Space required	more	less
5.	Use	continuous	intermittent
6.	Operating cost	less	more
7.	Period between overhauls	8000 hours	3200 hours

It shows that high speed engine though compact are more suitable for emergency backup power. While low speeds engine are suitable for continuous operation and have low operating cost and longer overhaul period.

7.6. TYPES OF FUEL USED IN DIESEL ENGINE

(*i*) **High Speed Diesel (HSD)**—It is used in high speed engines for power generation. Since, it is an expensive fuel, hence it is used for emergency power backup in industries, hospitals, malls, offices, hostels etc. Characteristics of high speed diesel are given in table 7.2

Table 7.2: Characteristics of high speed diesel

Parameter	***Value***
Density (at 15° C) (gm/ml)	0.78 – 0.80
Pour point(°C)	max + 6
Flash point (°C)	32
Kinematic viscosity (38°C)(cst)	2.0 – 7.5
Gross calorific value (kcal /kg)	10,500
Water content by volume(%)	max 0.2

(*ii*) **Light Diesel Oil (LDO)**—It is used in high speed diesel engines for emergency power backup. It is light yellow in colour with high calorific value and specific gravity. The characteristic of light diesel oil are given in table 7.3

Table 7.3 Characteristics of light diesel oil

Parameter	***Value***
Density (a 15°C)(gm/ml)	0.85 – 0.90
Pour point (°C)	12 – 18
Flash point °C)	66
Kinematic viscosity at 38°C (cst)	2.5 – 15.7
Gross calorific value (kcal/kg)	10,800
Water content by volume (max) (%)	0.25

(*ii*) **Fuel oils**—Fuel oils are higher distillates and are used as cheap fuel in low speed diesel engines of large capacity. These are used for power generation as well as for marine propulsion. Generally, these varieties are used for power generation viz low sulphur heavy stock (LSHS), furnace oil (FO) and heavy petroleum stock (HPS)oil. Characteristics of fuel oils are given in table 7.4

Table 7.4 Characteristics of fuel oil

Parameter	*Value*		
	LSHS	**HPS**	**HFO**
Density at 15°C (gm/ml)	0.90 – 0.96	0.96	0.95
Pour point(°C)	57	72	68
Flash point (°C)	75	75	66
Kinematic viscosity at 50°C (cst)	180	500	370
Gross calorific value (kcal/kg)	11000	9500	11000
Moisture content by volume (max)(%)	1.0	1.0	1.0

7.7. ELEMENTS OF DIESEL POWER PLANT

A diesel power plant consists of following systems—

(*i*) Engine start system. (*ii*) Air intake system.

(*iii*) Fuel system.

(*iv*) Cooling system.

(*v*) Lubrication system.

(*vi*) Exhaust system.

(*vii*) Electrical system.

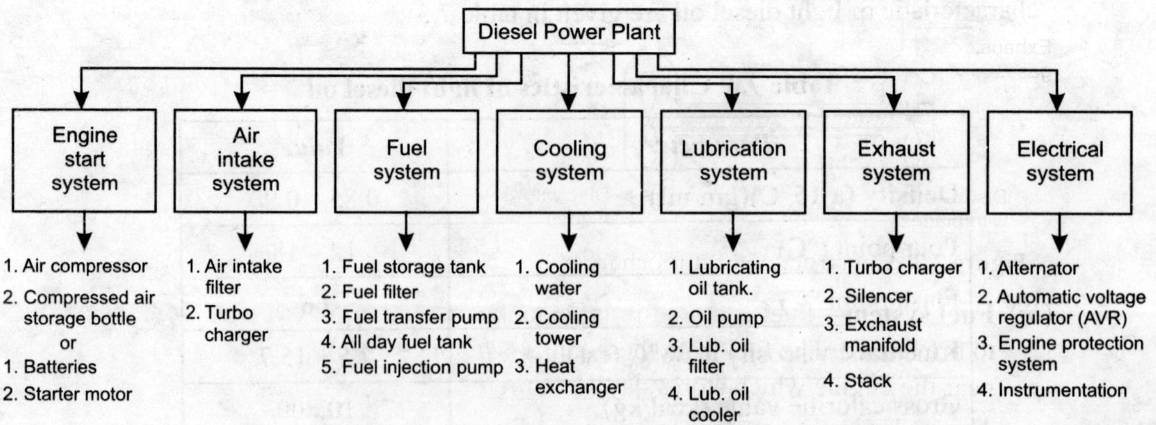

Fig. 7.1. Various systems in diesel engine

(*i*) **Engine start system**—It consists of either battery and starter motor (for small capacity engines) or air compressor and compressed air storage bottle (for large capacity engines). When start switch is pressed, a battery supplies power to the starter motor which makes engine crank with rotation, the suction valve of engine opens and admits air. This is followed by compression, fuel injection,expansion and exhaust.

In case of large capacity slow speed engines, compressed air at about twenty times the atmospheric pressure is used to crack the engine. This compressed air is provided by an air compressor and is stored in air bottles.

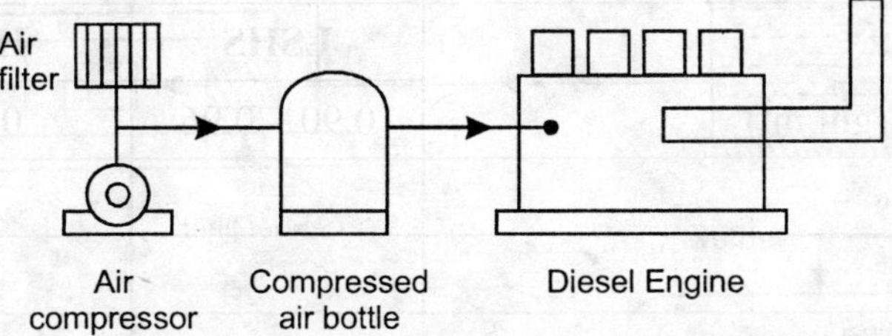

Figure 7.2. Engine start system

(*ii*) **Air intake system**—Air intake system supplies clean filtered air for combustion. Air is sucked through filter from atmosphere. This air then passes through an oil bath to the engine cylinder.

Air suction systems are of two types viz naturally aspirated engines and turbo-charged engines. Naturally aspirated engines suck air from atmosphere due to downward movement of piston. This system is used for smaller capacity engines. As the capacity of engine increases, the volume of air required for combustion also increases. Hence, turbo-charger is used. A turbo charger consists of disc having number of blades attached to it. The other end of this disc is connected through a shaft to another disc having set of blades. The exhaust gases from engine pass out through the first disc causing it to rotate at high speed. This inturn causes the shaft to rotate and the other disc attached to the shaft. This second disc forces air through the engine. In this way,the rate of flow of air into the engine is increased substantially.

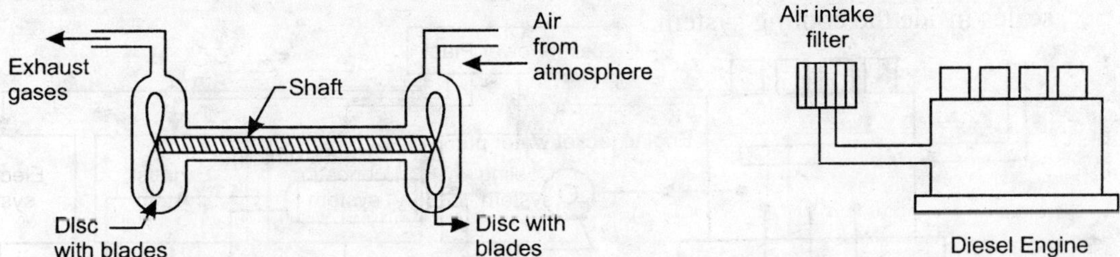

Figure 7.3. Construction of turbocharger

Figure 7.4. Air intake system

(*iii*) **Fuel system**—Fuel is stored in large tanks in tankfarm area away from the engines due to fire hazard. The fuel from these tanks is pumped to small capacity tanks called daytank near the engine which stores day's requirement.

The fuel injection system in engine comprises fuel filter,fuel measuring unit (PT pump) and injector. A small quantity of fuel is measured and injected into engine through injectors. Injectors atomise (i.e break into small droplets for easy combustion) fuel. The fuel is injected into engine cylinder at a very high pressure. Normally, three types of fuel injection systems are used viz—

(*a*) common rail injection system

(*b*) individual pump injection system

(*c*) distributer system

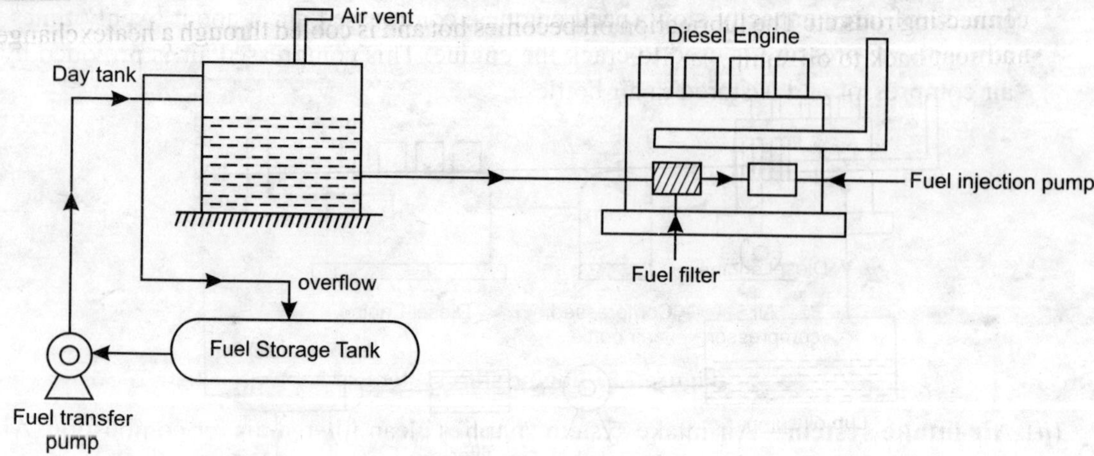

Figure 7.5. Fuel system

(*iv*) **Cooling system**—Cooling system consists of cooling water pump and cooling tower or spray pond. Heat is generated inside the engine cylinders due to combustion of fuel. This heat need to be dissipated to atmosphere otherwise piston seizure (piston gets stuck with cylinder due to extreme heat) will take place.

In order to remove heat from engine cylinder, a water jacket is provided around the cylinders. The heat from cylinders is conducted to water in the jacket. This hot water rejects heat to atmosphere through a cooling tower and a pump.

The water used for cooling purpose is soft water (soft water does not contain chlorides, sulphates and bicarbonates of calsium & magnesium). The soft water is supplied from a water softening plant. The purpose of using soft water is to prevent formation of hard scales inside the cooling system.

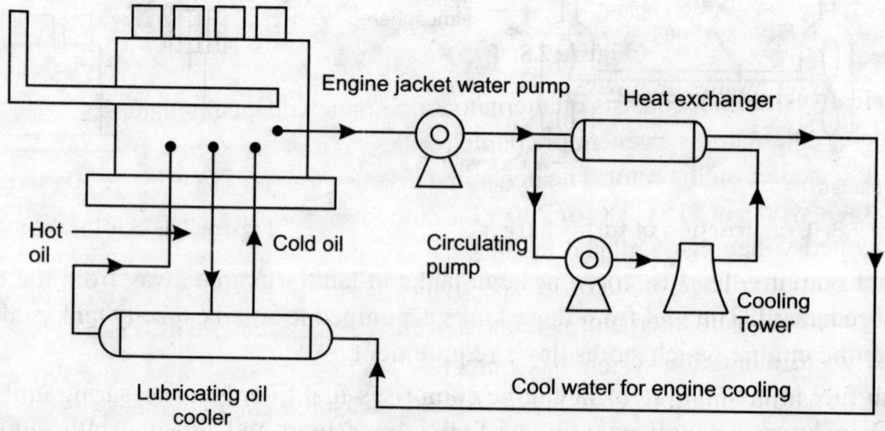

Figure 7.6. Cooling system

(*v*) **Lubrication system**—Purpose of engine lubrication system is reduce friction between moving parts, remove heat from cylinders and engine and to provide sealing between piston rings and cylinders. The oil is drawn from oil sump through a pump and a filter to various parts in a system such as pistons and cylinders,gears ,bearing, crankshafts and connecting rods etc The lubrication oil becomes hot and is cooled through a heatexchanger and sent back to oil sump.

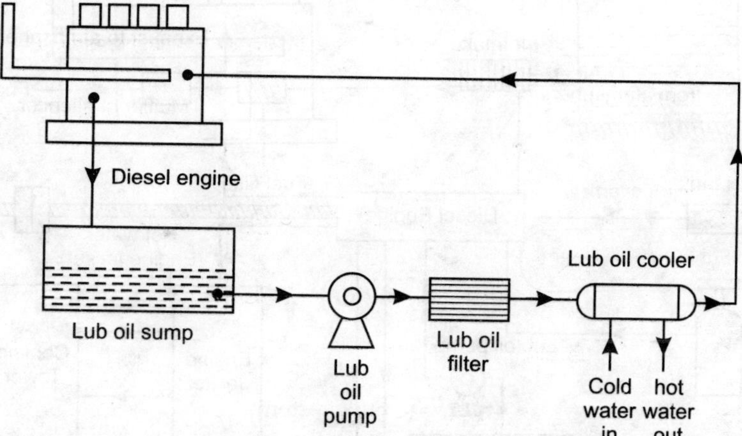

Figure 7.7. Lubrication system

(*vi*) **Exhaust system**—Function of exhaust system is to discharge product of combustion into atmosphere. It consists of exhaust manifold, turbo charger, silencer and stack. The stack is kept at sufficient height so that hot exhaust gases are easily dispersed into atmosphere.

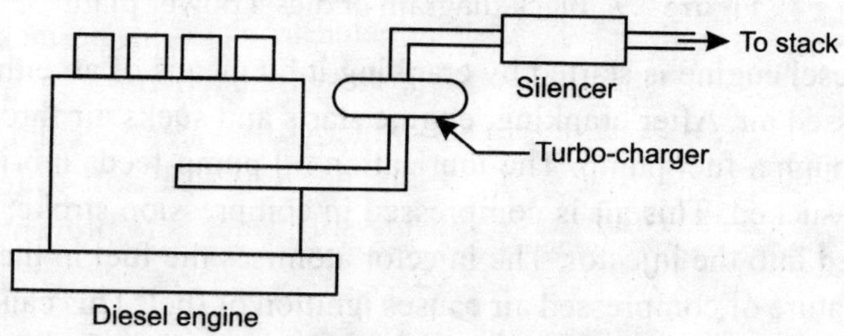

Figure 7.8. Exhaust system

(*vii*) **Electrical system**—It consists of alternator, automatic voltage regulator and various safety interlocks. Alternator is a generator coupled to the shaft of the engine. It has windings in the stator and exciter on the rotor. The generated voltages can be 415V, 50Hz to 6600V, 50Hz. The excitor works at 115V, DC or 220 VDC and is coupled to engine shaft. The magnitude of generated voltage is regulated by automatic voltage. regulator (AVR) which maintains constant output voltage of stator irrespective of variation in speed of engine or load. The power generated from alternator is fed to a panel having bus-bar with a circuit breaker.

The electrical instrumentation system has ammeters, voltmeters, wattmeters and synchronising system. The other instrumentation system consists of measurement of temperature of exhaust gases, lubrication oil temperature, cooling water jacket temperature etc. The pressure measurement system measures pressure in starting compressed air system, lubricating oil pressure before and after heat exchanger, cooling water pressure and fuel oil pressure.

For safety of engine,alarm and trip sensors are installed in the system. These are installed for high lubrication oil temperature, high cooling water temperature, low cooling water pressure, low lubrication oil pressure and high alternator winding temperature.

7.8. WORKING OF DIESEL POWER PLANT

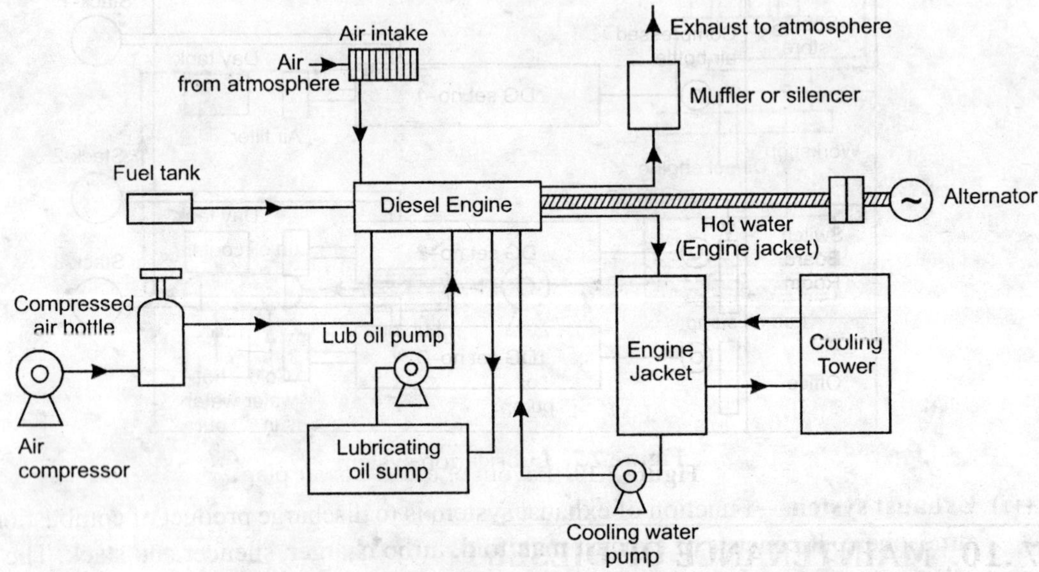

Figure 7.9. Black diagram of diesel power plant

Working—A diesel engine is started by cranking it by means of an either battery and electric motor or by compressed air. After cranking, engine starts and sucks air through air filter. The fuel is fed to injector through a fuel pump. The lubrication oil pump feeds lubrication system. During suction stroke, air is sucked. This air is compressed in compression stroke. Right quantity of fuel at right pressure is fed into the injector. The injector atomises the fuel in the compressed air in the cylinder. The temperature of compressed air causes ignition of fuel. This causes expansion of gases producing expansion stroke. This produces mechanical motion to the alternator which produces electricity. In expansion stroke, the exhaust gases are let out of the engine to the atmosphere through a silencer and a stack. The engine governor keeps the speed of engine constant irrespective of load variation. While automatic voltage regulator (AVR) keeps output voltage constant at set point.

Periodic maintenance requires cleaning of air filters, cooling system heat exchanger and lubricating filter replacement.

7.9. LAYOUT OF DIESEL POWER PLANT

A diesel power plant is composed of diesel engine and associated system,generator control panel, power control panel, bus bars, overhead travelling crane, workshop and office.

Each diesel generating set or DG set has its own compressed air system for starting, daytank for fuel storage and electric panel for alternator. The fuel is stored in tanks which are placed outside. The maintenance of all engine and alternator is carried out in adjoining workshop. A separate store keeps all necessary consumables and spares. Switchboard room houses electric panels which feeds power to main panel of the plant.

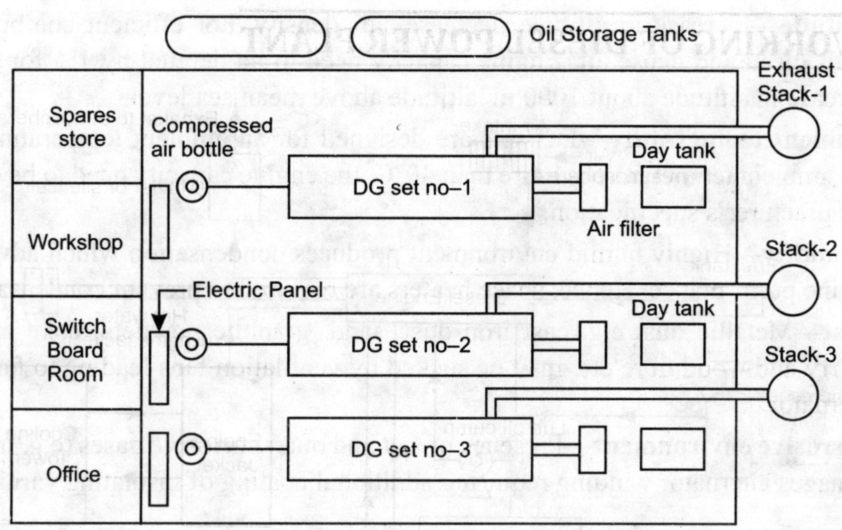

Figure 7.10. Layout of diesel power plant

7 .10. MAINTENANCE OF DIESEL ENGINE

A proper and timely maintenance of diesel engine enhances its life and also efficiency. Following steps need to be carried out for maintenance—

(*i*) **Fuel injectors**—Fuel injectors should be checked atleast once in three weeks for leakage and spray patterns.

(*ii*) **Exhaust valve**—The frequency of overhaul is dictated by exhaust gas temperature and impurities in air and fuel. The valve need to be cleaned and clearance is checked for excess oil consumption.

(*iii*) **Relief valve**—Relief valve is checked for operation at correct pressure and leakproof operation.

(*iv*) **Starting valves**—The valves need to be checked for proper closure.

(*v*) **Piston rings**—Piston rings are regularly inspected for wear & tear. The seats are also cleaned.

(*vi*) **Water and lubricating oil system**—Proper pressure and operation need to be checked periodically.

(*vii*) **Fuel system**—The filters need to be replaced regularly.

(*viii*) **Heat exchanger**—Heat exchanger in the water cooling system need to be cleaned once in 500 hours. The hardness and pH of the water need to be monitored on daily basis.

(*ix*) **Turbo-charger**—The internal surface should be cleaned once in 100 hours of operation.

7.11. SELECTION OF DG SETS

Diesel generation set (DG set) performance is impacted by environmental site conditions. Accordingly, selection and sizing of DG set is affected by following parameters.

(*i*) **Altitude**—Increase in altitude decreases air density. For efficient combustion, engine needs clean and dense air. Engine capacity need to be derated by 1% for every 100 m increase in altitude about 1000 m altitude above mean sea level.

(*ii*) **Ambient temperature**—DG sets are designed for an ambient temperature of 40°C. If the ambient temperature is more than 40°C, the engine capacity need to be derated as per manufacturer's specification.

(*iii*) **Humidity**—Highly humid environment produces condensation which adversely affects engine performance. Hence, space heaters are required to prevent condensation.

(*iv*) **Dust**—Metallic dust e.g. cast iron dust, sand, graphite powders, coke and lime dust, quarry and wood fibre etc. may be sucked by ventilation fans leading to flashover inside alternator.

(*v*) **Corrosive environment**—Presence of salt and other corrosive gases (e.g. in coastal area) damages alternator winding requiring additional coating of insulating varnish.

7.12. SIZING OF DG SETS

For right sizing of DG set, following information is required—

(*i*) total load to be supplied (wattage of all equipments).

(*ii*) block load requirement i.e maximum chunk of load that may come on DG set.

(*iii*) starting current requirement.

(*iv*) type of load (resistive /inductive/capacitive).

(*v*) future load (DG set capacity should by 10–20% more than maximum expected load).

A DG set is always operated at load above 30% of rated capacity as operation below this load affects overall performance.

As per norms of Central Pollution Control Board (CPCB), DG set with 1000 kVA and higher capacity need enclosures for meeting noise control norms (noise should be less than 75dB at 1m from the engine). 12V lead acid battery are selected for starting purpose. Following table gives number and ampere-hour capacity of batteries for different engine ratings.

Table 7.5: Sizing of lead acid batteries (high speed engine)

Sr.No	*Engine capacity(kVA)*	*Number and AH capacity of battery (12V)*
1.	up to 25	1 × 88 AH
2.	25 to 62.5	1 × 120 AH
3.	82.5 to 500	1 × 180 AH
4.	Above 500	2 × 180 AH

Height of exhaust stack of DG set as per CPCB norms is given by following expression.

$$H = h + 0.2\sqrt{KVA}$$

where, H = Total exhaust pipe stack height, m

h = height of building, m

For DG sets having capacity more than 1000 kVA, exhaust pipe height should be 30 m or 3m above height of building whichever is higher. A rain cap need to be provided at the end of exhaust pipe having diameter more than that of exhaust pipe.

7.13. ENERGY BALANCE OF DG SET

Energy balance provides detail of utilisation of input energy. A typical energy balance of a DG set is given below—

(*i*) Input energy = Thermal energy = 100%

→ Electrical output = 35%

→ Heatloss through chimney = 33%

→ Heat loss through coolant = 24%

→ Alternator losses = 4%

→ Radiation losses = 4%

It can be seen that major heat losses are (*i*) heat carried away by flue gases through chimney & (*ii*) heat taken away by engine cooling water. The heatloss through chimney can be recovered by using waste heat recovery system.

7.14. COMPARISON OF CONVENTIONAL POWER PLANTS

Table 7.7 gives comparison of various power plants viz. thermal power plant,hydro power plant,nuclear plant, gas turbine power plant & diesel power plant. Various parameters chosen for comparison are initial cost, running cost, efficiency, safety, time required for errection of plant, life of plant etc.

Table 7.6 gives efficiency of various types of co-generation systems.

Table 7.6: Comparison of co-generation system

Sr. No	*Type of co- generation*	*Overall efficiency (%)*
1.	Combined cycle	69–83
2.	Back pressure steam turbine	84–92
3.	Extraction cum condensing steam turbine	60–80
4.	Gas turbine	70–85
5.	Reciprocating engine	75–85

Table 7.7: Comparison of conventional power plants

Sr. No	Parameters	Thermal power plant	Hydroelectric power plant	Diesel power plant	Nuclear power plant	Gas based power plant
1.	Land required	large	very large	small	large	small
2.	Civil construction cost	medium	very high	low	very high	low
3.	Initial cost	medium	very high	low	highest	low
4.	Running cost	medium	nil	highest	low	high
5.	Life of plant	Long(70 years)	very long (100 years)	less (10 years)	medium (40 years)	less (20 years)
6.	Cost of fuel transportation	highest	nil	medium	very low	low
7.	Pollution	highest	nil	medium	clean	Better than diesel plant
8.	Cost of electricity	low	lowest	highest	medium	medium
9.	Time required for start up	very long time (60–600 minutes)	medium	quickest (1–5 minutes)	long time	quicker (10 – 20 minutes) combined cycle –30–60 minutes.
10.	Overall efficiency	least efficient (33–35%)	most efficient (85%)	moderately efficient(43–45%)	less efficient (33–36%)	less efficient [open cycle = 20%, combined cycle = 35 – 45%]
11.	Maintenace cost	very high	very less	high	highest	high
12.	Operating staff required	highest	very less	less	high	very less
13.	Time required for completion of plant	medium	highest	low	very high	low
14.	safety	medium	very safe	safe	very critical	safe
15.	Type of operation	Base load	Base load	peak load	Base load	Peak load
16.	Simplicity of operation	Complicated	Simplest	Simple	most complicated	Simple

Solved Examples

Example 7.1

Estimate the rating of a DG set in kVA with following details—

(*i*) Connected load =1600 kW

(*ii*) Percentage loading = 85%

(*iii*) Power factor = 0.80

(*iv*) Diversity factor = 1.88

Solution:

$$\text{Maximum demand} = \frac{\text{connected load}}{\text{Diversity factor}} = \frac{1600}{1.88} = 850 \text{ kW}$$

Given. Percentage loading = 85%

$$\therefore \quad \text{DG set rating} = \frac{850}{0.85} = 1000 \text{ kW}$$

$$\text{Rating in kVA at 0.8 power factor} = \frac{\text{kW}}{\cos\phi}\ \frac{1000}{0.8} = 1200 \text{ kW} \quad \textbf{Ans.}$$

Example 7.2

It is desired to utilize the heat energy of flue gases of a 1500 kVA DG set .The temperature of exhaust gases is 520°C at 100 kW load .The minimum temperature of exhaust gases is 180°C. below which condensation may cause corrosion. Specific heat of gases = 0.25

Solution:

The heat energy that can be recovered from exhaust gases

$$= 100 \times 8 \times 0.25 \times (520 - 180)$$

$$= 6.8 \times 10^5 \text{ kcal/hr} \quad \textbf{Ans.}$$

Example 7.3

A DG is rated at 1000 kVA, 415V, 50Hz, 3 phase, 1500 rpm,0.8 power factor. It produces 4 units of energy for every one litre of diesel consumed. Calculate diesel consumed for delivering full load for one hour.

Solution:

$$\text{Full load kW} = \text{kVA} \times \cos\phi = 1000 \times 0.8$$

$$= 800 \text{ kW}$$

Units generated in one hour = 800 kWh

Quantity of diesel consumed per hour when delivering 800 kWh

$$= \frac{800}{4.0}\ \frac{\text{kWh}}{\text{kWh/litre}} = 200 \text{ litres} \quad \textbf{Ans.}$$

Example 7.4

A DG set is planned to be installed in a hospital having height of 12m from ground level. The capacity of DG set is 1200 kVA. Calanlate the height of exhaust stack of engine as per CPCB norms.

Solution:

$$H = h + 0.2\sqrt{KVA}$$

$$H = 12 + 0.2\sqrt{1200}$$

$$H = 18.93 \text{ m}$$

Ans.

CHAPTER SUMMARY

Diesel engine based power generation is widely used for emergency backup power as well as for continuous requirement. Low speed diesel engines using cheaper heavy distillate fuels find wide application in captive power plants for continuous duty apart from marine propulsion. High speed diesel engine employing HSD are used extensively as emergency back-up power in industries, hospitals, hotels, malls, hostels, offices, shops etc. Due to higher speed, the size of engine is much smaller than slow speed engines. However, due to high cost of diesel, high speed engines are used only as back-up power. This power plant can be quickly started and loaded and hence can be used as peak load station. These engines have good part load efficiency but poor overload capacity. Large and heavy slow speed engines are started using compressed air as cranking method while for high speed engines, batteries are used. However, high speed engines are more maintenance prone than slow speed engines.

FORMULAE

1. DG set rating (kW) = $\dfrac{\text{Maximum demand}}{\text{percentage loading}}$
2. Heat energy that can be recoverd from exhaust gases = rated output of DG in kW × specific heat of exhaust gases × difference of minimum and maximum stack temperance × conversion factor (kW to kcal)
3. Diesel consumed per hour at rated load= $\dfrac{\text{full load kW}}{\text{units per litre}}$
4. Height of diesel engine stack, $H = h + 0.2\sqrt{KVA}$

   where, h = height of building in m, kVA = rated power of DG set.

REVIEW QUESTIONS

Q. 1. Discuss relative merits &demerits of diesel power plant.

Q. 2. State factors which govern the choice of a site for installation of diesel power plant.

Q. 3. Discuss classification of diesel engines.

Q. 4. What is the advantage of turbo-charged diesel engine over naturally aspirated diesel engine?

Q. 5. What are various types of liquid fuels which can be used in a diesel engine?

Q. 6. Explain with a neat sketch construction and working of a diesel power plant?

Q. 7. In which component of diesel power plant,maximum energy loss takes place?

Q. 8. Enumerate different methods of starting a diesel power plant.

Q. 9. Draw a neat sketch showing layout of 1500 kVA, 415V, 50Hz diesel based power plant.

Q. 10. Draw the maintenance tasks of various components of a diesel engine.

Q. 11. Disuses the criteria for selection of a diesel generating set.

Q. 12. Discuss the effect of ambient temperature and altitude on the power output of a diesel engine.

Q. 13. Write a brief note on sizing of DG set.

Q. 14. How the height of chimney of a DG set is selected?

Numerical Questions

Q. 1. Determine the rating of DG set in kVA based on following details—

(*i*) connected load = 200kW

(*ii*) percentage loading = 80%

(*iii*) power factor = 0.85

(*iv*) diversity factor =1.62 **[Ans:**1815 kVA]

Q. 2. A 2000 kVA DG set works with a flue gas heat recovery system. The temperature of exhaust gas is 485°C at 1600 kW load. The minimum allowable temperature of exhaust gas is 180°C. The specific heat of exhaust gas is 0.25. Find heat energy consumed per hour. **[Ans:** 9.76×10^5 kcal/hr]

Q. 3. A DG set is rated at 1500 kVA, 415 V, 50 Hz, 3 phase,1500 rpm,0.85 power factor. It generates 3.8 units of electricity for every litre of diesel consumed. Calculate diesel consumed for delivering full load for one hour. **[Ans:** 316 litres]

SHORT ANSWER TYPE QUESTIONS

Q. 1. What is the efficiency of a diesel engine?

Q. 2. State three fuels which can be used in a diesel engine.

Q. 3. What is the difference between a marine diesel engine and those used for power generation?

Q. 4. How does the speed of operation affects size of a diesel engine?

Q. 5. Why low speed diesel engines are preferred for large size ,continuous rated power plants?

Q. 6. Why high speed diesel engine is preferred over slow speed diesel engine for emergency power back-up in hospitals, hotels, malls etc?

Q. 7. What type of alternator is used for slow speed diesel engines?

Q. 8. What is the purpose of injectors in a diesel engine?

Multiple Choice Questions

Q. 1. Efficiency range of a diesel engine is

(*a*) 28–30% (*b*) 30–35%

(*c*) 35–44% (*d*) 44–46%

Q. 2. A diesel engine is a

(*a*) spark ignition engine (*b*) compression ignition engine

Q. 3. A diesel engine works on

(*a*) Brayton cycle (*b*) Otto cycle

(*c*) Rankine cycle (*d*) Diesel cycle

Q. 4. A high ambient temperature causes

(*a*) decrease in power output (*b*) increase in power output

(*c*) does not affect power output (*d*) none of these

Q. 5. A higher height of stack in a diesel engine.

(*a*) increase power output (*b*) decrease power output

(*c*) does not affect power output

Q. 6. A diesel engine uses following methods of cranking—

(*a*) batteries (*b*) compressed air

(*c*) both (*a*) & (*b*) (*d*) hand cranking

Answer to MCQ

1. (*d*) **2.** (*b*) **3.** (*d*) **4.** (*a*) **5.** (*b*)

6. (*c*)

Chapter

SOLAR THERMAL AND PHOTOVOLTAIC POWER GENERATION

Learning Objectives

After reading this chapter, reader will be able to

- Understand capture of solar energy through thermal and photovoltaic routes,various components involved & their comparative merits & demerits.
- Explore variety of usage of solar energy for residential, commercial, industrial, agricultural and rural areas.
- Update on solar power plants operating in India and in the world.
- Learn design of solar PV system.

"No problem can stand the assault of sustained thinking." — Voltaire

8.1. INTRODUCTION

Earth receives solar energy in the form of electromagnetic waves. The spectrum of this radiation ranges from cosmic radiation of very short wavelength to a very long wavelength. The range of radiation reaching earth consists of 8% ultraviolet radiation,46% visible light and 46% infrared radiation.

Sun is main source of energy on planet earth. Many renewable sources of energy on earth, such as geothermal, wind, biomass, ocean wave, ocean tidal, fossil fuels and organic chemicals find their origin in the sun. Sun's radiation contains heat and light. Both of these forms of energy are absorbed on earth and are stored and appear in different forms.

Sun has a diameter of 1.39×10^6 km and is 1100 times the diameter of earth (1.27×10^4 km). The mean distance between sun and earth is 1.5×10^8 km. This large distance subtends an angle of 32 minutes on earth's surface. So, the beam of radiation received from sun to earth is almost parallel. The brightness of sun varies from centre to its edge but for engineering calculation purpose, it is assumed to be constant. Sun's distance from earth and solar activity vary throughout the year, hence the amount of radiation reaching earth also varies. Sun is closest to earth during summer and farthest during winter.

Sun produces energy due to conversion of hydrogen into helium through fusion reaction. This generates huge amount of energy. The temperature of surface of sun is 6000°C. The radiation from Sun corresponds to a black body radiation at a temperature of about 5762K. The spectral distribution of solar radiation intensity consists of 7%in the range of 0 – 0.38 μm (95W/m^2 of energy), 47.3% in the range of 0.38 – 0.78 μm (640 W/m^2 of energy) and 45.7% in the range of 0.78 – 4.0 μm (618 W/m^2 of energy).It can be observed that 99% of Sun radiation is obtained upto a wavelength of 4 μm.

The solar energy received on earth is cyclic and intermittent and vary in power density from 0 to 1 kW/m^2. The direction of solar rays change during the day and with seasons. The amount of solar radiation received on earth is affected by scattering of rays due to collision with particles present in the atmosphere, absorption of rays by water vapour present in clouds and atmosphere, reflection of rays back into space by clouds, mountains etc. and diffusion of rays due to clouds. The solar radiation received on earth is also dependent upon latitude of location and time in a year. Nearly, all the ultraviolet radiation is absorbed by ozone and oxygen molecules. Carbon oxide and water vapour absorb some of the energy in infrared range. The output of Sun is 2.8×10^{23} kW while energy reaching the earth is 1.5×10^{18} kWh /year. India receives 4 – 7 kWh/m^2 for 250 – 300 sunny days in a year. Highest amount of solar energy is received in western part of the country while north eastern region of the country receives lowest amount of energy. This solar energy is harnessed by two routes-light (photovoltaic cells) and heat (solar thermal). This energy finds wide applications such as powers generation, cooking, heating, water pumping, water heating etc.

Advantages of solar energy are following

(*i*) it is an inexhaustible source of energy.

(*ii*) it is available throughout year.

(*iii*) solar photovoltaic system is useful for remote and rural areas.

(*iv*) solar thermal power plants can be used in deserts, mountaineous regions etc.

(*v*) solar energy has multiple uses such as drying, cooking, heating, power generation etc.

Limitations of solar energy are following—

(*i*) solar energy received on earth is of low power density (1 kw/m^2).

(*ii*) it requires large area to capture useful amount of energy.

(*iii*) it is intermittent, cyclical and changes with season.

(*iv*) direction of Sun changes throughout the day and hence requires continuous tracking.

(*v*) due to variation of solar energy received, there is need to store energy which increases the cost.

(*vi*) capital cost of solar energy to power conversion system is high.

8.2 TERMS RELATED TO SOLAR ENERGY AND GEOGRAPHY OF EARTH

Following terms find frequent use in solar energy utilization.

(*i*) **Solar Insolation:** It is total radiation received at any point on earth's surface. It is defined as the total solar radiation received on a horizontal surface of unit area on the ground in unit time. The insolation at a given location on earth's surface among other factors depends upon latitude of location, season and altitude of Sun (figure 8.2).

(*ii*) **Solar Constant (S):** It is defined as solar power received on unit surface area normal to sun-rays in the space outside the earth's atmosphere at a mean distance between sun and earth. Its value is 1353 W/m^2 (figure 8.2).

(*iii*) **Beam radiation or direct radiation (I_b):** It is the radiation received on earth's surface directly without change in direction which is not absorbed, scattered or reflected while passing through atmosphere.

(*iv*) **Diffuse radiation or scattered radiation (I_d):** It is the radiation received on earth's surface from all directions. The radiation is diffused due to atmospheric dust, gases and vapours. The average diffuse radiation is nearly 20% in the morning hours and decreases to 5–10% of the total radiation during a clear day but increases in hazy and cloudy conditions of sky.

(*v*) **Global or total radiation (I_T):** It is the sum of beam and diffuse radiation received on the surface of earth per unit area of location. The maximum value of global radiation is 1 kW/m^2 and is often called peak sun. The amount and intensity of radiation received is dependent upon sun angle, duration of day, path length, ground slope, and weather conditions among other factors. Due to curvature of earth, sunrays travel more distance at latitude than at equator.

Hence, Global radiation = Diffuse radiation + Beam radiation

$$I_T = I_d + I_b \cos\theta \qquad \text{...(8.1)}$$

where, θ = Zenith angle.

(*vi*) **Sun at zenith:** Position of sun directly over head.

(*vii*) **Concentration Ratio(C.R.):** It is defined as the ratio of solar power per unit area of the concentrator surface to the power per unit area on the line focus or point focus.

$$\text{Concentration ratio} = \frac{\text{Solar power per unit area of concentrator surface (kW/m}^2)}{\text{Power per unit area on the line focus or point focus (kW/m}^2)}$$

(*viii*) **Clarity Index (K_I):** It is the ratio of radiation received on earth's horizontal surface over a given period of time to radiation on equal surface area beyond earth's atmosphere in a direction perpendicular to beam. It lies between 0.1 to 0.7.

$$\text{Clarity Index }(K_I) = \frac{\text{Radiation received on earth's horizontal surface over a given period of time}}{\text{Radiation received on equal surface area beyond earth's atmoshphere in a direction perpendicular to beam}}$$

(*ix*) **Perihelion:** It is minimum distance between sun and earth. It is around 2nd January (figure 8.4).

(*x*) **Aphelion:** It is the maximum distance between sun and earth. It is around 3rd July (figure 8.4)

(*xi*) **Latitude:** These are imaginary lines on the surface of earth parallel to equitorial lines (figure 8.3). It is expressed in –90°to 90°. For northern hemisphere, latitude is positive.

(*xii*) **Longitude:** These are imaginary lines on the surface of earth between north and south pole (figure 8.3).

(*xiii*) **Angle of latitude:** It is the angle between the line joining the location to the centre of earth and the equatorial plane. For example, 40°N or 60°S.

(*xiv*) **Declination angle(δ):** It is the angle between line jointing sun to earth and the equatorial plane.

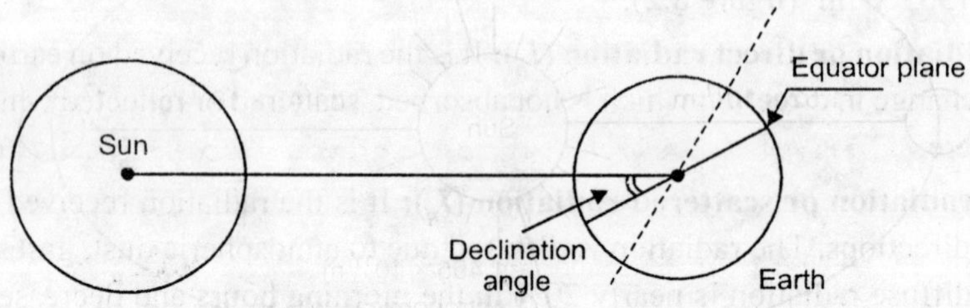

Fig. 8.1 Declination angle

This angle varies with season from minimum value of – 23.45° on December 21 to maximum value of + 23.45° on June 21. This angle is zero at two equinoxes i.e. March 21 and September 21.

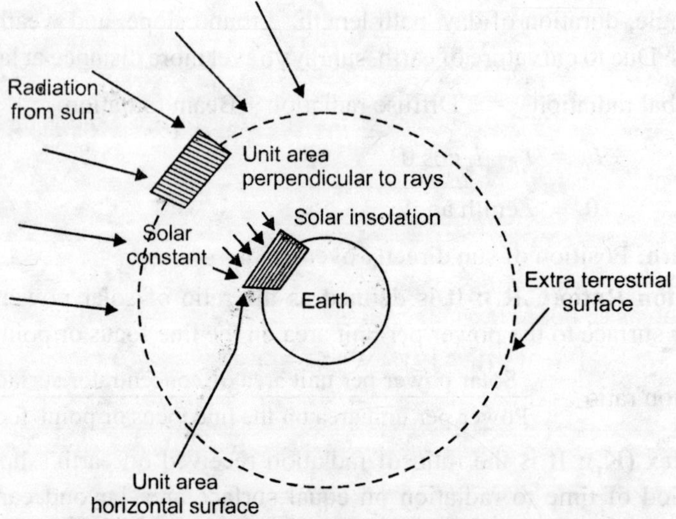

Fig. 8.2 Solar constant and solar insolation

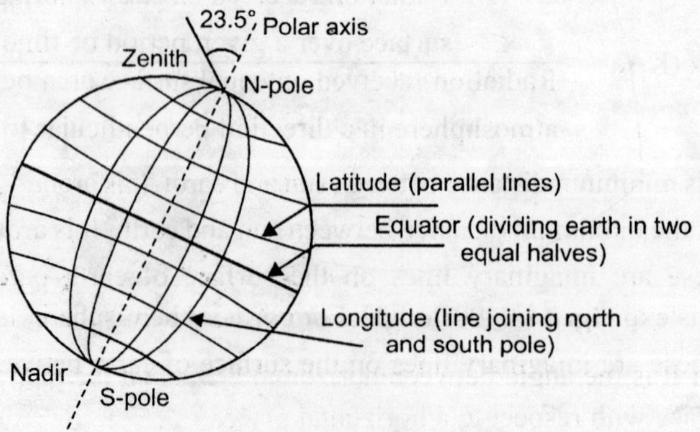

Fig. 8.3 Latitude and longitude

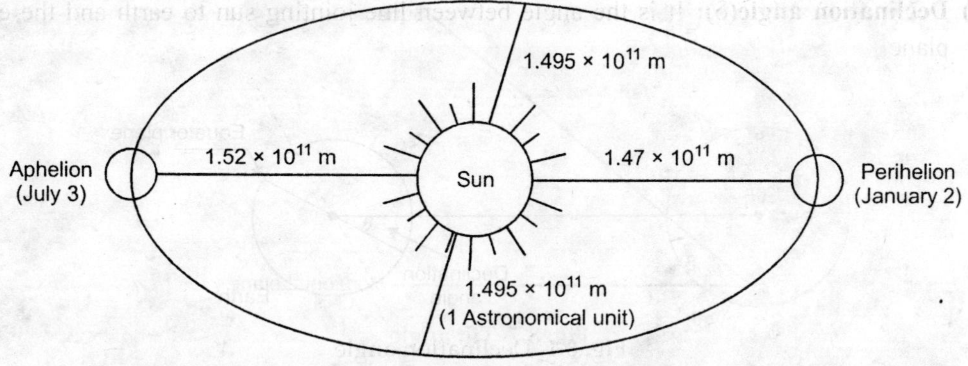

Fig. 8.4 Revolution of earth around the Sun

(*xv*) Angle of incidence (θ): It is angle between sunray and a line perpendicular to surface (figure 8.5).

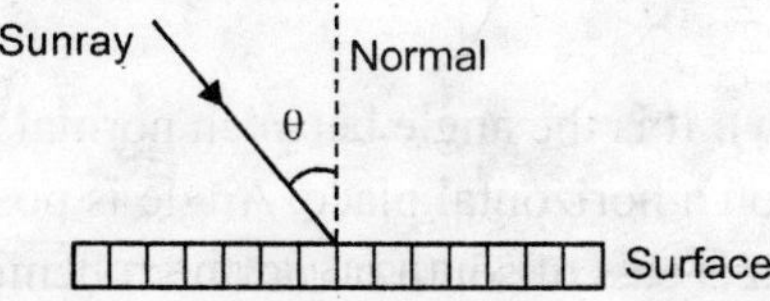

Fig. 8.5 Angle of incidence

(*xvi*) Hour angle (ω): It represents position of sun with respect to clock hour and with reference to sun's position at 12 noon. It changes at the rate of 15° per hour. Hour angle is given by—

$$\omega = 15\,(h - 12) \quad \text{Where h is current time of the day.}$$

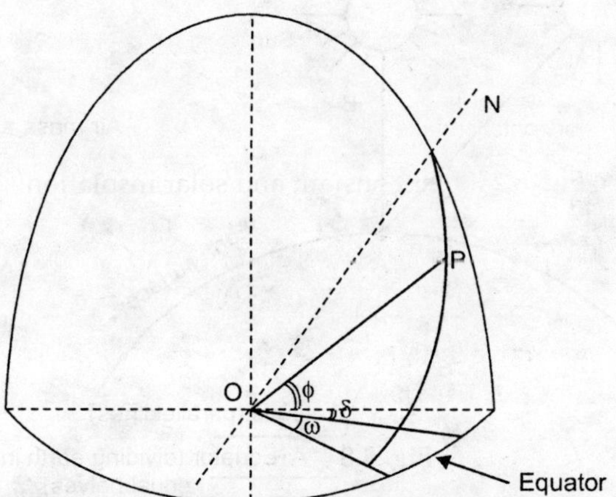

Fig. 8.6 Hour angle and declination angle

(*xvii*) Tilt angle (β): It is the angle between horizontal plane and the plane of surface. It measures slope of a surface with respect to a horizontal place.

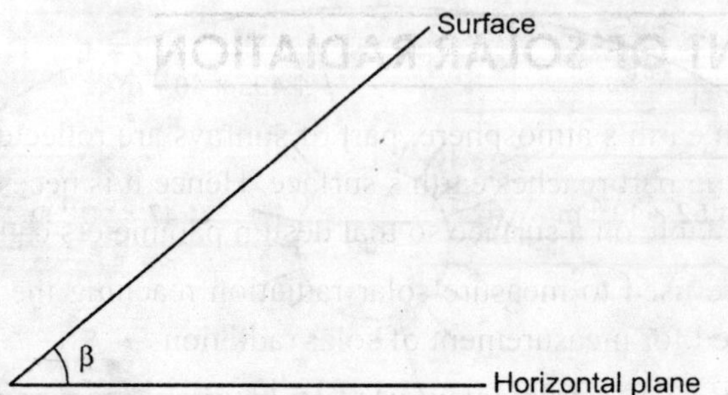

Fig. 8.7 Tilt angle

(*xviii*) **Zenith angle (θ_Z):** It is the angle of incidence for a horizontal surface. It is zero at solar noon and depends upon latitude, declination angle and time of day.

(*xix*) **Altitude angle (α):** It is angle between sunrays and the projection of rays on a horizontal plane.

$$\theta_Z = \frac{\pi}{2} - \alpha \qquad ...(8.2)$$

(*xx*) **Surface azimuth angle(γ):** It is the angle between normal to inclined plane and projection of normal inclined surface on a horizontal place. Angle is positive if projection is west of south and negative if projection is east of south on northern hemisphere.

(*xxi*) **Air mass:** It indicates attenuation of solar radiation reaching earth's surface. It is defined as ratio of distance through which radiation has to travel through the atmosphere to the distance it will travel when sun is at vertical location

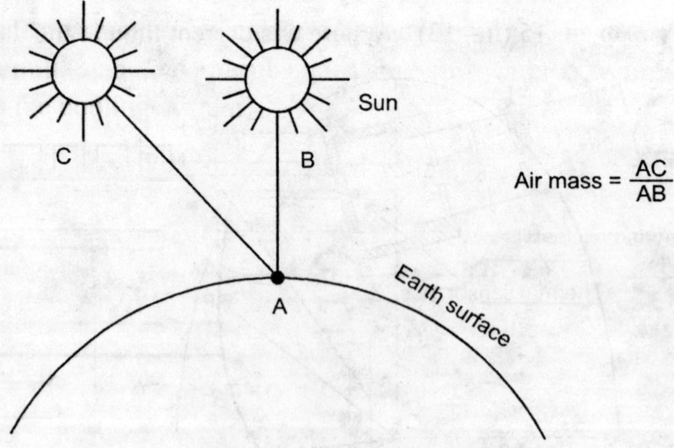

Fig. 8.8 Air mass

At noon, sun is vertically above so AC = AB or Air mass = 1. Value of air mass at noon time is a unit called standard air mass. Its value is higher in winter at December 21 and lower in the month of March 21 at northern hemisphere.

(*xxii*) **Irradiance:** It is the amount of solar energy received on a unit surface. Solar irradiance is solar insolation integrated with respect to time. The average daily value of solar irradiance worldwide on a optimally inclined surface is about 5 kWh/m^2.

8.3 MEASUREMENT OF SOLAR RADIATION

When sunrays pass through earth's atmosphere, part of sunrays are reflected back to space, a part of it are absorbed while remaining part reaches earth's surface. Hence,it is necessary to know the amount of radiation energy that is available on a surface so that design parameters can be decided.

Various instruments are used to measure solar radiation reaching the earth. Following two basic types of instruments are used for measurement of solar radiation—

(*i*) **Pyroheliometer:** This instrument is used to measure beam radiation at normal incidence using a collimated detector.

(*ii*) **Pyranometer:** This instrument is used to measure global and diffuse solar radiation.

8.3.1 Pyroheliometer

It measures direct or beam component of solar radiation at normal incidence. It is aimed directly at the sun and a tracking mechanism continuously follows the sun. Diffuse component of solar radiation is avoided by installing a collimeter tube over the sensor with a circular cone angle of about 5 degrees. It measures solar radiation from 280 to 3000 nm.

In order to prevent entry of diffuse radiation, the collimacting tube is fitted with five filters and continuously tracks the sun. The aperture angle of instrument is 5.7°. The sunrays pass through a crystal quartz window and is directed onto a cylindrical black body cavity containing a thermopile. This thermopile converts heat of sunrays into electrical signal which is measured by a milli voltmeter. With a calibration factor, the instrument gives radiant energy flux in W/m^2.

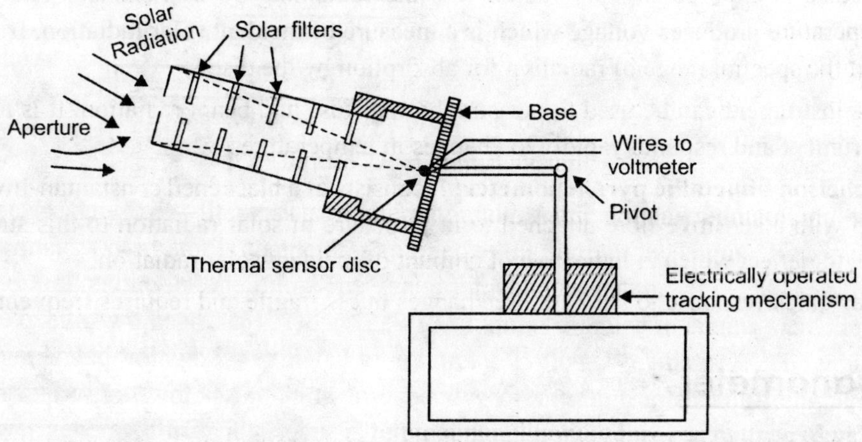

Fig. 8.9 Pyroheliometer

Pyroheliometer uses thermoelectric transducers to convert solar radiation into electrical signal. However, photovoltaic transducers due to low cost are used now widely. Five types of pyroheliometers are widely used viz. Angstrom pyroheliometer, Abbot silvers disc pyroheliometer, Eppley pyroheliometer, Linke -Fuessner pyroheliometer and Michelson bimetallic pyroheliometer.

(*i*) **Angstrom compensation pyroheliometer:** In this instrument, a thin blackened shaded manganin strip is electrically heated until it is at same temperature as a similar strip which receives solar radiation. The device uses thermocouple at the back of each strip and are connected in opposition through a sensitive galvanometer. Under balance condition, temperature of both the strips is same. The radiant solar energy is calculated by following expression—

Energy, $E = KI^2$ ...(8.3)

where, K = instrument constant

I = heating current, A

It needs to be calibrated against a primary standard. It is one of of the most accurate instrument with high degree of stability.

(*ii*) **Abbot silver disc pyroheliometer:** The instrument contains a blackened silver disc in a tube with diaphragms to limit aperture to 5.7°.A mercury glass thermometer is inserted in it to measure the temperature of the disc. The disc is thermally insulated from environment so that it receives energy only from the sun. A metallic shutter alternately shades and exposes the disc to solar radiation in a perfectly timed sequence. The rate of change of temperature of disc indicates energy flow. It is a very stable instrument but need to be calibrated.

(*iii*) **Eppley pyroheliometer:** It consists of a wire wound copper constantan plated thermopile with a blackened 9 mm diameter receiver. A thermopile which consists of series of thermocouples is used to measure the voltage that is produced by temperature difference due to incident solar radiation. The measured voltage is a measure of solar radiation falling on it. It is very stable instrument and is widely used.

(*iv*) **Linke-Fuessner pyroheliometer:** It consists of a thermopile (number of thermocouples connected in series) of manganin–constantan arranged in 1-cm diameter circle. 50% of this disc is exposed to solar radiation while remaining 50% is shaded. The difference in temperature produces voltage which is a measure of incident solar radiation. It uses filters to limit the spectral range of radiation for absorption by the disc

This instrument can be used to measure both diffuse and beam radiation. It is most sensitive instrument and responds rapidly to changes in temperature.

(*v*) **Michelson bimetallic pyroheliometer:** It consists of a blackened constantan-Invar bimetallic strip with a sensitive fibre attached to it. Exposure of solar radiation to this strip causes the fibre to deflect which is indicative of amount of incident solar radiation.

It has quick response to temperature changes but is fragile and requires frequent calibration.

8.3.2 Pyranometer

A pyranometer measures both diffuse and beam radiation or total radiation. To measurer diffuse radiation, a shading ring is used which prevents beam radiation falling on it. The sun's radiation falls on a black surface which is connected to hot junction of thermopile while the cold junction of thermopile does not receive solar radiation. The emf indued in thermopile is proportional to the solar radiation received. This measured voltage is solar radiation value.

The instrument essentially consists of two concentric discs, sensitive element, glass hemisphere and a radiation gauge. Outer disc is coated with magnesium oxide which has high reflectivity and reflects solar radiation falling on it. While inner disc is coated with absorbent black colour to absorb incident solar radiation. The inner disc absorbs solar radiation and heats up until its rate of heat gain is equal to rate of heat loss due to transfer of heat from inner disc to outer disc. The difference in temperature produced by solar radiation in the two discs is measured by thermocouples. The electrical voltage generated by thermocouples is measured by a voltmeter which indicates total radiation received by it. The whole assembly is encased in a glass hemisphere. The glass hemisphere prevents change in temperature of solar radiation due to rain, wind etc.

Diffuse radiation is measured by covering the sensor with a semi circular shading ring so that direct solar radiation on the sensor is blocked. The position of this shading ring is adjusted every few days to correct declination angle.

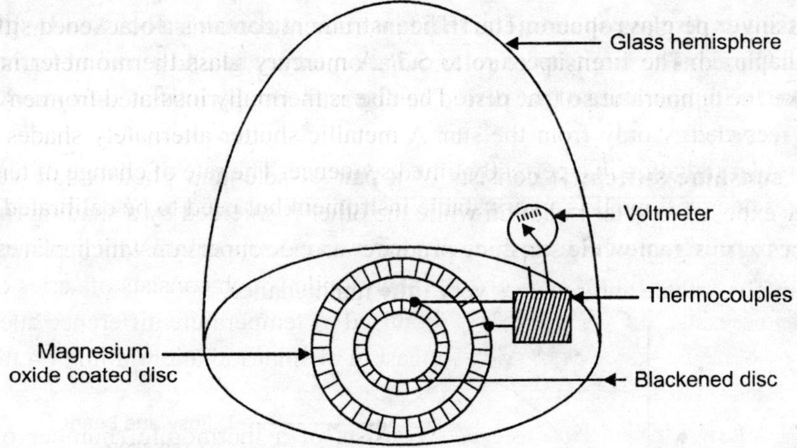

Fig. 8.10 Basic construction of a pyranometer

Various types of pyrometers are described below–

(*i*) **Eppley pyranometer:** It consists of two surfaces-one coated black which absorbs all solar radiation while another is coated with white surface which reflects all solar radiation. The incident solar radiation produces a temperature difference which is converted into electrical voltage by a copper-constantan thermopile. Hot junction is coated with black paint and cold junction with barium sulphate. The whole assembly is enclosed in a glass dome. The device is provided with a built in compensation.

(*ii*) **Moll-Gorczynski pyranometer:** It also consists of two discs painted black and white connected to 14 manganin -costantan thermocouples arranged in a rectangular configuration. It is widely used. Change in azimuth can introduce error.

(*iii*) **Yellot solarimeter:** This instrument uses photovoltaic cells as detectors. The incident solar radiation is converted into electrical current by photovoltaic cells. However, spectral response is non-linear.

(*iv*) **Rabitzsch bimetallic pyranometer:** It consists of a blackened bimetallic strip. Incident solar radiation causes the bimetallic strip to bend which moves a recorder pen. The chart is clock driven. It is very sensitive but has reduced level of accuracy.

(*v*) **Kipp and Zonen pyranometer:** It uses imprinted thermocouples on a ceramic substrate using thin film technology. The temperature difference induced due to solar radiation produces an emf which indicates amount of incident radiation.

It is temperature compensated and has less cosine and azimuth errors.

8.4 SUNSHINE RECORDER

This instrument is used to measure duration of bright sunshine in a day. It consists of a card strip placed in a spherical bowl. The sphere is used to focus sun's rays on the card strip. A bright sunshine is intense enough to burn a path along the card strip. The length of burnt path is proportional to the duration of sunshine.

The various types of sunshine recorders used are described below—

(*i*) **Campbell-Stokes sunshine recorder:** It consists of a special paste card board covered with a focussing type glass sphere. The incident solar radiation is focussed by glass sphere over the paste board. The intensity of solar radiation leaves behind a trail of burnt track. The card is marked with hourline so that period can be read. So, periods of sunny and cloudy duration can be recorded.

(*ii*) **Foster sunshine switch:** It consists of a pair of selenium photovoltaic cells. One cell is directly exposed to solar radiation while the other is shielded by a shading ring. Diffuse light produces zero signal while sunshine produces an electric signal which moves a recorder.

It is sensitive, stable and requires very little maintenance.

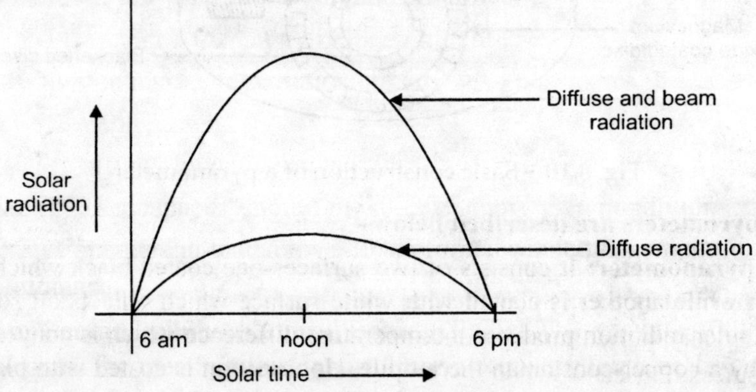

Fig. 8.11 Variation of total and diffuse radiation with solar time

8.5 OVERVIEW OF SOLAR ENERGY TECHNOLOGY

Sunrays or solar radiation are used for variety of applications including power generation. Classification of solar energy technology is explained in figure 8.12.

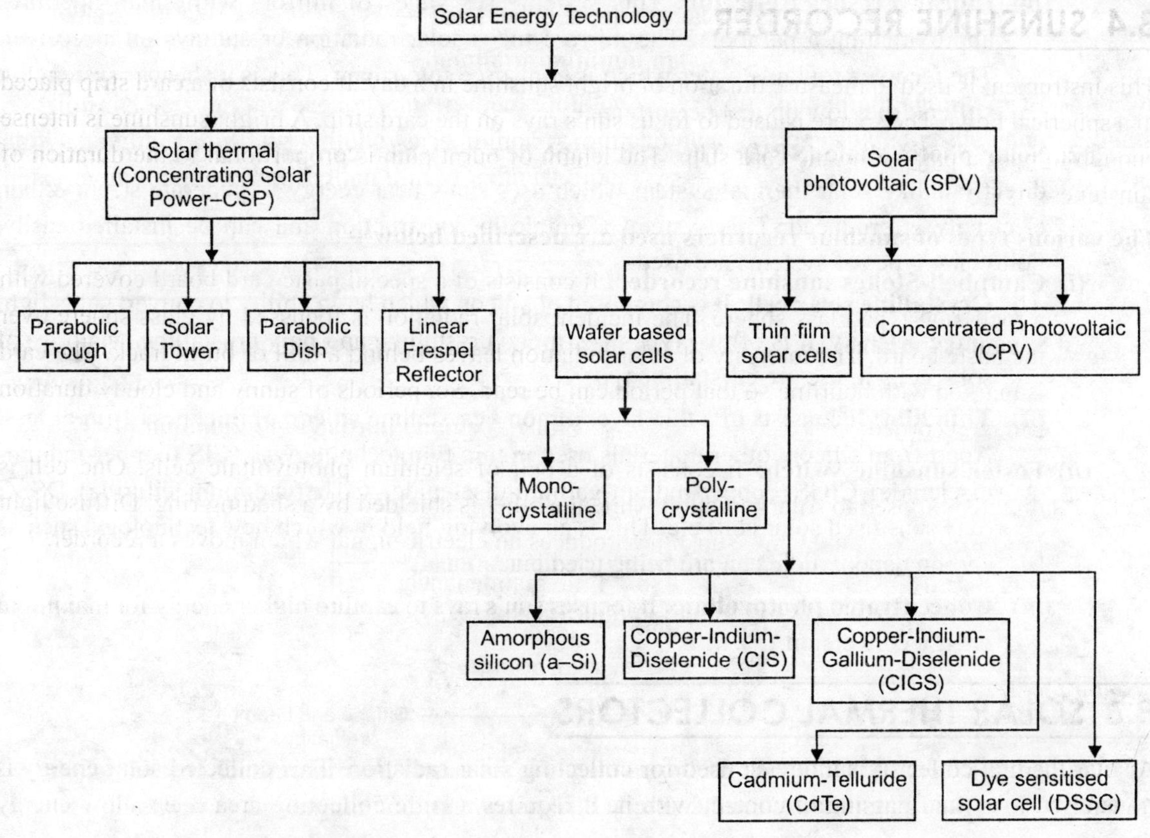

Fig. 8.12 Classification of solar energy technology

1. **Solar Thermal (CSP):** Solar thermal uses heat energy of sunrays to generate electricity, heat water, dry agricultural produce etc. For generation of electricity, following types of technologies are used—

   (i) **Parabolic Trough:** This system uses parabolic shaped mirrors to concentrate and receive solar radiation onto a receiver tube. The receiver tube is placed along the focal line of parabolic mirrors which contains thermic fluid (heat transfer fluid) to generate electricity through steam cycle. Parabolic mirrors track sun to capture maximum radiation& can provide about 400° C temperature to thermic fluid. This is a mature and widely used technology.

   (ii) **Solar Tower:** This system consists of circular array of heliostats focussing sunlight on a central receiver which is placed at the top of a tower. Heliostat track sun on two axes to capture maximum solar radiation. The system can produce very high temperature which is used to produce superheated steam. This steam is used to produce power using steam turbine and gas turbine. System is available upto 200 MW capacity.

   (iii) **Parabolic Dish:** It consists of parabolic shaped dish which focusses sunrays onto a receiver placed at its focal point. The dish tracks Sun. The focussed sunrays heat up fluid or gas in the receiver which is used to generate electricity in a stirrling engine or micro turbine. This system is costly and can generate small amount of power from 10–20 kW.

(*iv*) **Linear Fresnel Reflector:** This system uses slices of mirrors with small apertures approximating a parabola. The mirrors focus solar radiation or sunrays on a receiver. The receiver contains water which is converted into steam. This is a cheaper system but suffers from low optical performance.

2. **Solar photovoltaic (SPV):** These are static devices which convert sunlight into electricity directly unlike solar thermal system which uses sun's heat energy to generate steam &then electricity is produced. This system is simple in construction and can be installed easily. Following types of systems are used—

(*i*) **Crystalline solar cell:** It is composed of silicon which has a ability to convert sun's light into electricity. It is of two types viz. mono crystalline and poly crystalline. Majority of solar cells in use are crystalline type.

(*ii*) **Thin film:** It consists of a thin layer of non - crystalline silicon of thickness 1μm or less. Apart from silicon, other materials used in thin film techndogy are CIS (copper-indium-diselenide), CIGS (copper-indium-gallium-diselenide), CdTe (cadmium telluride), DSSC (day sensitised solar cell) etc. This is an evolving field in which new technology, such as carbon nanoparticle etc. are being tried out.

(*iii*) **Concentrated photovoltaic:** It focuses sun's rays to capture higher energy for maximum energy conversion.

8.6 SOLAR THERMAL COLLECTORS

A solar thermal collector is a device used for collecting solar radiation. This collected solar energy is transferred to a fluid passing in contact with it. It requires a large collecting area due to low energy density.

Solar collector are of two types viz. flat plate type solar collector and concentrating type solar collector. Uses of solar collector can be grouped into following three categories—

(*i*) **Low temperature system (less than 150°C):** This system is used for heating water for domestic use, swimming pool heating, space heating and cooling, solar desalination and crop drying purposes.

(*ii*) **Medium temperature system (150 – 400° C):** This system is used for industrial process heating and power plant (parabolic trough concentrating plant).

(*iii*) **High temperature system (400 – 1000° C):** These are used for industrial process heating and power generation (solar tower power plant and solar dish power plant).

8.6.1 Flat Plate Collectors

These collectors absorb both direct and diffuse solar radiation and consist of rectangular section in the shape of a panel. Size of the panel is 1.7 to 2.9 m^2 area. The solar energy is absorbed through a black coated plate made of metal or plastic which converts solar energy into heat. Tubes carrying heat transfer fluid are placed below the plates. The heat is transported by this fluid to the place of utilization of heat. To reduce heat losses, the collector surface facing the sun is covered with one or two layers of transparent glass sheet and sides of collector are equipped with thermal insulation.

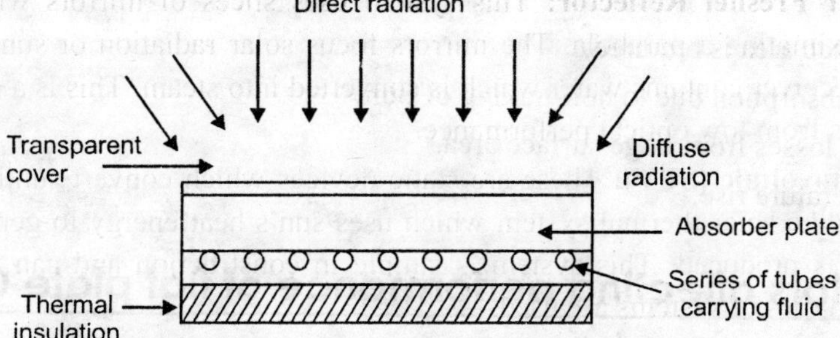

Fig. 8.13 Front view of flat plate collector

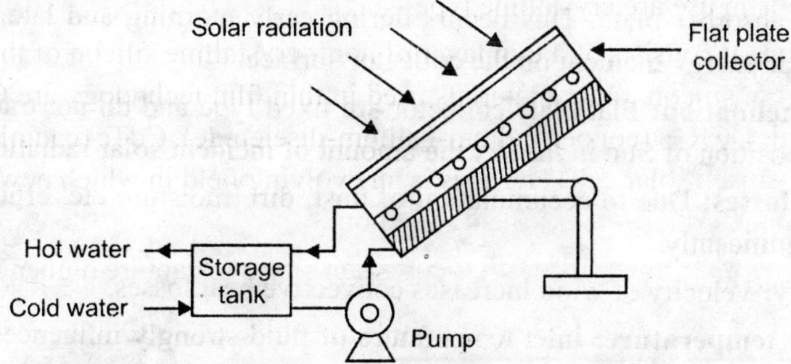

Fig. 8.14 Flate plate collector placed on an inclined plane

The complete system is placed on inclination to sun to absorb solar radiation. It gives a temperature upto 100°C with an efficiency of 30 – 50%. This type of collector is used for heating for residence, industry, hotels, solar cooker for cooking, drying and desalination applications. Air heating collectors are used for space heating and agricultural crop drying purposes.

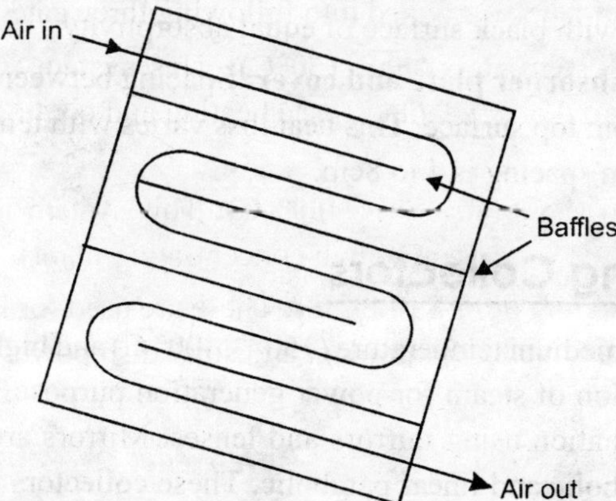

Fig. 8.15 Air heating flat plate collector

Advantages of flat plate collector are following—

(*i*) they use both direct and diffuse solar radiation.

(*ii*) they require low maintenance.

(*iii*) they do not require sun tracking.

(*iv*) they have simple design.

Disadvantages—

(*i*) large surface area is required.

(*ii*) less heat absorption due to non-traking of Sun.

(*iii*) large heat losses from large surface area.

(*iv*) low temperature rise.

8.6.1.1 Factors affecting performance of flat plate Collector

The efficiency of collector system is affected by following factors-

(*i*) **Shading:** When angle of elevation of Sun is less than 15°,the shadow of neighbouring panels fall on the absorber plate. This occurs during early morning and late evening hours. This reduces solar energy incident on the collector surface.

(*ii*) **collector inclination:** Flat plate collector are fixed type and do not track the Sun. With the change in position of Sun in the sky,the amount of incident solar radiation varies.

(*iii*) **Reflective losses:** Due to accumulation of dust, dirt, moisture etc, efficiency of collector is reduced significantly.

(*iv*) **Air velocity:** Velocity of wind increases convective heat losses.

(*v*) **Fluid inlet temperature:** Inlet temperature of fluid strongly influences the performance of the collector. A low temperature of inlet fluid decreases collector efficiency.

(*vi*) **Ambient temperature:** A low ambient temperature increases heat loss resulting in lower collector efficiency.

(*vii*) **Incident solar flux:** Collector efficiency increases with higher incident solar flux.

(*viii*) **Selective surfaces:** Absorber plate with selective surfaces show a high value of absorptivity for incoming solar radiation and low value of emissivity for outgoing re-radiation compared to a absorber plate with black surface of equal absorptivity.

(*ix*) **Spacing between absorber plate and cover:** Spacing between absorber plate and first cover affects heat loss from top surface. This heat loss varies with temperature difference and angle of tilt. The optimum spacing is 4 to 8cm.

8.6.2 Concentrating Collectors

These collectors are used for medium temperature (150° – 400° C) and high temperature (400° – 1000°C) applications such as production of steam for power generation purpose. High temperature is achieved through concentration of radiation using mirrors and lenses. Mirrors are cheaper than lenses. Shapes of mirrors are spherical parabolic and linear parabolic. These collectors require Sun tracking and have collector efficiency of 50 – 70%. These collectors are classified based on type of reflector, concentration ratio and type of tracking mechanism used. Various types of concentrating collectors are following—

(*i*) Parabolic dish concentrator.

(*ii*) Parabolic trough concentrator.

(*iii*) Fresnel lens type concentrator.

(*iv*) Central receiver with heliostat reflectors.

(*v*) Compound parabolic concentrator.

(*vi*) Flat plate collector with plane reflectors.

(*i*) Parabolic dish concentrator: This system uses large size paraboloidal dish to concentrate solar radiation. The reflecting surface of concentrator in made of silvered glass,thin electropolished anodized aluminium sheets or silver coated acrylic film. The rim angle ranges from 70° – 120° with a concentration ratio of 10 – 80. Only direct radiation can be collected by this type of collector and can achieve a temperature rise of 300° C. Tracking of Sun takes place in one plane only.

An absorber tube of steel or copper is located at the focal axis of parabolic concentrator carrying the fluid to be heated. The tublar surface is coated with selective coating for better absorption of concentrated incident solar radiation.

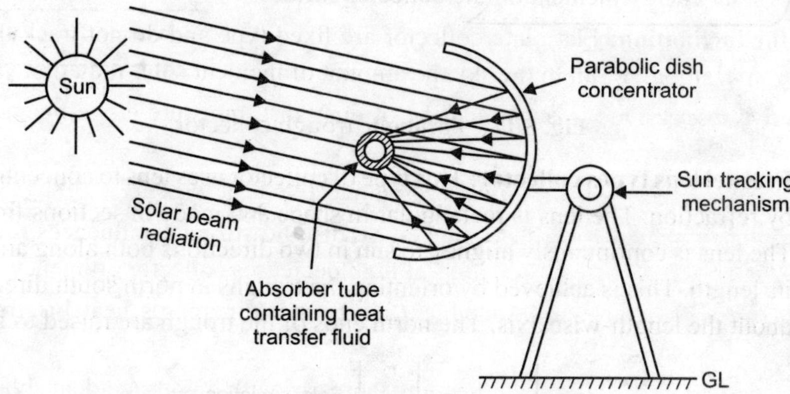

Fig. 8.16 Parabolic dish concentrator

Different types of heat transfer fluids used are described below—

(*i*) Water-steam: It is well established technology though less efficient. It can be used to raise steam to temperature of 540° to 600° C and at a pressure of 70 to 140 bar. It is used for central receiver system.

(*ii*) **Liquid metals:** It uses sodium which has high heat transfer coefficient. A cover gas such as argon is used to prevent oxidation. However, sodium freezes at 98°C hence requires auxiliary heating during shutdown.

(*iii*) **Gases:** Gases such as air, nitrogen and helium are used for heat transfer. These are used at a temperature of 840° C and above. Pressurisation is required to improve heat transfer rate.

(*iv*) **Thermic fluid or heat transfer oil:** Heat transfer fluids operate at a temperature range of 7 to 300°C beyond this temperature range decomposition of fluid takes place. These fluids are available under different commercial names and posses high mass flow rate and high heat transfer coefficient. These use pressurisation for the fluid flow.

(*ii*) Parabolic trough concentrator: Parabolic trough collectors are low cost, simple design and single plane Sun tracking type. The system consists of large fields of parabolic trough collectors through which a heat transfer fluid is circulated. The hot heat transfer fluid (at temperature of about 400°C) passes through a series of heat exchangers to generate steam

The system is provided with an optional thermal storage. The solar field consists of single axis tracking parabolic trough solar collector which are normally on a north-south horizontal axis. The collectors track the sun from east to west during the day to ensure that the sun is continuously focussed on the linear receiver.

A new variant of this technology called linear Fresnal reflector is available in the shape of a parabola using various mirror strips at different angles. These strips are mounted on horizontal surface and therefore need for heavy structures is alleviated.

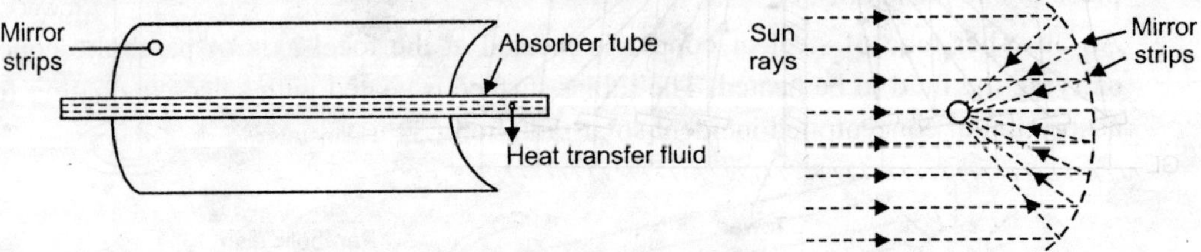

Fig. 8.17 Parabolic trough collector

(iii) **Fresnel lens types collector**: This type of collector uses lens to concentrate solar radiation by refraction. The lens is rectangular in shape and made in sections from acrylic plastic. The lens is continuously aligned to sun in two directions both along and perpendicular to its length. This is achieved by orienting the troughs in north south direction with rotation about the length-wise axis. The north ends of the trough are raised to increase the slope.

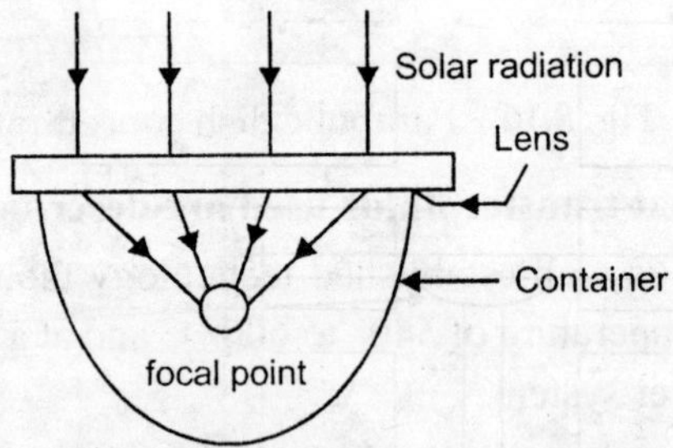

Fig. 8.18 Fresnel lens type collector

Solar radiation is concentrated on a receiver pipe placed at the focal point of lens. This hollow steel pipe carries heat transfer fluid The absorber pipe is usually enclosed in a pyrex glass jacket to reduce thermal losses by convection and radiation. The space between pipe jacket is sometimes evacuated to reduce convection loss.

(iv) **Cental receiver with heliostat reflectors:** This system consists of paraboloidal mirror using heliostat mirrors. A large number of mirrors called heliostat are distributed over an area on ground and can be steered independently about two axes. This results in reflected solar radiation always directed towards an absorber mounted on a tower. This design is mostly used in power plant for generation of electricity.

The central receiver is composed of many small mirrors each with its own heliostat to follow sun. The basic difference between single mirror concentrator and heliostat system is that heliostat system does not cover the land area by mirror, Each mirror acts as a parabolloid.

However, the heliostat mirrors require non-linear drive rate in two axes in areas to keep the reflected radiation on the fixed absorber. This system has highest efficiency of utilisation of reflected area and radiation losses are also less due to small area of absorber at the focus.

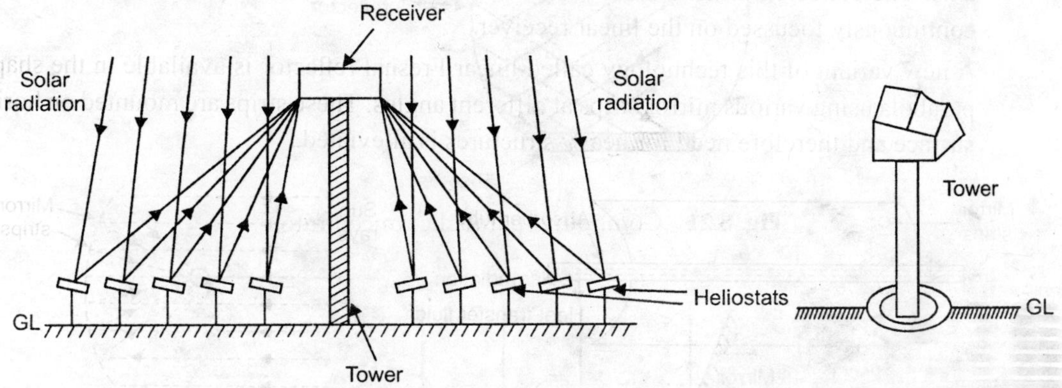

Fig. 8.19 Central receiver with heliostat reflectors

The working fluid is pumped from storage system upto the receiver where it is heated. A properly size receiver can generate a temperature of upto 1500° C.

In a system, several hundreds of heliostats are used which contribute to more than 50% of the total cost of the system.

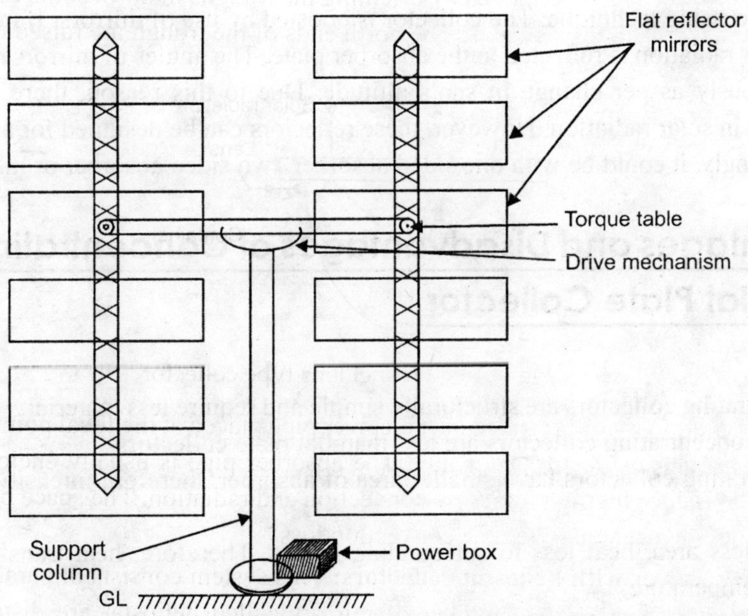

Fig. 8.20 Rear side of a heliostat

(v) Compound parabolic concentrator: It consists of two facing parabolic mirrors with a trough type arrangement. It is a non-focussing type directing radiations from many directions towards bottom of trough. This enables collection of direct and diffuse radiation. It provides moderately good concentration of solar radiation with sun tracking.

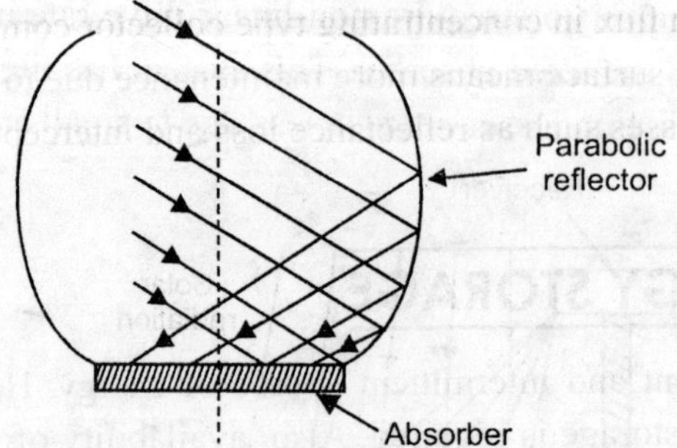

Fig. 8.21 Compound parabolic concentrator

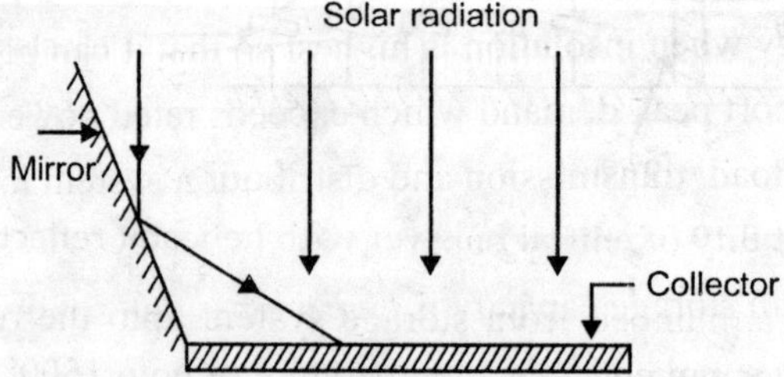

Fig. 8.22 Flat plate collector with plane reflector

(*vi*) **Flate plate collector with plane reflector:** It is simplest type of concentrating collector without using focussing technique. The collector is boosted by use of mirrors. If mirrors are properly set, solar radiation is reflected to the absorber plate. The angles of mirrors need to be adjusted continuously as per change in sun's altitude. Due to this reason, there is relatively small increase in solar radiation. However, these reflectors can be designed for any absorber shape. Accordingly, it could be with one sided absorber, two sided absorber or tubular absorber.

8.6.3 Advantages and Disadvantages of Concentrating Collector over Flat Plate Collector

Advantages—

(*i*) Concentrating collectors are structurally simple and require less material. Hence, cost per unit area of concentrating collectors are less than flat plate collectors.

(*ii*) Concentrating collectors have smaller area of absorber, therefore intensity of solar radiation is more.

(*iii*) Due to less area, heat loss to surrounding is less. Therefore, heat transfer fluid can attain higher temperature.

(*iv*) Due to small area of absorber, selective surface treatment required is less.

(*v*) Due to higher temperature attainable, heat energy storage costs are less.

(*vi*) Almost no antifreeze is required to protect the absorber in concentrating type.

Disadvantages—

(*i*) Concentrating collectors can not focus diffuse radiation Hence, it is lost.

(*ii*) Additional cost and maintenance of tracking system for concentrating collectors.

(*iii*) there is non uniform flux in concentrating type collector compared to flat plate collector.
(*iv*) additional reflecting surface means more maintenance due to dust, dirt etc.
(*v*) additional optical losses such as reflectance loss and intercept loss.
(*vi*) high initial cost.

8.7 THERMAL ENERGY STORAGE

Solar energy is time dependent and intermittent source of energy. Hence, to maintain continuity of supply, some form of energy storage is required. Also, availability of solar energy does not co-incide with demand for energy. There is also problem of clouds. Hence, storage of solar energy is required for following reasons—

(*i*) capture solar energy when insolation is highest so that it can be used later.
(*ii*) allows to supply short peak demand which exceeds rated power capacity of the plant.
(*iii*) due to nearness to load, transmission and distribution system loses are eliminated.
(*iv*) this improves reliability of energy supply.

The determination of optimum storage capacity is dependent upon following factors—

(*i*) nature of load to be supplied.
(*ii*) expected time dependence of solar radiation availability.
(*iii*) degree of reliability desired.
(*iv*) cost per unit of stored energy.
(*v*) capital cost of storage system.
(*vi*) environmental and safety issues.

8.7.1 Solar Energy Storage Systems

Various types of energy storage systems is given figure 8.23

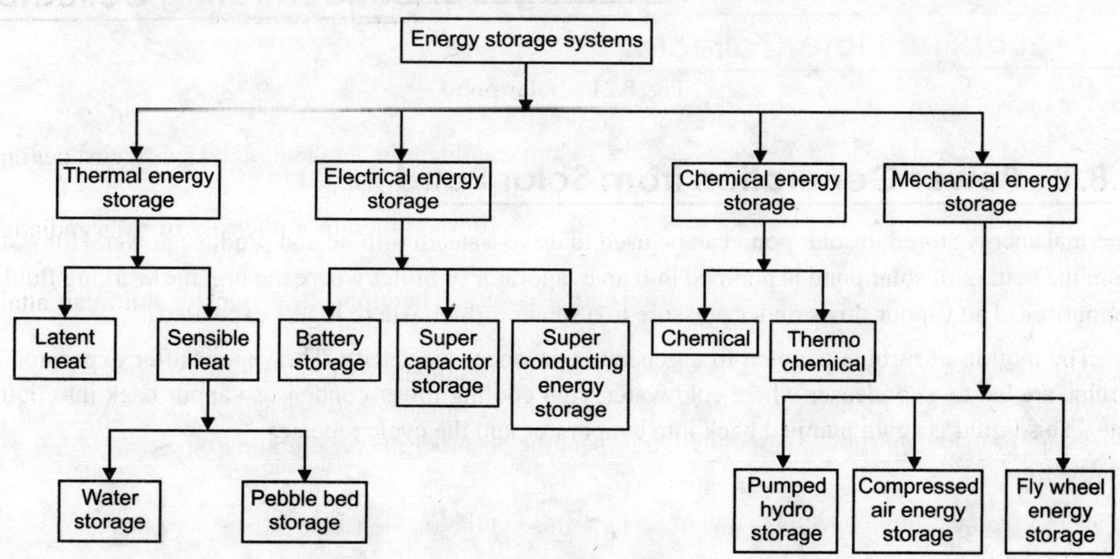

Fig. 8.23 Types of energy storage systems

8.8 SOLAR POND

Solar pond is a large body of still water used for absorption and storage of solar radiant energy. It provides effective means of large thermal storage. It is more economical than flat plate collector due to built in thermal storage, Although, this system does not concentrate solar radiation and hence, does not achieve high temperature. It can be used to produce electricity, provide heat for industrial process heating and desalination.

Solar pond consists of radiation absorbing black plastic bottom with a bed of insulating material underneath to minimize heat loss to ground. A curved cover made of transparent fibre glass allows transmittance of solar radiation and minimize radiation and convection losses due to air movement. Due to absorption of solar radiation, water becomes hot enough for suitable uses. There is variation of temperature at different layers of water and heat loss is more during night time. To minimize heat loss due to convection current setup in the water due to temperature difference, salt is used. With the usage of salt, bottom layer of water is more dense than top layer and hence, there is no convection current and consequent heat loss.

The temperature of pond reaches 60 to 100° C and is useful for industrial process heating and space heating. The addition of salt to pond water results information of three distinct zones viz upper convective zone, middle non-convective zone and lower convective zone. Salts, such as sodium chloride, magnesium chloride or sodium nitrate are dissolved. The concentration of dissolved salt is 20 to 30% at the bottom and zero at the top.

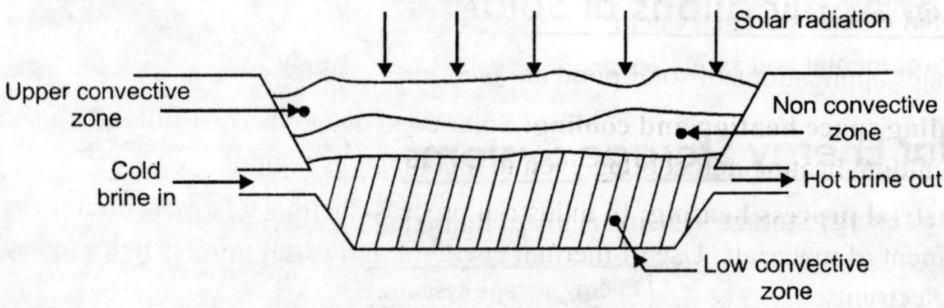

Fig. 8.24 Solar pond

8.8.1 Power Generation from Solar Pond

Thermal energy stored in solar pond can be used to drive a steam turbine and produce power. Hot water from the bottom of solar pond is pumped into an evaporator or boiler where the organic working fluid is vapourised. The vapour flows under pressure to a steam turbine where it gets expanded.

The motion of turbine coupled to a generator produces electricity. The vapour after expansion in turbine are led to a condenser where cold water from cooling tower condenses vapour back into liquid state. This liquid is again pumped back into evaporator and the cycle repeates.

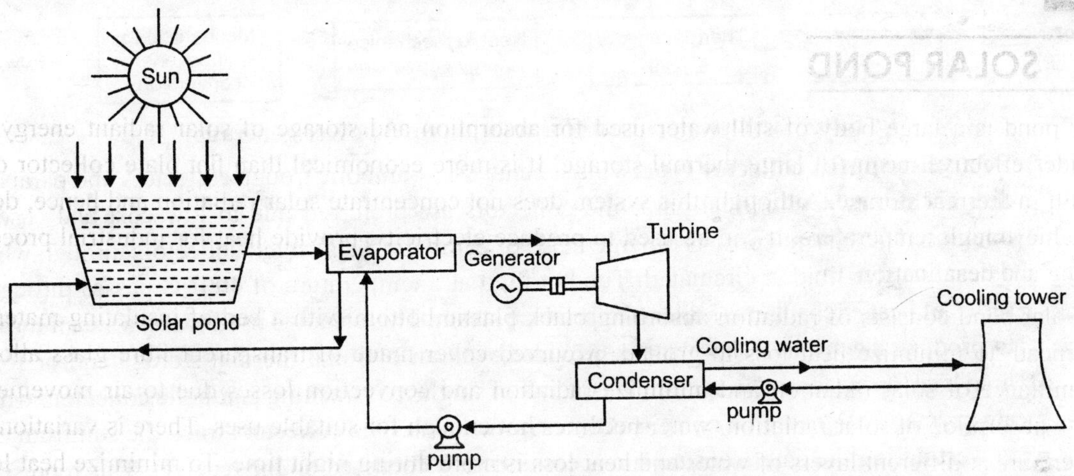

Fig. 8.25 Solar pond based power generation

Water can not be used as working liquid because maximum temperature of solar pond is 90 to 100°C. While working fluid can be heated from 85–95°C. The expansion of working fluid produces superheating rather than condensation. Moreover, due to high molecular weight of working fluid, friction losses are minimum.

Such plants are working in Israel on the shore of dead sea producing 5MW of power.

8.8.2 Other Applications of Solar Pond

Some of the major applications of solar pond are mentioned below—

(*i*) **Building space heating and cooling:** Solar pond due to thermal storage capacity can be used for building heating and cooling even in mountainous regions.

(*ii*) **Industrial process heating:** In industrial process, thermal energy is used for preparation and treatment of materials. Use of thermal energy in industrial process helps to save oil, coal,gas and electricity.

(*iii*) **Agricultural purpose:** Thermal energy is used in agriculture for the purpose of crop drying.

(*iv*) **Desalination:** Low cost thermal energy can be used to produce drinking water. It can also be used to purify sea water for irrigation purpose.

(*v*) **Biomass conversion:** Thermal energy can be used for conversion of biomass into alcohol or methane.

8.9 SOLAR THERMAL POWER GENERATION

Solar thermal power generation is one of the major applications of solar energy through thermal route. Solar thermal technologies use solar radiation to produce high temperature by focussing solar radiation from a larger area onto a smaller area and then generating electricity using a prime mover.

Solar thermal power projects can provide reliable electricity that can be fed to grid. A number of technology options are available to produce electricity using heat from solar radiation.

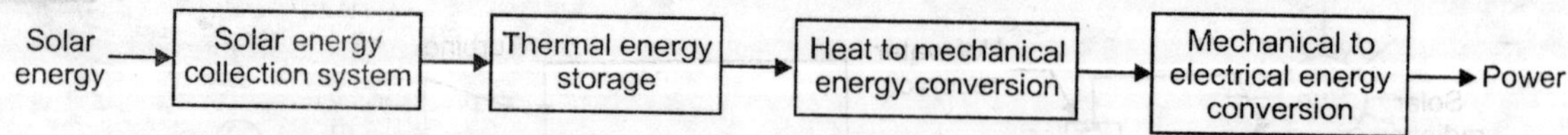

Fig. 8.26 General flow chart for solar thermal power generation

(*i*) **Solar distributed collector type:** This scheme uses parabolic trough collectors and parabolic dish collectors. Cylindrical parabolic collectors are preferred due to low cost and ease of tracking. The system consists of large fields of parabolic dish/trough collectors through which a heat transfer fluid is circulated. The hot fluid at a temperature of 400° C passes through a series of heat exchangers (boilers) to produce steam. This steam is used to run a steam turbine to produce electricity. The plant is provided with an optional thermal storage and or fossil fired back up system. The solar field consists of single axis tracking parabolic collectors which are normally aligned on a north -south horizontal axis. The collectors track the sun from east to west during the day to ensure sun is continuously focussed on the receiver. This represents most successfully tried technology world over.

A new variant of this technology called linear Fresnel reflector is also available where shape of parabola is achieved by organising various mirror strips at different angles. These strips are mounted on horizontal surface and therefore, the need for heavy structure is eliminated.

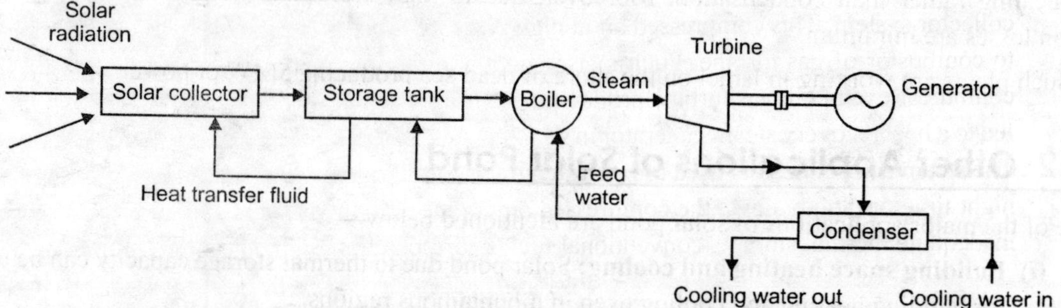

Fig. 8.27 Solar distributed collector type thermal power plant

(*ii*) **Solar central receiver type:** A solar tower is used to generate electricity from solar radiations by focussing concentrated solar energy on a tower in which heat transfer fluid flows. The solar tower configuration consists of field of heliostats or sun tracking mirrors which reflect solar energy to a tower mounted receiver. The concentrated heat energy absorbed by receiver is transferred to a circulating fluid that can be stored to produce power. These systems can operate at temperatures more than 500° C. Few plants have been built using molten salt (a mixture of 60% sodium nitrate and 40% potassium nitrate) and steam as the heat transfer fluid.

(*iii*) **Binary cycle solar thermal power plant:** A binary cycle plant has two cycles–water cycle and gas cycle. Solar thermal collectors concentrate the solar energy which is transferred to heat transfer fluid (water).The heat carried by water is transferred to ammonia (working fluid) through a heat exchanger. The hot ammonia vapour drive a gas turbine. The expanded ammonia vapour over gas turbine are condensed in a condenser. This liquid ammonia is pumped through heat exchanger in a closed cycle. The plant operates at low and medium temperature of heat transfer fluid (70 – 150° C).

Binary plant uses fixed type distributed solar thermal collectors or parabolic trough collectors.

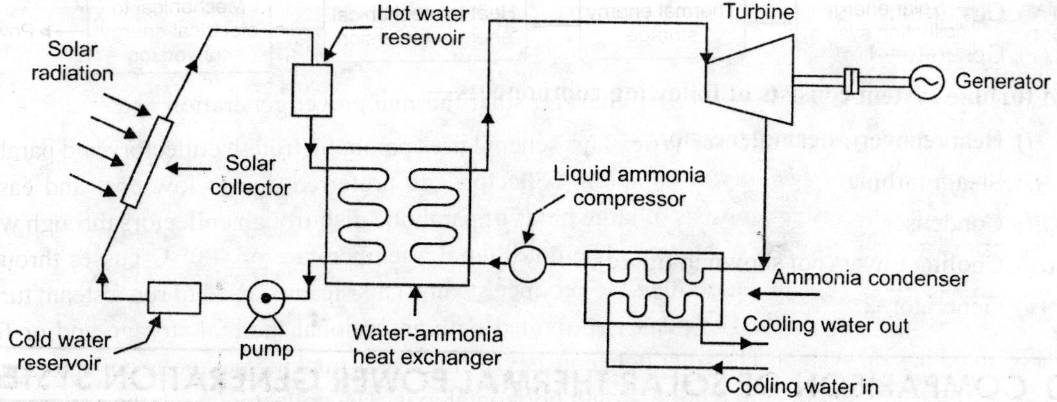

Fig. 8.28 Binary cycle solar thermal power plant

(*iv*) **Combined cycle solar thermal power plant:** A combined cycle power plant uses a gas turbine (Brayton cycle) and steam turbine (Rankine cycle). Solar central receiver thermal energy or solar distributed receiver thermal energy system provide heat input to the plant.

The atmospheric air is compressed by compressor of gas turbine into solar thermal heat collector system. This compressed air at high pressure is heated to about 815° C and is supplied to combustor of gas turbine. Fuel is also supplied to combustor of gas turbine. Hot gas from combustor expand in gas turbine producing electricity. Gases after expansion in gas turbine are fed to a heat recovery steam generator in which steam is produced from heat of the exhaust gases. The steam so produced is used to run a steam turbine which inturn produces electricity. During night time or cloudy days, the compressed air is heated in the thermal storage tank. In case of inadequate thermal storage, conventional fuel fired furnace is used to heat the compressed air.

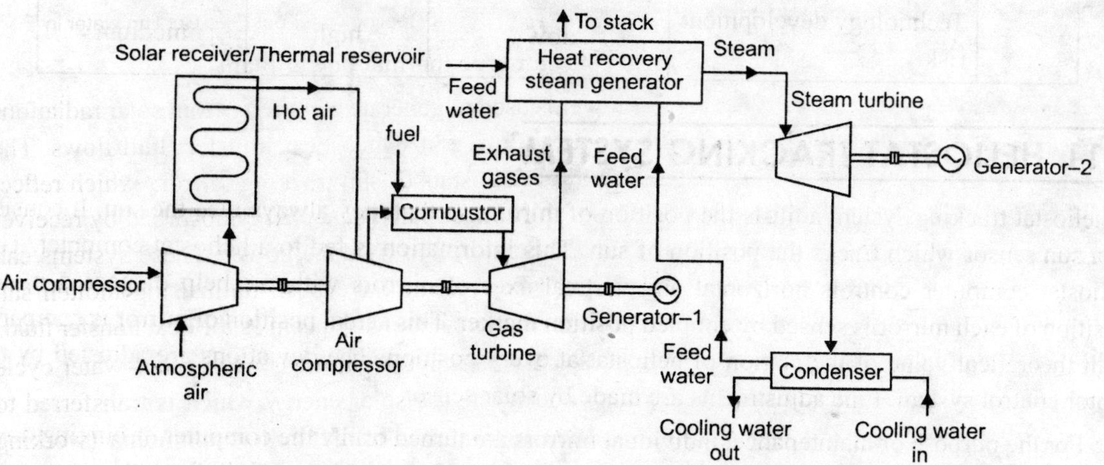

Fig. 8.29 Combined cycle solar thermal power plant

Gas turbine system consists of following components—

(*i*) Air compressor.

(*ii*) Solar receiver /Thermal reservoir.

(*iii*) Combustor.

(*iv*) Gas turbine.

(*v*) Generator–1.

Steam turbine system consists of following components—

(*i*) Heat recovery steam generator.

(*ii*) Steam turbine.

(*iii*) Condenser.

(*iv*) Cooling tower (not shown in figure).

(*v*) Generator–2.

8.10 COMPARISON OF SOLAR THERMAL POWER GENERATION SYSTEMS

Table 8.1: Comparison of various types of solar thermal power generation systems

Sr. No.	*Parameter*	*Parabolic trough*	*Dish trough*	*Power tower*
1.	Power plant capacity	30 to 300 MW	5 to 25 kW	10 to 200 MW
2.	Operating temperature	390° C	750° C	560° C
3.	Annual capacity factor	23 to 50 %	25 %	20 to 77 %
4.	Peak efficiency	20 %	29 %	23 %
5.	Net efficiency	11 to 16 %	12 to 25 %	7 to 20 %
6.	Storage	limited	battery	yes
7.	Technology development risk	low	high	medium

8.11 HELIOSTAT TRACKING SYSTEM

A heliostat tracking system adjusts the position of mirrors so that they always face the sun. It consists of a sun sensor which tracks the position of sun. This information is fed to a heliostat computer. This heliostat computer controls horizontal and vertical axes of mirrors with the help of geared motor. Position of each mirror is sensed by coupled position marker. This actual position of mirror is compared with theoretical value of inclination of heliostat at every position. The deviations are adjusted by the motor control system. Fine adjustments are made by solar sensor.

For the purpose of maintenance, individual mirrors are turned off by the computer or hinging down of mirror during bad weather is done by computer. In case of obstruction of fluid flow, the mirrors are turned away from the position. The degree of accuracy of tracking is $\pm$ 0.002°.

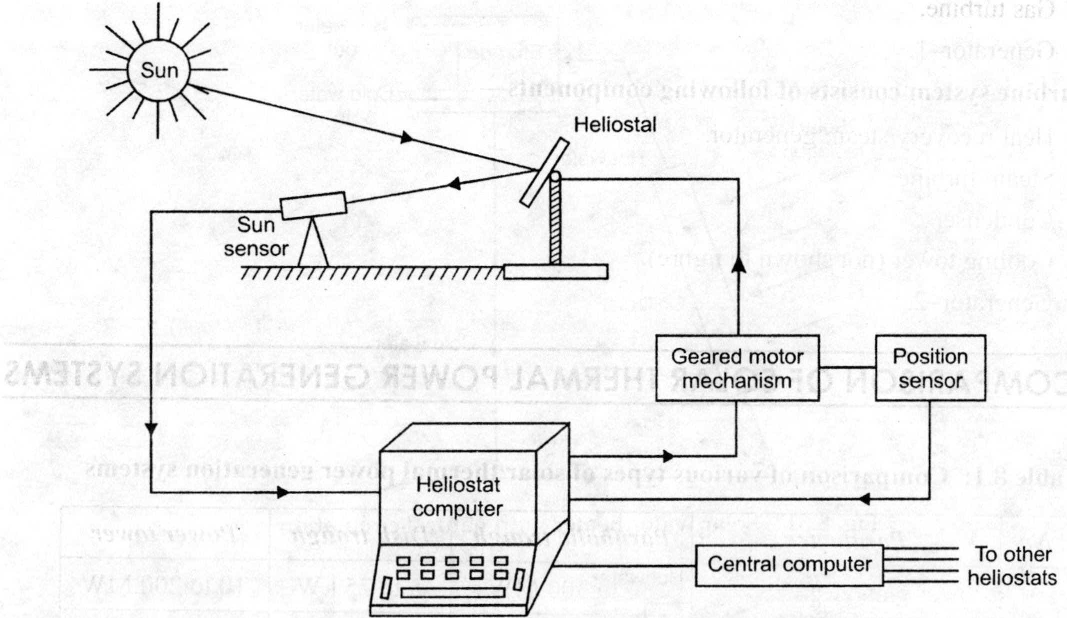

Fig. 8.30 Heliostat tracking system

8.12 APPLICATIONS OF SOLAR THERMAL ENERGY

(*i*) **Low temperature applications:** Applications which require operating temperature upto 80°C are classified as low temperature application. Some of the applications are disussed below—

(*a*) **Solar water heating system:** A solar water heating system is a device that uses solar energy for domestic, commercial and industrial purposes. Heating of water is the most common application of solar energy in the world. A typical domestic solar water heater of 100 litres per day capacity can save upto 1500 units of electrical energy year.

The water heating system consists of solar collectors, a hot water storage tank, arrangement of cold water supply and connecting pipes etc. The solar collector may be either flat plate type or evacuated glass tube type. For solar water heating systems of large capacity, an electric pump and a controller is also used. Solar collectors are installed facing due south in inclined position at a slope decided by the latitude of the place and seasonal load profile of hot water requirement. These system may be installed on roof top, on balcony or on ground. A continuous supply of cold water is provided from overhead tank. In solar water heating systems without pump, hot water storage tank is placed higher than top of solar collector.

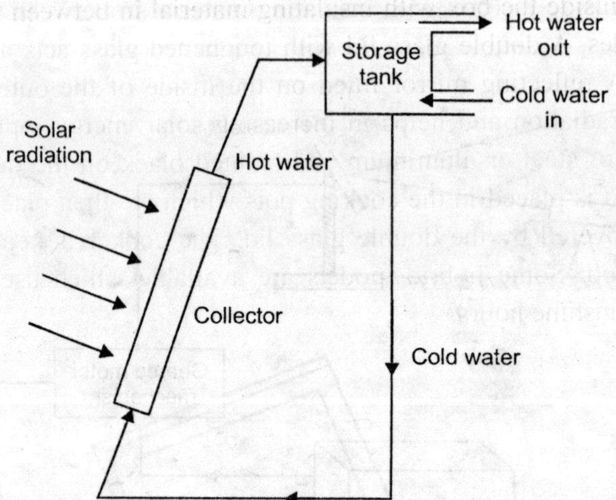

Fig. 8.31 Solar water heater with natural circulation

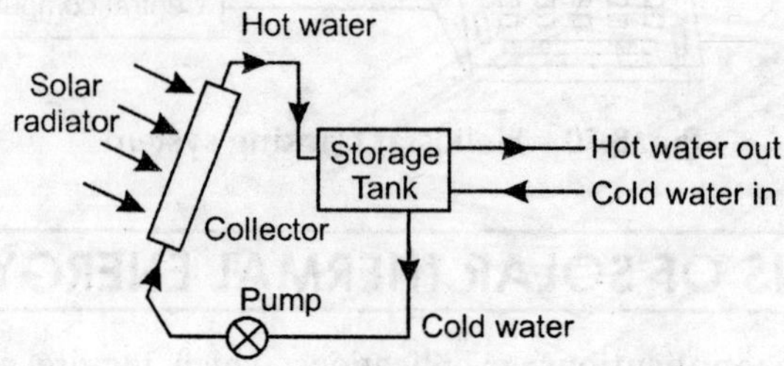

Fig. 8.32 Solar water heater with forced circulation

Another type of solar collector called evacuated tube collectors are increasingly being used instead of flat plate collectors. These are of two types viz. (*i*) all glass type and (*ii*) single glass envelope metal fin-in vacuum type. In this configuration, a special coating to absorb maximum solar radiation is applied on the outer surface of a glass tube which is inserted inside another tube of larger diameter. The open ends of the two tubes are sealed together and evacuation is done from other end. The water is circulated for heating inside the double glass tube assembly. The metal fin-in tube configuration may contain a heat pipe system connected to the absorber placed inside a glass tube. Air is removed from the tube to create the vacuum. It provides thermal energy at higher temperature of 80° C and is costlier than all glass evacuated tube construction.

The hot water so obtained can be used for various application at home, such as bathing, cleaning and washing. It can also be used in commercial purposes, such as hotels, dry cleaning etc. and for industrial process applications.

(*b*) Solar cooking: A large variety of solar cookers are available to suit different requirements. There are two types of solar cookers viz.—

(*i*) box type and (*ii*) solar dish type.

(*i*) Box type solar cooker: It consists of an outer box (in size of 600 mm × 600 mm) made of either fibre glass or aluminium sheet, a blackened aluminium tray, a double glass lid, a reflector, insulation and cooking pots. The blackened aluminium tray is fixed inside the box with insulating material in between to prevent heat loss from all sides. A double glass lid with toughened glass acts as a cover of the cooking tray. A reflecting mirror fitted on the inside of the outer box cover, reflects the solar radiation and helps in increasing solar energy input. The cooking pots are made of steel or aluminium and painted black on the outer side. The food to be cooked is placed in the cooking pots which are then placed in the aluminium tray and covered by the double glass lid. The cooker is kept facing the sun to cook the food. Some hybrid models are available which use electrical heater during non-sunshine hours.

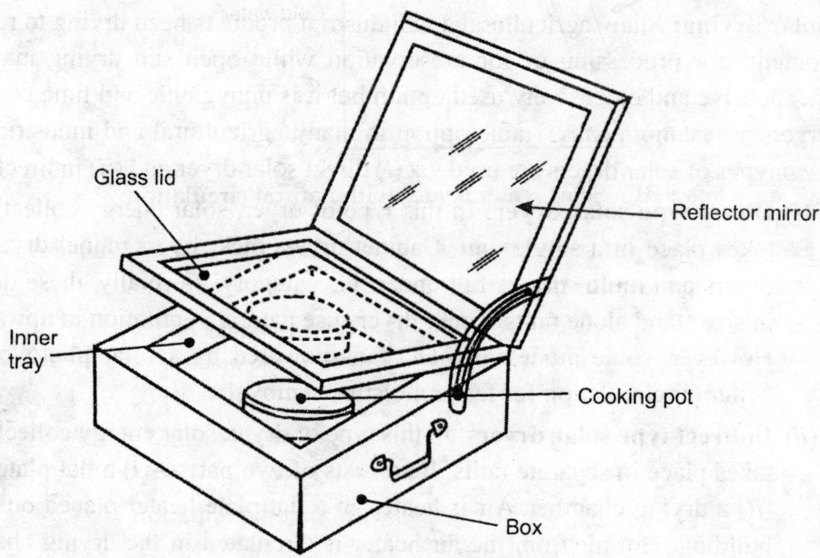

Fig. 8.33 Box type solar cooker

(*ii*) **Dish type solar cooker:** A dish solar cooker uses a parabolic dish to concentrate incident solar radiation. It has an aperture diameter of 1.4 m and a focal length of about 0.28 m. Other sizes and shapes are also available. Anodised aluminium sheet is used as a reflecting material which has a reflectivity of over 80 %. 350 – 400°C temperature is reached at the bottom of vessel which is sufficient for roasting, frying and the boiling. This cooker can meet the need of about of 10 – 15 people.

(*iii*) **Indoor cooking:** This type of system allows cooking inside the kitchen. It uses a large dish having 7 to 12 m^2 of aperture area. The dish is placed outside the kitchen so that it reflects solar rays into the kitchen through an opening in its north wall. A secondary reflector further concentrates the rays onto the bottom of cooking vessel. A mechanical clock work mechanism is provided for automatic tracking of sun. On a clear sunny day, a higher temperature of upto 400° C can be attained.

This system can be used for cooking food for 40 – 50 persons. Hence, it can be used in schools, institutional kitchens, canteens, religious ashrams, hotels, hospitals, armed forces etc.

(*iv*) **Solar steam cooking:** It is possible to cook large quantities of food using steam generated by solar heat. A solar steam generating system comprises automatically tracked solar concentrator, steam heater assemblies with receivers, steam pipelines, feed water pipings, steel structures, pressure gauges, temperature indicators, steam separators, steam traps etc. The system is generally hooked up with a conventional steam generating system already available with the user to make it reliable under all climatic conditions. A dish of 16m^2 area is most commorly employed.

These systems can be designed for large community kitchens for example in religious places, hotels, armed forces training centres etc.

(*c*) **Solar drying:** Many agricultural and industrial products need drying to reduce moisture contents for processing or for preservation while open sun drying may be the most inexpensive and extensively used option but it is unhygienic and time consuming. Solar dryers are economically viable option in many agricultural and industrial applications. Two types of solar dryers are used viz (*i*) direct solar dryer and (*ii*) indirect of solar dryer.

(*i*) **Direct type solar dryer:** In this type of dryer, solar energy collection and drying takes place in a single unit. Cabinet dryers,rack dryers,tunnel dryer, green house dryers and multi- dryers fall under this category. Normally, these dryers are small in size stand alone units. These dryers use natural ventilation in upward draft mode. However, some models use DC fans powered by a solar photovoltaic panel for better air circulation for faster moisture removal.

(*ii*) **Indirect type solar dryers**: In this type of dryer, solar energy collection and drying takes place in separate units. It consists of two parts—(*i*) a flat plate air heater and (*ii*) a drying chamber. Air is heated in a flat plate heater placed on the roof of the building. Hot air from the air heater is circulated in the drying chamber with the help of a blower. These dryers can be designed in different sizes with various configurations, depending upon the temperature of hot air, air flow rate, type of products to be dried etc.

Potential applications in industries include tea leaves, coffee beans, fruits, spices, cereals, mushrooms, vegetables, fish, sea food etc.

The temperature of 50–80° C can be achieved. Solar concentrating systems are also used to provide hot air at temperatures higher than 80° C.

(*iii*) **Mixed mode dryers:** These are solar dryers in which solar energy collection takes place in the drying unit as well as in the heating unit. The drying, however, takes place only in the drying unit. In large industrial systems, the solar heated air is combined with air heated by conventional energy. This increases system reliability and reduces conventional energy consumption.

(*d*) **Desalination:** Desalination is a water purification process which converts sea water or brackish water into pure form. For this purpose a conventional basin type solar stills are used where solar energy is absorbed and pure water is obtained through evaporation and condensation process in an enclosure containing raw water. These units produce 2–3 litres of water per square meter of solar collector area. This can be suitable for laboratories, battery topping up etc.

(*e*) **Industrial process heat applications:** According to an estimate, about 50% of energy needed in industry for production process is below 250° C. A large demand exists in paper, food, textile and chemical industries. Besides heating, solar cooling system for space and cold storage is another key area of industrial process requirements.

The thermal efficiency of flat plate collector based solar systems become quite low at temperature greater than 80° C. Concentrating solar collectors are employed to obtain higher temperatures. Presently, solar dish concentrators and parabolic trough concentrators are used. Typically, a 100 square meter concentrator saves about 8–10 tons of oil annually.

(*f*) **Solar air conditioning and refrigeration system:** In tropical countries, cooling is a necessity both for storing perishable products and for thermal comfort inside the building. Vapour absorption refrigeration systems are driven by thermal energy which can use solar energy. One of the important considerations in favour of these systems is that the need of refrigeration/cooling is maximum when the sun shines the most. The vapour absorption systems are based on water-lithium bromide and ammonia-water as working fluid. Water-lithium bromide system operates at temperatures compatible with selectively coated solar flat plate collectors having temperature of around 80° C. While ammonia-water system needs more than 150°C for economic operation.

(*g*) **Swimming pool heating:** A swimming pool heating requires low temperature of about 28°C. The low temperature level required can use cheap and simple thermal collectors. Swimming pool acts as heat energy storage.

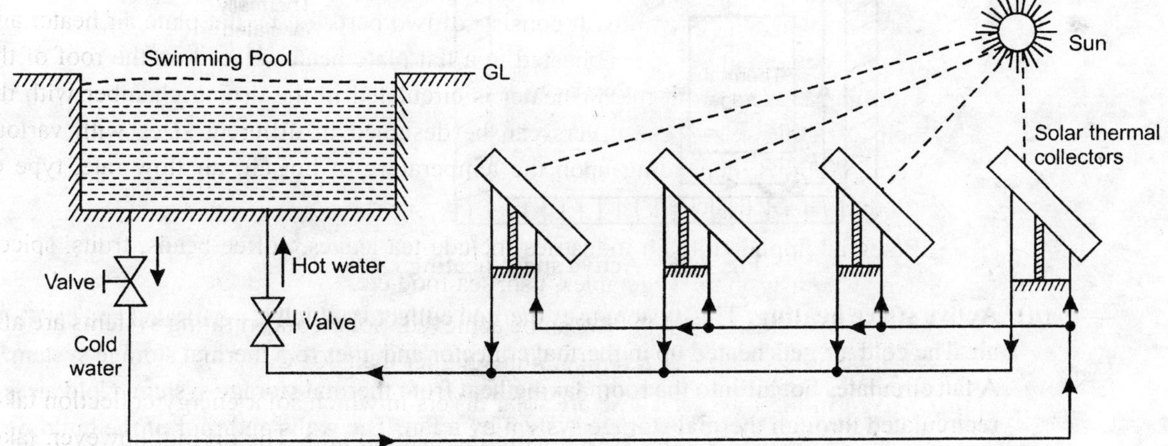

Fig. 8.34 Swimming pool heating using solar energy

(*h*) **Space heating:** Solar energy can be used to heat buildings in colder countries. This reduces heating load on air conditioning system. There are two types of space heating viz. (*i*) passive space heating and (*ii*) active space heating.

(*i*) **Passive space heating:** This method uses direct sunrays into living space through glass window and walls. The south facing wall of the building is painted black to absorb solar energy. Sunrays also enter through glass windows. A thermal storage system can be used to heat up the space.

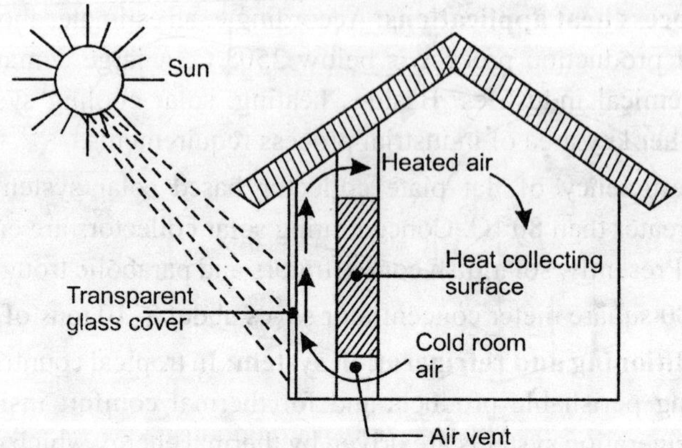

Fig. 8.35 Passive space heating

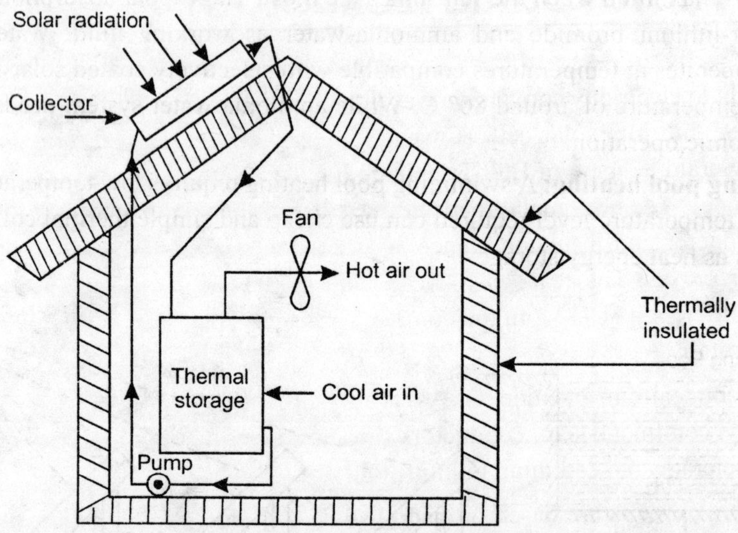

Fig. 8.36 Active space heating

(*ii*) **Active space heating:** This system uses thermal collector which is perforated and carries air. The cold air gets heated up in thermal collector and goes to a thermal storage system. A fan circulates hot air into the room taking heat from thermal storage system. Cold air is recirculated through thermal storage system by a fan. The walls and roof of the building are thermally insulated to prevent heat loss from the room. Due to presence of thermal storage, the system can be used even when sun is not shining.

(*i*) **Solar green house:** Green houses are used to maintain required environmental conditions to improve yield of crops, fish aquaculture etc. It is a covered structure of transparent plastic film or glass panes which allow short wavelength radiation and reflects infrared radiation producing a green house effect (similar to performed by earth's atmosphere).

An air vent at the top of roof allows natural circulation of air. Some part of solar radiation incident on the top of green house are transmitted to inside while a fraction of it are reflected back. The movement of air inside green house is due to convection and radiation which increase the temperature of space inside.

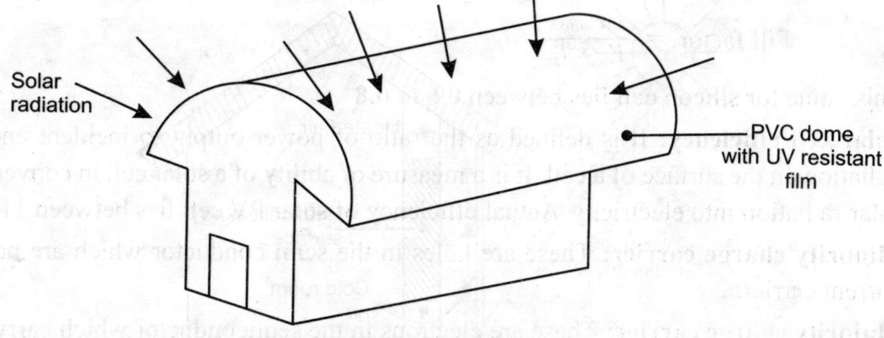

Fig. 8.37 Solar greenhouse

8.13 SOLAR PHOTOVOLTAIC TECHNOLOGY

Solar photovoltaic cells are used to convert solar radiation directly into electricity. This physical phenomenon of light to electricity conversion was first observed by Edmund Becquerel in 1839. In 1883, Fxitz fabricated first thin film solar cell. However, breakthrough came in 1954 when Darryl Chapin, Calvin Fuller and Gerald Pearson of Bell Telephone Laboratories in New Jersey, USA fabricated a PV cell with 6% efficiency. The non- metallic materials such as silicon and germanium had characteristics lying between conductor and insulator. Hence, a term semiconductor was coined. Efficiency of best single junction silicon cell has reached 24% in laboratory. The best silicon PV module available commercially has efficiency of 17%. In the coming years, efficiency of cells is going to increase while the price is going to fall.

Apart from silicon, gallium arsenide (Ga As) is also suitable material for construction of PV cells. In thin film technology, compound semi conductors such as copper indium diselenide (Cu In Se_2), copper indium-gallium-diselenide and cadmium tellulide (Cd Te) are also used.

Third generation PV cells are based on nano technology (first generation are crystalline PV cells and second generation are thin film PV cells). The technology aims to manipulate nano particles to form nano crystals consisting of very small collection of atoms called quantum dots.

8.13.1 Terms Associated with Photovoltaic Technology

(i) **Doping:** Addition of either trivalent or pentavalent impurity in a PV cell.

(ii) **PV modules:** Number of interconnected PV cells constitute a PV module.

(iii) **PV array:** Number of interconnected PV modules constitute a PV array.

(iv) **Peak watt:** It is the amount of power output obtained from a PV cell under standard test conditions (STC). Accordingly, power output from a solar cell is written as Wp.

(v) **Open circuit voltage:** It is the voltage of a PV cell when no load is connected across it.

(vi) **Short circuit current:** It is the maximum current at short circuit.

(vii) **Fill factor:** It is defined as the maximum power delivered by a cell to power obtained with product of open circuit voltage and short circuit current.

$$\text{Fill factor} = \frac{P_{mpp}}{V_{oc} \times I_{sc}} \qquad \text{...(8.4)}$$

This value for silicon cell lies between 0.6 to 0.8

(*viii*) **Solar cell efficiency:** It is defined as the ratio of power output to incident energy of solar radiation on the surface of a cell. It is a measure of ability of a solar cell in converting incident solar radiation into electricity. Actual efficiency of solar PV cell lies between 11–16%.

(*ix*) **Minority charge carrier:** These are holes in the semi conductor which are non- dominant current carrier.

(*x*) **Majority charge carrier:** These are electrons in the semiconductor which carry the current.

(xi) **Air mass:** It is defined as the ratio of the path length of the sun's rays to the path length when the sun is at the zenith.

8.14 PHOTOELECTRIC EFFECT

Solar cells convert sun light into electricity due to photoelectric effect. Sunlight is composed of tiny light particle called photon. These photons contain different level of energy corresponding to specific wavelength of solar spectrum. When a photon strikes a photovoltaic cell, the absorbed photons provide thermal energy to electrons to produce electricity. With absorption of sufficient solar energy, electrons break loose from the atoms and produce a flow of electrons or electric current.

According to Max Plank, photons possess energy proportional to the frequency of radiation.

$$\therefore \quad E = h\upsilon = \frac{hc}{\upsilon} \qquad \text{...(8.5)}$$

Where, h = Plank's constant

c = speed of light

υ = frequency of radiation

Electrons in a bond remain in valence band which is at lower energy level. Once some energy is absorbed by electrons, they move to higher energy state called conduction band. The difference of energy level between valence and conduction band is known as band gap energy.

Incident light on a photovoltaic cell generates electrons. If the incident light possess energy more than band gap energy (1.12ev for silicon), electrons from valence band move to conduction band and conduct electricity. Energy more than this results in heat. The wavelength of solar energy is from 0.3 μm to 3 μm. Wavelength more than 1.15 μm is not useful due to energy content less than band gap energy.

8.15 TYPES OF PV CELLS

Solar cells are composed of various semiconducting materials [semiconducting materials become electrically conductive when supplied with light or heat and remain insulator at low temperature. 95% of all solar cells produced worldwide are made of silicon, the second most abundant material on earth's crust. A semiconducting material is produced by doping a trivalent impurity (p-type semiconductor) or a pentavalent impurity (n-type semiconductor)]. A junction forms p and n type material called p-n junction constitutes a solar cell. Typical output of single PV cell when exposed to full sun is 0.45 V DC, 0.75 A DC and 0.33 W. Several solar cells need to be connected in series called strings and several such strings are connected in parallel called module. When several modules are connected in series, parallel and series parallel, an array is formed.

There are three types of PV cells based on crystalline structure viz mono crystalline silicon cell, poly-crystalline silicon cell and amorphous or thin layer cell.

(*i*) **Mono crystalline silicon cell:** To produce mono-crystalline silicon cell, absolutely pure semiconducting material is required. Silicon ingots are made by process of crystal growth or by casting in specially designed furnaces. The ingots are then sliced into thin wafers. These wafers are then processed to fabricate solar cells. A typical single crystal wafer is of 125×125 mm size.

(*ii*) **Poly crystalline silicon cell:** Production of poly-crystalline cell is most cost effective. It is produced by pouring liquid silicon into blocks that are subsequently sawed into plates. During solidification of material, crystal structure of varying sizes are formed. Poly crystalline cell is less efficient than mono-crystalline cell. However, manufacturing process of poly crystalline cell is less complex, less costly and has higher production speed.

(*iii*) **Amorphous or thin film silicon:** It is a non- crystalline silicon. Pure silicon without crystals is used. The layer thickness is less than 1 μm (thickness of human hair is 50–100 μm). These cells are least efficient but are low cost and easy to manufacture. These are used primarily in low power equipments, such as pocket calculator, watches etc. Materials are gallium arsenide, copper indium diselenide, cadmium telluride etc.

Fabrication process of PV cells is explained in following flow chart. (Fig. 8.38 (*a*))

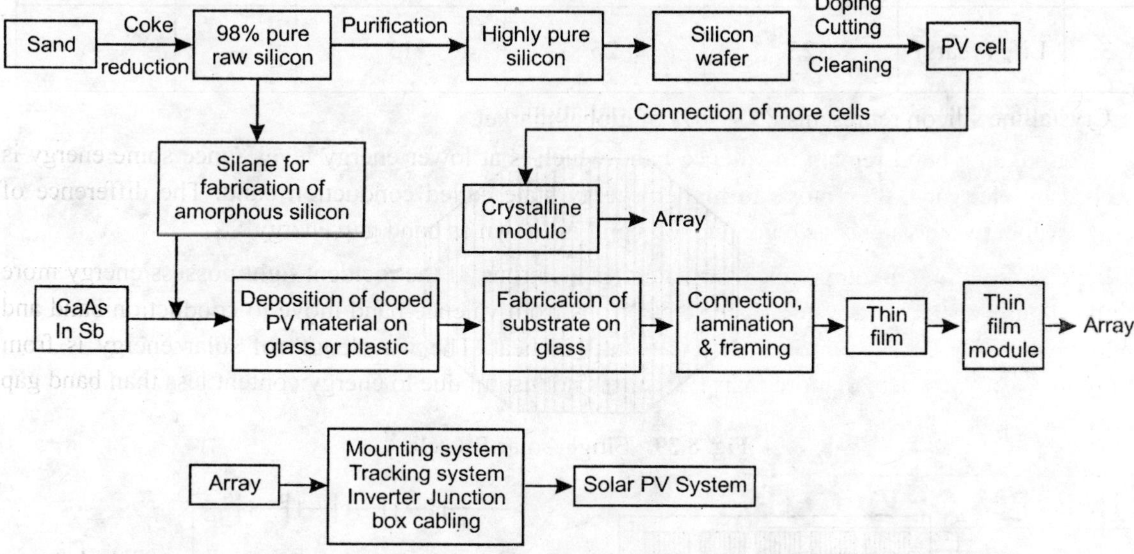

Fig 8.38 (*a*) Flow chart of crystalline and thin film solar cell fabrication process

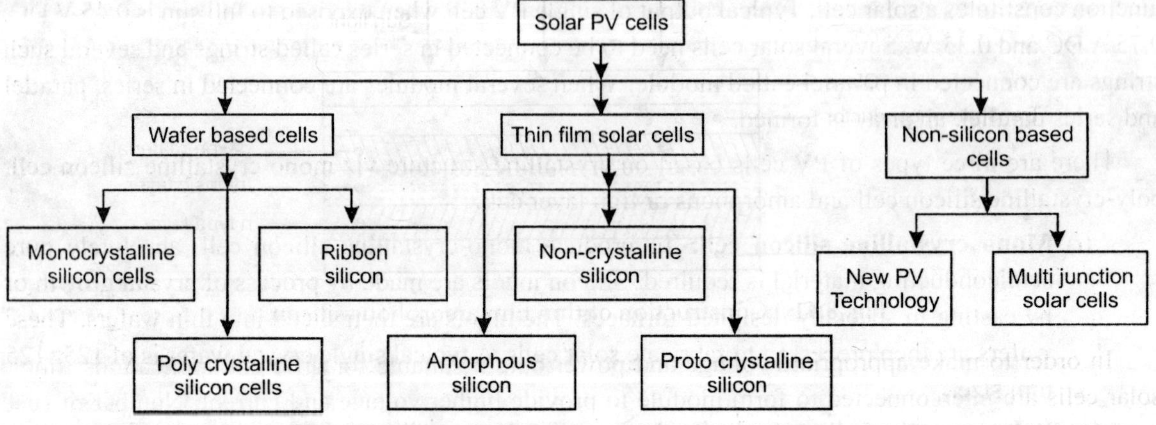

Fig 8.38 (*b*) Different types of solar cell technologies

Comparison of solar cells is given in table 8.2.

Table 8.2 Comparison of solar cells

Sr. No.	*Parameter*	*Si- mono crystalline*	*Si- Polycrystalline*	*Thin film*		
				Si- amorphous	*CdTe*	*CIS/CIGS*
1.	Efficiency	14 – 17%	13 – 15%	7 – 9%	9 – 11%	10 – 12%
2.	Peak Power (W/m^2)	160	140	120		
3.	Life (years)	25	25	15	–	–

Crystalline silicon represents 85 – 90% of global market.

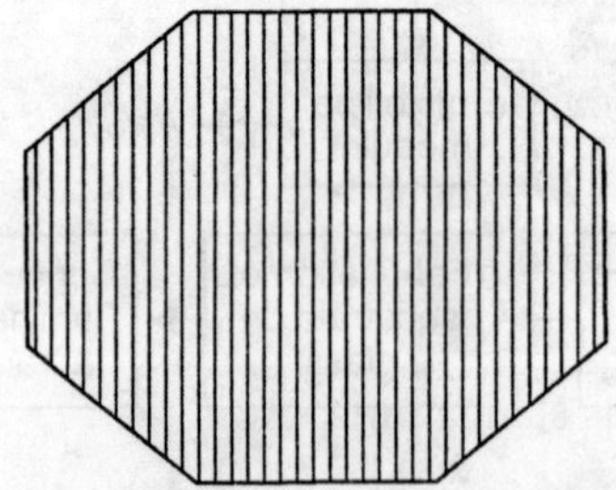

Fig. 8.39 Single solar PV cell

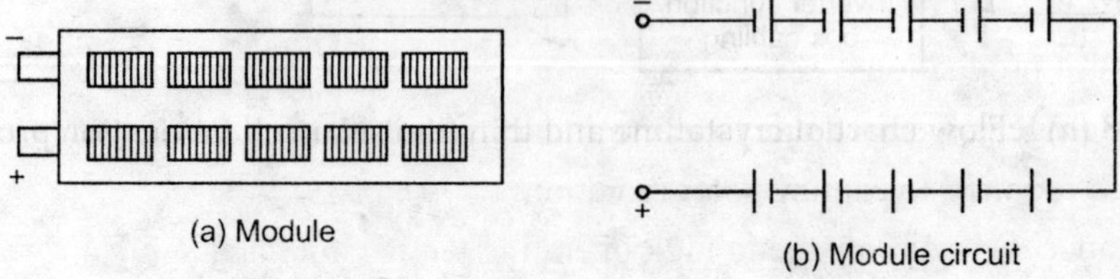

Fig. 8.40 Solar module

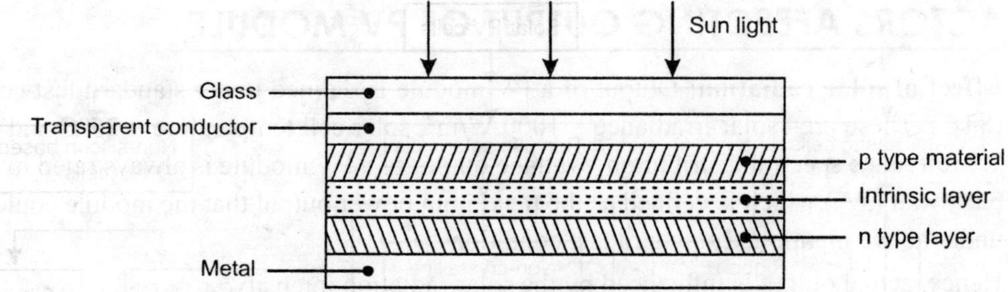

Fig. 8.41 Construction of thin film amorphous silicon

In order to make appropriate voltage and power output suitable for different applications, single solar cells are interconnected to form module to provide higher voltage and current. Number of such modules form array. The typical power ratings of solar modules are between 10 Wpeak and 100 Wpeak. This output refers to standard test conditions of 1000 W/m^2 solar radiation at a cell temperature of 25°C. The theoretical maximum level of efficiency for silicon crystal is 28%.

Reasons for low efficiency of solar cells are following—

(*i*) performance degradation due to high operating temperature.

(*ii*) recombination of electrons and holes.

(*iii*) light having low energy to liberate electrons.

(*iv*) shading produced by top surface electric contact.

(*v*) reflection from cell's surface.

(*vi*) resistance to current flow.

Advantages of photovoltaic systems are following—

(*i*) direct conversion of light to electricity.

(*ii*) modular structure of cells allow any size to be installed.

(*iii*) silicon used for making PV cells are abundantly available.

(*iv*) it has quick response.

(*v*) no moving parts, hence no maintenance.

(*vi*) it does not contain gases or liquids.

(*vii*) it has high power to weight ratio.

(*viii*) it requires no cooling or feed water.

(*ix*) can be used in remote area as standalone power source.

(x) long life.

(xi) due to modular construction, these are easily expandable.

Disadvantages—

(*i*) high cost of production.

(*ii*) energy storage is required due to intermittency of solar radiation.

(*iii*) large area required to capture solar radiation.

(*iv*) performance degradation due to high operating temperature and aging.

8.16 FACTORS AFFECTING OUTPUT OF PV MODULE

(*i*) **Effect of solar radiation:** Output of a PV module is defined under standard test conditions (STC). These are– solar irradiance = 1000 W/m^2, solar cell temperature = 25°C and air mass 1.5 reference spectral distribution. Wattage output of a PV module is always rated in terms of peak watt (W_P) which is defined as the maximum power output that the module could deliver under above mentioned standard test conditions.

Hence, actual output is influenced by the solar radiation intensity.

(*ii*) **Degradation due to aging:** Efficiency of energy conversion decreases with age.

(*iii*) **Presence of dust on cell surface:** Dust can accumulate on the surface of solar module which blocks the solar radiation from reaching the cell. This reduces the cell output.

(*iv*) **Module mismatch:** The maximum power output of a PV array is always less than sum of maximum output of individual modules. This is due to inconsistencies in performance of one module to next resulting in power loss.

(*v*) **Conversion losses:** Losses take place when dc power produced by PV cell is converted to ac power.

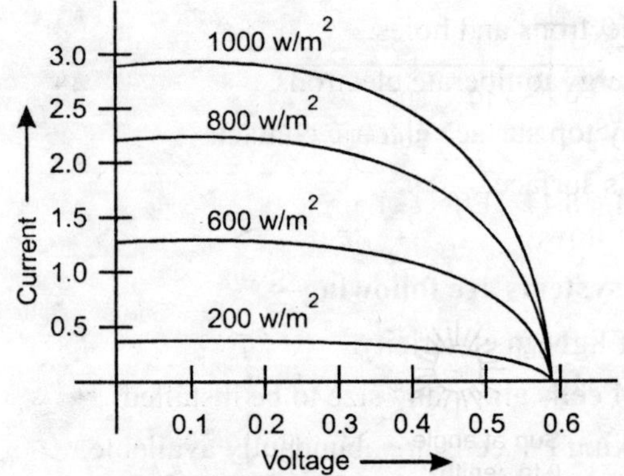

Fig. 8.42 Effect of solar radiation on output of PV cell

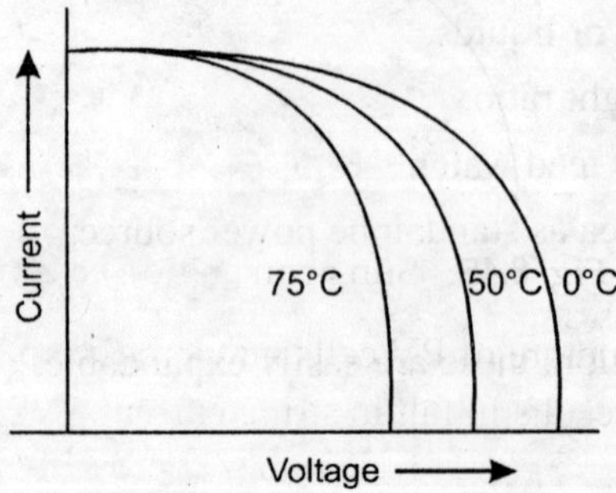

Fig. 8.43 Effect of cell temperature on output of PV cell

(*vi*) **Effect of cell temperature:** With increase in cell temperature, open circuit voltage and power output drops significantly. The voltage of the cell decreases by 2.2 mV for every 1°C rise in temperature.

$$V_{OC} = V_O(1 - \beta\Delta T) \quad ...(8.6)$$

Where, V_O is open circuit voltage at reference temperature, β is temperature co-efficient and ΔT is change in temperature.

(*vii*) **Effect of angle of Sun:** The angle of sun affects the cell current given by relationship—

$$I = I_O \cos\theta \quad ...(8.7)$$

Where, I_O is the current at reference position of sun and θ is the angle of sunline measured from the normal. This law holds good for angles between 0° to 50°. Beyond 50°, cell behaviour deviates significantly from cosine law.

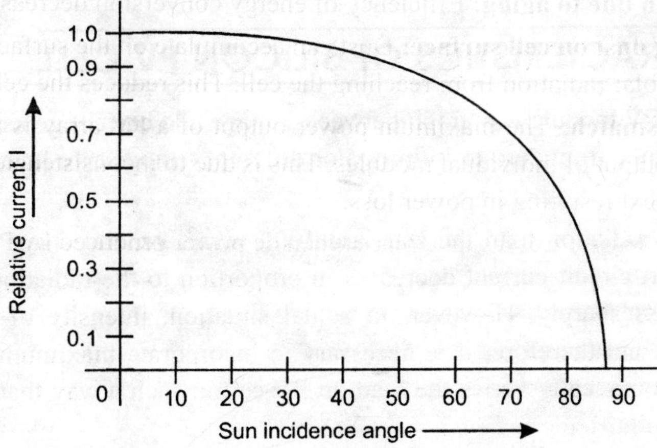

Fig. 8.44 Effect of angle of sun on PV cell current

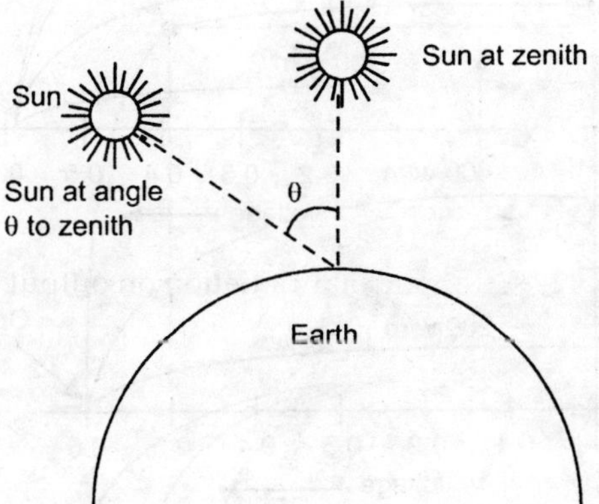

Fig. 8.45 Sun at an angle θ to zenith

(*viii*) **Effect of shadow:** Structure of PV cells may produce partial shadows on cells. This reduces output voltage which results in fall in string current.

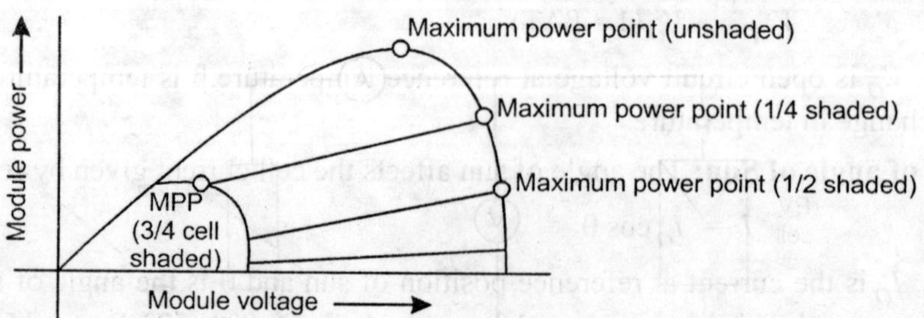

Fig. 8.46 Effect of shading on PV cell output

8.17 V–I CHARACTERISTICS OF SILICON PV CELL

V–I characteristic of a PV module is a graph between voltage and current generated by PV module by varying the load resistance from zero to infinity. For different temperature levels, different graphs are obtained.

At lower levels of radiation than the standard 1000 w/m^2, general shape of V–I characteristics remains same. But short circuit current decreases in proportion to the radiation intensity while open circuit voltage falls less sharply. However, in actual situation, intensity of solar radiation varies substantially over time and therefore, it is necessary to incorporate maximum power point tracking device. This device automatically varies the load on PV cell in such a way that it is always operating around the maximum point.

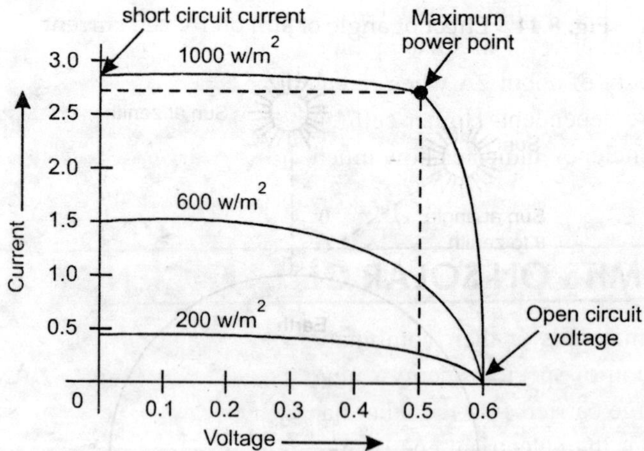

Fig. 8.47 V–I characteristics of a typical silicon PV cell at different levels of solar radiation

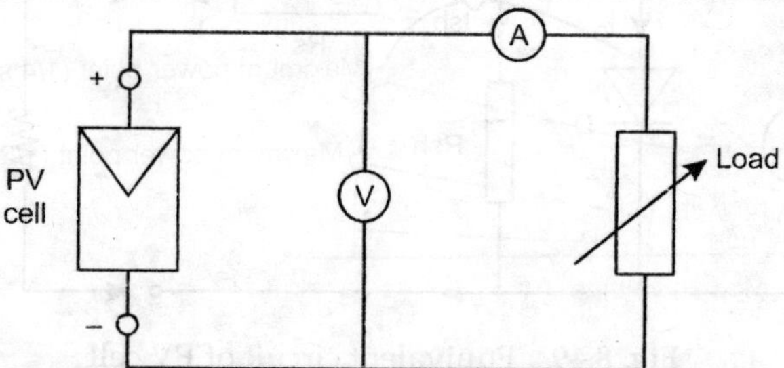

Fig. 8.48 Measurement of V–I characteristics of a silicon PV cell

8.18 MAXIMUM POWER POINT OPERATION

Level of solar radiation varies throughout the day due to change in orientation and altitude of the sun. Due to this change in level of solar radiation, output of a solar cell varies. In order to collect maximum radiation and hence maximum power, the PV module must operate at a certain voltage which corresponds to maximum power point under given operating condition. A maximum power point tracker (MPPT) senses the voltage and current output of a PV module and continuously adjusts the operating point to capture maximum power under given operating condition. Any excess power available than that needed by the battery is fed to dump heaters which may be used for space heating.

The usable voltage from solar cells depend on the semiconductor material. In silicon, it is approximately equal to 5 volts. Terminal voltage is weakly dependent on light radiation while current intensity increasers with higher level of solar radiation. For example, A 100 cm^2 silicon cell reaches a maximum current intensity of about 2A when radiated by 1000 W/m^2 of solar radiation. The output of solar cell is temperature dependent. Higher cell temperature lead to lower output and hence, lower efficiency. The level of efficiency indicates how much of the incident solar radiation is converted into electricity.

8.19 NATURAL LIMITS ON SOLAR CELL EFFICIENCY

Different semiconductor materials or their combinations are suited only for specific spectral ranges. Therefore, a specific portion of spectral energy cannot be used because photons do not have enough energy to activate the charge carriers. On the other hand, a certain amount of surplus photon energy is transformed into heat rather than electrical energy. In addition to this, there are optical losses, such as shadowing of cell surface through contact with the glass surface or reflection of incoming rays on cell. Other losses are electrical resistance losses in semiconductor material and connecting cables. Also, there is disruptive influence of material contamination, surface effects and crystal defects. These loesses cannot be further improved upon due to inherent physical limits imposed by materials themselves. This leads to a maximum level of efficiency of approximately 28% for crystal silicon.

8.20 EQUIVALENT CIRCUIT OF PV CELL

Equivalent circuit of PV cell is shown in figure 8.49.

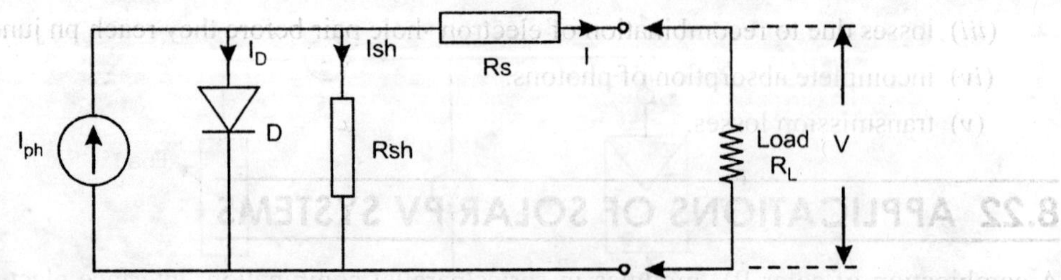

Fig. 8.49 Equivalent circuit of PV cell

Where,
I_{ph} = Insolation current
R_s = series resistance
I = cell current
R_{sh} = parallel resistance
V = cell output voltage
R_L = load sesistance

Incident solar radiation produces a constant photo current in the solar cell circuit. So, it can be considered as constant current generator. Without solar radiation, solar cell works as a semiconductor diode (D).Series and shunt resistances are due to structure of material. Good mono crystalline silicon cell does not have shunt resistance while poly crystalline and amorphous silicon cells do posses them.

Output current I is equal to photo current I_{ph} minus diode current I_D. Depending upon depth of p-n junction, impurities and contact resistance, series resistance (R_s) varies. The cell conversion efficiency is affected by series resistance R_s. In an ideal PV cell, $R_s = O$ and $R_{sh} = \propto$ (infinity)

(*i*) Open circuit voltage, $V_{oc} = V + IR_s$ ...(8.8)

(ii) Diode current, $I_D = I_s\left[\exp\left(\frac{eV_o}{AKT}\right)-1\right]$ ...(8.9)

Where,
I_s = saturation current of diode.
e = charge on an electron (1.6×10^{-19} coulombs).
V_{oc} = open circuit voltage.
A = curve fitting constant.
K = Boltz mann constant (1.38×10^{-23} J/k).
T = temperature in K.

(*iii*) Load current, $I = I_{ph} - I_s\left[\exp\left(\frac{eV_{oc}}{AKT}\right)-1\right] - \frac{V_{oc}}{Rsh}$ ...(8.10)

8.21 LOSSES IN A SOLAR CELL

The various losses taking place in a solar cell are following—

(*i*) losses due to internal resistance (ohmic loss).

(*ii*) losses due to reflection of incident solar radiation.

(*iii*) losses due to recombination of electron -hole pair before they reach pn junction.

(*iv*) incomplete absorption of photons.

(*v*) transmission losses.

8.22 APPLICATIONS OF SOLAR PV SYSTEMS

A combination of solar PV modules in series/parallel combination, interface electronics, mechanical support structure, cables, switches etc. constitutes a solar photovoltaic system (SPV). Storage batteries are used to store solar energy produced during the day for use in non-sunshine hours. A SPV system can be used to provide electricity for lighting, water pumping, battery charging and feeding power to grid. Advantages of solar PV system are reliability, low maintenance, low gestation period to set up system, no recurring expenditure and no pollution. A SPV system can be standalone or grid connected. Standalone system requires battery storage while grid connected does not require one.

Some popular SPV systems are following–

(*i*) **Solar lanterns:** It is a portable lighting device which can be used for indoor and outdoor usage. These lanterns are available with CFL/LED bulbs and a solar panel for charging purpose,

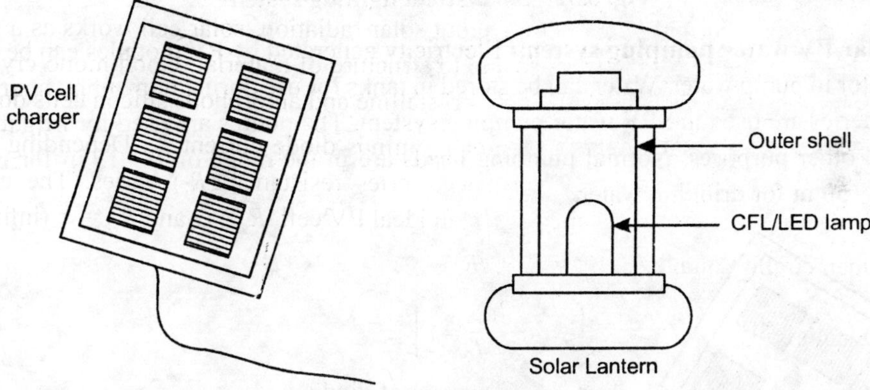

Fig. 8.50 Solar lantern

(*ii*) **Solar home lighting system:** A solar home lighting system (SHS) provides a comfortable level of illumination in one or more rooms of house. There are several SHS models featuring one, two or four CFLs/LEDs. It is also possible to run a small DC fan or a 12V DC television.

(*iii*) **Solar street lighting system:** A solar street lighting system is an outdoor lighting unit used to illuminate a street or an open area usually in a village. It automatically lights up when surroundings become dark and switch off around sunrise time.

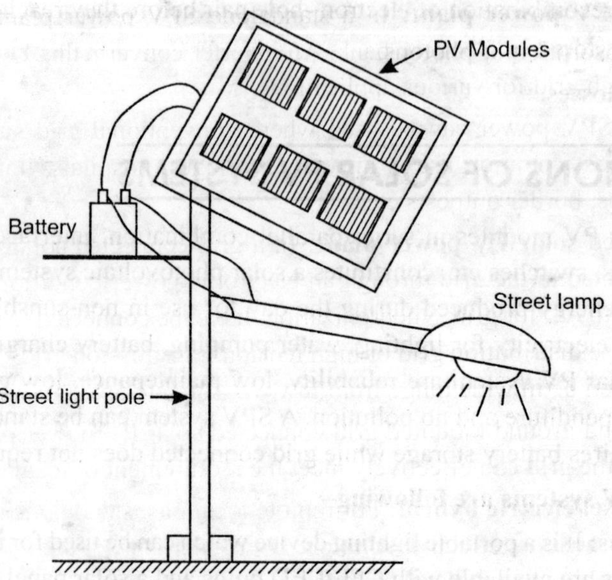

Fig. 8.51 Solar street lighting system

(*iv*) **Solar PV water pumping system:** Electricity generated by PV modules can be used to run a motor to pump water. Water can be stored in tanks for use during non-sunny hours. No storage batteries are used in SPV water pumping system. The pumps are used for irrigation, drinking and other purposes. Normal pumping heads are in the range of 7 – 15 m for irrigation and 10 – 50 m for drinking water.

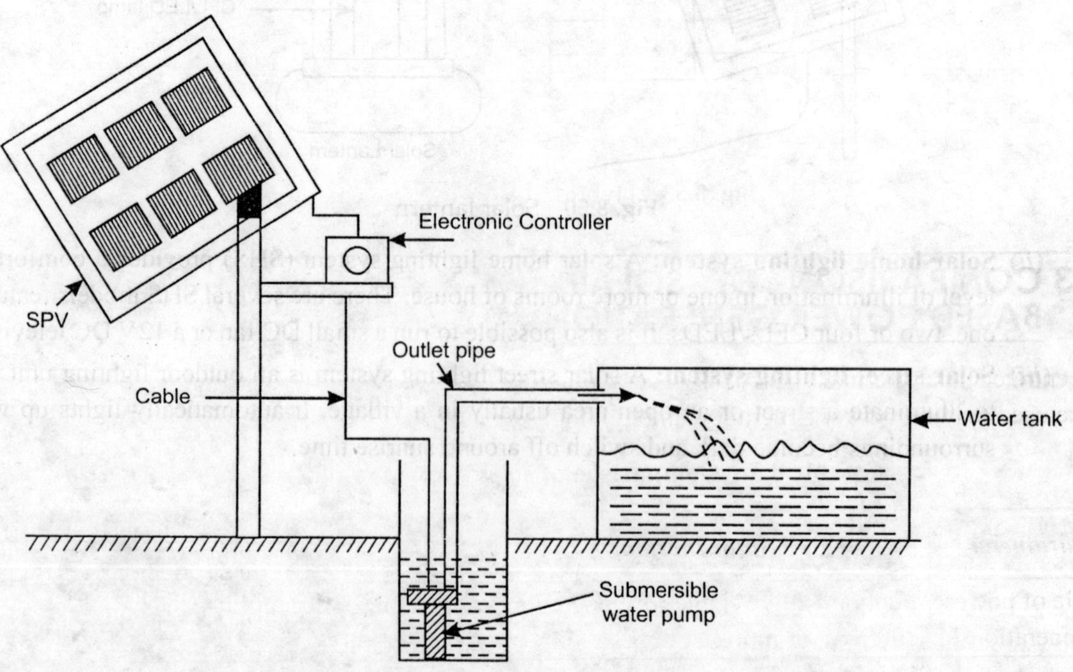

Fig. 8.52 SPV water pumping system

(*v*) **Standalone SPV power plant:** In a standalone SPV power plant, electricity is centrally generated and stored in a battery bank. An inverter converts this DC electricity into AC and supplies through grid for various applications.

A standalone SPV power can be used where conventional grid supply is not available or erratic. The most common use is in remote villages, hospitals, hotels, telecommunication, railway stations, border outposts etc.

(*vi*) **Grid connected solar PV power plant:** In a grid connected solar PV power plant, the PV array is connected to the grid through an electronic power conditioning unit which converts DC electricity to AC for grid synchronization. It can be connected to single phase low tension grid, three phase distribution grid or high tension transmission grid. The capacity of solar PV power plants can be in wide range from few watts to megawatts.

The roof top and ground mounted grid connected solar PV power plants when connected at the tail end of the grid can effectively meet the requirement of local communities.

(*vii*) **Solar PV–Diesel electric hybrid:** For remote locations, standalone solar PV -Diesel electric hybrid systems are cost effective solution. During day time, solar PV can deliver power and during non-sunshine hours diesel electric generator can feed power.

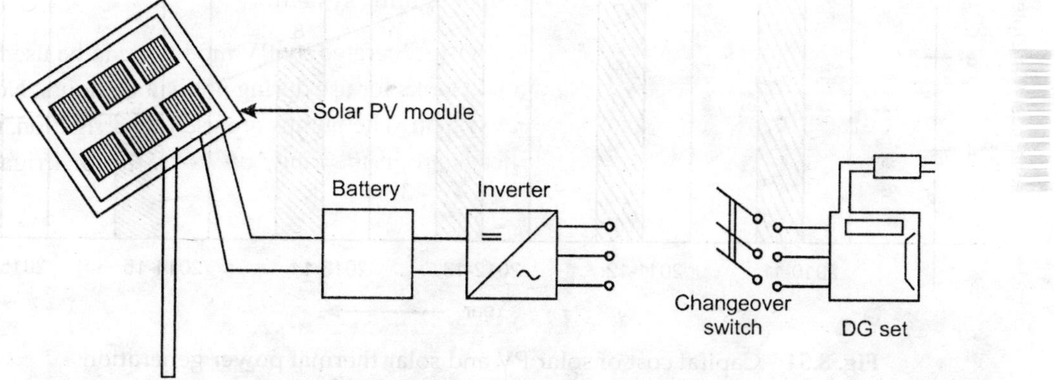

Fig. 8.53 Hybrid SPV-DG set system

8.23 COMPARISON OF SOLAR THERMAL AND PHOTOVOLTAIC BASED POWER GENERATION

Concentrated solar thermal energy has several other uses apart from power generation. While solar PV can be used only for power generation and lighting. A comparison of two systems is given below–

Table 8.3 Comparison of solar thermal and PV system

Parameter	*Solar thermal*	*Solar photovoltaic*
Scale of power generation	Economically viable if generation is 100 MW or more	Useful for decentralized generation
Energy storage	Easier to store thermal energy	Battery is needed to store energy which is most expensive part of installation

Hybrid power generation	It is convenient to introduce solar thermal technology in existing fossil full power plants.	PV system can generate power separately, there would not be any cost saving.
Uses	Besides producing electricity, it can be used for variety of applications.	Can be used only for producing electricity.

Capital cost of solar thermal power projects (Rs crore/MW)is higher than that of PV power plant, But there is a decreasing trend in the last 10 years.

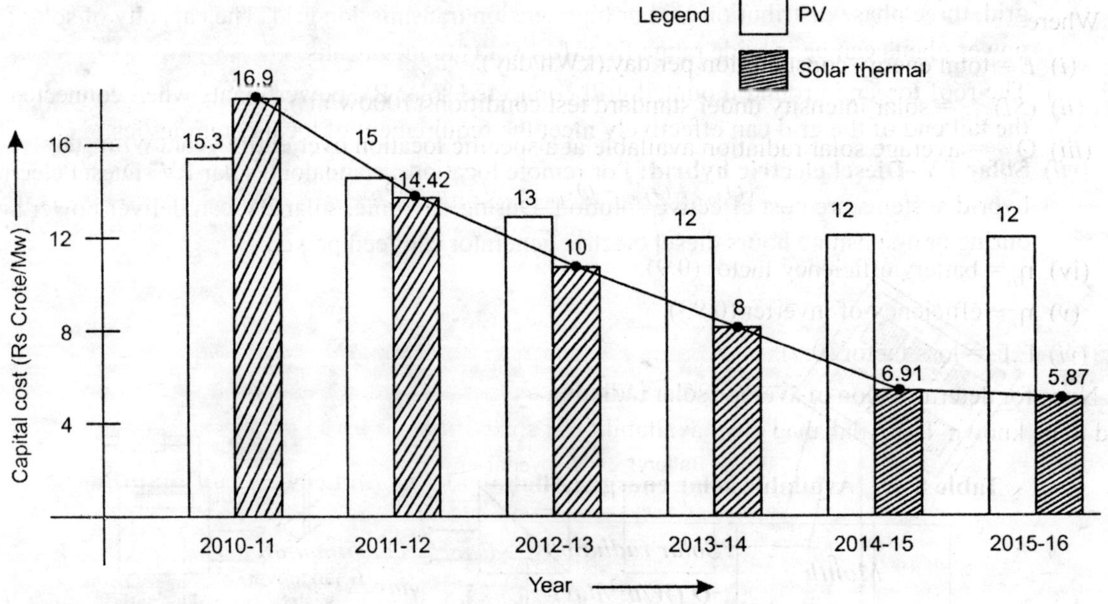

Fig. 8.54 Capital cost of solar PV and solar thermal power generation

8.24 DESIGN OF SOLAR PV SYSTEM

Various steps involved in calculation of average energy demand for a solar PV power plant is described below—

(*i*) estimation of total connected load.

(*ii*) estimation of duration of operation on battery.

(*iii*) estimation of average power generated from solar panels.

(*iv*) estimation of battery capacity.

This can be illustrated with the help of a suitable example.

Assumptions—

(*i*) total connected load = 5 kW

(*ii*) total unit consumption per day = 30 kW/day

(*iii*) system voltage = 48 V

(iv) duration of battery backup = 8 hours

(v) place of installation of PV plant = Allahabad city.

Design

Step (i) Total connected load = 5 kW.

Step (ii) Estimated duration of operation on battery = 8 hour

Step (iii) Estimation of average generation of electricity from solar panels

The average power generated from solar array = $\frac{E \times (SI)_{STC} \times 1000}{Qave \times \eta_B \times \eta_I \times (L.F.)}$ ...(8.11)

Where

(i) E = total energy consumption per day,(kWh/day).

(ii) $(SI)_{STC}$ = solar intensity under standard test conditions(1000w/m^2).

(iii) Q_{ave} = average solar radiation available at a specific location over entire year,(W/m^2/day).

$$= \frac{(Q_{Jan} + Q_{Feb} + Q_{Mar} + ...Q_{NOV} + Q_{Dec})}{12} \quad ...(8.12)$$

(iv) η_B = battery efficiency factor (0.9).

(v) η_I = efficiency of inverter (0.93).

(vi) L.F. = loss factor (0.9).

Now, for determination of average solar radiation over entire year, the data for a place of installation need to be known. For Allahabad city, availability of solar energy is given in table -8.4

Table 8.4: Available solar energy (Allahabad city) and energy consumption

Month	*Solar radiation Q (W/m²/day)*	*Energy consumption per day (kWh)*
January	3900	21.07
February	4870	21.07
March	6000	23.91
April	6520	23.91
May	6580	30.0
June	5710	30.0
July	4580	30.0
August	4380	30.0
September	4550	30.0
October	4840	30.0
November	4370	23.91
December	3780	21.07

Now,average solar radiation,

$$Q_{ave} = \frac{3900 + 4870 + 6000 + ... + 4370 + 3780}{12}$$

$$Q_{ave} = 5006.67 \text{ W/m}^2$$

Power generated from solar array for average solar radiation (Q_{ave}) calculated in previous step,

$$P = \frac{30 \times 1000 \times 1000}{5006.67 \times 0.9 \times 0.9 \times 0.93}$$

$$P = 7954.34 \text{ W}$$

Number of 250 W modules per panel required $= \frac{7954.34}{250}$

$= 31.8 \approx 32$

Given, output voltage of solar panel = 30.7 V

Therefore, number of panels to be connected in series for an output voltage of 48 V $= \frac{48}{32} = 1.5 \approx 2$

Assuming, number of panels =2

Number of panels to be connected in parallel $= \frac{28}{2} = 14$

Therefore, PV array will consist of two panels in series and 14 such panels to be connected in parallel.

Step (*iv*) Estimation of battery capacity: The capacity of battery for inverter is dependent upon rate and duration of discharge. The relationship can be expressed mathematically as (Peukert, 1897)—

A-h capacity of battery, $C = I^n T$

Where, I = discharge current, A

n = constant which depends upon construction of battery.

$= 1.05 < n < 2$

T = duration of discharge, hr

Now, for a total load of 5kW at voltage of 48V, the current drawn,

$$I = \frac{5000}{48} = 104.17 \text{ A}$$

Assuming, 8 hour of battery discharge, the capacity of battery,

$$C = (104.17)^{1.1} \times 8 \qquad (n = 1.1 \text{ assumed})$$

$= 1326.19$ Ah

Assuming a battery of 12 V, 150 Ah, number of batteries required for 8 hour full load backup

$$= \frac{\text{Ah of battery} \times \text{total battery voltage}}{\text{Ah of battery available} \times \text{battery voltage} \times \text{DoD}} \qquad ...(8.13$$

$$= \frac{1326.19 \times 48}{150 \times 12 \times 0.7}$$

$= 50.5 \approx 50$

Therefore, number of batteries each rated for 12 V, 150 Ah required = 50

8.25 SOLAR THERMAL AND SOLAR PV POWER PLANTS IN THE WORLD

Following is the selected list of solar thermal and solar photovoltaic power plants operating in the world.

(*i*) Table 8.5 Solar thermal power plants

Sr.No	*Country*	*Name of plant*	*Capacity of plant (MW)*
1.	USA	Ivanpah	377
2.	USA	SEGS	354
3.	USA	Solana	280
4.	USA	Genesis	250
5.	Spain	Solaben	350
6.	Spain	Palma Del Rio	100
7.	Spain	Manchasol	100
8.	Spain	Valle	100

(*ii*) Table 8.6 Solar PV power plants

Sr. No.	*Country*	*Name of plant*	*Capacity of plant (MW)*
1.	India	Charanka solar park	600
`2.	USA	Solar star– I and II	579
3.	USA	Topaz Solar farm	550
4.	USA	Desert sunlight solar farm	550
5.	USA	Copper mountain solar facility	484

The total installed capacity of solar PV in India (as on Nov, 2015) is 4680 MWp.

SOLVED EXAMPLES

Ex 8.1. For a photovoltaic system, effective illumination area = 0.136 m^2, V_{mp} = 15.6 V, I_{mp} = 1.4A. (For standard test condition of 1000 w/m^2, 25° C and air mass =1.5). Find the efficiency of solar panel.

Solution: Efficiency of solar panel,

$$\eta = \frac{\text{Fill factor} \times V_{OC} \times I_{SC}}{\text{Incident radiation} \times \text{Area}}$$

$$\text{Fill factor} = \frac{V_{mp}\, I_{mp}}{V_{OC} \times I_{SC}}$$

$$\Rightarrow \qquad \eta = \frac{\dfrac{V_{mp}\, I_{mp}}{V_{OC} \times I_{SC}} \times V_{OC} \times I_{SC}}{\text{Incident radiation} \times \text{Area}}$$

$$\eta = \frac{V_{mp} \times I_{mp}}{\text{Incident radiation} \times \text{Area}}$$

$$= \frac{15.6 \times 1.4}{1000 \times 0.136} \times 100$$

$$\eta = \mathbf{16.06\ \%} \quad \textbf{Ans.}$$

Ex 8.2. A thermal energy storage uses water as medium with 300 kW energy capacity. The temperature of stored water varies from 20°C to 80°C. Calculate (*i*) the volume and mass of stored water, (*ii*) energy density per unit mass (*iii*) energy density per unit volume.

Solution:

(*i*) Mean temperature of water $= \frac{20+80}{2} = 50°\text{C}$

Density and specific heat of water at 50°C = $\rho = 988\ \text{kg/m}^3$

$$C_p = 4181\ \text{J/kg K}$$

Energy stored, $Q = m\, C_p\, (T_1 - T_2)$

$$300 \times 3600 = m \times 4181\ (80 - 20)$$

$\therefore$ Mass of stored water, m = **4305 kg Ans.**

Volume of stored water $= \frac{m}{\rho} = \frac{4305}{988} = \mathbf{4.357\ m^3}$ **Ans.**

(*ii*) Energy density per unit mass $= \frac{Q}{m} = \frac{300}{4305} = \mathbf{0.07\ kWh/kg}$ **Ans.**

(*iii*) Energy density per unit volume $= \frac{Q}{\upsilon} = \frac{300}{4.357} = \mathbf{68.85\ kWh/m^3}$ **Ans.**

CHAPTER SUMMARY

Solar energy received on earth is in the form of electromagnetic radiation. Heat and light energy both are used for a variety of applications. Solar thermal route uses solar collectors, such as flat plate, parabolic trough, parabolic dish, Fresnel lens etc. Solar thermal energy is used for different applications such as heating, generation of steam, generation of power etc.

The thermal system consists of – (*i*) solar energy collection system (*ii*) heat transportation system (*iii*) heat receiver system (*iv*) thermal storage system and (*v*) supply system. It may include power generation system.

Solar thermal power plants are of three types viz (*i*) central receiver type (*ii*) distributed type and (*iii*) combination of two. The plant uses either binary cycle or steam cycle. Solar thermal energy can be used for residential, industrial, commercial, agricultural and rural applications.

Another route to utilize sun's energy is through PV cells. It uses sun's light energy to convert it into electricity using PV cells. PV cells use three types of systems viz (*i*) silicon wafer based PV cells employing mono crystalline and poly crystalline silicon cells (*ii*) thin film based employing amorphous silicon, cadmium telluride, copper-indium-diselenide, copper-indium-gallium diselenide, dye sensitised solar cells etc. (*iii*) nano particle based quantum dots. Conversion efficiency of these cells ranges from 7 to 16%. These are static system and hence, can be used on roof tops.

Solar PV cells find applications in residential, commercial, industrial and rural areas. Main uses are power generation and for lighting purposes. Batteries and inverters are used to store solar energy which is dc and convert it to ac for use.

Due to fast depletion of fossil fuel reserves, solar energy is being used increasingly to meet energy deficit. India has large number of sunny days in a year (300 – 330 days) which makes it suitable for usage of solar energy. Large number of solar PV and solar thermal power plants are coming up in India. The price differential between solar PV and solar thermal has narrowed down considerably.

REVIEW QUESTIONS

Q. 1. Distinguish between beam and diffuse solar radiation.

Q. 2. Define solar constant.

Q. 3. Why less amount of solar radiation is received on earth than received on the outer surface of atmosphere?

Q. 4. Define following terms–

(*i*) Zenith angle (*ii*) Incident angle (*iii*) Declination angle.

Q. 5. Differentiate between pyranometer and pyroheliometer.

Q. 6. What is sunshine recorder? Explain working of Campbell–Stokes sunshine recorder.

Q. 7. Discuss various solar energy technologies in use to harness solar energy.

Q. 8. Give a brief overview of solar thermal system.

Q. 9. Compare solar thermal and solar photovoltaic power generation system.

Q. 10. Explain the factors which affect the performance of flat plate collector.

Q. 11. Write a brief note on solar thermal energy storage.

Q. 12. Explain with a neat sketch–solar distributed collector type power plant.

Q. 13. What is a solar pond? How conduction and convections losses are kept minimum in a solar pond?

Q. 14. What are the various factors which affect the collection of solar energy through PV cells?

Q. 15. Discuss various applications of solar thermal energy.

Q. 16. Discuss various applications of solar PV in domestic area.

Q. 17. Compare flat plate and concentrating collector.

Q. 18. Write short note on following–

(*i*) solar pumping (*ii*) solar heating and cooling

(*iii*) solar cooking (*iv*) solar lighting

Q. 19. Explain construction and working of following type of collectors–

(*i*) parabolic trough (*ii*) parabolic dish

Q. 20. Explain with a schematic diagram working of distributed collector solar thermal power plant. How solar heliostats are arranged?

SHORT ANSWERS TYPES QUESTIONS

Q. 1. Solar thermal energy conversion route is more energy efficient than solar PV.

Q. 2. Why solar-hybrid system of power generation is preferable than standalone solar system?

Q. 3. Parabolic dish collector is more efficient than Fresnel system.

Q. 4. Solar tower is used for power generation.

Q. 5. Solar energy can be used for germicidal purpose in water purification.

Multiple Choice Questions

Q. 1. Sun generates energy by
- (*a*) fusion
- (*b*) fission
- (*c*) fusion and fission both
- (*d*) none of these

Q. 2. Ultraviolet radiation of sun is absorbed by
- (*a*) carbon dioxide and water vapour
- (*b*) ozone and oxygen molecule
- (*c*) reflected back to space
- (*d*) both (*a*) and (*b*)

Q. 3. Solar beam radiation is measured by
- (*a*) pyroheliometer
- (*b*) pyranometer
- (*c*) sunshine recorder
- (*d*) both (*a*) and (*b*)

Q. 4. Solar PV cells use sun's
- (*a*) heat energy
- (*b*) light energy
- (*c*) heat and light energy both
- (*d*) infrared radiations

Q. 5. Combined cycle solar thermal power plant uses
- (*a*) only steam turbine
- (*b*) only gas turbine
- (*c*) both steam and gas turbine
- (*d*) none of these

Q. 6. Following PV cells have highest conversion efficiency—
- (*a*) amorphous silicon
- (*b*) poly crystalline silicon
- (*c*) cadmium telluride
- (*d*) gallium arsenide

True/False Questions

Q. 1. On a cloudy day, diffuse and beam radiation both are present.

Q. 2. Solar thermal energy conversion has higher conversion efficiency than PV cells.

Q. 3. Fresnel optical collectors have lower efficiency than flat plate collector.

Q. 4. Poly crystalline PV cell is more efficient than mono crystalline cell.

Q. 5. Life of amorphous silicon is more than poly-crystalline cell.

Answer to MCQ

1. (*a*) **2.** (*b*) **3.** (*a*) **4.** (*b*) **5.** (*c*) **6.** (*b*)

Answer to True/False

1. False **2.** True **3.** True **4.** True **5.** False

Chapter

Wind Power Generation

Learning Objectives

After reading this chapter, reader will be able to

- Understand process of wind power generation,effect of various parameters affecting wind power generation and methods employed to reduce variability of wind resource.
- Explore various schemes of power generation employing synchronous and induction generators.
- Explore latest trends in wind power generation in off-shore windfarms.
- Update on operating wind power plants in India and in the world.

"Art without engineering is dreaming.
Engineering without art is calculating".

— Steven Roberts

9.1. INTRODUCTION

Wind is air in motion and is formed due to earth's rotation and uneven heating of surface of earth due to sunrays. This uneven heating creates pressure difference or different pressure zones. The resulting pressure difference causes wind to flow from high pressure to low pressure zone. About 2%of sun's energy reaching earth gets converted into wind energy. Earth's rotation causes a coriolis force producing easterly wind velocity component in the northern hemisphere. During day–time surface heats up rapidly compared to ocean or water bodies thereby generating surface wind flow from surface to water bodies. At night time, wind flows from water bodies to surface due to faster cooling of land surface compared to water bodies. The speed of wind increases with height e.g. wind speed at a height of 10 m are 20–25% more than that at close to surface.

This kinetic energy of wind is converted into mechanical or electrical energy. The mechanical energy is generally used for pumping water while electrical energy is either used locally or fed to the grid.

Use of wind energy dates back to 5000 years ago when wind energy was used to propel boats in Egypt. First wind mill was built in ancient Babylon in 2000 BC.Use of wind energy for milling grain in western countries dates back to 12th century. Wind mills were used in Netherland to pump water from sea to reclaim land. By latter half of 19th century,wind mills were being used in United States. The process of producing electricity using wind energy started by the end of 19th century. Now, wind energy generation process has become a mature technology. India occupies 5th place in terms of wind power installed capacity in the world. About 80%of world's installed capacity in wind energy sector is located in USA, Denmark, Spain and India.

14 Indian states and union territories are found to have mean annual wind power density of more than 200W/m^2at 50m height,These locations are considered suitable for wind power generation. These states are Gujarat, Maharashtra, Odisha,Tamil Nadu, Rajasthan, Andhra Pradesh, Madhya Pradesh, Karnataka, Kerala, West Bengal, Lakshdweep, Andaman & Nicobar, Jammu & Kashmir and Uttarakhand.

Advantages of wind energy are following—

(*i*) there is no fuel cost as wind is freely available in nature.

(*ii*) pollution free and environment friendly resource.

(*iii*) low gestation period (less than 6–8 months) for building wind power plant.

(*iv*) low operation and maintenance cost of wind power generation system.

(*v*) it is available on- shore as well as off-shore.

(*vi*) mature technology.

(*vii*) part of wind energy which is not converted into electrical energy does not appear as heat (happens with fossil fuels).

Disadvantages of wind energy are following—

(*i*) availability of wind is variable,irregular and intermittent.

(*ii*) it is low energy density source.

(*iii*) due to intermittent nature, it requires energy storage which increases cost.

(*iv*) large land is required for wind farms.

(*v*) high capital cost.

(*vi*) high overall weight of generating system.

(*vii*) low efficiency of wind turbine generator system (overall efficiency 10–30%).

(*viii*) prediction of wind velocity, changes etc. is not accurate.

9.2. SELECTION OF SITE FOR WIND POWER GENERATION

Major considerations for selection of site for wind powers generation are following–

(*i*) the site should have high annual average wind speed as wind power generated is proportion to cube of wind velocity.

(*ii*) it should be located away from cities and forests.

(*iii*) it should be near to roads or railways so that heavy machinery and structures could be transported to site.

(iv) altitude of proposed site should provide sufficient velocity. (relation between velocity and height is $V \propto H^{1/7}$ for heights between 50 to 250m).

(v) ground conditions,type of soil etc. should be stable to allow heavy construction.

(vi) the site should be above the flood level of the area.

(vii) it should be near to load centre which will mimimize length of transmission line ,cost and losses.

(viii) sufficient land should be available at low cost.

(ix) site specific conditions, such as dust, snow etc should not be present.

(x) it should be away from flight path of migratory birds, bird sanctuary etc.

(xi) site selected should have no history of cyclones as equipment may get damaged/uprooted during cyclonic storms.

(xii) there should be no physical obstruction to location, such as mountains etc.

Sites with annual mean wind speed of 20 km/hour at a hub height of 30m and power density of $150 W/m^2$ are economically viable.

9.3. TERMS RELATED TO WIND POWER GENERATION

(i) **Nacelle**–It is an enclosure above the tower that houses low speed shaft, gear box, high speed shaft, generator ,controller and brake. Purpose is to provide protection from weather. Large nacelles have helipad for helicopter landing.

(ii) **Low speed shaft**–It is the main shaft connecting rotor to gear box and transfers rotary motion to gear box.

(iii) **Gear box**–It is used to increase the speed of electric generator. It receives low rpm from low speed shaft and delivers high rpm to high speed shaft. Typical speed conversions are 30 to 60 rpm to 1000 to 18000 rpm. It is of either planetary gear box or parallel shaft gear box.

(iv) **High speed shaft**–It transmits rotary motion from gearbox to generator.

(v) **Tip speed**–It is the tangential velocity of rotor at the tip of the blade of wind turbine.

(vi) **Tip speed ratio(TSR)**–It is ratio of rotor tip speed to wind speed.

$$\text{TSR}(\lambda) = \frac{\textit{Rotor tip speed}}{\textit{Wind speed}} = \frac{\omega r}{v} \quad \text{...(9.1)}$$

ω = rotational speed, r = radius of blade

A higher tip speed ratio means higher resistance of blades to wind. While a lower tip ratio means lesser extraction of power from wind.

Table 9.1: Comparison of low and high TSR

Sr. No	*Parameter*	*Low TSR (1–2)*	*High TSR(more than10)*
1.	Blade profile	Large	Small
2.	Aerodynamics	Simple	Complex
3.	Aerodynamic stress	Less	More
4.	Centrifugal Stress	Less	More
5.	Torque	High	Low
6.	Efficiency	Low	High
7.	Use	Wind mill for pumping water	Power generation

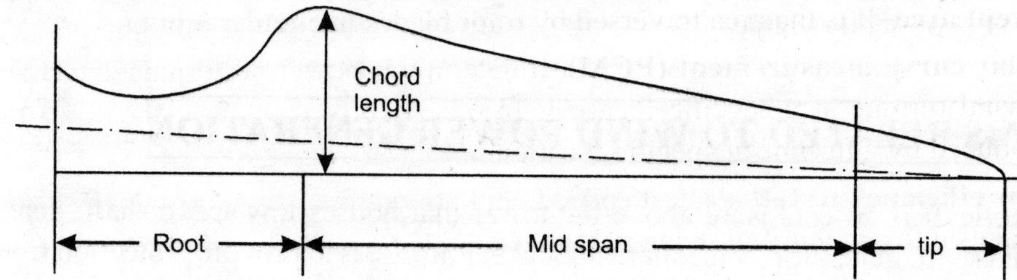

Figure 9.1. Cross-section of rotor blade of wind turbine

$$\text{Optimal value of TSR} \approx \frac{4\pi}{n} \quad ...(9.2)$$

Where, n = number of blades

For three bladed turbine, optimum TSR = 4.19

The range is 9.42 to 3.14 for wind speed of 5m/s to 25m/s.

(*vii*) **Capacity factor**–A wind turbine is unable to produce power continuously due to intermittent nature of wind. Capacity factor provides a measure of actual power output in a given period.

It is defined as a ratio of actual power output in a given period to power output if the turbine had operated 100% of time.

$$\text{C.F.} = \frac{\text{Average annual output of wind turbine}}{\text{Maximum or rated output of wind turbine}}$$

It usually lies between 0.25 – 0.40.

(*viii*) **Availability factor**–It is percentage of time that a plant is ready to generate. It is a measure of reliability of plant.

(*ix*) **Yaw control**–It is steering of axis of turbine in the direction of wind. The purpose is to maximize wind power output and minimize asymmetric load acting on rotor blades and tower. Yaw control system is driven either through electric motor or through hydraulic system. It is needed for horizontal axis wind turbine only.

(*x*) **Pitch angle**–It is the angle between direction of wind and a direction perpendicular to the plane of blade.

(*xi*) **Pitch control**–It is control of pitch angle of blades of horizontal axis wind turbine. Purpose is to capture more power from wind and protect the blades from high wind speed. Pitch control is operated either electrically or hydraulically.

(*xii*) **Stall control**–It is used to regulate the power output of wind turbine by stalling the blades after rated speed is achieved. Pitch control is preferred over stall control.

(*xiii*) **Cut -in speed**–It is the minimum wind speed at which wind turbine starts generating usable power. The typical range is 10 – 16 km/hr.

(*xiv*) **Cut-out speed**–It is the maximum speed at which wind turbine stops operating due to safety reasons. The typical range is 72 – 128 km/hr.

(*xv*) **Rated wind speed**–It is the minimum wind speed at which wind turbine generates power. The typical range is 40–55 km/h.

(*xvi*) **Swept area**–It is the area traversed by rotor blades in circular motion.

(*xvii*) **Polar curve measurement (PCM)**–It determines power performance characteristics of a wind turbine at a specific location. In other words,it is the estimated annual energy produced by a turbine at specific location.

(*xviii*) **Yaw efficiency test**–It is a test carried out to determine ability of turbine to follow wind. It takes into account following parameters—

(*a*) air temperature.

(*b*) air pressure.

(*c*) relative humidity

(*d*) wind direction.

(*e*) Yaw direction.

(*f*) wind speed at reference height.

(*g*) hub height.

(*xix*) **Betz limit**–It is the theoretical maximum amount of energy in the wind that can be captured by a wind turbine rotor. This value is 59.2% and is known as Betz limit named after German phycist Albert Betz. In practice, actual efficiency of rotor lies between 35 to 45%. A complete wind energy system comprising rotor,transmission system ,generator and energy storage devices deliver 10 to 30% of available energy in wind.

(*xx*) **Turbulence**–It is a measure of change in speed of wind within a period of 10 minutes. This fluctuation in wind speed leads to fatigue in components of wind turbine. Turbulence reduces with increase in height above ground. It reduces life of turbine components.

(*xxi*) **Wind shear**–It is change in average wind speed with increase in height. This causes additional load on blades of rotor of wind turbine.

(*xxii*) **Extreme wind speeds**–A wind turbine is designed to withstand very high wind speeds especially during storms. It is defined as maximum 10 minute average wind speed and maximum 3 second gust wind speed expected at a turbine hub height over a 50 year period. It is designed to withstand maximum wind speed of 50m/s for 10 minutes and gust wind speed upto 70m/s for 10 minutes,

Wind speeds are classified based on Beaufort scale as per table: 9.2

Table 9.2: Classification of wind speeds

Beaufort scale number	*Description of wind*	*Wind speed at 10m height above open flat ground (m/s)*
0	Calm	0 – 0.2
1	Light air	0.3 – 1.5
2	Light breeze	1.6 – 3.3
3	Gentle breeze	3.4 – 5.4
4	Moderate breeze	5.5 – 7.9
5	Fresh breeze	8.0 – 10.7
6	Strong breeze	10.8 – 13.8
7	Near gale	13.9 – 17.1
8	Gale	17.2 – 20.7
9	Strong gale	20.8 – 24.4
10	Storm	24.5 – 28.4
11	Violent storm	28.5 – 32.6
12	Hurricane	32.7 and more.

(*xiii*) **Solidity**–It is ratio of rotor platform area to swept area.

$$\text{Solidity} = \frac{\text{Total rotor platform area}}{\text{swept area}}$$

Low solidity (0.1) results in high speed and low torque while high solidity (> 0.8) results in low speed and high torque.

9.4. COMPONENTS OF WIND TURBINE

Wind turbine size ranges from 10 kW with a rotor diameter of 1 m to 5 MW with a diameter of 150 m. Following are the components of wind turbine-generator system—

(*i*) **Rotor**–Assembly of blades and hub is known as rotor,It is a rotating element which converts kinetic energy of wind into mechanical energy. By regulating the orientation or pitch of blades, the power, aerodynamic and efficiency can be altered.

(*ii*) **Blade**–Blades are rotating elements designed aerodynamically to work on the principle of lift and drag. Number of blades are two or three for power generation application. For mechanical power applications such as pumping,grinding etc more number of blades are used due to higher torque requirement. Length of blades affects power generation capacity.

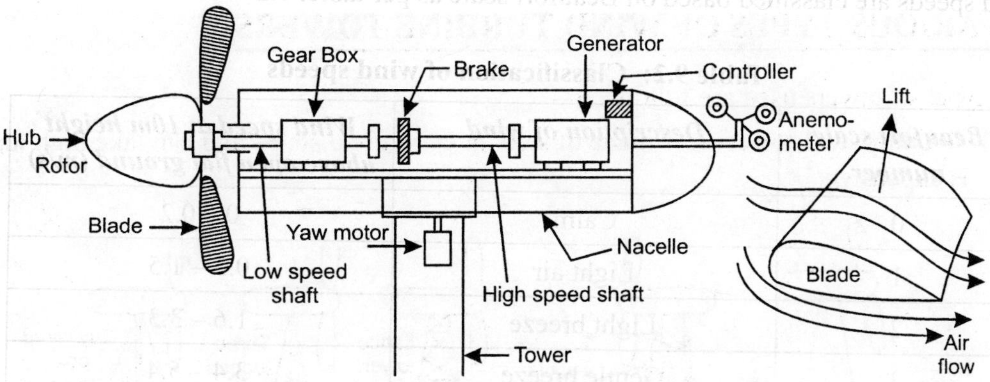

Figure 9.2. Cross-sectional view of wind turbine

(*iii*) **Nacelle**–It is an enclosure on the top of a tower that houses gearbox,generator,low speed shaft ,high speed shaft,controller and brake. It is a protective enclosure against weathering effects which also reduces gearbox and generator noise.

(*iv*) **Low speed shaft**–It connects rotor to gearbox and supports weight of the rotor.

(*v*) **Gearbox**–It increases the speed of low speed shaft so as to match the speed requirement of generator to produce power at 50 Hz. It increases speed from 30 to 60 rpm to 1000 to 1500 rpm. It is expensive and heavy component. However, some designer have no gearbox as generators are directly coupled. Usually,either parallel shaft gear or planetary gear box configurations are used.

(*vi*) **High speed shaft**–It transmits rotational energy from gearbox to generator.

(*vii*) **Brake**–Brake is used to stop the wind turbine from rotation at the time of strong winds for safety reasons or for maintenance purpose. Usually, mechanical clutch brakes or disc brakes are used.

(*viii*) **Tower**–It is a tall metallic structure which supports nacelle. Different types of towers are used, such as tubular tower, lattice tower ,guy wired tower etc.

(*ix*) **Yaw motor**–It is used to keep the turbine blades facing the wind flow direction.

(*x*) **Controller**–It is used to start and shut down the turbine at preset velocities.

(*xi*) **Anemometer**–It is used to measure the wind velocity.

(*xii*) **Wind vane**–It is fixed at the tail end of turbine which measures the direction of wind and makes yaw drive to align turbine blades facing the wind flow.

(*xiii*) **Generator**–It converts mechanical energy of rotating blades into electrical energy. Synchronous and induction both types are used.

(*xiv*) **Foundation**–It supports entire wind turbine structure. Type of foundation is dependent on soil condition and water table. For good soil condition, concrete foundation is preferred. For poor soil condition, pile foundation is used.

9.5. VARIOUS TYPES OF WIND TURBINE TOWERS

Various types of towers used are following—

(*i*) **Tubular steel tower**–It is made of steel in cylindrical shape and can take high loads but is expensive.

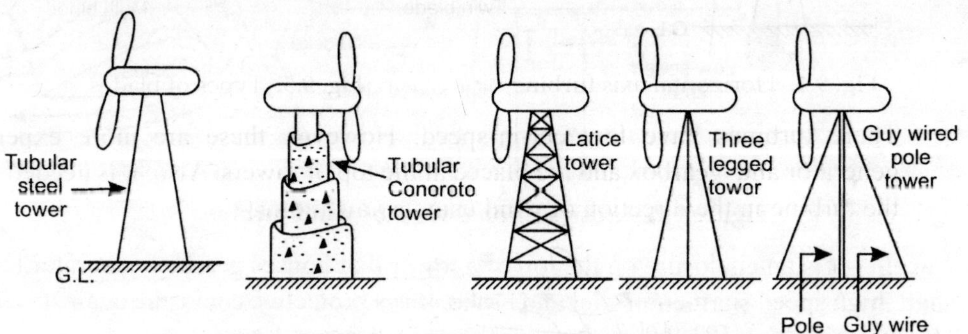

Fig. 9.3. Various types of wind turbine towers

(*ii*) **Tubular concrete tower**—It is made of concrete and possesses high elasticity and high load carrying capacity.

(*iii*) **Lattice tower**—It is made of steel strips and can take relatively less load but can be fabricated easily.

(*iv*) **Three legged tower**—It consists of three legs of steel which can take lesser load. But fabrication and transportation is easy.

(*v*) **Guy wired tower**—It is made of steel but additionally tethered with steel ropes. It can take less load and is not preferred for heavy wind turbine. However,fabrication and transportation is easy.

(*vi*) **Hybrid tower**—It is a combination of tubular and latticeless construction. It can take high load.

9.6. CLASSIFICATION OF WIND TURBINES

(*i*) According to direction of axis—

(*a*) **Horizontal axis wind turbine (HAWT)**–It has rotating axis parallel to ground .Most of the wind turbines are horizontal axis type. The axis of rotation of blade is parallel to the flow of wind. A wind vane connected at the end of turbine is used to make the blades face the wind .The number of blades are two,three or more with a span of 60 m. The capacity varies from 15 kW to 3 MW.

Two and three blade turbines have low swept area and optimum tip speed ratio of 6 to 20. These are used for power generation. While multi blade turbines have high swept area and have high solidity. These are used for supplying power to mechanical devices, such as pumps.

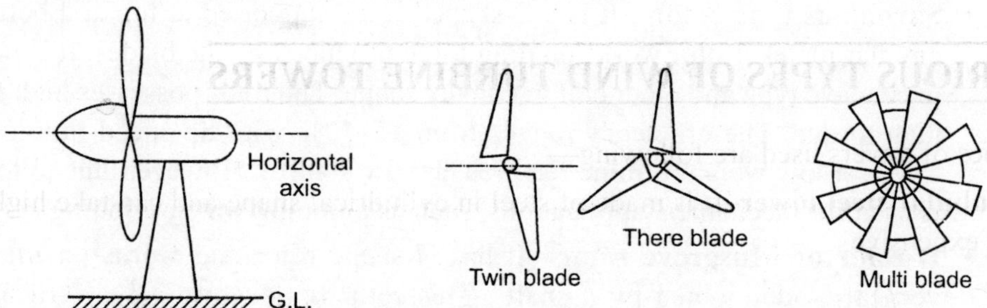

Fig. 9.4. Horizontal axis turbine **Fig. 9.5.** Types of blades

There turbines have low cut-in-speed. However, these are more expensive as generator and gearbox and are placed at the top of towers. Also, it is needed to orient the turbine in the direction of wind using a yaw motor.

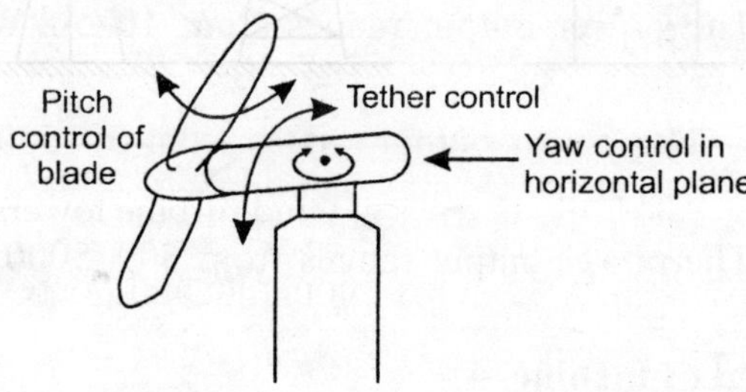

Fig. 9.6. Controls of wind turbine

(*b*) **Vertical axis wind turbine**—It this turbine, axis of rotation is perpendicular to the direction of wind. The blades go from top to bottom. These are of large size viz 4 MW and above and are 30 m tall and 15 m wide. These are lighter in wight and cheaper and do not need yaw control to orient the rotor axis in the direction of wind. These turbines are used where direction of wind changes frequently.

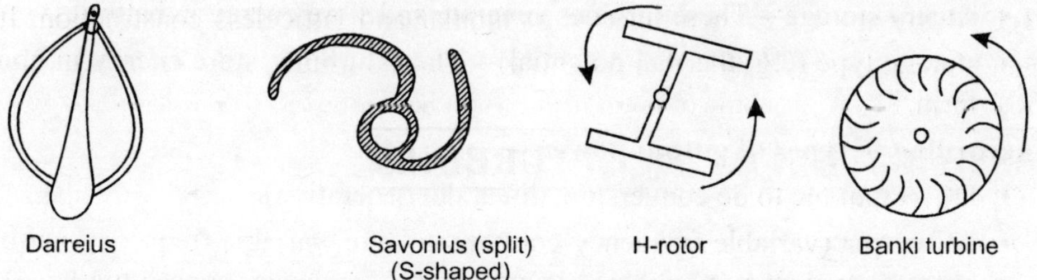

Fig. 9.7. Different types of vertical axis wind turbine blades

Following are the three types of designs that are commonly used—

- **Darrieus rotor**—This type of rotor works due to lift forces generated by set of air-foil. The shape of rotor blades is of two or three convex blades which can have wind from any direction. The vertical shaft is hollow and mounted on upper and lower bearing. The top part is supported by guy wire. The generator and gearbox are placed on ground and does not require yaw control. These are low cost machine with capacity of 4MW and higher. The efficiency lies between 35–40%. These are not self starting.

- **Savonious type rotor**—It is a S-shaped rotor supported at top and bottom by two circular plates. Rotor works on drag force produced by the blades. It is half cylinder in concave type and other half in convex shape. The rotor possesses high solidity and high torque. The efficiency ranges from 15–30% with tip speed ratio of 1–2. This low cost low weight turbine requires no yaw control. However, due to low speed, it is used for mechanical applications, such as pumping water, grinding grain etc.
- **H-rotor or Musgrove rotor**—It has H-shape rotor and works on lift force (two vertical blades joined by a shaft). This rotor revolves round a vertical axis. The generator and gearbox are located at the upper portion. Fixed blade designs are used for lower rating (upto 450kW).While variable shape blade design is used for higher rating (80kW and above).

(*ii*) **According to capacity of turbines**—Based on power generating capacity from wind, wind turbines can be classified as per following—

- **Small size**—The power output ranges from 10–50kW with a blade diameter of 1–16m.
- **Medium size**—The power output ranges from 50–500kW with blade diameter of 16–50m.
- **Large size**—The power output ranges from 500–5000 kW with blade diameter of 50–130m.

(*iii*) **According to speed of turbine**—

- Constant speed with variable pitch blades (using synchronous generator).
- Nearly constant speed with fixed pitch blade (using induction generator).
- Varible speed with fixed pitch blades (using field modulated system, AC commutator, generator, AC – DC – AC link).

(*iv*) **According to end use**—

- grid interactive—These are connected to electricity grid and feed power to it.
- battery storage—These turbines generate and store energy in batteries.
- storage type (e.g. thermal potential)—These turbines store energy in non-electrical form.

(*v*) **According to types of output power**—

- DC output (ac to dc conversion, direat dc generation).
- AC output (variable frequency-constant voltage, variable frequency-varible voltage, constant frequency-variable voltage,constant frequency-constant voltage).

(*vi*) **According to power control**—

- Stall regulated (fixed rotor blades).
- Pitch regulated (adjustable rotor blades).

(*vii*) **According to location**—

- on-shore–These are situated on land.
- off-shore–These are situated mid sea/ocean.

(*viii*) **According to type of hub—**

- rigid
- tethered
- hinged blades
- gimbaled

(*ix*) **According to yaw orientation**

- Free yaw
- driven yaw
- fixed yaw

(*x*) **According to transmission**

- with gear
- without gear

(*xi*) **According to number of blades**

- one bladed
- two bladed
- three bladed
- multi bladed

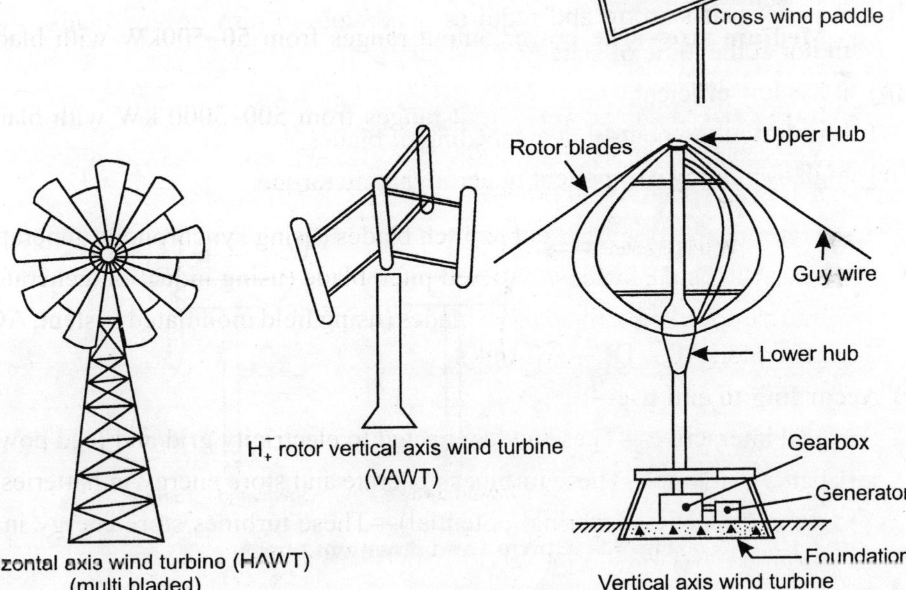

Fig. 9.8. Types of wind turbine

9.6.1. Advantages and Disadvantages of Horizontal Axis and Vertical Axis Wind Turbines

(*a*) Horizontal axis wind turbine(HAWT)

Advantages—

(*i*) It has high efficiency.

(*ii*) It is possible to turn blades of rotor (pitchable blades) which helps to generate more power and also prevent damage during storms.

(*iii*) it has low cost to power ratio.

Disadvantages—

(*i*) heavy equipments such as generator and gearbox are mounted on the tower.

(*ii*) difficult to carryout maintenance.

(*iii*) need to be aligned along the wind by yaw control which makes design complex.

(*b*) vertical axis wind turbine (VAWT)

Advantages—

(*i*) heavy equipments such as generator and gearbox are mounted on the ground.

(*ii*) easy to carryout maintenance.

(*iii*) can receive wind from any direction and hence yaw control is not required resulting is simpler design.

(*iv*) simple blade design as no pitching is provided.

(*v*) low cost of fabrication.

Disadvantage—

(*i*) it is not self starting and requires generators to turn turbine blades by running as motor at the time of start.

(*ii*) it has low efficiency.

(*iii*) it is difficult to control overspeeding of blades.

(*iv*) high oscillating component in aerodynamic torque.

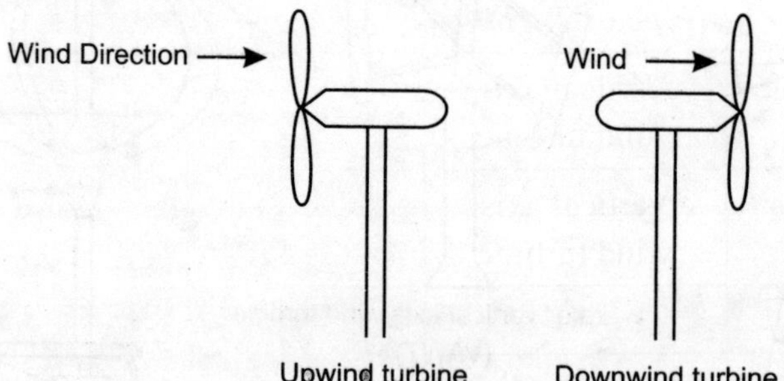

Fig. 9.9. Upwind and downwind turbine

9.6.2. Comparision of blades of HAWT

Table 9.3: Comparision of blades of HAWT

Sr. No.	*Parameter/item*	*Single blade*	*Double blade*	*Three blade*
1.	Rotor speed	Higher rotor speed required to capture same amount of wind power.	Same as single blade.	Lower rotor speed can capture more wind power.
2.	Gearbox	Lower cost of gearbox due to higher speed.	Same as single blade.	Higher cost of gearbox due to lower speed.

3.	Noise	Higher speed produces more noise.	Same as single blade.	Lower speed produces less noise.
4.	Chances of bird strike	Higher due to higher speed.	Same as single blade.	lower due to lower speed
5.	Counter balance	Required.	Required.	Not required.
6.	Ease of rotor installation	Easy.	Need teethering hub due to gyroscopic imbalance.	Gyroscopic forces are balanced.
7.	Energy capture	Captures 10% less energy than two blade.	Captures 5%less energy than three blades.	—

9.6.3. Comparision of type of propulsion and peak efficiency

Table 9.4: Comparision of propulsion and peak efficiency of HAWT and VAWT

Sr. No	*Design*	*Type of Turbine*	*Propulsion*	*peak efficiency*
1.	Darrieus rotor	Vertical axis wind turbine	Lift	40%
2.	Savoniur rotor	Vertical axis wind turbine	Drag	16%
3.	Cup	-do-	Drag	8%
4.	Three bladed	Horizontal axis wind turbine	Lift	50% (Single blade –43%) (Double blade–47%
5.	Dutch mind mill	-do-	Lift	27%
6.	American farm wind mill	-do-	Lift	31%

9.7. EXPRESSION FOR WIND POWER OUTPUT

Let m = mass of air flow, kg

v = velocity of air mass, m/s

ρ = density of air, kg/m^3

Q = volume of air flow, m^3

A wind turbine extracts power from wind by slowing down the wind. Hence,power produced by wind turbine is net kinetic energy change across the turbine blades.

∴ Kinetic Energy, $$E = \frac{1}{2} mv^2 \quad ...(9.3)$$

Power generated, $$P = \frac{dE}{dt} = \frac{d}{dt}\left[\frac{1}{2} mv^2\right] \quad ...(9.4)$$

$$P = \frac{1}{2}\frac{d}{dt}[(\rho.Q) \times v^2] \quad (\because \text{mass} = \text{density} \times \text{volume}), = \rho.Q \quad (9.5)$$

$$P = \frac{1}{2}\rho\frac{dQ}{dt}v^2 \quad ...(9.6)$$

Now, $\frac{dQ}{dt}$ = discharge = area of cross section of rotor blade × velocity of air

$$= A_s \times v$$

∴ $$P = \frac{1}{2}.\rho.(A_s.v).v^2 \quad ...(9.7)$$

$$P = \frac{1}{2}.\rho.A_s.v^3 \quad ...(9.8)$$

This is the expression for theoretical power .However, due to spillage loss taking place between blades through the gap, actual power generated is less than the theoretical power. To account for this loss, co-efficient of power (Cp)is defined as follows—

$$\text{Coefficient of power, } C_p = \frac{\text{Actual power}}{\text{Theoretical power}} = \frac{P_{actual}}{P_{theoretical}}$$

Value of Cp is unique to each turbine type and is a function of wind velocity.

∴ $$P_{actual} = C_P.\frac{1}{2}.\rho.A_s v^3 \quad ...(9.9)$$

Taking into account,efficiency of gearbox (η_{GB})and generator (η_{Gen}), The actual power generated is given by following expression—

$$P_{actual} = \frac{1}{2}C_p.\rho.\frac{\pi D^2}{4}.v^3.\eta_{GB}.\eta_{Gen} \quad ...(9.10)$$

$$P_{actual} = \frac{\pi}{8}.C_p.\rho.D^2 v^3.\eta_{GB}.\eta_{Gen} \quad ...(9.11)$$

It is observed that actual output of wind turbine depends upon following factors—

(*i*) wind speed (v).

(*ii*) diameter of rotor blades.

(*iii*) conversion efficiency of rotor or coefficient of power(C_p).

(*iv*) efficiency of generator (η_{Gen}).

(*v*) efficiency of gearbox (η_{GB}).

Wind speed has highest influence on power output as it varies in cubic power.

Actual efficiency of wind turbine generator system is 35–45% which reduces to 10 – 30% considering gearbox efficiency, generator efficiency and efficiency of energy storage system.

9.7.1. Factors Affecting Power Output of Wind Turbine

Power output of a wind turbine depends upon following factors—

(*i*) wind speed, v

(*ii*) diameter of rotor blades (swept area), D.

(*iii*) co-efficent of power, C_p.

(*iv*) air density, ρ.

(*v*) height of tower, H.

(*vi*) capacity factor, C_F.

(*vii*) Betz limit.

(*i*) **Wind speed**—Power output of wind turbine increases with increase in wind speed in cubic relation.

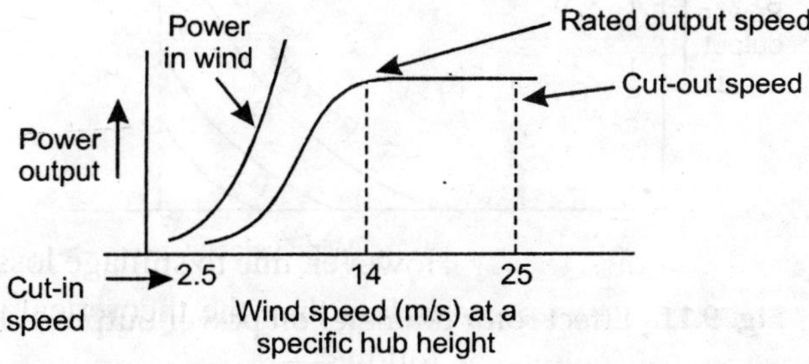

Fig. 9.10. Wind speed -power output characteristics

Usable power generation starts at 2.5m/s wind speed called cut-in speed. With further increase in wind speed,power output increases. The maximum operating wind speed limit is 25 m/s called cut-out speed due to safety reasons. Hence, in order to produce more, the site should have high value of wind speed throughout the year. Doubling of wind speed increases power output 8 times. Cut-in-speed depends upon design and inertia of machine.

(*ii*) **Diameter of rotor blades (D)**—A large diameter of blade has more swept area ($\pi D^2/4$) and hence generates more power. A small increase in blade length produces higher output power. Table 9.2 gives generated rated power output for a given diameter of blade.

Since, $P \propto D^2$

$$\therefore \quad \frac{P}{P_o} = \left(\frac{D}{D_o}\right)^2 \qquad ...(9.12)$$

Table 9.5: Rotor diameter and generator rated power output

Rotor diameter(m)	*Generator rated power output (kW)*
27	225
33	300
40	500

44	600
48	750
54	1000
64	1500
72	2000
80	2500
116	5000

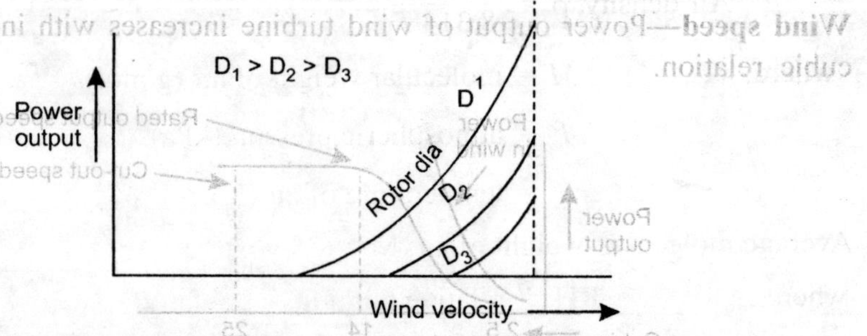

Fig. 9.11. Effect rotor diameter on power output

It is observed that power output increases sharply with increase in rotor diameter. Material used for rotor blades are glass fibre reinforced plastic(GRP–it is fibre reinforced polyester or epoxy), Carbon fibre, Kevlar, wood fibre epoxy and wood. Use of steel blades increases the weight of blades while aluminium alloy have fatigue strength problem. However, these are used for small wind turbines. For large size wind turbine, GRP is preferred choice,

(*iii*) **Co-efficient of power(C_p)**—It is the fraction of power in wind that is converted by turbine into mechanical output.

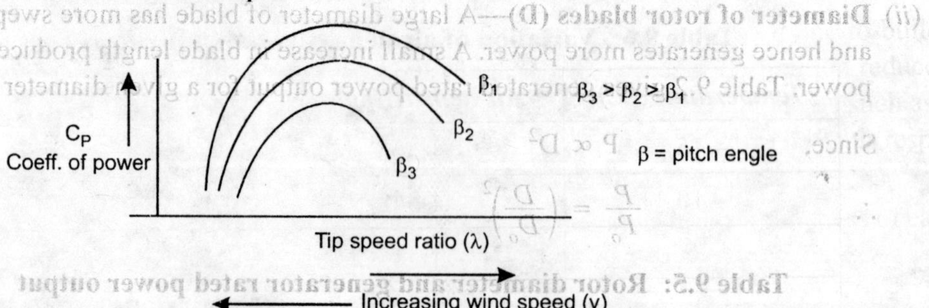

Fig. 9.12. C_p-TSR characteristics

With increase in wind speed, co-efficient of power increases. But after peak value is reached, power output starts decreasing.

$$\text{Tip speed ratio (TSR)} = \frac{\text{Rotor tip speed}}{\text{wind speed}} = \frac{\pi DN}{60v} \qquad ...(9.13$$

where, N = rpm of rotor blades.

v = wind speed.

D = diameter of rotor blades.

(*iv*) **Air density (ρ)**—A higher value of air density results in more power output. Air density varies with ambient temperature and height above ground. Air density is less at higher elevation. Also, cold air is more dense than warm air. So, output of wind turbine is more at lower height and lower average temperature.

Air density is given by following expression—

$$\text{Air density, } \rho = \frac{M.P.}{8.314\,T} \quad ...(9.14)$$

where, M = molecular weight of air (g/mol).

P = atmospheric pressure(kPa).

T = temperature of air (K).

Average molecular weight of air, M = (28.964 g/mol-RH)

where RH = relative humidity of air. ...(9.15)

$$\therefore \quad \text{Air density, } \rho = \frac{[28.964 - 0.253\,(RH)]\,P}{8.314\,T} \quad ...(9.16)$$

ρ = 1.225 kg/m^3 at 15°C and 1 atmospheric pressure given by following expression-

$$\rho = 1.225 K_T K_A \quad ...(9.17)$$

where, K_T = Density ratio (for temperature correction).

K_A = Pressure ratio (for altitude correction).

Following table 9.6 gives density of air at different temperature and corresponding temperature correction factor.

Table 9.6: Variation of air density with temperature

Temperature(°C)	*Air density (kg/m^3)*	*Density ratio(K_T)*
–15	1.368	1.12
– 10	1.342	1.10
– 5	1.317	1.07
0	1.293	1.05
5	1.269	1.04
10	1.247	1.02
15	1.225	1.00
20	1.204	0.98

25	1.184	0.97
30	1.165	0.95
35	1.146	0.94
40	1.127	0.92

Variation of atmospheric pressure with altitude is given in table 9.7—

Table 9.7: Variation of atmospheric pressure with altitude

Altitude (m)	*Pressure(atm)*	*Pressure ratio* K_A
0	1.000	1.000
200	0.977	0.977
400	0.954	0.954
600	0.931	0.931
800	0.910	0.910
1000	0.888	0.888
1200	0.868	0.868
1400	0.847	0.847
1600	0.827	0.827
1800	0.808	0.808
2000	0.789	0.789
2200	0.771	0.771

(*v*) **Height of tower, H**—Wind on the surface of earth are slowed down due to buildings, forests or other structures. As the altitude increases, the affect of obstruction reduces and wind speed increases resulting in higher output power. On smooth surfaces such as calm sea, very low resistance is offered to wind and variation of wind speed with respect to altitude is modest. Tall buildings, forests etc. create turbulence in air.

Hellman's exponential law is used which takes into account surface roughness of earth on wind speed.

$$\frac{v}{v_0} = \left(\frac{H}{H_0}\right)^{\alpha} \qquad ...(9.18)$$

where, v = Wind speed at new height H.

v_o = Wind speed at original height H_o.

H = New height.

H_o = Original height.

α = Wind shear exponent.

($\propto$ is a measure of surface roughness)

Following table 9.8 gives various value of $\propto$ for different ground conditions

Table 9.8: Values of friction coefficient (α)

Type of landscape	*Friction coefficient* (α)
Smooth surface–ocean, ice	0.07
Lakes,smooth and hard ground	0.10
Grassland	0.15
Tall crops,hedges, shrubs	0.20
Heavy forest	0.25
Small town with trees	0.30
City area with tall buildings	0.40

Following graph shows variation of altitude with wind velocity for different values of friction coefficient (α).

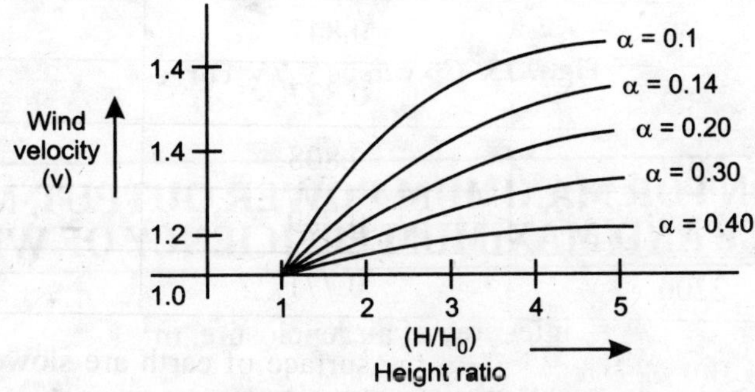

Fig. 9.13. Wind velocity-height ratio curve

Small wind turbines of capacity (10–100kW) are located at a height of 30–50 m. Higher capacity wind turbines of capacity 1–5 MW are located at 60–100 m height. The length of blades go upto 150 m.

Following graph gives relationship between wind velocity and altitude.

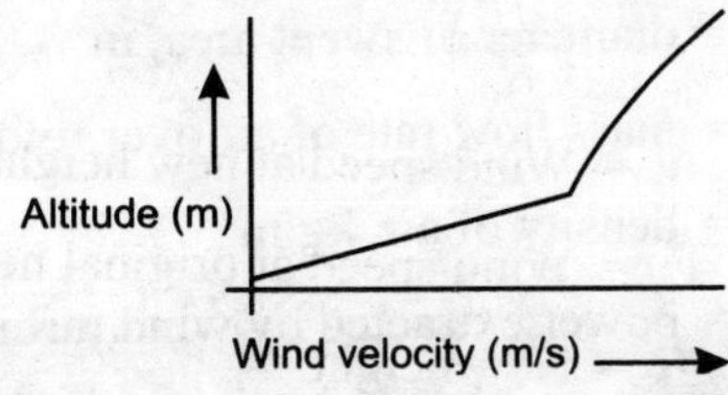

Fig. 9.14. Altitude-wind velocity characteristic

(*vi*) **Capacity factor (C_F)**–It is a measure of actual output of a wind turbine in given period. As the wind flow is intermittent in nature ,the power output varies accordingly. A higher value of average wind velocity results in higher power output.

$$\text{Capacity factor, } C_F = \frac{\text{Actual annual energy produced}}{\text{maximum plant rating} \times 8760}$$

Capacity factor is 12% for a wind speed of 5m/s. This increase to 30% for a wind speed of 7m/s. That is, **a 2m/s increase in wind velocity results in 18% increase in capacity factor.**

(*vii*) **Betz limit**–Maximum efficiency of all types of wind turbine is limited by Betz limit. This value is 59.25%.This limitation is due to aerodynamic imperfections of rotor blades and mechanical losses.

The curve shows variation of coeff. of power w.r. to velocity ratio due to Betz limit.

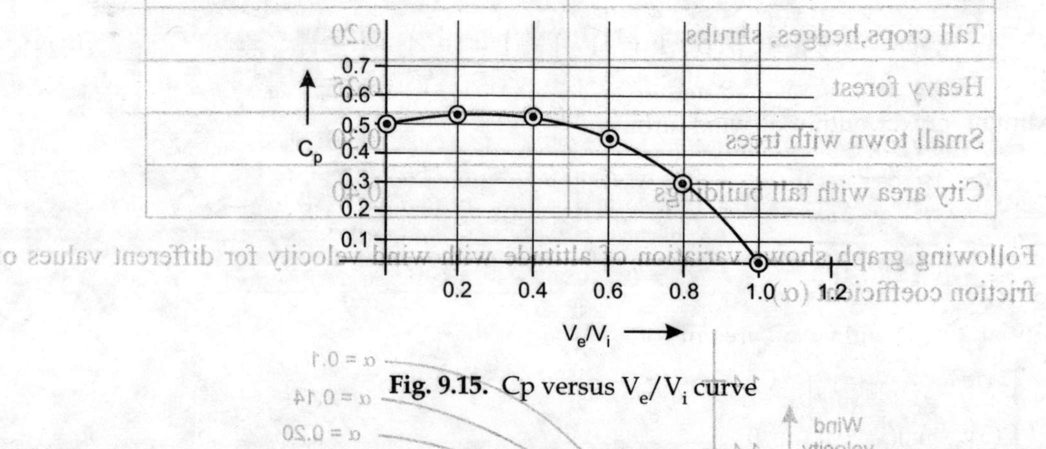

Fig. 9.15. Cp versus V_e/V_i curve

9.8. EXPRESSION FOR MAXIMUM POWER OUTPUT, MAXIMUM AXIAL FORCE AND MAXIMUM EFFICIENCY OF WIND TURBINE

Let A_i = inlet area of air enclosure, m^2

A_e = exit area of air enclosure, m^2

V_i = velocity of wind at inlet, m/s.

V_e = velocity of wind at exit, m/s.

V_r = velocity of rotor,m/s.

A_s = rotor swept volume, m^3.

D = diameter of swept area, m^2.

m = mass flow rate of air over rotor, kg/s.

ρ = density of air, kg/m^3

P_T = power extracted by wind turbine, W.

Power extracted by wind turbine is net change in kinetic energy across the wind turbine.

$$P_T = \frac{1}{2} m\,(v_i^2 - v_e^2) \qquad \text{...(9.19)}$$

Since mass flow rate, $m = \rho\, A_s\, V_r$

$$\therefore \quad P_T = \frac{1}{2} . \rho . A_s . v_r . (v_i^2 - v_e^2) \qquad \text{...(9.20)}$$

Rotor speed (v_r) is the average of inlet and output speed.

$$\therefore \quad v_r = \frac{1}{2}(v_i + v_e)$$

$$\therefore \quad P_T = \frac{1}{2} . \rho . A_s . \frac{1}{2}(v_i + v_e) . (v_i^2 - v_e^2) \qquad \text{...(9.21)}$$

$$P_T = \frac{1}{4} \rho . A_s [v_i^3 - v_e^3 - v_i v_e^2 + v_i^2 v_e] \qquad \text{...(9.22)}$$

$$P_T = \frac{1}{4} . \rho . A_s\, v_i^3 \left[1 - \left(\frac{v_e}{v_i}\right)^3 - \left(\frac{v_e}{v_i}\right)^2 + \left(\frac{v_e}{v_i}\right)\right] \qquad \text{...(9.23)}$$

For maximum power output of wind turbine, $\frac{dP_T}{dv_e} = 0$

$$\therefore \quad \frac{dp_T}{dv_e} = 0 = \frac{1}{4} . \rho A_s . V_i^3 \left[1 - \left(\frac{V_e}{V_i}\right)^3 - \left(\frac{V_e}{V_i}\right)^2 + \left(\frac{V_e}{V_i}\right)\right] \qquad \text{...(9.24)}$$

$$\text{or} \quad \frac{1}{4} . \rho\, A_s . [-3v_e^3 - 2v_e v_i + v_i^2] = 0 \qquad \text{...(9.25)}$$

As density of air (ρ) and swept area of rotor blades (A_s) can not be zero, therefore—

$$[-3v_e^2 - 2v_e v_i + v_i^2] = 0 \qquad \text{...(9.26)}$$

$$\text{or} \quad (3v_e - v_i)(v_e + v_i) = 0 \qquad \text{...(9.27)}$$

Now, $v_e = -v_i$ is not possible. Hence,

$$v_e = \frac{1}{3} v_i \qquad \text{...(9.28)}$$

Substituting above in eq. 9.23, we get,

$$(P_T)_{\text{Max}} = (0.5925) . \frac{1}{2} (\rho . A_s . v_i^3) \qquad \text{...(9.29)}$$

So, the maximum efficiency of a wind turbine is 59.25% due to imperfections in aerodynamic structure and mechanical losses. This is known as **Betz limit** (named after German physcist Albert Betz in 1926).

Axial force exerted by wind stream on blades of turbine is given by—

$$F = m\,(v_i - v_e) \qquad \text{...(9.30)}$$

$$F = \rho . A_s \left(\frac{v_i + v_e}{2}\right)(v_i - v_e) \qquad \text{...(9.31)}$$

$$F = \rho . \frac{\pi D^2}{4} \left(\frac{v_i^2 - v_e^2}{2}\right) \qquad \text{...(9.32)}$$

$$F = \frac{\pi}{8} \rho D^2 (v_i^2 - v_e^2) \quad ...(9.33)$$

Substituting $v_e = \frac{1}{3} v_i$ to get maximum axial fore in eq. (9.33)

$$(F)_{Max} = \frac{\pi}{9} \rho D^2 v_i^2 \quad ...(9.34)$$

Therefore, maximum axial force on blade of a wind turbine is proportional to square of inlet velocity and square of diameter of swept area.

9.9. AERODYNAMICS OF WIND TURBINE

The blades of wind turbine have aerofoil cross-section. Depending upon aerodynamic performance desired, width and length of blades are designed. Power extracted by wind turbine depends upon lift force and drag force. Lift force acts at right angle to air flow while drag force acts in the direction of air flow. Change in velocity of air flow over lifting surface produces lift force. This change in velocity causes difference in pressure across the lifting surface resulting in production of a force which is directed from high pressure side to low pressure side.

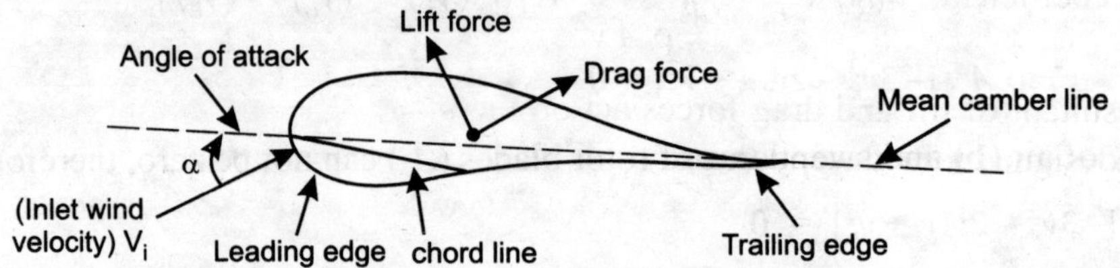

Fig. 9.16: Aerofoil section

Drag force is due to viscous friction force at the surface of aerofoil and unequal pressure at the aerofoil surface. Lift force is stronger than drag force. Both lift and drag forces are proportional to wind speed, area of aerofoil and density of air. Both these forces causes the rotor blades to spin due to resultant force.

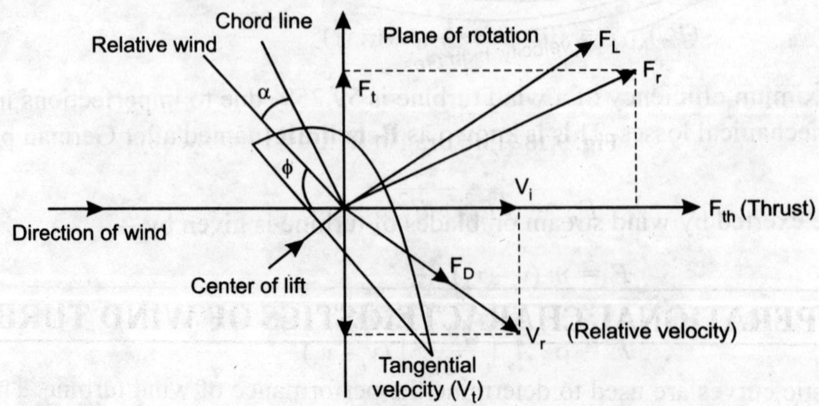

Fig. 9.17: Forces acting on an aerofoil section

When wind attacks the blade with velocity v_i, its tangential component v_t acts along the plane of rotation and relative velocity component at angle ϕ to the direction of wind velocity v_i. Relative force has two components–tangential force (F_t) and thrust (F_{th}) at right angle to each other. The lift and drag forces are given by—

Lift force, $$F_L = \frac{1}{2} C_L \rho A v_i^2 \quad ...(9.35)$$

Drag force, $$F_D = \frac{1}{2} C_D \rho A v_i^2 \quad ...(9.36)$$

where, A = Surface area of blades.

ρ = density of air

Lift coefficient, $$C_L = \frac{L/A_L}{\frac{1}{2}\rho v^2} = \frac{\text{Lift force/cross. section of aerofoil}}{\frac{1}{2} \times \text{air density} \times (\text{wind speed})^2}$$

Drag coefficient, $$C_D = \frac{D/A_D}{\frac{1}{2}\rho v^2} = \frac{\text{Drag force/effective area of aerofoil in drag direction}}{\frac{1}{2} \times \text{air density} \times (\text{wind speed})^2}$$

Thrust coefficient, $$C_T = \frac{T}{\frac{1}{2}\rho A v^2} = \frac{\text{Thrust force}}{\text{Dynamic foce}}$$

The resultant of lift and drag forces act on the blade. The structural members viz. tower and blades are designed to withstand thrust.

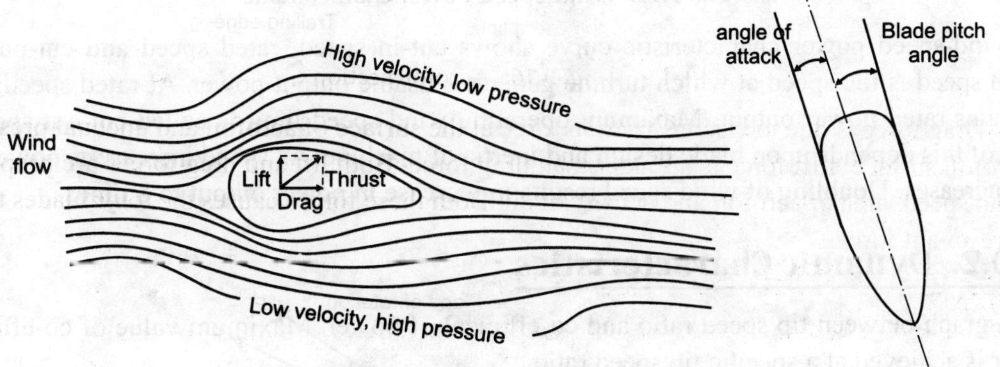

Fig. 9.18. Lift, drag and thrust on an aerofoil

$$F_R = \sqrt{F_L^2 + F_D^2} \quad ...(9.34)$$

9.10. OPERATIONAL CHARACTERISTICS OF WIND TURBINE

Characteristic curves are used to determine the performance of wind turbine. These are explained below—

9.10.1. Wind speed–Power characteristics

Output of wind turbine varies with wind speed. Various factors which determine the shape of this curve are following—

(i) rotor swept area.
(ii) shape of blade.
(iii) number of blades.
(iv) tip speed ratio (TSR).
(v) cut-in speed.
(vi) rated speed.
(vii) cut-out spccd.

The cut-in speed is 2.5m/s and cut-out speed is 25m/s.

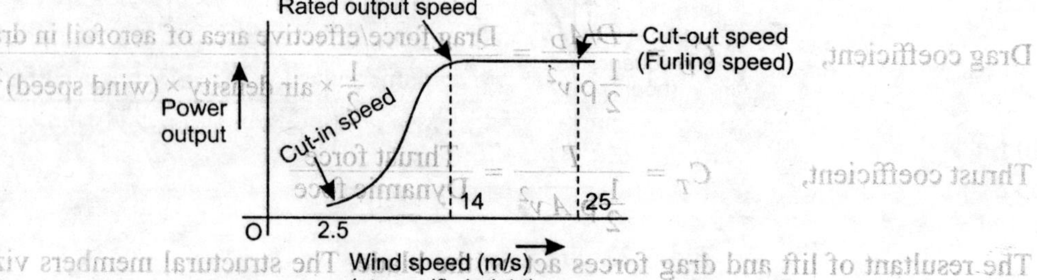

Fig. 9.19. Wind-speed Power characteristic

Wind-speed power characteristic curve shows cut-in speed, rated speed and cut-out speed. Cut-in speed is the speed at which turbine generates usable output power. At rated speed, turbine generates rated power output. Maximum operating wind speed limit is called cut-out speed. The value of this depends upon blade design and inertia of machine. As speed increasers, power output also increases. Doubling of wind speed results in increase in power output to 8 times.

9.10.2. Dynamic Characteristics

It is a graph between tip speed ratio and co-efficient of power. Maximum value of co-efficient of power is achieved at a specific tip speed ratio.

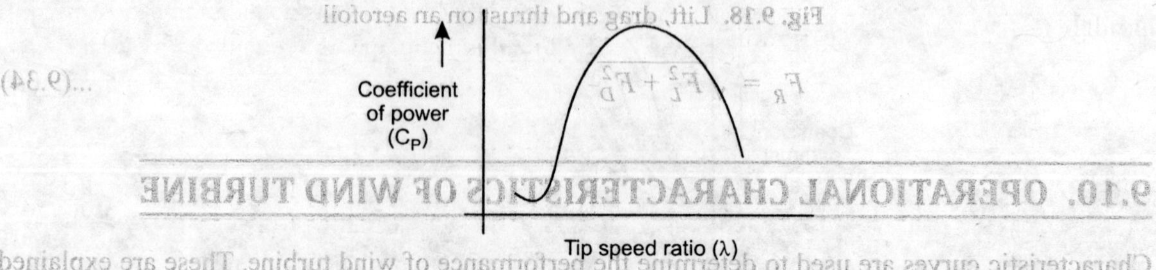

Fig. 9.20. C_p–λ curve

9.10.3. Velocity duration curve, Power duration curve and frequency duration curve

Velocity duration curve is a graph between mean wind velocity and hours in a year.

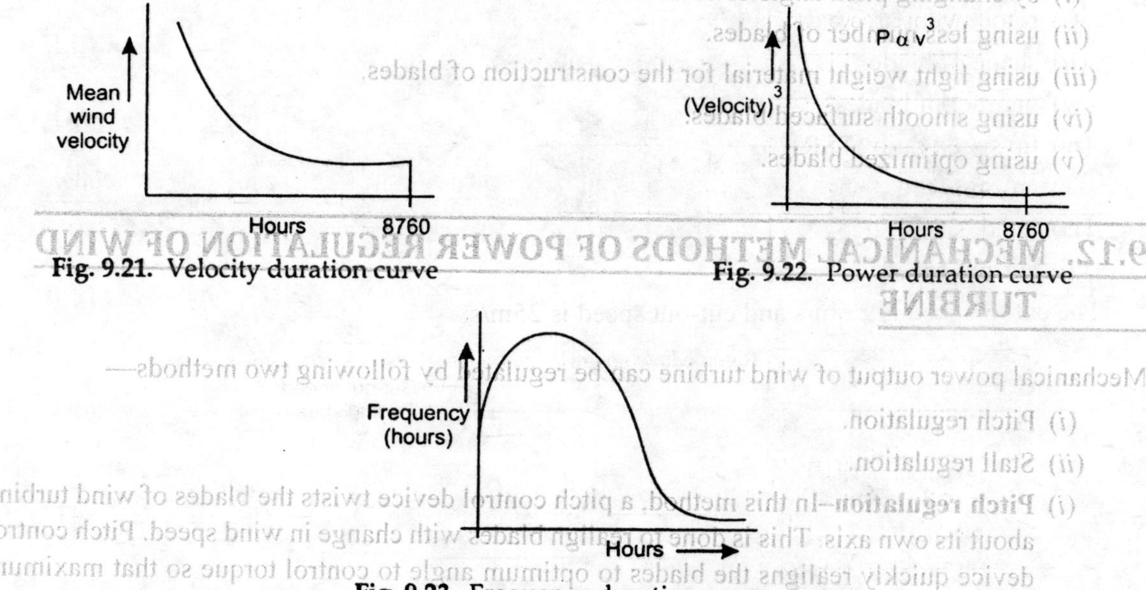

Fig. 9.21. Velocity duration curve

Fig. 9.22. Power duration curve

Fig. 9.23. Frequency duration curve

Power- duration curve is graph between cube of wind velocity and duration(v^3 is proportional to power output).Frequency duration curve is a graph between number of hours for which mean wind velocity of particular value is available.

These curve are useful in deciding a particular types of wind turbine. These curve are site specific. These data is also useful in estimating actual energy output of turbine.

9.10.4. Axial force characteristic

It is a graph between thrust force coefficient (C_F) and tip speed ratio (λ). At a particular tip speed ratio, the thrust increases with increased solidity. This information is needed for structural design of tower.

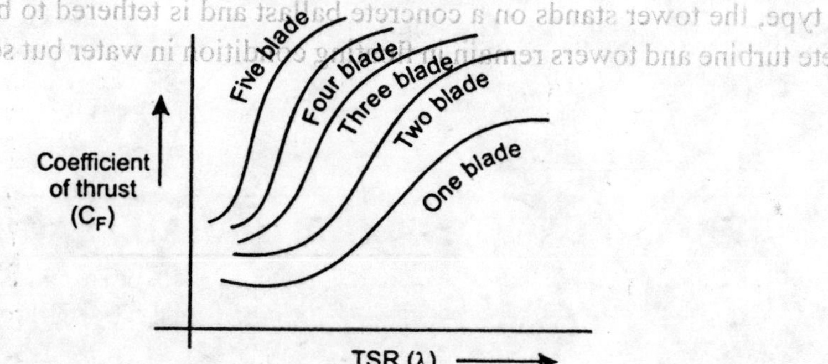

Fig. 9.24. Axial force coefficient-tip speed ratio curve

9.11 METHODS OF REDUCING DRAG ON WIND TURBINE

Following are the methods used for reducing drag on wind turbine—

(*i*) by changing pitch angle of blades.

(*ii*) using less number of blades.

(*iii*) using light weight material for the construction of blades.

(*iv*) using smooth surfaced blades.

(*v*) using optimized blades.

9.12. MECHANICAL METHODS OF POWER REGULATION OF WIND TURBINE

Mechanical power output of wind turbine can be regulated by following two methods—

(*i*) Pitch regulation.

(*ii*) Stall regulation.

(*i*) **Pitch regulation**–In this method, a pitch control device twists the blades of wind turbine about its own axis. This is done to realign blades with change in wind speed. Pitch control device quickly realigns the blades to optimum angle to control torque so that maximum energy of wind can be trapped.

(*ii*) **Stall regulation**–It this method, design of wind turbine blades are such that aerofoil produces reduced aerodynamic force due to high wind speed which ultimately leads to stalling of turbine. This feature protects the wind turbine from high speed wind.

9.13. OFF-SHORE WIND POWER GENERATION

Flow of wind is obstructed by buildings, forest and other construction resulting in low wind velocity. On seas and coastal areas,the velocity of wind is high due to absence of any obstruction. A higher wind velocity translates into higher power output. Construction of wind power farms is preferable in off-shore area. Off-shore wind turbines are of two types-fixed bottom construction and floating construction. In fixed bottom construction, the wind turbine tower is installed on the sea bed. While in floating type, the tower stands on a concrete ballast and is tethered to bed through ropes so that the complete turbine and towers remain in floating condition in water but secured to seabed through ropes.

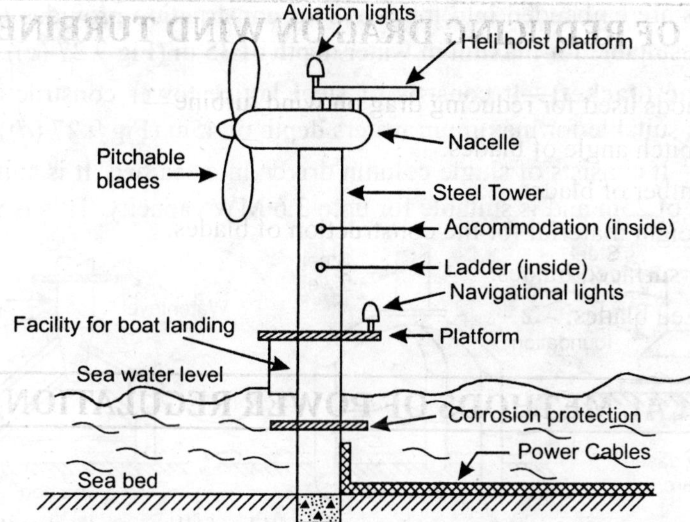

Fig. 9.25. Construction of off-shore wind turbine structure (fixed bottom type)

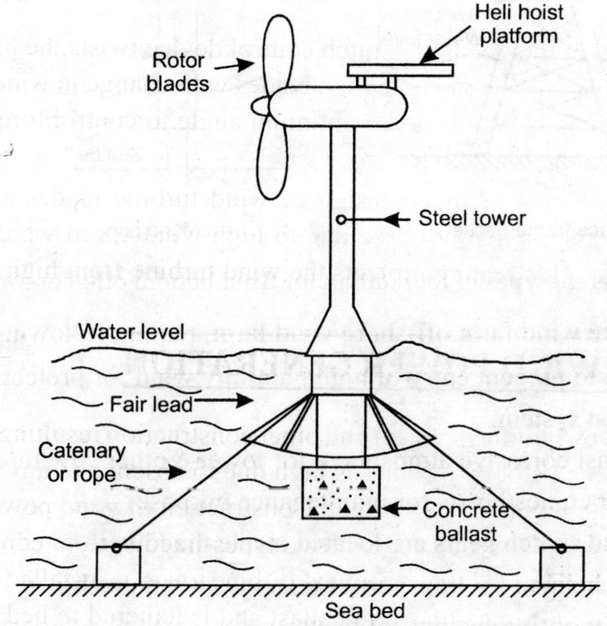

Fig. 9.26. Construction of floating type wind turbine structure

Foundation for off-shore fixed bottom wind turbine are of following types—

(*i*) **Gravity based structure**—It is used for fixed wind turbine construction and steel tower is directly driven into seabed .It is limited to maximum waters depth of 30 m and is suitable for 5MW capacity (Fig 9.27 (*a*)).

(*ii*) **Space frame (tri-pile)**—The tower is supported on three legs embedded into seabed (Fig,9.27 (*b*)).

(*iii*) **Space frame (tri-pod)**—The tower is supported on three legs which are interconnected and the legs are embedded into the sea. This construction provides more rigidity to the towers. It is suitable for maximum water depth of 35 m (Fig 9.27 (*c*)).

(*iv*) **Space frame (Jacket)**—It consists of steel lattice tower construction embedded into seabed. It is suitable for maximum waters depth of 45m (Fig 9.27 (*d*)).

(*v*) **Mono pile**—It consists of single column driven into sea bed .It is suitable for maximum water depth of 25m and is suitable for upto 3.6 MW capacity. This is widely used.

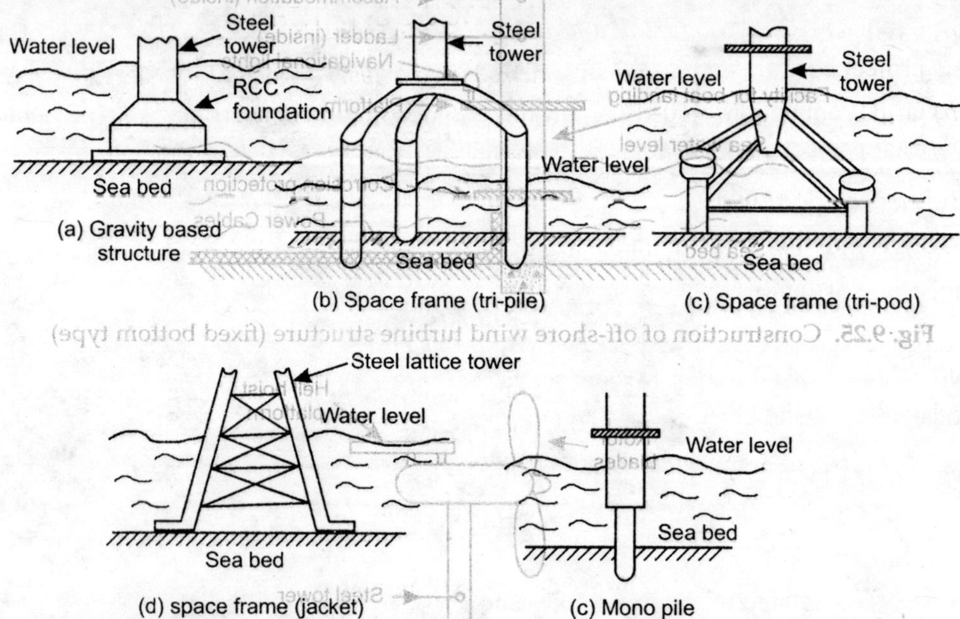

Fig. 9.27. Different types of foundation for fixed bottom off-shore wind turbine

Compared to on-shore wind farm,off-shore wind farm, require following special systems—

(*i*) air tight nacelle to prevent entry of high humidity wind for protection against corrosion .

(*ii*) dehumidification system.

(*iii*) protection against corrosive atmosphere for tower &other structures.

(*iv*) arrangement for cranes/hoists for maintenance purpose.

(*v*) transformers and switch gears are located inside the tower.

(*vi*) construction of helipad for transport of manpower and machinery.

(*vii*) construction of mooring facility for boats.

(*viii*) aviation and navigational lights.

Following is the comparison of on-shore and off-shore wind farms—

Table 9.9: Comparison of on-shore and off-shore wind farms

	On -shore		***off-shore***
1.	Availability of large, clear space is a constraint.	1.	Large space with no obstruction are available.

2.	Low wind velocity and hence, low output power.	2.	High wind velocity and hence, high output power.
3.	Unrestricted 24 hours a day access.	3.	Restricted access due to high waves and storms.
4.	Low construction cost (*a*) Civil works = 7 – 9% of the total project cost. (*b*) Grid connection =10–12% of the total project cost.	4.	High construction cost (*a*) Civil works = 21 – 25% of the total project cost. (*b*) Grid connection = 10 – 12% of the total project cost.
5.	Built on solid ground.	5.	Soil conditions vary (sandy, rocky or clay).
6.	Problem of shadow flicker, audible noise and asthetics.	6.	No problem of shadow flicker, noise and asthetics as theses are located upto 70 km from shore.
7.	No problem of corrosion (except those located at coastal belt).	7.	Severe problem of corrosion of structure and machinery.

Advantages of off-shore wind farms are following—

(*i*) high average wind velocity due to obstruction free smooth surface.
(*ii*) wide choice of location.
(*iii*) no issues related to shadow flicker and noise.
(*iv*) potential for industrial growth in coastal area.

Disadvantages—

(*i*) difficult access for maintenance purpose.
(*ii*) highly corrosive environment affecting life of structure & equipment.
(*iii*) high cost of foundation and submarine cables.
(*iv*) issues of social acceptance from fisherman and other marine users.
(*v*) obstruction to ships, boats, oil pipelines etc.

9.14. CONSTRAINTS IN OFF-SHORE WIND FARM CONSTRUCTION

Selection of site has following issues—

(*i*) **Shipping lanes**–While selecting suitable site for location of off-shore wind-farms,route of ships need to be considered. The selected location should be away from such routes.

(*ii*) **Naval exercise area**–Chosen location has to be away from navel exercise area due to security reasons.

(*iii*) **Slope of seabed**–Condition of seabed and soil type decides the cost of foundation for tower. A sloping seabed is not fit for tower foundation.

(*iv*) **Obstruction due to oil platforms, pipelines and cables**–The location of windfarms should be away from oil drilling rig platforms,under sea oil and gas pipelines and submarine cables.

(*v*) **Dumping area for hazardous waste**–The selected location should be away from dumping area for hazardous waste, ammunition etc. due to safety reasons.

9.15. FLOATING WIND TURBINES

A floating wind turbine is more economical in construction and shipping .It consists of a wind turbine mounted on a floating platform which is tethered to seabed using chains upto 30–1000m depth.

Advantage of floating wind farms is low visibility from land .Following expression gives coastal zone of visual influence—

$$L = \sqrt{2\,HR} \qquad \text{...(9.37)}$$

where, L = distance of turbine from shore to be visible.

H = maximum height of turbine blade tip (155m).

R = radius of earth (~6,370 km).

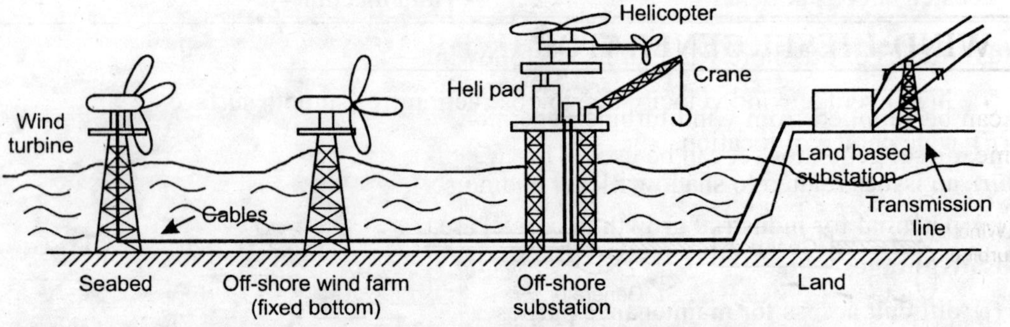

Fig. 9.28. Off-shore fixed bottom wind farms with substation

9.16. CONTRA ROTATING WIND TURBINE

This type of structure has two oppositely rotating blades mounted on same shaft. This construction has 6–16% higher efficiency than normal turbine. The two set of blades rotate in opposite direction and are coupled to two different generators.

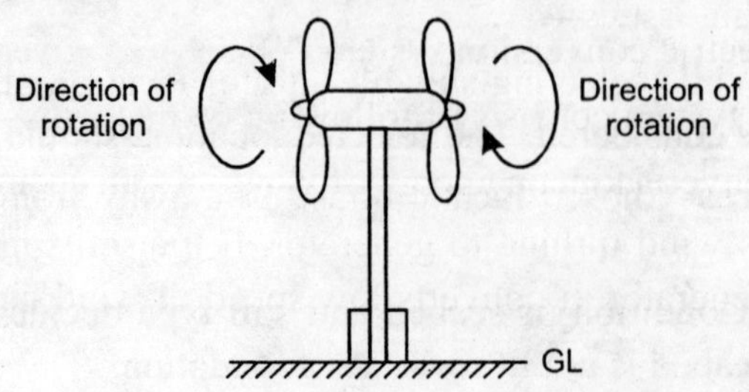

Fig. 9.29. Contra rotating wind turbine

9.17. WIND-SOLAR HYBRID SYSTEM

Due to intermittent nature of wind, it can be combined with solar PV cells to minimize variation of power output. Also, some sites have both sun and wind for several months of year. When favourable wind is available, power is generated from wind turbine. During daytime, solar PV cells can be used to generate power. System can be complimented with storage system, such as batteries.

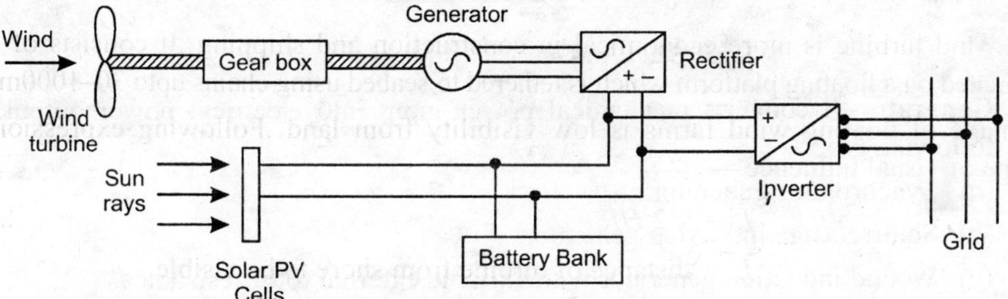

Fig. 9.30. Wind-solar hybrid system

9.18. WIND-DIESEL GENERATOR HYBRID SYSTEM

Energy can be supplied from wind turbine generator during favourable wind condition. While at other time, diesel generator set can be used. This system is useful for remote areas.

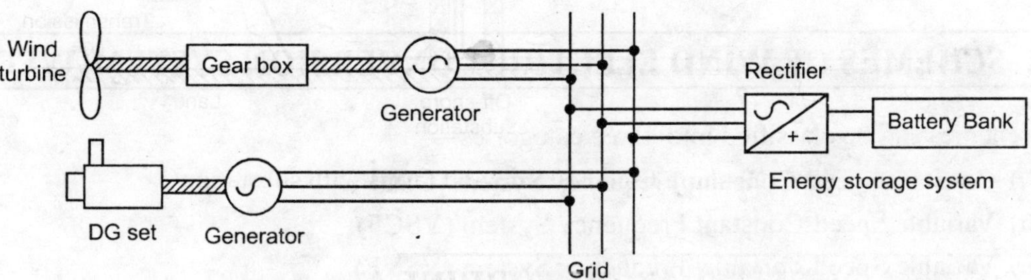

Fig. 9.31. Wind-diesel generator hybrid system

9.19. ELECTRIC POWER GENERATION FROM WIND TURBINE

Basic components of wind electric conversion system (WECS) are given below—

Wind electric conversion system consists of following components—

(*i*) **Wind turbine**–It converts kinetic energy of wind into mechanical energy .

(*ii*) **Gearbox**–It couples wind turbine to generator. It transmits mechanical energy of wind turbine to electric generator. It converts low speed of wind turbine to high speed which drives generator.

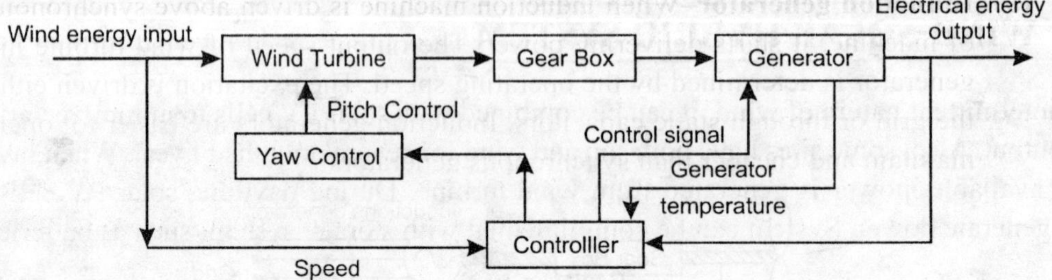

Fig. 9.32. Wind electric conversion system

(*iii*) **Generator**–It converts mechanical power input into electrical power output. It is of following types—

(*a*) Synchronous generator.

(*b*) Squirrel cage induction generator.

(*c*) Wound induction generator with variable external rotor resistance.

(*d*) Doubly fed induction generator.

(*iv*) **Controller**–It takes wind speed as feedback signal and gives necessary control output to yaw control so that wind turbine blades are aligned to the direction of wind flow to capture maximum power from wind. It receives feedback signal from output and gives necessary control output to generator control system

(*v*) **Yaw control**–Purpose of yaw control is to align the wind turbine in the direction of wind to capture maximum wind energy.

9.20. SCHEMES OF WIND ELECTRIC CONVERSION SYSTEM(WECS)

These schemes can be classified into three categories—

(*i*) Constant Speed-Constant Frequency System (CSCF).

(*ii*) Variable Speed-Constant Frequency System (VSCF).

(*iii*) Variable Speed-Variable Frequency System (VSVF).

(*i*) **Constant Speed-Constant Frequency system (CSCF)**–This system uses constant speed drive for large generators connected directly to the grid where constant frequency operation is needed. The system uses either synchronous generator or induction generator.

(*a*) **Synchronous generator**–This type of generator requires constant speed input by using variable pitch blade wind turbine.

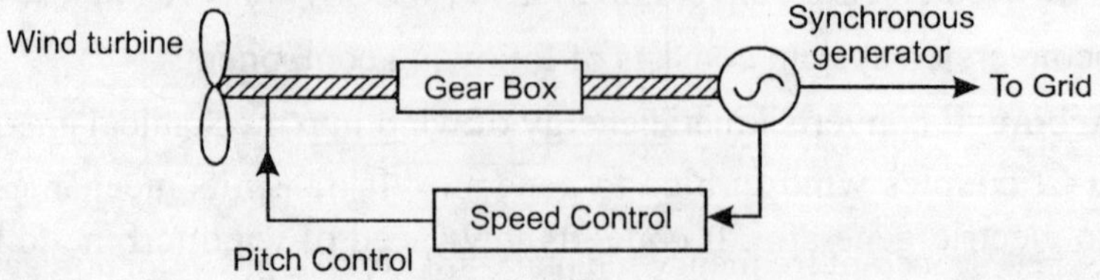

Fig. 9.33. Constant Speed-Constant Frequency system using synchronous generator

(*b*) **Induction generator**–When induction machine is driven above synchronous speed of machine, it starts delivering power. The output speed of wind turbine induction generator is determined by the operating speed. The excitation is driven either from the grid or through static capacitors. Induction generators are easier to operate and maintain and cheaper than synchronous generators.

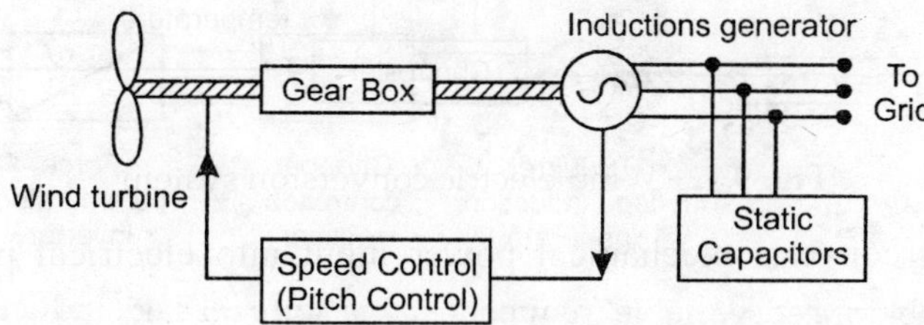

Fig. 9.34. Constant Speed-Constant Frequency system using induction generator

(*iii*) **Variable Speed-Constant Frequency speed scheme (VSCF)**–Variable speed operation of wind electric system gives higher output for both low and high speed wind. Constant frequency output is obtained by following schemes—

(*a*) **Induction generator with full converter interface**–The a.c. output of three phase induction generator is rectified using bridge rectifier and converted to ac using line commutated inverter or synchronous inverter whose frequency is fixed by the power line.

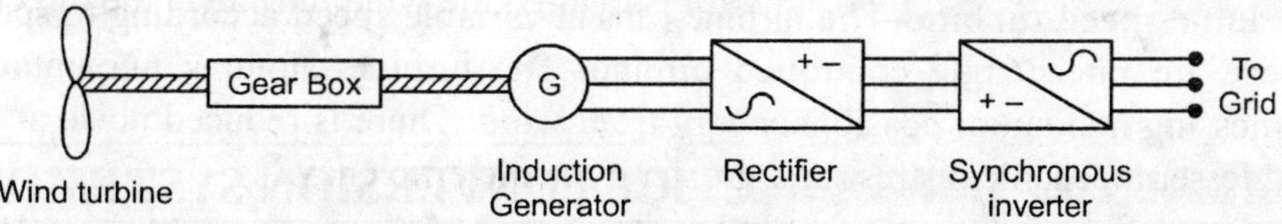

Fig. 9.35. Variable speed-constant frequency scheme using induction generator with full converter interface

(*b*) **Doubly fed induction generator with full converter interface**-Doubly fed induction generator (DFIG) is a wound rotor induction generator with slip rings. The rotor power output at slip frequency is converted to line frequency power by rectification and inversion which is then fed to the grid. The stator output which is at grid frequency is fed to the grid.

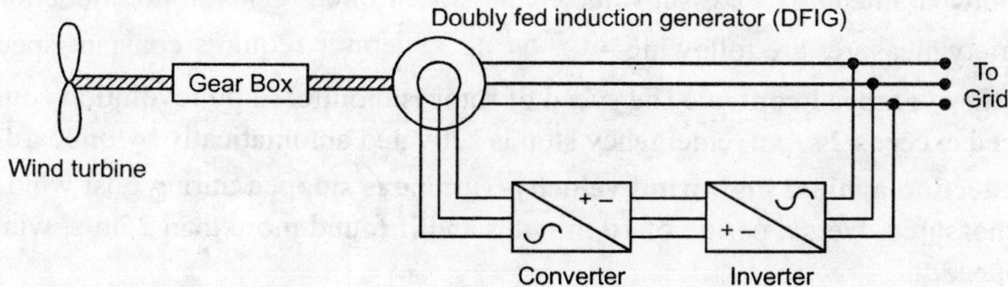

Fig. 9.36. Variable speed-constant frequency scheme using doubly fed induction generator using full converter interface with rotor circuit

(*iii*) **Variable Speed-Variable Frequency scheme (VSVF)**–This system uses squirrel cage induction generator whose voltage magnitude and frequency depends upon prime mover speed, excitation capacitance and load impedance. Such systems find application in standalone wind power application. The varying output voltage can be converted to constant dc voltage by using chopper controlled rectifier and force commutated inverters.

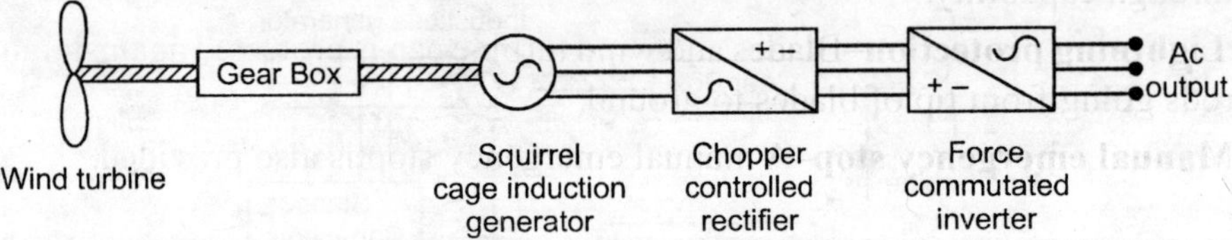

Fig. 9.37. Variable speed-variable frequency using squirrel cage induction generator

Fixed speed of turbine is obtained by using stall regulated wind turbine. Variable speed is obtained by pitch regulated wind turbine.

9.21. TYPES OF WIND-TURBINE GENERATOR

(*i*) **Constant speed turbine**–The turbine runs at one constant speed regardless of wind speed. These are fixed blade stall controlled turbine. These are low cost and easy to operate but prone to noise and mechanical stress.

(*ii*) **Variable speed turbine**–The turbine runs at variable speed according to speed of wind. These are pitch angle controlled turbine. The turbine captures maximum power by harnessing maximum possible energy from wind. There is reduced noise at lower speed and lesser mechanical stress and greater dynamic efficiency.

(*iii*) **Variable speed direct drive turbine**–These turbines run at variable speed (pitch angle regulated) without gearbox. These are very expensive.

9.22. PROTECTION OF WIND TURBINE GENERATOR SYSTEM

Following safety features are incorporad into wind turbine-generator system—

The complete system is computer controlled which monitors all system parameters and initiates shutdown if any parameter exceeds set value.

Major safety measures are following—

(*i*) **Rotor overspeed control**–The speed of rotor is monitored by revolution counters. If the speed exceeds 24 rpm, emergency stop is activated automatically by onboard computer.

(*ii*) **Protection against high wind velocity**-Turbine is stopped during gust wind. Gust wind is measured overs a period of 10 minutes and if found more than 25m/s, wind turbine is stopped.

(*iii*) **Protection against high blade tip speed**–If wind turbine speed is more than 28 rpm, a parachute attached to each blade tip opens thereby reducing the speed of turbine.

(*iv*) **Over voltage/under voltage protection of generator**–Generator is protected against set over and under voltage. In case, the set value is exceeded, a trip is initiated by the on -board computer.

(*v*) **Fault ride through capability**–To stabilize wind turbine during electrical fault and minimize current in rotor converter, active power flow is ramped down for a pre determined time and then ramped up again to pre fault value. This is known as fault ride through capability.

(*vi*) **Lightning protection**–Blades and wind turbine cap is protected against lightning through rods going from tip of blades to ground.

(*vii*) **Manual emergency stop**–A manual emergency stop is also provided.

9.23. WIND ENERGY STORAGE SYSTEM

Operation of wind turbine system is highly intermittent. Consequently, sometimes power is not available. Hence, some form of energy storage system is required to ensure continuity in power output. Sometimes power generated exceeds the demand so excess power could be stored for use at other time. Peak demand of short duration can be met from storage system. However, addition of energy storage system increases the overall cost. Several energy storage systems are available. some are listed below—

(*i*) **Pumped storage system**–The plant operates as normal hydro-electric power plant but excess energy is available water, from tail race is pumped back to reservoir at head race by running hydro turbine as pump. The stored water in reservoir can be used to meet higher demand. This is a high capacity, low cost energy storage system but require special site.

(*ii*) **Batteries**–Batteries are electro-chemical means of energy storage and are widely used. The electrical energy can be stored in the battery as chemical energy by charging them at the time of low energy demand. The same can be released at the time of high energy demand. A variety of batteries are available for use, Relative merits and demerits are listed below—

Table 9.10: Relative merit and demerit of various types of batteries

Sr. No	*Type of battery*	*Merit*	*Demerit*
1.	Lead-acid	Low capital cost	Limited life-cycle
2.	Nickel-Cadmium	High power density, high efficiency, long life	high cost,requires special charging circuit
3.	Lithium-ion	-do-	-do-
4.	Metal-air	Very high energy density.	Electric charging is difficult

5.	Zinc Bromide	high capacity.	Low energy density,
6.	Polysulphide-Bromide	-do-	-do-
7.	Vanadium-Redox	-do-	-do-
8.	Sodium-Sulphur	High power density, high efficiency.	High cost,

(*iii*) **Compressed air system**–Excess energy is used to drive air compressor which can be used at the time of excess energy demand. These are high capacity,low cost system which require special site for compressed air storage.

(iv) **Super capacitors**–Super capacitors can be used to store energy. These possess high efficiency and long life-cycle but have low energy density.

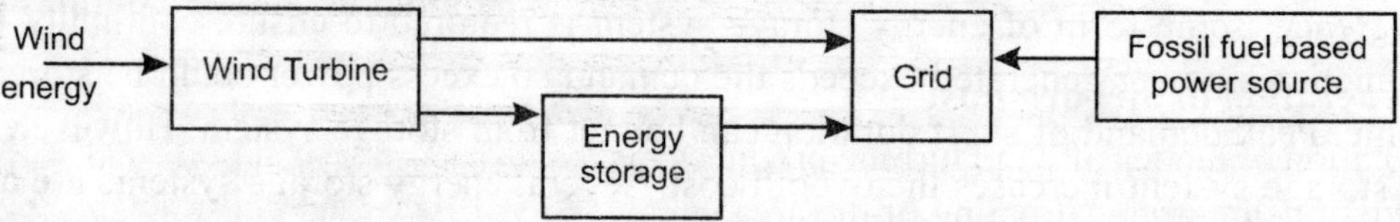

Figure 9.38. Wind energy conversion system with energy storage

9.24. ENVIRONMENTAL IMPACT OF WIND POWER GENERATION

Wind power generation is not entirely free from environmental concerns. Following are the main effects of wind turbine power generation–

(*i*) **Noise**

Wind turbine power generation system produces noise. This noise emanates from two sources-mechanical noise and aerodynamic noise. Mechanical noise is produced by gearbox and generator. Aerodynomic noise is produced by movement of wind turbine blades in air. Typical noise of a 0.5–3.6 MW wind turbine is 97–100dB(A) at a distance of 10 m from base of tower. This reduces to 35–45 dB(A) at a distance of 350 m. This low frequency noise emission may cause sleep disturbance, headache, tinnitus (constant ringing sound in ear in the absence of external stimulus), balance and equalibrium disturbance, anxiety, nausea, concentration disturbance etc.

Mechanical noise can be reduced by mounting equipment on resilient or sound and vibration absorbing mounts, using accoutstic enclosures etc. Operation of wind turbine at lower speed minimize aerodynamic noise emission.

(*ii*) **Electromagnetic interference**—

A wind turbine can reflect electromagnetic radiation if positioned near radio, television or microwave transmitter and receiver. This reflected wave interferes with original signal and may lead to significant distortion in received signal. The extent of disturbance depends upon of blade material and shape of the tower. Chances of interference is more if the blade is of metal or contains metal component.

Laminated timber blade in wind turbine absorb rather than reflect radio waves, smooth rounded tower reflect less due to their flat surface.

(*iii*) **Shadow flicker—**

Rotation of wind turbine blades produce shadow flicker(rotating blades produce a shadow on a stationary observer). This causes annoyance and in very specific case may lead to photo epileptic seizure.

(*iv*) **Visual impact—**

Changes to visual appearance of landscape leads to public opposition. However, visual perception depends upon lot of factors, such as turbine size ,number of blades, colour, number of turbines in a wind farm, layout of turbine, turbine design etc. An individual perception depends upon his level of understanding of technology, opinion on sources of energy,influence others opinion on the subject etc.

The visibility issue can be mitigated by using subdued colours for wind turbine & structure.

(*v*) **Generation of airborn dust—**

Rotation of blades of wind turbine produces localised airborn dust. This is generally taken care of using grass carpeting of the area which also enhance the appearance.

(*vi*) **Hazard to birds—**

Running blades of wind turbine present a potential hazard to birds and bats due to fatal collision. However, incidence of bird fatalities is relatively low. More birds die due to collision with vehicles, tall buildings, tall communication towers etc.

A thorough study conducted by National Environmental Research Institute, Denmark on off-shore wind farm at Tuno Knob concluded that there were no significant impact on water birds.

(*vii*) **Interference to military radar—**

Armed forces have voiced theirs concern over interference to military radars caused by wind turbine. Moreover, large diameter tall towers may intrude into theirs low flying zones used by military aircrafts.

Some studies indicate that some software based technical solutions could be retrofitted in radars located in nearby area of wind farms.

(*viii*) **Safety to human and animals—**

Rotating blades present a potential hazard to human beings and grazing animals which may lead to fatal accidents.

9.25. CURRENT STATUS OF WIND POWER GENERATION IN INDIA

Major areas suitable for wind power generation are–coastal regions of Gujarat, Andhra Pradesh, Tamil Nadu, Odisha, West Bengal, plains and hills in Rajasthan, UP and MP. The estimated potential of wind power at 50 m height is 49,130 MW. This is 1,02,788 at 80 m height.

The total installed capacity in wind power generation (as on 31/3/15)is 24,376 MW. India stands at fifth position in terms of installed capacity in the world. Other leading countries are China, USA, Germany and Spain.

Following are the statewise break up of wind power installed capacity (as on 31/3/15).

(*i*) Tamil Nadu = 7455.2 MW
(*ii*) Gujarat = 3645.3 MW
(*iii*) Maharashtra = 4450.8 MW
(*iv*) Rajasthan = 3307.2 MW
(*v*) Karnataka = 2638.4 MW
(*vi*) Andhra Pradesh = 1031.4 MW
(*vii*) Madhya Pradesh = 879.7 MW
(*viii*) Kerala = 35.1 MW

Major wind turbine manufacturers are ABB, Siemens, Gamesa, Vestas, Windmatic, Suzlon, Micon, Polenko etc.

The maximum capacity of single unit wind turbine operating in the world is 6 MW while in India, the highest capacity is 1.5 MW

Following are the technical details of 6 MW wind turbine—

(*i*) Capacity = 6 MW
(*ii*) Diameter of rotor = 154 m
(*iii*) Speed = 5 – 11 rpm
(*iv*) Voltagę = 690 V
(*v*) Frequency = 50 Hz
(*vi*) Cut-in speed = 3 – 5m/s
(*vii*) Cut-out speed = 25m/s
(*viii*) Maximum 3 second gust speed withstand = 70m/s
(*ix*) Generator = Permanent magnet synchronous generator
(*x*) Type of drive = Direct drive.

9.26. OPERATING WIND POWER PLANTS IN THE WORLD

Some of the operating on-shore wind farms are listed below—

Table 9.11: Select list of on-shore wind farms in the world

Sr. No	*Location*	*Capacity (MW)*
1.	Gansu, China	5160
2.	Muppandal, India	1500
3.	Jaisalmer, India	1064

4.	Alta,USA	1020
5.	Shepherds Flat ,USA	845
6.	Roscoe,USA	781.5
7.	Horse hollow,USA	735.5
8.	Capricorn Ridge,USA	662.5

Following is the list of off-shore windfarms—

Table 9.12: Select list of off-shore windfarms in the world

S. No	*Location*	*Capacity (MW)*
1.	London array, U.K.	630
2.	Gwynty Mor, U.K.	576
3.	Greater Gabbard, U.K.	504
4.	Anholt, Denmark	400
5.	Bard off-shore -1, Germany	400
6.	West of Duddon Sands, U.K.	389
7.	Walney,U.K.	367
8.	Thornton Bank, Belgium	325
9.	Sheringham Shoal, U.K.	315
10.	Thanet, U.K.	300

SOLVED EXAMPLES

Ex 9.1: Determine the power output of wind turbine having 150 kW rating. Details of wind turbine are following-

(*i*) Blade diameter of wind turbine = 20 m

(*ii*) Average wind speed = 15 m/s

(*iii*) Efficiency of generation = 95%

(*iv*) Efficiency of gearbox = 90%

Given,density of air = 1.2kg/m^3, Coefficient of performance of blade = 0.3

Solution: Power output of wind turbine, $P = \frac{1}{2} \rho A C_p \eta_G \eta_{GB} V^3$ watt

$$P = \frac{1}{2} \times (1.2) \times \left(\frac{\pi \times (20)^2}{4}\right) \times 0.3 \times 0.95 \times 0.90 \times (15)^3$$

$$P = 163 \text{ kW}$$ **Ans.**

Ex 9.2: Speed of wind at a place in coastal Gujarat is 30 km/hr and wind swept area is 25 m^2. Determine the power generated by the wind turbine. Given, co-efficient of power = 0.45.

Solution: Power output of wind turbine $P = \frac{1}{2} \rho A_s C_p V^3$ watt

$$P = \frac{1}{2} \times 1.2 \times 25 \times 0.45 \times \left(\frac{30 \times 1000}{3600}\right)^3$$

$$P = 3902 \text{ watt}$$ **Ans.**

Ex 9.3: A wind turbine has a diameter of 15 m and cut in speed of 4 m/s develops a power of 3kW. Determine—

(*i*) efficiency of wind turbine.

(*ii*) effect of wind velocity of 15 m/s on wind turbine power and axial force.

Given, density of air = 1.2 kg/m^3

Solution: (*i*) Swept area are of turbine, $A_s \frac{\pi D^2}{4} = \frac{\pi \times (15)^2}{4} = 176.6 \text{ m}^2$

Wind velocity $v = 4$ m/s

Wind power $P = \frac{1}{2} \rho A_s v^3 = \frac{1}{2} \times 1.2 \times 176.6 \times (4)^3 \eta_T$

$$3000 = \frac{1}{2} \times 1.2 \times 176.6 \times (4)^3 \times \eta_T \Rightarrow \eta_T = \frac{3000}{\frac{1}{2} \times 1.2 \times 176.6 \times (4)^3}$$

$$\eta_T = 44.2\%$$ **Ans.**

(*ii*) Power developed at 15m/s velocity, $P = \frac{1}{2} . \rho . A v^3$

$$P = \frac{1}{2} \times 1.2 \times 176.6 \times (15)^3 = 2.3841 \text{ kW}$$ **Ans.**

Axial force on turbine, $F = \rho Av(v - v_c)$

$$= \rho Av [v - v\sqrt{1 - \eta_T}]$$

$$= 1.2 \times 176.6 \times 15 [15 - 15\sqrt{1 - 0.442}]$$

$$= 12063 \text{ N}$$ **Ans.**

Ex 9.4: Coastal area of Karnataka has a horizontal shaft propeller type wind turbine operating at speed of 12 m/s at 15°C and 1 atm. Determine—

(*i*) density of air.

(*ii*) total power density in wind stream.

(*iii*) maximum possible power density.

(*iv*) actual power density.

(*v*) power output from wind turbine if diameter of turbine is 120 m.

(*vi*) axial thrust and torque acting on wind turbine revolving at 40 rpm.

Given: maximum efficiency = 40%

Solution: (*i*) $\rho = \dfrac{P}{RT}$

where, ρ = density of air, P = pressure of air (Pa),

T = temperature of air (K),

R = Gas constant (287 J/kg at 1 atm)

Given P = 1 atm

$= 1.01325 \times 10^5$ Pa

$T = 15°C = 15 + 273.515 = 378.15$ K

$R = 287$ J/kg K.

$$\therefore \quad \rho = \frac{1.01325 \times 10^3}{287 \times 378.15} = 1.226 \text{ kg/m}^3$$ **Ans.**

(*ii*) Total power density in wind stream $\dfrac{P_d}{A} = \dfrac{P}{A} = \dfrac{1}{2}\rho v^3$

$$= \frac{1}{2} \times 1.226 \times (12)^3 = 1059 \text{ W/m}^2$$ **Ans.**

(*iii*) Maximum possible power density

$$\frac{P_{max}}{A} = \frac{8}{27}\rho v^3 = \frac{8}{27} \times 1.226 \times (12)^3 = 627.71 \text{ W/m}^2$$ **Ans.**

(*iv*) Actual power density

$$= \frac{P}{A} = \eta_T \frac{P_d}{A} = 0.40 \times 1059 = 423 \text{ W/m}^2$$ **Ans.**

(*v*) Power output of wind turbine, $P = \dfrac{1}{2}\rho\left(\dfrac{\pi d^2}{4}\right)V^3$

$$= \frac{1}{2} \times 1.226 \times \left(\frac{\pi \times 120}{4}\right)^2 \times (12)^3$$

$$= 9.4 \text{ MW}$$ **Ans.**

(*vi*) Maximum Torque, $T_{max} = \dfrac{2}{27} \times \dfrac{\rho D V^3}{N} = \dfrac{2}{27} \times \dfrac{1.226 \times 120 \times (12)^3}{(40/60)}$

$$= 28532\text{N}$$ **Ans.**

Axial thrust $F_{max} = \dfrac{\pi}{9}\rho D^2 V^2$

$$= \frac{\pi}{9} \times 1.226 \times (120)^2 \times (12)^2 = 886.96 \text{ kN}$$ **Ans.**

Ex 9.5: A wind turbine has a diameter of 1.2 m and rotates at 15 rpm. If the wind speed is 3 m/s, determine tip speed ratio of the rotor.

Solution: Tip speed ratio $= \dfrac{\text{Rotor tip speed}}{\text{Wind speed}} = \dfrac{\pi D n}{v}$

$$= \frac{\pi \times 12 \times 15/60}{3} = 3.14$$ **Ans.**

Ex 9.6: A horizontal wind turbine operating in coastal area of Karnataka has 20 blades each 0.30 m wide. The diameter of rotor is 12 m. Determine solidity.

Solution: Solidity $= \frac{NB}{\pi D} = \frac{\text{No. of blades} \times \text{average width of blade}}{\pi \times \text{diameter of rotor}}$

$$\frac{20 \times 0.30}{\pi \times 12} = 0.1592 \text{ or } 15.92\%$$ **Ans.**

Ex 9.7: Determine the power output and axial force on a wind turbine having wind velocity of 5m/s. The swept volume of rotor blade is 100 m^2. Given, coefficient of power, $C_p = 0.44$ and density of air = 1.2kg/m^3.

Solution: Power output $= \frac{1}{2} C_p \rho . A_s . V^3$

$$= \frac{0.44}{2} \times 1.2 \times 100 \times (5)^3 = 3.3 \text{ kW}$$ **Ans.**

$$\text{Axial force} = F = \rho A_s V(V - V\sqrt{1 - \eta_T})$$

$$= 1.2 \times 100 \times 5\,(5 - 5\sqrt{1 - 0.44})$$

$$= 755\text{N}$$ **Ans.**

Ex 9.8: Average wind speed of 10 m/s provide output of 100 W/m^2. Calculate power generated by wind turbine if the wind speed is 40 m/s.

Solution : Since power generated by wind turbine αV^3

$$\therefore \quad \frac{P_2}{P_1} = \left(\frac{V_2}{V_1}\right)^3 \Rightarrow P_2 = P_1\left(\frac{V_2}{V_1}\right)^3$$

$$P_2 = 100\left(\frac{40}{10}\right)^3$$

$$P_2 = 6.4 \text{ kW}$$ **Ans.**

Ex 9.9: Quotations are received from two different wind turbine manufacturers for wind power generation project. The site has average wind speed of 6 m/s and wind is available for 2000 hours per year. Given-cost/unit = 6 ₹/kWh, life of turbine = 20 years, density of air = 1.225 kg/m^3

Select most economical wind turbine with following specifications

Table 9.13: Wind turbine specifications

Parameter	*Manufactures-A*	*Manufactures-B*
Capital cost	₹ 50,00,000	₹ 56,00,000
Maintenance cost /year	₹ 65,000	₹ 65,000
Rotor diameter	25m	28m

Power coefficient	0.38	0.35
Gearbox efficiency	0.90	0.88
Generator efficiency	0.98	0.95

Solution :Powers output of turbine = $\frac{1}{2} C_p \rho \frac{\pi D^2}{4} V^3 \eta_{GB} \eta_{Gen.}$

Powers output of turbine-A at 6 m/speed,

$$P_A = \frac{1}{2} \times 0.38 \times 1.225 \times \pi \times \frac{(25)^2}{4} \times (6)^3 \times 0.90 \times 0.98$$

$$P_A = 21755 \text{ W}$$

Units generated by turbine A/year = 21755 × 2000 kWh

Power output of turbine = B at 6 m/s, speed

$$P_B = \frac{1}{2} \times 0.35 \times 1.225 \times \pi \times \frac{(28)^2}{4} \times (6)^3 \times 0.88 \times 0.95$$

$$P_B = 23{,}824 \text{ W}$$

Units generated by turbine-B/year = 23.824 × 2000 kwh

Difference in energy generated per year = (23.824 – 21.755) × 2000

= 4138 kWh

Difference in cost for 20 years (life of turbine) = 4138 × 20

= ₹ 82, 760.

It is observed that although capital cost of turbine –B is more than turbine-A but the number of units generated over its life is more with turbine –B. Hence, turbine –B is most economical offer.

Ex 9.10: Under standard condition, rating of a wind turbine is 100 kW at a wind velocity of 10 m/s. Power output of wind turbine is directly proportional to air density. Determine the power output of turbine at a wind velocity of 10 m/s at 20°C. Given, atmospheric pressure is 79.4 k P_a at an elevation of 2000 m above sea level.

Solution : Density of air at 20° C (293K) is given by following expression

$$\rho = \frac{mP}{RT} = \frac{3.484P}{T} \text{ kg/m}$$

where ,

m = mass of one kilo mole of air,

P = pressure of air, kPa

T = ambient temperature, K

R = universal gas constant

$$\therefore \quad \rho = \frac{3.484 \times 79.4}{293} = 0.944 \text{ kg/m}^3$$

It is given that power output of wind turbine is directly proportional to density of air.

$$\therefore \quad \frac{P_2}{P_1} = \frac{\rho_2}{\rho_1} \quad \Rightarrow \quad P_2 = P_1 \times \frac{\rho_2}{\rho_1}$$

$$P_2 = 100 \times \left(\frac{0.944}{1.293}\right) = 73 \text{ kW}$$

It is observed that power output of wind turbine has reduced from 100 kW to 73 kW at same wind velocity.

CHAPTER SUMMARY

Wind flows due to atmospheric temperature difference and rotation of earth. A wind speed of 4 to 30 m/s is used to generate power. Wind power generated is proportional to cube of wind speed and square of diameter of turbine blades. With increase in height, wind speed increases. Compared to vertical axis wind turbine, three blade horizontal axis wind turbine is widely used. The single largest capacity of turbine unit is 6 MW.

Synchronous and induction generators both types are used in wind power generation.

Horizontal axis wind turbine use stall and pitch control for mechanical power regulation (much like governors of a steam turbine). Yaw control is needed to keep horizontal axis wind turbine oriented towards the wind. Major weight of horizontal axis wind turbine consists of gearbox. turbine & generator. While in vertical axis wind turbine,gearbox and generator are placed at ground level thereby eliminating need for a nacelle at a height. This makes accessibility for maintenance easier. Moreover, no yaw mechanician is needed thereby simplifying the turbine design. However, vertical axis turbine are not self-starting.

Due to variability of wind resource, wind -diesel or wind solar hybrid power generation system is preferred. Due to higher wind velocity in off-shore area, a large number of off -shore wind farms are being constructed.

Indian has 13 GW installed capacity and ranks 5th in the world.

FORMULAE

1. Electrical power output from wind -turbine $= \frac{\pi}{8} C_p \cdot \rho D^2 . v^3 \;\; \eta_{GB}\eta_{Gen}$.
2. Tip speed ratio (TSR) $= \frac{\pi DN}{60\, v}$

   where $D =$ dia. of rotor blades, m

   $N =$ rpm of rotor, rpm

   $v =$ wind speed, m/s
3. Air density, $\rho = \frac{MP}{8.314\, T}$

   where, $M =$ Molecular weight of air, g/mol

   $P =$ Atmospheric pressure (kPa)

   $T =$ Temperature of air (K)

4. Air density, $\rho = \dfrac{[28.964 - 0.253\,(RH)]\,P}{8.314\,T}$

5. Air density, $\rho = 1.225\,K_T K_A$

where, K_T = Density ratio (for temperature correction).

K_A = Pressure ratio (for altitude correction).

6. $$\frac{v}{v_0} = \frac{H}{H_0}$$

where, v = wind speed at new height (m/s)

v_0 = wind speed at original height (m/s)

H = new height (m)

H_0 = original height (m)

7. Maximum power output, $(P_T)_{max} = \dfrac{(0.5925)\,.\,\rho\,.\,A_s\,.\,v_i^3}{2}$

where, ρ = density of air, kg/m^3

A_s = swept area, m^2

v_i = inlet velocity, m/s

8. Axial force, $F = \dfrac{\pi}{8}\,\rho\,.\,D^2\,(v_i^2 - v_e^2)$

where, v_i = inlet velocity, m/s

v_e = exit velocity,m/s

9. Maximum axial force, $(F)_{max} = \dfrac{\pi}{9}\,.\,\rho\,D^2\,v_i^2$

10. Average molecular weight of air, $M = 28.964$ g/mol

11. Density of air at 15°C and 1 atmospheric pressure = 1.225 kg/m^3

REVIEW QUESTIONS

Q. 1. Explain the principle of wind energy conversion.

Q. 2. Discuss the factors to be considered for location of wind power generation plant.

Q. 3. Explain with a neat sketch various components of a wind turbine.

Q. 4. Discuss classification of wind turbines.

Q. 5. Compare horizontal and vertical axis wind turbine.

Q. 6. Derive the expression for power output of wind turbine.

Q. 7. What is Betz limit? Why efficiency of wind turbine can not exceed Betz limit?

Q. 8. Define coefficient of power.

Q. 9. Discuss various factors affecting power output of wind turbine.

Q. 10. Derive the expression for power output of a wind turbine.

Q. 11. Derive the expression for maximum axial force exerted by wind stream on blades of a wind turbine.

Q. 12. Describe various forces which act on a aerofoil section with a diagram.

Q. 13. Discuss *(a)* velocity duration curve *(b)* power duration curve and *(c)* frequency duration curve.

Q. 14. What are various methods employed to reduce drag on wind turbine blades?

Q. 15. Discuss pitch regulation and stall regulation.

Q. 16. Compare off-shore and on-shore wind farms.

Q. 17. How the impact of variability of wind power is reduced?

Q. 18. Discuss various schemes of wind power generation.

Q. 19. What is yaw control? Why is it needed?

Q. 20. Explain various protection scheme employed for wind-generator system.

Q. 21. Explore limitations of wind power generation.

NUMERICAL QUESTIONS

Q. 1. A wind turbine with a diameter of 120 m rotates at 40 r.p.m. at maximum efficiency. Wind is blowing at 10 m/s, with 15°C and atmospheric pressure. Determine—*(i)* total power produced *(ii)* torque and axial thrust.

Ans. *(i)* 2770 kW *(ii)* 16347 N, 616255 N

Q. 2. A wind turbine operating at 1 kW has rotor dia of 3 m. The average wind velocity is 10 m/s. Determine coefficient of power. Efficiency of generator & gearbox is 80%. Given, density of air is 1.2 kg/m^3. **[Ans:** 0.295]

Q. 3. A wind turbine generates 15 kW at 12 m/s wind velocity. The twine blade turbine has diameter of 7 m. Calculate *(i)* efficincy of wind turbine *(ii)* tip speed ratio, if blade speed is 240 rpm. Given, air density = 1.23 kg/m^3. **[Ans:** *(i)* 36.69% *(ii)* 7.33]

Q. 4. A horizontal axis wind turbine has a rotor diameter of 15 m. Wind speed is 8 m/s. and efficiency of generator is 85% . Determine power output of wind turbine if rotor extracts 35% of energy of wind. Given ,air density =1.23 kg/m^3. **[Ans:** 5.269 kW]

SHORT ANSWERS TYPES QUESTIONS

Q. 1. Wind generator output is largely dependent on wind velocity.

Q. 2. Yaw control is not required in vertical axis turbine.

Q. 3. A three blade turbine generates more power than twine blade turbine.

Q. 4. Off-shore windfarms generate more power than on-shore turbine.

Q. 5. Hybrid power system can minimize variability of wind power.

Multiple Choice Questions

Q 1. Wind power output increases with

(*a*) increase in height (*b*) decrease in height
(*c*) remains same. (*d*) none of these

Q. 2. Power output of wind turbine can never exceed

(*a*) 49% (*b*) 59%
(*c*) 69% (*d*) 50%

Q. 3. With increase in air density, wind power output

(*a*) decreases (*b*) remains same
(*c*) increase (*d*) none of these

Q. 4. The maximum force is exerted on

(*a*) hub of turbine (*b*) structure of turbine
(*c*) on nacelle (*d*) blade tip

Q. 5. Vertical wind turbines are

(*a*) self starting (*b*) require starting
(*c*) none of these (*d*) none of these

Answer to MCQ

1. (*a*) **2.** (*b*) **3.** (*c*) **4.** (*d*) **5.** (*b*)

Chapter 10

BIO-MASS POWER GENERATION

Learning Objectives

After reading this chapter, reader will be able to

- Understand the types of biomass, their composition and various energy conversion routes.
- Explore various schemes of power generation using biomass.
- Grasp different techniques used for energy conversion process including types of reactions taking place.
- Explore suitability of different routes for power generation.
- Update on operating biomass based power plants in India and the world.

"Perfection is beyond us,for it means the end.
We are always journeying trying to achieve
something that is ever receding"

— Rabindranath Tagore

10.1. INTRODUCTION

Biomass in an organic matter of recent origin produced by plants, animals and micro-organisms in land and in water. Biomass includes forest crops and residue, agricultural crops, animal manure, urban and rural organic waste, aquatic crops, agro-industrial waste etc. The most widely used form of biomass are sugarcane bagasse, pulp and paper residue, rice husk, saw dust, stalks of corn, soya bean, sorghum, sunflower, barley, wheat etc. Biomass material is categorised as—

(*i*) Dry biomass.
(*ii*) Wet biomass.
(*iii*) Municipal solid waste.
(*iv*) Forest waste and.
(*v*) Agricultural waste.

The average composition of biomass is $C_6H_{10}O_5$.

Biomass is considered as a renewable source of energy which is generated by every day. Green plants generate biomass by photosynthesis process in the presence of sun light. Other living organisms such as humen, animals, micro organisms generate biomass by consuming green plants or their byproducts. Similarly, fossil fuels (coal, natural gas and petroleum oil) are produced from buried biomass. However, fossil fuels are not included in the category of biomass.

Most parts of the world have abundant biomass resources which can be used to produce energy. The main reason for use of biomass energy generation is due to numerous favourable factors such as wide availability, renewable nature, source of cleaner fuel and CO_2 neutral (CO_2 produced due to combustion is balanced by CO_2 extracted during photosynthesis).

Biomass can be converted to energy by three routes viz –

(*i*) Thermal conversion process.

(*ii*) Chemical conversion process and

(*iii*) Bio-chemical conversion process. So, biomass can be used in solid, liquid or gaseous form.

Biomass has a wide range of applications such as

(*i*) rural areas.

(*ii*) urban and industrial applications and

(*iii*) for electrical power generation

Typical capital cost of biomass power project range from ₹ 4 crores/MW to ₹ 5 crores/MW depending upon the cost of biomass plant load factor (PLF) and the efficiency of conversion. The cost of generated electricity varies from ₹ 3.25 /kWh to ₹ 3.75/kWh depending upon the plant load factor and interest on term loans. The life of biomass plant is 20 years and can be further extended by 10 years by major overhauling. The land requirement for a typical 10 MW plant is about 10 acres. All major sugar producing industries use sugarcane bagasse as biomass fuel to raise steam in a high pressure boiler. This steam is used to generate power for captive use and excess power is exported to electricity grid.

In this chapter, focus will be on conversion of biomass into various forms of energy resource including electricity generation.

10.2. PHOTOSYNTHESIS AND ORIGIN OF BIOMASS

Photosynthesis is a chemical reaction of sunlight and chlorophyll (present in green plants). Chlorophyll, water and carbon dioxide react in the presence of sunlight (0.4 μm to 0.7 μm wavelength of sun's spectrum) to produce carbohydrate and oxygen. The temperature range of this reaction is limited to 0 to 60°C. The complete photosynthesis process takes place in two stages viz light reaction and dark reaction.

In light reaction stage, energy carrier molecules are formed in the presence of sunlight. Reaction produces adenosin Triphosphate (ATP) and Nicotinamide Adenine Dinucleotide Phosphate (NADPH) in the presence of sunlight (0.4 – 0.8 μm). This results in production of sugar, starch and cellulose. This reaction takes place in the grana of chloroplast. In the dark reaction stage (i.e. independent of light) takes place in stroma of chlorophyll. ATP and NADPH that are produced in the light reaction stage create carbohydrate which is final organic product of photosynthesis process. The plant draws energy from stored carbohydrate.

$$\text{Light reaction: } 2H_2O + \text{Energy} \longrightarrow O_2 + 4H^- + 4e^- \qquad ...(10.1)$$

$$\text{Dark reation: } 4H^+ + 2\,CO_2 \xrightarrow{\text{ATP}} 2\,[CH_2O] \qquad ...(10.2)$$

$$\text{Overall reaction: } CO_2 + 2H_2O \xrightarrow{\text{Sun light}} O_2 + [CH_2O] + H_2O \qquad ...(10.3)$$

$[CH_2O]$ represents basic unit of carbohydrate.

For glucose production, the following is the reaction—

$$6\,CO_2 + 6\,H_2O \xrightarrow{\text{Sun light}} 6\,O_2 + C_6H_{12}O_6 - 672 \text{ kcal} \qquad ...(10.4)$$

It is to be noted that 672 kcal is needed to fix one molecule of CO_2.

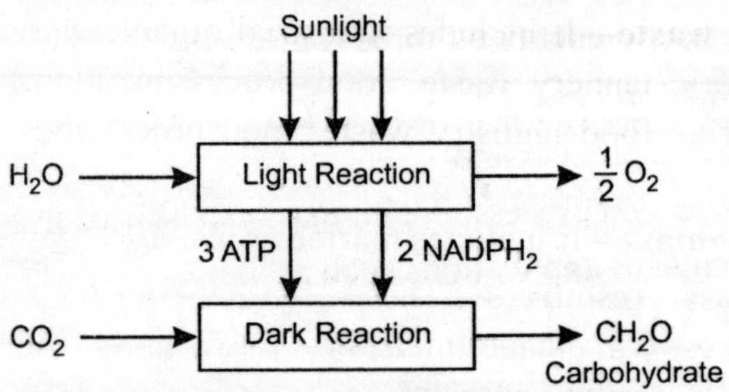

Figure 10.1. Photosynthesis reaction

Non-green plants, micro-organisms and animals derive organic matter from green plants as food.

10.3. TYPES OF BIOMASS RESOURCES

Biomass resources are mainly of three categories—

(*i*) solid (*ii*) liquid and (*iii*) gas.

(*i*) **Solid biomass resources**—Following are the solid biomass resources—

(*a*) energy crops. (*b*) dung.
(*c*) forest residues. (*d*) cereal residues.
(*e*) sugarcane residues. (*f*) urban refuge.
(*g*) municipal sewage. (*h*) firewood.
(*i*) industrial waste. (*j*) marine biomass.

(*a*) **Energy crops**—These are crops specially grown in energy plantation for obtaining biomass. Genetic research is used to develop special plant species. These are fast growing trees, aquatic crops, algae etc. which have high energy density. These crops are mentioned as below—

(*i*) sugarcane crops, sweet beet, sweet sorghum crops.

(*ii*) forest crops.

(*iii*) Others specially grown species are Casuarina Equisilifolia(calorific value 20,725kJ/kg), Leucaena Leucocephala (17,585 to 20,100 kJ/kg), Albizia Lebbek (21,770 kJ/kg) Acavia Auriculi form is (20,100 to 20,515 kJ/kg).

(*b*) **Dung**—These include cow dung, horse dung, sheep dung, poultry droppings, slaughter house waste, piggery dung, fishery waste etc.

(*c*) **Forest residue**—It consists of branches, tops, culled logs, stubs, stalks etc.

(*d*) **Cereal residue**—It includes rice husk,wheat straw, bagasse of sugarcane, groundnut shells, coconut shells, wheat husk, rice straw, coconut husk, waste fruits etc.

(*e*) **Sugarcane residue**—It includes stubs, bagasse etc.

(*f*) **Urban refuge**—It includes municipal waste.

(*g*) **Municipal sewage**—It consists of human excreta.

(*h*) **Firewood**—It is obtained from forests.

(*i*) **Industrial waste**—It includes industrial organic waste, process waste, waste from sugar factory, tannery waste, food processing industry waste, furniture industry waste, marine food industry waste, food processing industry waste, tyre industry waste etc.

(*j*) **Marine biomass**—It includes marine crops, fishery waste, algae etc.

(*ii*) **Liquid biomass resources**—These are obtained through chemical/biochemical conversion process e.g. ethanol,methanol, butanol, isopropanol etc

(*iii*) **Gaseous biomass resources**—These are obtained the chemical from biochemical conversion process.

Following table 10.1 gives calorific value of dried biomass materials—

Table 10.1: Calorific value of dried biomass materials

Biomass material	*Calorific value (MJ/kg)*
Waste paper	17.0
Sugar cane	15.0
Vegetable oils	39.0
Algae	15.0
Textile and rubber	21.0
Pinewood	20.2
Oak wood	18.3

10.4. COMPOSITION OF BIOMASS

Biomass is composed of following constituents—

(*i*) Cellulose, (*ii*) Hemi cellulose, (*iii*) lignin, (*iv*) minerals and (*v*) others

(*i*) **Cellulose**—It is main constituent (40–50%)of biomass which provides a frame for wood cells. It is composed of polymer chain of sugar.

(*ii*) **Hemi cellulose**—It constitutes 20 – 30% of biomass and is composed of polymers of five types of sugars.

(*iii*) **Lignin**—It constitutes 20 – 30% of biomass and is of non-carbohydrate material. It acts as a bonding material for cells resulting in formation of hard structure.

(*iv*) **Others**—Small amount of lipids, proteins, simple sugar, starch,inorganic matter and moisture.

10.5 METHODS OF ENERGY GENERATION FROM BIOMASS

There are various conversion processes used to convert biomass into useful heat/bio gas/bio chemical fuels. Type of particular method used depends upon the end use. The conversion process results in higher energy density (J/kg) of the final product as compared to raw biomass and also allows easy storage and transportation to long distances for further use. The biomass finds extensive use in rural applications (cooking, lighting etc), urban and industrial application and large scale electrical power generation. This helps in rural development, waste disposal, energy generation and maintenance of environmental balance.

Various routes of biomass conversion is given below—

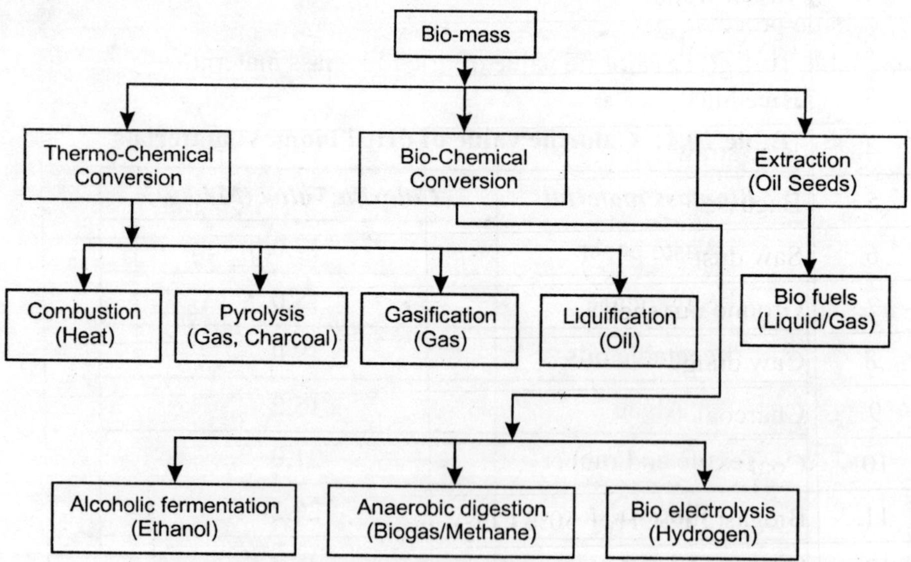

Figure 10.2. Methods of biomass energy conversion

(*i*) **Thermo-chemical conversion**—

The process uses thermal energy to convert biomass into other energy form. Following are the processes used for thermo-chemical conversion—

(*a*) **Combustion**—

In this process, biomass is burnt in the presence of oxygen which produces heat, light and others products. Solid biomass materials, such as crop residue, wood, animal dung, cultivated biomass etc. is used. The heat thus obtained can be used for several useful purposes, such as cooking, industrial heating, steam generation etc. However, this has very low thermal efficiency. The process of burning biomass to ashes is called incineration. This is well established process of disposal of solid waste e.g. medical waste in hospitals, municipal waste, industrial waste etc. Municipal waste to energy power plants can generate electricity from 1 to 200 MW. Sugar plants use bagasse (waste after extraction of sugarcane juice) to generate steam and electricity by combustion in a boiler. The steam is used in process partly for heating and remaining is used for power generation.

To improve the bulk density of biomass material for transportation, storage and increased heat value, it is converted into small blocks called briquette or converted into small cubes or rods of small diameter (5 – 12 mm) called pellets. Both the process require removal of moisture to improve heat content of the biomass material. Heat content of different biomass is given in table 10.2.

Table 10.2: Heat of combustion in biomass materials

Sr. No	*Biomass type*	*Gross heat value (MJ/kg)*
1.	Green wood	8
2.	Dry wood	10 – 11
3.	Rice husk	11 – 12.2
4.	Rice straw	12 – 13.8
5.	Bagasse	7 – 8.8
6.	Saw dust	24 – 27
7.	Ground nut shell	16 – 17.6
8	Caw dung	12 – 15
9.	Charcoal	32
10.	Coal	27
11.	Biogas(50%CH_4 + 50% CO_2)	28
12.	Methane	56
13.	Butane	50
14.	Crude oil	44
15.	Petrol	47

Following table 10.3 gives efficiency of combustion for different combustion systems—

Table 10.3: Combustion efficiency of different systems

Process	*Efficiency (%)*
Open fire	5–10
Open fireplace	10–20
Cooking oven	40–50
Fire oven	60–70
Under fire oven	60–80

Biomass materials with moisture have low calorific value as some energy is wasted in vaporising the water content. Also, bulk density of biomass material is considered to be low, hence these are compacted in the shape of pellets etc. to increase bulk density.

Burning of biomass in the shape of pellets in ovens or boiler increases combustion efficiency due to excess oxygen supply. However,this method of extraction of energy from biomass materials have low efficiency.

(*b*) **Pyrolysis**—It is a process of chemical decomposition of organic matter brought about by heat. In this process, the organic matter is heated in the absence of air until the molecules thermally breakdown to become a gas comprising smaller molecules or synthesis gas. Gasification can also take place as a result of partial combustion of organic matter in the presence of a restricted quantity of air or oxygen. This gas is known as producer gas. The gases produced by pyrolysis mainly comprise of carbon monoxide (25%), a combination of hydrogen and hydrocarbon (15%) and also carbon dioxide and nitrogen (60%).The synthesis gas so produced is cleaned and burnt in an engine or in a boiler to run steam turbine.

Advantages of pyrolysis are-low pressure operation, use of simple equipments, generation of negligible waste and high conversion efficiency (about 83%)

(*c*) **Gassification**—It is a process of converting a solid biomass into combustible gas mixture. This process uses various types of biomass, such as agricultural waste, wood waste, wood, crop residue etc. The gas produced in gasifier is the producer gas with a heating value of 950–1200 kcal/m^3. The main constituents of producer gas are-hydrogen (18 – 20%)and carbon monoxide (18 – 24%). This gas can be used in a gas engine to produce motive power or burnt directly in a boiler to produce power from steam turbine. Gasifiers are reliable, easy to operate and require low maintenance.

Gassifiers are classified depending upon the type of draft (upward draft, downward draft and cross draft gassifiers), capacity of gasifiers (small upto 10 kW, medium 10 – 50 kW, large 50 – 300 kW and very large more than 300 kW) and type of bed in gassifiers (fixed bed, fluidized bed).

(*i*) **Fixed bed gassifier**—In a fixed bed upward draft gassifiers, air enters the combustion zone from the bottom. Biomass is fed from the top. The gases produced after combustion leave the gassifiers at the top. The gassifier has following zones–

- **Drying zone**—In this zone, moisture of biomass is removed by incoming hot gases. The moisture gets converted into steam. The temperature of this zone is 120°C.
- **Pyrolysis zone**—In this zone,biomass breaks down to various gases and liquids. The temperature is 400°C.
- **Reduction zone**—In this zone,reaction takes place in the absence of air and results in generation of CH_4, CO and H_2. Temperature of this zone is 900°C.
- **Oxidation zone**—In this zone, char reacts with atmospheric air and forms CO_2 and water vapour. The temperature of this zone is 700 – 1300°C.

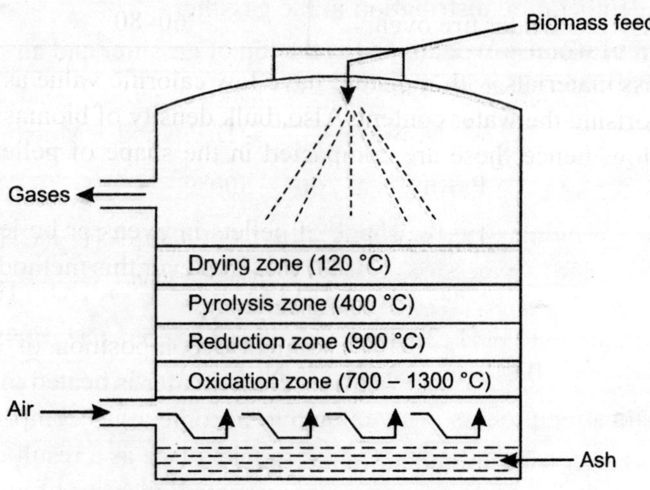

Figure 10.3. Fixed bed gassifier (updraft)

Following reactions take place in a gassifier—

(*i*) Drying zone → $H_2O \text{ (moisture)} \rightarrow H_2O \text{ (steam)}$ ...(10.4)

(*ii*) Reduction zone → $C + 2H_2 \rightarrow CH_4$ ...(10.5)

$C + H_2O \rightarrow CO + H_2$ ...(10.6)

$C + CO_2 \rightarrow 2CO$ ...(10.7)

(*iii*) Oxidation zone → $C + O_2 \rightarrow CO_2$ ...(10.8)

Gas produced from gassifier can be burnt in a gas engine to produce motive power or electricity. It can be burnt in a boiler to produce steam which can be used for heating need and for producing power in a steam turbine.

(*ii*) Fluidized bed gassifier—

This type of gassifier is suitable for burning any type of biomass due to high efficiency and low pollution. It consists of bed of inert material which are held in suspension by upward flow of air. This enables rapid mixing and high turbulence resulting in better combustion and high heat release. Fluidised bed can handle biomass with high ash content. The bed uses inert material (such as sand) as well as reactive material (such as limestone).The bed is kept in fluid state by circulating the air. The operating range of bed is 750–950°C so that there are no chances of clinker formation.

Advantages of fluidized bed gassifiers are following–

(*a*) any type of biomass can be burnt.
(*b*) quick start up.
(*c*) high rate of heat output.
(*d*) quick response to change in fuel input.
(*e*) biomass with high moisture content can be burnt.
(*f*) low operating temperature reduces corrosion and stress.
(*g*) reduced pollution (low No_x and So_x).
(*h*) uniform temperature distribution in the gassifier.

- **Gassification of wood**—Wood is fed at the top of gassifier and air and steam are charged at the base. Following reactions take place—

$$\text{Moist wood} \xrightarrow{\text{Heat}} \text{Dry wood} + \text{Moisture}$$

Pyrolysis at 200° – 500°C

$$\text{Dry wood} \xrightarrow{\text{Heat}} CO + CO_2 + H_2 + CH_4 + \text{char} + \text{tar} \quad ...(10.9)$$

$$\text{Char} + O_2 + H_2O \xrightarrow{\text{Gassification}} CO + H_2 + CO_2 \quad ...(10.10)$$

Gassified wood contains—18% H_2,22.8% CO,9.2% CO_2,2.5% CH_4, 0.9% other hydrocarbon, 0.8% oxygen, 45.8% N_2.

Flow chart of gassification process is given below–

(*i*) Heating of biomass with limited air or oxygen.

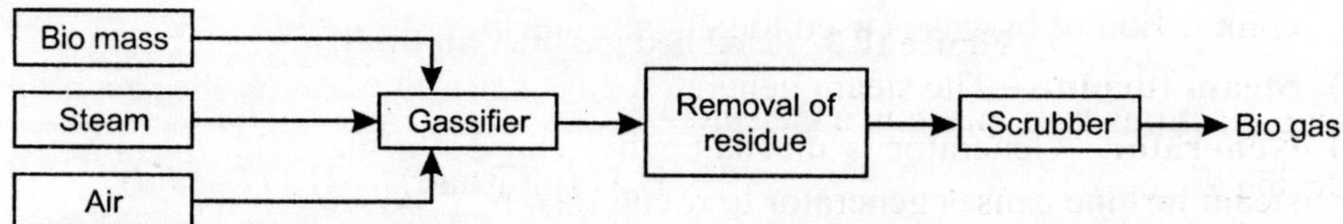

Figure 10.4. Bio gas generation with limited air or oxygen.

(*ii*) Heating of biomass at high temperature and pressure in the presence of steam and oxygen.

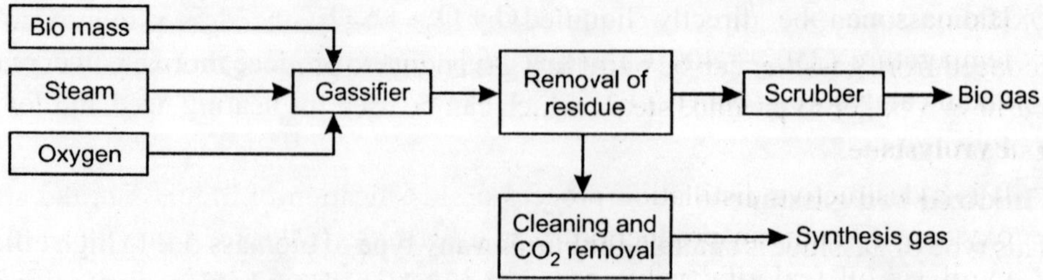

Figure 10.5. Bio gas generation at high temperature and pressure

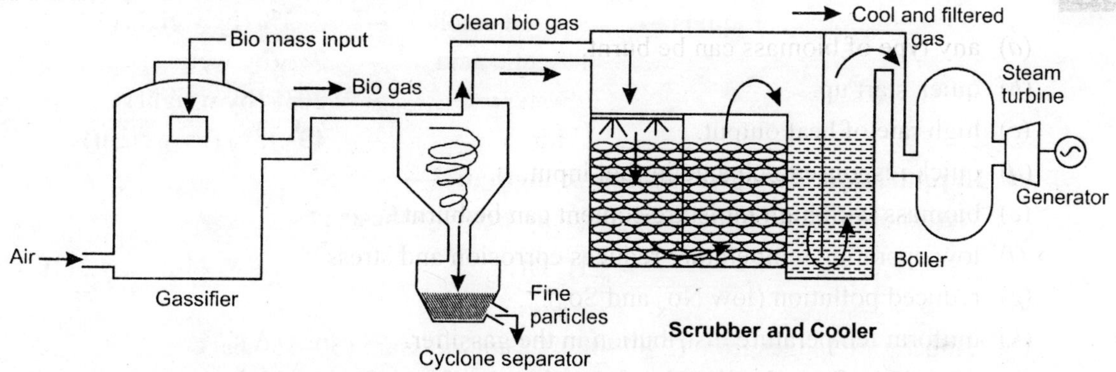

Figure 10.6. Biomass gassifier based power generation

Biomass gassifier based power generation consists of following components–

(i) **Gassifier**—Depending upon power output, gassifiers are classified as of four types-small size gassifier (upto 10 kW), medium size gassifier (10 – 50 kW), large size gassifiers (50 – 300 kW) and very large size gassifiers (above 300 kW).

(ii) **Cyclone separator**—It separates solid particles from biogas generated from gassifiers by cyclonic separation principle. This gas free from solid particles is passed onto scrubber & cooler.

(iii) **Scrubber and cooler**—It consists of a packed bed with water sprinkler which traps the remnant particles and reduces temperature of biogas.

(iv) **Boiler**—The filtered and cooled biogas is burnt in the boiler. The heat produced by combustion of biogas is used to generate steam from water.

(v) **Steam turbine**—The steam generated in boiler is used to run the steam turbine.

(vi) **Generator**—Generator is mechanically coupled to the steam turbine. Rotation of steam turbine causes generator to rotate thereby producing electricity.

(d) **Liquification**—Liquification of biomass is carried out by three methods viz by chemical reduction, by pyrolysis and by methanol synthesis with gasification.

- **Liquification by chemical reduction—**

  Biomass can be directly liquified by reacting with carbon monoxide at high temperature (250° – 400°C) and at high pressure(140–280 bar)in the presence of alkali catalyst (e.g. Na HCO_3).

- **Pyrolysis—**

  It is a destructive distillation process or gassification of biomass in the absence of oxygen. It results in production of pyrolysis gas (calorific value 20 – 30 MJ/m^3), pyrolysis oil (calorific value 23 – 30 MJ/kg). Volume of final products depends upon–*(i)* temperature *(ii)* heating rate *(iii)* composition of biomass and *(iv)* residence time in reactor. Composition of final product of pyrolysis depends upon temperature, process and type of biomass. A typical composition of pyrolysis of wood with a temperature range of 400°–600°C produces following final products—

Solid →	charcoal	–	35% (by weight)
Gases →	Gas	–	15–20% (by weight)

Liquids →	wood alcohol	–	2–3% (by weight)
	Acetic acid	–	7% (by weight)
	water	–	20% (by weight)
	Tar	–	13–15% (by weight)

- **Liquification through synthesis of methanol—**
  Methanol is manufactured catalytically from synthesis gas.

$$\underbrace{CO + 2\,H_2}_{\text{synthesis gas}} \xrightarrow{\text{Catalyst}} \underbrace{CH_3\,OH}_{\text{Methanol}} \qquad ...(10.11)$$

The temperature ranges from (230°–400°C) and pressure (50–360 bar).

Methanol is used with petrol (15%maximum) as transportation fuel. However,it has low calorific value. It is poisonous and corrosive.

(*iii*) **Biochemical conversion**—This process converts biomass into liquid or gaseous fuel through the action of micro-organisms by breakdown of biomass.

(*a*) **Alcoholic fermentation**—It is a process of converting the carbohydrates into alcohol and carbon dioxide by using yeast or bacteria or both under the anaerobic condition. Essentially, this process converts sugar into alcohol using micro-organism. This process is used to produce ethyl alcohol from grains, molasses, fruits, waste liquor,sweet sorghum,beet root etc. Chemical reaction of conversion of starch to ethyl alcohol by fermentation is given below—

$$\underbrace{(C_6\,H_{10}\,O_5)_n}_{\text{(Starch)}} + nH_2O \xrightarrow{\text{Enzyme}} \underbrace{n\,C_6\,H_{12}\,O_6}_{\text{(Dextrose)}}. \qquad ...(10.12)$$

$$\underbrace{(C_6\,H_{12}\,O_6)_n}_{\text{(Dextrose)}} \xrightarrow{\text{Yeast}} 2C_2H_5OH + 2CO_2 \qquad ...(10.13)$$

Sugar are — (*a*) Glucose = $C_6H_{12}O_6$

(*b*) Fructose = $C_6H_{12}O_6$

(*c*) Dextrose = $C_6H_{12}O_6$

(*d*) Sucrose = $C_{12}H_{22}O_{11}$.

Ethanol can be obtained from sugars (cane sugar, beet sugar, fruits, molasses, grapes), starches (potatoes, grains,root crops) and cellulose (wood, agricultural waste, waste liquors from pulp and paper mills).

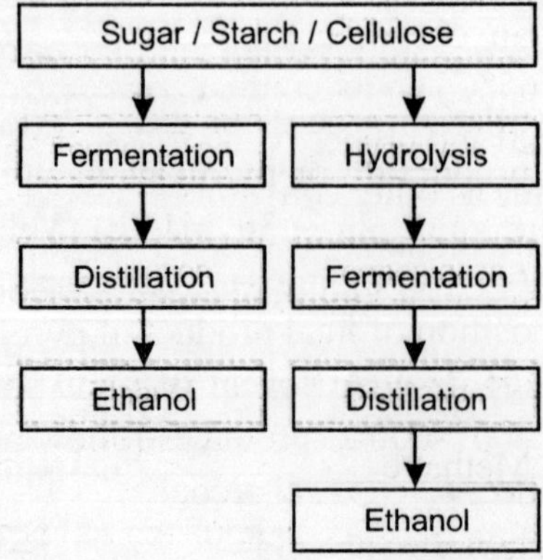

Figure 10.7. Ethanol production steps

Fermentation process depends upon—(*i*) sugar content (*ii*) temperature (*iii*) yeast concentration (*iv*) pH value and (*v*) fermentation time.

(*i*) **Sugar content**—The optimum range is 10 – 18% by weight.

(*ii*) **Temperature**—Suitable temperature range is 30° – 40°C.

(*iii*) **Yeast concentration**—It is kept 40 – 60 gm of yeast per litre of substrate.

(*iv*) **pH value**—The range is 3.0 to 6.0.

(*v*) **Fermentation time**—Fermentation process takes near about 36–48 hours.

Ethanol finds extensive uses, such as solvent, organic chemical, plastics, lacquers, liquid detergents, sprays, automotive fuel additives etc.

Table 10.4: Various types of raw materials used for fermentation

Raw materials	***Fermented product***
Cane sugar, beet root, fruit juices, molasses, grains, potatoes, wood, sweet sorghum	Ethyl alcohol
Sugars, carbohydrates, fats, proteins, organic waste	Methyl alcohol
Carbohydrates, mixed solvents	Butanol, Isopropanol

(*b*) An aerobic Digestion—In this process, organic matter (agricultural, animal, domestic and industrial organic waste) is fed to a closed container called biogas digester. In the digester, organic matter undergoes biodegradation in the presence of methanogenic bacteria under anaerobic condition producing methane rich biogas and sludge. This biogas can be used either for cooking or for generating motive power or electricity through dual fuel or gas engine or low pressure gas turbine or steam turbine. The sludge from anaerobic digestion can be used as manure.

Anaerobic digestion consists of three steps. These are given below—

- Decomposition (hydrolysis)of plant, animal or other biomass matter to breakdown complex organic materials into simple organic substances.
- Conversion of decomposed matter into organic acids.
- Conversion of acids into methane gas.

As the process temperature affects the rate of digestion,it is maintained in the mesophilic range(30° – 40°C) with an optimum of 35°C. It is also possible to operate in the thermophilic range (55° – 65°C) under controlled conditions. Composition of gas depends upon quality of feed material and process conditions. The percentage of methane in the gas determines its calorific value as other constituents do not contribute to the energy content. Major contents of biogas are methane, carbon dioxide, hydrogen sulphide, hydrogen and nitrogen. A typical composition of biogas is given below in table 10.5.

Table 10.5: Typical composition of biogas

Methane	55 to 60%
Carbon dioxide	35 to 40%

Hydrogen	5%
Hydrogen sulphide, Nitrogen and Oxygen	Traces.

The content of methane in biogas can be enhanced upto 97%by employing enrichment and purification technologies. Factors affecting biogas generation are given below–

(*i*) **Temperature**—Temperature strongly influences anaerobic digestion of organic matter. Rapid production of gas takes place between 29° to 40°C or between 49° to 60°C due to operation of two different types of bacteria. However, continuous production of methane takes place between 32° to 35°C.

(*ii*) **Carbon-nitrogen ratio**—Carbon/nitrogen ratio ensures either fertilizer quality or methane content. A high C/N ratio causes rapid consumption of nitrogen by methanogens and further reaction of leftover carbon does not take place. The optimum C/N ratio is maintained from 20 to 30%.

(*iii*) **pH Value**—pH affects the speed of fermentation. Higher basic or acidic pH results in slower rate of fermentation. The optimum pH range is 6.8 to 8.0. A pH higher than 8.5 produces toxic effect on methanogen bacteria.

(*iv*) **Retention time**—The duration for which an organic matter stays inside digester is known as retention time. Retention time depends upon temperature and volume of feedstock added. The retention time varies from few weeks to few months depending upon type of feedstock and temperature.

(*v*) **Feeding rate**—It is the amount of organic material fed per unit volume of digester per day. Gas production reduces if the feeding rate is above or below the recommended value.

(*vi*) **Volatile solids**—Presence of higher amount of volatile solid content increases the gas production rate.

(*vii*) **Agitation of biomass**—Biomass need to be agitated otherwise a hard layer forms on the surface,inhibiting production of gas.

(*viii*) **Heavy metals**—Heavy metals, such as stones, Fe, Cu, Cr, Pb, Cd etc. produces poisonous effect on bacteria and also consumes useful space in digester. Hence, these materials need to be removed from feeding material.

Advantages of anaerobic digestion are following–

(*a*) easy storage and supply of gas.

(*b*) reduction of waste going to landfills.

(*c*) efficient way of energy conversion to clean gaseous fuel.

(*d*) production of enriched organic manure which can supplement chemical fertilisers.

(*e*) improvement in sanitation, hygiene and environment.

(*f*) source of decentralized electrical/mechanical power generation.

(*g*) improves quality of life in rural area by providing cooking gas and lighting.

(*h*) reduction of BOD (Biological Oxygen Demand) of waste water.

Composition of different biomass technologies is given in Table 10.6.

Table 10.6: Composition of different biomass technologies

Sr. No	*Parameter*	*Combustion*	*Anaerobic digestion*	*Gassification*	*Pyrolysis*
1.	Raw material	Solid biomass	Wet biomass	Solid biomass	Solid biomass
2.	Drying	Not essential but helps	Not essential	Necessary	Necessary
3.	Temperature (°C)	700–1400	30–65	500 – 1300	380 – 530
4.	Pressure (MPa)	> 0.1	—	> 0.1	0.1 – 0.5
5.	Advantages	—	Suitable for high moisture content biomass.	High efficiency 25–50%.	Main product liquid-easy to store and transport.

(*c*) **Bio- electrolysis**—In a microbial fuel cell, electrogenic micro-organisms consume a source of energy, such as a acetic acid,lactic acid etc. and produce protons and electrons. This results in the creation of electric potential. This generates hydrogen from protons.

(*iii*) **Extraction**—It is a process of conversion of oil seeds, such as soya bean, sunflower, rapeseed etc. into vegetable oils. Most of these oils are edible and find other uses in manufacturing of colours, paints, soaps, cosmetic items etc. apart from the usage as energy source.

One of the major use of oils from the oil seeds is production of bio-diesel. Rapeseed oil is suitable for conversion into bio-diesel. Bio-diesel produced by crushing,refining and transesterification of vegetable oil extracted from oil seed. The process of bio-diesel production is given in a flow chart. (Figure 10.8).

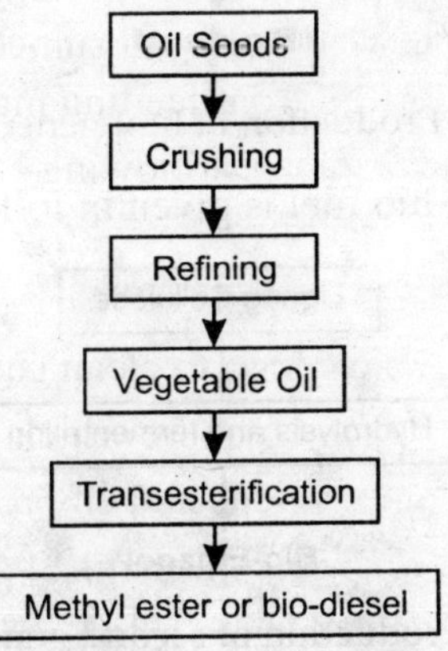

Figure 10.8. Production of bio-diesel

Calorific value of some important oil seeds is given in the table 10.7

Table 10.7: Calorific value of oil seeds

Oil seed	*Calorific value (MJ/litre)*
Rape seed	33.9
Palm seed	35.1
Ground nut	33.7
Sunflower seed	34.0
Soya bean	34.0
Cotton seed	33.7

10.6. BIO FUELS

It is a process of conversion of plant and animal matter into liquid or gaseous fuel. Some biofuels are used in transportation and power generation. In transportation, bio ethanol is used as the partial replacement for petrol and bio-diesel is used in diesel engines.

First generation bio-fuels are made from sugar, starch and vegetable oils. However, large scale production of first generation bio fuel will impact upon food supply. Hence,second generation bio-fuels are made from sustainable feedstock which have minimum impact on green house gas emission, bio-diversity, land use etc. It minimizes the impact on food supply.

Production process of first generation bio fuel is given in following flow chart (Figure 10.9).

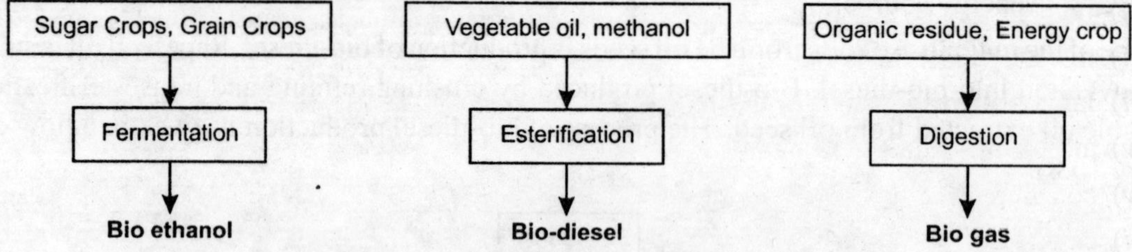

Figure 10.9. Production of first generation bio fuel

Production of second generation bio fuel is given in following flow chart. (Figure 10.10).

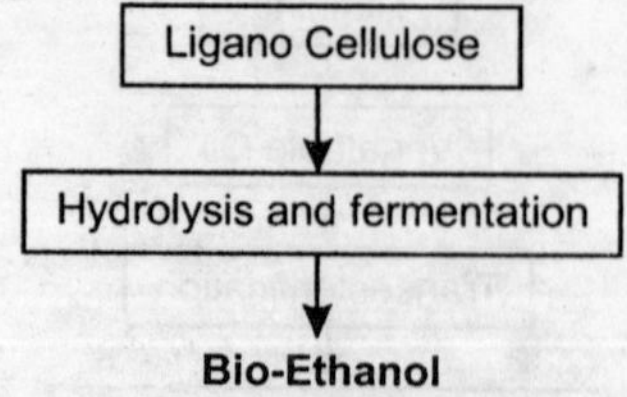

Figure 10.10. Production of second generation bio fuel

Following table 10.8 gives some first and second generation bio fuels

Table 10.8: First and second generation bio fuels

First generation	*Second generation*
Methanol	Cellulose ethanol
Ethanol	Algae fuel
Propanol	Bio hydrogen
Butanol	Bio methanol
Vegetable oil	wood diesel
Bio gas	Fischer Tropsch diesel
Synthesis gas	Bio hydrogen diesel

Various feed stocks for bio-fuels are-sugarcane, sugar beet, corn, soya bean, Jatropha, algae, cassava, palm oil, rapeseed, groundnut, certain fungi, animal fat, camelina, wheat, miscanthus, switchgrass, willow, poplar etc.

Advantages of bio fuels are following—

(*i*) clean source of fuel.
(*ii*) reduces green house gases.
(*iii*) increased energy security.
(*iv*) bio-degradable.
(*v*) reduces fossil fuel consumption.
(*vi*) rural development.
(*vii*) safe due to higher flash point.

Disadvantages—

(*i*) high capital cost.
(*ii*) nitrous oxide emission.
(*iii*) large area is required for cultivation which competes with food grain production.
(*iv*) affects food supply system.
(*v*) consume precious water resource.
(*vi*) causes deforestation.

Energy density of some bio fuel is given in the following table 10.9—

Table 10.9: Feedstock and energy density of bio-fuels

Sr. No	*Type of bio-fuel*	*Feed stock*	*Energy density (MJ/kg)*
1.	**Bio-alcohol**-Ethanol, Propanol, Butanol	Wheat, Corn, Sugar cane, Molasses, Potatoes, Fruits	Ethanol-30.0 Propanol-34.0 Butanol-36.6
2.	**Bio-diesel**	Animal fat, vegetable oil, algae	37.8
3.	**Bio gas**	organic matter	55.0

4.	**Solid bio fuel**-Wood Bagasse, manure	Wood, Saw dust, Garbage, Agricultural waste	Wood-16.0–21.0 Bagasse-10.0 Manure-10.0

Biogas is produced from agro industrial residues, sewage, municipal solid waste etc. It can be produced in digestor, anaerobic reactor etc.

- **Bio-gas Generation through Thermophilic Digestion–**

  In this process, bio gas is produced by thermophilic bacteria at a temperature of 50°C using agro-industrial residues.

Advantages—

(*a*) higher digestion efficiency.

(*b*) shorter residence time.

(*c*) more destruction of pathogens (disease causing bacteria).

Disadvantages—

(*a*) temperature sensitive.

(*b*) higher feeding rate.

(*c*) good mixing required for digester.

(*d*) additional heat required for digester.

- **Bio-gas Generation through Anaerobic Reaction—**

  In this process,methane is produced by the action of bacteria on agro-industrial residue. The reactor is a packed bed reactor with immobilized bacteria. The feed liquid is supplied from top of reactor. The upward movement of gas bubbles due to anaerobic reaction keeps the sludge fully mixed .High gas generation rates are achieved.

- **Bio-gas from Sewage–**

  Anaerobic digestion of municipal solid waste produce biogas. The bio-gas so generated can be used for cooking, lighting and power generation. The gas can be used in gas turbine and exhaust of gas turbine can be used to run steam turbine (combined cycle operation).

Biogas can also be generated from human excreta (nightsoil) in septic tanks.

Comparison, composition and properties of bio gas w.r. to other fuels are given in table 10.10.

Table 10.10: Composition and properties of bio gas

Sr. No	*Gas*	*Composition (%)*	*Calorific value (kWh/m³)*
1.	Bio gas	$CH_4/CO_2 = 60/40$	5.96
2.	Natural gas	$CH_4/H_2 = 65/35$	7.52
3.	Methane	$CH_4 = 100$	9.94
4.	Propane	$C_3H_8 = 100$	25.96
5.	Butane	$C_4H_{10} = 100$	34.02

10.7. BIO GAS PLANTS

A bio gas plant converts biomass into bio gas by anaerobic digestion. Bio gas is a mixture of 50–65% methane,30–40% carbon dioxide and the balance is made up of H_2, H_2 S and N_2. It is produced by decomposition of animal, plant and human waste. It is a clean gas having calorific value of 5000–5550 kcal/kg. Cow dung, piggery waste, poulry dropping, crop residue, kitchen waste, human waste, waste from sugar cane industry, water hyacinth etc. are used as feed material.

Bio chemical process inside digester occurs in three stages—

(*a*) insoluble biodegradable material, such as cellulose is broken down to soluble carbohydrates and fatty acids. This occurs at 25°C. It also takes one day.

(*b*) acid forming bacteria produces acetic and propionic acid. This occurs at 25°C. It also takes one day.

(*c*) methane producing bacteria takes 14 days at 25°C. During this process, 70% methane, 30% CO_2 and small quantities of H_2 and H_2S are produced.

A bio gas plant consists of following components—

(*i*) **Mixing tank**—Feed material is collected in mixing tank. Biomass and waste water are added to 50:50 ratio and thoroughly mixed till a homogeneous mixture is formed.

(*ii*) **Inlet pipe**—Slurry from mixing tank is discharged into the digester.

(*iii*) **Digester**—It is an enclosed air and water tight vessel where anaerobic digestion of biomass takes place. In this,slurry is added with seeding matter (bacteria rich substance) so that fermentation reaction takes place in the absence of oxygen.

(*iv*) **Gas storage dome**—This drum is made up of mild steel, fibre reinforced plastic (FRP) etc. and is of cylindrical shape and conical top. It fits the digester at top. This drum is of either fixed or floating type. In floating type, as the gas gets collected, it floats freely over the slurry.

(*v*) **Slurry tank**—Digested slurry after sufficient residence time (20–30 days) is discharged into slurry tank from the opening provided in the digester.

(*vi*) **Gas pipeline**—It carries the gas to the point of usage e.g. gas stove for cooking, lamp for lighting or gas engine for generation of electricity.

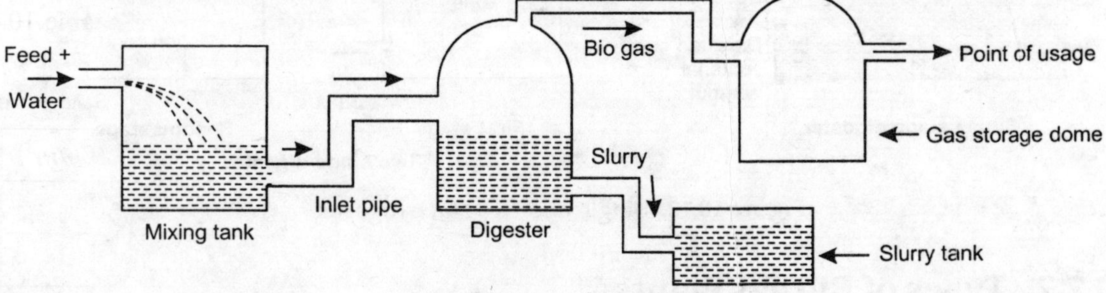

Figure 10.11. Bio gas plant

Benefits of bio gas are following—

(*i*) It is clean and sustainable source of energy.

(*ii*) It saves village women and children from drudgery of collecting and carrying firewood for cooking purpose.

(*iii*) It provides clean and smokefree cooking gas.

(*iv*) It provides source of lighting in rural area having no electricity.

(*v*) It generates enriched organic manure for agriculture.

(*vi*) It is efficient and environmental friendly way of disposing off organic waste.

(*vii*) It provides source of decentralized power generation.

10.7.1. Bio Digester

It is the heart of a biogas plant where decomposition of biomass material takes place. It is an air and water tight cylindrical structure where various chemical and microbiological reactions take place. It creates the necessary conditions for microbiological reactions to take place.

Feeding of biomass takes place either in batches (for solid biomass) or in continuous form (for slurry biomass). Bio gas digesters are of two types-single stage and two stage. In single stage digester, biomass is charged into an active zone where anaerobic reaction takes place. The decomposed solids being heavier settle down at the bottom of digester from where these are taken out. Bio gas produced due to anaerobic reaction rises through layers of scum and gets collected at the top of the digester. A thick layer of scum prevents the release of gas. Since, the retention time is more, hence this is considered as the inefficient digester.

By reducing retention time, gas output is increased in a two stage digester. Anaerobic digestion process takes place in two separate chambers. Bio gas is collected in second chamber where bio-methanation takes place. The first chamber is continuously fed, completely mixed and temperature controlled while the second stage is unstirred and is meant for solid separation and low volume of gas collection. However, This type of plant is more expensive, difficult to operate and maintain.

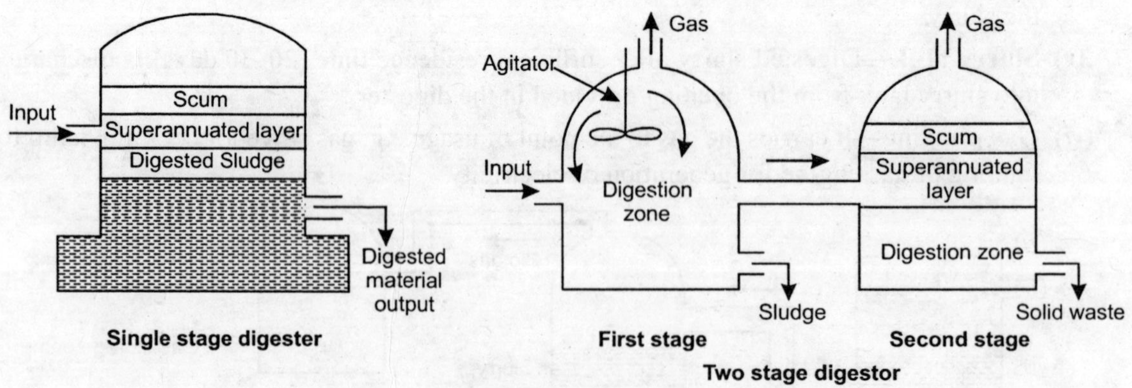

Figure 10.12. Single and two stage digester

10.7.2. Types of Bio gas Plants

Following are the types of bio gas plants—

(*i*) Continuous and batch type.

(*ii*) Fixed dome and floating drum type.

(*i*) **Fixed Dome Type Biogas Plant**—It consists of underground brick masonry fermentation chamber with a fixed dome on the top of it for gas collection. Both the digester and gas holder units are combined .This design is suitable for batch type process for small daily feedings. An additional chamber is provided for collection of slurry .The life of this type of plant is 20–50 years.

Due to fermentation of biomass,gas is formed which rises upward and collects in the hemi-spherical dome. This gas exerts pressure by pushing the slurry to another chamber. Diameter and height digester is 1.75 : 1 ratio.

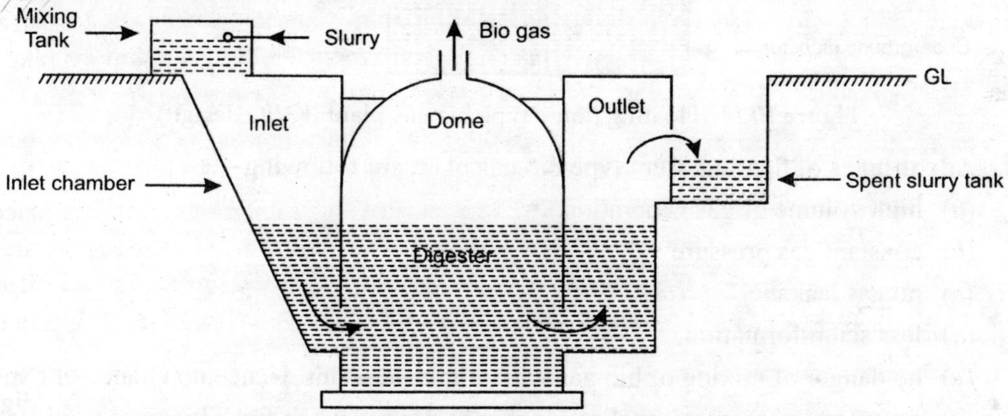

Figure 10.13. Fixed dome type bio gas plant (Janata model)

Advantages of fixed dome types bio gas plant are given as following—

(*a*) low cost.

(*b*) no corrosion problem.

(*c*) longer operating life.

(*d*) due to underground construction,thermal insulation is better which helps to maintain temperature.

(*e*) no maintenance.

Disadvantages—

(*a*) skilled masons are needed for construction.

(*b*) due to absence of stirring arrangement, scum formation may be considered as a problem.

(*c*) gas pressure is variable.

(*d*) low volume of gas production.

(*ii*) **Floating Drum Type Bio gas Plant**—It consists of a mild steel or fibre glass drum which floats along a guide frame and acts as gas reservoir. The main digester moves up and down according to pressure and volume of bio gas. The digester can be constructed over ground or underground. The digester is divided into two equal halves. This type of digester is more expensive.

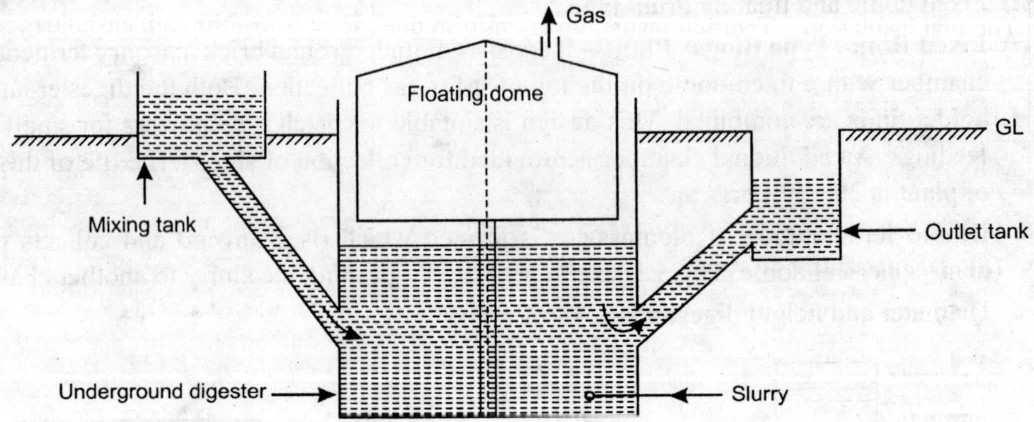

Figure 10.14. Floating dome type bio gas plant (KVIC design)

Advantages of floating drum type bio gas plant are following—

(*a*) high volume of gas generation.

(*b*) constant gas pressure.

(*c*) no gas leakage.

(*d*) less scum formation.

(*e*) no danger of mixing of bio gas with atmospheric air .Hence,no chance of explosion.

(*f*) no separate pressure equalisation device needed when fresh biomass is added.

Disadvantages—

(*a*) higher cost of dome.

(*b*) heat escapes through metal gas holder.

(*c*) gas holder requires periodic painting for protection against corrosion.

(*d*) flexible pipe joining gas holder and man gas pipe both require maintenance.

Comparison of fixed dome and floating drum type bio gas plants is given in table 10.11.

Table 10.11: Comparision of is fixed dome and flooating drum type biogas plant

Sr.No	*Parameter*	*Fixed dome type plant*	*Movable drum type plant*
1.	Construction	Digester and gasholder are of masonary or concrete construction.	Digester is of masonry while gas holder is of mild steel or fibre glass.
2.	Gas pressure	Variable gas pressure	Constant gas pressure
3.	Cost	Low	High
4.	Digestion period	30 – 60 days	40–60 days
5.	Reliability	Low due to underground construction	High due to prefabricated structure.
6.	Masonary skills needed	High	Low

7.	Thermal insulation	Thermal insulation is uniform due to underground construction.	Heat is lost through gasholder.
8.	Life	20 – 50 years	20 – 30 years
9.	Maintenance	High	Low

***(iii)* Other Bio gas plants**—Some widely used models of bio gas plant are described below—

(*a*) Deenbandhu Biogas Plant—

It is a low cost, fixed dome type bio gas plant. It consists of brick masonry work with a concave bottom and spherical top .Inlet pipe carries raw material from mixing tank to the digester. The outlet pipe conveys bio gas to the point of usage. Slurry is taken to a displacement chamber.

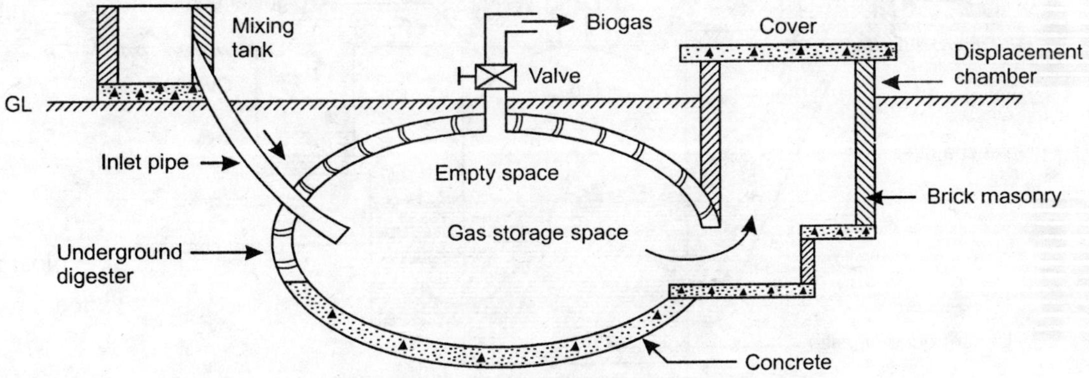

Figure 10.15. Deenbandhu Bio gas plant

(*b*) KVIC Bio gas plant

KVIC is acronym for Khadi and Village Industries (KVIC).

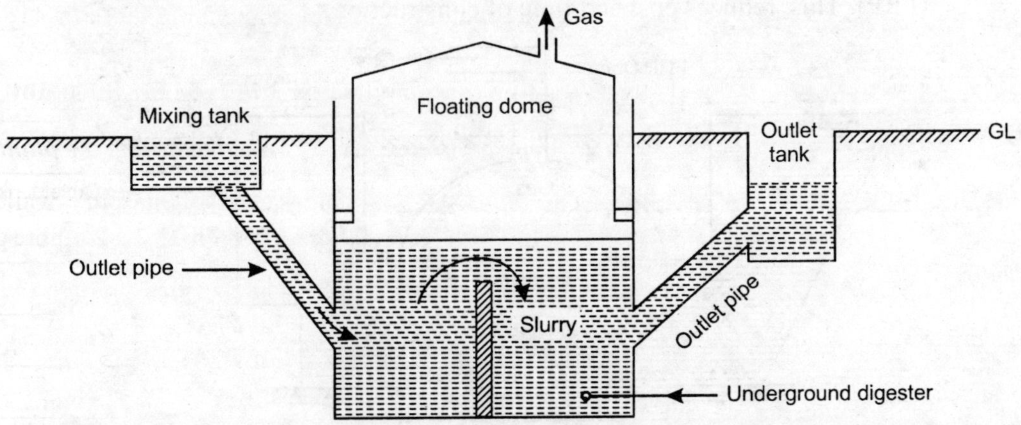

Figure 10.16. KVIC bio gas plant

This plant is also known as gobar gas plant. It is a floating drum bio digester. It has one mixing tank with an inlet pipe feeding to digester. The digester is separated by separation wall that is 3/4th of its height. The slurry from digester goes to the outlet tank. The bio gas gets collected in the upper portion of floating drum. This plant is available in sizes from one cubic metre to 140 cubic meter capacity. The bio gas is stored in the mild steel drums at a pressure of about 10 cm of water column.

(c) Janata bio gas plant

It is a fixed dome types bio gas plant based on Chinese technology. Digester and gas holder are made up of single unit. Brick masonary is used for construction. Entire construction is done underground. Digester is of cylindrical shape and holds dung slurry for gas generation. Gas gets collected at the top end of the digester. Inlet pipe caries slurry from mixing tank to the digester.

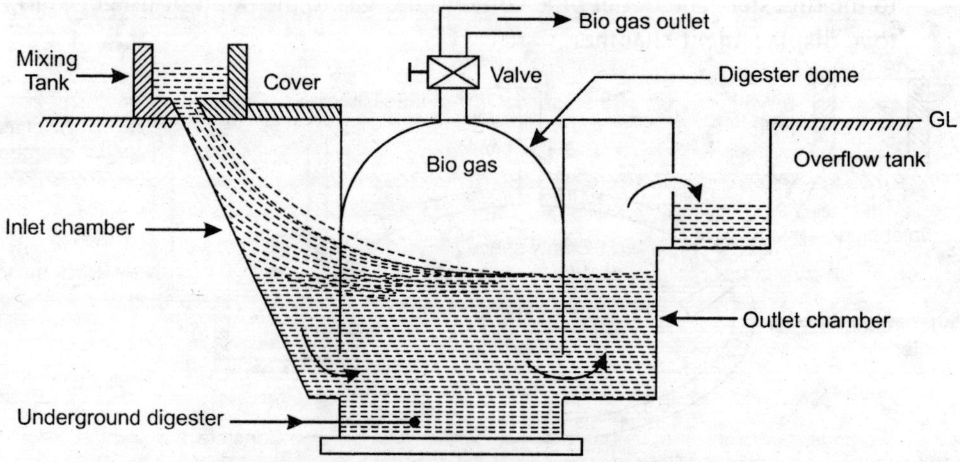

Figure 10.17. Janata Bio gas plant

(d) Gayatri bio gas plant

The digester of this biogas plant is made up of pre fabricated fibre reinforced plastic (FRP). This reduces cost and time of construction.

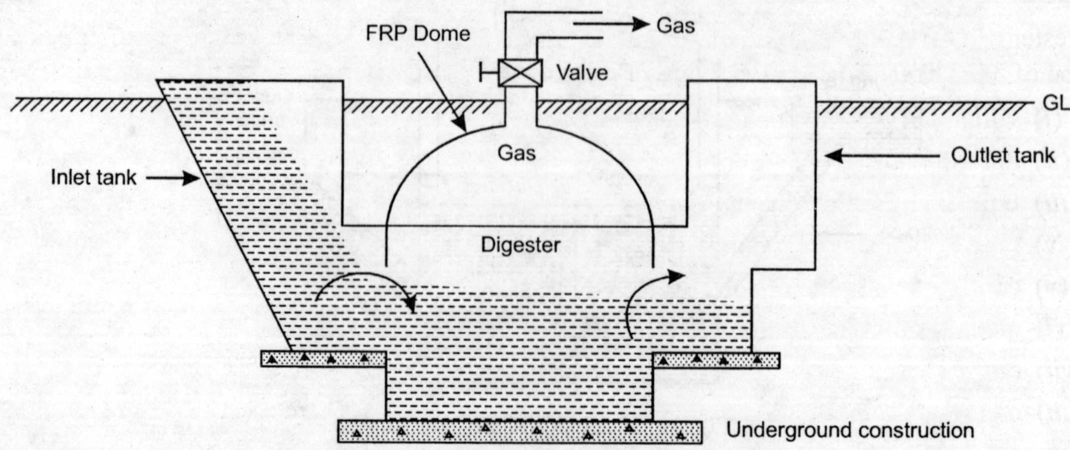

Figure 10.18. Gayatri bio gas plant

(*e*) **Flexible Bag type Bio gas plant**

The digester is made of plastic and hence it is cheap and easy to install. However, plastic is affected by ultraviolet rays thereby reducing its life.

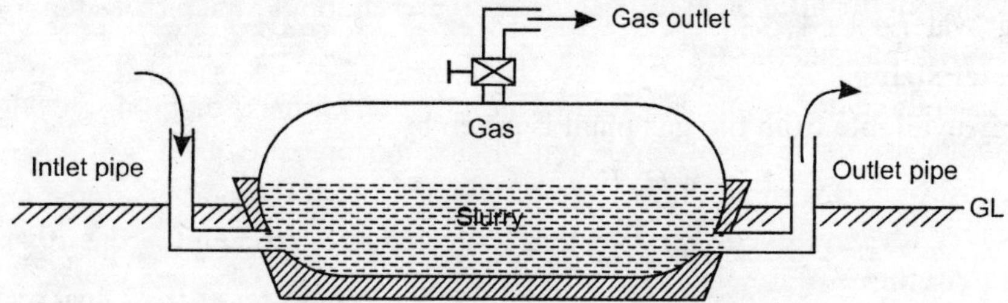

Figure 10.19. Flexible bag bio gas plant

(*f*) **Manipal Bio gas plant**

It consists of rectangular shaped digester with RCC roof. The top of the digester stores bio gas. The base and sidewalls are of brick masonry.

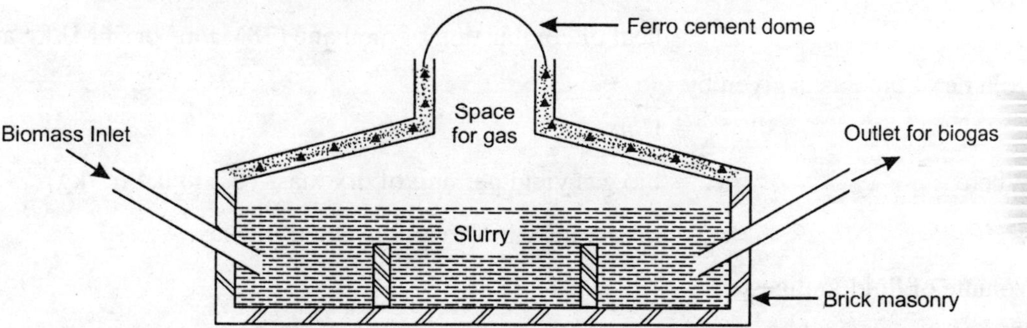

Figure 10.20. Manipal bio gas plant

10.7.3. Design of Digester

A digester can be designed to be of any shape, such as cylindrical, rectangular etc. The top cover may be of fixed or floating type. Design of digester is affected by following factors—

(*i*) volume of waste to be used per day.

(*ii*) duration of digestion period.

(*iii*) type of entry for raw material and exit.

(*iv*) type of biomass available.

(*v*) condition and type of sub soil.

(*vi*) method of biogas usage.

(*vii*) climatic conditions.

(*viii*) method of agitation required.

The optimum temperature range required inside digester is 15°C to 35°C. Process of anaerobic digestion slows down beyond this range. The capacity of digester is taken equal to 2/3rd of organic matters in the slurry. Following parameters need to be maintained for optimum gas output—

(*i*) C/N ratio – 30 to 35

(*ii*) Temperature – 15° to 35°C

(*iii*) Dung: vegetable mixture – 1.2 : 1

(*iv*) Dung: water – 1 : 4

- **Digester sizing**

Energy available from bio gas plant is given by

$$E = \eta H_b V_b \quad ...(10.14)$$

$$= \eta f_m H_m V_b \quad ...(10.15)$$

Where, η = Combustion efficiency of burner (about 60%).

H_b – heat of combustion of bio gas per unit volume at 0.01 atmospheric pressure (20MJ/m^3).

V_b = volume of bio gas (m^3).

f_m = fraction of methane in biogas (0.70).

H_m = heat of combustion of methane (28MJ/m^3 or 56MJ/kg at STP)

Volume of bio gas is given by

$$V_b = C\, m_d \quad ...(10.16)$$

Where, C = bio gas yield per unit of dry mass (0.2 to 0.4 m^3/kg)

m_d = mass of dry biomass consumed per day.

Volume of fluid in digester,

$$V_f = \frac{m_d}{\rho_d} \quad ...(10.17)$$

Where, ρ_d = Density of dry mass in fluid (about 50kg/m^3)

Volume of digester, $V = V_f\, t_r$. ...(10.18)

Where, t_r = retention time in digester

V_f = volume of fluid in digester

10.8. POWER GENERATION FROM BIOMASS

India generates about 500 million tons of biomass material in agricultural, agro-industrial and forestry operation. Majority of it is used as fuel and fodder. A significant portion of this biomass goes waste due to lack of any avenue for productive use. Current potential for biomass power generation is 17,538 MW (as on 31-3-2014). Current installed capacity of grid interactive biomass power generation is 4013.55MW. Off grid waste to energy installed capacity is 106.58 MW.

During 2011 alone, 25 rice husk based gassifier system for industrial generation were installed in 70 remote villages of Bihar. The largest biomass gas plant is at Sirohi, Rajasthan of 20MW capacity. In 2011, biomass gassifier of 1.2 MW was installed in Gurjarat and 0.5 MW in Tamil Nadu. In Kakadpara, Nasik district of Maharashtra, a pilot project of 10 kW gasifier was commissioned on 16th April, 2011 to feed power to 85 households in the village. The power supplied meets the need of domestic lighting, street lighting and other entertainment activities. Power is supplied from 7 pm to 2 am at night.

Typical capital cost of biomass power projects ranges from ₹ 4 crores /MW to ₹ 5 crores/MW. Cost of generation depends upon cost of biomass, plant load factor and efficiencies of conversion. Life of power plant is about 20 years which may be further extended by another 10 years after major overhaul.

Following are various types of power generation schemes based on biomass—

(*a*) Biomass gassifier based distributed/off grid power generation for rural areas to provide power from lighting, irrigation and other commercial establishments.

(*b*) Biomass gassifier based captive power generation, such as in sugar mills (bagasse), rice mills (rice husk), wood /paper mills (wood waste), palm oil mill (empty fruit bunches, shells), cassava (root, stem), corn (corn waste) etc.

(*c*) Biomass gassifer based grid connected power projects having either 100% producer gas engines or boiler-turbine-generator.

(*d*) Power generated from urban waste (landfill gas, incineration, digestion).

Advantages of biomass based power generation are described below—

(*i*) raw material is abundant and environmentally sustainable.

(*ii*) it reduces dependency on fossil fuels.

(*iii*) it provides fuel diversity providing flexibility in operation.

(*iv*) suitable for distributed power generation especially in rural areas.

(*v*) it is carbon neutral.

(*vi*) efficient utilization for renewable biological resources.

(*vii*) efficient disposal of toxic biomass waste.

(*viii*) it is domestically produced.

(*ix*) it is reliable and continuous source of energy unlike solar and wind.

(*x*) biomass power generation is attractive to industry (sugar mills, rice mills, parer industry etc).

(*xi*) due to proximity to rural areas, these projects improve quality of life in rural area by providing electricity, cooking gas etc.

(*xii*) equipment for these projects are similar to those for coal based thermal power plants, hence no new technological developments are needed.

Disadvantages of biomass based power generation are given as follows—

(*i*) high cost of raw material.

(*ii*) inefficient as compared to fossil fuel.

(*iii*) availability & security of feedstock supply is not guaranteed.

(*iv*) unstable price of raw material.

(*v*) useful agri waste suitable for cooking and fodder is diverted for power generation.

(*vi*) problem of disposal of ash & sludge.

(*vii*) variation of fuel quality with season.

(*viii*) requirement of expensive pollution control equipments.

10.8.1. Technologies used for Biomass Power Generation

Biomass resources are used for generation of power, heat, combined heat and power. Following are various techniques used for generation of power, heat and combined heat and power.

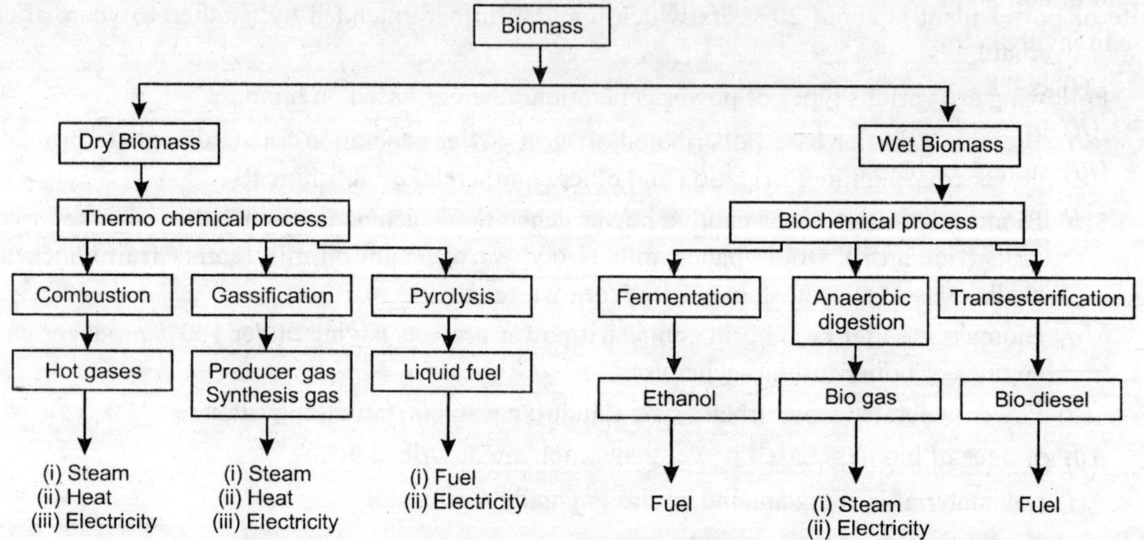

Figure 10.21. Technology used for biomass power generation

1. **Power generation by Combustion or Incineration**—It is a process of burning solid organic waste matter, such as industrial waste, agricultural waste, municipal waste etc.

(*a*) **Agricultural waste**— These are Bagasse, palm kernel shells, coconut shells, coca shells, almond shells, cashew shells, coffee husk and shells, rice husk, sunflower husk, soya husk, olive cake, grap seeds, cherry pits, corn etc.

(*b*) **Municipal wastes**— These are—

(*a*) Domestic waste—Food waste, garden waste, newsprint, paper, plastic, metal, glass, discarded items etc.

(*b*) Commercial waste—Packaging materials, office supplies, food waste etc.

(*c*) Institutional waste—Similar to domestic and commercial waste, hospital waste (includes hazardous medical waste).

(*d*) Construction and demolition waste—Soil, stone, bricks, concrete, wood, ceramic materials, packaging material etc. Usually this is not suitable for incineration. Typical composition of muncipal waste are-food and organic waste –45%, plastic – 23%, textile –3.5%, paper and cardboard –1.4%, leather and rubber –8%, wood – 4.1%, glass –1.3%, others –1.5%. The composition of municipal waste depends upon economic strata of society, geographical location, season etc.

(*e*) Industrial waste—paper, plastic, packing material, metal item, hazardous process waste, agro-industrial waste, such as bagasse, rice husk, energy crops etc.

10.8.1.1. Power generation from agri waste/ agri-industrial waste

This process produces power by burning agri and agri-industrial waste. Combustion or incineration technique is used to generate hot gases. These gases are used to generate steam in a boiler. The steam of boiler is used to run a steam turbine thereby producing electricity.

In involves following steps–

(*i*) collection of biomass feedstock.

(*ii*) transportation of biomass to power plant.

(*iii*) storage of biomass.

(*iv*) pretreatment of biomass—It involves conversion of biomass into bales, pellets or briquettes so as to make them suitable for use in furnace. The process involves following steps—

Figure 10.22. Pretreatment process of biomass

(*v*) Combustion in a furnace/boiler—

Treated biomass is burnt in a boiler which has following methods of burning of biomass—

(*a*) Grate firing—It involves feeding biomass pellets or briquetts into a travelling chain called grate. The grate travels at slow speed allowing the biomass material to burn. The ash produced after combustion falls to the bottom of furnace. The hot gases so produced are led into a boiler to produce steam. This method is suitable for power plant capacity of upto 50 MW.

(*b*) Pulverised fuel firing—It involves burning of biomass in combination with pulverised (powdered) coal or lignite in a boiler. It is basically co-combustion of coal and other fossil fuels with treated biomass material .This method allows conventional fossil fuel based power plants to use biomass material as partial fuel substitution thereby generating 3–15% of input energy from biomass. Also,it avoids construction of new biomass power plant. This process is also known as mixed fuel burning or co-firing. Different schemes of co- firing are given in the flowchart below (Figure 10.23).

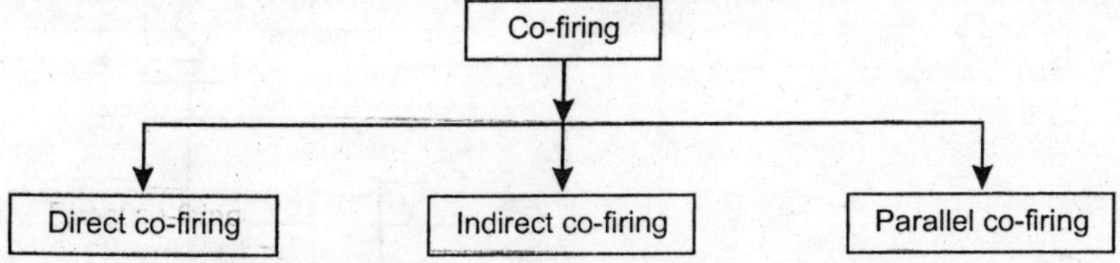

Figure 10.23. Various methods of co-firing

(*i*) Direct co-firing—It involves mixing of pulverised coal and prepared biomass .The combined fuel is burnt in a boiler .

(*ii*) Indirect co-firing—This method is suitable for combustion of biomass material having different characteristics than fossil fuel. The biomass material is burnt separately.

(*iii*) Parallel firing—This method is suitable for combustion of biomass material having high alkali and chlorine content. The biomass material is burnt in a separate power plant.

(*c*) Fluidised bed combustion—It is a special type of vessel consisting of vertical refractory lining inside with a bed of grannular material, such as limestone, sand, ceramic material etc. These grannular materials are mixed with fuel and are fluidised by air. This results in good combustion at comparatively lower temperature. The heat energy so released is used to raise steam in a boiler which is further expanded in steam turbine to generate electricity. The advantages of fluidised bed firing are low capital and maintenance cost, high thermal efficiency upto 90% and suitability for wide range of fuels. Disadvantages are strict demand on size and composition of biomass.

(1) Combustion Based Biomass power plant—

It consists of following components—

(*i*) **Biomass pretreatment plant**—It converts raw biomass into pellets, bales or briquetts.

(*ii*) **Fuel storage and handling**—It stores treated biomass in the form of pellets, bales or briquetts.

(*iii*) **Combustor (furnace /boiler)**—Pellets, bales or briquetts are burnt here to generate steam.

(*iv*) **Steam turbine**—Steam is expanded here to produce motive power.

(*v*) **Generator**—It converts mechanical motion of steam turbine into electricity.

(*vi*) **Condenser**—It condenses steam after expansion in turbine to be feedback as feed water to boiler.

(*vii*) **Cooling tower**—It removes heat of exhaust steam.

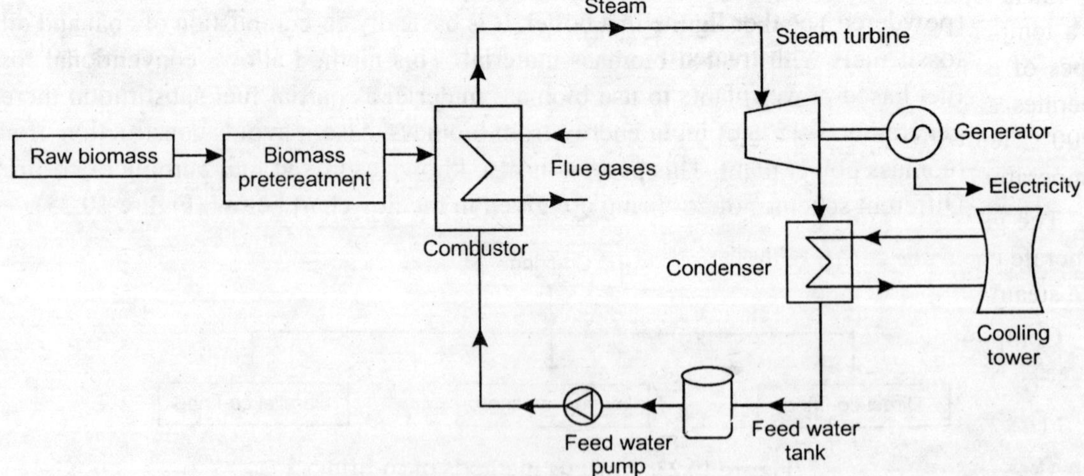

Figure 10.24. Combustion based biomass power plant (steam turbine)

Combustion reaction → $\underbrace{C_6H_{10}O_5}_{\text{Biomass}} + 6O_2 \rightarrow 6CO_2 + 5H_2O + 17.5\text{MJ/kg}$. ...(10.19)

Combustion process are designed to recover energy from waste in the form of electricity, heat or both. Following table 10.12 gives efficiency of these usage.

Table 10.12: Efficiency and usage of combustion process

Output	*Efficiency*	*Usage*
Heat	80–90%	Process heating, building heating.
Power	14–27%	For local consumption, for feeding to grid.
Combined heat and power	Dependent upon particular scheme used	As above

Combustion based method of power generation is similar to coal or thermal power plant as plant and equipments are similar (working on Rankine cycle).

Advantages of power generation from combustion are given below—

(*i*) valuable energy recovered from waste.

(*ii*) energy substitution leading to conservation of fossil fuels.

(*iii*) avoids landfill.

Disadvantages—

(*i*) low efficiency.

(*ii*) generation of green house gases.

(*iii*) expensive method of energy generation.

(*iv*) despite pollution control measures,pollutants contaminate air, water and soil.

(2) Gassifier Based Biomass Power Plant–

Gasification involves reaction of biomass feedstock with oxygen, air, steam or carbon dioxide at a temperature of 800°C and above. The main output is synthesis gas (CH_4, H_2, CO). Three types of gassifiers are used viz fixed bed, fluidised bed and entrained flow. Fixed bed gassifier operates at 800–1000°C and pressure of 1–10 MPa. Fluidised bed gassifiers operated at 800–1000°C temperature and 1–2.5 MPa pressure. Entrained flow gassifier operates at 1500–1900°C temperature and 2.5–4 MPa pressure.

The gas produced from gassification of biomass is burned in a gas turbine, or gas engine to generate electricity. It can also be burnt in a boiler to produce steam. This steam is then expanded in a steam turbine to generate electricity.

Components of gassifier based power plant (gas turbine)are mentioned below—

(*i*) **Biomass pretreatment plant**—It converts raw biomass into pellets, bales or beiquetts.

(*ii*) **Fuel storage and handling**—Pretreated biomass are stored here.

(*iii*) **Biomass gassifier**—It converts biomass into gaseous form.

(*iv*) **Gas cooler**—It reduces temperature of gases from gassifier.

(*v*) **Gas filter**—It removes suspended particulate matter in the gases.

(*vi*) **Gas scrubber**—It further removes suspended matter through water.

(*vii*) **Gas turbine**—It burns gases and produces motive power.

(*viii*) **Generator**—It converts mechanical motion of gas turbine into electricity.

(*ix*) **Stack**—It discharges exhaust gases from gas turbine to atmosphere.

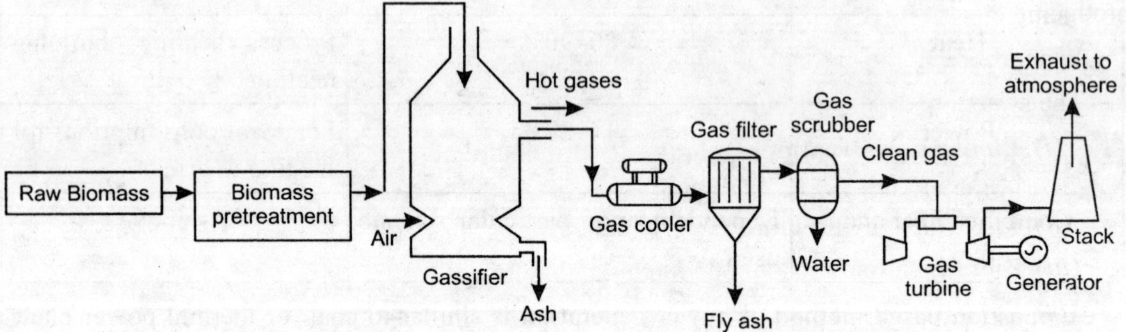

Figure 10.25. Gassifier based biomass power generation (gas turbine)

$$\text{Gassification reaction} \rightarrow \underbrace{C_6H_{10}O_5}_{\text{Biomass}} + \frac{1}{2}\ O_2 \rightarrow 6CO + 5H_2 + 1.85\ \text{MJ/kg}. \qquad ...(10.20)$$

Electricity can be produced by burning the gas in a gas engine.

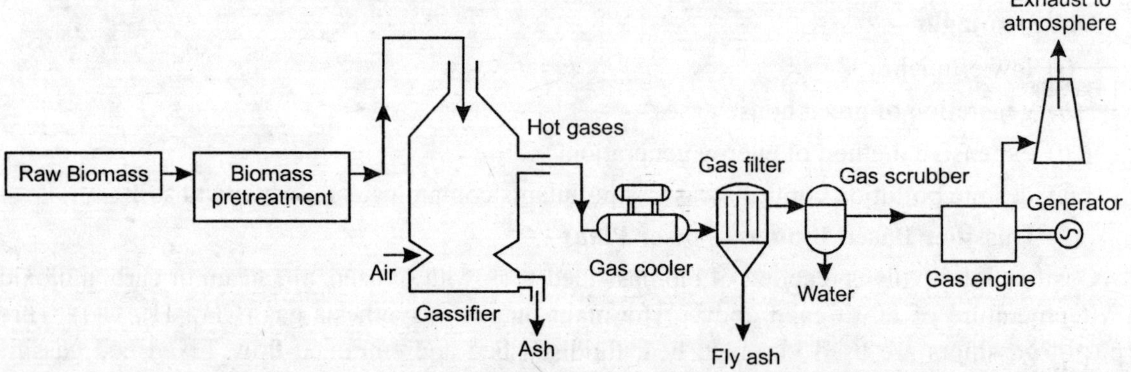

Figure 10.26. Gassifier based biomass power generation (gas engine)

Combined cycle power plant uses gas turbine and a steam turbine (Brayton cycle and Rankine cycle).

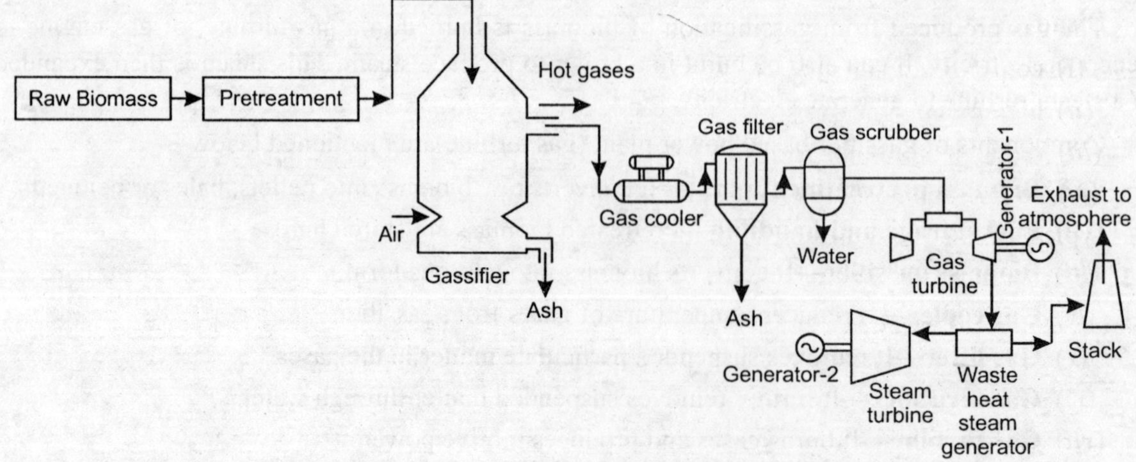

Figure 10.27. Gassifier based biomass power generation (combined cycle)

Combined cycle power generation plant uses exhaust of gas turbine into a waste heat recovery steam generator. The steam out of this steam generator is used to run a steam turbine thereby producing electricity.

In another scheme,gas engine is used to generate electricity.

The system consists of following components—

(*i*) **Biomass pretreatment plant**—It sorts and converts biomass into pellets or balles or briquetts.

(*ii*) **Fuel storage and handling**—Pellets, bales or briquetts are stored here.

(*iii*) **Biomass gassifier**—It converts biomass into hot gases.

(*iv*) **Furnace**—Gases are burnt here to release heat energy.

(*v*) **Gas engine**—It produces motive power.

(*vi*) **Generator**—Mechanical motion of gas engine is converted into electricity.

(*vii*) **Stack**—It discharges exhaust gases from gas engine to atmosphere.

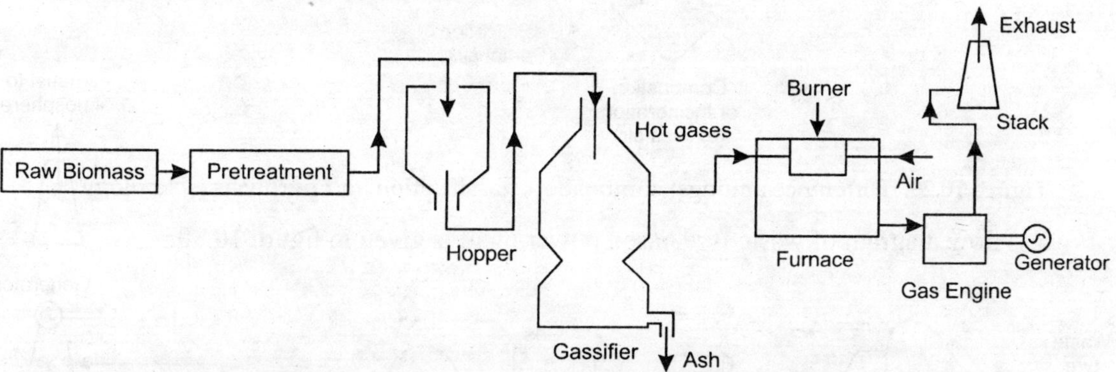

Figure 10.28. Gassifier based biomass power generation (gas engine)

Advantages of gassifier based power generation are given below–

(*i*) high efficiency at small scale.
(*ii*) flexible capacity.
(*iii*) low investment needed.
(*iv*) can use any biomass source.

Disadvantages—

(*i*) complex equipment.

(*ii*) high maintenance cost.

(*iii*) requires more time to start.

(*iv*) composition,energy content and impurities of producer gas vary from time to time.

Typical efficiency and capacity of different scheme are given below (table 10.13).

Table 10.13: Efficiency and capacity of various combustion schemes

Technology	*Typical sizes (MW)*	*efficiency(%)*
Co-firing	10 – 50	35 – 40

Steam turbine	5 – 25	30 – 35
Gassifier + Engine	0.2 – 1	25 – 30
Gas engine(CHP)	< 0.1	11 – 20

(3) Pyrolysis Based Biomass Power Plant

Pyrolysis is the chemical decomposition of organic matter in the absence of air. Difference amongst the three processes viz. Combustion, Gassification and Pyrolysis is given in following figure 10.29.

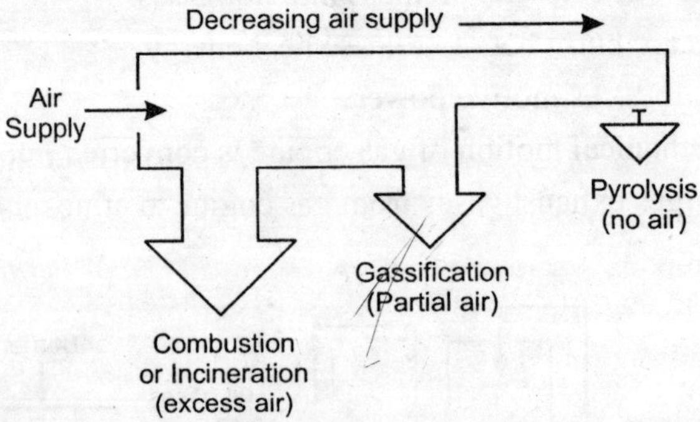

Figure 10.29. Difference amongst combustion, gassification and pyrolysis technology

Process flow diagram of waste tyre based power plant is given in figure 10.30.

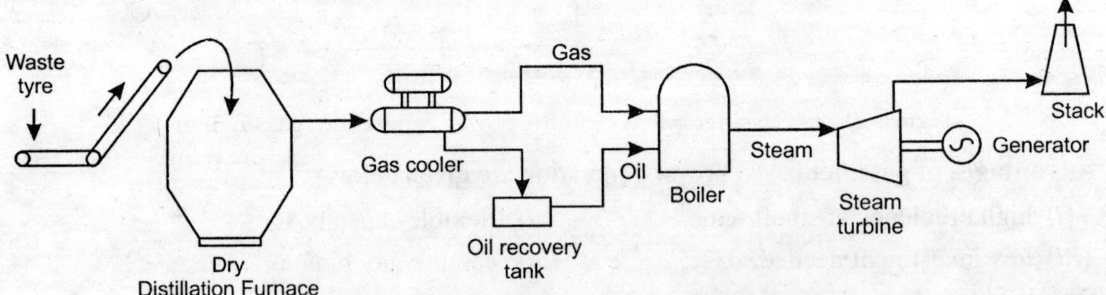

Figure 10.30. Pyrolysis based biomass power plant

Pyrolysis based biomass power plant consists of following components–

(*i*) **Dry distillation furnace**—It is used to generate hot gases from biomass.

(*ii*) **Gas cooler**—It is used to reduce the temperature of hot gases.

(*iii*) **Oil recovery tank**—Oil content in gas is collected here.

(*iv*) **Boiler**—Steam is raised by using heat of gases.

(*v*) **Steam turbine**—Steam is expanded here to produce motion.

(*vi*) **Generator**—Mechanical motion of steam turbine is used to generate electricity.

(*vii*) **Stack**—It discharges exhaust gases to atmosphere.

10.8.1.2. Power Generation from Municipal Waste

Power can be produced from municipal waste. Following diagram gives energy routes from municipal waste.

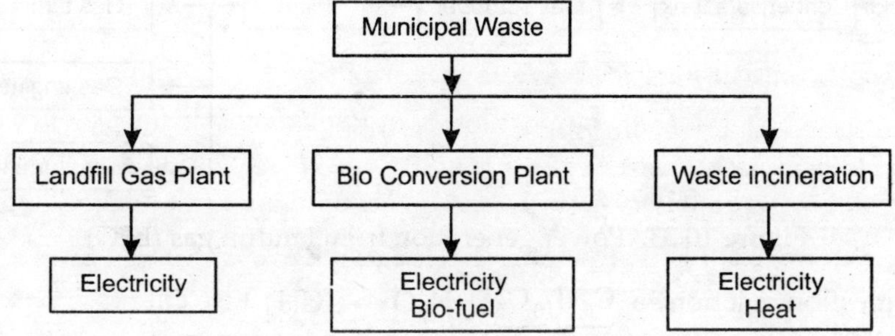

Figure 10.31. Methods of production of electricity from municipal waste

(*i*) Power generation from landfill gas (LFG)—

Landfilling is a method of disposal of municipal waste to wasteland. The landfill generates landfill gas due to operation of micro-organisms on organic matter. Landfill gas is composed of 60% methane and 40% carbon dioxide. This gas is collected by drilling wells into landfill area and collecting gas through wells. This gas can be used in gas turbine or gas engine. The efficiency of gas engine is 33% and gas turbine is 28% on landfill gas.

Collection of landfill gas consists of drilling number of holes in landfill and collecting gas through pipelines to a tank.

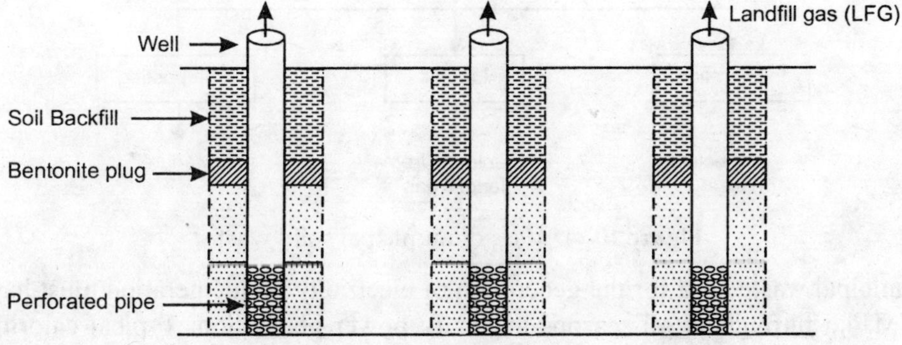

Figure 10.32. Landfill gas (LFG)well drilling

In less than one year, the anaerobic condition are established and methane producing bacteria decompose the municipal waste and produce methane. The landfill gas (LFG) can be burnt in a gas turbine or gas engine to generate electricity. The calorific value (LCV) of LFG is 3 – 6 MJ/Nm^3. This gas generation continues for 10–15 years. The rate of methane generation depends upon moisture in waste,volume of waste ,density of solid waste, presence or absence of sewage sludge etc.

Advantages of power generation from LFG are given below—

(*i*) it is a reliable source of energy as it is generated about 24 hrs a day:

(*ii*) methane emission (green house gas) can be reduced.

(*iii*) it generates jobs due to new power plants.

(*iv*) energy substitution (consumption of fossil fuel is reduced).

The flow chart for electricity generation from landfill gas is given in figure 10.33.

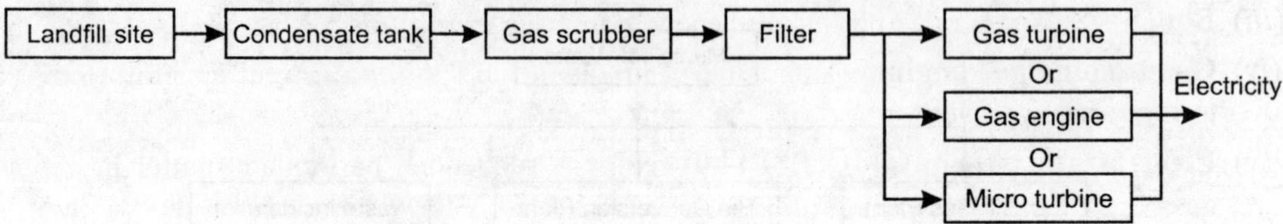

Figure 10.33. Power generation from landfill gas (LFG)

Anaerobic digestion reaction $\rightarrow \underbrace{C_6H_{10}O_5}_{\text{Biomass}} + H_2O \rightarrow 3CH_4 + 3CO_2$. ...(10.21)

Capacity of micro-turbine working on LFG ranges from 30 kW – 250 kW, gas engine from 10 kW – 3 MW and gas turbine 800 kW to 10.5 MW.

(*ii*) Power generation from incineration of municipal waste—

It is the combustion of solid organic waste matter in municipal waste. This process of incineration is used for disposal of medical waste, certain hazardous waste where pathogens (disease causing bacteria)and toxins are destroyed by high temperature. This process yields heat energy which can be used to generate electricity.

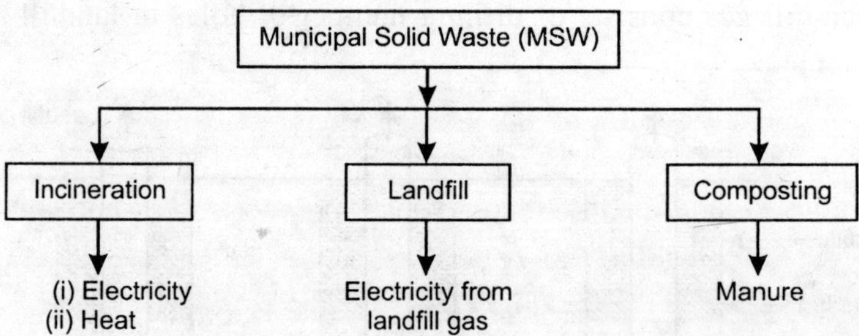

Figure 10.34. Uses of municipal solid waste

The municipal waste used for the generation of electricity by incineration must have calorific value of 6 MJ/kg throughout all seasons to justify power generation. Typical calorific value of municipal solid waste (MSW) is 10 MJ/kg.

Power generation process from municipal solid waste is given in following flow chart (figure 10.35).

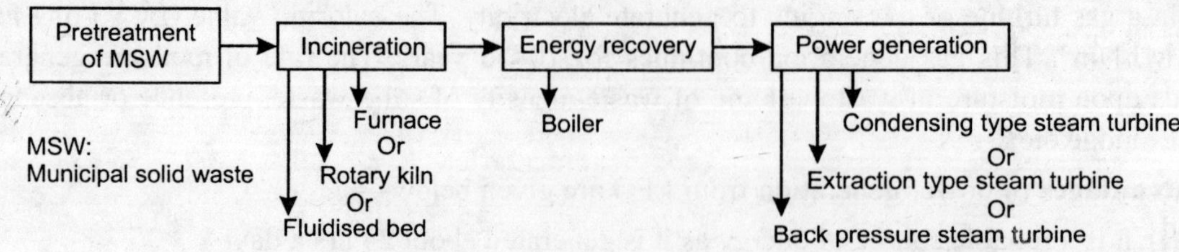

Figure 10.35. Process flow chart of power generation from MSW

Major components of municipal solid waste power plant consists of following components–

(*i*) **Pretreatment plant**—It is used to convert raw biomass into pellets.

(*ii*) **Furnace**—Treated biomass is burnt here to generate hot gases.

(*iii*) **Boiler**—Steam is raised by using heat of hot gases from furnace.

(*iv*) **Gas turbine/gas engine**—Gas is burnt in gas turbine/gas engine and generator coupled to it produces power.

(*v*) **Electrostatic precipitator (ESP)**—It removes suspended particulate matter in exhaust gas.

(*vi*) **Scrubber**—It cleans gas by bringing it in contact with water.

(*vii*) **Stack**—It discharges clean exhaust gases to atmosphere.

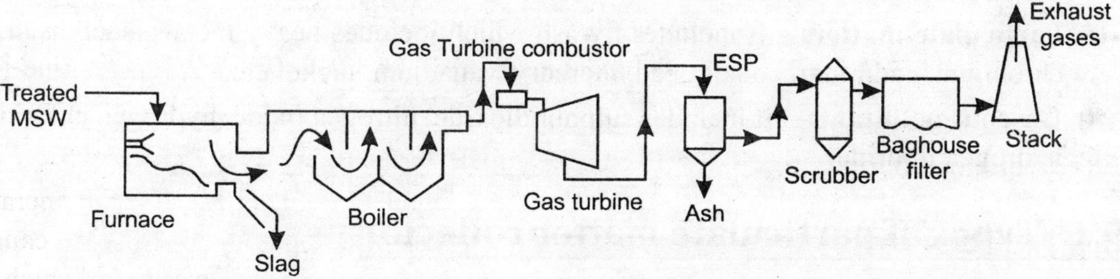

Figure 10.36. Power generation from municipal solid waste

Purpose of electrostatic precipitator is to remove suspended particulate matter in exhaust gas. Gas scrubber further removes acid forming gases by a water sprinkler.

Urban local bodies spend around ₹ 500 to ₹ 1500 per ton on solid waste management, out of which 60 to 70% of the amount is on collection & 20 to 30%on transportation. After segregation of waste, about 45% goes to landfills. Most solid waste goes to landfill and water bodies causing pollution. Also, locating a new landfill site is a challenging task. So, permanent and eco-friendly solution lies in conversion of this garbage into energy (waste to energy).

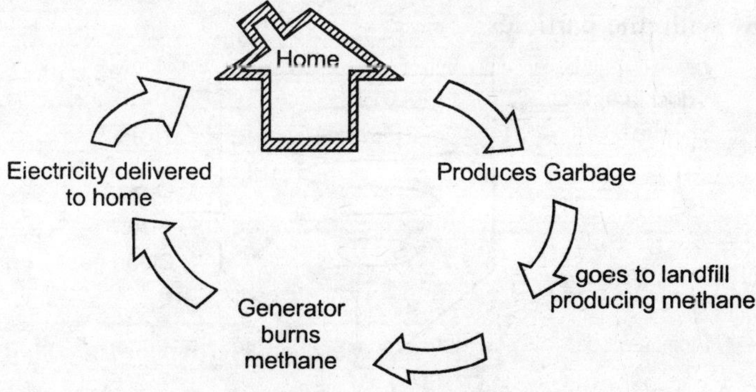

Figure 10.37. Waste to energy cycle

Today, more than 900 waste to energy plants operate around the globe. These plants treat estimated 200 million tons of municipal solid waste with an estimated output of 130 tera watt hours of electricity.

Shadnagar facility of 6 MW in Andhra Pradesh is the first operational waste to energy plant in India. APTRANSCO buys power at ₹ 3.48/kWh and feeds grid through a 33/11 kV substation. The plant is operating since November 2003. Timarpur okhla municipal solid waste management project in Delhi is first commercial waste to energy facility in North India. This plant can treat one third of Delhi garbage into electricity.

10.9. POLLUTION CONTROL TECHNIQUES

Gas produced due to incineration of municipal solid waste contains particulate matter and gaseous pollutants. These pollutants need to be removed before these are exhausted to atmosphere. Composition of pollutants are given below—

(*i*) **Particulate matters**—It includes fly ash which includes heavy metals, such as arsenic, chromium, cadmium, cobalt, lead, mercury, vanadium, nickel etc.

(*ii*) **Gaseous pollutants**—It includes sulphur dioxide, nitrogen oxide, hydrogen chloride and hydrogen flouride.

10.9.1. Types of particulate matter collector

The various types of particulate matter collectors are following—

(*i*) Cyclone Separator.
(*ii*) Venturi Scrubber.
(*iii*) Fabric Filters.
(*iv*) Electrostatic Precipitator

(*i*) **Cyclone Separator**—When dust lader gas enters tangentially into cyclone separator,the centrifugal forces cause those dust particles present in the gas to strike the wall of separator and fall into the bottom from where these are removed. Clean gas leaves the cyclone separator. These are low cost,robust and maintenance free devices. However, efficiencies becomes low with fine particles.

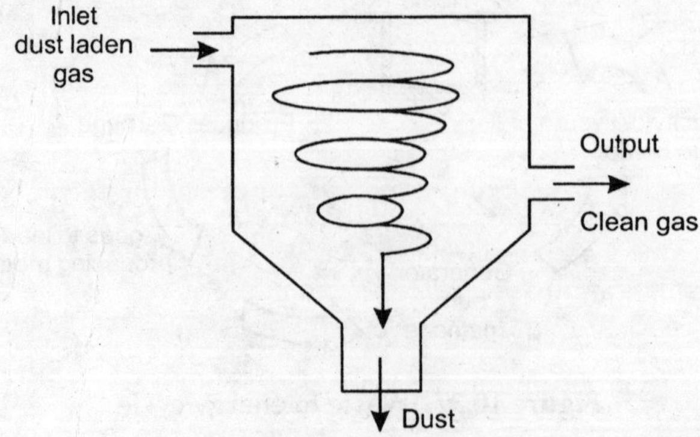

Figure 10.38. Cyclone Separator

(*ii*) **Venturi Scrubber**—This scrubber uses water to remove dust particles from gas .When dust laden gas accelerates through a venturi (throat), it atomises the water that is being injected. These atomised waster droplets collect dust particles and are precipitated in a cyclone chamber. These are low cost devices but generate salty waste water and have high operation and maintenance cost.

(iii) **Fabric Filter**—These are fabric filters which retain the dust particles on the outer surface of the filler so that clean filtered gas leaves the filler house. The layer of dust deposited on the outer surface of filter are removed by different types of shaking mechanisms .These filters possess high efficiency and dust layer can remove acid gases but vulnerable to spark and moisture.

(iv) **Electrostatic Precipitator (ESP)**—It consists of a chamber having a number of earthed electrodes that are suspended. Negatively charged electrodes are placed near these earthed electrodes. This produces an electric field such that the charging particles force them to migrate to the earthed electrodes,The dust deposited on earthed electrodes are removed by mechanically shaking them so that these are collected at the bottom of a dust collection hopper.

10.9.2. Types of Pollution Control Systems

Following are the types of pollution control systems used—

(i) Simple Wet System.

(ii) Dry System.

(iii) Advanced Wet System.

(i) **Simple Wet System**—This system can remove particulate matter, hydrogen chloride, hydrogen flouride and heavy metals. The system consists of an electrostatic precipitator, quencher and a scrubber. Advantages of this system are – low cost, low maintenance and low chemical consumption. Disadvantages are-generation of waste water, corrosion and production of dense white plume at the output of stack.

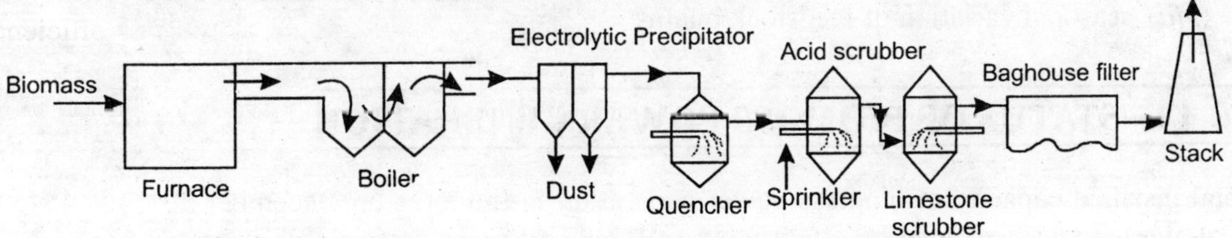

Figure 10.39. Simple wet system for pollution control

(ii) **Dry System**—This system is suitable for the removal of dust particles,hydrogen chloride, hydrogen fluoride and heavy metals. System uses reactor and baghouse filter. Advantage of this system is that hydrogen produces no waste water, less vulnerable to corrosion and produces no visible plume at the outlet of stack. Disadvantages are high chemical consumption [expensive $Ca(OH_2)$] and more solid residue.

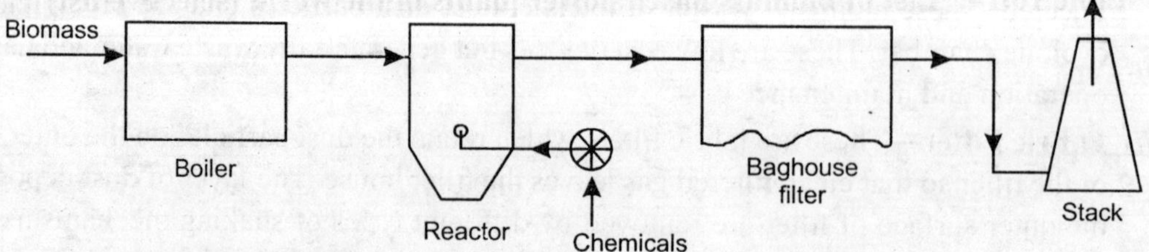

Figure 10.40. Dry system of pollution control

(*iii*) **Advanced wet system**—This system removes dust particles, sulphur dioxide, nitrogen oxides, dioxins, hydrogen chloride, hydrogen flouride and heavy metals. Advantages of this system are-cheap method of removal of nitrogen oxides, sulphur dioxide and dioxins. Disadvantages are high initial cost, waste water discharge, production of white plume in humid weather.

10.10. ISSUES IN BIOMASS POWER GENERATION

Biomass power though appears sustainable and low cost suffers from following challenges—

(*i*) escalation of biomass resource price after completion of power project.

(*ii*) transport cost forms significant part of input raw material cost.

(*iii*) continuous availability and security of feedstock supply is a major concern.

(*iv*) problem of disposal of sludge and ash.

(*v*) competition for scarce land and water from food grain production.

(*vi*) objection to installation of municipal waste incineration and landfill based power plant by public.

(*vii*) expensive biomass pretreatment.

(*viii*) seasonal variation of feedstock quality

10.11. STATUS OF BIOMASS POWER GENERATION

Total installed capacity of biomass power generation in India (as on December 2015) is 4545.63 MW. Waste to energy generation is 106.58 MW while the total potential for biomass based power generation is 17,538 MW excluding bagasse based generations which is 5000 MW.

Major Indian states leading in biomass power generation are – Karnataka, Andhra Pradesh and Maharashtra. Countries, such as USA, Germany, Brazil, Japan, Finland, Denmark, Spain and Canada are leaders in biomass based power generation in the world.

Following is the select list of biomass based power plants operational in the world—

Table 10.14: List of biomass based power plants in the world (selective list)

Sr. No	*Country*	*Capacity (MW)*	*Type of input*
1.	U.K,Tilbury B	750	Wood pellet
2.	U.K., Drax	660	Wood pellet
3.	U.K., Iron bridge	600	Wood pellet
4.	Finland, Alholmens Kraft	265	Forest residue
5.	Poland,Polaniec	205	Wood chips
6.	Belgium,Rodenhuize	180	Wood chips
7.	U.K.,Ashdown paper mill	157	Black liquor

10.12. CASE STUDY OF BIOMASS POWER GENERATION IN INDIA

A biomass gassifier based power plant was commissioned in Chhottomolla Khali village of West Bengal in Sundarbans island. The details are given below—

(*i*) Population of village = 28,000

(*ii*) Capacity and type of power plant = 4 × 125 MW, biomass gassifier.

(*iii*) Date of commissioning = 29 June, 2001.

(*iv*) Hours of operation = 5 pm to 11 pm.

(*v*) Energy plantation area = 40 hectares.

(*vi*) Fuel consumption = 70%biomass, 30% diesel.

Solved Examples

Example 10.1

A cow consumes 3 kg of dry biomass everyday. Cowdung of ten cows is fed to a biogas digester. Calculate—

(*i*) volume of biogas in digester.

(*ii*) power available from biogas plant if burner efficiency is 0.75 and retention time of biomass is 30 days.

Solution:

(*i*) Total dry biomass fed per day to digester = 3 × 10 = 30 kg/day

Assuming, 50 kg/m^3 density of dry biomass in the fluid, volume of fluid

$$V_f = \frac{mass}{density} = \frac{30}{50} = 0.6 \text{ m}^3/\text{day}$$

Volume of digester $V = V_f \times t_r$

Where, V_f = Volume of fluid

t_r = Retention time

$V = 0.6 \times 30 = 18 \text{ m}^3$ **Ans.**

(*ii*) Volume of biogas yield/day, $V_b = C\, m_d$.

Where, C = Biogas yield per unit of dry mass (0.2 – 0.4 m^3/kg)

m_d = mass of dry input consumed by cattle/day

Assuming, 0.2 m^3/kg as biomass yield per unit of dry mass

$$V_b = 0.2 \times 30$$

$$= 6 \text{ m}^3.$$

∴ Energy available from digester,

$$E = \eta f_m H_m V_b.$$

Where, η = combustion efficiency of burner.

f_m = fraction of methane in biogas (0.7)

H_m = heat of combustion of methane (28 MJ/m^3 or 56 MJ/kg at STP)

$$E = 0.75 \times 0.7 \times 28 \times 6$$

$$= 88.2 \text{ MJ/day}$$ **Ans.**

Example 10.2

Following data are given for a family biomass digester suitable for the output of five cows: retention time is 20 days,temperature 30°C, dry matters consumed per day is 2 kg, biogas yield is 0.24 m^3/kg, Efficiency of burner is 60%, methane proportion is 0.8, heat of combustion of methane is 28 MJ/m^3. Calculate the volume of digester and power available from digester.

Solution:

Total dry biomass fed per day to digesters = 5 cows × 2kg/cow = 10 kg

(*i*) Volume of digester, $V = V_f \times t_r$

Where, V_f = Volume of fluid in digester, t_r = retention time.

$$= 0.24 \text{ m}^3/\text{kg} \times 20 \text{ days} \times (5 \times 2) \text{ kg/day}$$

$$= 48 \text{ m}^3$$ **Ans.**

(*ii*) Volume of bio gas yield/day = 0.24 m^3/kg × (5 × 2) kg/day

Burner efficiency, η = 0.6, H_m (heat of combustion of methane) = 28 MJ/m^3

f_m (fraction of methane in biogas) = 0.8

∴ Energy produced $= \eta f_m H_m V_b$

$$= 0.6 \times 0.8 \times 28 \times (0.24 \times 5 \times 2)$$

$$= 32.256 \text{ MJ/day}$$ **Ans.**

CHAPTER SUMMARY

Biomass is generated by plants, animals, micro-organisms and human beings. Plants produce organic matter due to photosynthesis process. Biomass is an important renewable energy source especially for rural areas. It is used for cooking, and heating applications in rural areas.

Biomass is converted to useful energy through various energy conversion process, such as—

(*i*) incineration of biomass producing heat.

(*ii*) anaerobic digestion of wet biomass producing methane.

(*iii*) biochemical reactions producing biogas and chemicals.

(*iv*) fermentation process producing alcohols.

Biomass is derived from waste (municipal waste,agricultural waste, industrial waste etc.), from energy crops, forest residue and aqua farms.

A biomass based power generation uses different routes, such as gasification, pyrolysis, anaerobic digestion, etc. Community based bio gas plants, called gobar gas plants are popular in rural areas for cooking fuel, lighting fuel, high quality manure and for power generation purpose through internal combustion engines. Urban area uses incineration of municipal waste and landfill gas for power generation.

With fast depleting fossil fuels, biomass is expected to produce renewable energy in the next century.

FORMULAE

1. Average density of biomass = 50 kg/m^3

2. Bio gas yield per unit of dry biomass = 0.2 – 0.4 MJ/kg

3. Heat of combustion of methane = 28 MJ/m^3 or 56 MJ/kg at STP

4. Volume of fluid in a bio gas digester,

$$V_f = \frac{Mass}{Density}$$

5. Volume of digester, $V = V_f \times t_r$

where V_f = volume of fluid in digester.

t_r = retention time for biomass in digester.

6. Energy available from digester,

$$E = \eta f_m H_m V_b$$

where, η = Combustion efficiency of burner.

f_m = fraction of methane in bio gas (60%to 70%).

H_m = heat of combustion of methane (28 MJ/m^3 or 56 MJ/kg).

V_b = volume of biogas yield per day.

= Bio gas yield per unit of dry biomass × mass of dry input consumed by cattle per day

$= C \times m_d$

Total dry biomass fed per day to digester = No. of cows × weight of dry biomass consumed by each cow.

REVIEW QUESTIONS

Q. 1. Explain various routes of biomass conversion.

Q. 2. What is the origin of biomass energy? Differentiate between biomass energy resource and fossil fuels.

Q. 3. Explain the process of photosynthesis. What are the conditions that need to be satisfied?

Q. 4. Write a brief note on various types of biomass resources.

Q. 5. Differentiate between thermo chemical conversion and biochemical conversion.

Q. 6. Explain the process of pyrolysis of biomass. What are the merits and demerits of this process?

Q. 7. Discuss the process of gassification. What are the merits and demerits of this process?

Q. 8. Explain with a neat diagram working of fixed bed gassifier.

Q. 9. What is difference between fixed bed and fluidized bed gassifier? Discuss relative merits and demerits.

Q. 10. Explain the working of a biomass gassifier based power plant. Indicate the function of each component of the plant.

Q. 11. Differentiate between alcholic fermentation and anaerobic digestion.

Q. 12. What are the various factors which affect the process of biogass generation?

Q. 13. What is bio-electrolysis? What are the advantages of this process?

Q. 14. Write a brief note on extraction and application of oil from oil seeds.

Q. 15. Discuss classification of bio-fuels. What are the advantages and disadvantages of bio-fuels?

Q. 16. Explain the process of bio gas generation through—

(*i*) thermophilic digestion and (*ii*) anaerobic reaction.

Q. 17. Discuss the composition and properties of biogas generated from municipal waste.

Q. 18. What is a community bio gas plant? Explain with a neat sketch, various components of bio gas plants.

Q. 19. Discuss various types of bio gas digesters.

Q. 20. Compare fixed dome type and movable dome type bio gas plant.

Q. 21. What are the advantages and disadvantages of biomass based power plant?

Q. 22. Discuss various technologies used for biomass based power generation.

Q. 23. What is co-firing? What are types of co-firing?

Q. 24. Explain the construction and working of a combustion based biomass power plant.

Q. 25. Write brief note on power generation from municipal waste.

Q. 26. Discuss various techniques of pollution control measures adopted in a incineration power plant.

Numerical Questions

Q. 1. A community based bio gas plant uses cow dung from five cows. The retention time is 25 days,temperature is 32°C,dry matter consumed per day is 2 kg, bio gas yield is 0.26 m^3/kg, the efficiency of burner is 60%, methane proportion is 0.8, heat of combustion of methane is 28 MJ/m^3. Determine (*i*) volume of digester (*ii*) power available.

[**Ans:** (*i*) 230.4 m^3 (*ii*) 144.5 MJ/day]

Q. 2. A cow consumes 3.2 kg of dry biomass everyday. Cowdung of 12 cows is fed to a community based biogas digesters. Determine (*i*) volume of biogas in digester (*ii*) power available from biogas plant. Given: efficiency of burner is 70% and retention time of biomass is 25 days. [**Ans:** (*i*) 19.2 m^3 (*ii*) 105.4 MJ/day]

SHORT ANSWER TYPE QUESTIONS

Q. 1. What is light and dark reaction in photosynthesis process?

Q. 2. What is energy crop?

Q. 3. What is the composition of biomass?

Q. 4. Write the reaction of methanol production from synthesis gas.

Q. 5. How bio-diesel is produced?

Q. 6. What are the applications of alcohol?

Multiple choice Questions

Q. 1. Origin of biomass is

(*a*) sun (*b*) carbon dioxide
(*c*) photosynthesis (*d*) sun, carbon dioxide and water.

Q. 2. Highest energy is contained in

(*a*) green wood (*b*) bagasse
(*c*) cow dung (*d*) methane

Q. 3. Process of pyrolysis produces

(*a*) only solid (*b*) only liquid
(*c*) only gas (*d*) all of these.

Q. 4. Alcoholic fermentation requires pH value of

(*a*) 0 – 3 (*b*) 3 – 6
(*c*) 6 – 8 (*d*) 8 – 10.

Q. 5. Which of the following has maximum calorific value?

(*a*) biogas (*b*) natural gas

(*c*) methane (*d*) butane.

Q. 6. A fixed dome biogas plant has

(*a*) constant gas pressure (*b*) variable gas pressure

(*c*) it depends on raw biomass (*d*) none of these

Answer to MCQ

1. (*c*) **2.** (*d*) **3.** (*d*) **4.** (*c*) **5.** (*d*)

6. (*b*)

Chapter

Geothermal Power Generation

Learning Objectives

After reading this chapter, reader will be able to

- Understand process of capture of geothermal energy, types of geothermal sources, relative merits and demerits of geothermal energy usage.
- Examine the process of power generation through various schemes, understand relative merits and demerits and area of application.
- Explore variety of uses of geothermal energy other than power generation.
- Update on geothermal power plants operating in the world.

"Whenever you see what seems to be the end, do not lose faith for beneath the despair may lie a glowing new opportunity."

— Rabindranath Tagore

11.1 INTRODUCTION

Geothermal energy is a renewable source of energy buried deep inside the earth. This source of energy is independent of any terrestrial source, such as solar, wind, biomass etc. The molten rock or magma is present at a depth of 24 km to 40 km and this heat energy rises from the core of earth to the surface of the earth through cracks in the rocks .The temperature of these resources lie in the ranges of 180°–200°C (in the form of water and steam), 100°–180°C (as hot water) and less than 100°C (as hot water).The economic operational life of geothermal power plant is typically 20 to 30 years. For every 100 m below ground, the temperature of rock increases by about 3°C.

The hot magma when reaches the surface of earth, it solidifies as igneous rock. The magma below this layer transmits heat to it. The ground water finds it way into this hot region through some crevices in the rock. The water is heated by the heat of the rocks and rises upwards through porous and permeable reservoir above these rocks. This hot water is trapped by an impermeable layer of rocks and a small fissure provides an outlet for this resulting in a continuous stream of hot spring called geysers. So, core of the earth acts as a huge boiler producing steam and hot water through the internal heat trapped inside the earth.

Historically, the first use of geothermal energy was in Iceland way back in 1300. In 1897 in Italy, this energy was used to produce steam in a boiler to run steam engine. The first use of this energy to produce power was in 1904 in Italy. In USA, geysers were tapped to produce electricity in 1960. The unit size was 11 MW. The other countries using geothermal energy are Japan, Mexico, New Zealand, Phillippines, Indonesia etc.

India lies in low geothermal potential region with a temperature range of 100°–180°C and less than 100°C. According to Geological Survey of India, the estimated geothermal potential in India is 10,000 MW. As per international report, a Geothermal power plant of 1 MW capacity generates about 8.3 Million units per MW per annum compared to 1.6 MU per MW for solar, 1.9 MU per MW for wind and 3.9 MU per MW for hydro. A comparison with other renewable energy sources is given in table 11.1.

Table 11.1 Comparison of Geothermal energy with other renewable energy sources

Sr. No.	*Renewable source*	*Cost per MW*	*Average units produced per MW per year*	*Ratio of capital cost to the total generation*
1.	Geothermal	₹ 30 Cr.	8.3 MU	36.1
2.	Solar PV	₹ 6.91 Cr.	1.66 MU	41.6
3.	Solar Thermal (with storage)	₹ 25 Cr.	2.01 MU	124.3
4.	Wind	₹ 6.03 Cr	1.93 MU	31.2
5.	Hydro	₹ 7.35 Cr	3.90 MU	18.8

Geological Survey and studies have identified 340 hot springs in India. The various geothermal belts in India are– Himalayas, West Coast, Cambay, Son-Narmada-Tapi, Godavari and Sohna. The potential states are– Jammu & Kashmir, Himachal Pradesh, Chhatisgarh, West Bengal, Gujarat, Maharashtra, Madhya Pradesh, Bihar, Jharkhand, Andhra Pradesh, Odisha and Haryana.

The largest group of Geothermal power plant is located at California, USA. Five countries viz Iceland, Phillippines, Costa Rica, El Salvador and Kenya generate more than 15% of their total electrical energy from geothermal sources. Total 24 countries generate electricity from geothermal sources in the world.

11.2 GEOTHERMAL FIELDS

Earth's surface can be classified into there major groups—

(*i*) **Non thermal area:** It has a temperature gradient of 10° – 40°C per km depth.

(*ii*) **Semi thermal area**: It has a temperature gradient of 70°C per km depth.

(*iii*) **Hyper thermal area**: The temperature gradients are many times greater than non-thermal area.

Geothermal fields are further classified into following—

(*i*) **Hyper thermal fields-**

(*a*) **Wet fields:** In this field, the water has temperature of above 100°C and is in pressurised state .When it reaches surface of earth , a part of it is converted into steam and remaining is boiling water.

(*b*) **Dry fields**: In these fields, dry saturated steam or super heated steam at above atmospheric pressure is released from surface of earth.

(*ii*) **Semi thermal fields**: These can produce hot water at a temperature of 100°C and above.

11.3 GEOTHERMAL SOURCES

There are five types of geothermal resources viz.—

(*i*) Hydrothermal convective systems

(*a*) Vapour dominated or dry steam fields.

(*b*) Liquid dominated or wet fields.

(*c*) Hot water fields.

(*ii*) Geopressured resources.

(*iii*) Petro-thermal or hot dry rocks (HDR).

(*iv*) Magma resources.

(*v*) Volcanoes.

(*i*) **Hydro-thermal convective systems**: In this system, water is heated by hydrothermal convection by contact with hot rock.

These are further sub-classified as per following—

(*a*) **Vapour dominated or dry steam fields**: These fields contain steam in a dry state at a temperature of 200°C and at a pressure of 7 kg/cm^2 or below. This steam is useful for generation of electricity. However, the system contains corrosive gases and abrasive materials. This leads to early wear and tear of pipelines and turbine parts. Such systems are less in number and are used in USA and Italy.

(*b*) **Liquid dominated systems:** This system contains circulating hot water at a temperature of 175°–315°C. The geothermal energy is tapped by drilling holes into the earth which cause the water to reach to the surface or is pumped out, if required .The hot water may partially flash into steam but the mixture is mainly liquid dominated. However, the water has high total dissolved solid (TDS) of 3,000–25,000 ppm which leads to precipitation, scaling and erosion of metal parts, such as pipelines and heat exchangers etc.

Liquid dominated systems are more in number than vapour dominated systems.

(*ii*) **Geopressured resources**: These resources are available at deep sedimentary basins. The basin contains high temperature brine or water at a high pressure. The water contains large amount of dissolved methane which releases when pressure is reduced.

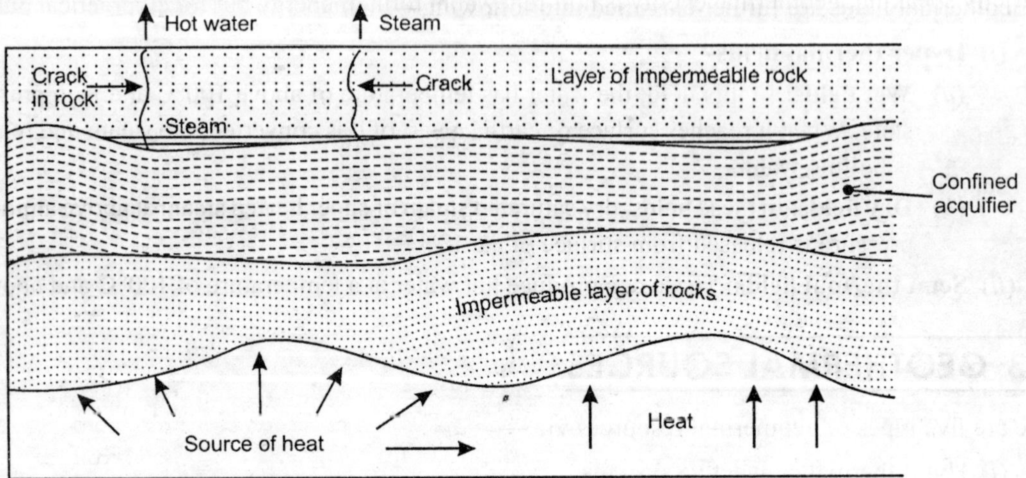

Fig, 11.1 Cross-section of a geothermal site

Geopressured water is available at a depth of 2.4 to 9 km. The water is at a low temperature of 160°C but at a very high pressure of about 1000 kg/cm^2. The total dissolved solid is high causing the water to convert into a brine solution. Such resources are available in large numbers and are suitable for generation of electricity.

(*iii*) **Petro thermal or hot dry rocks (HDR)**: These are low permeability rocks containing no water but have very high temperature occurring at moderate depth. The temperature of rocks range from 150° to 290°C. In order to recover the heat energy of rocks, cold water need to be pumped which will carry the heat of the rocks to the earth's surface. Such fields are available in plenty. The trapped heat energy of rocks is taken out by drilling wells and fracturing it by high pressure water jet. This helps to increase the exposure of hot surface area of rocks to water.

(*iv*) **Magma Resources**: Partially or completely molten rocks contain a temperature of 650°C or more. Such sites are available at moderate depths near active volcanoes. Such resources possess large heat content so much so that it may be difficult to extract heat energy due to very high temperature. Hence, these sites present a technological problem preventing extraction of geothermal heat.

(*v*) **Volcanoes**: These resources present a very high source of heat energy. The volcanic erruptions are caused by extremely high gas pressure. The magma solidifies at a depth if 1–5 km, Recovering energy from such sources require technology which are still not available and are extremely hazardous though such experiments had been conducted in Iceland and USA in the past.

11.4 ESTIMATES OF GEOTHERMAL POWER

Earth was formed 4600 million yeas ago. The exterior surface cooled rapidly compared to the interior. The temperature at the centre is estimated to be 7000°C. The amount of heat energy flowing through the surface of the earth is 8×10^{21} Joules at a depth of 3 km .This is 4×10^{22} Joules at a depth of 10 km. Although, energy inside earth is much less than massive solar radiation received on the surface of the earth but still it is too significant quantity of energy to be ignored.

Strictly speaking, geothermal energy is non-renewable form of energy but for all practical purposes it is taken as renewable form of energy.

The average thermal gradient is 30°C per km depth. The geothermal energy released through earth's crust is 0.06 W/m^2 (this is $\frac{1}{1000}$th of solar energy received on earth's surface). About 4 × 10^{12} EJ of geothermal energy is stored in the earth. About 4 × 10^3 EJ of renewable energy is available in 3 km zone.

11.5 ADVANTAGES AND LIMITATIONS OF GEOTHERMAL ENERGY

Advantages—

(*i*) geothermal energy has multiple uses.

(*ii*) it is cheaper source of energy as compared to obtained from fossil fuels.

(*iii*) it is a continuous form of energy unlike wind or solar which are intermittent in nature.

(*iv*) it provides relatively higher amount of net energy compared to other renewable and non -renewable sources.

(*v*) geothermal power plant has higher load factor of 85–90% compared to 35–40% for fossil fuels plants.

(*vi*) it is least polluting compared to other conventional energy sources.

(*vii*) it has high energy density.

(*viii*) geothermal power plant requires much less space (0.75 – 1.2 acres/MW) compared to solar (5 – 8 acres MW).

Limitations—

(*i*) efficiency of power generation is about 15% which is much lower compared to 35–40% of fossil fuel plants.

(*ii*) extraction of large amount of steam and hot water may result in differential settlement of soil.

(*iii*) the hot water contains high dissolved salts and abrasive particles which erodes and corrodes the pipeline , surface of heat exchangers etc. thereby shortening life of equipments.

(*iv*) steam and hot water contains gases, such as H_2S, NH_3, CO_2 etc. which are released to atmosphere. This results in air pollution.

(*v*) drilling of holes produces noise and vibration.

11.6 CLASSIFICATION OF GEOTHERMAL POWER PLANTS

Classification is based on types of geothermal fluids used. Accordingly, Geothermal power plants are of following types—

(*i*) **Steam Geothermal Power Plant:** Power plant uses steam as geothermal fluid. Steam turbine is used to produce power.

(*ii*) **Hard Rock or Petro Thermal Geothermal Power Plant:** The power plant uses thermal energy extracted from hot dry rocks by circulating water through manmade fractures in hot dry rock .Steam turbine is used to produce power.

(*iii*) **Flashed Steam Geothermal Power Plant:** Power plant uses mixture of hot water and steam at a temperature of more than 180°C having low dissolved solids. The Geothermal liquid is flashed to produce steam which drives steam turbine.

(*iv*) **Binary Cycle Liquid Dominated Geothermal Power Plant:** Power plant uses mixture of hot water and steam at a temperature of 150°C and below. This is circulated through a heat exchanger to transfer heat to a working fluid (composed of Isobutane, Freon-12, Ammonia and Propane). This working fluid of low boiling point expands in a gas turbine to produce power.

(*v*) **Binary Cycle Geothermal Power Plant with Hot Brine:** Power plant is similar in operation to that in sr. (iv) except that the liquid has high dissolved solids.

(*vi*) **Total Flow Geothermal Power Plant:** The total geothermal fluid is passed though a special turbine. Such system is used when geothermal fluid has high total dissolved solids, mud and other impurities.

The starting of geothermal power plant requires few hours as the initial geothermal fluid contains high particulate matter which reduces gradually after some time. The thermal components, such as turbine, heat exchanger etc. are loaded gradually to allow thermal expansion of metal. The unit size of plant ranges form 5MW to 800MW. Such plants are located at geothermal sites.

The power rating of turbine depends upon mass flow rate of geothermal fluid, temperature and type of geothermal fluid (e.g. dry steam, hot water and steam etc.). Accordingly, a production well has a rating of about 6MW for a steam flow rate of 10 kg/s at 200°C. Usually production wells are separated by a distance of 0.5 km and have a life of 6 to 15 years. When steam production from a well falls drastically, a new well is drilled. These are used as base load power plants.

11.7 TYPES OF GEOTHERMAL POWER PLANTS

(*i*) **Dry Steam Geothermal Power Plant:** The geothermal fluid used in this system is steam or vapour dominated resource without liquid .The reservoir supplies superheated steam at a temperature of 180°–230°C and pressure of 4–8MPa. Sometimes, steam is available at higher temperature and pressure.

Since the steam contains very low dissolved impurities, hence it can be directly admitted to the turbine or through a centrifugal separator if it contains small amount of dissolved impurities. The steam after expansion in turbine is sent to a condenser. The condensate is reinjected into a well. The low pressure exhaust steam is condensed by circulating cooling water in a cooling tower. The generator coupled to the turbine produces electricity.

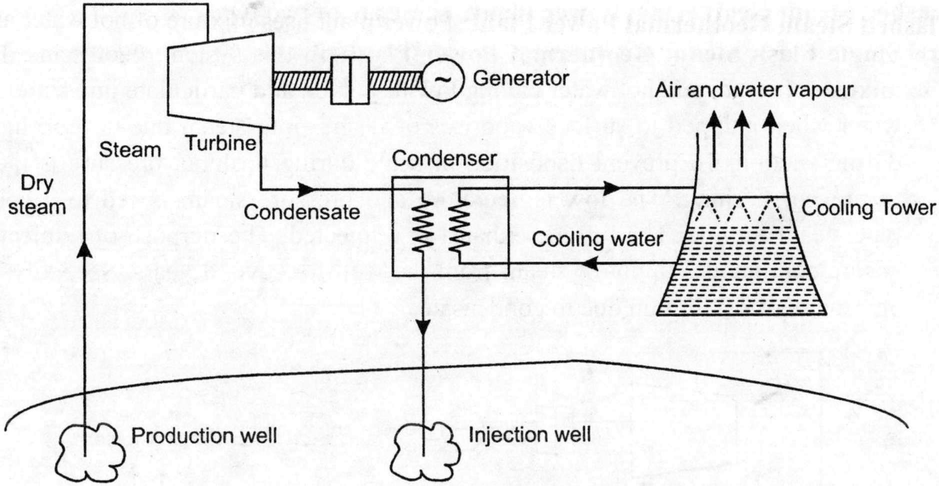

Fig. 11.2 Dry steam Geothermal power plant

(*ii*) **Petro Thermal Geothermal Power Plant:** In this system, thermal energy of hot dry rocks is extracted by circulating water or other fluid into artificial fractures in hot dry rock. The water is injected at a temperature of 65°C and at a pressure of 110 bar. This water takes heat from hot rocks and gets converted into steam (typically 280°C and 138 bar) which is fed to a steam turbine. The exhaust steam from steam turbine is condensed in a condenser. This condensate is then reinjected into reinjection well. Hence, the system works in a closed loop mode. Fracture is created in the dry rooks by drilling using high pressure water jet or by chemical explosion .These power plants are typically in the range of 50–150 MW.

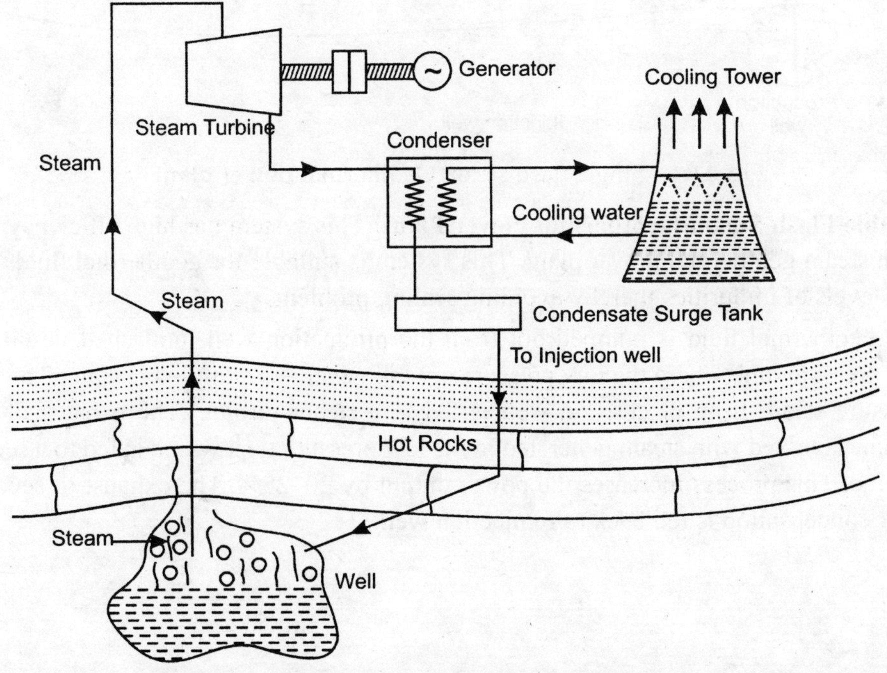

Fig. 11.3 Petro Thermal Geothermal power plant

(*iii*) **Flashed Steam Geothermal Power Plant:** These are of two types viz—

(*a*) **Single Flash Steam Geothermal Power Plant:** In this system, geothermal fluid is a mixture of steam and hot water having low dissolved and particulate impurities. The hot water when pumped to surface vaporises or flashes into steam due to drop in pressure during suction. To prevent deposition of scale during flashing, pressure is maintained to prevent flashing. The low temperature and pressure steam is fed to a condensing type steam turbine. The turbine exhaust is reinjected. The purpose of reinjection is to ensure continuous supply of steam from the well for several years. Secondly, to avoid environmental pollution due to condensate.

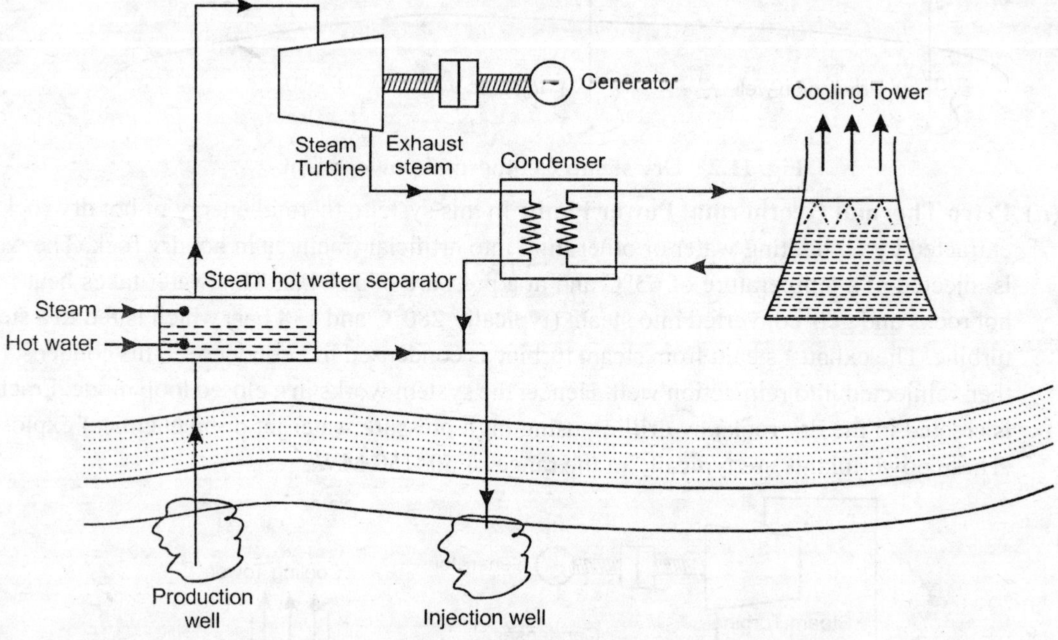

Fig. 11.4 Single flash steam Geothermal power plant

(*b*) **Double Flash Steam Geothermal Power Plant:** This system has high efficiency than single flash steam geothermal power plant. This system is suitable for geothermal fluids containing low levels of impurities thereby avoiding scaling problem.

The geothermal fluid is pumped out from the production well, unflashed liquid flows into low pressure tank where the low pressure of tank generates additional steam. The initial high pressure steam from production well is fed to a steam turbine .The exhaust of this steam turbine is mixed with steam generated in the low pressure tank which is fed to a second steam turbine. This process increases the power output by 20–25%. The exhaust of second turbine after condensation is fed back to reinjection well.

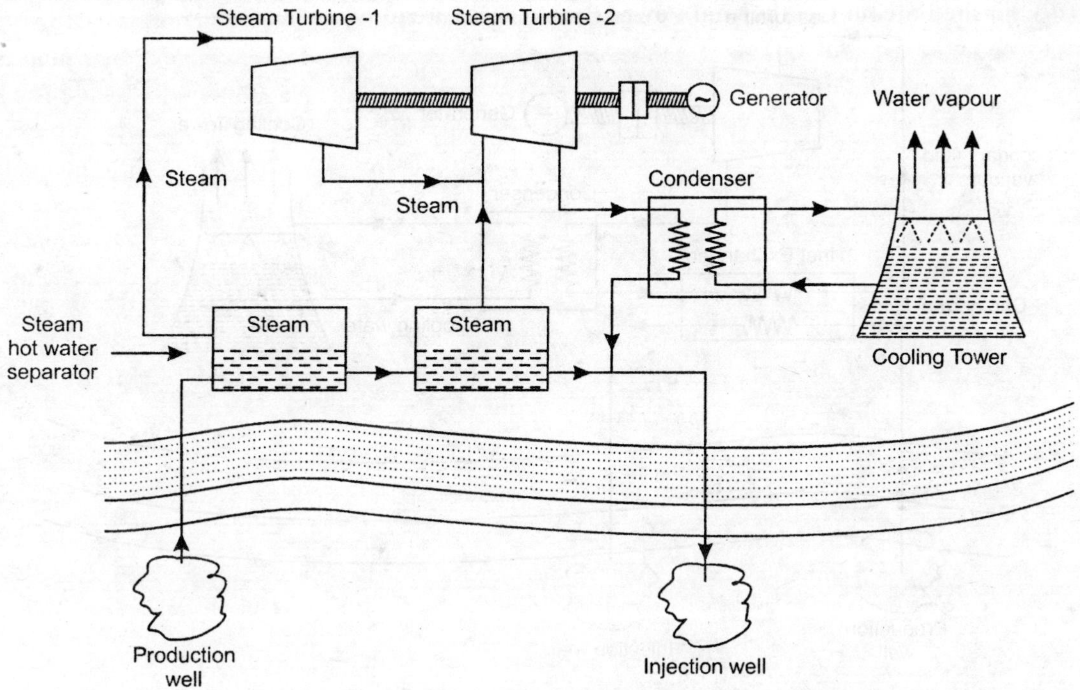

Fig. 11.5 Double flash steam Geothermal power plant

(*iv*) **Binary Cycle Liquid Dominated Geothermal Power Plant:** Binary cycle power plants use primary working fluid and secondary working fluid.

Primary working fluid: It is a geothermal fluid consisting of steam and hot water or brine which is extracted from production well.

Secondary working fluid: It is a working fluid having low boiling point. For example, Isobutane, Freon–12, Ammonia, Propane, Pentane etc. This system is useful where single flash system is unsatisfactory. Also, this system allows to use chemically impure geothermal fluid. The primary working fluid or geothermal fluid transfers heat to secondary working fluid through a heat exchanger. This working fluid turns into a superheated vapour. This superheated vapour is expanded in a gas turbine. The exhaust of the gas turbine i.e. the superheated vapour after expansion is condensed in a condenser. The gas turbine drives the generator to produce electricity. Disadvantage is that the secondary fluid needs to be repressurised which consumes extra energy.

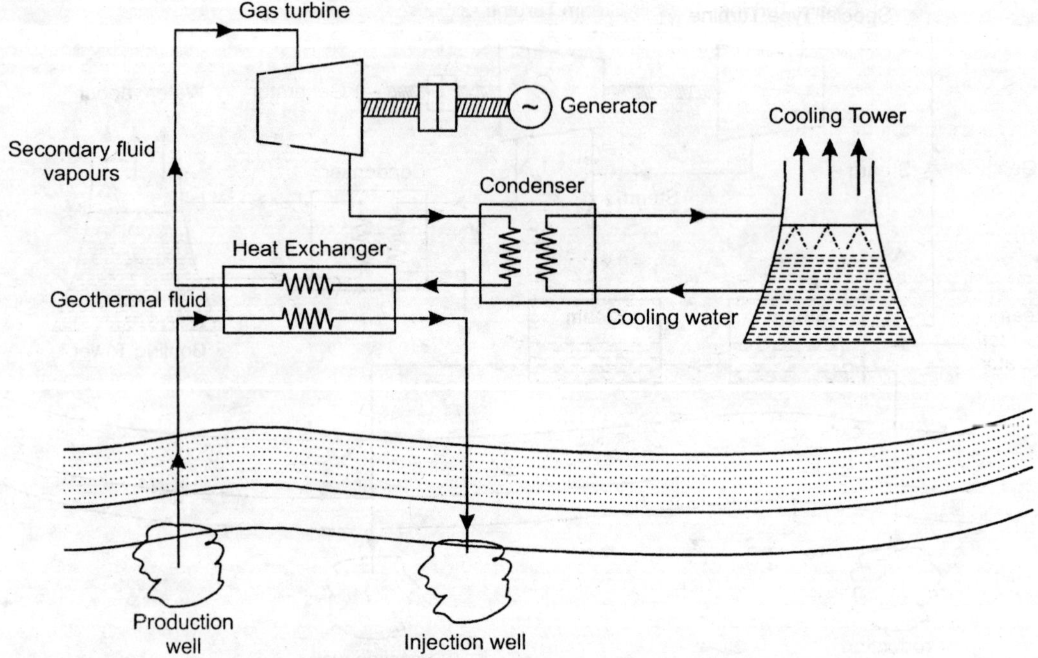

Fig. 11.6 Binary cycle liquid dominated Geothermal power plant

Advantages of Binary Cycle Geothermal Power Plant are following—

(*a*) Corrosion and scaling of turbine parts, condenser and piping is avoided by using a secondary working fluid which is free of dissolved solids, particulate matter etc.

(*b*) Geothermal energy in low temperature brine can be extracted.

(*c*) There is no environmental pollution as geothermal fluid is returned to the earth.

Example of this types of power plant is 24 MW East Mesa Binary Geothermal power plant in California, USA.

(*v*) Total Flow Geothermal Power Plant: In this system, geothermal brine is passed through a special type of turbine, such as radial impact turbine, bladeless turbine and helical screw expander turbine. The geothermal fluid from the well passes through turbine thereby expanding total head of the production well. The geothermal fluid is then passed through condenser. The turbine which is coupled to the generator produces electricity. The cooling water used for cooling turbine exhaust is operated in a closed loop mode. The condensed brine is then reinjected into the ground.

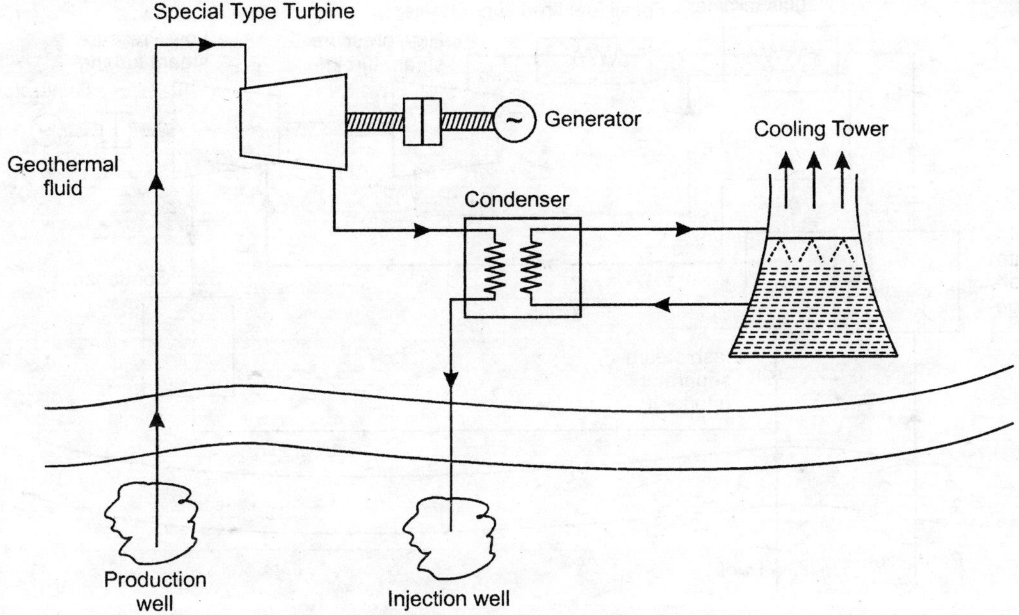

Fig. 11.7 Total flow Geothermal power plant

11.8 GEOTHERMAL HYBRID POWER PLANTS

Hybrid system uses geothermal heat in a conventional system to reduce consumption of fuel. There are two types of hybrid power plant viz. Fossil Super Heat Hybrid system and Geothermal Preheat Hybrid system.

(*i*) **Fossil Super Heat Hybrid System:** In this system, vapour dominated steam obtained from geothermal system is superheated using fossil fuel. Steam obtained from flash steam separator is heated by the exhaust of high pressure turbine. It is further heated by fossil fuel fired superheater. It is expanded in high pressure turbine. Thereafter, it is led to regenerator where it is mixed with low pressure steam obtained from second stage flash steam separator. This steam is then expanded in low pressure steam turbine. The condensate obtained from this turbine is injected into the earth.

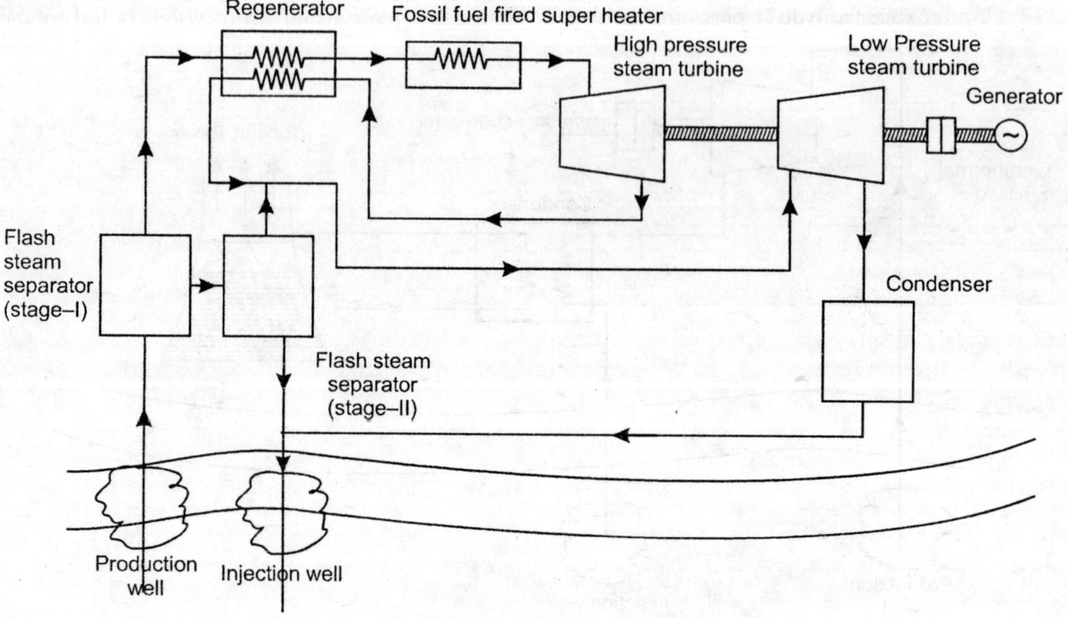

Fig. 11.8 Fossil fuel super heat hybrid system

(*ii*) **Geothermal Preheat Hybrid System:** This system is suitable for low temperature liquid dominated geothermal fluid. It utilizes geothermal heat to heat feed water in a conventional fossil fuel power plant.

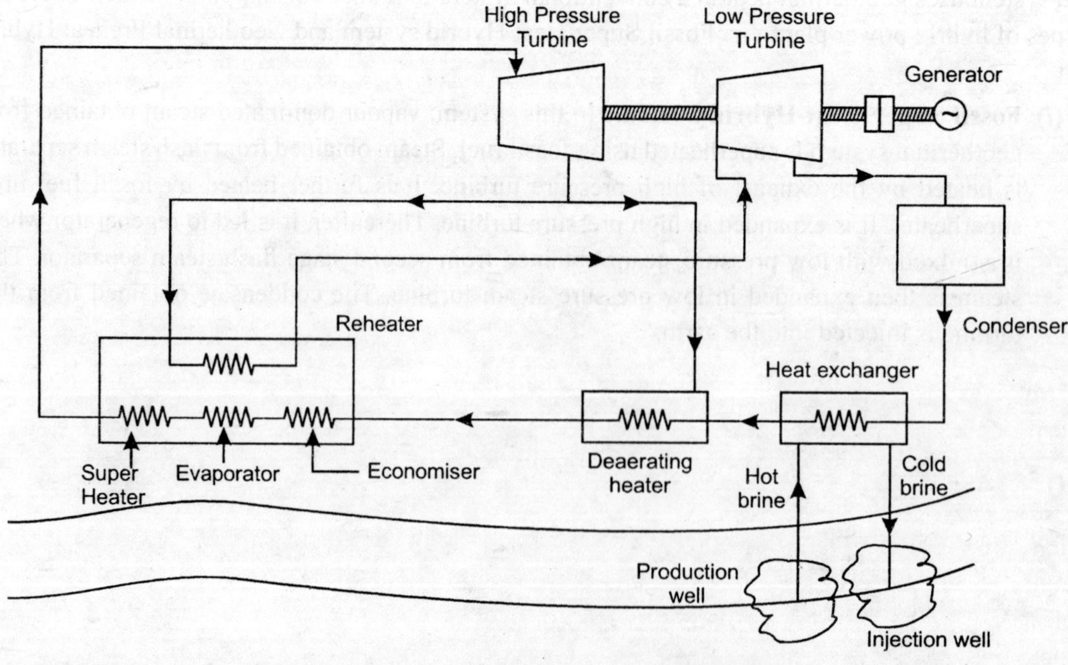

Fig. 11.9 Geothermal preheat hybrid system

Condensate from low pressure turbine is heated by geothermal fluid which is led to second stage feed water heater. The second stage feed water heating is provided by exhaust steam of high pressure turbine. This feed water is fed to economiser, evaporator and superheater where it is heated by exhaust steam of high pressure turbine. This exhaust steam from superheater is led to low pressure turbine. The low pressure and high pressure turbines are coupled to the generator which produces electricity.

11.9 GROUND SOURCE HEAT PUMP (GSHP)

Ground Source Heat Pump utilises geothermal heat to provide heating, cooling and hot water for homes and commercial buildings (i.e. non-power plant application). The system uses temperature of 16°–24°C at a depth of 20 feet. The system uses heat absorbed by earth's surface from solar radiation. At a depth of 20 feet, the ground temperature is approximately equal to mean annual air temperature at that latitude at the surface.

GSHP system is very efficient having 50 to 70% higher efficiency than other heating systems. Cooling efficiency is also 40–50% higher than conventional air conditioners. The average capital cost of this system is about ₹ 1 lakh to 1.5 lakh per tonnes.

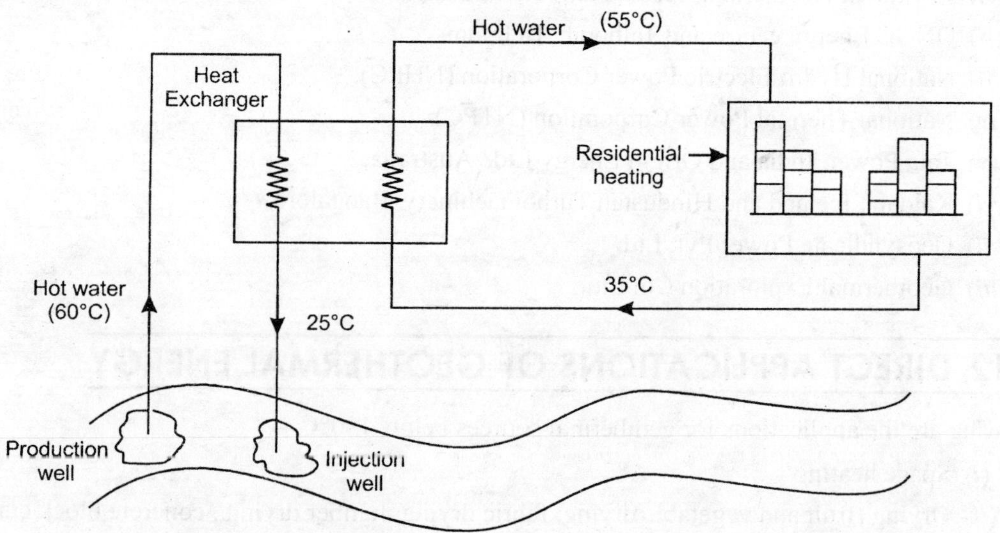

Fig. 11.10 Residential heating and cooling system using Ground Source Heat Pump

11.10 STATUS OF GEOTHERMAL POWER GENERATION IN THE WORLD

Electricity is being generated from geothermal sources in 24 countries in the world. Out of these, five countries viz. Iceland, Phillippines, El Salvador, Kenya and Costa Rica generate 15–30% of their electricity demand from geothermal sources. There are about 11 geothermal power plants under construction in various parts of the world. Iceland is leader in generation of power through geothermal route and produces 30% of total power requirement through this route. This is followed by Phillippines which produces 27% of total power. While El Salvador generate 25% of total demand using geothermal sources.

Other countries generating more than 1% of total electricity demand are Nicaragua (10%), Kenya (11.2%), New Zealand (10%), Indonesia (3.7%), Mexico (3%) and Italy (1.5%).

11.11 SCOPE OF GEOTHERMAL POWER GENERATION IN INDIA

India has few geothermal sites having low to moderate temperature of geothermal fluids. Some are in the form of hot water springs with temperature ranging from 40°–98°C. Some of the prominent geothermal sites are Puga Valley in Jammu & Kashmir (hot water springs, 50°–84°C temperature). Some sites in Maharashtra and Gujarat (hot water springs 34°–72°C temperature) and Tattapani field in Madhya Pradesh (hot water springs , 50°–98°C temperature).

At Puga Valley, a space heating pilot project was undertaken at an altitude of 4500 m using 125°C, 2.8 kg/cm^2 steam in 1975.

Another, cold plant was commissioned in Manikaran in Himachal Pradesh for fruit and potato storage. Hot water at 90°C from a geothermal site and 10°C water from Parbati river was utilized.

Following are some of the Indian organizations working in collaboration with foreign companies for power production using geothermal sources—

(*i*) Reykjavik Geothermal, Iceland and Thermax, India.
(*ii*) ONGC Energy centre and Talboom, Belgium.
(*iii*) National Hydro Electric Power Corporation (NHPC).
(*iv*) National Thermal Power Corporation (NTPC).
(*v*) Tata Power, India and Origin Energy Ltd, Australia.
(*vi*) Kaldara, Iceland and Hindustan Turbomachinery, Bangalore.
(*vii*) Geosyndicate Power Pvt. Ltd.
(*viii*) Geothermal Exploration Co. Ltd.

11.12 DIRECT APPLICATIONS OF GEOTHERMAL ENERGY

Following are the applications for geothermal sources below 150°C—

(*i*) Space heating.
(*ii*) Drying (fruit and vegetable drying, fabric drying, lumber drying , concrete block curing)
(*iii*) Industrial processes.
(*iv*) Air conditioning.
(*v*) Aqua culture.
(*vi*) Poultry and fish farming.
(*vii*) Mushroom farming.
(*viii*) Horticulture.
(*ix*) Cold storage.
(*x*) Tourist resorts and pools.
(*xi*) Melting snow.
(*xii*) Bio gas and bio-fuel production.

11.13 ENVIRONMENTAL IMPACT OF GEOTHERMAL POWER PLANTS

Geothermal process can pollute the surroundings if sufficient precautionary measures are not observed. Various sources of environmental pollution emanating from utilization of geothermal resources are explained below—

(*i*) **Non-condensable gases and solid particles:** Geothermal fluid (steam and water) contains non-condensable gases and solid particles. These solid particles are removed by centrifugal separators and strainers before feeding to turbine. The non-condensable gases are carbon dioxide, methane, hydrogen, nitrogen, ammonia and hydrogen sulphide. About 80% is carbon dioxide and remaining are varying amount of other gases. Presence of these gases lower vacuum in condenser and hence gas ejectors are needed to remove these gases. Secondly, these gases in wet condition cause corrosion of shaft seals, condenser lining, condenser piping, pumps and metal parts in cooling towers. Thirdly, turbine nozzles are made of chrome steel which gets corroded due to presence of hydrogen sulphide. Hydrogen sulphide gas has adverse effect on electrical equipments, crops and marine life. High dissolved carbon dioxide in water affects weeds growth in water.

(*ii*) **Land subsidance:** Removal of large quantity of water from underground resources may lead to land subsidence. Hence, reinjection into the well minimizes this. Also, discharge of large quantity of geothermal fluid into rivers or ocean is hazardous to marine life and may intoxicate water bodies.

(*iii*) **Land erosion:** Drilling of geothermal wells lead to land erosion.

(*iv*) **Noise pollution:** Noise is generated by centrifugal separaters and exhaust blowers. To minimize this noise pollution, silencers need to be installed.

(*v*) **Water pollution:** Wet fields sometimes contain toxic substances, such as mercury, arsenic, ammonia etc. which if discharged into water stream may cause water pollution affecting marine life, flora and fauna. This can be minimized by reinjection.

(*vi*) **Heat pollution:** In wet fields, discharge of large amount of hot and unwanted water into water bodies may cause heat pollution leading to death of fishes and water weeds.

(*vii*) **Possibility of seizmic activity:** Persistent exploitation of geothermal reserves could trigger earthquakes.

(*viii*) **Silica:** Reinjection of water containing large amount of silica chokes the fine pores in underground strata. This necessitates frequent change of reinjection wells.

(*ix*) **Release of Flash steam:** Release of large amount of flash steam leads to dense fog in nearby areas affecting the climate.

11.14 OPERATING GEOTHERMAL POWER PLANTS IN THE WORLD

The mammoth plant in California produces 40 MW and is in operation since late 1980s. It is a binary cycle plant (isobutane) with geothermal fluid flow rate of 900 kg/s. Due to high flow rate of geothermal fluid and to reduce pollution, reinjection is carried out. This is a self contained emission free plant.

Creil district heating scheme in Paris was commissioned in 1976. The scheme uses geothermal energy to heat 2000 appartments by under floor heating. The system uses water from geothermal well at a temperature of 60°C and returns at 25°C. A heat exchanger transfers this heat to water operating between 55°C and 10°C.

East Mesa plant in southern California, USA was commissioned in 1988. It generates 37 MW from 16 wells. Brine flow rate is 1000 kg/s.

A health centre at St. Mary's Isles of Scilly, UK, uses 25kW reversible heat pump to supply hot water for building heating and cooling. This unit is working since 1988.

A geothermal power plant in Imperial valley, California, USA generates 40 MW.

Krafla well in Iceland covers an area of 50 km^2 and generates 60 MW.

Larderello Geothermal Power Station, Italy has a capacity of 769 MW. It started operation in 1913 with 250 MW.

Some of the biggest geothermal power plants are located in Philippines (three), US (two), Indonesia (two), Italy (two), Mexico (one) and Iceland (one).Ten biggest geothermal power plants are listed below—

(*i*) The Geysers Geothermal Complex, California, USA , has installed capacity of 1517 MW and operating production is 900 MW.

(*ii*) Larderello Geothermal Complex, Italy has 34 plants totalling 769 MW.

(*iii*) Cerro Prieto Geothermal Power Station, Mexicali, Baja California, Mexico has a capacity of 720 MW.

(*iv*) Makban Geothermal Complex , Batangas, Phillippines has capacity of 458 MW.

(*v*) Salton Sea Geothermal Plant, Southern California, USA has capacity of 340 MW.

(*vi*) Hellisheidi Geothermal plant, Mount Hengil, Iceland has capacity of 303 MW.

(*vii*) Tiwi Geothermal Complex, Albay, Phillippines has capacity of 289 MW.

(*viii*) Maltibog Geothermal Power Station, Phillippines has capacity of 232.5 MW.

(*ix*) Wayang Windu Geothermal Power Plant, West Java, Indonesia has capacity of 227 MW.

(*x*) Darajat Power Station, West Java, Indonesia has capacity of 259 MW.

Other operating geothermal power plants in the world are listed below—

(*i*) Wairakei Power Station, New Zealand, 157 MW.

(*ii*) Valle Secolo Power Station, Italy, 120 MW.

(*iii*) Bacman Power Station, Phillippines, 110 MW.

(*iv*) Miravalles Power Station, Costa Rica, 100 MW.

(*v*) BLM Geothermal Station, USA, 100 MW.

(*vi*) Svartsengi Power Station, Iceland, 77 MW.

(*vii*) San Jacinto Tizate Geothermal Power Station, Nicaragua, 72 MW.

(*viii*) Linhir Geothermal Power Plant, Papua New Ginea, 55 MW.

Installed capacity of Geothermal power plants of some countries is given in table 11.2.

Table 11.2 Installed capacity of Geothermal Plant(2013)

Country	*Installed Capacity (MW)*
USA	3,389
Phillippines	1,848
Mexico	1,017.4
Indonesia	1,341
Italy	8,755
Japan	537
New Zealand	842.6
Iceland	664.4
Costa Rica	207.1
El Salvador	204.4
Kenya	248.5
Russia	81.9
Nicaragua	149.5
Guatemala	48.0
China	27.0
Papua New Ginea	56.0
Turkey	166.6
Portugal	28.8

SOLVED EXAMPLES

Ex 11.1. In a heat exchanger, the inlet and outlet temperature of cooling water in a condenser of a geothermal power plant are 30°C and 36°C respectively. The flow rate of cooling water is 400 litres/hr. The working fluid enters the heat exchanger at 60°C and leaves at 45°C. Find out the flow rate of working fluid. Given: C_p of working fluid = 0.8 kcal/kg°C.

Solution: Heat transferred by working fluid to cooling water = m Cp dt

$$= 400 \times 1 \times (36 - 30) = 2400 \text{ kcal/hr}$$

$$\text{Flow rate of working fluid} = \frac{\text{Heat gained by working fluid}}{\text{Cp dt}}$$

$$= \frac{2400}{0.8 \times (60-45)} = \mathbf{200\ kg/hr}\quad \textbf{Ans.}$$

CHAPTER SUMMARY

Geothermal energy can be tapped from four sources viz. steam, hot water, hot dry rocks and mixture of these. Earth's surface can be categorised into three groups viz. non-thermal area, semi thermal area and hyper thermal area.

For power generation purpose, geothermal wells are drilled upto 3km in depth. The well may contain steam, hot brine or hot dry rock. The thermodynamic cycle used are steam cycle and binary cycle. Steam cycle uses steam from geothermal sources either directly or indirectly. While binary cycle uses geothermic fluid indirectly. About 24 countries generate electricity using geothermal sources in the world. Iceland, Italy , USA, Phillippines, Indonesia, New Zealand and Japan are leaders in this field.

REVIEW QUESTIONS

Q. 1. Explain types of geothermal fields.

Q. 2. What are various sources of geothermal energy?

Q. 3. What is hot dry rock (HDR)?

Q. 4. Discuss the classification of geothermal power plants based on types of geothermal fluid used.

Q. 5. Explain with a neat sketch binary cycle geothermal power plant using hot brine.

Q. 6. Discuss operation of dry steam geothermal power plant.

Q. 7. Why injection wells are required in a geothermal power plant?

Q. 8. Write a brief note on (*i*) Petro thermal power plant (*ii*) Flashed steam geothermal power plant.

Q. 9. What is ground source heat pump?

Q. 10. What is the current status of geothermal power plants in the world?

Q. 11. Discuss the scope of geothermal based power generation in India.

Q. 12. Discuss direct applications of geothermal energy.

Q. 13. Discuss in detail the environmental impact of geothermal power plants.

Q. 14. Discuss advantages and disadvantages of geothermal power.

SHORT ANSWER TYPE QUESTIONS

Q. 1. What is the source of geothermal energy?

Q. 2. What are wet and dry fields?

Q. 3. What is the purpose of condenser in a geothermal power plant?

Q. 4. What are the disadvantages of geothermal power plants?

Q. 5. How the efficiency of geothermal power plant can be increased?

Multiple Choice Questions

Q. 1. Dry fields produce

(*a*) wet steam (*b*) saturated steam

(*c*) superheated steam (*d*) both (*b*) and (*c*).

Q. 2. Rise in temperature of rock for every 100 m below ground is

(*a*) 1°C (*b*) 2°C

(*c*) 3°C (*d*) 5°C

Q. 3. Which power plant has lowest capital cost?

(*a*) Geothermal (*b*) Solar PV

(*c*) Solar thermal (*d*) Wind

(*e*) Hydro

Q. 4. Temperature range for hot dry rocks is

(*a*) 100–150°C (*b*) 150–300°C

(*c*) 300–400°C (*d*) 400–450°C

Q. 5. Power output of a geothermal power plant depends on

(*a*) temperature of fluid (*b*) mass flow rate

(*c*) type of fluid (*d*) all of these

Answer to MCQ

1. (*d*) **2.** (*c*) **3.** (*d*) **4.** (*b*) **5.** (*d*)

Chapter 12

OCEAN THERMAL, TIDAL AND WAVE POWER GENERATION

Learning Objectives

After reading this chapter, reader will be able to

- Understand process of capture of energy from ocean.
- Examine the technology of power generation from ocean thermal, ocean tidal and ocean waves.
- Explore relative merits, demerits and complexities involved in the capture of these energy.
- Update on powers plants operating on these principles in the world.

"Failure is the opportunity to begin again more intelligently". — Henry Ford

12.1. INTRODUCTION

Ocean is a huge reservoir of energy. It covers 70% of earth's surface. The energy that can be generated from ocean largely encompasses–ocean thermal energy, ocean tidal energy, ocean wave energy,current energy and salinity gradient energy.

The temperature of water layer is different at different depths in ocean. The upper layer is warm due to solar radiation. A temperature difference of about 20°C can be obtained within a depth of 1000 m. This temperature gradient is used to convert thermal energy into electrical energy. Usually, open and closed cycle technologies are used. In closed cycle, a working medium such as ammonia is pumped into an heat exchanger. The media gets vaporised and the vaporized steam turns a turbine. The cold water at a depth in ocean converts this vapour into liquid state where it returns to heat exchanger. In open cycle, warm surface water of ocean is pressurised in a vacuum chamber to produce steam. This steam is used to run a turbine. The steam is condensed from the cold water at ocean depth. India has potential installed capacity of 1,80,000 MW of ocean thermal power.

Tides in ocean occur due to gravitational pull exerted by the moon. The level of ocean water rises periodically during high tide and falls during low tide. This tide cycle happens every 12 hours.

This difference in head of water during high tide and low tide is used to generate electrical energy. In order to generate sufficient energy, height of high tide must be atleast 5 m greater than low tide .There are about 20 locations in the world where difference in head is more than 5 m. In India, Gulf of Cambay and Gulf of Kutch in Gujarat on west coast have an average tidal range of 6.77 m and 5.23 m while maximum tidal range is 11 m and 8 m respectively. The estimated potential for tidal energy in India is 9000 MW.

The waves in ocean take water to the shore. Waves occur due to rotation of earth and the winds over the ocean surface and take place at an interval of 4 to 12 seconds. The energy contained by these waves is harnessed to generate electrical energy. Wave power can be captured through oscillating water column .The changes in air pressure introduced by trapped wave in a column drives a turbine. The wave energy potential in India is 40,000 MW.

Current in ocean move in one direction. This ocean current is called Gulf stream, The kinetic energy of stream can be captured by submerged turbine to generate electrical energy.

These technologies can generate power 24 hours a day and 365 days a year. The energy supplied from other renewable sources, such as solar and wind are not predictable and consistant. Geothermal is site specific and biomass renewable energy consumes precious agricultural resources.

12.2. SOURCES OF ENERGY IN OCEAN

(*a*) **Ocean thermal energy**—All water bodies, such as ocean, sea, river, lake etc. absorb solar radiation during the day. This thermal energy is stored in water at low temperature (about 27°C).The surface of water can be considered as heat source and water layer at a depth of about 1 km can be considered as heat sink. The temperature of water at a depth of 1 km is about 10°C. The potential of ocean thermal power in the world is 10^7 MW. The power output is proportional to heat transfer rate. Density of water decreases with an increase in temperature and at 4°C the density is maximum which again decreases below this temperature. This results in no convection currents between top warmer layer and bottom cold layer. Therefore, these two layers present an infinite source of heat energy. This trapped energy can be harnessed to generate electrical power. Although surface temperature of water layer vary depending on season and latitude. This is maximum in tropical, sub-tropical and equatorial water. The power generation system uses either open cycle system or closed cycle system. In open cycle system,steam obtained from warm water is used to drive a turbine which is coupled to an electric generator and produces electric power.

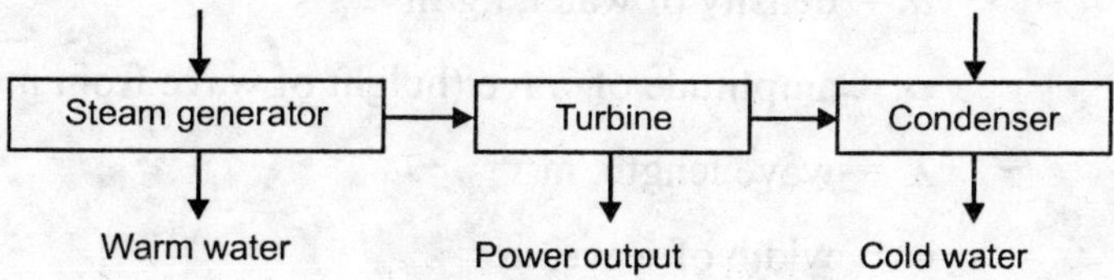

Fig. 12.1. Open cycle ocean thermal energy converter

The exhaust steam from turbine is passed through a condenser which is cooled by cold water from bottom layers. The closed cycle uses low boiling point liquids, such as propane and ammonia. The warm ocean water transfers heat to working fluid which drive a special turbine to produce power. This fluid is then condensed in a condenser using cold water from bottom layers.

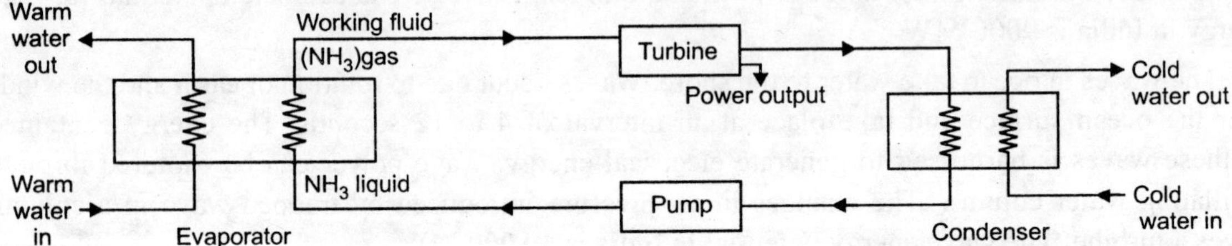

Fig. 10.2. Closed cycle ocean thermal energy converter

The achievable net energy conversion efficiency is about 2.5 percent in closed cycle system.

(*b*) **Tidal energy**—There is periodic rise and fall of water level in ocean due to the influence exerted by moon. The difference in level of water provides a "head" or potential energy which can be harnessed to produce electricity. The potential for tidal power plant in the world is 2×10^5 MW. Out of this total,a small part is recoverable due to economic reasons. Usually, the high tide available is 2 to 4 m only.

A basin containing hydro turbine is constructed at a higher level. Water during high tide is led into the basin and allowed to go back into the ocean during low tide thereby generating power due to the difference of head.

In one year, there are about 705 full tidal cycles.

(*c*) **Wave energy**—Waves in ocean is generated indirectly by sun through wind, ocean thermal energy and rotation of earth. The level of ocean waves reach from few centimetre to about 10 m for a period of 4 to 12 seconds. The potential for wave power generation in the world is 5×10^6 MW.

The energy contained in waves is utilized in two ways. The kinetic energy i.e. energy of forward motion of wave can be harnessed to generate power. The second is potential energy of wave due to raised level of water.

The potential energy contained in wave is given by following expression—

$$\text{Potential energy} = \frac{1}{4} da^2 \lambda \text{ Wg} \qquad ...(12.1)$$

where, d = density of water, kg/m^3

a = amplitude of wave (height of wave from mean sea level)

λ = wave length, m

w = width of wave, m

g = acceleration due to gravity, m/sec^2

The kinetic energy contained in the wave is given by following expression—

$$\text{Kinetic energy} = \frac{1}{4}\, da^2\, \lambda\, Wg \qquad ...(12.2)$$

Expression for potential energy and kinetic energy are identical. Hence, energy contained in waves is proportional to the square of amplitude of wave, wave length and width of wave.

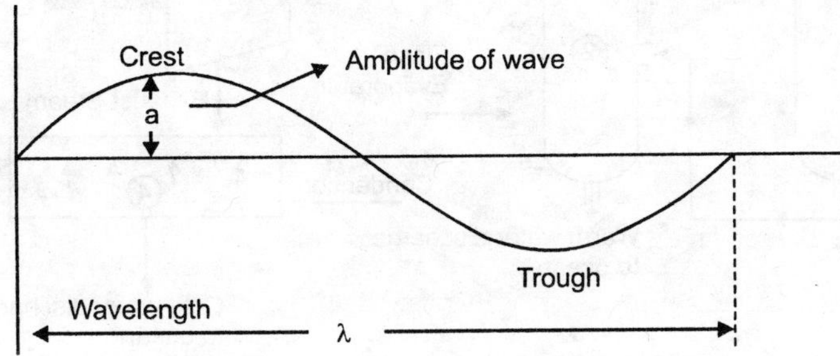

Fig. 12.3. Parameters of wave

12.3. OCEAN THERMAL ENERGY CONVERSION SYSTEM (OTEC)

Ocean thermal energy conversion system uses difference in temperature of different layers of water in ocean for generation of electric power. The average surface temperature of surface water is 24° C to 27°C. The average temperature gradient is 4°C to 6°C per km depth. However, this temperature gradient is not uniform. The maximum theoretical efficiency or carnot cycle efficiency is about 7% while practically achievable is only 2%. There is variation of temperature of layers of water due to variation in season and latitude. Surface temperature of water is higher during summer months and in tropical zones.

Following are the two types of OTEC system in operation—

(*a*) **Open cycle system**—Warm water of ocean is used to generate steam to drive a steam turbine to produce power.

(*b*) **Closed cycle system**—Warm water of ocean is used to vapourise a liquid working fluid, such as Propane, Ammonia, Freon etc. This working fluid vapour drives a turbine to generate power. The working fluid after exhaust is condensed by cold water of ocean for recirculation.

12.3.1. Open Cycle OTEC system

Open cycle OTEC system uses water as working fluid. Warm ocean water is used to produce steam in evaporator. This low pressure steam so produced is used to drive a steam turbine. The exhaust steam from steam turbine is condensed into water by passing cold water from deeper layers of ocean. This water is then discharged into ocean. As the steam generated is of very low pressure size of the turbine is large.

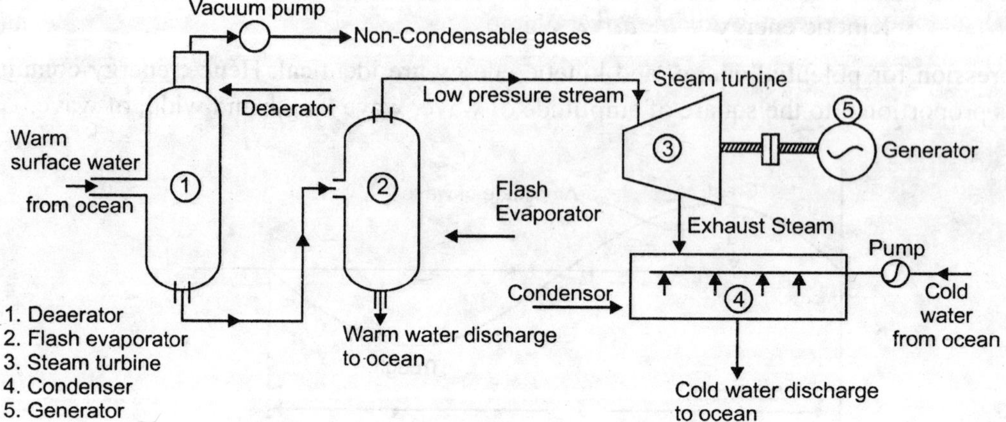

Fig. 12.4. Schematic of open cycle OTEC power plant

Components of open cycle OTEC power plant consists of following—

1. **Deaerator**—Function of deaerator is to remove non-condensable gases from warm water drawn from the surface of ocean through a pump.
2. **Flash evaporator**—It generates steam from warm surface water under vacuum. Vacuum inside the flash evaporator is maintained by a vacuum pump. Under vacuum, boiling point of water reduces thereby producing steam. The steam so produced is saturated steam and remaining water is discharged into ocean.
3. **Steam turbine**—Steam turbine converts thermal energy of steam into mechanical energy by expanding the steam over a series of blades.
4. **Condenser**—It condenses the exhaust steam into water by direct spray of cold water from depth of ocean. This condensed steam is discharged into ocean. The temperature and pressure inside condenser is 15°C and 0.17 bar respectively.
5. **Generator**—Generator is mechanically coupled to steam turbine. It converts mechanical energy of steam turbine into electrical energy.

- **Working of open cycle OTEC power plant—**

Warm water from surface of ocean is introduced to deaerator through a pump. Non-condensable gases are removed from warm water by having vacuum inside the deaerator. Vacuum inside deaerator is maintained by a vacuum pump. This warm water is then fed to a flash evaporator where warm water is converted into low pressure saturated steam. This flash steam is produced due to boiling of warm water under vacuum. This low pressure saturated steam so produced is fed to a steam turbine. The steam expands overs a series of bucket shaped blades which causes rotation of steam turbine. The steam after expansion in turbine is condensed in a direct contact spray type condenser. The steam, thus, condensed into water is discharged to ocean.

12.3.1.1. Advantages and limitations of open cycle OTEC power plant

Advantages—

(*i*) it is a renewable source which provides continuous output unlike wind or solar plant.

(*ii*) quantity of energy available is very large.

(*iii*) useful for remote island, light houses, oil rigs etc

Limitations of open cycle OTEC system—

(*i*) very low overall efficiency (about 2%).

(*ii*) turbine operates at low steam pressure, hence size of turbine is very large.

(*iii*) high cost of plant due to large turbine and heat exchanger.

(*iv*) high cost of electricity produced.

(*v*) plant is subjected to high waves, storms etc. causing severe stress on plant equipments.

(*vi*) maintenance of plant is difficult and expensive.

(*vii*) plant size is limited due to large size of plant components.

(*viii*) problem of bio-fouling of heat exchanger (deposition of micro-organisms on cooling water side of heat exchanger).

(*ix*) saline water causes corrosion of metal parts. Impact of particle flowing in water causes erosion of metal parts.

(*x*) deposition of salt, algae etc. in pipe and equipments obstructs water flow.

12.3.2. Closed cycle OTEC system

Closed cycle OTEC system utilizes working fluid of low boiling point which circulates in closed system heat exchanger, turbine and condenser. Low boiling point working fluid is chosen due to very low density of steam at ocean water temperature. Ammonia, Propane, Butane etc. are used as working fluid .This working fluid extracts heat from warm sea water in evaporator and gets vapourised. These vapours of working fluid expand over turbine causing it to rotate. A generator coupled to turbine also rotates thereby producing electricity. The working fluid after expansion in turbine is condensed into liquid form in a condenser by taking away the heat by cooling sea water. A feed pump then increases the pressure of liquid working fluid to that of evaporator. This completes the cycle.

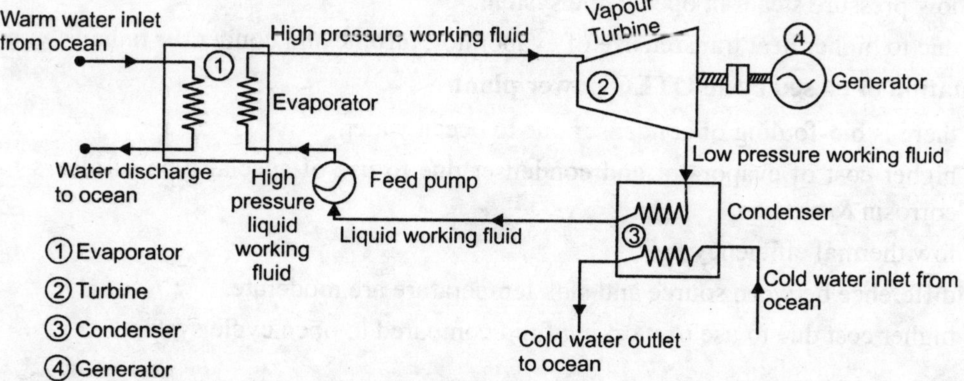

Fig. 12.5. Schematic of closed cycle OTEC power plant

Components of closed cycle OTEC power plant—Closed cycle OTEC power plant consists of following components—

(*i*) **Evaporator**—It converts liquid working fluid into high pressure vapour. The heat required for evaporation is extracted from sea water which is pumped into the evaporator at a high rate. In order to minimize corrosion and erosion due to ocean water, 90/10 Copper Nickel alloy, Titanium based heat exchanger is used.

(*ii*) **Turbine**—The vaporised high pressure working fluid is allowed to expand in a vapour turbine. This causes turbine to rotates and generator coupled to it also rotates thereby producing electricity.

(*iii*) **Condenser**—Surface type condenser is used to condense low pressure working fluid into liquid state. The heat is extracted by cold water from ocean. The water after heat absorption is discharged into ocean. It is also composed of 90/10 Copper-Nickel alloy or special stainless steel, such as Al –29 –4C and Al –6X.

(*iv*) **Generator**—It converts mechanical motion of vapour turbine into electrical energy by electro-magnetic induction. The electricity so produced is transported to on-shore through submarine cables.

• **Working of closed cycle OTEC power plant**—

It is a binary cycle power plant using a low boiling point working fluid, such as ammonia,propane butane etc. though ammonia is preferred. The heat energy of warm sea water causes the liquid working fluid to evaporate into high pressure vapours in a evaporator. The high pressure vapours are led into a vapour turbine where high pressure working fluid expands making the turbine to rotate. The working fluid after expansion has low pressure. This low pressure working fluid is condensed into liquid state by passing it through a condenser. This liquid working fluid is again pressurised by a feed pump to let into evaporator, thus, completing the cycle.

12.3.2.1. Advantages and limitations of closed cycle OTEC power plant

Advantages—

(*i*) closed cycle power plant has better efficiency than open cycle plant.

(*ii*) due to use of low boiling point working fluid,heat transfer is higher compared to that by low pressure steam in open cycle system.

(*iii*) due to higher heat transfer,size of evaporator, turbine and condenser reduces.

Limitation of closed cycle OTEC power plant—

(*i*) there is bio-fouling of condenser due to ocean water.

(*ii*) higher cost of evaporator and condenser due to use of special type of alloys to reduce corrosin & erosion.

(*iii*) low thermal efficiency.

(*iv*) difference between source and sink temperature are moderate.

(*v*) higher cost due to use of working fluid compared to open cycle system.

12.3.3. Hybrid cycle OTEC power plant

Hybrid cycle is a variation of standard open cycle OTEC power plant. This cycle combines advantages of open and closed cycle system and avoids their limitations.

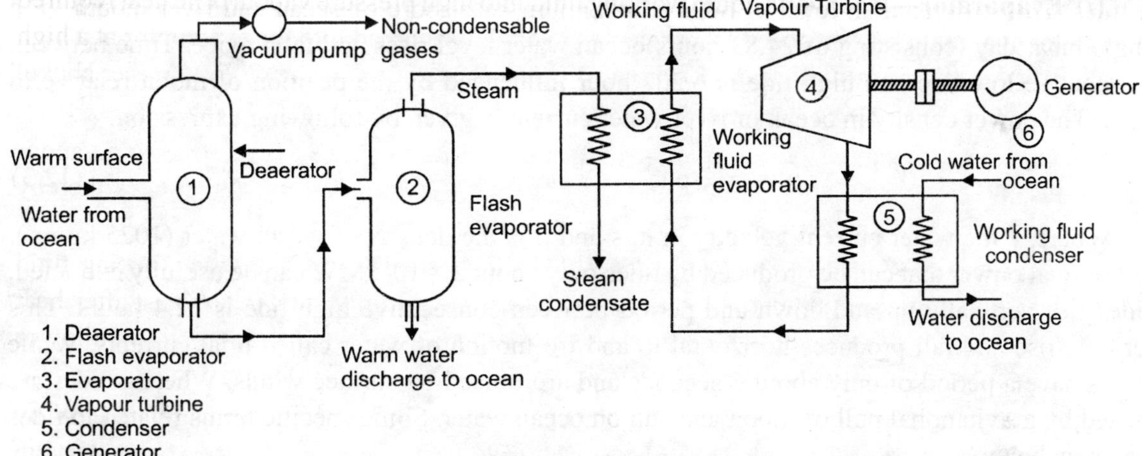

Fig. 12.6. Schematic of hybrid cycle OTEC power plant

In hybrid system, warm water is pumped into a deaerator to remove non-condensable gases. This warm ocean water is then fed to a flash evaporator where low pressure steam is generated by taking heat from warm ocean water.

The flash steam, so produced is fed to an evaporator where working fluid, such as ammonia is vapourised. This vapourised working fluid is fed to a vapour turbine where the working fluid expands causing the turbine to rotate. The exhaust working fluid after expansion is fed to a surface condenser where it is condensed into liquid state by passing cold ocean water. This liquid working fluid is again pumped into working fluid evaporator to complete the cycle.

Components of hybrid OTEC power plant—

It consists of following components—

(*i*) **Deaerator**—It is used to remove non-condensable gases from sea water. It is maintained under vacuum by a vacuum pump.

(*ii*) **Flash evaporator**—It produces steam from warm ocean water under vacuum .Vacuum causes reduction of boiling point of water producing steam.

(*iii*) **Working fluid evaporation**—The flash steam produced by flash evaporator is used to vapourise working fluid by transferring heat to it. It is a heat exchanger.

(*iv*) **Vapour turbine**—The pressurised working fluid generated in working fluid evaporator is expanded in vapour turbine producing motion.

(*v*) **Working fluid condenser**—Working fluid after expansion in vapour turbine is condensed into liquid in this condenser. Cold ocean water is used to remove the heat.

(*vi*) **Generator**—It produces electricity as it is coupled to the vapour turbine.

12.4. TIDAL POWER GENERATION

Tides are periodic rise and fall of ocean water level due to gravitational pull exerted by moon, sun and spinning of earth around its axis. This periodic rise and fall of water level represents an unlimited source of energy which can be used to generate electricity by tapping potential energy of tides. This difference in level of tides is maximum near shore of ocean and river mouth. In a single lunar day (consisting of 24.83 hours)ocean water level rises and falls twice. Time between consecutive low tide and high tide is 6.207 hour influenced by the position of moon relative to earth. The power density in ocean or river water current is given by following expression.

$$p = = \frac{1}{2} \rho v^3 \quad ...(12.3)$$

Where, v the water current velocity in m/s and ρ is the density of ocean water (1025 kg/m^3). Out of total power that can be produced by tides,only about 2×10^{12} MW can be usefully extracted. Tides rise vertically up and down and period between consecutive high tide is 12.4 hours. This periodic rise and fall produces horizontal to and fro motion of water called tidal currents. While waves have a period of only about 6 seconds and are caused by surface winds. Whereas tides are caused by gravitational pull of moon and sun on ocean water. Some specific terms related to tides are given below.

(*i*) **Tidal range**—It is the difference of water level between consecutive high tide and low tide.

(*ii*) **Diurnal tide**—It consists of two low tides and two high tides for one rotation of moon around earth.

(*iii*) **Spring tides**—These are tides on full moon or new moon. Tidal range is maximum during this period.

(*iv*) **Neap tides**—Tidal range on first quarter and third quarter moon. Tidal range is minimum during this period.

(*v*) **Single effect**—Power is generated during low tide after filling of basin during high tide.

(*vi*) **Double effect**—Power is generated during low tide and high tide.

(*vii*) **Pool**—It is a basin which retains water.

(*viii*) **Estuary**—It is part of ocean or river which is influenced by tide in the main ocean.

(*ix*) **Tidal basin**—Basin which gets filled up during high tide by opening of gates in the dam or barrage.

(*x*) **Sluice gates**—Sluice gates allow water to flow through turbine.

(*xi*) **Tidal turbine**—This is underwater turbine whose blade is turned by tides to produce electricity such as Bulb turbine, Straflo turbine, Tubular turbine etc

12.5. TYPES OF TIDAL ENERGY GENERATION SCHEMES

Tidal energy generation schemes are classified based on number of basins and operating modes of turbine-generator. Accordingly, various tidal power generation schemes are following.

(i) Single basin scheme

  (*a*) Single effect scheme.

  (*b*) Double effect scheme.

(*ii*) Two basin scheme.

(*iii*) Multiple basin scheme.

(*iv*) Pumped storage scheme—A tidal energy generation plant consists of a barrage with sluice gate, duct for passage of water through barrage, turbine–generator unit in duct and associated electrical and mechanical auxiliaries.

12.5.1. Principle of Tidal Power Generation

Potential energy of tides (due to difference in level during high tide and low tide) is converted into kinetic energy by passing water through a turbine. This spinning of turbine drives a generator to produce electricity. The power output is proportional to the square of the tidal range.

A tidal plant essentially consists of a barrage with a sluice gate which allows entry of water during high tide. The water leaves the turbine during low tide by passing through the turbine thereby producing power.

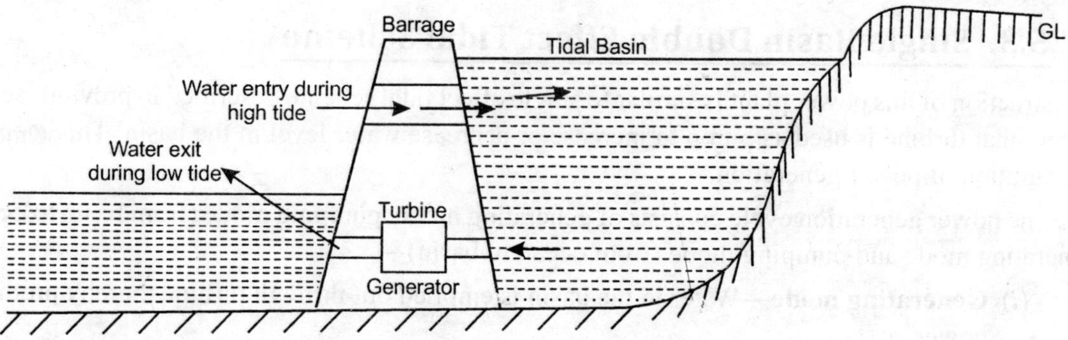

Fig. 12.7. Tidal power generation

So, power is generated during low tide and is intermittent in nature.

12.5.2. Single Basin Single Effect Tidal Scheme

This type of power generation scheme has only one barrage and generates power with one way flow of water through turbine–generator set.

The basin allows entry of water during high tide so that basin is full of water. The energy is stored in the basin in the form of tidal range. Water is released during low tide thereby producing electricity. The turbine is designed one way operation. The cycle of power generation consists of waiting mode, generating mode, waiting mode and refilling mode—

(*i*) **Waiting mode**—It begins with falling water level to allow ocean water level to reduce. This increases water head in the basin. This period lasts approximately for 1.5 hours. The basin remains full of water during this period .

(*ii*) **Generating mode**—When ocean water level falls to desired level, sluice gates are opened to release the water to ocean. The water passes through turbine-generator set thereby producing power. This period lasts for approximately 4.5 hours.

(*iii*) **Waiting mode**—This is second waiting mode waiting for high tide.

(*iv*) **Refilling mode**—The water is allowed to enter the barrage to fill the basin again during high tide. This period lasts approximately 4 hour.

It can be observed that power generation period per tide is only 4 hours in every 12.4 hours. The plant is idle during rest of the time.

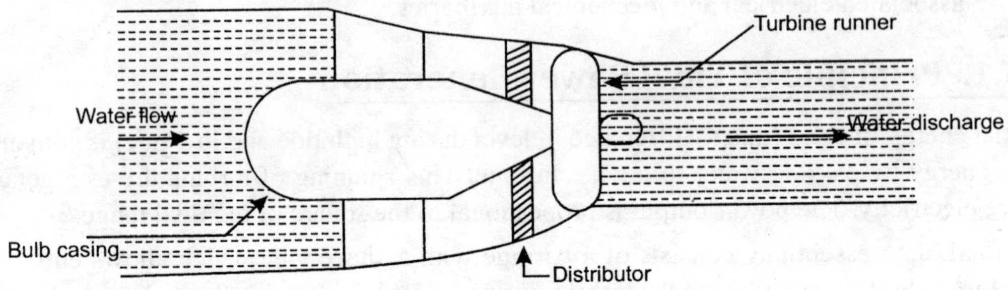

Fig. 12.8. Bulb turbine

12.5.3. Single Basin Double Effect Tidal Scheme

Construction of this power plant is similar to single effect tidal scheme described in previous section except that turbine is used as pump to increase or decrease water level in the basin. This increases the duration of power generation.

The power generation cycle consists of generating mode, pumping mode (from basin to ocean), generating mode and pumping mode (from ocean to basin)—

(*i*) **Generating mode**—Water in the basin is emptied out through turbine thereby producing power.

(*ii*) **Pumping mode (from basin to ocean)**—The basin is emptied faster by operating turbine in pumping mode(consuming power).

(*iii*) **Generating mode**—The filling of basin takes place thereby producing power.

(*iv*) **Pumping mode (from ocean to basin)**—Turbine is used as pump to accelerate filling of basin.

It can be observed that there are two generating modes in this scheme compared to previous scheme in a cycle. This is done by reducing waiting time using turbine as pump to accelerate filling and emptying of basin.

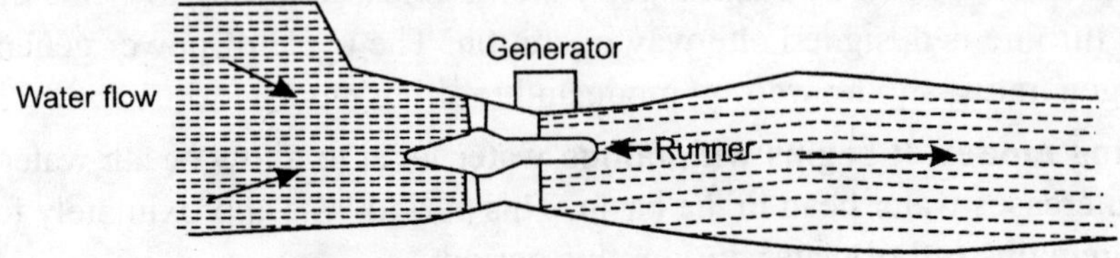

Fig. 12.9. Straflo turbine

12.5.4. Two Basin Scheme

This scheme has advantage of generating power continuously but at a variable rate. The scheme uses two separate basins, one at a higher level called upper basin while other basin at a lower level called power basin. There is a difference of head between upper and lower basin which permits continuous generation of electricity. The turbine is housed between two adjacent upper and lower basin.

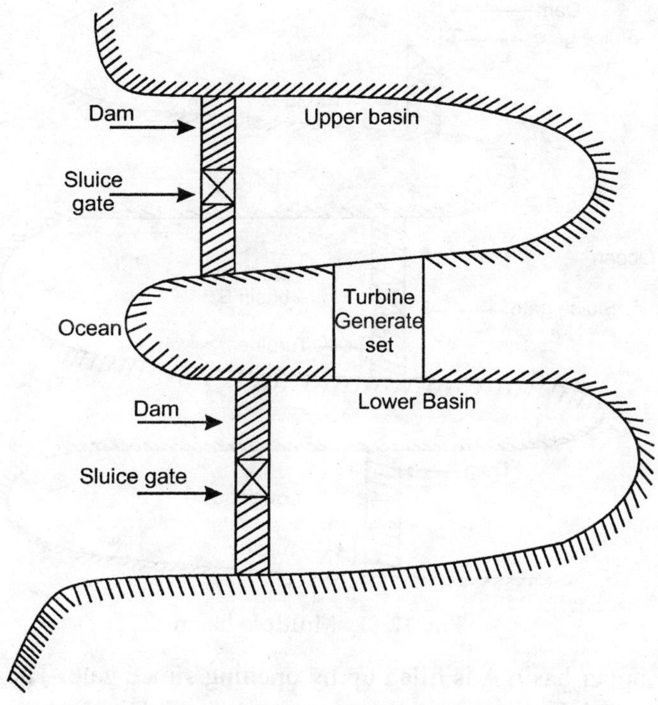

Fig. 12.10. Two basin tidal power plant

At high tide, water is allowed to enter upper basin by opening the sluice gate. The turbine remains in stopped condition. The sluice gate of lower basin are closed. So, water fills up upper basin and lower basin remains empty. Once the level of water in upper basin provides sufficient head, water from upper basin is allowed to enter lower basin by starting the turbine thereby generating power. So, water continues to enter upper basin from ocean and also in lower basin from upper basin. Once high tide in ocean is over and water level is maximum in upper basin, sluice gate of upper basin is closed. Again, when the water level of low tide in ocean is lower than the level in lower basin, sluice gate of lower basin is opened to let the water go back to ocean. This process is continued till there is sufficient water head in upper basin to run the turbine. This process is repeated with next high tide. The tandem operation of water flow between two basins allows longer operation of generator thereby reducing the intermittency or gap in power generation.

In order to match the time during which peak power demand in the system occurs, during off-peak period water can be pumped back to upper basin which can be used during peak power demand period. The power required to run turbine as pump can be drawn from some alternate sources.

12.5.5. Multiple Basin Schemes

A multiple basin scheme uses more than two basins which either operate paired or in cascade mode.

In paired basin scheme, number of basins are located apart and water amongst them are never exchanged. So, each basin generates power independently thereby producing dependable and continuous power.

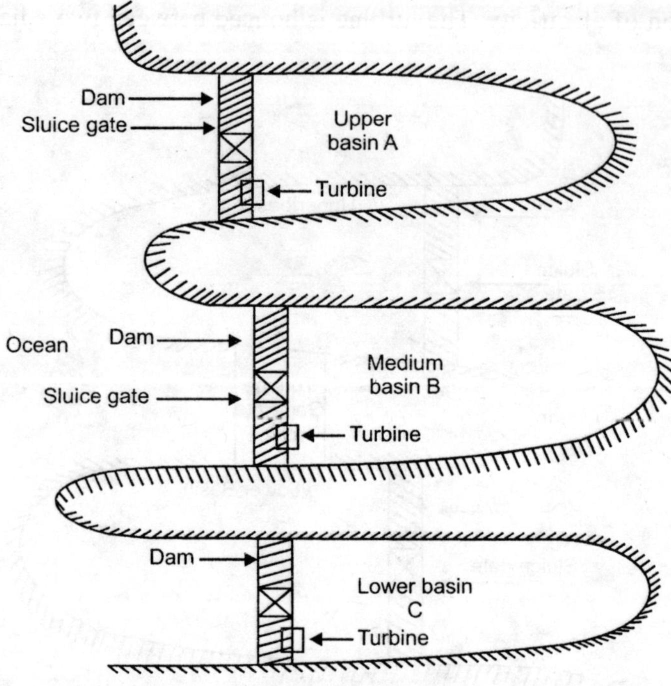

Fig. 12.11. Multiple basin

During high tide,upper basin A is filled up by opening sluice gate. The water filing process is continued till the end of high tide then sluice gates are closed. During low tide, water from upper basin A is allowed to go back to ocean through turbine thereby generating power.

During rising low tide, medium basin B and lower basin C are filled through turbines thereby generating power. When low tide is at the bottom of cycle, water from basin B and C are released through sluice gate to ocean. This cycle is then repeated. This process takes the advantage of producing power during low and high tide independently thereby increasing reliability and continuity of power.

12.5.6. Pumped Storage Scheme

Pumped storage scheme has a reservoir at high level and uses reversible turbine-pump. During peak generating period, turbine works as pump and lifts water from basin to high level reservoir. During non-generating period, the stored water in high reservoir is used to drive turbine and generate power.

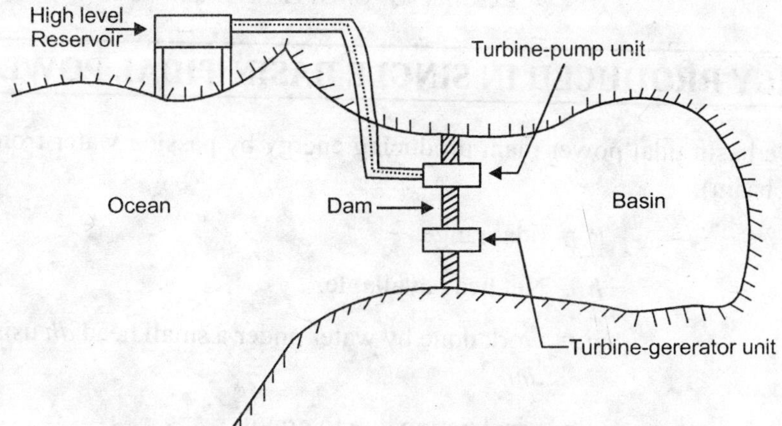

Fig. 12.12. Pumped storage scheme

12.6. COMPONENTS OF TIDAL POWER PLANT

A tidal power plant has following components—

(*i*) **Dam or barrage**—A dam or barrage is a barrier between ocean and basin or between basins. It allows the water to enter or leave the basin through turbine or sluice gates. The dam has to withstand impact of the waves where pressure changes continuously. Normally, head of tidal power plant is much less than that of a hydro power plant where the dam has to withstand high static head. In case of tidal power plant, the head is usually upto 20 m. Dam is made of concrete and is located near a bay or estuary having good head.

(*ii*) **Sluice gates and locks**—Gates allow entry and exit of water from basin. This is housed in the concrete dam. Gates need to be opened and closed quickly. Vertical lift gates are also used for control of water flow.

(*iii*) **Turbine**—Due to availability of small heads in tidal power plants, large size turbine are used. Bulb type & Rim type turbines are used.

A Bulb type turbine is an axial flow turbine consisting of o–give shaped steel shell housing a Kaplan turbine and an alternator. It is placed horizontally in the water duct. The Kaplan turbine consists of four mobile blades and guide vanes. The unit can be used as pump as well.

In Rim type turbine, generator is attached peripherally to the turbine blades. The rotor surrounds the turbine runner.

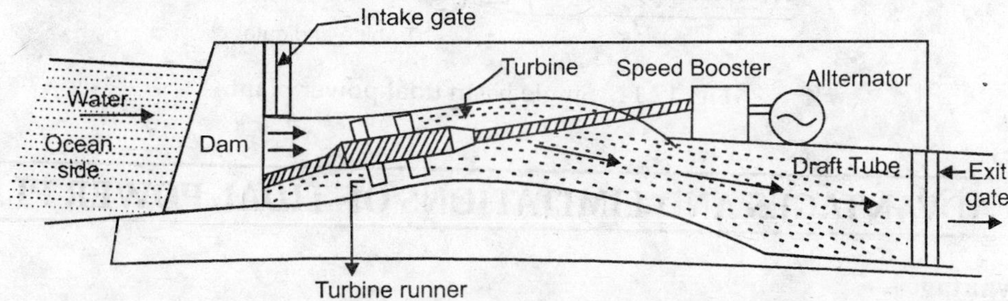

Fig. 12.13. Tidal power plant

12.7. ENERGY PRODUCED IN SINGLE BASIN TIDAL POWER PLANT

Consider a single basin tidal power plant producing energy by passing water from basin to ocean (i.e emptying of basin).

Let R = tidal range.

h = Net head available.

dw = work done by water under a small head dh using mass of water dm.

g = acceleration due to gravity.

m = mass of flowing water.

ρ = density of water.

A = surface area of basin.

$\therefore \quad dm = dm \,.\, g \,.\, h$ (potential energy = mgh) ...(12.3)

also, $dm = -\rho \,.\, A \,,\, dh$ ...(12.4)

$\therefore \quad \text{dw} = -\rho \,.\, A.\, dh.\, g.\, h$ (12.5)

Total work done, $W = \int_R^o dw = -\rho A g \int_R^o h\, dh$ ...(12.6)

$$W = \frac{1}{2} \rho g A R^2$$

Therefore, workdone is proportional to square of tidal range and area of basin. For double effect scheme (filling and emptying), following is the expression—

$$W = \rho g A R^2 \quad \text{...(12.8)}$$

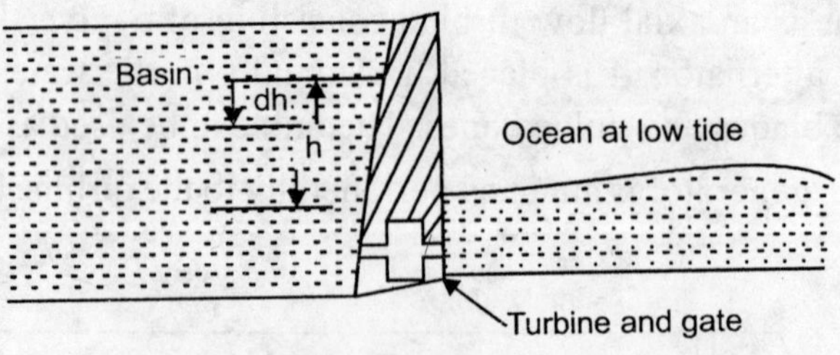

Fig. 12.14. Single basin tidal power plant

12.8. ADVANTAGES AND LIMITATIONS OF TIDAL POWER PLANT

Advantages—

(*i*) power generated by tidal power plant does not depend upon rain (output of hydro power plant depends upon rain).

(*ii*) tidal power plant does not cause pollution.

(*iii*) tidal power plant does not require expensive land, deforestation or migration and resettlement of people.

(*iv*) development of region takes place on both sides of dam.

(*v*) tidal power plant becomes place of tourist attention.

(*vi*) a pumped storage tidal power plant can produce power during peak demand.

Limitations—

(*i*) variable output power.

(*ii*) variable tidal range.

(*iii*) intermittent operation.

(*iv*) corrosive sea water affects life of plant and machinery.

(*v*) construction of power plant estuary is difficult and expensive.

(*vi*) presence of tidal power plant affects marine animals and navigation.

12.9. ENERGY GENERATION FROM WAVES

Ocean and sea waves are periodic up and down movement of water which can be converted into electrical energy. Ocean and sea waves are caused by surface winds, solar heating and rotation of earth. These waves possess potential and kinetic energy.

The forward motion of wave possesses kinetic energy and higher level of water contains potential energy. The height of waves is affected by wind velocity, depth of ocean, contour of shore etc. The energy content of waves is proportional to square of amplitude of wave, wavelength and width of wave (pl .see eq 12.1 and 12.2). Potential for wave energy is better than solar, biomass and wind power. Power generation from wave uses up and down movement of waves. Accordingly, three basic methods of wave energy conversion are used viz. float system, oscillating water column devices and tapered channels or tap chan.

12.9.1. Expression for power generated from waves

Let,

V = velocity of wave, m/s

λ = wavelength, m

d = density of water, kg/m^3

a = amplitude of wave, m

W = width of wave, m

g = acceleration due to gravity, m/s^2

Expression for kinetc energy associated with wave,

$$\text{KE} = \frac{1}{4} d a^2 \lambda \text{Wg} \qquad \text{...(12.9)}$$

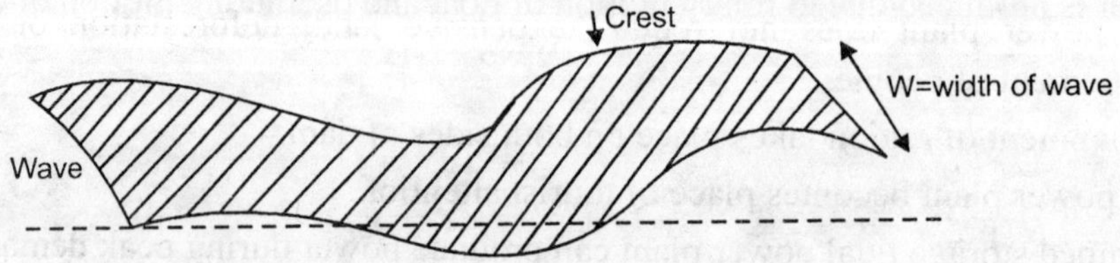

Fig. 12.15. Progressive ocean wave

Potentail energy associated with wave,

$$PE = \frac{1}{4}\, d\, a^2\, \lambda\, Wg \quad ...(12.10)$$

Total energy associated with wave,

$$TE = KE + PE$$

$$= \frac{1}{2}\, d\, a^2\, \lambda\, Wg \quad ...(12.11)$$

Power of wave per unit area per unit time or power density

$$= \frac{\text{Total energy of wave}}{\lambda\, WT}$$

$$= \frac{1}{2}\, d\, a^2\, gf\, W/m^2 \quad ...(12.12)$$

Where, wave period, $T = \frac{1}{f}$

wavelength, $\lambda = 1.56\, T^2$ ...(12.13)

12.9.2. Wave Energy Conversion Devices

Following are the wave energy conversion devices used for conversion of wave energy into electrical energy—

(*i*) **Float systems**—In these devices rise and fall of water level is used to drive hydraulic pump. It is a kind of buoy that is fixed to ocean bed or to floating raft. The float or buoy rises and falls with the movement of waves. This up and down movement of float is used to produce electricity.

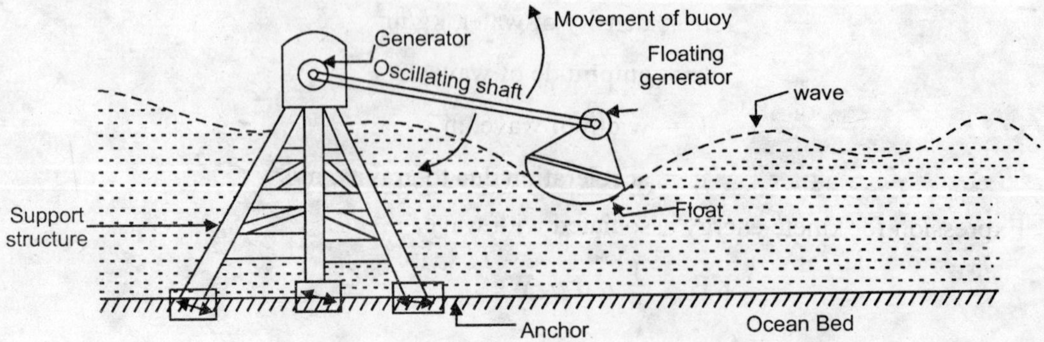

Fig. 12.16. Float wave power generation

Power is produced due to rotary motion of float and oscillating motion of connecting rod. The float is made of a cylindrical rollar. A ratchet and wheel mechanism at the end of connecting rod converts oscillating motion into rotary motion .A dolphin rollar type wave energy converter produces power given by following expression—

$$P = 1740\, A^2 T \text{ W/m} \qquad \text{...(12.14)}$$

where, A = amplitude of wave, metre

T = period of wave, second

(*ii*) **Oscillating water column devices**—In these devices, when waves at shores enter a column, air inside the column is compressed and when wave receeds, air inside the column expands. This oscillating air column is used to drive an air pump or water pump or turbine. The device consists of oscillating water column partly submerged in ocean. The structure is made of concrete or steel having an opening to the ocean. The wave when hits the device,water column inside rises and falls. The rise and fall of water volume compresses and decompresses the air column inside. The air is allowed to enter a turbine which runs the generator. Normally,axial flow well air turbine is used.

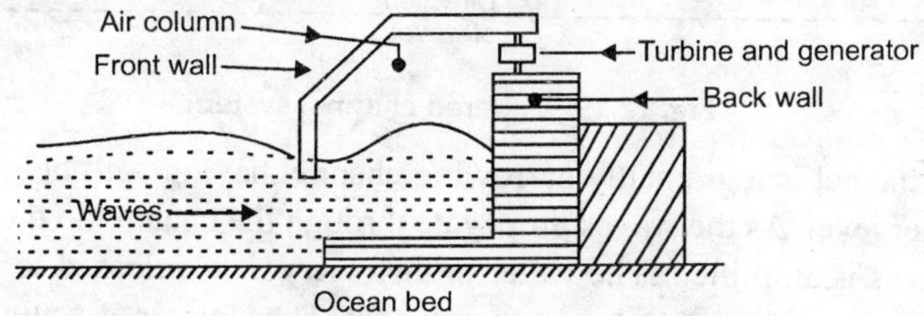

Fig. 12.17. Oscillating column device

In some designs, number of air pumps are mounted on a float. A piston and a cylinder arrangement is mounted on the float. The cylinder is stationary and piston can move inside the cylinder to compress the air. The piston and cylinder compresses the air and deliver it to an air turbine. The turbine is coupled to a generator which produces electricity. In order to increase the input, a number of piston and cylinder arrangements can be connected in parallel.

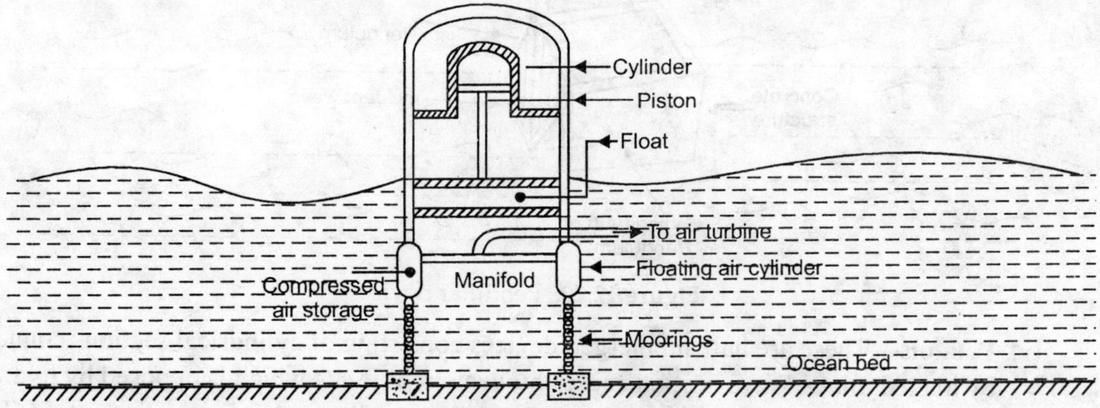

Fig. 12.18. Oscillating float air pump

Similarly, a hydraulic piston cylinder arrangement can be used which compresses the water in an accumulator. The high pressure water drives a hydro-turbine. The turbine inturn runs electrical generator to produce electricity. The large volume of water in accumulator ensures continuous motion of turbine.

(*iii*) **Tapered channel system**—A structure on the shore takes waves through a channel to an elevated reservoir. The water flowing out of this reservoir drives a hydro turbine which inturn drives a generator producing electricity.

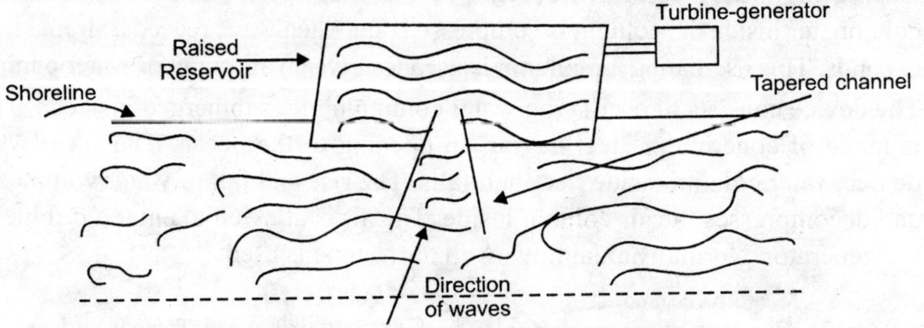

Fig. 12.19. Tapered channel system

Tapered channel is a gradually narrowing channel having wall height of 3 to 5 m above mean water level. As the waves propagate through the channel to the reservoir, the height of the waves is amplified .The water in the reservoir is released to ocean through a low head conventional hydro-turbine generator set. The storage of water in reservoir helps to generate constant output.

(*iv*) **Pendular device**—This device converts motion of waves into pendulum type swinging motion to generate electricity. The system consists of a rectangular box with only one side opening. The open side has a hinged flap connected to it. As the waves strike the hinged flap, it moves back and forth .This motion is converted to electricity by a hydraulic pump and generator.

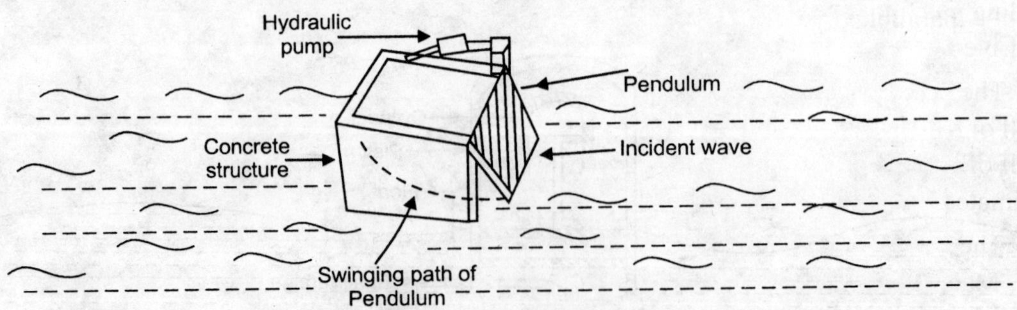

Figure 12.20. Pendular device

(*v*) **Pelamis**—These are half submerged devices consisting of cylindrical sections connected by hinged joints. Wave motion causes movement of joints which is opposed by hydraulic rams. These rams are used to pump high pressure oil through hydraulic motors. These hydraulic motors are used to drive electrical generator to produce electricity.

12.9.3. Advantages and Limitations of Wave Energy

Advantages—

(*i*) power generated from waves is more predictable.

(*ii*) wave energy has more kinetic energy (about 1000 times) than wind.

(*iii*) wave energy is available 24 hours a day unlike solar and wind.

(*iv*) wave energy has higher energy density than solar and wind energy.

(*v*) wave power generation is more smoother and consistent than solar or wind and hence, has higher capacity factor.

(*vi*) wave energy can be used in remote islands, light houses, oil drilling rigs etc.

(*vii*) wave energy has less infrastructure cost.

Limitations—

(*i*) unavailability of data pertaining to wave height with time and directional properties of wave.

(*ii*) difficult and expensive construction work in ocean.

(*iii*) corrosion of plant and machinery by sea water.

(*iv*) growth of algae,water hyacinth etc. in the plant requiring periodic cleaning.

(*v*) obstruction to ship movement.

(*vi*) storms in ocean can damage plant.

(*vii*) transmission of power from ocean is expensive and complicated.

12.10. POTENTIAL OF OCEAN ENERGY GENERATION IN INDIA

India has a very long coastline of 7500 km extending from one end of Gujarat to West Bengal on the other end. This presents a vast ocean based energy resource that remains to be tapped.

IIT, Madras had conducted a preliminary investigation on establishment of a 1MW ocean thermal energy plant at Minicoy in Lakshadeep island. It was based on binary cycle having a low boiling point chemical which can be vapourised by ocean water .This vapourised chemical is used to drive a turbine. The energy was tapped upto a depth of 800–1000 m.

The potential sites for tidal power generation are gulf of cambay (Bhavnagar, Sonrai, Gujarat), Gulf of Kutch (Kandla and Navalakhi, Gujarat) and Hoogly river (Diamond Harbour, West Bengal). Gulf of Kutch and Gulf of Cambay have a mean per meter tidal range of 5 and 7 respectively. The estimated installed capacity are 900 MW (Gulf of Kutch) and 700 MW (Gulf of Cambay).

The wave energy generation potential along coastline is 5 – 10 kW/m. Wave energy group at IIT, Madras had carried out research on wave energy devices (Raju, Ravindran 1989) viz single float system, double float system and oscillating wave column. It was found that oscillating wave column technology has maximum potential. A Caisson was constructed for 150 kW prototype in Vizhinjam, Thiruvantapuram in 1990. A successful trial was carried out. Based on this,it was proposed to build 10 caissons of 1.1 MW each in Thangassery on west coast of India.

It can be seen that despite potential for ocean based power generation, there is not much progress beyond prototype testing stage. Hence, India need to explore and expliot this vast source of energy lying untapped.

12.11. OPERATIONAL OCEAN ENERGY BASED POWER PLANTS IN THE WORLD

A tidal energy based power plant was constructed at La Rance in France from 1961 to 1967. The plant employed 24 reversible pump turbines of each 10 MW capacity. The operating tidal range was upto 12 m. The plant is functional with 90% availability producing 480 GWH annually. Another tidal based operational power plant is Kislaya Guba tidal power plant in Kislaya bay near Murmansk, Russia. The plant uses 8×10kW units having average tidal range of 2.37 m. The surface area of pool is 1.25 km with a channel of 40 m wide × 4 m deep. The bulb turbines used are reversible blade type (similar to La Rance, France)with a runner diameter of 3.8 m and speed of 69 rpm (generator speed 600 rpm).

A wave based power plant working on oscillating water column is working in Dawanshan island in China. It is a 3 kW plant being upgraded to 20 kW.

Another wave based power plant working on tapered channel device employing Kaplan turbine is working near university of Aalborg, Denmark since June 2003.

An oscillating wave column power plant of 500 kW is located in Pico island, Portugal. It produces average output of 124 kW with a maximum instantaneous value of 525 kW. The turbine operates between 750 and 1500 rpm.

It is proposed to build 1MW floating ocean thermal based power plant near Tuticorin, India by National Institute of Ocean Technology, Govt. of India (warm water temperature 29°C, cold water temperature 7°C at a depth of 1000 m).

Other demonstration plant working on ocean thermal principle are given below—

(*i*) 1 MW, closed cycle, floating plant,Hawaii, USA,1980.

(*ii*) 210 kW, open cycle, shore based plant,Hawaii, USA,1992.

(*iii*) 120 kW, closed cycle,shore based plant, Nauru, 1982.

(*iv*) 75 kW, closed cycle, Lab model, Saga, Japan,1984.

(*v*) 53 kW, closed cycle, floating plant, Hawaii, USA, 1979.

(*vi*) 22 kW, open cycle, shore based plant, Cuba,1930.

(*vii*) 9 kW, closed cycle, Lab model, Saga, Japan, 1995.

Wave based power plants in operation are listed below—

(*i*) 2.25 MW, Agucadoura, Portugal

(*ii*) 0.5 MW, Islay Limpet, U.K.

(*iii*) 0.3 MW, Matriku Break water, Spain.

(*iv*) 0.04 MW ,SDE Sea, Israel.

Tidal based power plants in operation are listed below—

(*i*) 254 MW, sihwa Lake, South Korea.

(*ii*) 20 MW, Annapolis Royal, Canada.

(*iii*) 3.9 MW, Jiangxia, China.

Solved Examples

Example 12.1

Determine the overall efficiency of an OTEC plant if the temperature of warm water is 32°C and the temperature of water in the depth is 7°C. Relative efficiency factor of the power plant may be taken as 0.5.

Solution:

Temperature of warm water = 32°C = 32 + 273 = 305 K

Temperature of water in depth = 7°C = 7 + 273 = 280 K

$$EF = 0.5$$

Efficiency,
$$\eta = \frac{T_1 - T_2}{T_1} \times 100$$
$$= \frac{305-280}{305} \times 100$$
$$= \frac{25}{305} \times 100$$
$$= 8.197\%$$

Efficiency of OTEC, $\eta_{OTEC} = EF \times \eta$
$$= 0.5 \times 0.08197$$
$$= 0.040985$$
$$= 4.099\%$$ **Ans.**

Example 12.2

A single of basin type tidal power plant has following data—

(*i*) Area of basin = 25×10^6 m^2

(*ii*) Tidal range = 10 m

(*iii*) Density of sea water = 1025 kg/m^3

The turbine stops generating when water head falls below 2 m. Determine energy and power produced in one cycle of filling .

Solution:

Total work done,
$$W = \frac{1}{2} \rho g A(R^2 - r^2)$$

Where, $R = 12$ m and $r = 2$ m

$$\therefore \quad W = \frac{1}{2} \times 1025 \times 9.81 \times 25 \times 10^6 \, [(12)^2 - (2)^2]$$

$$= 17596687.5 \times 10^6 \text{ joules}$$

$$= 17896687.5 \text{ MJ}$$

Ans.

Average power generated,

$$P_{ave} = \frac{W}{T} = \frac{17596687.5 \times 10^6}{10 \times 3600}$$

$$= 488.796 \times 10^6$$

$$W = 4\,88.796 \text{ MW}$$

Ans.

Example 12.3

A tidal power plant has an installed capacity of 2276 MW. The head at rated output is 5.55 m and embankment is 6.5 km long. The turbine generator efficiency is 95% each. If generation is 5 hours twice a day, determine—

(*i*) basin capacity.

(*ii*) annual energy of generated.

Assume, density of sea water = 1025 kg/m^3

Solution:

Maximum energy available per tidal cycle (assuming single basin plant),

$$E = \frac{1}{2} \rho g A R^2$$

$$E = \frac{1}{2} \times 1025 \times 9.81 \times A \times (5.55)^2$$

$$E = 154863.419 \times A \text{ Joules}$$

Average energy potential,

$$E_1 = \frac{E}{T}$$

$$2276 \times 10^6 = \frac{154863.419 \times A}{5 \times 2 \times 3600}$$

$$2276 \times 10^6 = 4.302 \times A$$

$$A = \frac{2276 \times 10^6}{4.30}$$

$$= 529.056 \times 10^6 \text{ m}^2$$

$$\text{Basin Capacity} = \text{Area} \times \text{Range}$$

$$= 529.056 \times 10^6 \times 5.25$$

$$= 2936.26 \text{ m}^3$$

Ans.

(*ii*) Energy generated per hour = Installed Capacity×turbine efficiency×generator efficiency

$$= 2276 \times 0.95 \times 0.95$$

$$= 2054.09 \text{ MWh}$$

$$\text{Energy generated per day} = 2054.09 \times 10 = 20540.9 \text{ MWh}$$

$$\text{Energy generated per year} = 20540.9 \times 365$$

$$= 7497.429 \times 10^6 \text{ MWh}$$

Example 12.4

In Gulf of Cambay, the observed difference between high and low water tide was 10.8 m. The estuary having an area of 10 sq km can generate power for three hours in each cycle. Assuming averge available head to be 10m and overall efficiency of the generation to be 75% . Calculate the total energy generated in the year. Take specific density of sea water 1025 kg/m^3.

Solution:

$$A = 10 \text{ km}^2,\ t = 3 \text{ hours},\ h = 10 \text{ m},\ \eta_{T+G} = 0.75$$

$$E = ?,\ d = 1025 \text{ kg/m}^3,\ R = 10.8 \text{ m}$$

$$\text{Volume of basin} = A.\,h = 10 \times 10^6 \times 10 \text{ m}^3$$

$$= 10^8 \text{ m}^3$$

$$\text{Average discharge, } Q = \text{volume of water/time}$$

$$= \frac{10^8}{3 \times 3600}$$

$$= 9259.26 \text{ m}^3/\text{s}$$

$$\text{Power generated} = \frac{\eta Q h d}{75} \times 0.736$$

where,

Q = discharge

h = head

d = density of water

η = turbine-generater efficiency

$$= \frac{0.75 \times 9259.26 \times 10 \times 1025 \times 0.736}{75}$$

$$= 698.52 \text{ kW}$$

$$\text{Energy generated per tidal cycle} = 698.52 \times 3$$

$$= 2095.56 \text{ kWh}$$

$$\text{No. of tidal cycles in a year} = \frac{8760 \text{ hours in a year}}{12.4166 \text{ hours/cycle}} = 705$$

($\because$ Tidal cycle repeats after 12 hr and 25 minutes or 12.4166 hrs)

$$\text{Yearly power generated} = 2095.56 \times 705$$

$$= 1477.37 \times 10^3 \text{ kWh}$$ **Ans.**

Example 12.5

An ocean wave is of amplitude 1 m period 6 seconds width 100 m. Calculate wavelength, velocity, energy density and power. Take density of water 1025 kg/m^3.

Solution:

$$\text{wavelength } \lambda = 1.56\, T^2$$

$$= 1.56 \times (6)^2 = 56.16 \text{ m} \qquad \textbf{Ans.}$$

$$\text{Wave velocity } e = \frac{\lambda}{T} = \frac{56.16}{6} = 9.36 \text{ m/s} \qquad \textbf{Ans.}$$

$$\text{Energy density, } \frac{E}{(\lambda)} = \frac{1}{2}\, d\, a^2\, g \qquad (\lambda W = \text{wave area})$$

$$= \frac{1}{2} \times 1025 \times (1)^2 \times 9.81$$

$$= 5027.63 \text{ J/m}^2 \qquad \textbf{Ans.}$$

$$\text{Energy} = \frac{E}{(\lambda W)} \times \lambda W = \frac{1}{2}\, d\, a^2\, \lambda\, \text{Wg}$$

$$= 5027.63 \times 56.16 \times 100 \text{ J}$$

$$= 2823.517 \times 10^4 \text{ J}$$

$$\text{Power} = E \times f \times W = 2823.517 \times 10^4 \times \frac{1}{6} \times 100$$

$$= 470.586 \times 10^6 \text{ W} \qquad \textbf{Ans.}$$

Example 12.6

An ocean wave energy plant converts energy from 100 m area of ocean surface with wave amplitude of 2 m and wave period of 5 seconds. The efficiency of energy conversion is 30%. Calculate the power rating in kW. Density of water is 1025 kg/m^3.

Solution:

$$\text{Energy} = \frac{1}{2}\, d\, a^2\, \lambda\, \text{wg}$$

$$d = 1025 \text{ kg/m}^3,\ a = 2 \text{ m},\ w = 100,\ g = 9.81 \text{ m/s}^2\ 2,\ T = 5\text{s}$$

$$\lambda = 1.56\, T^2$$

$$= 1.56 \times (5)^2 = 39 \text{ m}$$

$$\text{Energy} = \frac{1}{2} \times 1025 \times (2)^2 \times 39 \times 100 \times 9.81$$

$$= 7843.095 \times 10^4 \text{ J}$$

$$\text{Power} = E \times f \times W \Rightarrow E \times \frac{1}{T} \times \text{W}$$

$$= 7\,843.095 \times 10^4 \times \frac{1}{5} \times 100$$

Actual power produced $= \lambda \times E \frac{1}{T} \times \text{W}$

$= 0.30 \times 7843.095 \times 10^4 \times \frac{1}{5} \times 100$

$= 470.586 \times 10^6$ W

$= 470586$ kW **Ans.**

CHAPTER SUMMARY

Ocean thermal energy conversion system utilises heat energy of ocean to generate power. It is of two types viz open cycle and closed cycle. Closed cycle OTEC plant uses binary system having low boiling working fluid. This vapourised fluid drives a turbine to generate power.

Tidal energy conversion system uses rise and fall of water level in ocean to generate power. The small head of rising water is utilized to generate power in turbine. In one year, there are about 705 full tidal cycles.

Wave energy uses level of ocean waves to generate power. The wave are of few centimetres to about 10 m in height and appear periodically with an interval of 4 to 12 seconds.

FORMULAE

(*i*) Efficiency of OTEC power plant = Efficiency factor $\times \left[\frac{(T_1+273)-(T_2+273)}{(T_1+273)}\right]$

Where, T_1 = temperature of warm water in °C.

T_2 = temperature of water at depth in °C.

(*ii*) Energy of generated from single basin tidal power plant $= \frac{1}{2} \rho g A R^2$

Where, ρ = density of water, kg/m³

g = acceleration due to gravity, 9.81 m/s²

A = surface area of basin, m²

R = tidal range, m

(iii) Energy generated from single basin double effect tidal power plant

$= \rho g A R^2$

(*iv*) Average power generated,

$$P = \frac{\text{Energy generated}}{\text{Time duration}}$$

(*v*) Energy available per hour = Installed capacity of power plant $\times \eta_T \times \eta_G$

Where, η_T = efficiency of turbine.

η_G = efficiency of generator.

(*vi*) Power generated in a tidal power plant $= \frac{\eta_T \cdot \eta_G \cdot Qhd \times 0.736}{75}$

Where, Q = discharge, m^3/s

h = head, m

d = density of water, kg/m^3

(*vii*) Energy generated by waves = $\frac{1}{2}\, d\, a^2\, \lambda\, Wg$

Where, d = density of water, kg/m^3

a = amplitude of wave, m

λ = wavelength, m

W = width of wave, m

g = acceleraion due to gravity, 9.81 m/s^2

(*viii*) Wavelength, $\lambda = 1.56\, T^2$

Where, T = Wave period, s

REVIEW QUESTIONS

Q. 1. What are various sources of energy available from ocean?

Q. 2. Discuss ocean based open cycle thermal energy conversion system with schematic diagram.

Q. 3. Differentiate between open cycle and closed cycle thermal energy conversion system.

Q. 4. Explain how energy is tapped from ocean tides?

Q. 5. Explain how energy is tapped from ocean waves?

Q. 6. Compare power generated from tides and waves.

Q. 7. List limitations of open cycle OTEC system.

Q. 8. Explain with diagram, operation of hybrid OTEC power plant.

Q. 9. Explain the working of single basin single effect tidal power plant.

Q. 10. Explain the working of single basin double effect tidal power plant.

Q. 11. Explain the operation and advantages of multi basin tidal scheme.

Q. 12. Derive the expression for energy produced in a single basin tidal power plant.

Q. 13. Discuss advantages and limitations of tidal power plant.

Q. 14. Derive the expression for power generated from waves.

Q. 15. Write a note on wave energy conversion devices.

Q. 16. Discuss advantages and limitations of wave energy.

Q. 17. Write a brief note on potential of ocean energy generation in India.

Q. 18. Compare ocean thermal, tidal and wave power generation.

Numerical Questions

Q. 1. Calculate the efficiency of ocean thermal power plant if the temperature of warm water is 30°C and temperature of water in depth is 8°C. Efficiency of power plant is 0.42.

[**Ans:** 3.05%]

Q. 2. A single basin tidal power plant has following data—

(*i*) basin area = 28×10^6 m^2 (*ii*) tidal range =12 m

(*iii*) density of sea water = 1025 kg/m^3.

Turbine stops generating when water head falls below 2 m. Calculate energy produced if generation is 10 hours per day. [**Ans:** 27028512 MJ]

Q. 3. A tidal power plant has an installed capacity of 2500 MW. The head at rated output is 6m and embankment is 6.9 km long. The efficiencies of turbine and generator may be taken as 90% and 95 % respectively. If the generation of power lasts 4 hours twice a day, calculate—

(*i*) basin capacity. (*ii*) annual energy generated

Assume density of sea water = 1025 kg/m^3

[**Ans:** (*i*) 2386.8×10^6 m^2 MWh, (*ii*) 6241500 MWh]

Q. 4. An ocean wave based power generation plant converts energy from 90 m area of ocean surface with wave amplitude of 3.2 m and wave period of 5 seconds. The efficiency of energy conversion is 33%. Calculate the power rating. Assume density of water as 1025 kg/m^3. [**Ans:** 1073.4 MW]

SHORT ANSWER TYPE QUESTIONS

Q. 1. What are the working fluids used in binary cycle OTEC power plant?

Q. 2. What is the duration between consecutive high and low tide?

Q. 3. Where do you get maximum height of tide in a river?

Q. 4. Define diurnal tides.

Q. 5. What is pelamis?

Multiple choice Questions

Q. 1. A temperature difference of about 20°C can be obtained at a depth of

(*a*) 1 km (*b*) 2 km

(*c*) 3 km (*d*) more than 5 km.

Q. 2. Time duration of a wave is

(*a*) 1 to 5 seconds (*b*) 10 to 15 seconds

(*c*) 4 to 12 seconds (*d*) 15 to 20 seconds

Q. 3. In a year, there are about

(*a*) 205 full tidal cycles (*b*) 405 full tidal cycles

(*c*) 505 full tidal cycle (*d*) 705 full tidal cycles.

Q. 4. The average temperature gradient in an ocean is

(*a*) 2 to 3° C per km (*b*) 3to 4°C per km
(*c*) 4 to 6°C per km (*d*) 8 to 10°C per km.

Q. 5. Maximum theoretical efficiency of OTEC plant is

(*a*) 4% (*b*) 5%
(*c*) 6% (*d*) 7%

Q. 6. Power density in a river or ocean is proportional to

(*a*) v (*b*) v^2
(*c*) v^3 (*d*) v^4

Answer to MCQ

1. (*a*) **2.** (*c*) **3.** (*d*) **4.** (*c*) **5.** (*a*)
6. (*c*)

Fuel Cell, MHD and Hydrogen Based Power Generation

Learning Objectives

After reading this chapter, reader will be able to

- Understand construction and operation of fuel cells and MHD generation.
- Examine different types of fuel cells, difference in construction, efficiency, operating parameters and applications.
- Update on current status on fuel cell based and MHD based generation in the world.
- Understand various process of hydrogen generation, storage and use including safety precautions.

"Many of life's failures are people who did not realise how close they were to success."

— Thomas A .Edison

13.1 INTRODUCTION

A fuel cell is an electro-chemical device which converts chemical energy of conventional fuels directly into electrical energy. The cell consists of a cathode, anode and an electrolyte. It is like a battery except that chemical energy is stored in the battery and supplied as electrical energy to external circuit. While in fuel cell chemical energy of fuels is directly and continuously converted into electrical energy.

Operation of fuel cell was first successfully reported by Sir William Grove in 1939. He used reaction of oxygen and hydrogen to produce water and electricity. The various energy sources are hydrogen, carbon mono-oxide, alcohol, aldehydes etc. The rate of reaction in a full cell is influenced by temperature and pressure of fuels fed into the cell. The efficiency of energy conversion of fuel cell varies from 30 to 75%.

Fuel cells are used for generation of electric power in space vehicles, submarine propulsion, emergency standby power source, remote signal lights etc.

13.2 ADVANTAGES AND LIMITATIONS OF FUEL CELLS

Following are the advantages of fuel cells–

(*i*) since no combustion takes place, hence there is no pollution.

(*ii*) no moving parts and hence, little maintenance is required.

(*iii*) good conversion efficiency (about 70%).

(*iv*) quiet operation and quick startup.

(*v*) flexibility of fuel usage.

(*vi*) good efficiency at partial loads.

(*vii*) modular construction to suit load.

(*viii*) good response to variable load.

(*ix*) unattended operation.

(*x*) flexibility in size.

Limitations—

(*i*) it is expensive.

(*ii*) poor reliability at higher temperature.

(*iii*) it is a new technology and hence, reliability need to be established.

(*iv*) unsafe to handle hydrogen and oxygen due to fire hazard.

13.3 PRINCIPLE OF WORKING OF FUEL CELL

A fuel cell essentially consists of an anode (fuel electrode), a cathode (oxidant) and an electrolyte. Both fuel and oxidizing agents are fed through porous electrodes and are brought in contact with electrolyte. When an external load is connected to anode and cathode a current flows through it. The electric current continue to flow as long as fuel is fed to the cell. Voltagé produced per cell is 1 volt. Hence, in order to increase voltage, number of cells are connected in series to form what is known as module. A number of such modulas are connected in series or in parallel.

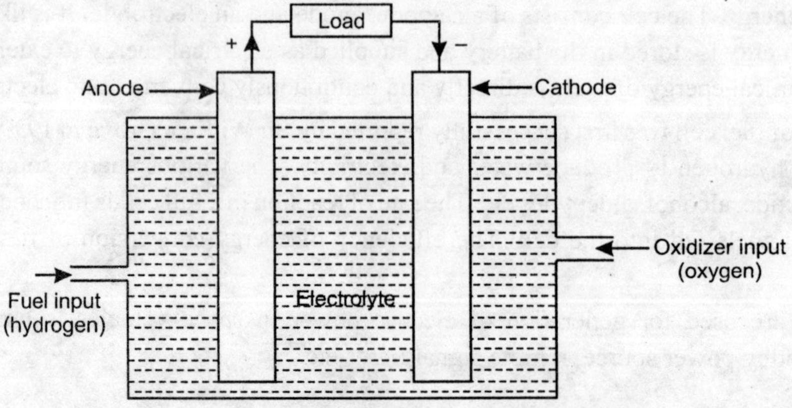

Fig. 13.1 Hydrogen-oxygen fuel cell

The amount of energy produced depends on rate of cell reaction, working temperature and nature of electrolyte. However, electrical output could be less if intermediate product is produced due to chemical reaction between fuel and oxidiser. The electrolyte used in hydrogen-oxygen fuel cell is either sulphuric acid or potassium hydroxide. The electricity produced from a single cell is 100–200 A/cm^2 at a voltage of 1 volt dc. The overall reaction is given below–

Anode reaction: $$H_2 + 2\,OH^- \rightarrow H_2O + 2e^- \quad ...(13.1)$$

Cathode reaction: $$\frac{1}{2}O_2 + 2e^- + H_2O \rightarrow 2\,OH \quad ...(13.2)$$

Overall reaction: $$H_2 + \frac{1}{2}O_2 \rightarrow H_2O + \Delta H \quad ...(13.3)$$

13.4 CLASSIFICATION OF FUEL CELLS

Fuel cells are classified based on following parameters—

(*i*) **based on operating temperature**

(*a*) Low temperature

(*a-i*) Hydrogen – Oxygen fuel cell.

(*a-ii*) Hydrogen – Halogen fuel cell.

(*a-iii*) Metal – Oxygen fuel cell.

(*a-iv*) Organic compound – Oxygen fuel cell.

(*a-v*) Nitrogenous compound – Oxygen fuel cell.

(*b*) Intermediate temperature

(*b-i*) Hydrogen – Oxygen fuel cell.

(*b-ii*) Ammonia – Oxygen fuel cell.

(*b-iii*) Organic compounds – Oxygen fuel cell.

(*c*) High temperature

(*c-i*) Carbon monoxide – Oxygen fuel cell.

(*c-ii*) Hydrogen – Oxygen fuel cell.

(*ii*) **based on method of feeding fuel–**

(*a*) Direct fuel cell: fuel is directly fed to anode.

(*a-i*) Hydrogen – Oxygen fuel cell.

(*a-ii*) Hydrogen – Halogen fuel cell.

(*b*) Indirect fuel cell: Fuel is first converted to hydrogen or hydrogen rich gas and then fed to cell.

(*b-i*) Reformer fuel cell.

(*b-ii*) Bio-chemical fuel cell.

(*iii*) **based on regeneration–** Fuel cell product is reconverted into its reactant by following methods–

(*a*) Electrical. (*b*) Thermal.

(*c*) Chemical. (*d*) Radio -chemical. (*e*) Phyto-chemical.

(*vi*) **based on type of electrolyte used—**

(*a*) Alkaline fuel cell (AFC).

(*b*) Phosphoric acid fuel cell (PAFC).

(*c*) Molten carbonate fuel cell (MCFC).

(*d*) Solid oxide fuel cell (SOFC).

(*e*) Direct methanol fuel cell (DMFC).

(*f*) Proton exchange membrane fuel cell (PEFC).

13.5 WORKING OF VARIOUS TYPES OF FUEL CELLS

13.5.1 Phosphoric Acid Fuel Cell (PAFC)

In this fuel cell, Phosphoric acid is used as electrolye. This is commercially successful first generation fuel cell. Anode consists of a porous graphite with platinum or platinum alloy as catalyst. Cathode is similar to anode with noble metal catalyst. Anode current collector ribs conduct electrons from anode separator plate. The space between the ribs provide path for hydrogen gas distribution to anode. Cathode current colletor rib is similar to anode current collector rib with noble metal catalyst. Separation between anode current collector ribs and cathode current collector ribs is provided by graphite or carbon separator to prevent short circuit.

A variety of fuel can be used such a direct coal, hydrogen, indirect methanol, indirect hydrocarbon etc. The fuel gas is passed through a passage between anode and separator/anode ribs The oxidizer or air is passed between cathode and the separator/cathode rib. The operating temperature range is 150° to 220°C. At higher temperature, materials, such as carbon, platinum etc. have low stability while at low temperature electrolyte (phosphoric acid) has poor conductivity. Efficiency range is 37–42%.

13.5.2 Molten Carbonate Fuel Cell (MCFC)

This type of fuel cell uses electrolyte consisting of alkali metal molten carbonate salt mixture suspended in a porus chemically inert ceramic lithium aluminium oxide ($LiAlO_2$) matrix. The operating temperature is between 600°–700°C. Conduction in the electrolyte is by carbonate ions. Nickel and Nickel oxide are used as catalyst .The efficiency range is 40–50%.

The cathode and anode reactions are following—

Cathode: $\frac{1}{2}O_2 + CO_2 + 2e^- \rightarrow CO_3^{-2}$ ...(13.4)

Anode: $CO_3^{-2} + H_2 \rightarrow H_2O + CO_2 + 2e^-$ ...(13.5)

Overall reaction: $H_2 + \frac{1}{2}O_2 \rightarrow H_2O$ ...(13.6)

Disadvantages—

(*i*) carbonates are corrosive.

(*ii*) high temperature is needed to keep electrolyte carbonate in liquid form.

(*iii*) it requires recycling of carbon dioxide from anode zone to cathode zone.

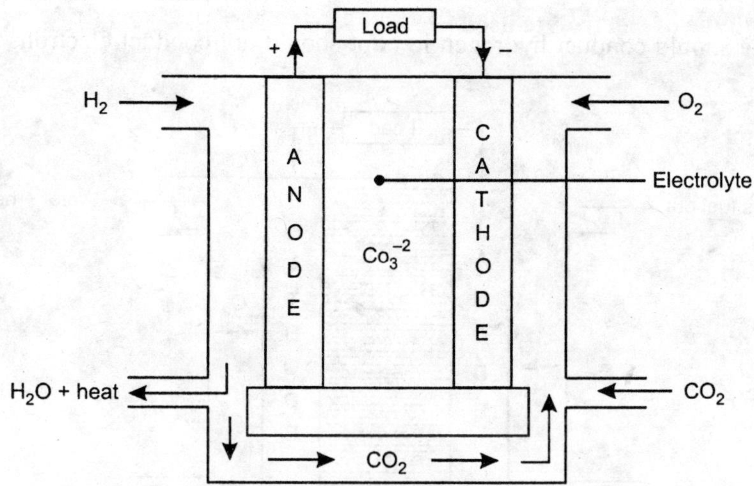

Fig. 13.2 Molten carbonate fuel cell (MCFC)

13.5.3 Solid Oxide Fuel Cell (SOFC)

This type of fuel cell uses non porous metal oxide electrolyte. Ionic conduction takes place by migration of oxide ions through crystal lattice. The material of electrolyte is known as Yittria stabilized Zirconia (a ceramic material) .The operating temperature range is 800°C to 1000°C. Typical efficiency is 60%.

The negatively charged oxygen ions travel from cathode to anode. Oxygen ions travel through the electrolyte to react with hydrogen gas at anode. The reactions at cathode and anode are given below—

Anode: $2H_2 + 2O^{-2} \rightarrow 2H_2O + 4e^-$ ...(13.7)

Cathode: $O_2 + 4e^- \rightarrow 2O^{-2}$ ...(13.8)

Overall reaction: $2H_2 + O_2 \rightarrow 2H_2O$ ...(13.9)

Any fuel e.g. methane, propane, butane etc. first need to be converted into hydrogen by internal reforming.

Disadvantages—

(*i*) slow start up time rendering it unfit for mobile application .

(*ii*) gradual buildup of carbon dust on anode slow down reforming process.

13.5.4 Proton Exchange Membrane Cell (PEMC)

This type of cell uses proton conducing polymer membrane as electrolyte (a solid electrolyte). The operating temperature range is 80° to 120°C. A stream of hydrogen is delivered at anode. This hydrogen is split into protons and electrons by platinum catalyst .The cell reactions are give below—

Anode: $H_2 \rightarrow 2H^+ + 2e^-$ ...(13.10)

Cathode: $\frac{1}{2}O_2 + 2H^+ + 2^-e \rightarrow H_2O$ ...(13.11)

Overall reaction: $H_2 + \frac{1}{2}O_2 \rightarrow H_2O$ ...(13.12)

The membrane should conduct hydrogen ion but should not conduct electrons as it will result in short circuit.

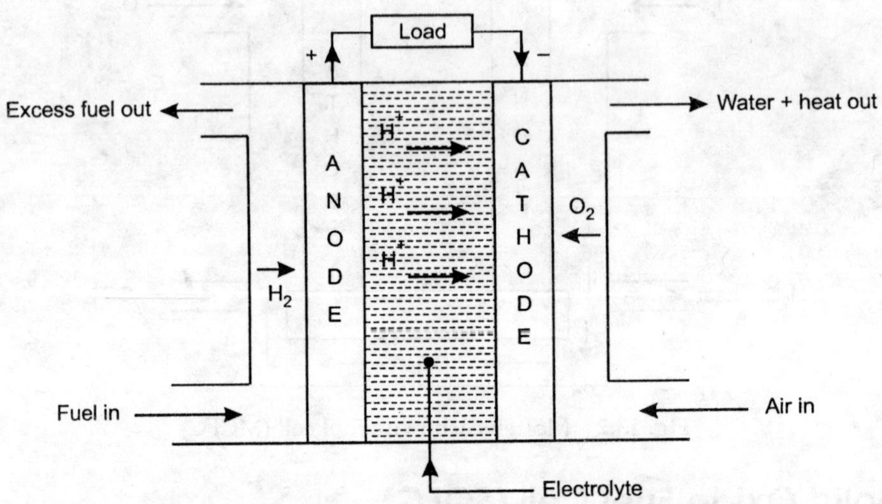

Fig. 13.3 Proton exchange membrane fuel cell (PEMFC)

13.5.5 Direct Methanol Fuel Cell (DMFC)

This fuel cell uses methanol (CH_3 OH)as fuel. Although this type of fuel cell can be used in portable and mobile application but it suffers from poor efficiency and low power density.

Methanol reacts with water and generates carbon dioxide and hydrogen ions at anode. Hydrogen ions are conducted through electrolyte and react with oxygen at cathode and produce water.

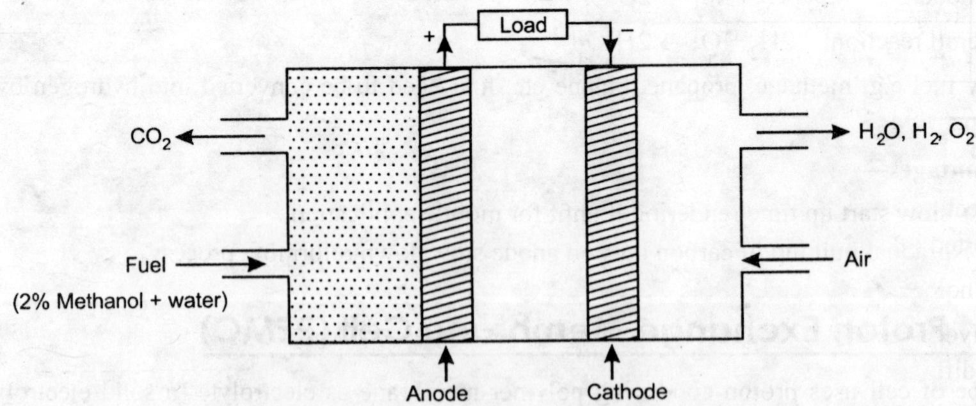

Fig. 13.4 Direct methanol fuel cell (DMFC)

At Anode: $CH_3\,OH + H_2O \rightarrow CO_2 + 6H^+ + 6e^-$ ...(13.13)

At Cathode: $\frac{3}{2}O_2 + 6H^+ + 6e^- \rightarrow 3H_2O$ ...(13.14)

Overall reaction: $CH_3OH + H_2O + \frac{3}{2}\,O_2 \rightarrow CO_2 + 3H_2O$ ...(13.15)

Voltage of cell is 0.4 to 0.6 V. The maximum power density varies 20–50 mw/m^2.

13.5.6 Alkaline Fuel Cell (AFC)

Alkaline fuel cell contains solution of potassium hydroxide as electrolyte. It can use wide range of metals as catalyst at anode and cathode. The operating temperature range is between 100° to 250°C. The maximum possible efficiency attained till date is 60%.

These cell are easily affected by CO_2 in air. Moreover, these are expensive.

Table 13.1 Comparison of various types of fuel cells

Sr. No.	*Types of Fuel cell*	*Electrolyte*	*Operating temperature range (°C)*	*Efficiency (%)*	*Applications*
1.	Phosphoric acid fuel cell (PAFC)	Phosphoric acid	150–200	45–50	–power generation in distributed mode.
2.	Molten carbonate fuel cell (MCFC)	Solution of lithium sodium and/ or potassium	600–700	45–50	–power generation in distributed mode.
3.	Solid oxide fuel cell (SOFC)	Yittria stabilized Zirconia	700–1000	60%	–power generation in distributed mode.
4.	Proton exchange membrane fuel cell (PEMFC)	Polymer membrane	80–120	35%	–portable power –transportation –backup power
5.	Alkaline fuel cell (AFC)	Aqueous solution of potassium hydroxide	90–100	60%	–space application –military application

13.6 FUELS USED IN FUEL CELLS

In direct type fuel cells, fuel is directly fed into the cell. But in indirect types fuel cells, fuel need to be converted into an intermediate form before it can be fed to the cell.

Choice of a particular fuel is dependent upon cost, availability, transportability, reactivity etc.

Hydrogen fuel is costlier and highly reactive. Other fuels called compromise fuels are cheaper but more difficult to oxidize and require expensive catalyst at high temperature.

Table 13.1 Hydrocarbons and compromise fuels

Hydrocarbon fuels	Methane, Ethane, Propane, Butane, Ethylene, Acetylene, Propylene, Pentane, Hexane, Octane, Nonane, Decane, Benzene, Toulene, Kerosene.
Compromise fuels	Hydrazine, Ammonia, Methanol.

Ammonia is readily available and easier to handle but has low reactivity. Hydrazine is highly reactive, does not require expensive catalyst but more expensive than hydrogen. Methanol has comparable cost to that of hydrogen and is readily available and undergoes direct electro-chemical reaction at electrode.

13.7 ELECTRODES USED FOR FUEL CELLS

Generally porous electrodes are used due to higher current density compared to smooth electrodes. For low temperature applications, a composite structure consisting of platinum catalyst on surface with carbon black and PTFE (polytetra-fiuoro ethylene) is used as binder. Carbon black provides higher surface conductivity.

MCFC type uses ceramic electrolyte matrix of Li AlO_2. In SOFC type, solid polymer membrane is used.

13.8 PERFORMANCE CHARACTERISTICS OF FUEL CELLS

Performance of fuel cell is judged by following parameters—

(*i*) voltage versus current density characteristics.

(*ii*) power developed per cell.

(*iii*) cell efficiency.

(*i*) Voltage versus current density characteristics: Voltage of cell decreases with increase in current density due to polarisation effect. Polarisation is internal chemical,thermal and electrical effect causing energy loss. It is measured in terms of polarisation voltage (V_p).

$$\Delta V_p = V_{no} - V_{fl} \quad ..(13.16)$$

Where ΔV_p = voltage drop due to polarisation.

V_{no} = voltage of cell at no load.

V_{fl} = voltage of cell at full load.

The polarisation curve or voltage-current density curve is shown in figure 13.5.

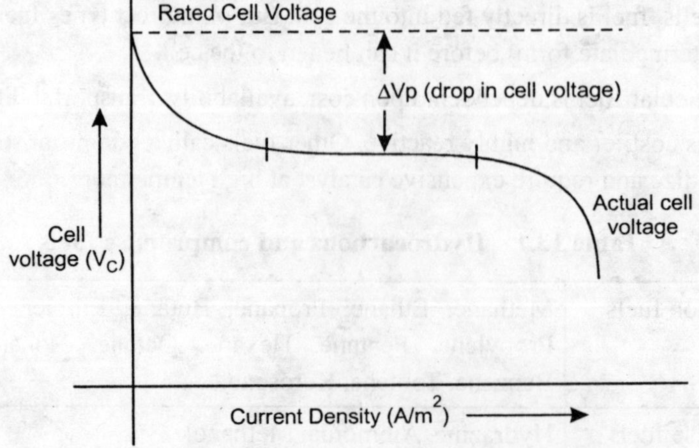

Fig. 13.5 Voltage-Current density characteristics

As shown in figure 13.5, with increase in load (indicated by increase in current density), the cell voltage drops due to higher polarisation effect.

(*ii*) Power Developed per cell: Power developed in a cell is a product of cell current and cell voltage.

$$P_c = V_c \times I_c \qquad ...(13.17)$$

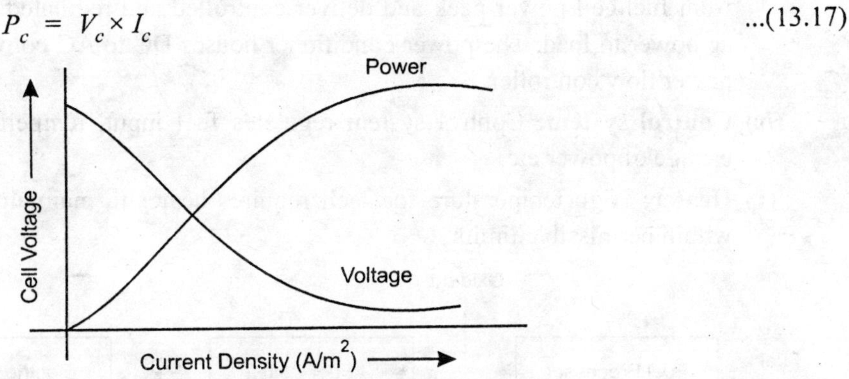

Fig. 13.6 Power-current density characteristics

As shown in figure 13.6, power output of cell increases with increase in current density. But, due to polarisation effect, power flow reaches a saturation level.

(*iii*) Cell Efficiency: Efficiency of fuel cell is given by following expression—

$$\text{Efficiency} \qquad (\eta) = \frac{\text{Cell voltage at full load}}{\text{Cell voltage at no load}}$$

Fig. 13.7 Efficiency curve of fuel cell

Efficiency of cell decreases with increase in load and reaches a saturation value and thereafter it starts decreasing. At this stage, loss increases and appears as heat.

13.9 FUEL CELL POWER PLANT

A fuel cell power plant consists of following sections—

(*i*) Fuel processor: This section receives, purifies and stores the fuel to be fed to the fuel cell. Depending upon the type of fuel, method and steps of processing changes. For example, hydrogen is simply stored and directly fed to the cell. In case of natural gas, it is first desulphurised i.e. sulphur content from gas is removed. The gas is then converted to H_2 and CO in a steam reforming reactor. Liquid fuels, such as naphtha, diesel, heavy fuel oil etc. are converted to H_2 in partial oxidation reformers.

(*ii*) **Fuel cell power pack:** Fuel from fuel processor alongwith air or oxidant is fed to fuel cell power pack. It delivers DC power at low voltage. A variety of fuel cells are used to produce power which are described in the previous sections.

(*iii*) **Electric power conditioner:** Purpose of electric power conditioner is to receive dc power from fuel cell power pack and deliver controlled and regulated three phase or single phase ac power to load. The power conditioner houses DC to AC converter, voltage regulator and power flow controller.

(*iv*) **Control system:** Control system regulates fuel input, temperature of electrolyte, rate of change of power etc.

(*v*) **Heater:** High temperature fuel cell requires heater to maintain temperature of electrolyte within permissible limits.

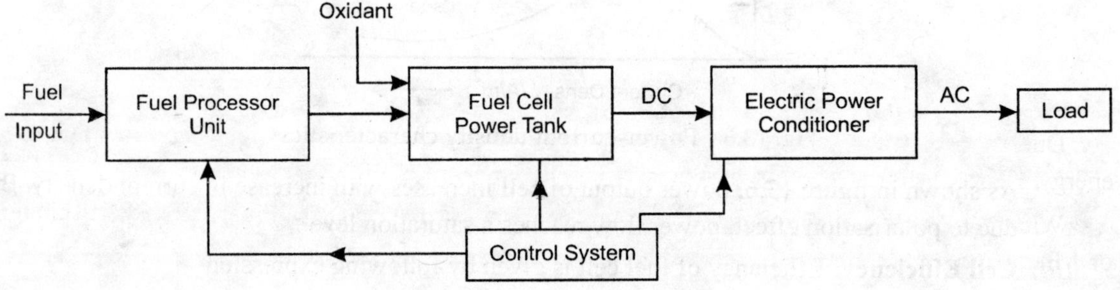

Fig. 13.8 Fuel cell power plant

13.10 LOSSES IN FUEL CELL

The energy conversion from chemical energy to electrical energy results in some losses. Following are various losses taking place in a fuel cell—

(*i*) **Active polarisation losses:** These losses are due to energy lost in breaking ions from electrodes where these are formed. The energy is consumed to overcome the potential barrier of fuel and oxygen ions. These losses are proportional to rate of electro-chemical reaction. These are influenced by temperature and pressure of reactants and fuel cell design.

(*ii*) **Ohmic polarisation losses:** These losses are due to resistance offered to flow of ions in the electrolyte solution and electrons in electrodes. These losses are equal to product of cell current and cell resistance. These losses are influenced by conductivity of electrolyte and distance between the electrodes.

(*iii*) **Concentration polarisation losses:** As the electrochemical reaction proceeds in a cell, there is a drop in initial concentration of electrolyte. This results in drop in potential at the electrodes. This loss in influenced by rate of diffusion and load. Higher the load or slower the rate of diffusion, higher is the drop.

13.11 PERFORMANCE ANALYSIS OF FUEL CELL

In a fuel cell, oxidation and reduction reaction takes place. As a result of this, electrode potential develops. The cell potential E^0 is the difference of cathode potential E^0_C and anode potential E^0_a.

$\therefore$ Cell potential $E^0 = E^0_c - E^0_a$ ...(13.18)

In a fuel cell, potential is always positive while in a electro-chemical cell, it is negative.

During a reaction in a fuel cell, the change in Gibbs free energy is given by (called Gibbs – Helmholtz equation).

$$\Delta G = \Delta H - T\,\Delta S \qquad ...(13.19)$$

Where, ΔG = change in Gibbs free energy.

ΔH = enthalpy change in reaction(KJ/mole).

$$\Delta H = \Sigma\,\Delta H_g - \Sigma\,\Delta H_p \qquad ...(13.20)$$

$\Sigma\,\Delta H_g$ = enthalpy of formation of reactants (KJ/mole).

$\Sigma\,\Delta H_p$ = enthalpy of formation of products (KJ/mole).

$T\Delta S$ = thermal losses of energy (KJ/mole).

Due to irreversible thermal losses taking plane in a cell, all the energy is not converted into electrical energy. Hence, electrical energy produced is less than change in Gibbs free energy (ΔG).

When 1 kg mole of electron passes through a circuit then the energy is equal to 9.65×10^7 Coulombs or 1 Faraday. The electric energy of cell is then given by—

$$E = \eta\, FE_g \qquad ...(13.21)$$

Where, E = electric energy produced.

E_g = internal cell voltage.

η = moles of electrons released during cell reaction.

The ideal conversion efficiency of cell is defined as ratio of change in free energy to heat generated due to reaction .

$$\therefore \quad \eta_{max} = \frac{E_{max}}{\Delta H} = 1 - \frac{T\Delta S}{\Delta H} = 1 - \frac{\text{Heat rejected}}{\text{Enthalpy change}}$$

Actual conversion efficiency, $\eta = \dfrac{\eta.F.V_L}{\Delta H}$ ...(13.22)

Where, V_L = output voltage of cell.

Power output of fuel cell, $P = \dfrac{\Delta G.m}{M}$ ...(13.23)

Where, M = molar mass of hydrogen = 2.016 kg/mole

m = mass flow rate of hydrogen (kg/s)

13.12 APPLICATIONS OF FUEL CELL

A fuel cell has low voltage (0.3 to 1.23 V DC) and low current (100 – 400 mA/cm^2 of electrode surface). However, by connecting several cells in series and parallel, the required power rating can be obtained. The range of power ratings are 1.5 KW to 10 MW.

Various potential applications are following—

(*i*) **As source of power in remote locations:** These may be weather stations, military applications, off-shore drilling rigs, remote signalling systems etc.

(*ii*) **Emergency power source:** These include hospitals, civil defence installations, radio and T.V. services, infiltration detection systems installed at border etc.

(*iii*) **Source of portable of power:** These include emergency communication systems used during disasters, for search and rescue operations, lighting etc.

(*iv*) **Propulsion applications:** Such as urban automobiles, forklift trucks, underwater rescue operation, boats, mass transit vehicules etc.

(*v*) **Source of base load power:** Power generating stations for centralised utilities as well as for industrial and commercial applications.

13.13 MHD POWER GENERATION

MHD or **Magneto Hydro Dynamics** deals with flow of electrically conducting fluid in a magnetic field. It is a method of conversion of thermal energy into electrical energy directly. It requires a strong magnetic of 5 to 6 T and flow of ionized fluid at high temperature (2500 K). MHD plant uses gasified coal as a fuel and has efficiency of 40 to 55% as compared to 30 to 40% of conventional coal fired plants. However, plant causes higher level of pollution due to generation of NO_x and SO_x. This can be used as a topping unit i.e. after generation of power using MHD generator, the high temperature gases can be used to produce power in a steam power plant.

13.13.1 Principle of Operation of MHD Generator

An MHD generator consists of a duct through which a hot ionized gases are made to flow. A strong magnetic field is applied at right angle to the direction of motion of flow. The hot electrically conducting gas is expanded in a divergent duct. If magnetic field is applied at right angle to the flow of ionized gases, emf is produced at right angle to the magnetic filed. The emf produced is DC.

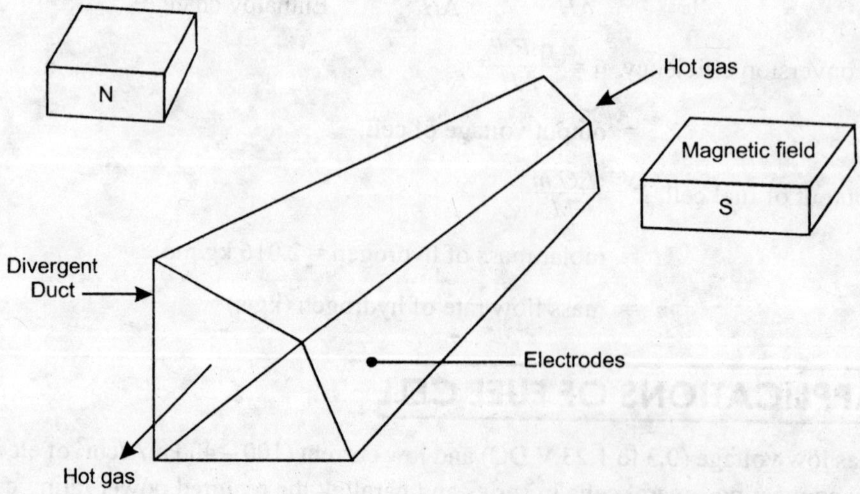

Fig. 13.9 MHD generator

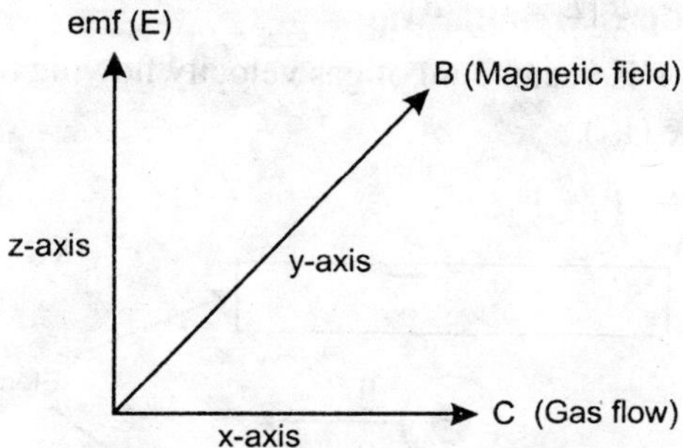

Fig. 13.10 Emf, field and current in a MHD generator

If the direction of flow of gas is along x-axis, then direction of applied magnetic filed is at right angle to flow of gas along y-axis. The induced emf generated due to interaction of conducting gas with magnetic filed is along z-axis. The current flow is from lower electrode through the gas to the upper electrode and external load.

Emf is induced in transverse as well as in the direction of fluid flow. Transverse emf is produced due to Faraday's law. While axial emf is due to Hall effect. In order to increase electrical conductivity of ionized gas, a small quantity of $K_2 CO_3$ or Cesium or KO H is added as seed material (ionizing agent).

13.13.2 Advantages and Disadvantages of MHD Generation

Following are the **advantages** of MHD generation—

(*i*) direct conversion of heat into electricity with higher efficiency (50%) which is more than conventional power plants.

(*ii*) can be loaded quickly.

(*iii*) better utilization of fossil fuels.

(*iv*) no hot, stressed and moving parts therefore no maintenance.

(*v*) suitable for generation of large power.

(*vi*) no noise and vibration.

(*vii*) can use all kinds of heat sources, such as coal, oil, gas, solar, nuclear etc.

(*viii*) simple construction of generator.

(*ix*) generator has low specific weight and high power density.

Disadvantages—

(*i*) high frictional and heat transfer losses.

(*ii*) it operates at high temperature.

(*iii*) requires large expensive magnets.

(*iv*) if coal is used as fuel, molten ash may short circuit electrodes.

13.13.3 Expression for Power Generated by MHD Generator

Consider an ionized gas particle of charge q is moving with a velocity V in perpendicular magnetic field with flux density B and electric field E. Force acting on the charged particle is given by—

$$F = q\,[E + V \times B] \qquad ...(13.24)$$

Velocity of ionized particle V is vector sum of gas velocity flowing between two electrodes (V_1) and drift velocity of charged particle (V_2).

$$\therefore \quad V = V_1 + V_2 \qquad ...(13.25)$$

Fig. 13.11 Charged particle moving between two electrodes

Therefore,
$$F = q\,[E + V_1 \times B + V_2 \times B] \qquad ...(13.26)$$

Let
$$E' = V_1 \times B + V_2 \times B$$

$$\therefore \quad F = q\,[E + E'] \qquad ...(13.27)$$

If gas is moving in x-axis, magnetic field in y-axis, then the force acting on the particle is in z-axis. If two electrodes are connected through a resistance, electric current flows. The electric intensity between the electrodes is given by—

$$E_z = \frac{-V}{d} \qquad ...(13.28)$$

Where, V = Voltage across load resistance.

d = distance between two electrodes.

Total electric filed,
$$E'_z = E_z + BV \qquad ...(13.29)$$

Or
$$E'_z = \frac{-V}{d} + \text{BV} \Rightarrow E'_z = \frac{BVd - V}{d} \qquad ...(13.30)$$

Magnetic field B and electric field E_z produce same force as magnetic field B and electric field E'_z with zero average velocity.

$\therefore$ Open circuit voltage, $V_o = BVd$

If the internal resistance of the generator is R_g, then maximum output power is obtained when $R_g = R_L$ where R_L is external load resistance.

$$\therefore \quad P = V_o I = (IR_g)\, I$$

$$P = I^2 R_g \qquad ...(13.31)$$

But
$$I = \frac{V_o}{R_g + R_L}$$

$$\therefore \quad P = \left(\frac{V_o}{R_g + R_L}\right)^2 R_g \qquad ...(13.32)$$

For maximum power output, $R_g = R_L$

$$\therefore \quad P_{max} = \frac{V_o^2}{4 R_g}$$

Internal resistance of the generator, $R_g = \dfrac{d}{\sigma A}$

Where, σ = Conductivity of gas.

A = area of cross-section of electrode

$$\therefore \quad P_{max} = \frac{B^2 V_o^2 \sigma\, da}{4} \quad (\because V = Bvd) \qquad \text{...(13.33)}$$

$$\text{Maximum power per unit volume (d.A)} = \frac{B^2 V_o^2 \sigma}{4} \qquad \text{...(13.34)}$$

Since $V_o = BVd$

$$\therefore \quad P_{max} = \frac{B^2 V^2 d^2}{4R_g} \qquad \text{...(13.35)}$$

13.13.4 Open Cycle MHD Power Plant

In open cycle MHD power plant, the hot gases are discharged to atmosphere.

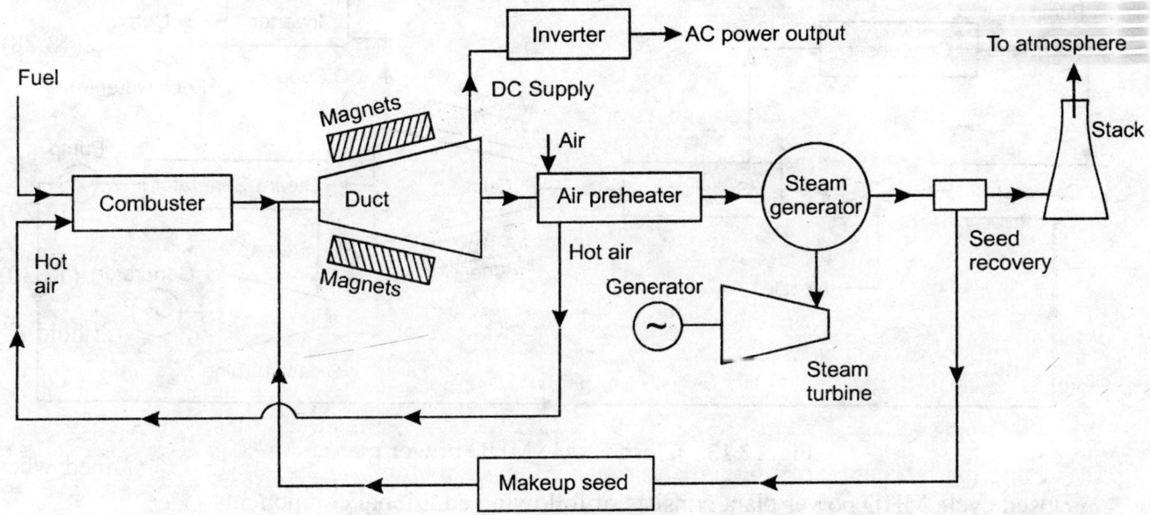

Fig. 13.12 Open cycle MHD power plant

MHD power plant consists of following components—

(i) **Duct:** Hot ionized gases pass through a convergent divergent duct. The gases attain supersonic velocity in divergent section of the duct. The cross-section of duct could be circular or rectangular.

(ii) **Combuster:** Combuster produces hot air by burning fuel and air. The temperature of hot gases are in the range of 2500–3000K. A seeding material or ionizing agent is also introduced

to the gas to increase electrical conductivity. The seeding materials are $K_2 CO_3$, KOH or ceasium. The fuels used are natural gas, gasified coal and coal.

(*iii*) **Electromagnetic field coils:** Field coils are used to produce strong magnetic field (5 to 6 Tesla) at right angle to the direction of hot gas flow. DC supply for field coils is obtained from rectifier set. Generally, super conducting magnets are used .

(*iv*) **Air heater:** Purpose of air heater is to heat air before feeding to the combustor. This increases efficiency of combustion.

(*v*) **Seed recovery:** Since the seed material is expensive, hence it is necessary to recover it before gases are discharged to atmosphere.

(*vi*) **Electrodes:** Segmented electrodes are provided in the direction of electric field but at right angle to magnetic field. The electrodes collect DC power produced.

(*vii*) **Inverter:** It converts DC supply at the electrodes to 3 phase AC supply for feeding to load.

In order to utilise temperature of hot gases,a steam generator is used to produce steam. This steam is used to generate power through a turbine-generator set. Purpose is to improve cycle efficiency by extracting heat from gases before being exhausted to atmosphere.

13.13.5 Closed Cycle MHD Power Plant

In closed cycle MHD power plant,the hot gases are recirculated and not discharged to atmosphere.

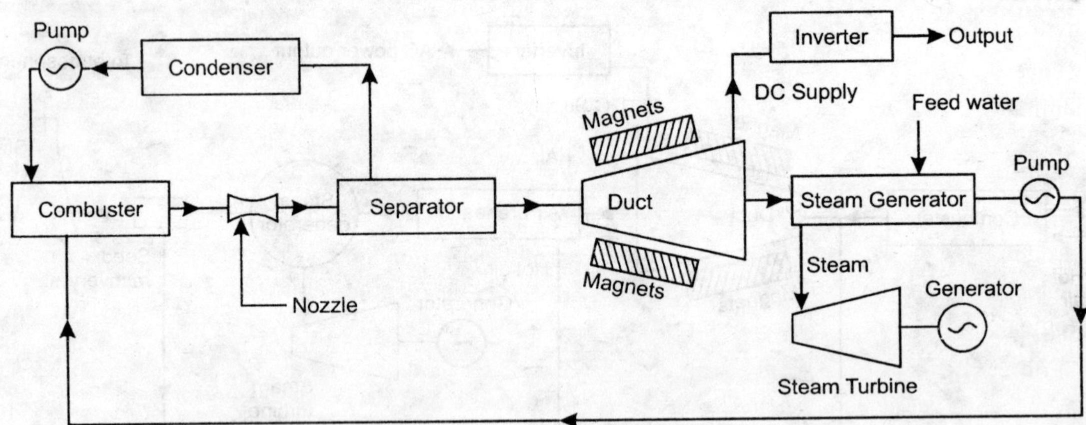

Fig. 13.13 Closed cycle MHD power plant

A closed cycle MHD power plant consists of following additional components–

(*i*) **Nozzle:** It is used to increase the velocity of hot gases.

(*ii*) **Condenser:** Vapour formed due to nozzle is separated and condensesd in a condenser and fed back to combustor.

After raising steam in a steam generator, the gases are sent back to combuster thereby completing a closed loop.

13.13.6 Losses in MHD Generator

The various losses taking place in MHD generator are following—

(*i*) **Friction and heat transfer losses:** The fluid flowing through a MHD generator has high velocity with high turbulence. This turbulence increases frictional loss in fluid flow which also results in heat losses.

(*ii*) **Eddy current losses:** Eddy current losses take place in the duct section due to rapid variation of velocity of gases, magnetic field and electric field. These losses can be minimized by streamlining the gas flow through installation of guide vanes at inlet and exit points.

(*iii*) **Hall effect loss:** Lorentz force which is due to original electric field and generated field of current, causes a drift force to be applied on charged ion. The force causes the electrons to move in circular arc resulting in very large current on collecting electrode. This produces more ohmic losses thereby lowering the plant efficiency.

(*iv*) **Electrode loss:** Cool electrode causes increase in resistivity of fluid resulting in high voltage drop across the gas film.

13.14 HYDROGEN BASED POWER GENERATION

Hydrogen is considered energy source of the future. It releases good amount of energy upon combustion. 2 kmol of hydrogen when burnt with 1 kmol of oxygen releases 241.8 MJ of energy. The calorific value of hydrogen is 1,41,790 kJ/kg, one of the highest amongst all fuels.

One of the major applications of hydrogen is in transportation sector. However, it is highly inflammable.

13.14.1 Methods of Production of Hydrogen

Hydrogen can be produced by using a wide variety of fuels available, such as natural gas, oil, coal, biomass etc. The processes used for generation of hydrogen could be photovoltaic, chemical, biological, thermo chemical, electrolytic etc.

Following are various methods of generation of hydrogen—

13.14.1.1 Steam Reforming

This method uses methane and water vapour to produce hydrogen. The process is endothermic i.e. requires heat.

$$CH_4 + H_2O + \text{Heat} \rightarrow CO + 3H_2 \quad ...(13.36)$$

The reaction takes place at 700°–850°C and at a pressure of 3–25 bar.

Carbon mono oxide can be further converted into CO_2.

$$CO + H_2O \rightarrow CO_2 + H_2 + \text{Heat} \quad ...(13.37)$$

Hydrogen can also be produced by another process. When steam is passed over hot sponge iron at 550°C to 800°C, hydrogen is produced.

$$\underset{\text{(Spong iron)}}{3Fe} + \underset{\text{(steam)}}{3H_2O} \rightarrow Fe_2O_3 + 3H_2 \quad ...(13.38)$$

Another method of producing hydrogen is by using coal.

$$\underset{\text{(coal)}}{C} + H_2O + \text{heat} \rightarrow CO + H_2 \quad ...(13.39)$$

$$CO + H_2O \rightarrow CO_2 + H_2 + \text{heat} \quad ...(13.40)$$

13.14.1.2 Electrolysis of Water

Hydrogen can be produced by electrolysis of water.

$$H_2O \xrightarrow{\text{Electricity}} H_2 + \frac{1}{2} O_2 - 2.87 \text{ MJ/kg} \quad ...(13.41)$$

13.14.1.3 Polymer Electrolyte Membrane Electrolysis

This method uses acidic polymer membrane.

Anode: $$H_2O \rightarrow \frac{1}{2} O_2 + 2H^+ + 2e^- \quad ...(13.42)$$

Cathode: $$2H^+ + 2e \rightarrow H_2 \quad ...(13.43)$$

The advantage of this method is suitability for stationary as well as mobile applications due to absence of liquid electrolyte, compact design, higher operating pressure and good part load efficiency. Disadvantage is high cost , poor efficiency and short life of membrane.

13.14.1.4 Hydrogen from biomass

In this method, biomass is converted into producer gas ($CO + H_2$) using biomass gassifier.

Gassification and pyrolysis are two commercially successful methods of hydrogen production.

13.14.1.5 Thermo Chemical Method of Hydrogen Production

The overall efficiency for conversion for primary energy from fossil and nuclear fuels into hydrogen by electrolysis is dependent on the net efficiency of generation of electricity. The overall efficiency of hydrogen production would be only 20 to 30%. Higher conversion efficiency might be possible if the heat produced by the primary fuel could be used directly to decompose water, without the intermediary of electrical energy. A sequential chemical reaction series can be devised in which hydrogen and oxygen are produced, water is consumed and all other chemical intermediates are recycled. Such operation is called thermo-chemical cycle. A reaction sequence as follows—

$$2\,Cr\,Cl_2 + 2HCl \rightarrow 2Cr\,Cl_3 + H_2 \quad (325°C) \quad ...(13.44)$$

$$2Cr\,Cl_3 \rightarrow 2Cr\,Cl_2 + Cl_2 \quad (875°C) \quad ...(13.45)$$

$$H_2O + Cl_2 \rightarrow 2HCl + \frac{1}{2} O_2 \quad (850°C) \quad ...(13.46)$$

In above reactions, only water is split, all other chemicals are completely recycled.

13.14.1.6 Solar Energy Methods

There are two such approaches—

(*i*) Bio photolysis.

(*ii*) Photo electrolysis.

(*i*) **Bio photolysis:** This method uses living systems or materials derived from such systems to split water into hydrogen and oxygen. In normal photosynthesis process in green plants, the green pigment chlorophyll absorbs energy from sunlight and in a series of complex reactions breaks up water molecules into oxygen gas, hydrogen ions and electrons. Oxygen is evolved from the green plant but hydrogen ions and electrons are removed by interaction with carbon dioxide to produce sugars.

Certain single cell green algae can make enzyme called hydrogenase. These algae can eliminate carbon dioxide thereby circumventing second stage of photosynthesis. The hydrogen ions and electrons then combine in the presence of hydrogenase to produce hydrogen gas.

Chloroplast (small bodies containing chlorophyll in green plants) retain their photosynthetic activity when extracted from plant. Hydrogen and oxygen then can be obtained from water by exposing chloroplast to sunlight together with hydrogenase and ferredoxin (an electron carrier of biological origin).

(*ii*) **Photo electrolysis:** In normal electrolysis, water is decomposed into oxygen and hydrogen by passing an electric current from external source. In photo electrolysis, one or both electrodes are exposed to sunlight to produce electric current. Oxygen and hydrogen gases are liberated at respective electrodes due to decomposition of water. Atleast, one of the electrodes in photo electrolysis is a semi conductor.

The solar electricity needed for electrolysis can be produced either photo electrically or thermo chemically .Both these technologies are available today.

13.14.2 Hydrogen Storage

In energy system, there is a need to store energy before utilisation. The location of energy storage should be close to the point of usage. Hydrogen can be stored. Following are the various schemes of hydrogen storage—

(*i*) compressed gas storage.

(*ii*) liquid storage (cryogenic storage in insulated tanks).

(*iii*) line pack system (allowing pressure in the distribution system to vary).

(*iv*) underground storage (in depleted oil and gas fields).

(*v*) storage as metal hydride.

(*i*) **Compressed gas storage:** Hydrogen can be easily stored in high pressure cylinders for variety of applications. However, this method of storage is expensive and bulky.

(*ii*) **Liquid storage:** Liquefied hydrogen is stored in vacuum insulated or super insulated storage tanks at cryogenic temperatures (below –150°C).

(*iii*) **Line pack system:** This system is used in natural gas industry but provides small storage capacity .However, it can respond quickly to demand variation.

(*iv*) **Underground storage:** It is cheap method of storage. Hydrogen can be stored in depleted oil and gas reservoirs, underground aquifiers etc.

(*v*) **Metal hydrides:** A number of metals and alloy react with hydrogen and form solid compounds called metal hydride. When hydride is heated, hydrogen gas is liberated and original metal or alloy is recovered for further use. An important feature of this type of storage system is that the pressure of gas release is dependent upon the temperature of heat source and gas pressure remains practically constant until it is exhausted.

13.14.3 Hydrogen Transportation

It is possible to transport hydrogen through pipelines similar to natural gas pipeline. However, energy required to compress hydrogen is more than that required for natural gas (because of density difference).

Another method of bulk transport of hydrogen is as liquid. Usually, double walled insulated tanks can be store liquid hydrogen and can be transported by road vehicles.

Yet another method of transport is as solid metal hydride. However, the weight of hydrogen relative to hydride is much less.

13.14.4 Utilization of Hydrogen Gas

Hydrogen can be used for numerous applications, such as—

(*i*) for residential use (cooking, heating,electricity generation etc).

(*ii*) for industrial use (heating, in chemical reactions, electricity generation etc)

(*iii*) an alternative transport fuel (hydrogen gas driven vehicles).

(*iv*) an alternative fuel for aircraft.

(*v*) for electric power generation.

(*i*) **Residential use:** Fuels cells using hydrogen gas can be used to generate electricity to operate domestic appliances. Hydrogen can also be used as cooking fuel in place of natural gas or LPG.

(*ii*) **Industrial use:** It could be used as a fuel or as a reducing agent (i.e. oxygen removal). It could be used to reduce oxide ores (e.g. iron ore to metal).

(*iii*) **Transportation use:** Hydrogen can be used in internal combustion engines of automobiles, such as buses, trucks, farm machinery etc.

(*iv*) **Aircraft use:** Liquid hydrogen could be used in aircraft as fuel. Main advantage is low weight of hydrogen. However, volume of hydrogen would be greater than regular fuel (aviation turbine fuel).

(*v*) **Electric power generation:** Hydrogen can be used in fuel cells to produce electricity. Chemical combination of oxygen and hydrogen produces water and electricity. The electrodes act as catalyst due to different potentials during the reaction. This potential difference of electrodes causes electric current to flow in the external circuit. The water produced due to reaction is extracted by evaporation.

13.14.5 Safety Measures

Hydrogen is highly inflammable gas and hence, need to be handled with care. However, precaution in handling,storage and usage can avoid danger of fire or explosion. In a closed space, a minor leakage could be a cause of explosion or fire as hydrogen leaks three times faster than natural gas.

Liquid hydrogen presents another safety issue. The low temperature of liquid hydrogen cause surrounding air to liquify thereby forming an oxygen rich mixture which is a greater fire and explosion hazard.

Usually, hydrogen leaks from flanges and valves. While filling hydrogen in liquid form,it is necessary to purge the vessel of any remnant hydrogen gas. Hydrogen and oxygen must be kept separate in a electrolysis cell and in the gas collection system. It is preferable to store hydrogens in open space so that any minor leakage of gas is quickly dispersed in the surroundings.

13.15 OPERATING FUEL CELL AND MHD POWER PLANTS IN THE WORLD

(i) **Fuel cell power plant:** A demonstration fuel cell power plant of 2 MW capacity was commissioned in 1990. The fuel cell was molten carbonate type. Toshiba Electric Company, Japan has installed 11 MW GOI power station. Fuel cell was based on phosphoric acid. Westinhouse Electric Corporation, USA has installed a high temperature solid oxide fuel cell plant of 600 to 1200 kW capacity range.

Largest fuel cell based power plant, Gyeonggi Green Energy Facility (hydrogen based fuel cell) of 59 MW capacity has been commissioned in Hwasung city, South Korea in 2015.

(ii) **MHD power plant:** A demonstration MHD power plant of 25 MW capacity was commissioned in erstwhile USSR in 1970. The plant was able to produce and feed electricity to Moscow grid successfully.

Indian research programme in MHD power generation was started in 1977. Bhabha Atomic Research Centre (BARC), Bharat Heavy Electrical Ltd (BHEL) and Institute of High Temperature (Russia) Collaborated to develop 5MW MHD power plant. It was installed in march 1985 at Tiruchirapally, Tamil Nadu. It was open cycle plant with field magnet of 2 Tesla having ceramic lined water cooled combustor which can withstand temperature of 2500°C. Experimental run was carried out successfully in August 1985.

SOLVED EXAMPLES

Ex 13.1 An MHD generator with plate area of 0.2 m^2 and flux density of 2 wb/m^2 has average gas velocity of 800 m/s conductivity as 10 mho/m. The distance between the plates is 0.4 m. Calculate the open circuit voltage and maximum power output.

Solution:

Given, $A = 0.2\ m^2$, $B = 2 wb/m^2$

$V = 800$ m/s, $\sigma = 10$ mho/m

$d = 0.4$ m

Open circuit voltage, $V_o = B\,Vd$

$$= 2 \times 800 \times 0.4 = \mathbf{640\ V} \quad \textbf{Ans.}$$

Resistance of generator,

$$R_g = \frac{d}{\sigma A} = \frac{0.4}{10 \times 0.2} = 0.20 \text{ ohm}$$

Maximum power $\quad P_{max} = \dfrac{V_o^2}{4\,R_g} = \dfrac{(640)^2}{4 \times 0.2} = \mathbf{512W} \quad \textbf{Ans.}$

Ex 13.2 The specifications of an MHD generator are: plate area = 0.15 m^2, distance between plates = 0.5 m, flux density = 2.5 T, average gas velocity = 1.5 × 10^3m/s, gaseous conductivity = 10 mho/m. Calculate (*i*) open circuit voltage (*ii*) maximum power output.

Solution:

(*i*) Open circuit voltage

$$V_o = B\,V\,d.$$

$$= 2.5 \times 1.5 \times 10^3 \times 0.5$$

$$= \mathbf{1875\ Volts} \quad \textbf{Ans.}$$

(*ii*) Maximum power output

$$P_{max} = \frac{V_o^2}{4\,Rg}$$

$$R_g = \frac{d}{\sigma A} = \frac{0.5}{10 \times 0.15} = 0.33 \text{ Ohm}$$

$$P_{max} = \frac{(1875)^2}{4 \times 0.33} = \mathbf{266.34\ kW} \quad \textbf{Ans.}$$

Ex 13.3 Calculate the efficiency of a fuel cell having open circuit voltage of 1.23 V and cell terminal voltage 1.09 V and loading of 210 mA/cm^2.

Solution:

$$\text{Efficiency of fuel cell} = \frac{\text{Actual voltae}}{\text{Open circuit voltage}} \times 100$$

$$= \frac{1.09}{1.23} \times 100$$

$$= \mathbf{88.6\%} \quad \textbf{Ans.}$$

Ex 13.4 A hydrogen fuel operates at 298 K. Find (*i*) voltage output from cell (*ii*) efficiency (*iii*) output electrical work (*iv*) heat rejected by cell for per mole of hydrogen consumed.

Given: ΔH = –285.8 KJ/mole and ΔG = –237.14 KJ/mole.

Solution:

$$\text{Cell reaction} \rightarrow H_2 + OH^- \rightleftharpoons 2H_2O + 2e^-$$

$$\therefore \quad n = 2$$

(*i*) Cell voltage, $\quad E = \dfrac{\Delta G}{nF} = \dfrac{-273.14}{2 \times 96.5} = \mathbf{1.229\ V} \quad \textbf{Ans.}$

(*ii*) Cell efficiency $= \dfrac{\Delta G_{298k}}{\Delta H_{298K}} = \dfrac{-237.14}{-285.8} \times 100 = \mathbf{83\%}$ **Ans.**

(*iii*) output electrical work $= -\Delta G = -$ **237.148 KJ/mole of H_2/H_2O** **Ans.**

(*iv*)Heat rejected $= T\Delta S$

$$= \Delta H_{298k} - \Delta G_{298k}$$

$$= -285.8 - (-237.14)$$

$$= \mathbf{-0.485\ kJ/mole}$$ **Ans.**

CHAPTER SUMMARY

Fuel cell is an electro-chemical device used for conversion of fuels into electrical energy. These cells have high efficiency, quick start up and have no moving parts. Depending upon the fuel used, a variety of fuel cells are available.

MHD power generation deals with conversion of thermal energy into electrical energy directly in the presence of magnetic field. It consists of flow of ionized fluid at high temperature through a strong magnetic filed. It can be used either in open cycle or in closed cycle mode.

Hydrogen is fuel of next century ("hydrogen economy"). It can be used for power generation through fuel cell, as transport fuel, as fuel in furnaces for heat generation etc. It can be produced from variety of available fuels,from biomass, by electrolysis of water, by chemically, by bio photolysis and by photo electrolysis. However, due to explosive nature of hydrogen, extra care is needed for storage, transportation and usage.

FORMULAE

1. Open circuit voltage of MHD generator,

$$V = B\,Vd$$

Where, B = flux density, wb/m^2

d = distance between plates, m

V = gas velocity, m/s

2. Maximum power output of MHD generator,

$$P_{\max} = \frac{V^2}{4R_g}$$

Where, R_g = internal resistance of MHD generator, ohm

$$P_{\max} = \frac{B^2 V^2 d^2}{4\,R_g}$$

3. Electric energy of a cell,

$$E = \eta F E_g$$

Where, η = number of moles of electrons released during cell reaction.

E_g = internal cell voltage

4. Maximum cell efficiency,

$$\eta_{mas} = 1 - \frac{\text{Heat rejected}}{\text{Enthalpy change}}$$

5. Power output of fuel cell,

$$P = \frac{\Delta G.m}{M}$$

Where, M = molar mass of hydrogen,

m = mass flow rate of hydrogen,

ΔG = Gibbs free energy

REVIEW QUESTIONS

Q. 1. Differentiate between a fuel cell and a battery.

Q. 2. What are the advantages and limitation of fuel cell?

Q. 3. Discuss classification of fuel cells.

Q. 4. Explain with a neat sketch the working of phosphoric acid fuel cell (PAFC).

Q. 5. Discuss working and demerits of molten carbonate fuel cell (MCFC).

Q. 6. Draw diagram of solid oxide fuel cell (SOFC) and explain its working.

Q. 7. Discuss with a sketch operation of proton exchange membrane cell (PEMC).

Q. 8. Explain construction and working of direct methanol fuel cell (DMFC).

Q. 9. Elaborate on various fuels used in fuel cells.

Q. 10. Write a brief note on electrodes used in fuel cells

Q. 11. Discuss various performance and characteristics and of fuel cells.

Q. 12. Explain construction and working of fuel cell power plant.

Q. 13. What are the various losses that take place in a fuel cell?

Q. 14. Discuss briefly applications of fuel cell.

Q. 15. Explain the principle of MHD power generation.

Q. 16. Derive the expression for power generated by MHD generator.

Q. 17. Obtain an expression for maximum power generated in a MHD generator.

Q. 18. Explain with a diagram working of a open cycle MHD plant.

Q. 19. Explain with a neat sketch operation of closed cycle MHD plant.

Q. 20. Discuss various types of losses taking place in a MHD generator.

Q. 21. Discuss various methods of generation of hydrogen.

Q. 22. Write a brief note on (*i*) bio photolysis (*ii*) photo electrolysis

Q. 23. Explain in detail methods of hydrogen storage.

Q. 24. What are various applications of hydrogen gas?

NUMERICAL QUESTIONS

Q. 1. An MHD generator has following data—

(*i*) plate surface are = 0.25 m^2

(*ii*) flux density = 2.1 wb/m^2

(*iii*) average gas velocity = 700 m/s

(*iv*) conductivity = 10 mho/s

(*v*) distance between plates = 0.4 m

Determine voltage and maximum power output of MHD generator.

[Ans: (*i*) 588 V (*ii*) 540.23 kW]

Q. 2. Calculate the voltage output,cell efficiency and heat rejected by a hydrogen fuel cell operating at 298 K.

Given $\Delta H = -285.8$ KJ/mole, $\Delta G = -237.14$ KJ/mole.

[Ans: (*i*) 1.23 V (*ii*) 83% (*iii*) – 485 J/mole]

SHORT ANSWER TYPE QUESTIONS

Q. 1. What are the types of fuels used in solid oxide fuel cell?

Q. 2. What is the range of efficiency of phosphoric acid fuel cell?

Q. 3. What is the magnitude of voltage of single cell of a direct methanol fuel cell?

Q. 4. List compromise fuels used in fuel cell.

Q. 5. What are different electrodes used in fuel cells?

Multiple Choice Questions

Q. 1. Operating temperature range of phosphoric acid fuel cell is

(*a*) 100° to 120°C (*b*) 150° to 220°C

(*c*) 160°C (*d*) 210° to 300°C

Q. 2. Power output of a fuel cell increase with

(*a*) decrease in current density (*b*) increase in current density

(*c*) remains same. (*d*) none of these

Q. 3. With increase in load, fuel cell voltage

(*a*) increase (*b*) deceases

(*c*) remains same. (*d*) all of these

Q. 4. Cell efficiency increase with

(*a*) increase in load (*b*) decrease in load

(*c*) neither of these two (*d*) none of these

Q. 5. Power output of MHD generator is inversely proportional to

(*a*) open circuit voltage (*b*) conductivity of gas

(*c*) flux density (*d*) internal resistance of generator

Q. 6. Hydrogen can be produced from

(*a*) coal (*b*) biomass

(*c*) oil (*d*) natural gas

(*e*) all of these

Answer to MCQ

1. (*b*) **2.** (*b*) **3.** (*b*) **4.** (*b*) **5.** (*d*) **6.** (*e*)

Chapter

Thermo-Electric, Thermionic and Small Hydro Power Generation

Learning Objectives

After reading this chapter, reader will be able to

- Understand process of power generation using thermo-electric and thermionic process.
- Explore the types of materials suitable for thermo-electric and thermionic generation, their relative merits and demerits including desirable characteristics of materials.
- Understand process of power generation using small hydro power plant including classification and application of hydro turbines.
- Update on small hydro power generation in India.

14.1 INTRODUCTION

The concept of power generation based on thermo-electric effect was discovered by Thomas J. Seeback in 1821. It is based on conversion of thermal energy into electrical energy directly. The thermo-electric power generation is based on Seeback effect, Fourier effect, Peltier effect and Thomson effect. The best efficiency that can be achieved using Bi Te is 6%. Normally, the generation efficiency range from 5 to 10% and is dependent upon the type of material used.

Due to low efficiency of generation, there is no generation of power for commercial purpose. However, it is a good method of converting waste heat into useful electrical energy. These are specifically developed for space craft, military applications, under sea installations and remote sites.

The commercial application is not viable due to low power output, high cost and low conversion efficiency. Development of cheaper and superior thermo-electric materiels are expected to make it commercially viable in near future.

14.2 PRINCIPLE OF OPERATION

The conversion of thermal energy into electrical energy using dissimilar conductor material is based on Seeback effect, Peltier effect, Joul effect, Fourier and Thomson effect.

(*i*) **Seeback effect:** If two dissimilar metals are subjected to a difference in temperature at its two end, a voltage is produced. The cold side becomes negatively charged with respect to hot side. The voltage generated is called 'Seeback voltage'. The voltage so generated is dependent upon temperature difference and nature of material used.

This effect can be explained. As one side of material is heated, then free electrons move towards cooler side. The addition of heat increases the kinetic energy of electrons causing them to move towards cold side. This higher concentration of free electruns at cold junction produces an electrical charge gradient. Hence, a potential difference is established between a hot and cold junction causing an electric current to flow in the external load.

Lesser the number of free electrons in a material, more is the accumulation of electrons at the cool side. Hence, the potential difference generated is higher. Thr output of way thermo-electric material is inversely proportional to the number of free electrons in that material.

If open circuit voltage produced in thermo- electric material is V, then—

$$V = \int_{t_c}^{t_h} s\,d\,T. \qquad \text{...(14.1)}$$

Where, t_h = temperature of hot side

t_c = temperature of cold side

s = seeback co-efficient

dT = temperature difference of junctions.

(*ii*) **Peltier Effect:** At any isothermal junction of dissimilar conductors, there is absorption or release of heat due to change in heat capacity of carriers when they move from one medium to another. The absorption of heat causes current to flow in one direction while release of heat causes the current to flow in reverse direction.

The Peltier heat transferred is proportional to the current flow, I

$$\therefore \quad Q_p \propto I$$

$$\text{or} \quad Q_p = \pi I \qquad \text{...(14.2)}$$

Where π is Peltier co-efficient. The co-efficient π is function of temperature. A relationship exists between Peltier co-efficient and Seeback co-efficient and temperature.

$$\pi = sT \qquad \text{...(14.3)}$$

(*iii*) **Thomson effect:** A temperature gradient causes electrons to flow thereby producing electric current flow.

$$\frac{dQ_T}{dx} = \tau I \frac{dT}{dx} \qquad \text{...(14.4)}$$

Where $\frac{dP_T}{dx}$ is heat flow per unit time per unit length of conductor, α is Thomson coefficient, I is current and $\frac{dT}{dx}$ is temperature gradient.

Seeback, Peltier and Thomon effects are more pronounced in semiconductor materials than metals.

(iv) Joule Effect: When current passes through a resistance, a part of electrical energy is converted into heat.

$$\therefore \quad Q_J = I^2 R \quad ...(14.5)$$

(v) Fourier Effect: When two ends of a material are at two different temperature T_H and T_C ($T_H > T_C$), an amount of heat Q_{HF} enters through hot junction at T_H and amount Q_{CF} leaves the cold junctions at T_C. If the remaining portion of material is so insulated that heat can neither enter nor leave, then .

$$Q_{HF} = Q_{CF} = A\,(T_H - T_C) \quad ...(14.6)$$

Where, A is the heat conducted per unit temperature.

14.3 THERMO-ELECTRIC MATERIALS

A number of thermo-electric material are available. The conversion efficiency ranges from 5 – 10% over a temperature ranging from room temperature to 600°C. These materials are evaluated by a parameter called figure of merit (Z). Figure of merit is given by-

$$Z = s^2 \rho k \quad ...(14.7)$$

Where, s = Seeback coefficient of material.

ρ = electrical resistivity of material.

k = thermal conductivity of material.

A good thermo-electric material has higher value of Z. However, Z is temperature dependent and is maximum at certain temperature.

A good thermo-electric material should have high value of Z and good thermal stability. Table 14.1 gives list of promising thermo-electric materials for power generation.

Table 14.1 List of thermoelectric materials

Material	*Composition*	*Conduction type*	*Optimum temperature (°C)*	*Figure of merit Z*
Silicides	Mn–Si	*p*	300 – 600	0.80
	Mg–Si	*p*	300 – 600	1.07
Si–Ge based	Sio_8 Ge_2	*p*	730	0.70

Oxide based	Na Co_2O_4	*p*	30 – 500	1.20
	$(CaSrBi)_2CO_2O_5$	*p*	330 – 730	–
	$(Z_nO)_5(Ino._{97}Yo.o_3)_2O_3$	n	430 – 800	0.31
Pb–Te based	Pb Te	*n*	230 – 577	0.70
TA Gs based	Ge Te–Ag Sb Te_2	*p*	430	1.40
Zn_4 –Sb_3 based	Zn $(Sbo_{97}$ Sno.03$)_3$	*p*	230 – 480	1.00
	Zn_4Sb_3	*p*	230 – 480	1.22

Bismuth Telluride (Bi Te) is most promising material which gives an efficiency of 6%. Other materials, such as Pb Te is used but is less efficient and need to be used at 600°C on hot side and these are expensive.

A good thermo-electric material must possess following properties—

(*i*) high electrical conductivity to minimize ohmic losses.

(*ii*) low thermal conductivity so as to maintain large temperature gradient.

(*iii*) high Seeback co-efficient (voltage per unit temperature difference)so as to generate high voltage.

(*iv*) good figure of merit (figure of merit $Z = \frac{S^2}{\rho k}$ where 'S' is Seeback co-efficient, ρ is electrical resistivity and k thermal conductivity).

(*v*) Stable at high temperature.

(*vi*) high resistance to corrosion.

14.4 THERMO-ELECTRIC GENERATOR

Thermo-electric generators produce power based on Seeback effect. A thermo-electric generator consists of *p* and *n*-type semiconductor material. Hot sides of conductors are joined by a metallic strip. The other cold ends are connected to load.

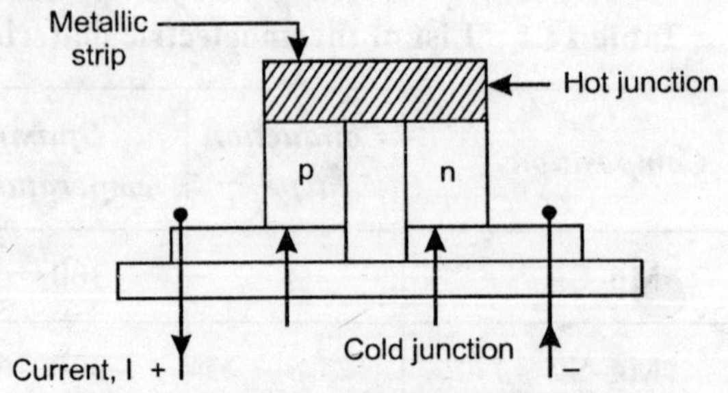

Fig. 14.1 Thermo-electric generator

A pair of *p* type and *n* type material forms a thermocouple. A number of thermocouples are connected in series or in parallel forming an array. When heat and cold are applied,electricity is produced. The magnitude of voltage produced is directly proportional to number of thermo-couples,temperature difference between hot and cold side and Seeback co-efficient of thermo-electric material.

$$V \propto N.\,dT.\,s \qquad ...(14.8)$$

Where, N = no. of thermocouples

dT = temperature difference between hot and cold side

s = Seeback co-efficient

Thermo-electric generators are used for following applications–

(*i*) as power supply in spacecrafts where solar PV cells cant be used.

(*ii*) generator in oil and gas industry.

(*iii*) power supply in automobiles using waste heat of engine.

(*iv*) power supply for circulating fan at the time of power failure.

Advantages of thermoelectric generation are following—

(*i*) no moving parts.

(*ii*) compact and long life.

(*iii*) portable.

Disadvantages are following—

(*i*) high cost.

(*ii*) low efficiency.

(*iii*) low output.

14.5 THERMIONIC GENERATION

Thermionic emission was discovered by Thomas Edison in 1885. It is a process of direct conversion of thermal energy into electrical energy. This effect is produced when metals or semiconductors are heated and electrons are emitted from the heated materials.

Thermionic devices are widely used in electronic devices, such as high powered radio and television transmitters, cathode ray tubes in oscilloscopes, computes monitors, radar screens etc. However, cathode ray based monitors are being replaced by high resolution LCD (liquid crystal display) and plasma panels. Thermionic devices are also used in microwave devices, such as klystron, Magnetron and travelling wave tubes (TWT).

Any heat source, such as fossil fuel, nuclear, solar etc. can be used to provide heat to generate electrons. However, problem is to tackle material that can be withstand hot corrosive gases.

14.6 PRINCIPLE OF THERMIONIC EMISSION

Free electrons move in metals and semiconductors at any temperature above absolute zero. These electrons do not have sufficient kinetic energy to overcome the forces exerted by nucleus of the atom.

The energy required to extract an electron from the atom is called 'work function'. Once an energy equal to or more than work function is supplied to material, electrons are emitted from it. There are different ways to provide energy to electrons, such as by increasing temperature of surface of material (thermionic emission), by bombardment of light (photo electric emission), by impact of ions or electrons (secondary emission), by intense electric field produced by nearby positively charged source (field emission) etc.

The electron beam (J_o) emitted through thermionic emission is proportional to work function exponentially.

$$J_o = \frac{4\pi\, meK^2}{h^3} T^2 \exp\left(\frac{-\phi}{kT}\right) \tag{14.9}$$

Where, m is the mass of electron in kg, e is the charge on electron (1.60210×10^{-19} J), k is the Boltzmann constant (1.38054×10^{-23} J/K), h is Planck's constant in Joule-sec, T is temperature in Kelvin and ϕ is the work function in eV. This equation is known as Richardson-Dushman equation.

The electrons are easily emitted in a vacuum because, these can not travel far in air. These emitted electrons are collected at the collector plate. Table 14.2 shows work function of different materials

Table 14.2 Work function of some selected materials

Sr. No	*Material*	*Work function ϕ (ev)*	*Melting point (K)*
1.	W	4.52	3683
2.	Mo	4.20	2890
3.	Cr	4.60	2130
4.	Ni	4.61	1726
5.	Pt	5.32	2045

The work function (ϕ) is sensitive to material of emitter and condition of its surface.

A good emitter material must possess following properties—

(*i*) the emitter material should posses high melting point so that it is able to release more electrons at high temperature.

(*ii*) the material should have low work function so that electrons are released with low temperature or energy input.

(*iii*) the material should possess high mechanical strength.

Advantages of thermionic generators are following—

(*i*) direct generation of electricity without any intermediate conversion.

(*ii*) due to operation at high temperature, carnot cycle efficiency is high.

(*iii*) due to high power density, size is small.

(*iv*) heat is rejected at high temperature resulting in simplified heat sink design.

(*v*) no moving parts, hence no wear & tear or maintenance.

The limitations of thermionic generators are following—

(*i*) low efficiency (about 15%).

(*ii*) high operating temperature of anode.

(*iii*) requires caesium vapours to reduce space charge.

(*iv*) metal used as anode is expensive.

14.7 THERMIONIC GENERATOR

A thermionic generator consists of two flat plate electrodes viz. anode and cathode held in vacuum. Cathode or emitter is heated so that electrons are released from its surface. These electrons travel in vacuum and reach anode or collector through external circuit.

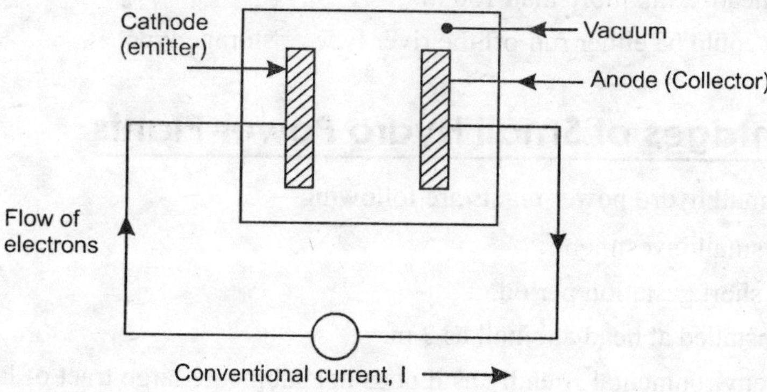

Fig. 14.2 Thermionic generator

Due to emission of electrons from cathode, electrons accumulate around cathode called space charge. This space charge repels electrons from cathode thereby preventing their escape from cathode surface. This effect of space charge can be minimized by restricting the space between two electrodes.

The operating life of these generators is limited.

14.8 SMALL HYDRO POWER PLANT

Small hydro power generation system has highest energy density amongst all renewable sources of energy. The global installed capacity is about 50 GW and estimated potential is 180 GW. These power plants are ideally suited for rural electrification in hilly and mountainous regions, especially where availability of grid supply is absent.

Cost/MW of small hydro plant is ₹ 7 to 8.5 crore/MW depending upon location and site topology. Payback period is 5–7 years depending upon capacity utilization factor.

14.8.1 Definition of Small Hydro and its Classification

According to Ministry of Renewable Energy Sources, a hydro power upto 25 MW is considered as small hydro.

Small hydro projects are further classified as per following–

(*i*) Small hydro projects are classified as mini, micro and pico as per following–

(*a*) Large hydro. .... More than 100 MW installed capacity.

(*b*) Medium hydro. .... 25–100 MW installed capacity.

(*c*) Small hydro. .... 1–25 MW installed capacity.

(*d*) Mini hydro. .... 100 kW–1 MW installed capacity.

(*e*) Micro hydro. .... 5 kW–100 kW installed capacity.

(*f*) Pico hydro. .... up to 5 kW installed capacity.

(*ii*) Small hydro projects are classified according to head available.

(*a*) Low head. .... 2 m to 20 m

(*b*) Medium head. .... 20 m to 150 m.

(*c*) High head. .... more than 150 m.

The small hydro could be either run-off the river type or storage type.

14.8.2 Advantages of Small Hydro Power Plants

Advantages of small hydro power plants are following—

(*i*) it requires small investment.

(*ii*) it requires short gestation period.

(*iii*) it can be installed at head as small as 2 m.

(*iv*) it is more environmental friendly as it does not submerge large tract of land and hence, does not displace population or causes deforestation.

(*v*) it provides off-grid electricity to rural areas, especially far-flung or hilly areas.

(*vi*) it has long life of 60 yeas.

(*vii*) water for irrigation and drinking purpose can be used.

(*viii*) it has very high efficiency (85 – 90%) compared to solar PV (15%), wind energy (40%), Biomass power (35%) and co-generation (60%).

(*ix*) it can use locally manufactured equipments e.g. HDPE (high density poly ethylene) penstocks can be used.

(*x*) easy operation and maintenance (by village residents).

(*xi*) it avoids expensive transmission and distribution lines & hence, losses.

(*xii*) local materials can be used for civil works.

(*xiii*) low cost connection to domestic users in local area.

(*xiv*) use of local labour for construction, operation and minor maintenance.

(*xv*) good planning can help to achieve high load factor and balanced load pattern.

14.8.3 Selection of Site for Small Hydro Power Plant

Following are the factors to be considered for selection of site for a small hydro power plant—

(i) the project should be technically and environmentally sustainable.

(*ii*) a verifiable power demand data should be available.

(*iii*) cost of transportation of equipment and materials should be as low as possible.

(*iv*) availability of local people for construction and subsequently training for operation and maintenance should be present.

(*v*) geological condition of site should permit installation of power plant.

(*vi*) chances of damage to turbine through rapid silting should be minimal.

(*vii*) ease of access to site for transportation of construction materials, plant and machinery and manpower should be possible.

14.8.4 Components of Small Hydro Power Plant

A small hydro power plant has a capacity of 5 kW to 25,000 kW with head ranging from 2 m to 150 m. various components of small hydro plants are following—

(*i*) Intake or Reservoir: Water is usually drawn from a storage reservoir by building dam across the stream. Type, shape and dimension of dam is decided by local engineering considerations. The dam could be of earth or bricks.

(*ii*) Penstock: penstock is pipe that carries water from forebay to turbine. The velocity of water is restricted to 0.8m/sec for earth filled dam and 1.5m/sec for concrete dam. Penstock is usually made of steal or HDPE plastic tubing.

(*iii*) Forebay: It is a basin located before entry to penstock.

(*iv*) Surge Tank: It is a tank located along the penstock to control sudden changes in water flow.

(*v*) Trash Rack: It is a mesh that prėvents entry of rocks, twigs or any floating material into the penstock. This need to be cleaned regularly.

(*vi*) Settling Tank: It allows sedimentation of small particles before entry into turbine. If allowed to enter, these particles have abrasive action on turbine blades causing erosion of blade material.

(*vii*) Intake Gate: It allows water to enter hydraulic turbine. It is used to protect the turbine against rise in water level of river or to isolate the turbine.

(*viii*) Hydraulic Turbine: A hydraulic turbine converts hydro energy into mechanical energy. The turbine consists of runner with blades attached to it. The water entering a turbine casing is directed through guide vanes to the turbine runner. This causes the runner to rotate due to pressure head or impulse of impinging water jet. The selection of type of turbine is based on head and power output. This is given in table 14.3.

Table 14.3 Selection of type of hydro turbine

	Turbine type	*Head (m)*	*Power output(kW)*
IMPULSE TURBINE	Micro Pelton	30 – 70	5 – 15
	Pelton	100 – 550	50 – 6000
	Micro Turgo	10 – 75	3 – 45
	Turgo	30 – 200	15 – 3000

REACTION TURBINE	Franics	15 – 250	15 – 7000
	Kaplan	2.5 – 30	500 – 7500
	Semi Kaplan	2.5 – 25	10 – 6000
	Propeller	2.5 – 30	10 – 6000
	Bulb	2 – 12	100 – 2600

Hence, for low head application Kaplan or semi Kaplan turbine is preferred. For medium and high, Francis turbine is preferred. For high head, Micro Pelton and Turgo are also used.

(*ix*) **Draft Tube:** It is used to carry water from turbine runner to tail race.

(*x*) **Regulator:** It is a kind of governor that ensures constant speed of turbine irrespective of power demand.

(*xi*) **Alternator:** Alternator is mechanically coupled to the turbine. Generally, alternator can be any of the following types—

(*a*) Permanent magnet DC generator.

(*b*) Synchronous generator.

(*c*) Induction generator.

(*d*) Synchronous reluctance generator.

Synchronous generator is used for isolated off-grid application while asynchronous generator or induction generator is used for gird connected applications.

14.8.5 Portable Micro–Hydel Power Generation

Portable micro hydel power generation sets have capacities of 5 to 15 kW. These can be easily installed and operated by local communities and NGOs. Such units are installed in hilly regions which are not connected by electricity grids or it is uneconomical to extend the grid to such regions.

Requirement for installation of portable micro hydel unit is characterised by following factors—

(*i*) availability of sufficient discharge of water at moderate to high heads.

(*ii*) small village or cluster of villages with small population.

(*iii*) remote high altitude or inaccessible area making it extremely difficult to transport, install and maintain a generating unit.

(*iv*) electricity is needed to meet basic need of the people, such as lighting, heating, cooking, grinding etc.

(*v*) it is difficult to locate and train skilled manpower for operation and maintenance of generating unit.

(*vi*) there is no hope of electricity grid extension in future.

These are small, compact, light weight sets which can be installed by semi-skilled workers. The head ranges from 30m to 70m. The maximum weight and volume of largest single set is 300 kg and 1.25 m^3 respectively.

These sets of 5 to 10 kW are installed in Uttar Pradesh, Himachal Pradesh, Arunachal Pradesh, Meghalaya, Bihar, West Bengal and Jammu and Kashmir.

Normally, micro Pelton wheel is used as hydro turbine alongwith synchronous generator. Turbine and generator shafts are coupled through a belt. Electronic load controller is used to maintain balance between demand of power and water flow. When the load on the turbine reduces, a heater load is switched on to maintain balance between generated power and load consumption. This way constant power output is maintained thereby avoiding mechanical movement of turbine governing. The turbine, generator and control board are placed at site as plug in unit. The unit can be easily removed and transported to a different site.

14.8.6 Turbines Used for Mini and Micro Hydro Plants

Choice of hydro turbine is governed by hydraulic conditions (head, discharge etc.) at site, operating requirements and economic considerations. All turbines can be broadly categorised as reaction turbine and impulse turbine.

(*i*) **Reaction Turbine:** A reaction turbine converts linear and angular momentum of water into shaft power. The blades are totally immersed in water. The pressure of the water leaving the runner is reduced to atmospheric or lower.

(*a*) Axial flow turbine → Tube turbine, Bulb turbine and straflo turbine.

(*b*) Kaplan turbine.

(*c*) Francis turbine.

- **Tube Turbine:** Tube turbines are axial flow propeller type turbines. The turbine is encased in a tube which acts as a water passage and generator is mounted outside the water passage in horizontal plane. The turbines are suitable for water head ranging from 2 to15 m. The turbine has fixed or adjustable guide vanes to take care of varying load, head or flow conditions. This results in better efficiency over wide range. Automatic co-ordination of guide vanes are used under special operating conditions.

  Guide vane house is made of cast iron and consists of casing, hub and guide vanes. Guide vane regulates the flow of water. Runner is made of polished cast steel. Shaft of turbinc connecting the generator is made of carbon steel. The draft tube is fabricated from mild plates. Draft tube allows passage to water after passing through turbine blades. For low head applications, a good design is required to ensure efficient recovery of hydraulic energy.

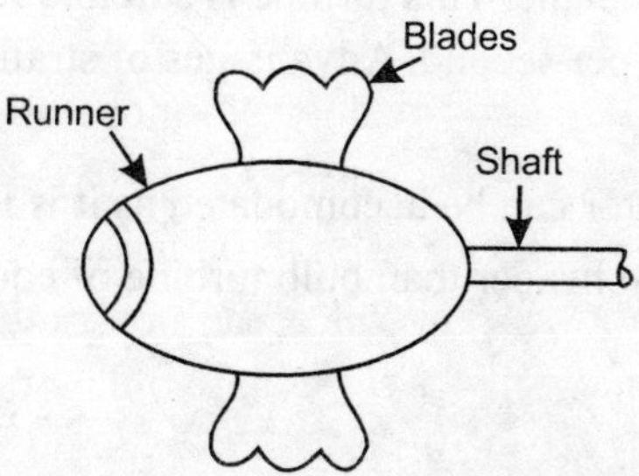

Fig. 14.3 Tube turbine

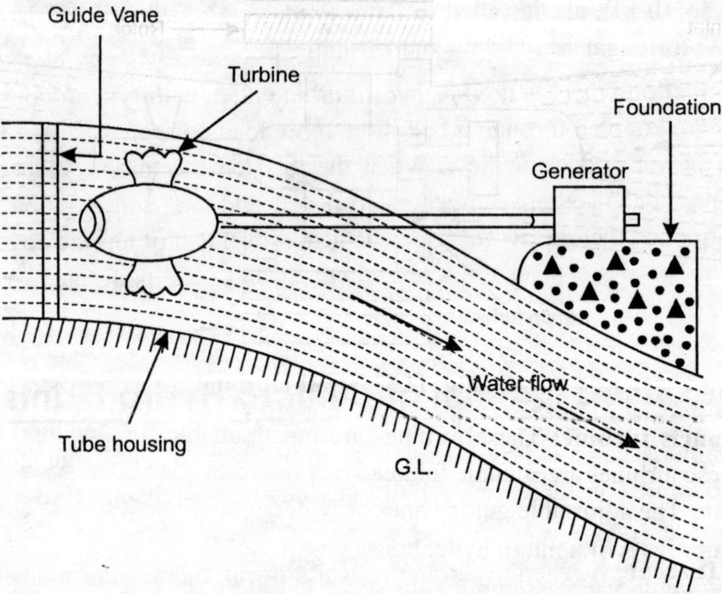

Fig. 14.4 Tube turbine generator

- **Bulb Turbine:** It is an axial flow horizontal turbine which remains submerged in the water passage. Generator is placed ahead of the rotor in a steel capsule or bulb in the passage. It is suitable for water head of 1.25 to 25 m and a discharge of 3 to 70 cubic meter per second.

  Advantages of bulb turbine are following–
  - ➢ bulb unit can be used as reversible pump motor unit.
  - ➢ construction time required is very less.
  - ➢ higher efficiency.
  - ➢ higher specific speed and specific output.
  - ➢ less affected by cavitation.
  - ➢ reduction in foundation depth, power house height and width and hence, economical.
  - ➢ straight draft tube, hence less friction loss.
- **Straflo Turbine:** This turbine is extremely compact in size. The runner blades are contained in another ring which acts as generator rotor hub. The generator stator is then installed in the runner plane. This turbine is suitable for head of 2 to 50 m and discharge of 3to 20 cubic meter per second. Advantages of straflo turbines are following—
  - ➢ no driving shaft.
  - ➢ large size generator can be accomodated as it is located on the outer periphery.
  - ➢ these turbine are cheaper than bulb turbine of equal rating and hydraulic condition.

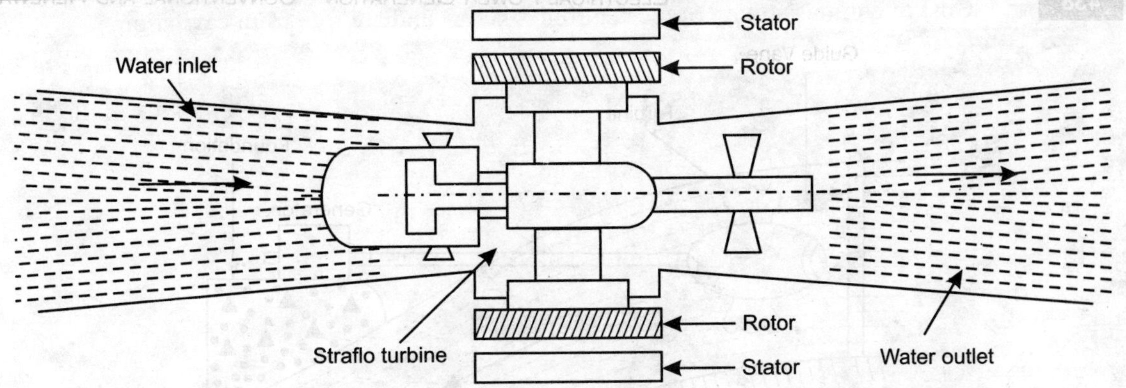

Fig. 14.5 Straflo turbine

- **Francis turbine:** These turbines are most suitable for medium and low head plants. These turbines are suitable for head ranging from 15 to 20 m. These are built with vertical shaft. The adjustable guide vanes provide good efficiency over wide range.

  Major parts of a micro hydel house consists of following—
  - ➢ guide vane assembly consists of guide vanes, outlet casing, guide vane operating ring and ring supporting bracket.
  - ➢ runner shaft assembly consists of shaft runner, stuffing box with ball bearing, thrust bearing and coupling.
  - ➢ outlet casing flange, draft tube bend and draft tube extension.
  - ➢ inlet valve with servo motor control to supply water to turbine.
  - ➢ generator and a flywheel.
  - ➢ governor with oil pump and guide vane operating mechanism.
  - ➢ control panel containing circuit breaker, ammeter, voltmeter, frequency meter, energy meter and automatic voltage regulator.

(*ii*) Impulse turbine: An impulse turbine converts kinetic energy of a jet of water striking turbine blades into motion. There is no pressure reduction as water pressure is atmospheric on both sides of impeller.

Four types of impulse turbines are used for ultra low head to high head generation. These are following–

(*a*) Ossberger Cross Flow tubine. (*b*) Lotte Schneider engine.
(*c*) Turgo turbine. (*d*) Pelton turbine.

(*a*) Ossberger Cross Flow turbine: It is an impulse turbine with two stage velocity compounding. The water jet strikes a cylindrical runner and the runner blades. The water then passes from the periphery towards the centre and then after crossing the open centre moves outward. This turbine is suitable from 1 kW to 1000 kW with discharge ranging from 0.03 to 9 cubic meters per second under heads varying from 1 to 200. The turbine is of horizontal shaft type having a runner in the form of rotor of fixed diameter fitted with number of blades. The blades are curved only in radial direction and produce no axial thrust. A metering guide vane at the intake maintains high efficiency (about 85%) over a wide range of water flow.

Cost of commissioning of these turbines is low and are free from cavitation.

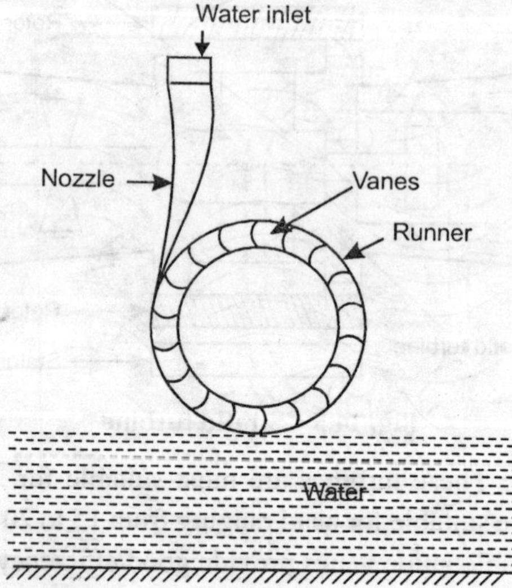

Fig. 14.6 Ossberger cross flow turbine

(*b*) **Lotte Schneider Engine:** It is named after its inventer Dr. Daniel J. Schneider and is useful for low head plant. The range of water head can be as low as 0.5 m to upto 15m. The flow rate range is 0.1 to 50 cubic meter per second with a power output of 0.2 kW to 5000 kW.

Design of the engine causes the water to strike the cross-section of the Schneider engine at a uniform velocity. As the water flows into throat section, it meets the first stage guide vanes. The first stage guide vanes direct the water flow to lift downward on the first stage hydro foils by directing the flow to optimally match the velocity of the hydro foils. This velocity matching achieves a high recovery efficiency.

Once the water flow leaves the first stage hydro foils, it comes into contact with the second stage vanes. The second stage guide vanes redirect the water velocity in an upward direction, lifting the second stage hydro foils at a matched velocity.

The linear movement of hydro foils is used to drive chains attached to each end of hydro foils. The drive chain turns sprocates located at the top and bottom of the engine. The top sprocates are attached to shaft leading to the speed increase and the shaft's rotation drives the generator.

After leaving the second stage hydro foils, the water simultaneously enters the tube and third stage guide vanes to the channel. The third stage guide vanes and draft tube are designed to minimize head losses. The efficiency ranges from 72.7% to 86.5%.

(*c*) **Turgo Turbine:** It is a high capacity, medium head, free jet impulse turbine. A jet of water impinges on a runner cup at one side and is discharged at the other end falling by gravity to tail race. This turbine is suitable for head ranging from 30 to 200 m. The specific speed for a given head and output is nearly double of Pelton wheel, thus making it compact and economical. The types of turbine finds applications between ranges of Francis turbine and high head single jet Pelton wheel.

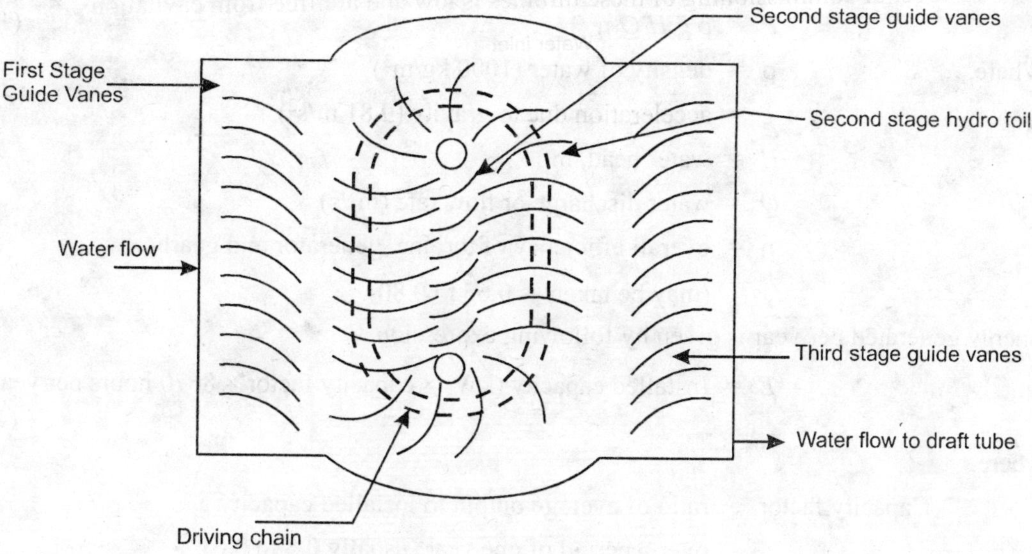

Fig. 14.7 Lotte Schneider engine

Advantages of turgo turbine are following—

(*i*) horizontal split casing of turbine makes inspection and maintenance easier.

(*ii*) efficiency curve is almost flat for a wide range of load resulting in efficient part load operation.

(*iii*) being a free jet turbine, there is no cavitation damage on the runner.

(*iv*) governing of turgo turbine with long penstock is possible without the need of a surge tank or relief valve.

(*d*) **Pelton turbine:** It is used for high head ranging from 100 to 550m suitable for low discharge application. This type of turbine can be single jet or multi jet.

The water flow control mechanism can either be deflector or spear control or both. The performance curve is almost flat and hence, has high efficiency irrespective of load variation. Due to split casing, turbine maintenance and inspection is easy

14.8.7 Turbine Regulators

Turbine control is a function of system frequency, load and water head. The function of turbine governor is to adjust automatically the turbine gate opening according to load and thus, attain regulation.

Speed frequency regulation is required only in case of isolated operation. In case of inter connected system, speed and voltage regulation is undertaken by large machines. Regulator is used with adjustable guide vane and/or ranner blades. No regulator is used with fixed guide vane and runner blades.

Now-a-days, micro processor based governors are used with PID (proportional integral derivative) control features for speed regulation. It can also perform level regulation, flow regulation, storage volume regulation and power regulation.

14.8.8 Power Output and Energy Generated in Small Hydro Plant

Power output of small hydro power plant is given by following expression—

$$P = \rho\, g\, H\, Q\, \eta \qquad (14.10)$$

Where, ρ = density of water (1000 kg/m^3)

g = acceleration due to gravity (9.81 m/s^2)

H = water head, m

Q = water discharge or flow rate (m^3/s)

η = overall efficiency of turbine, generator and gearbox (may be taken as 0.65 to 0.80).

Energy generated per year is given by following expression

$$E = \text{Installed capacity (kW)} \times \text{capacity factor} \times 8670 \text{ hours per year} \qquad (14.11)$$

where,

Capacity factor = ratio of average output to installed capacity over a period of one year (usually 0.5 to 0.6).

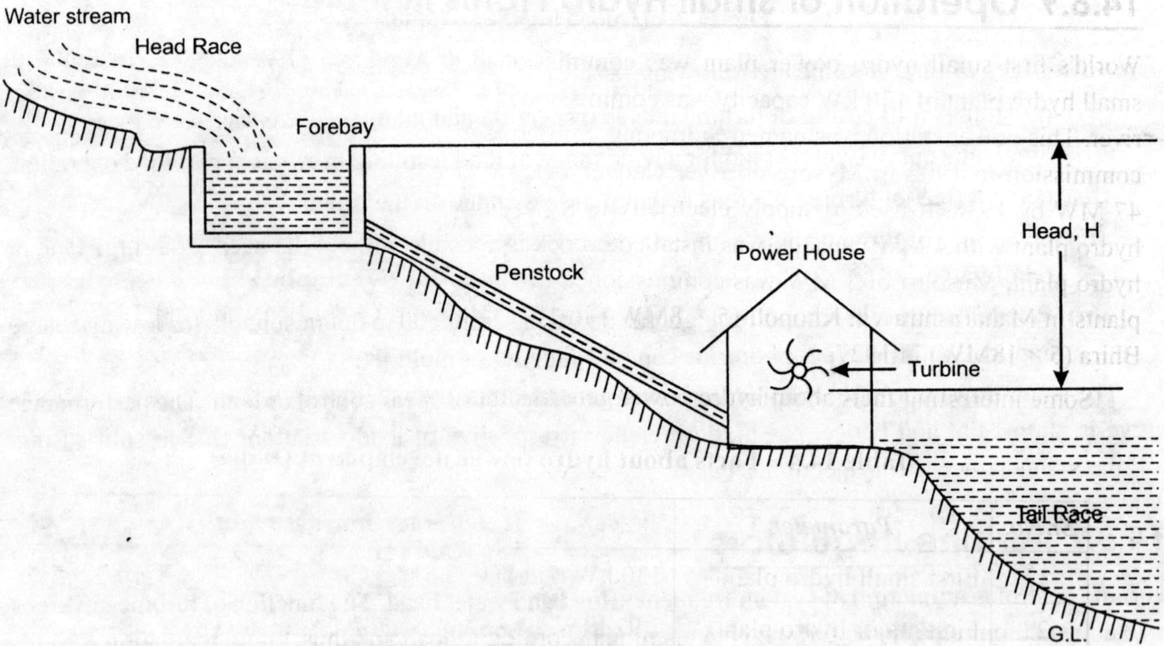

Fig. 14.8 Small Hydro plant

14.8.8 Case Studies of Low Head Mini Hydel Plant

(*a*) Kakroi mini hydel power plant is located near Sonepat in Haryana on Western Yamuna Canal. It is lowest head mini hydel power plant in India designed by Alternate Hydro Energy Centre, Roorkee University. It is a joint venture of Department of Non-conventional and Renewable Energy Sources, Govt. of India, Haryana Irrigation and Haryana State Electricity Board. Salient features of the project are following—

Designed head = 1.6 to 1.9 m

Designed discharge = 31.6 cubic meter per second.

Total installed capacity = 3 × 100 kW

The first unit consists of tube turbine coupled to induction generator of 100 kW 61.5 rpm, BHEL make. The magnetising current for induction generator is supplied by the grid. Induction generator operates at super synchronous speed. The second unit consists of straflo turbine coupled to synchronous generator supplied by Voest Alpine, Austria. Third unit consists of Schneider engine coupled to synchronous generator suppled by Loll Schneider Engine Company, Seoul, South Korea.

(*b*) Shansha micro hydel project is located at a height of 3005 m in Lahaul valley in Himachal Pradesh. Vertical Francis turbines operate under a head in 25 m generating 56 kW at a speed of 1000 rpm. A governor operates guide vanes mounted on the runner to control flow of water into turbine. Power is generated at 415 V, 3 phase, 50Hz, 6 pole generator.

A steel penstock pipe of 61 cm diameter carries water to turbine with a total head of 60 m.

14.8.9 Operation of Small Hydro Plants in India

World's first small hydro power plant was commissioned at Appleton, USA in 1882. In India, first small hydro plant of 130 kW capacity was commissioned in Darjeeling, West Bengal in 1897 on Teesta river. This power station was named Sidrapong. Subsequently, Shiva Samudram small hydro plant was commission in 1902 in Mysore on river Cauvery. It was of 7.92 MW capacity which was raised to 47 MW by 1938. It used to supply electricity to Kolar Gold mine, 25 km from power plant. Mohora hydro plant with 4 MW capacity was installed on river Jhelum in 1905 in Jammu and Kashmir. Golgoi hydro plant, Musouri of 3 MW was commissioned in 1907. Tata power established three major hydro plants in Maharashtra viz Khopoli (5 × 8MW) in 1915, Bhivpuri (4 × 12 MW)during 1922 – 25 and Bhira (5 × 18MW) in 1927.

Some interesting facts about hydro power generation is given below—

Table 14.4 Facts about hydro power development (India)

Sr.No.	*Parameter*	*Location of hydro plant*
1.	First small hydro plant	130 kW, Sidrapong, Darjeeling in 1897
2.	First major hydro plant	7.92 MW,Siva Samudram, Mysore in 1902
3.	First private hydro plant	32 MW, Tata Khopoli, Maharashtra,1915
4.	Largest tunnel diameter	15 m, Srisailam (770 MW) in Andhra Pradesh
5.	Longest tunnel	27 km, Nathpa Jhakri (1500 MW), HP
6.	Highest dam	206 m,Tehri (1000 MW), Uttarakhand
7.	Highest head	1026 m, Pykara (59.2 MW) Tamil Nadu
8.	Largest unit size	250 MW, (*i*) Koyna–IV (*ii*) Nathpa Jhakri (*iii*) Tehri
9.	Maximum plant capacity	1500 MW, Nathpa Jhakri, HP

Table 14.5 Comparison of Renewable Power Plants

Sr. No	Parameter	Solar PV	Solar Thermal	Wind	Biomass	Geothermal	Ocean based	Fuel cell	MHD
1.	Land required	Large	Moderate	Large	Small	Moderate	– N.A. –	Small	Small
2.	Capital cost	Large	Large	Moderate	Moderate	Small	Tidal, OTEC, Wave } Enormous	High	Moderate
3.	Operating cost	Small	Moderate	Small	Small	Small	Tidal, OTEC } Negligible	Moderate	Small
4	Cost of electricity	Very high	High	Low	Low	High	Very high	High	High
5.	Efficiency	[upto 15%]	[14 – 23%]	[upto 35%]	[30 – 40%]	[upto 15%] For 190°C	[OTEC-7% Tidal-25%]	[40–52%]	upto 35%
6.	Environmental impact	Large	Moderae	Small	Small	Small	Tidal-Large OTEC- Small	Small	Small

Efficiency of conventional and renewable power plants in order of decreasing efficiency is given below—

(*i*) Large hydro.
(*ii*) Small hydro.
(*iii*) Tidal.
(*iv*) Combined cycle gas turbine (CCGT).
(*v*) Molten carbonate fuel cell.
(*vi*) Thermal plant (super critical technology).
(*vii*) Solid oxide fuel cell.
(*viii*) Large gas turbine based plant.
(*ix*) Large steam turbine based thermal plant.
(*x*) Wind power plant.

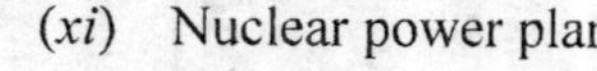
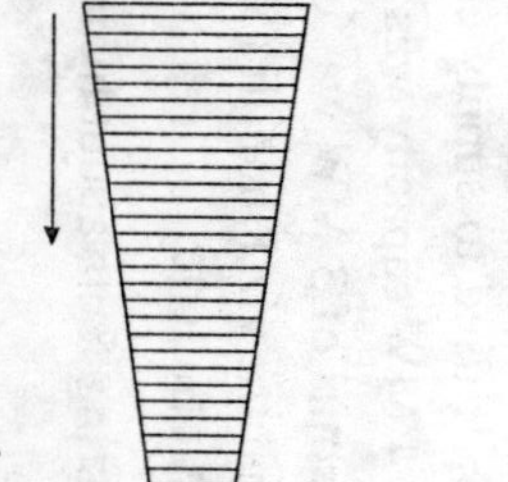
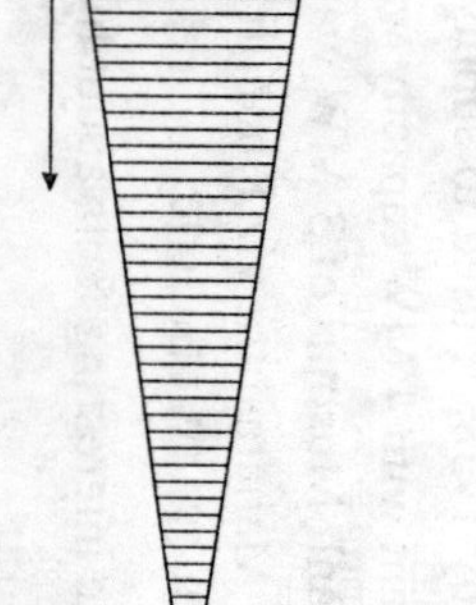

(*xi*) Nuclear power plant.
(*xii*) Biomass and bio gas power plant.
(*xiii*) Waste to electricity power plant.
(*xiv*) Diesel power plant.
(*xv*) Solar PV
(*xvi*) Geothermal power plant.

SOLVED EXAMPLES

Ex 14.1 A small hydro power plant operates at a head of 32 m and 25 m^3/s discharge. The efficiency of turbine, generator and gearbox is 68 %. Given: density of water = 1000 kg/m^3. Determine the power output and select a suitable hydro turbine for the power plant.

Solution: $H = 32$ m, $Q = 25\ m^3/s$, $\rho = 1000\ kg/m^3$, $\eta_{overall} = 68\%$

Power output, $P = \rho g H Q \eta$

$$= 1000 \times 9.81 \times 32 \times 25 \times 0.68$$

$$= \mathbf{5336.6\ kW\ Ans}$$

Based on head of water available at site i.e. 32m, suitable hydro turbines are (*i*) micro Pelton (*ii*) micro Turgo.

Ex 14.2 Station capacity of a small hydro power plant is 3500 kW at a head of 38 m. Determine the water discharge. Assume combined efficiency of generator, turbine and gearbox as 70%.

Solution: $P = 3500 \times 10^3$ W, $H = 38$m, $\eta_{overall} = 70\%$, $\rho = 1000\ kg/m^3$

$$P = \rho g H Q \eta$$

$$3500 \times 10^3 = 10^3 \times 9.81 \times 38 \times Q \times 0.70$$

$$Q = \frac{3500 \times 10^3}{10^3 \times 9.81 \times 38 \times 0.70} = \mathbf{13.4\ m^3/s\ Ans.}$$

Ex 14.3 A small hydro power plant located in the hills of Himachal Pradesh has following data: Power output = 750 kW, head = 10 m, discharge = 12 m^3/s, efficiency of gearbox = 90%, efficiency of generator = 88%.

Determine– (*i*) efficiency of hydro turbine.

(*ii*) propose a suitable hydro turbine for the plant.

Solution:

(*i*) $P = \rho g H Q \eta_{gen} \cdot \eta_{tur} \cdot \eta_{gb}$

Where, η_{gen} = efficiency of generator

η_{tur} = efficiency of turbine

η_{gb} = efficiency of gearbox

$$750{,}000 = 1000 \times 9.81 \times 10 \times 12 \times 0.88 \times 0.90 \times \eta_{tur}$$

$$\eta_{tur} = \frac{750{,}000}{1000 \times 9.81 \times 10 \times 12 \times 0.88 \times 0.90} \times 100$$

$$= \mathbf{80.4\%\ \ Ans.}$$

(*ii*) Suitable turbine is bulb turbine.

CHAPTER SUMMARY

Thermo-electric power generation is based on Seeback effect and directly converts thermal energy into electrical energy. Efficiency of energy conversion ranges from 5 to 10% and depends upon the type of material used. Due to low conversion efficiency, this technology does not find commercial application. However, it used in military applications, space applications, under sea installation etc.

Thermionic generator uses thermal energy to liberate electrons from metals or semi-conductors. It is used to generate flow of electrons in high powered radio and television transmitters, CRO, radar screens etc.

Small hydro power plants have capacity ranging from 1 to 25 MW. The scheme could be run off the river type or storage type. These are ideally suited for remote areas away from conventional grid. Due to no environmental impact, easy and cheaper construction, these plant are preferred. In fact, portable micro-hydel power systems are also available.

A wide variety of hydro turbines are used, such as tube turbine, bulb turbine, straflo turbine, turgo turbine, minor pelton turbine,propeller turbine etc.

FORMULAE

1. Figure of merit, $Z = s^2 \rho k$

   Where, s = Seeback co-efficient of material.

   ρ = electrical resistivity of material.

   k = thermal conductivity of material.

2. Richardson-Dushman equation–

   Electron beam due to thermionic emission. $J_o = \frac{4\pi\, mek^2}{h^3} T^2 \exp\left(\frac{-\phi}{KT}\right)$

   Where, m = mass of electron

   e = charge on electron

   h = planck's constant

   T = temperature in kelvin

   ϕ = work function.

3. Power output of a small hydro plant, $P = \rho\, g\, H\, Q\, \eta$

   Where, ρ = density of water.

   g = acceleration due to gravity.

   H = head of water.

   ϕ = water flow rate.

   η = efficiency of turbine × efficiency of generator×efficiency of gearbox

REVIEW QUESTIONS

Q. 1. Explain methods of generation of electrical energy using– (*i*) Seeback effect (*ii*) Peltier effect (*iii*) Thomson effect and (*iv*) Fourier effect.

Q. 2. Write a brief note on thermo-electric materials.

Q. 3. Describe operation of thermo electric generator.

Q. 4. Explain the principle and operation of thermionic generation.

Q. 5. Write down the characteristics of a good emitter material.

Q. 6. What are the properties of a good thermo-electric material?

Q. 7. Compare thermo-electric and thermionic power generation.

Q. 8. Discuss the applications of thermo-electric power generation.

Q. 9. List possible applications of thermionic power generation.

Q. 10. Discuss classification of hydro-electric power plants.

Q. 11. What is the basis on which small hydro-electric power plants are classified?

Q. 12. What are the advantages of small hydro power plants over large hydro power plants?

Q. 13. Discuss the factors which govern the selection of site for a mini hydro power plants.

Q. 14. Discuss in detail various components of a small hydro power plant.

Q. 15. Describe the function of–(*i*) Forebay (*ii*) surge tank (*iii*) settling tank in a small hydro power plant.

Q. 16. What is a portable micro hydel power plant? What are possible applications?

Q. 17. Write an exhaustive note on various types of hydraulic turbines used in small hydro power plants.

Q. 18. What is the purpose of using a turbine regulator in a small hydro power plant?

Q. 19. Discuss various factors which affect the power output of a small hydro power generation.

Q. 20. Write a brief note on status of small hydro power development in India.

NUMERICAL QUESTION

Q. 1. Calculate the power output of a small hydro power plant having 18 m head, 60 m^3/s discharge. Overall efficiency of turbine, generator and gearbox may be taken as 0.75. Density of water is 1000 kg/m^3. [**Ans:** 7.95 MW]

SHORT ANSWER TYPE QUESTIONS

Q. 1. What is the conversion efficiency of thermo-electric materials?

Q. 2. State Richardson- Dushman equation.

Q. 3. What is the conversion efficiency of thermionic generators?

Q. 4. State capacity of pico, mini hydro stations in kW.

Q. 5. What is the function of trash rack in a small hydro power station?

Q. 6. Name various reaction turbines used in small hydro power plant.

Q. 7. What are major factors which affect the capacity of small hydro plants?

Multiple Choice Questions

Q. 1. A good thermo-electric material has

(*a*) low figure of merit (*b*) high figure of merit

(*c*) both (*a*)and(*b*) (*d*) none of these

Q. 2. A thermionic generator converts

(*a*) heat energy into electricity (*b*) mechanical energy into electricity

(*c*) solar energy into electricity (*d*) both (*a*) and (*c*)

Q. 3. Electrons are emitted from a material if energy supplied is

(*a*) less than work function (*b*) more than work function

(*c*) equal to work function (*d*) none of these.

Q. 4. Purpose of regulator in a small hydro plants is to

(*a*) increase speed of turbine (*b*) decrease the speed of turbine

(*c*) both(*a*) and (*b*) (*d*) keep the speed of turbine constant.

Q. 5. For very low head hydro plant, following turbine is used (head 2 to 12m)—

(*a*) Micro Pelton (*b*) Francis

(*c*) Turgo (*d*) Bulb

Q. 6. Power output of micro Pelton lies in the rage of

(*a*) 5 – 15 kW (*b*) 3 – 45 kW

(*c*) 100 to 2600 kW (*d*) 10 to 6000 kW

Q. 7. Induction generator is used in small hydro plant for

(*a*) isolated off grid application (*b*) grid connected system

(*c*) both (*a*) and (b) (*d*) none of these.

Q. 8. Straflo hydro turbine is

(*a*) impulse turbine (*b*) radial flow turbine

(*c*) axial flow turbine (*d*) mixed flow turbine.

Answer to MCQ

1. (*b*) **2.** (*a*) **3.** (*b*) **4.** (*d*) **5.** (*d*) **6.** (*a*)

7. (*a*) **8.** (*c*)

Chapter

Co–ordinated Operation of Power Plants

Learning Objectives

After reading this chapter, reader will be able to

- Understand the importance, necessity and advantages of co-ordinated operation of power plants.
- Examine advantages of operation of different combinations of power plants.
- Understand process of economic operation of power plants and significance of unit commitment.
- Understand impact of transmission losses in power plant operation.

"No amount of experience can prove me right;
a single experiment can prove me wrong."

— Albert Einstein.

15.1 INTRODUCTION

Installation of a power generating station requires huge investment. The tariff is controlled by the government so the return on the investment is small. Hence, it is necessary that power plants are operated as economically as possible to reap good return. Moreover, certain power plants, such as thermal, diesel, gas etc. can be built near the load centres while hydro plants are location specific. So, to obtain optimum benefit, it is necessary that different plants are run in a co-ordinated manner so as to derive benefit of combined operation. Thermal, hydro and nuclear power plants are best suited as base load plants. While diesel and gas turbine plants are used as peak load plants. By combined operation of these different plants, overall economy in operation can be achieved. Such operation allows reduced spare capacity requirement, optimization of generator unit size and efficient loading based on minimum fuel consumption. This leads to higher reliability, more flexibility and better contingency operation.

15.2 ADVANTAGES OF COMBINED OPERATION OF POWER PLANTS

Following are the advantages of combined operation of power plants—

(*i*) **Better reliability:** Availability of power from hydro power plants is dependent upon stream flow which is greatly affected during summer months. Hence, combined operation with a thermal power plant can tide over with the crisis during summer months. This greatly enhances power reliability. Similarly, solar photovoltaic power plant can supply power during daytime. If this system is combined with diesel power plants, the power reliability and availability is improved. So, by combining best of both power sources,reliability and availability can be improved.

(ii) **Reserve capacity:** Any power system requires certain amount of reserve capacity to meet unforeseen situations, such as forced outage of units,unscheduled/scheduled maintenance of units, weather effects, festivals etc. Under such situations, continuity of supply can be maintained from other power sources in combined operation. This advantage greatly reduces requirement of reserve capacity.

(iii) **Flexibility in operation:** Power demand varies through the day and from season to season. This calls for efficient and optimum loading of generating units so as to keep operating expenses minimum. So, units with higher efficiency are loaded first and subsequent units are loaded in order of their decreasing efficiency. The unit with higher operating cost is loaded during emergency or during peak load requirements. Hydro power plants have very low operating cost compared to thermal power plant. While a nuclear power plant can not tolerate load variations and need to be operated as base load plant. Similarly,gas based power plants and diesel power plants can be quickly started and stopped and are most suited for peak load operation. The cold startup time required for thermal power plant is very high compared to hydro power plant. Hence, by combined operation of different power plants, advantages of different types of power plants can be utilised for flexible operation.

(iv) **Better utilization of hydro resources:** Hydro power plants have quick startup and low operating cost benefit. So, during heavy stream flow, hydro power plants can be loaded more thereby permitting lesser load on thermal power plants. This helps to save fossil fuels.

(v) **Optimum operation and maintenance expenses:** A thermal and a nuclear power plant requires high operation and maintenance expenses and gas turbine plant requires less operation and maintenance expenses. Combined operation of these plants ensure optimum operation and maintenance expenses.

15.3 BASE LOAD AND PEAK LOAD OPERATION

Total load on a power station is composed of a fixed or constant load and a variable load. A constant load on a power plant is called base load while a variable load is called peak load. A power plant must be able to meet the entire load demand. But, a power plant designed to meet the entire load equal to peak load is uneconomical. Because peak load occurs for a short duration in a year and the installed capacity remains idle during rest of the year. Hence, the load on power station is split into two parts. Some power stations supply base load while others are used to supply peak load. Hence, a combined operation of power plant is necessary.

The characteristics of base load plant should be following—

(i) the plant must be able to meet the load continuously.
(ii) the capital cost of the plant should be minimum.
(iii) the operation cost of the plant should be minimum.
(iv) maintenance requirement of plants should be minimum.

(*v*) spare parts should be easily available.

(*vi*) total plant personnel required should be minimum.

(*vii*) it should be possible to install the plant near the load centre.

The characteristics of peak load plant should be following—

(*i*) the capital cost of plant should be minimum.

(*ii*) the operation cost of plant should be minimum.

(*iii*) the plant should be able to start and stop quickly.

(*iv*) the plant should be able to respond to load variations quickly

Characteristics of some conventional power plants are following—

(*i*) Hydro electric power plant: The characteristics of hydro electric power plants are following—

(*a*) it can be quickly started from cold condition.

(*b*) as the fuel cost is zero, the plant can be used as base load plant.

(*c*) at the time of lean season with limited water supply, plant can be used as peak load plant.

(*d*) plant requires few personnel and low maintenance.

Hence, hydro-electric power plant is suitable for base load as well as peak load operation.

(*ii*) Nuclear power plant: The characteristics of nuclear power plants are following—

(*a*) the fuel cost is low.

(*b*) requirement of fuel is less.

(*c*) it can not respond to load variations.

(*d*) it can not be started and stopped quickly.

(*e*) maintenance is expensive and time consuming.

Hence, nuclear power plant is suitable for base load operation.

(*iii*) Thermal power plant: The characteristics of thermal power plants are following—

(*a*) when used as base load, the plant gives minimum cost of generation per unit.

(*b*) it can not be started quickly.

(*c*) it can be installed near load centre.

(*d*) it can respond to load variations.

(*e*) maintenance is expensive.

Hence, thermal power plant is suitable as base load plant.

(*iv*) Gas turbine power plant: Characteristics of gas turbine power plants are following—

(*a*) it can be started quickly from cold condition.

(*b*) it can respond to load variations.

(*c*) it can be installed near load centres.

(*d*) cost per unit is higher than thermal power plant but lesser than diesel power plant.

(*e*) maintenance is expensive.

Hence, gas turbine plants can be used as peak load power plants.

(*v*) Diesel power plant: Characteristics of diesel power plants are following—

(*a*) it can be quickly started from cold condition.

(*b*) it can respond to load variations.

(*c*) cost per unit of generated power is most expensive.

(*d*) it can be installed near load centre.

(*e*) maintenance is frequent.

Due to very high cost per unit, diesel power plants are not much used for bulk power generation. Their use is limited for captive power generation or as emergency power backup.

The order of preference for various conventional power plants is given below—

Preference	Power plant	Type
Most referred	1. Run off the river hydro power plants.	Base load plant
	2. Nuclear power plants.	Base load plant
	3. Thermal power plants.	Base load plant
Preference	4. Hydro power plant with limited storage.	peak load plant
	5. Pumped storage hydro power plant.	peak load plant
	6. Gas turbine power plant.	peak load plant
Least referred ↓	7. Diesel power plant.	peak load plant

15.4 COMBINED OPERATION OF RUN OFF THE RIVER HYDRO POWER PLANT AND THERMAL POWER PLANT

Run off the river plant has small water storage and water flow varies widely throughout the year. During drought or lean water flow,thermal power plant can be used to supply load. While during heavy run -off in hydro plant, it can be used as base load plant and thermal power plant as peak land plant. This allows the load to be adjusted on thermal power plant. This type of operation results in better utilisation of water flow in hydro and saving in fuel of thermal power plant.

15.5 COMBINED OPERATION OF STORAGE HYDRO POWER PLANT AND THERMAL POWER PLANT

A hydro power plant with ample storage can supply more power and can act as base load power plant. Thermal power plant can be used as peak load plant to minimize fuel cost. However, depending upon water availability, the role can be reversed. The hydro and thermal generation is scheduled as to keep the cost per unit of power generated to minimum value.

15.6 COMBINED OPERATION OF PUMPED STORAGE PLANT AND NUCLEAR POWER PLANT

A pumped storage hydro electric power plant stores water during off-peak hours by working as pump. During peak hours,the stored water is allowed to flow causing turbine to produce power and meet peak load demand. While a nuclear power plant can be run as base load plant. The combined operation gives operational economy.

15.7 COMBINED OPERATION OF HYDRO ELECTRIC AND GAS TURBINE POWER PLANTS

A gas turbine plant can be used as peak load plant especially where the load factor is very low (15% or less). Hydro power plant(run-off-the -river or with sufficient storage) can be used as base load plant.A gas turbine plant has advantages of quick startup, lesser space requirement, very little cooling water requirement and faster response to load changes. Although running cost of gas turbine is high but it is compensated by lower operating and maintenance cost and less requirement of plant personnel.

Example 15.1

A power system has a straight time load duration curve with a minimum load of 24 MW and a maximum load of 120 MW. The cost of operation of a base load and a peak load plant are given below—

$$\text{Peak load plant} = 60 \text{ ₹/kW} + 0.12 \text{ ₹/kWh}$$

$$\text{Base load plant} = 240 \text{ ₹/kW} + 0.06 \text{ ₹/kWh}$$

Calculate– (*i*) load shared by base load and peak load plants for minimum cost.

(*ii*) annual load factor of base load and peak load plants.

Solution: The operating cost of base load and peak load plant are given by following—

$$\text{For base load plant} = A \text{ kW} + B \text{ kWh}$$

$$\text{For peak load plant} = C \text{ kW} + D \text{ kWh}$$

$$A = 240, \quad B = 0.06$$

$$C = 60, \quad D = 0.12$$

(*i*) For minimum overall cost, if h is the number of hours for which base load plant be operated then,

$$h = \frac{A - C}{D - B} = \frac{240 - 60}{0.12 - 0.06} = 3000 \text{ hours.}$$

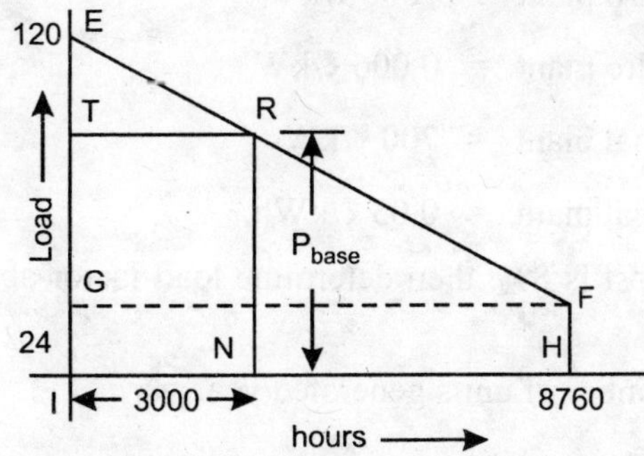

Fig. 15.1 Base load and peak load operation

Now,
$$P_{base} + P_{peak} = 120 \text{ MW}$$

$$P_{peak} = 120 - P_{base}$$

Triangles ERT and EFG are similar.

$$\therefore \quad \frac{ET}{EG} = \frac{TR}{GF}$$

$$\frac{120-P_{base}}{120-24} = \frac{3000}{8760} \Rightarrow \mathbf{P_{base} = 87\ MW} \quad \textbf{Ans.}$$

$$\therefore \quad P_{peak} = 120 - 87 = \mathbf{33\ MW} \quad \textbf{Ans.}$$

(*ii*) Annual load factor for base load and peak load plant

$$[\text{L.F}]_{\text{base laod}} = \frac{\text{Average load} \times 8760}{\text{Peak load} \times 8760} \Rightarrow \frac{\text{Area } TRFHIT}{P_{base} \times 8760}$$

$$= \frac{\text{Area } TRFGT + \text{Area } GFHIG.}{P_{base} \times 8760.}$$

$$= \frac{\frac{1}{2}(3000 + 8760) \times (87 - 24) + 24 \times 8760}{87 \times 8760}$$

$$= \mathbf{76.2\%} \quad \textbf{Ans.}$$

$$[\text{L.F}]_{\text{peak laod}} = \frac{\text{Area ERT}}{\text{P}_{\text{peak}} \times 8760}$$

$$= \frac{\frac{1}{2} \times 3000 \times 33}{33 \times 8760}$$

$$= \mathbf{17.1\%} \quad \textbf{Ans.}$$

Example 15.2

A cement manufacturing company has a peak demand of 150 MW. The load demand can be met either through a thermal power plant or through a hydro power plant. The cost of both power plant are given below-

Capital cost of hydro plant = 1600 ₹/kW

Operating cost of hydro plant = 0.006 ₹/kW

Capital cost of thermal plant = 700 ₹/kW

Operating cost of thermal plant = 0.03 ₹/kWh.

If the interest on capital cost is 8%, then determine load factor above which hydro plant will be economical.

Solution: Assume total number of units generated/year = x

For thermal power plant—

$$\text{Capital cost} = 700\ ₹/\text{kW} \times 150 \times 10^3\ \text{kW} = ₹\ 105 \times 10^6$$

$$\text{Interest charges} = 105 \times 10^6 \times \frac{8}{100} = ₹\ 8.4 \times 10^6$$

$$\text{Fixed cost} = ₹\ \frac{8.4 \times 10^6}{x} \text{ per kWh}$$

$$\text{Given, operating cost} = ₹\,0.03 \text{ per kWh.}$$

$$\text{Overall cost} = \text{Fixed cost} + \text{operating cost} = \left(\frac{8.4 \times 10^6}{x} + 0.03\right) ₹/\text{kWh.}$$

Hydro power plant

$$\text{Capital cost} = ₹\,1600 \text{ kW} \times 150 \times 10^3 \text{ kW} = ₹\,240 \times 10^6$$

$$\text{Interest charges} = 240 \times 10^6 \times \frac{8}{100} = ₹\,19.2 \times 10^6$$

$$\text{Fixed cost} = \frac{₹\,19.2 \times 10^6}{x} \text{ per kWh}$$

Given,

$$\text{operating cost} = ₹\,0.006 \text{ kWh}$$

$$\text{overall cost} = \text{Fixed cost} + \text{operating cost}$$

$$= \left(\frac{19.2 \times 10^6}{x} + 0.006\right)$$

$$\text{If overall cost of hydro plant} = \text{overall cost of thermal plant}$$

$$\frac{19.2 \times 10^6}{x} + 0.006 = \frac{8.4 \times 10^6}{x} + 0.03$$

or

$$x = 450 \times 10^6 \text{ kWh}$$

$$\therefore \quad \text{Unit generated by hydro plant} = 450 \times 10^6 \text{ kWh}$$

$$\text{Load factor} = \frac{\text{Total units produced}}{\text{Maximum demand} \times 8760} = \frac{450 \times 10^6}{150 \times 10^3 \times 8760}$$

$$= 0.342 \text{ or } \mathbf{34.2\%} \quad \textbf{Ans.}$$

Hence,hydro power plant will be more economical at load factor of 34.2% or more.

Example 15.3

A fertilizer plant has load demand varying from 10 MW to 50 MW. The load curve can be assumed to be linear. A hydro power plant can supply a peak load of 60 MWh per day during lean water flow period. However, power from thermal power plant during off-peak hour can be used to pump water back to reservoir by the hydro plant at 100% load factor. With efficiency of thermal plant as 60%, determine maximum capacity of both type of plants.

Solution:

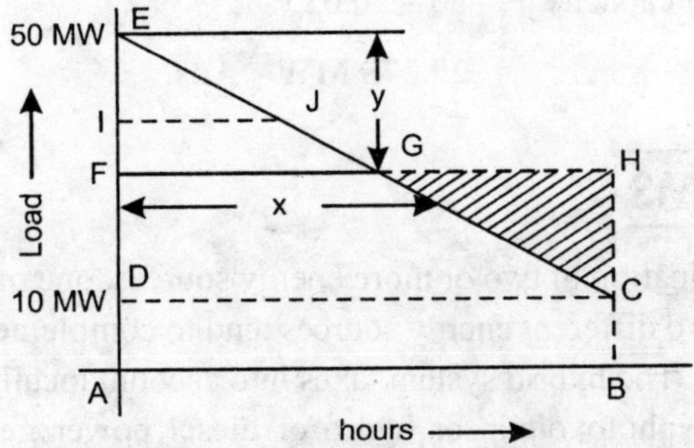

Fig. 15.2 Load duration curve

The maximum demand $AE = 50$ MW

Minimum demand $AD = 10$ MW

Δ CGH represents capacity of thermal power plant used to pump water back to reservoir during off peak hours.

Δ EIJ represents hydro power available during lean flow period.

The energy supplied by thermal power plant to hydro power plant is represented by FGJI with efficiency of 60%.

$$\therefore \quad \text{Area of FGJI} = 0.60 \times \text{area of CHG}$$

But

$$\text{area of FGJI} = \text{Area of EFC} - \text{Area of EJI}$$

$$= \text{Area of EFG} - 60000$$

$$= \frac{1}{2} xy - 60000$$

$$\text{Area of EFB} = \frac{1}{2}(24 - x)(40000 - y)$$

or

$$\frac{1}{2}xy - 60000 = \frac{1}{2}(24 - x)(40000 - y) \times 0.60$$

Triangles EFG and CDE are similar.

$$\therefore \quad \frac{y}{40000} = \frac{x}{24} \Rightarrow y = \frac{40000\,x}{24}$$

or

$$\frac{1}{2}x^2 \frac{40000}{24} - 60000 = \frac{1}{2}(24 - x)\left(40000 - \frac{40000\,x}{24}\right) \times 0.60$$

$$x^2 - 72 = (x^2 - 48x + 576) \times 0.60$$

$$x^2 + 72x - 1044 = 0$$

$$x = \frac{-70 \pm 96.75}{24} = 12.375$$

$$\therefore \text{ The hydro plant capacity,} \quad y = \frac{40000 \times 12.75}{24}$$

$$= \textbf{20.625 MW} \quad \textbf{Ans.}$$

$$\text{Thermal power plant capacity} = 50 - 20.625$$

$$= \textbf{29.375 MW} \quad \textbf{Ans.}$$

15.8 HYBRID SYSTEMS

Hybrid system refers to combination of two or more energy sources, one of which is a renewable energy source. The combination of two different energy sources tend to complement each other by overcoming shortcomings in either system. The hybrid system takes into account locally available renewable energy sources, such as wind, solar, photovoltaic or hydro or diesel power generation. These systems are preferred for off-grid application *i.e.* as standalone source of power in remote area. In some applications, inherent limitations of one type of renewable energy source is compensated by other renewable source. For example, solar PV can be supply power during daytime while wind system can be used to supply power during night time. Hence, hybrid system is a combination of conventional energy source and /or renewable source which offers advantages, such as optimized overall plant cost and improved reliability of supply.

Features of hybrid systems are following–

(*i*) there is flexibility of fuel to be used.

(*ii*) due to combined operation, overall efficiency is increased.

(*iii*) reliability of supply is improved.

(*iv*) it acts as means of rural electrification for off-grid application.

(*v*) lower emission due to minimized usage of fossil fuel.

(*vi*) high reliability can be achieved through energy storage or redundant technologies.

(*vii*) hybrid system can be designed to achieve desirable characteristics, such as lowest maintenance cost, long life, lower operations cost etc.

15.8.1 Solar PV and Wind Hybrid System

This hybrid system uses two types of renewable sources viz solar PV and wind. The system consists of solar PV cells, a controller, wind turbine, AC to DC converter, battery banks for energy storage, and DC to AC inverter.

The wind generator produces AC voltage with variable voltage and frequency. This variable voltage and variable frequency AC supply is converted into DC voltage to charge the battery banks. An inverter converts DC voltage from batteries to AC voltage at 220 V and 50 Hz frequency. A controller is provided which protects the battery from over charging and deep discharging.

The solar PV cells produce DC voltage when solar radiation is incident on it. This DC voltage is fed to the controller which inturn charge batteries.

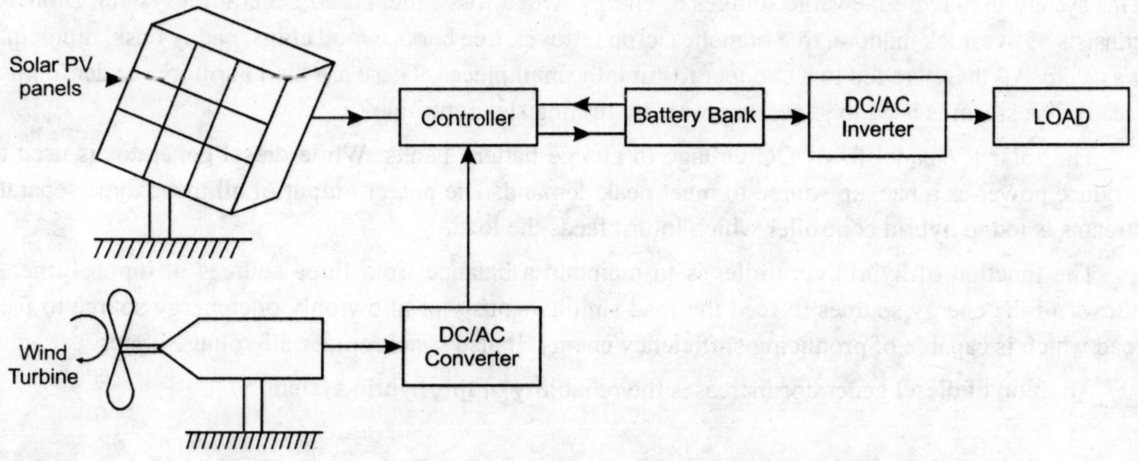

Fig. 15.3 Block diagram of solar PV/Wind hybrid system

15.8.2 Solar PV and Hydro Hybrid System

In a solar PV and hydro hybrid system, the hydro system has small reservoir capacity to store water. The water head and discharge depends upon specific site condition. The hydro power is normally installed on small streams as run-off the river scheme.

The system is composed of solar PV cells, a controller, battery banks, DC to AC inverter, mini hydro system and AC to DC converter. Hydro turbine produces AC output voltage of variable magnitude and variable frequency. This is then converted to DC voltage to charge battery banks. The inverter converts DC voltage of battery to 220 V AC and 50 Hz supply for the load.

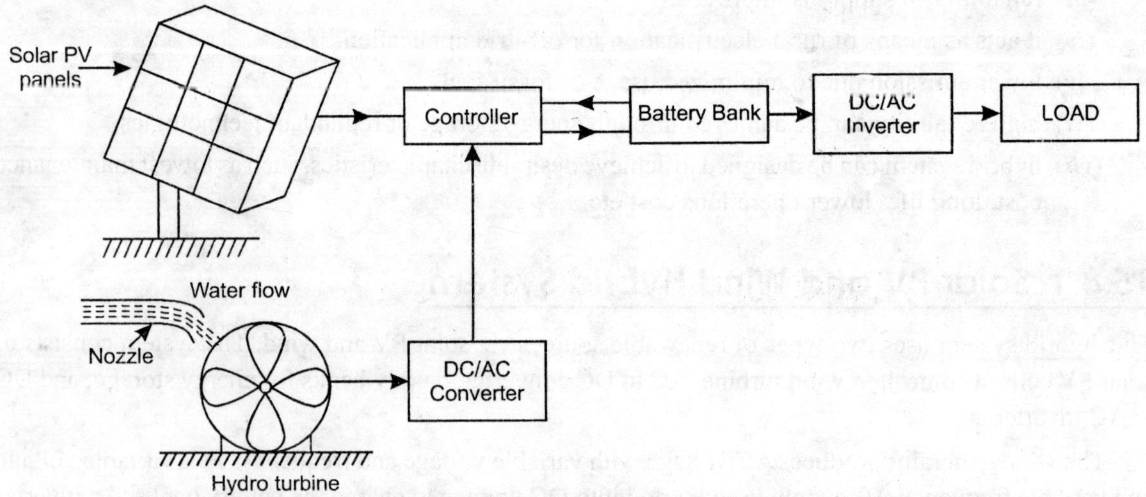

Fig. 15.4 Block diagram of solar PV/hydro hybrid system

15.8.3 Biomass-Solar PV-Diesel Hybrid

This system uses two renewable sources of energy with a fossil fuel based generation system. Biomass consists of livestock manure, tree branches, crop leftover, tree barks, wood chips, paddy husk, municipal waste etc. All these are fed to a chopper to cut into small pieces. These are then burnt in a boiler to raise steam. The steam is used to generate power by turning steam turbine.

The solar PV panel feeds DC voltage to charge battery banks. While diesel generator is used to produce power as a backup source to meet peak demand. The power output of all these three separate streams is fed to hybrid controller which inturn feeds the load.

The function of hybrid controller is to maintain a balance from three sources of input. Either it allows all the energy sources to feed the load simultaneously or allow only one energy source to feed load which is capable of producing sufficiency energy. It also synchronizes all voltage inputs.

Addition of diesel generator increases the reliability of this hybrid system.

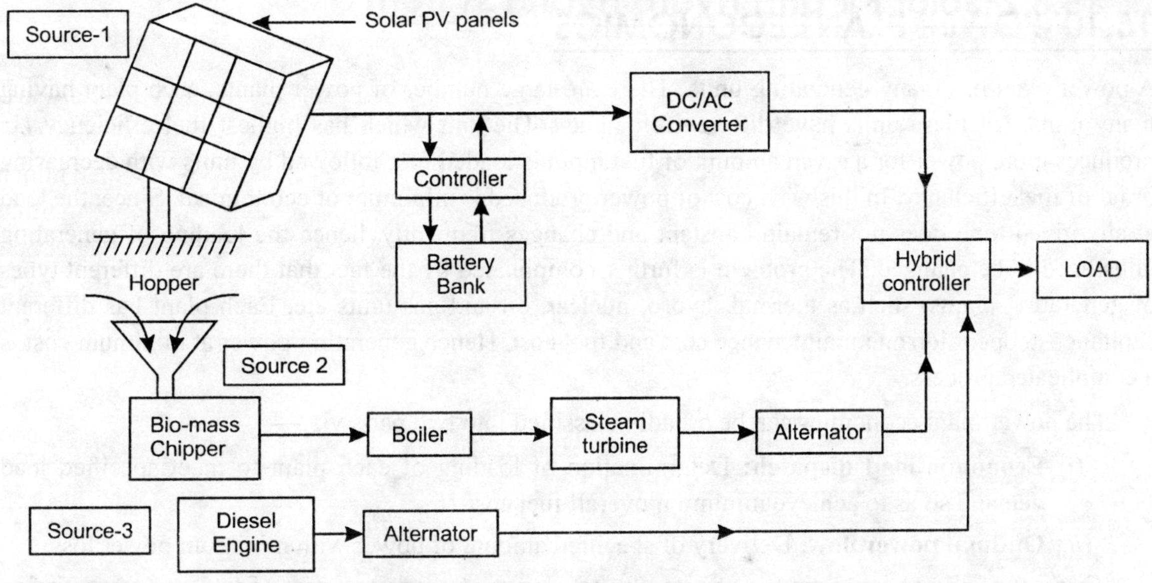

Fig. 15.5 Block diagram of biomass-solar PV-diesel hybrid system

15.9 SHORT TERM HYDRO-THERMAL CO-ORDINATION

The economic operation of combined hydro-thermal system depends upon following factors–

(*i*) incremental fuel cost of thermal plant.

(*ii*) incremental transmission loss characteristics.

(*iii*) load pattern.

(*iv*) expected inflow of water during operating period.

(*v*) hydro-generation as a function of water storage.

(*vi*) reservoir elevation as a function of water storage.

(*vii*) tail race elevation as a function of water discharge.

(*viii*) water intake losses, evaporation, seepage etc.

The above mentioned factors vary widely making task of scheduling very difficult. Co-ordination of combined system is carried out assuming a fixed quantity of water at a constant head over a certain operating period. The problem is to supply load as per load pattern during the operating period so as to minimize generation cost. The operating fuel cost of hydro plant is zero while that of thermal power plant constitutes as sizable sum. Hence, hydro-thermal scheduling is a problem of optimal control with certain constraints. The constraints are following—

(*i*) total amount of water available for hydro generation over a given period of time.

(*ii*) total generation minus losses must be equal to load at any instant of time

15.10 POWER PLANT ECONOMICS

A power plant has many generating units. There are large number of power plants, each plant having many units. All these units have different efficiency. The unit which has highest fuel efficiency *i.e.* produces more power for a given amount of fuel input is loaded first followed by units with decreasing order of fuel efficiency. In this way, cost of power produced is minimum or economical. Since, the load at any given time does not remain constant and changes frequently, hence the loading of generating units need to be changed. The problem is further complicated by the fact that there are different types of generating plants, such as thermal, hydro, nuclear, oil and gas units etc. Each plant has different capital cost, operation and maintenance cost and fuel cost. Hence,generating power at minimum cost is a complicated process.

The power plant economics can be broadly classified into two parts viz.—

(*i*) **Economic load dispatch:** Determination of loading of each plant to meet specified load demand so as to achieve minimum overall fuel cost.

(*ii*) **Optimal power flow:** Delivery of specified amount of power with minimum power loss.

The cost of power generation is affected by efficiency of generator, cost of fuel and transmission losses. For example, even if generator is efficient but located far from load centre, then it may lead to high transmission losses and hence operation becomes uneconomical. Similarly, if fuel cost is high, the most efficient generator may not give minimum cost. Fuel cost does not include capital cost, deprecation cost, start up and shutdown cost, maintenance cost etc.

In the subsequent sections, we shall concentrate on economic dispatch problem determining power output of each plant and power output of each generating unit in a plant with a view to minimize overall fuel cost without considering transmission losses. Again, this exercise is repeated considering transmission losses.

15.10.1 Performance Curves

(*i*) **Input-output curve:** Fuel cost in a thermal power plant is a major cost and it can be controlled. Hence, minimization of fuel cost is chosen for economic operation. The fuel input is measured in Tonnes/hr or Million of Btu/hr. If the cost of fuel in ₹/Tonne or ₹/Millions of Btu is known, input cost of generating unit in ₹/hours can be calculated. A typical input–output curve of generating unit is shown below—

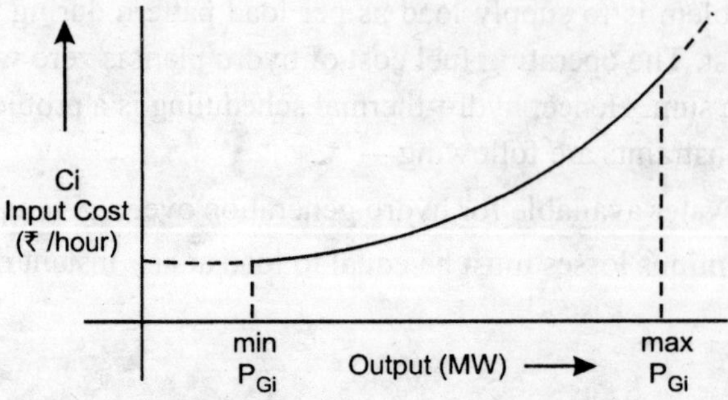

Fig. 15.6 Input-output characteristics

Where, F_i = Input cost of generating power P_{Gi} MW in ₹/hour.

P_{Gi}^{min} = Minimum power generated by i^{th} unit.

P_{Gi}^{max} = Maximum power generated by i^{th} unit.

The input output curve is quadratic then,

$$F_i = a_i + b_i P_{Gi} + c_i\, p_{Gi}^2 \text{ ₹/hour} \quad ...(15.1)$$

Where a_i, b_i and c_i are co-efficients.

Each generating unit has different input-output curve. Hence, for a given input cost, power generated will be different for different units.

(ii) **Heat rate curve:** Heat rate is defined as ratio of fuel input in kcal to energy output in kWh. The slope of input-output curve gives heat rate at any point. Reciprocal of heat rate is fuel efficiency.

(*a*) $$\text{Heat rate} = \frac{\text{Fuel input in kcal}}{\text{Energy output in kWh.}}$$

(*b*) $$\text{Fuel efficiency} = \frac{\text{Energy output in kWh}}{\text{Fuel input in kcal}}$$

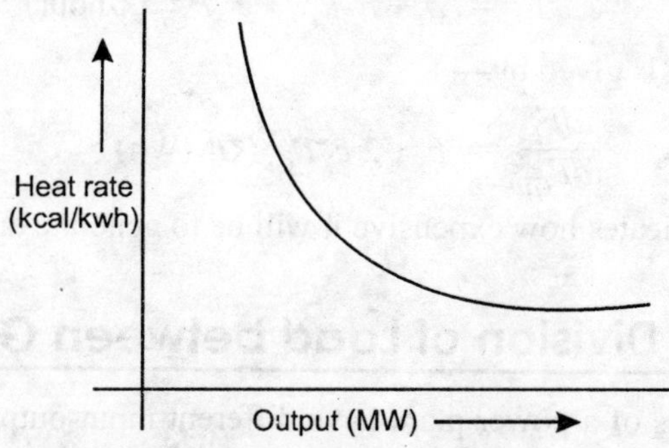

Fig. 15.7 Heat rate curve

(iii) **Incremental fuel rate curve:** Incremental fuel rate is defined as ratio of small change in input fuel to the corresponding change in output power.

$$\therefore \quad \text{Incremental fuel rate} = \frac{\text{Change in input fuel}}{\text{Chagne in output power}}$$

Fig. 15.8 Incremental fuel rate curve

(*iv*) **Incremental cost curve:** The product of incremental fuel rate and fuel cost is known as incremental cost (₹/MWh)

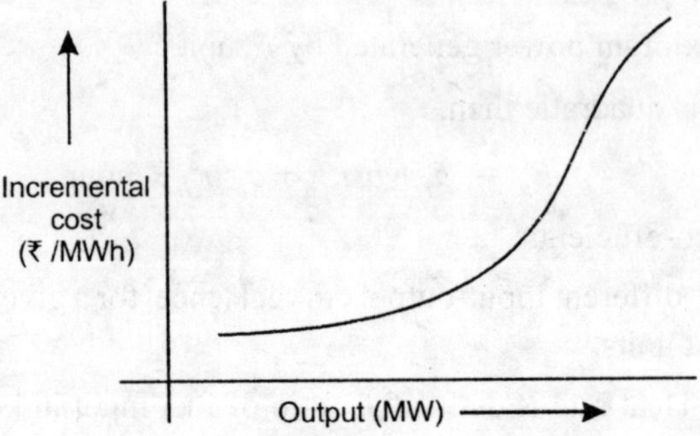

Fig. 15.9 Incremental cost curve

Criterion for distributing total load on any two generator is based on the fact that increase of load on one unit and corresponding decrease of load on the other unit changes the total cost. The total cost may increase or decrease.

If fuel cost F_i of a plant is given by following–

$$F_i = a_i + b_i P_{Gi} + c_i P_{Gi}^2 \text{ (₹/hour)} \quad ...(15.2)$$

The incremental fuel cost is given by—

$$\frac{dF_i}{dP_{Gi}} = b_i + 2c_i P_{Gi} \text{ (₹/MWh)} \quad ...(15.3)$$

Incremental fuel cost indicates how expensive it will be to generate an increment of power.

15.10.2 Economic Division of Load between Generating Units

Generally, all generating units of a power plant have different input-output characteristic curve (unless units are identical). Consider a case, where total load is to be shared by two generating units such that incremental cost of one unit is higher than other unit. If a part of the total load is shifted from one unit having lower incremental cost, then there will be overall reduction of total cost. This shifting of load from one unit to the other can be continued till incremental cost of both the unit are equal. Consider increment cost curve of two units such that $\frac{dF_2}{dP_{G2}} > \frac{dF_1}{dP_{G1}}$

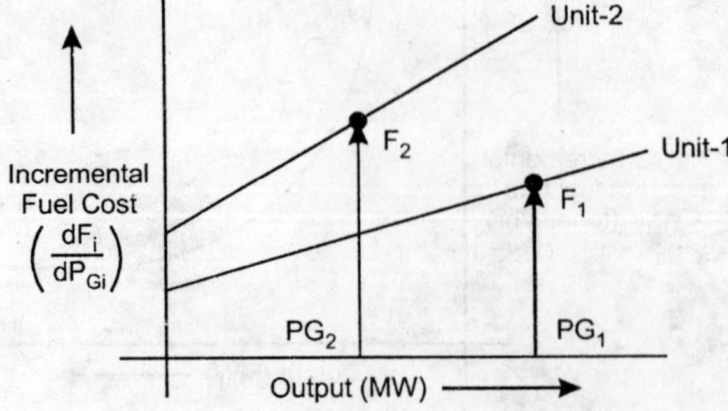

Fig. 15.10 Cost curve of two units

If output power of unit-2 is decreased by ΔP_G and output power of unit-1 is increased by ΔP_G, so that $\frac{dF_2}{dP_{G2}}\Delta P_G > \frac{dF_1}{dP_{G1}}\Delta P_G$. The change is continued till $\frac{dF_1}{dP_{G1}} = \frac{dF_2}{dP_{G2}}$.

Hence,total cost will be minimum when incremental cost of both units are equal.

15.10.3 Economic Generation Scheduling Neglecting Losses And Generation Limits

Let us consider a simple case of economic dispatch where transmission losses are neglected.

Let there be N_g number of generators supplying a total demand P_D. The incremental cost of generators be,

$F_i(P_{G1}), F_2(P_{G2}), F_3(P_{G3}) \ldots F_i(P_{Gi})$.

We have to find set of P_{Gi} which minimizes total cost for a given load demand.

$$\text{Total cost, } F_T = F_1(P_{G1}) + F_2(P_{G2}) + F_3(P_{G3}) + \ldots + F_i(P_{Gi}) \qquad \ldots(15.4)$$

or

$$\text{Minimize } F_T = \sum_{i=1}^{Ng} Fi \qquad \ldots(15.5)$$

Subject to condition—

$$P_D - (P_{G1} + P_{G2} + P_{G3} + \ldots + P_{Gi}) = 0 \qquad \ldots(15.6)$$

or

$$P_D = \sum_{i=1}^{Ng} P_{Gi} = 0 \qquad \ldots(15.7)$$

or

$$P_D - \sum_{i=1}^{Ng} P_{Gi} = 0 \qquad \ldots(15.8)$$

This is an optimization problem with equality constraint and can be solveu by method of Lagrangian multiplies.

Hence, augmented cost function is given by—

$$L = F_T + \lambda\left(P_D - \sum_{i=1}^{Ng} P_{Gi}\right) \qquad \ldots(15.9)$$

$$\text{Minimum is obtained when } \frac{\partial L}{\partial P_{Gi}} = 0 \text{ and } \frac{\partial L}{\partial \lambda} = 0 \qquad \ldots(15.10)$$

$$\therefore \quad \frac{\partial L}{\partial P_{Gi}} = \frac{\partial F_T}{\partial P_{Gi}} - \lambda = 0 \qquad \ldots(5.10)$$

And

$$\frac{\partial L}{\partial \lambda} = \mathrm{P_D} - \sum_{i=1}^{Ng} P_{Gi} = 0 \qquad \ldots(15.11)$$

It can be seen that above *eq* is nothing but the constraint of the problem.

Hence,cost of a plant (F_T) depends only on its output (P_{Gi}).

$$\therefore \quad \frac{\partial F_T}{\partial P_{Gi}} = \frac{\partial F_i}{\partial P_{Gi}} = \frac{dF_i}{dP_{Gi}}$$

Again, $$\frac{\partial F_i}{\partial P_{Gi}} = \frac{dF_i}{dP_{Gi}} = \lambda$$

So, $$b_i + 2\,c_i\,P_{Gi} = \lambda \qquad ...(15.12)$$

This is known as **co-ordination equation**. It shows that for economic generation scheduling, all plants must work at equal incremental cost neglecting transmission losses and generation limit.

For above equation, $$P_{Gi} = \frac{\lambda - bi}{2ci} \qquad ...(15.13)$$

For a lossless system $$\sum_{i=1}^{Ng} P_{Gi} = P_D \qquad ...(15.14)$$

$$\therefore \quad \sum_{i=1}^{Ng}\left(\frac{\lambda - bi}{2ci}\right) = P_D \qquad ...(15.15)$$

or $$\lambda = \frac{P_D + \sum_{i=1}^{Ng} \frac{bi}{2ci}}{\sum_{i=1}^{Ng} \frac{1}{2ci}} \qquad ...(15.16)$$

It is observed that λ is a function of demand P_D and cost co-efficients (b_i and c_i).

Example 15.4

Consider the fuel cost of two units–

$$F_1 = 1.6 + 25\,P_{G1} + 0.1\,p_{G1}^2 \text{ ₹/h}$$

$$F_2 = 1.8 + 35\,P_{G2} + 0.1\,P_{G2}^2 \text{ ₹/h.}$$

Where P_{G1} and P_{G2} are in MW. Neglecting transmission losses, determine the optimal schedule when total load to be shared is 200 MW.

Solution:

$$\frac{dF_1}{dP_{G1}} = 25 + 0.2\,P_{G1} \qquad \text{₹/MWh}$$

$$\frac{dF_2}{dP_{G2}} = 35 + 0.2\,P_{G2} \qquad \text{₹/MWh}$$

$$P_D = P_{G1} + P_{G2} = 200 \text{ MW} \qquad \text{given}$$

For economic schedule,

$$\frac{dF_1}{dP_{G1}} = \frac{dF_2}{dP_{G2}} = \lambda$$

$$25 + 0.2\,P_{G1} = 35 + 0.2\,(200 - P_{G1})$$

$$25 + 0.2\,P_{G1} = 35 + 40 - 0.2\,P_{G1}$$

$$0.4\,P_{G1} = 10 \Rightarrow P_{G1} = \frac{10}{0.4} = \mathbf{25\ MW} \quad \textbf{Ans.}$$

$$\therefore \quad P_{G2} = 200 - 25 = \mathbf{175\ MW} \quad \textbf{Ans.}$$

$$\lambda = 25 + 0.2\,(25) = 30\ ₹/\text{MWh}.$$

Example 15.5

The fuel cost in ₹/*h* for two 100 MW plants is given by—

$$F_1 = 300 + 6.0\,P_{Gi} + 0.004\,P_{G1}^2$$

$$F_2 = 600 + b_2 P_{G2} + c_2\,P_{G2}^2$$

Determine- (*i*) optimal generation schedule neglecting losses when total demand is 600 MW and incremental cost of power (λ) is ₹ 8/MWh

(*ii*) optimal generation schedule neglecting losses when the total demand is 1500 MW and incremental cost of power (λ) is ₹ 10/MWh.

(*iii*) Find co-efficients b_2 and c_2

Solution:

(*i*)

$$P_{G1} = \frac{\lambda - b_1}{2c_1} = \frac{8-6}{2\times 0.004} = \mathbf{250\ MW} \quad \textbf{Ans.}$$

$$P_{G2} = P_D - P_{G1} = 600 - 250 = \mathbf{350\ MW} \quad \textbf{Ans.}$$

(*ii*)

$$P_{G1} = \frac{\lambda - b_1}{2c_1} = \frac{10-6}{2\times 0.004} = \mathbf{500\ MW} \quad \textbf{Ans.}$$

$$P_{G2} = P_D - P_{G1} = 1500 - 500 = \mathbf{1000\ MW} \quad \textbf{Ans.}$$

(*iii*)

$$P_{G2} = \frac{\lambda - b_2}{2c_2}$$

From (*i*)

$$P_{G2} = \frac{\lambda - b_2}{2\,c_2} \Rightarrow 350 = \frac{8 - b_2}{2\,c_2}$$

From (*ii*)

$$1000 = \frac{10 - b_2}{2\,c_2}$$

Solving above two equations, we get

$$\mathbf{b_2 = 6.92, \quad c_2 = 0.0015} \quad \textbf{Ans,}$$

Example 15.6

A power plant has three units with following cost characteristics—

$$F_1 = 4000 + 216\,P_1 + 0.5\,P_1^2\ ₹/h$$

$$F_2 = 6000 + 275\,P_2 + 1.0\,P_2^2\ ₹/h$$

$$F_3 = 8000 + 165\,P_3 + 0.7\,P_3^2\ ₹/h$$

P_1, P_2 and P_3 are in MW. The minimum and maximum load allowed on each unit are 40 MW and 160 MW. Determine economic scheduling for total demand of 350 MW.

Solution: The incremental cost of all the three units is given by—

$$\frac{dF_1}{dP_1} = 216 + 1.0\,P_1 \text{ ₹/MWh}$$

$$\frac{dF_2}{dP_2} = 275 + 2.0\,P_2 \text{ ₹/MWh}$$

$$\frac{dF_3}{dP_3} = 165 + 1.4\,P_3 \text{ ₹/MWh}$$

For optimal scheduling

$$1.0\,P_1 + 216 = \lambda; \quad 2.0\,P_2 + 275 = \lambda; \quad 1.4\,P_3 + 165 = \lambda$$

Since $P_1 + P_2 + P_3 = 350$ MW (given)

$$\text{or} \quad \left(\frac{\lambda - 216}{1.0}\right) + \left(\frac{\lambda - 275}{2.0}\right) + \left(\frac{\lambda - 165}{1.4}\right) = 350$$

$$\text{or} \quad \lambda\left(\frac{1}{1.0} + \frac{1}{2.0} + \frac{1}{1.4}\right) = 350 + \frac{216}{1.0} + \frac{275}{2.0} + \frac{165}{1.4}$$

$$2.2143\,\lambda = 821.3571$$

$$\text{or} \quad \lambda = 370.93$$

Therefore,

$$P_1 = \frac{\lambda - 216}{1.0} = \frac{370.93 - 216}{1.0} = \mathbf{154.93\ MW} \quad \textbf{Ans.}$$

$$P_2 = \frac{\lambda - 275}{2} = \frac{370.93 - 275}{2} = \mathbf{95.93\ MW} \quad \textbf{Ans.}$$

$$P_3 = \frac{\lambda - 165}{1.4} = \frac{370.93 - 165}{1.4} = \mathbf{147.09\ MW} \quad \textbf{Ans.}$$

P_1, P_2 and P_3 all are with in minimum and maximum limits of generation.

Example 15.7

Incremental cost of two units in a plant are given below—

$$\frac{dF_1}{dP_1} = 0.8\,P_1 + 160 \text{ ₹/MWh}$$

$$\frac{dF_2}{dP_2} = 0.9\,P_2 + 120 \text{ ₹/MWh}$$

The load varies minimum of 50 MW to maximum of 250 MW. The minimum and maximum allowable load on each unit are 20 and 125 MW respectively. Determine incremental cost and optimal allocation of loads for various total loads.

Solution:

It can be observed that incremental cost of unit-1 is higher than unit-2. Hence, unit-1 need to be loaded to minimum allowable value *i.e.* $P_1 = 20$ MW, therefore $P_2 = 50 - 20 = 30$ MW.

$$\frac{dF_1}{dP_1} = 0.8 \times 20 + 160 = 176 \text{ ₹/MWh}$$

$$\frac{dF_2}{dP_2} = 0.9 \times 30 + 120 = 147 \text{ ₹/MWh.}$$

As the load is increased from 50 MW, load on unit-2 can be increased upto ₹ 176 MWh so that load on unit-2 is $P_2 = \dfrac{176-120}{0.9} = 62.2\text{MW}$.

When λ is increased above ₹ 176 MWh then,

$$P_1 = \frac{\lambda - 160}{0.8} \text{ MW and } P_2 = \frac{\lambda - 120}{0.9} \text{ MW}$$

Following table 15.1 shows allocation of load on two units.

Table 15.1 Load allocation

Load on unit-1 P_1*(MW)*	*Load on unit-2* P_2 *(MW)*	*Incremental cost (λ)*	*Total load* $P_1 + P_2$ *(MW)*
20	30	147	50
20	62.2	176	82.2
25	66.6	180	91.6
37.5	77.7	190	115.2
50	88.8	200	138.8
62.5	100.0	210	162.5
75	111.1	220	186.1
87.5	122.2	230	209.7

As the load on unit-2 approaches maximum value of 125 MW then $\lambda = 0.9 \times 125 + 120 = 232.5$ ₹/MWh.

Since λ tends to increase further hence P_2 is kept at 125 MW and load on unit-1 is increased $\left(P_1 = \dfrac{\lambda - 160}{0.8}\right)$. The corresponding load allocation is shown in table 15.2

Table 15.2 Load allocation with $P_2 = 125$ MW

P_2*(MW)*	P_1*(MW)*	$P_1 + P_2$ *(MW)*	*λ (₹/MWh)*
125	90.62	215.62	232.5
125	100	225	240
125	112.5	237.5	250
125	125	250	260

15.10.4 Derivation of Transmission Loss Formula (B co-efficients)

Power system consists of several power plants widely dispersed geographically. These plants are inter-connected by transmission lines. When power is transmitted over these lines, power loss takes place. This power loss depends upon three parameters viz. line parameters (resistance, inductance, capacitance), bus voltages and power flow. An expression for determination of transmission loss can be derived for N number of power plants with some reasonable approximation (exact derivation by Kron is elaborate).

Following assumptions can be made—

(*i*) same X/R ratio for all network branches.

(*ii*) same phase angle of all load current with respect to a common reference. Consider case of two generating plants connected to loads through transmission network

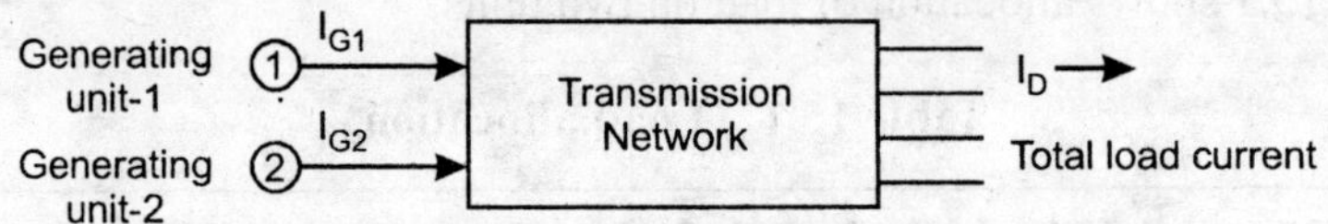

Fig. 15.11 Two generating plants connected to loads

Assume that load is supplied by generator-1 only.

Let the current in any branch M be I_{M1}.

$$N_{M1} = \frac{I_{M1}}{I_D} \quad \text{...(15.17)}$$

Here, $I_{G1} = I_D$

Again, when generator-2 supplies total load I_D then,

$$N_{M2} = \frac{I_{M2}}{I_D} \quad \text{...(15.18)}$$

Here, $I_{G2} = I_D$

N_{M1} and N_{M2} are current distribution factors whose magnitude depends upon line impedances and network connection and are independent of I_D. When both generator-1 and generator-2 are supplying total I_D then,

$$I_M = N_{M1} I_{G1} + N_{M2} I_{G2} \quad \text{...(15.19)}$$

As assumed earlier, I_{M1}, I_{M2} and I_D currents have same phase angles. Hence, current distribution factors are real and not complex,

Let $I_{G1} = |I_{G1}| \angle \theta_1$ and $I_{G2} = |I_{G2}| \angle \theta_2$

Now,

$$|I_M|^2 = (N_{M1} |I_{G1}| \cos\theta_1 + N_{M2} |I_{G2}| \cos\theta_2)^2 + (N_{M1} |I_{G1}| \sin\theta_1 + N_{M2} |I_{G2}| \sin\theta_2)^2 \quad \text{...(15.20)}$$

$$|I_M|^2 = N_{M1}^2 |I_{G1}|^2 + N_{M2}^2 |I_{G2}|^2 + 2N_{M1} N_{M2} |I_{G1}||I_{G2}| \cos(\theta_1 - \theta_2) \quad \text{...(15.21)}$$

We know,

$$|I_{G1}| = \frac{P_{G1}}{\sqrt{3}\,|V_1|\cos\phi_1}, \quad |I_{G2}| = \frac{P_{G2}}{\sqrt{3}\,|V_2|\cos\phi_2}$$

where, P_{G1} = three phase real power output of generator–1

P_{G2} = three phase real power output of generator–2

V_1 = line to line bus voltage of generator–1

V_2 = line to line bus voltage of generator–2

ϕ_1 = power factor angle of generator–1

ϕ_2 = power factor angle of generator–2

Total transmission loss in the system is given by

$$P_L = \sum_M 3\,|I_M|^2 R_M \quad ...(15.22)$$

Where, R_M = branch resistance

Substituting value of I_M in above equation.

$$P_L = \frac{P_{G1}^2}{|V_1|^2(\cos\phi_1)^2}\sum_M N_{M1}^2 R_M + \frac{2\,P_{G1}\,P_{G2}\cos(\theta_1-\theta_2)}{|V_1||V_2|\cos\phi_2|\cos\phi_1}\sum_M N_{M1}N_{M2}R_M + \frac{P_{G2}^2}{|V_2|^2(\cos\phi_2)^2}\sum_M N_{M2}^2 R_M \quad ...(15.23$$

or we can write above equation as —

$$P_L = P_{G1}^2\,B_{11} + 2P_{G1}P_{G2}B_{12} + P_{G2}^2\,B_{22} \quad ...(15.24)$$

Where,

$$B_{11} = \frac{1}{|V_1|^2(\cos\phi_1)^2}\sum_M N_{M1}^2 R_M$$

$$B_{12} = \frac{\cos(\theta_1-\theta_2)}{|V_1||V_2|\cos\phi_1\cos\phi_2}\sum_M N_{M1}N_{M2}R_M$$

$$B_{22} = \frac{1}{|V_2|^2(\cos\phi_2)^2}\sum_M N_{M2}^2 R_M$$

B_{11}, B_{12} and B_{22} are called loss coefficients or *B*-coefficients and have unit of MW^{-1}.

For a large system having *n* generators, the transmission loss is given by—

$$P_L = \frac{P_{G1}^2}{|V_1|^2(\cos\phi_1)^2}\sum_M N_{M1}^2 + ... + \frac{P_{Gn}^2}{|V_n|^2(\cos\phi_n)^2}\sum_M N_{Mn}^2 R_M + 2\sum_{\substack{a,b=1\\a\neq b}}^{n}\frac{P_{Ga}\,P_{Gb}\cos(\theta_a-\theta_b)}{|V_a||V_b|\cos\phi_a\cos\phi_b}\sum_M N_{Ma}N_{Mb}R_M \quad (15.25)$$

In a generalised form–

$$P_L = \sum_{a=1}^{n}\sum_{b=1}^{n} P_{Ga}\,B_{ab}\,P_{Gb} \quad ...(15.26)$$

where,

$$B_{ab} = \frac{\cos(\theta_a-\theta_b)}{|V_a||V_b|\cos\phi_a\cos\phi_b}\sum_M N_{Ma}N_{Mb}R_M$$

B-coefficients are treated as constants over load cycle.

In matrix form, loss equation can be represented by

$$P_L = [P_1\ P_2 \ldots P_n] \begin{bmatrix} B_{11} & B_{12} & \cdots & B_{1n} \\ B_{21} & B_{22} & \cdots & B_{2n} \\ \vdots & \vdots & \vdots & \vdots \\ B_{n1} & B_{n2} & \cdots & B_{nn} \end{bmatrix} \begin{bmatrix} P_1 \\ P_2 \\ \vdots \\ P_n \end{bmatrix} \quad \ldots(15.27)$$

Example 15.8

Determine loss co-efficients in MW^{-1} and pu for a base of 50 MVA with following detail (given in pu)

$I_A = 1.2 - j0.4$ $\quad Z_A = 0.02 + j0.08$

$I_B = 0.4 - j0.2$ $\quad Z_B = 0.08 + j0.32$

$I_C = 0.8 - j0.1$ $\quad Z_C = 0.02 + j0.08$

$I_D = 0.8 - j0.2$ $\quad Z_D = 0.03 + j0.12$

$I_E = 1.2 - j0.3$ $\quad Z_E = 0.03 + j0.12$

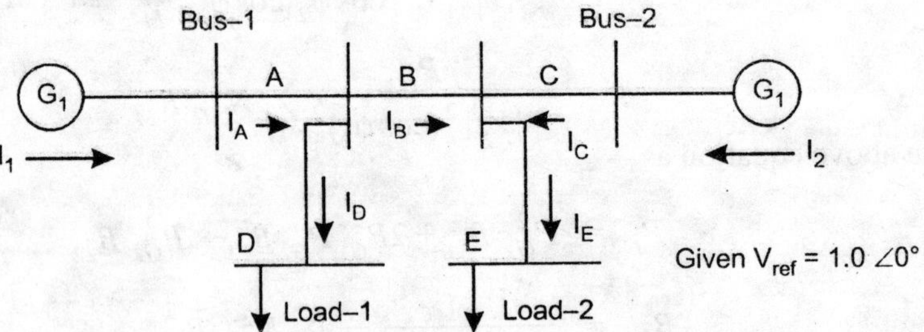

Fig. 15.12 Example 15.8

Solution:

Total current $\quad I_L = I_D + I_C = 2.0 - j0.5 = 2.061 \angle -14.3°$ A

$$I_{L1} = I_D = 0.8 - j0.2 = 0.825 \angle -14.03° \text{A}$$

$$\frac{I_{L1}}{I_L} = 0.4, \quad \frac{I_{L2}}{I_L} = 1.0 - 0.4 = 0.6$$

Assume, only generator–1 supplies entire load then $I_1 = I_L$

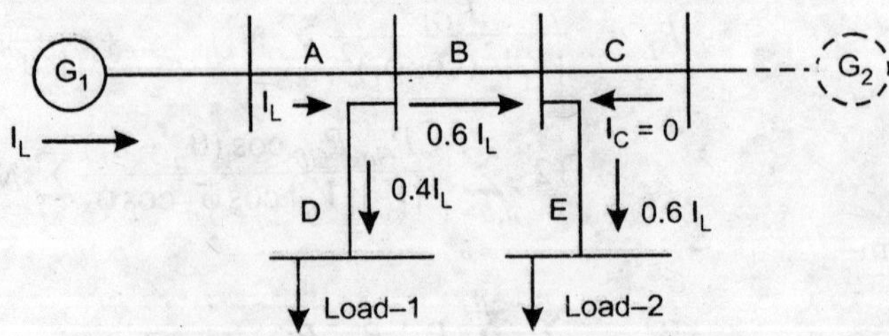

Fig. 15.13 Generator-1 supplying entire laod

$$N_{A1} = \frac{I_A}{I_L} = 1.0,\ N_{B1} = \frac{I_B}{I_L} = 0.6,\ N_{C1} = 0,\ N_{D1} = 0.4,\ N_{E1} = 0.6$$

Now, assume only generator–2 supplies entire load then $I_2 - I_L$

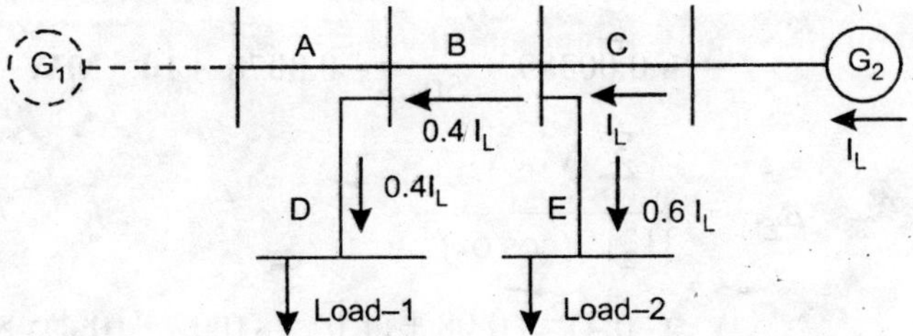

Fig. 15.14 Generator–2 supplying entire load

$$N_{A2} = 0, N_{B2} = -0.4. N_{C2} = 1.0, N_{D2} = 0.4, N_{C2} = 0.6$$

Now, $V_1 = V_{ref} + I_A Z_A = 1.0 \angle 0° + (0.02 + j0.08)(1.2 - j0.4)$

$$= 1.06 \angle 4.78° \text{ pu}$$

$$V_2 = V_{ref} - I_B Z_B + I_C Z_C$$

$$= 1.0 \angle 0° - (0.4 - j0.2)(0.08 + j0.32) + (0.8 - j0.1)(0.02 + j0.08)$$

$$= 0.93 \angle -3.10° \text{ pu}$$

Current phase angles,

Now $\theta_1 = \text{angle of } I_1 = I_A = \tan^{-}\left(\frac{-0.4}{1.2}\right) = -18.43°$

$$\theta_2 = \text{angle of } I_2 = I_C = \tan^{-1}\left(\frac{-0.1}{0.8}\right) = -7.13°$$

$$\cos(\theta_1 - \theta_2) = 0.98$$

Therefore, Power factor angles—

$$\phi_1 = 4.78° + 18.43° = 23.21°, \text{Cos}\phi = 0.92$$

$$\phi_2 = 7.13° - 3.10° = 4.03°. \text{Cos}\phi = 0.998$$

Loss co-efficient $B_{11} = \dfrac{\sum N_{M1}^2 R_M}{|V_1|^2 (\cos\phi_1)^2}$

$$B_{11} = \frac{(1.0)^2 \times 0.02 + (0.6)^2 \times 0.08 + (0.4)^2 \times 0.03 + (0.6)^2 \times 0.03}{(1.06)^2 (0.920)^2}$$

$$= 0.0677 \text{ pu}$$

$$= 0.0677 \times \frac{1}{50} = \mathbf{0.1354 \times 10^{-2}\ MW^{-1}} \quad \textbf{Ans.}$$

$$B_{12} = \frac{\cos(\theta_1 - \theta_2)}{|V_1| V_2 | \cos\phi_2} \sum_M N_{M1} N_{M2} R_M$$

$$B_{12} = \left(\frac{0.98}{1.06 \times 0.93 \times 0.998 \times 0.92}\right)$$

$$(-0.4 \times 0.6 \times 0.8 + 0.4 \times 0.4 \times 0.03 + 0.6 \times 0.6 \times 0.03)$$

$$= -0.00389 \text{ pu}$$

$$= -0.00389 \times \frac{1}{50} = \mathbf{-0.0078 \times 10^{-2}\ MW^{-1}}\quad \textbf{Ans.}$$

$$B_{22} = \frac{\sum_M N_{M2}^2 R_M}{|V_2|^2 (\cos\phi_2)^2}$$

$$B_{22} = \frac{(-0.4)^2 \times 0.08 + (1.0)^2 \times 0.02 + (0.4)^2 \times 0.03 + (0.6)^2 \times 0.03}{(0.93)^2 \times (0.998)^2}$$

$$= 0.056 \text{ pu}$$

$$= 0.056 \times \frac{1}{50} = \mathbf{0.112 \times 10^{-2}\ MW^{-1}}\quad \textbf{Ans.}$$

15.10.5 Economic Dispatch Considering Transmission Losses

Let us consider economic dispatch problem including transmission losses, then total power supplied by generating plant is given by—

$$P_T = P_1 + P_2 + P_3 + \ldots + P_n - P_{\text{Loss}} \qquad \text{...(15.28)}$$

Where, P_{Loss} = total transmission line loss and is assumed constant.

Differentiating above equation

$$0 = dP_1 + dP_2 + dP_3 + \ldots + dP_n - dP_{\text{Loss}} \qquad \text{...(15.29)}$$

dP_{Loss} includes power loss due to each generator

$$\therefore \quad dP_{\text{Loss}} = \frac{\partial P_{Loss}}{\partial P_1} dP1 + \frac{\partial P_{Loss}}{\partial P_2} dP_2 + \frac{\partial P_{Loss}}{\partial P_3} dP_3 + \ldots + \frac{\partial P_{Loss}}{\partial P_n} dP_n \qquad \text{...(15.30)}$$

For minimum generation cost, $dF_T = 0$

Multiplying above two equations (15.29 and 15.30) by λ and combining, we get,

$$0 = \left(\frac{\lambda \partial P_{Loss}}{\partial P_1} - \lambda\right) dP_1 + \left(\frac{\lambda \partial P_{Loss}}{\partial P_2} - \lambda\right) dP_2 + \ldots + \left(\frac{\lambda \partial_{Loss}}{\partial P_n} - \lambda\right) dP_n \qquad \text{...(15.31)}$$

Also, in order to minimize total fuel cost F_T

$$dF_T = \frac{\partial F_T}{\partial P_1} dP_1 + \frac{\partial F_T}{\partial P_2} dP_2 + \ldots + \frac{\partial F_T}{\partial P_n} dP_n = 0 \qquad \text{...(15.32)}$$

Adding equation (15.31)and (15.32), we get,

$$0 = \sum_{i=1}^{n} \left(\frac{F_T}{\partial P_i} + \frac{\lambda P_{Loss}}{\partial P_i} - \lambda \right) dP_i \qquad \text{...(15.33)}$$

The above equation is true if

$$\frac{\partial F_T}{\partial P_i} + \frac{\lambda \partial P_{Loss}}{\partial P_i} - \lambda = 0, \text{ for } i = 1, 2, \ldots n \qquad \text{...(15.34)}$$

From above equation

$$\lambda = \frac{dF_1}{dP_1} L_1 = \frac{dF_2}{dP_2} L_2 = \ldots = \frac{dF_n}{dP_n} L_n \quad \text{...(15.35)}$$

Where $L_1, L_2, \ldots L_n$ are called penalty factors.

$$L_i = \frac{1}{1 - \frac{\partial P_{Loss}}{\partial P_i}} \quad \text{for } i = 1, 2, \ldots, n \quad \text{...(15.36)}$$

The above equation means that minimum fuel cost is obtained when incremental cost of each plant multiplied by its penalty factor is same for the plants.

If power generated by various units are represented by following—

$$P = [P_1 \, P_2 \ldots P_n] \quad \text{...(15.37)}$$

Then transmission loesses can be expressed as,

$$P_{\text{Loss}} = P^T B P \quad \text{...(15.38)}$$

Where B is symmetric matrix given by—

$$B = \begin{bmatrix} B_{11} & B_{12} & \cdots & B_n \\ B_{12} & B_{22} & \cdots & B_{2n} \\ \vdots & \vdots & \vdots & \vdots \\ B_{1n} & B_{2n} & \cdots & B_{nn} \end{bmatrix}$$

B-co-efficients are not constant but vary with plant loading. However,for simplicity,these co-efficients can be assumed to be constant so as to calculate penalty factors.

In actual practice, incremental costs are non-linear equations which require iterative solution for optimal generator loading.

15.10.6 Algorithm for Optimum Loading of Plants

It is an iterative process and requires three things viz. (*i*) total load, (*ii*) incremental cost and (*iii*) loss co-efficient matrix.

1. Step-1: Initially, assume that transmission losses are zero and plants are loaded equally.
2. Step-2: Calculate $\frac{dF_i}{dP_i} = 2c_i P_i + b_i$. Put value of λ

   into $$\frac{dF_i}{dP_i} + \lambda \frac{\partial P_L}{\partial P_i} = \lambda \quad \text{...(15.39)}$$

   $$(2\, c_i\, P_i + b_i) + \lambda \sum_{i=1}^{n} 2\, B_{ab}\, P_b = \lambda \quad \text{...(15.40)}$$

   Solve above simultaneous equations to get values of P_i.
3. Step-3: Determine transmission loss, $P_L = [P]\,[B]\,[P^T]$

   Where $$P = [P_1 \, P_2 \ldots P_n]$$

4. Step-4: Check power balance by comparing $\sum_{i=1}^{n} P_i$ With $(P_D + P_L)$. If power balance is satisfied, it is the optimal loading. Otherwise change value of λ. For the first time, λ can be changed as per following—

   λ is to be increased by about 5% if $\sum_{i=1}^{n} p_1 < P_D + P_L$

   λ is to be decreased by about 5%if $\sum_{i=1}^{n} P_i > P_D + P_L$

   In subsequent iterations, linear interpolation can be used to find new value of λ as per following expression—

$$\lambda^{K+1} = \lambda^{K} + \frac{\lambda^{K} - \lambda^{K-1}}{\sum_{i=1}^{n} P_i^{K} - \sum_{i=1}^{n} P_i^{K-1}} [P_D + P_L^K - \sum_{i=1}^{n} P_i^k] \quad ...(15.41)$$

Where, K = present iteration count.

$K-1$ = previous iteration count.

$K+1$ = next iteration count.

5. Step-5: Go back to step-2 and proceed by taking steps 2, 3, 4 till power balance equation is met with desired accuracy.

Example 15.9

In a power system, two plants have following incremental costs—

$$\frac{dF_1}{dP_1} = 1.0\ P_1 + 200 \text{ ₹/MWh}, \quad \frac{dF_2}{dP_2} = 1.0\ P_2 + 150 \text{ ₹/MWh}$$

Loss co-efficient matrix, $B = \begin{bmatrix} 0.001 & -0.0005 \\ -0.0005 & 0.0024 \end{bmatrix}$

Determine optimum loading and total transmission loss for a total load of 100 MW.

Solution: Initially, the problem will be solved assuming no transmission loss and equal loading on generators.

So, $P_1 = 50$ MW, $P_2 = 50$ MW. Therefore, $\lambda = (1.0 \times 50) + 200 = 250$.

$$\therefore \quad \frac{dF_i}{dP_i} + \lambda \frac{\partial P_L}{\partial P_i} = \lambda \quad \Rightarrow \quad (2\, c_i P_i + b) + \lambda \sum_{n=1}^{N} 2\, B_{mn} P_n = \lambda$$

$$\Rightarrow \quad (1.0\ P_1 + 200) + 250\ (0.002\ P_1 - 0.001\ P_2) = 250$$

$$(1.0\ P_2 + 150) + 250\ (-0.001\ P_1 + 0.0048\ P_2) = 250$$

or $\quad 1.5\ P_1 - 0.25\ P_2 = 50$ and $-0.25\ P_1 + 2.2\ P_2 = 100$

Solving, $\quad P_1 = 41.6988$ MW, $P_2 = 50.1931$ 1MW

Now, $\quad P_L = P^T B P \quad$ where $P = [P_1 P_2 \ldots P_n]$

$$P_L = [P_1 \quad P_2]\begin{bmatrix} B_{11} & B_{12} \\ B_{21} & B_{22} \end{bmatrix}\begin{bmatrix} P_1 \\ P_2 \end{bmatrix}$$

$$P_L = [41.6988 \quad 50.1931]\begin{bmatrix} 0.001 & -0.0005 \\ -0.0005 & 0.0024 \end{bmatrix}\begin{bmatrix} 41.6988 \\ 50.1931 \end{bmatrix}$$

$$P_L = 5.6919 \text{ MW}$$

Now, $P_1 + P_2 = 41.6988 + 50.1931 = 91.8919$ MW

$$P_D + P_L = 100 + 5.6919 = 105.6919 \text{ MW}$$

Since, $P_1 + P_2 < P_D + P_L$ therefore, λ could be increased, Let it be increased by 4%.

$\therefore$ New value of $\lambda = 1.04 \times 250 = 260$ ₹/MWh

Substituting new values in co-ordination equations,

$$\frac{dF_i}{dP_i} + \lambda \frac{\partial P_L}{\partial P_i} = \lambda$$

$$(1.0\, P_1 + 200) + 260\,(0.002\, P_1 - 0.001\, P_2) = 260$$

$$(1.0\, P_2 + 150) + 260\,(-0.001\, P_1 + 0.0048\, P_2) = 260$$

or $1.52\, P_1 - 0.26\, P_2 = 60$ and $-0.26\, P_1 + 2.248\, P_2 = 110$

Solving, $P_1 = 48.8093$ MW, $P_2 = 54.5776$ MW

Now, $P_L = P^T B P$

$$P_L = [48.8093 \quad 54.5776]\begin{bmatrix} 0.001 & -0.0005 \\ -0.0005 & 0.0024 \end{bmatrix}\begin{bmatrix} 48.8093 \\ 54.5776 \end{bmatrix}$$

$$P_L = 6.8673 \text{ MW}$$

Now, $P_1 + P_2 = 48.8093 + 54.5776, \quad P_D + P_L = 100 + 6.8673$

$$P_1 + P_2 = 103.3869 \text{ MW}, \quad P_D + P_L = 106.8673 \text{ MW}$$

Now, $P_1 + P_2 < P_D + P_L$

The new value of λ can be calculated as per following—

$$\lambda^{K+1} = \lambda^K + \frac{\lambda^k - \lambda^{k-1}}{\sum_{i=1}^{n} P_i^k - \sum_{i=1}^{n} p_i^{k-1}}\left[P_D + P_L^k - \sum_{i=1}^{n} P_i^k\right]$$

$$\lambda = 260 + \frac{260 - 250}{103.3869 - 91.8918}(106.8673 - 103.3869)$$

$$= 263 \text{ ₹/MWh}$$

With new value of λ,the same procedure can be repeated.

with $\lambda = 263$, $P_1 = 50.9119$, $P_2 = 55.8769$, $P_L = 7.2405$, $P_1 + P_2 = 106.789$, $P_D + P_L = 107.2405$

$\lambda = 263.3$, $P_1 = 51.1061$, $P_2 = 55.9878$, $P_L = 7.2737$, $P_1 + P_2 = 107.0939$, $P_D + P_L = 107.2737$

$\lambda = 263.5$, $P_1 = 51.2636$, $P_2 = 56.0768$, $P_L = 7.3003$, $P_1 + P_2 = 107.3404$, $P_D + P_L = 107.3003$

$\lambda = 263.467, P_1 = 51.2401, P_2 = 56.0659, P_L = 7.2969, P_1 + P_2 = 107.3060, P_D + P_L = 107.2969$

The optimum loading is $P_1 = 51.2401$ MW, $P_2 = 56.0659$ MW, $P_L = 7.2969$ MW

15.10.7 Unit Commitment

Economic dispatch gives optimum schedule or loading of generating units giving lowest fuel cost of generators. Optimal power flow gives delivery of power with minimized losses in the system. Unit commitment means which generator to switch on or which generator to switch off.

The total load in a power system varies throughout the day and night. Hence, loading on generators needed to be adjusted so that total generation is always equal to total load at any instant of time. When the load increases the generators are switched on in sequence. Similarly, When load decreases, generators are switched off sequentially. A utility need to know in advance the switching on and switching -off sequence of units. However, in doing so, the total operating cost should be minimum. So,the order in which units are switched on and the order in which the units are switched off over a period of time known as unit commitment. Hence, in short, unit commitment is a economic dispatch problem over a complete day. However, for unit commitment, the period may be week, month or a year.

Unit commitment is a complex problem due to possibility of variety of combinations (consider sheer size of power network involving so many plants and each plant having so many generators) and also due to variety of constraints.

Some of the constraints are following—

1. **Requirement of spinning reserve:** Some generating units are kept in running condition ready to take load in anticipation of sudden increase in load or unexpected outage or breakdown of running unit. So, it is necessary to keep some units in continuous running condition.
2. **Minimum start up time required:** When a thermal unit it started, it can not be switched off suddenly because it requires some time to switch on. Hence, once it is committed, the unit will remain in the system for a specified time.
3. **Minimum shutdown time:** Similarly, when a thermal unit it to be shut down, it can be not be done suddenly as it requires a certain minimum time. Same is the case with nuclear power plants.
4. **Manpower constraint:** Availability of manpower affects operation. For example, during festival time or during marriage season,availability of manpower is affected.
5. **Changeover cost:** Whenever status of units are change *i.e.* stopped units are started or running units are stopped, some cost is always involved.
6. **Hydro-constraints:** Operation of hydro plant is affected by availability of sufficient water. Moreover, most of the hydro plants are multi-purpose plants which affects the operation schedule of plants.
7. **Must run units:** Some units need to be run regardless of cost concern due to requirement of voltage support and stability.
8. **Fuel availability concern:** Some times scheduled units could not be run due to non-availability of fuel,due to strike, riots, natural disaster etc.
9. **Transmission system constraint:** The reserve capacity need to be dispersed in a power

network to aviod power system limitation. This prevents availability of these units for regular commitment.

15.10.8 Priority List Method of Unit Commitment

In this a priority list of switching on or off of units is prepared based on full load average production cost of each unit.

$$\text{Full load average production cost} = \frac{\text{Producion cost corresponding to full load}}{\text{full load}}$$

The load pattern i.e whether increasing or decreasing is observed every hour. thereafter, it is calculated if switching off next unit on priority list will leave sufficient generation to meet load demand plus spinning reserve. If this condition is not met, unit continues to run.

If a unit is needed after some time say h_1 and the shutdown time of this unit is h_2 such that $h_2 > h_1$ then unit is continued to run.

Example 15.10

Determine the priority list of unit startup and shutdown for the following units-

$$P_1 = \text{Maximum permissible load} = 600 \text{ MW}$$

$$F_1 = 0.01562\, P_1^2 + 79.2\, P_1 + 5610 \text{ ₹/hour}$$

$$P_2 = \text{Maximum permissible load} = 400 \text{ MW}$$

$$F_2 = 0.0194\, P_2^2 + 78.5\, P_2 + 3100 \text{ ₹/hour}$$

$$P_3 = \text{Maximum permissible load} = 200 \text{ MW.}$$

$$F_3 = 0.05784\, P_3^2 + 95.64\, P_3 + 936 \text{ ₹/hour}$$

Solution:

1. Full load average production cost of unit-1

$$= \frac{0.01562 \times (600)^2 + 79.2 \times 600 + 5610}{600}$$

$$= 97.922 \text{ ₹/hour}$$

2. Full load average production cost of unit-2

$$= \frac{0.0194 \times (400)^2 + 78.5 \times 400 + 3100}{400}$$

$$= 94.01 \text{ ₹/hour}$$

3. Full load average production cost of unit-3

$$= \frac{0.05784 \times (200)^2 + 95.64 \times 200 + 936}{200}$$

$$= 111.888 \text{ ₹/hour}$$

Arranging the priority list based on increasing average production cost

Table 15.3 Priority List for Unit commitment

Unit no.	*Average cost*	*Max MW*
2	94.01	400
1	97.922	600
3	111.888	200

Therefore, unit-2 will be loaded first (having lowest average cost amongst all thee units) followed by unit-1 and unit-3 in order of increasing average cost.

For shutdown of units following priority list is to be followed-

Table 15.1 Priority list for unit shut down.

Unit no.	*Total load demand*
2 + 1 + 3	1000 MW $\leq P_D \leq$ 1200 MW
2 + 1	400 MW $\leq P_D \leq$ 1000 MW
2	$P_D \leq$ 400 MW

When the load demand lies between 1200 to 1000 MW, all the three units will be run. When load reduces and lies between 1000 to 400, unit-3 to be shutdown and load to be carried by units-2 and 1. When load reduces below 400 MW, unit-1 to be shutdown and entire load to be on unit-2 only.

CHAPTER SUMMARY

Co-ordinated operation of plant means operation of different types of power plants, such as thermal, hydro, nuclear, solar, biomass, diesel etc. to improve system reliability, flexibility, higher reserve capacity, optimum operation and minimize maintenance expenses etc. Depending upon type of plant, it is run as base load or peak load plant. A base load plant is run continuously having low operation and capital cost. While a peak load plant should have the ability of quick startup and shutdown and should be able to respond to load variations quickly. Some base load plants are-run off the river hydro plant, nuclear plant, thermal plant etc. Peak load plants are -pumped storage hydro plant, gas turbine plant and diesel power plant.

Loading of power plants is decided by among other factors-minimum overall fuel cost and minimum power loss. The division of total load between generating units is decided on the basis of minimum incremental fuel cost. The total load to be shared by various units is decided by a scheduling process known as unit commitment. It is carried out a day ahead of actual loading lased on load forecast. Optimal generator loading requires solution of non-linear equations through iterative process. So, the aim of operation of power plant is to meet the load demand at the same time meeting other constraints, such as active power limits, reactive power limits etc. Also, this power need to be supplied at lowest cost and with minimum losses.

FORMULAE

1. Fuel cost, $F_i = a_i + b_i P_{Gi} + C_i P_{Gi}^2$

where a_i, b_i, c_i = Coefficient

F_i = input cost of P_{Gi}

P_{Gi} = power generated by i^{th} unit.

2. For a loss less system, $\lambda = \dfrac{P_D + \sum_{n=1}^{Ng} \dfrac{b_i}{2\,c_i}}{\sum_{i=1}^{Ng} \dfrac{1}{2\,c_i}}$

3. Power loss matrix, $P_L = [P_1\,P_2 \dots P_n] \begin{bmatrix} B_{11} & B_{12} & \cdots & B_{in} \\ \vdots & & & \\ B_{n1} & B_{n2} & \cdots & B_{nn} \end{bmatrix} \begin{bmatrix} P_1 \\ \vdots \\ P_n \end{bmatrix}$

4. Power loss, $P_L = \sum_{a=1}^{n} \sum_{b=1}^{n} P_{Ga}\,B_{ab}\,P_{Gb}$

$$B_{ab} = \frac{\cos(\theta_a - \theta_b)}{|V_a||V_b|\cos\phi_a \cos\phi_b} \sum_M N_{Ma}\,N_{Mb}\,R_M$$

Where n = number of genrators

θ = impedance angle

ϕ = power factor angle

R_M = Branch resistance

5. $P_L = P_{G1}^2\,B_{11} + 2\,P_{G1}\,P_{G2}\,B_{12} + P_{G2}^2\,B_{22}$

$$B_{11} = \frac{1}{|V_1|^2(\cos\phi_1)^2} \sum_M N_{M1}^2\,R_M$$

$$\mathrm{B}_{12} = \frac{\cos(\theta_1 - \theta_2)}{|V_1|\,V_2|\,(\cos\phi_1\,\cos\phi_2)} \sum_M N_{M1} N_{M2} R_M$$

$$B_{22} = \frac{1}{|V_2|^2(\cos\phi_2)^2} \sum_M N_{M2}^2\,R_M$$

6. New value of λ, $\lambda^{K+1} = \dfrac{\lambda^k - \lambda^{k-1}}{\sum_{i=1}^{n} P_i^K - \sum_{i=1}^{n} P_i^{k-1}} \left[P_D + P_L^K - \sum_{i=1}^{n} P_i^k \right]$

REVIEW QUESTIONS

Q. 1. Enumerate advantages of combined operation of power plans.

Q. 2. What is base load and peak load operation?

Q. 3. How a thermal power plant and run off the river hydro plant can be run together?

Q. 4. Discuss combined operation of nuclear power plant and pumped storage hydro plant. What are the merits and demerits?

Q. 5. Describe with a schematic diagram solar PV and wind hybrid system.

Q. 6. Explain the operation of Biomass-PV-Diesel hybrid system with a neat sketch.

Q. 7. Distinguish between short term and long term hydro-thermal co-ordination.

Q. 8. Explain the terms- (*i*) economic dispatch (*ii*) optimal power flow.

Q. 9. Discuss various performance curves of thermal power plant.

Q. 10. Discuss economic division of load between generating units.

Q. 11. Derive the expression for transmission loss formula.

Q. 12. Derive the expression for economic dispatch considering transmission losses.

Q. 13. Discuss the significance of penalty factor.

Q. 14. How optimal loading of power plants is carried out?

Q. 15. Discuss the importance of unit commitment.

Q. 16. What are various constraints in unit commitment?

Q. 17. Explain with suitable example priority list method of unit commitment.

Q. 18. What are the constraints in co-ordinated operation of power plants.

NUMERICAL QUESTION

Q. 1. Fuel cost of unit-A and unit-B are given below-

$$F_A = 1.65 + 26\, P_{GA} + 0.2\, P_{GA}^2 \text{ ₹/h}$$

$$F_B = 1.79 + 32\, P_{GB} + 0.2\, P_{GB}^2 \text{ ₹/h}$$

Where P_{GA} and P_{GB} are in MW,

Neglecting transmission losses, calculate optimal load sharing between units-A and B when total load is 250MW. **[Ans:** $P_{GA} = 132.5$, $P_{GB} = 117.5$ MW, $\lambda = 79$ ₹/MWh]

Also calculate incremental cost of power.

Q. 1. The fuel cost in ₹\h for two 800 MW plants is given by

$$F_1 = 256 + 5.8\, P_{G1} + 0.004 P_{G1}^2 \text{ ₹/h}$$

$$F_2 = 610 + b_2\, P_{G2} + c^2\, P_{G2}^2 \text{ ₹/h}$$

Calculate- (*i*) Neglecting losses, optimal generation schedule when total demand is 600 MW and incremental cost of power(λ)is Rs10/MWh.

(*ii*) Neglecting loses, optimal generation schedule when the total demand is 1400 MW and incremental cost of power (λ) is Rs12/Mwh.

(*iii*) Coefficients b_2 and c_2.

[Ans: (*i*) 525 MW, 75 MW (*ii*) 77 MW, 625 MW (*iii*) $b_2 = 9.89$, $c_2 = 0.00075$]

SHORT ANSWER TYPE QUESTIONS

Q. 1. List three base load power plants.

Q. 2. List three peak load power plants.

Q. 3. Define economic load dispatch.

Q. 4. What is optimal power flow?

Q. 5. Why unit commitment is needed?

Q. 6. Why spinning reserve is required?

Q. 7. Why combined operation of fossil fuel fired power plant and renewable energy generation plants are beneficial?

Multiple Choice Questions

Q. 1. Advantage of combined operation of power plants is

(*a*) higher reserve (*b*) improved reliability

(*c*) flexible operation (*d*) all of these.

Q. 2. Nuclear and gas turbine power plants are

(*a*) peak load, peak load (*b*) base load, base load

(*c*) peak, load base load (*d*) base load, peak load.

Q. 3. Priority of loading of units is decided on the basis of

(*a*) total load (*b*) incremental fuels cost

(*c*) capacity of unit (*d*) both (*a*) and (*c*)

Q. 4. Economic division of loads between generating units is decided by

(*a*) capacity of units (*b*) heat rate of units

(*c*) fuel cost (*d*) none of these.

Q. 5. Unit of loss co-efficient in transmission loss formula is

(*a*) MW^{-1} (*b*) MW

(c) MVA (*d*) MVA^{-1}

Q. 6. Generation must be equal to

(*a*) load demand + losses (*b*) load demand

(*c*) active power demand (*d*) reactive power demand

Q. 7. Unit to be run depends on

(*a*) manpower availability (*b*) voltage support required

(*c*) need for spinning reserve (*d*) all of these

Answer to MCQ

1. (*d*) **2.** (*d*) **3.** (*b*) **4.** (*c*) **5.** (*a*) **6.** (*a*)
7. (*d*)

Chapter

ELECTRICAL ENERGY CONSERVATION

Learning Objectives

After reading this chapter, reader will be able to

- Appreciate the meaning, advantages, need and process of energy conservation.
- Know the applicable legal framework.
- Explore various techniques of electrical energy conservation.
- Update on new technologies being used in improving energy conservation and energy efficiency improvement.

"Nothing is too wonderful to be true if it be consistent with the laws of nature."

–Michael Faraday

16.1. INTRODUCTION

Energy is a major driver for economic development of a country. Economic progress of a country is measured by several indices among them is per capita electricity consumption. However, economic growth and energy demand are non-linearly connected. A 6 % increase in India's Gross Domestic Product (GDP) imposes an increased demand of 9% on its energy resources. Developed countries follow lower energy intensive routes to maintain less than one energy to GDP ratio.

Conventional energy sources, such as coal, oil, gas etc. are depleting very fast. With limited reserve available, it is imperative that these resources are conserved and also alternate sources of energy are explored. This chapter focuses on ways and means to conserve energy through reduction in electrical energy consumption.

16.2. NEED FOR ENERGY CONSERVATION

Following are the need for energy conservation—

(*i*) to conserve limited energy resources.
(*ii*) to improve energy security.
(*iii*) to reduce energy consumption bill.
(*iv*) to reduce environmental emission.
(*v*) to improve organisational profit.
(*vi*) to improve productivity.
(*vii*) to ensure compliance with energy conservation act.
(*viii*) to ensure compliance with Environment Protection act.
(*ix*) to reduce cost of heating/cooling of machines.
(*x*) to reduce import bill of petroleum products.

16.3. ENERGY EFFICIENCY

There is a difference between energy conservation and energy efficiency. Energy conservation means reduction in consumption of energy. This may be due to reduction of wastage, increase in productivity, change in process technology etc. While energy efficiency means reduction in energy intensity in a product or process without affecting output, consumption or comfort level. Hence, energy efficiency promotes energy conservation.

The difference can be illustrated with an example. A 100 watt incandescent lamp can be replaced by a 15 watt compact flourescent lamp (CFL) without affecting light output. Again, 15W CFL lamp can be replaced with a 9 watt LED (light emitting diode) lamp. Hence, consumption of electricity is reduced without affecting light output. Use of CFL and LED technology demonstrates the use of energy efficient technology for energy conservation.

16.4. ENERGY CONSERVATION OPPORTUNITIES IN ELECTRICAL SYSTEM

Following are the area of energy conservation in electrical system—

(*i*) **by improvement of power factor:** By installing automatic power correction equipment, high power factor can be maintained. This reduces overall energy bill.

(*ii*) **by using energy efficient motors:** Energy efficient motors possess 3 to 4% higher efficiency than standard motors.

(*iii*) **by using energy efficient lighting:** By using LED and CFL lamps in indoor, lighting energy consumption can be reduced. Similarly, light dimmers can be used to reduce energy consumption.

(*iv*) **by controlling energy peak demand:** Peak energy demand can be controlled by rescheduling loads to off peak hours, shedding non-essential loads, storage of products (chilled water, hot water etc).

(*v*) **by voltage optimization:** Maintaining correct voltage reduces current drawn by motor and improves motor efficiency.

(*vi*) **by optimum loading of transformers and generators:** Transformers and generators should be optimally loaded for higher efficiency

(*vii*) **by using variable speed drive motors:** Variable speed drive motors conserve energy at lesser than rated speed.

(*viii*) **by using amorphous metal distribution transformer:** Amorphous metal transformer reduces no load losses upto 80% as compared to CRGO silicon steel (cold rolled grain oriented silicon steel) or conventional transformer.

(*ix*) **by connecting lightly loaded motors to star connection:** All motors operating at less than 50% load, should be connected in star. This reduces energy consumption.

16.5. ENERGY EFFICIENT MOTORS

Energy efficient motors possess 3 to 4% higher efficiency than standard motors (typical efficiency of a standard motor is 83 to 92%). Energy efficient motor gives same output but at reduced input energy. However, these motors cost 25 to 30% more than standard efficiency motors. These motors possess fairly flat performance characteristics over wide range of speed.

Following are the factors affecting efficiency of electric motors—

(*i*) **Overload:** Overload increases operating temperature of motor due to higher loss thereby reducing the life of insulation of windings.

(*ii*) **Temperature:** High operating temperature of motor reduces efficiency and life of motor.

(*iii*) **Age:** Normal wear and tear causes deterioration of efficiency of motor.

(*iv*) **Slip:** A low slip motor is more efficient than high slip motor.

(*v*) **Rewinding:** Rewinding of burnt motor results in poor efficiency due to use of poor quality material and bad workmanship.

Advantages of energy efficient motors are following—

(*i*) reduced power consumption and hence, lower operating cost.

(*ii*) lower temperature rise and hence, longer life.

(*iii*) constant efficiency over a broad band (from 50 % to 100 % of load).

(*iv*) high power factor.

(*v*) longer insulation and bearing life.

(*vi*) less vibration.

(*vii*) less failure rate.

(*viii*) extended lubrication cycle due to cooler operation.

(*ix*) less starting thermal stress.

Improvement in energy efficiency of motor is due to following changes—

(*i*) to reduce iron loss, steel with improved properties is used. Standard motors use low carbon laminated silicon steel for rotor and stator. Such steel typically has iron losses at

606 watt/kg. High efficiency motors are built with high grade silicon steel with iron losses of about 3.3 watt /kg.

(*ii*) iron losses are reduced by using thinner laminations. Reduced thickness of lamination lowers eddy current losses. Improved insulation between laminations further reduces these losses. The use of thinner lamination result in reduction of iron losses from 10% to 25% depending upon the method of processing of lamination steel and method of assembling the magnetic core.

(*iii*) iron losses are reduced by using longer core which reduce the losses due to lower operating flux densities.

(*iv*) use of higher cross-section of copper conductors in stator and rotor windings reduce stator and rotor copper loss. Older standard motors employ aluminium or copper conductors of size no longer than that needed to deliver the required horse power. High efficiency motors utilize bigger copper conductors to lower the winding resistance. Size of conductor is 35% to 45% larger than needed to satisfy motor output horse power requirement.

(*v*) more efficient fan design reduces windage losses due to air movement.

(*vi*) use of better quality bearing and lubricating material reduces friction losses.

(*vii*) stray losses are reduced by optimized design, strict quality control, proper proportioning of stator & rotor slots and small slot opening.

(*viii*) optimized air gap reduces magnetising current and associated losses resulting in improved power factor.

There are two classes of energy efficient motors viz high efficiency (efficiency class eff 1) and improved efficiency (efficiency class eff 2). Comparison of efficiencies of standard and energy efficient motors is given in table 16.1

Table 16.1: Comparison of efficiencies of standard and energy efficient motors

Output (4 Pole)	*Standard efficiency (IS 8789)*	*Improved efficiency -eff 2 motor (IS 12615)*	*High efficiency eff 1 motor (IS 12615)*
0.075 kW	71.0 %	73.0 %	82.5 %
1.5 kW	76.0 %	78.5 %	85.0 %
3.7 kW	83.0 %	84.0 %	88.3 %
11 kW	85.5 %	88.4 %	91.0 %
18.5 kW	87.0 %	90.0 %	92.2 %
37 kW	88.5 %	92.0 %	93.6 %
75 kW	Not specified	93.6 %	94.7 %
110 kW	Not specified	94.4 %	95.2 %
160 kW	Not specified	95.0 %	95.8 %

Figure 16.1 shows efficiency range of standard and high efficiency motors

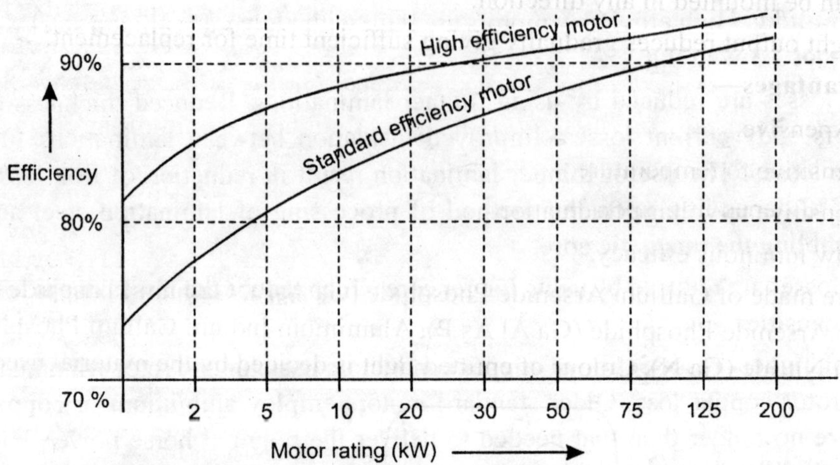

Fig. 16.1. Efficiency range for standard and high efficiency motor

16.6. AMORPHOUS METAL TRANSFORMER

Standard distribution transformer uses CRGO silicon steel (Cold Rolled Grain Oriented) as core. Amorphous metal transformers can reduce no load losses by 70% compared to CRGO silicon steel transformer.

The amorphous metal is an alloy of Fe–Si–B (iron, silicon and Boron) which is produced by rapid solidification of molten alloy. This results in non-crystalline structure which is easy to magnetise leading to lower hysteresis losses. Due to low thickness, eddy current losses are also reduced (it has high electrical resistivity of 130 $\mu\ \Omega$–cm compared to 51 $\mu\ \Omega$–cm in CRGO silicon steel). However, material is more expensive and saturation magnetic flux density is lower than CRGO silicon steel. But higher initial cost is compensated by reduced losses over lifetime of transformer. These type of transformers are extensively used as distribution transformers in India.

16.7. ENERGY EFFICIENT LIGHTING

Conventional incandescent bulb, flourescent lamp and CFL lamps can be replaced by LED (light emitting diode) lamps. Advantages of LED lamps are following—

(*i*) very long life (50,000 hours).

(*ii*) no ultra violet or infra red light emission and hence, can be used for artifact display lighting.

(*iii*) no flicker like all discharge lamps (HPMV, HPSV, CFL, Fluorescent lamp).

(*iv*) light dimming is possible for energy saving purpose.

(*v*) highly energy efficient.

(*vi*) free from toxic mercury.

(*vii*) does not generate heat.

(*viii*) very compact.

(ix) can be mounted in any direction.

(x) light output reduces gradually giving sufficient time for replacement.

Disadvantages—

(i) expensive.

(ii) sensitive to temperature.

(iii) sensitive to voltage fluctuations.

(iv) low luminous efficacy.

LED are made of Gallium Arsenide Phosphide (Ga AsP), Gallium Phosphide (Ga P), Gallium Aluminium Arsenide Phosphide (Ga Al As P), Aluminium Indium Galium Phosphide (Al In GaP) and Galium Nitride (Ga N). Colour of emitted light is decided by the material used.

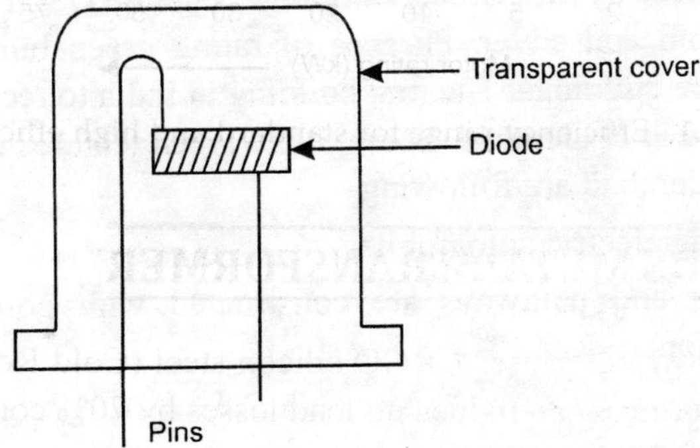

Fig. 16.2. Light emitting diode

16.8. ENERGY EFFICIENT BUILDINGS

Energy efficient or green building uses minimum natural resources for construction and uses energy efficient devices to minimize energy consumption. It employs renewable energy sources, water and waste water management and uses materials with high recycle content for construction.

Benefits of green buildings are following—

(i) 30% to 40% reduction in energy cost.

(ii) 20% to 30% reduction in water consumption.

(iii) recycling of waste e.g. use of fly ash bricks.

(iv) environmental friendly construction & operation.

Some salient features of green buildings are following—

(i) use of renewable energy sources to meet energy requirement of the building.

(ii) use of energy efficient air-conditioning and lighting system.

(iii) use of building management system (BMS) for efficient operation and control.

(iv) segregation, collection and disposal of water stream at source.

(v) use of salvaged or refurbished material.

(vi) use of low volatile organic compound (VOC) paints and adhesives.

(*vii*) use of daylight to minimize lighting energy consumption.

(*viii*) rain water harvesting.

(*ix*) recycling of 100% grey water (waste water from kitchen and wash basins and bathrooms) and treatment.

(*x*) use of energy efficient motors and variable frequency drives for air handling unit of air conditioning.

(*xi*) use of fly ash based cement.

(*xii*) use of autoclave aerated concrete blocks.

(*xiii*) installation of carbon dioxide sensors to monitor indoor air quality.

Green buildings are rated through Leadership in Energy and Environmental Design (LEED), a green building rating system by US Green Building Council (USGBC). There are three kinds of ratings viz platinum, gold and silver. Purpose of rating green buildings is to develop high performance and sustainable buildings. The first building in India to receive platinum rating is CII Godrej green building centre in Hyderabad. Some of the green features incorporated in CII Godrej Green Business Centre, Hyderabad are following—

(*i*) facility for charging electric automobiles.

(*ii*) all paved parking and pathways are constructed with porous material to recharge underground aquifers.

(*iii*) rain water cycling.

(*iv*) solar orientation of building so as to receive maximum daylight.

(*v*) recycling of 100 % grey water.

(*vi*) daylight lighting dimmer control.

(*vii*) recycle of construction waste material.

16.9. BUILDING MANAGEMENT SYSTEM (BMS)

All large buildings, such as corporate offices, malls, hospitals, hotels, airports, appartment blocks etc requires variety of services like heating, ventilation and air conditioning (HVAC), voice and data communication, lighting, power (normal and emergency), fire detection monitoring and fire fighting systems, security and access control etc. Generally, all such services are controlled manually by specific personnel including maintenance. However, in BMS all such operation and control functions are automatically synchronized resulting in efficient utilization of available resources, reduced operation and maintenance cost and improved performance. So, BMS is an automated centralized control of all building services with a view to optimize performance, investment and operating cost.

Salient features of such buildings are following—

(*i*) automatic control of lighting, ventilation and temperature inside building by tracking movement of human beings.

(*ii*) distribution of electric power to loads as per demand and activation of emergency generators is case of power failure.

(*iii*) sensing, monitoring and control of fire.

(*iv*) automatic lifts with sensors and memory.

(*v*) safety and energy management systems.

(*vi*) logging of data from various sub-systems as to provide a base for detection of impending failures and for the purpose of scheduling of maintenance activities.

(*vii*) reduced dependency on human beings.

16.10. VARIABLE SPEED DRIVES

Variable speed drives are devices used for varying the speed of a driven equipment to exactly match the requirement of the driven equipment and achieve energy savings. For example, in many applications, variable flow of liquids is required. So, instead of throttling the flow through a valve, by reducing the speed of the motor, required flow can be achieved. Also, it can result in significant energy savings.

Some of the variable speed drives are following—

(*i*) **DC Drive:** DC drive is an electronic controller which rectifies incoming ac supply to dc supply. The speed of dc motor can be varied by varying the output dc voltage of the controller. The variable dc voltage can be used to vary the speed of the motor by applying to the field or armature.

(*ii*) **Variable Frequency AC Drive:** It is a frequency changer which varies the frequency and voltage of ac supply fed to an induction motor. Hence, AC drive improves energy savings by variable speed operation.

(*iii*) **Eddy Current Drive:** It is a combination of a constant speed ac induction motor coupled to an eddy current clutch. It operates on principle of eddy currents to transmit torque from a fixed speed ac motor to the load. The function of an eddy current clutch is to transmit a controlled torque from the induction motor to the load.

(*iv*) **Rotor Resistance Control:** This method is used to vary the speed of a slip ring induction motor. An external resistance is inserted into rotor circuit to control the speed of the motor.

(*v*) **Slip Power Recovery Scheme:** This method recovers rotor slip energy of slip ring induction motor.

(*vi*) **Variable Fluid Coupling:** This method uses hydraulic coupling filled with an oil to transmit power from drive to a driven equipment. The variable speed is obtained by controlling the oil flow in the hydraulic circuit of the coupling.

16.11. VARIOUS METHODS OF IMPROVING ENERGY SAVINGS

1. **Peak clipping:** Peak clipping is peak load reduction i.e. using equipment during off peak hours.

2. **Valley filling:** Load over entire day is maintained as constant as possible by shifting peak load to low load period

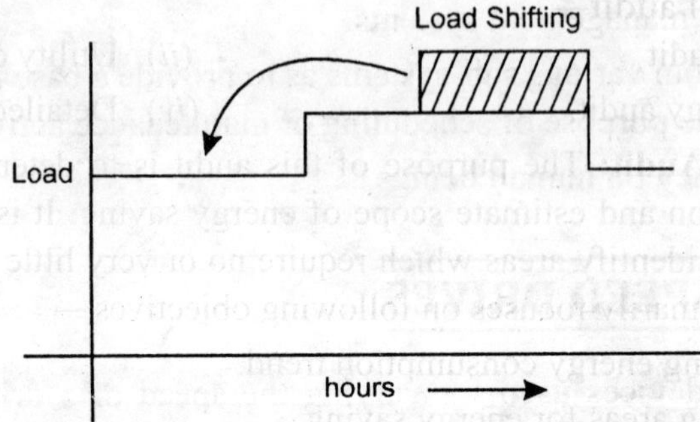

Fig. 16.3. Valley Filling in load duration curve

3. **Use of star rated appliances:** Bureau of Energy Efficiency under Ministry of Power does energy efficiency labelling of appliances. Rating of upto five stars are given to most energy efficient appliance followed by four star, three star and single star in that decreasing order of energy efficiency. So, one must choose five star appliance for higher energy saving.

16.12. ENERGY AUDIT

As per Energy Conservation Act, 2001; energy audit is defined as "Verification, monitoring and analysis of use of energy including submission of technical report containing recommendations for improving energy efficiency with cost benefit analysis and an action plan to reduce energy consumption." Purpose of energy audit is to control wastage of energy and improve efficiency of energy usage.

16.12.1. Need for Energy Audit

The need for energy audit are following—

(*i*) to measure and record energy consumption.

(*ii*) to improve energy efficiency.

(*iii*) to reduce energy cost.

(*iv*) to conserve depleting fossil fuel.

(*v*) to establish norms for checking consumption of different category of consumers.

(*vi*) to forecast energy demand.

(*vii*) to provide input for system expansion.

(*viii*) to set benchmark in energy consumption.

16.12.2. Types of Energy Audit

There are four types of audit—

(*i*) Preliminary audit (*ii*) Utility cost analysis audit.
(*iii*) Standard energy audit. (*iv*) Detailed audit.

(*i*) Preliminary Audit: The purpose of this audit is to determine energy consumption in the organisation and estimate scope of energy saving. It is simplest form of audit. This audit helps to identify areas which require no or very little investment for energy saving projects. It primarily focuses on following objectives—

(*a*) establishing energy consumption trend.
(*b*) identifying areas for energy saving.
(*c*) establishing benchmark in energy consumption (by comparing with similar industry).
(*d*) identifying areas for detailed audit.

(*ii*) Utility Cost Analysis Audit: The purpose of this audit is to audit utility (section of organisation producing power, compressed air, steam, hot water, chilled water, air conditioning, raw water, processed water, demineralised water etc). The audit helps to identify energy wastages and determine potential for energy efficiency retrofits.

(*iii*) Standard Energy Audit: This audit provides detailed analysis of energy systems of an organisation. It takes into account preliminary audit and utility cost analysis audit.

(*iv*) Detailed audit: This audit evaluates all major energy systems. It estimates energy savings and cost of implementation of energy saving projects including payback period. This audit consists of three stages—

- *Pre audit stage:* It involves site visit, familiarisation with plant process, issue of questionnaire to each department for data collection, collection of design and operating data.
- *Audit stage:* It involves collection of basic, energy generation and consumption data by actual measurement to establish base line data.
- *Post audit stage:* It involves preparation of proposals for energy saving projects with justification and payback period calculation.

16.12.3. Procedure for Conducting Energy Audit

The procedure for conducting audit consists of following steps—

(*i*) measurement and collection of data pertaining to type of energy sources and consumption areas on a specially designed format.
(*ii*) establishing benchmark by comparing collected data with other similar industry.
(*iii*) study of plant operation practices, maintenance practices and equipment performance to estimate potential for saving.
(*iv*) recommendations for energy saving projects with detailed technical and financial analysis.
(*v*) monitoring of progress and course correction.
(*vi*) training of plant operating and maintenance personnel for implementation.

16.12.4. Energy Conservation Act, 2001

Government of India has enacted Energy Conservation Act, 2001. Bureau of Energy Efficiency (BEE) under ministry of power is the nodal agency for implementation and monitoring of this act. The energy conservation programmes have been targeted for various types of industries, such as steel, sugar, aluminium, chemical etc. The objective is to promote energy efficiency in industrial as well as in commercial establishments by benchmarking their own levels of efficiency with the best available in India.

The salient features of the act are following—

(*i*) to carry out mandatory energy audits in specified industries and designated consumers .

(*ii*) to prescribe energy consumption norms.

(*iii*) to subject appliances and equipments to labeling regime.

(*iv*) to prohibit manufacture, sale, import or deal in appliances and equipments not meeting standards and labeling requirements.

(*v*) to inspect and enforce compliance.

(*vi*) to give direction for appointment of energy manager.

(*vii*) to prescribe energy conservation building codes.

(*viii*) to levy penalties.

(*ix*) to certify energy auditors and energy managers.

(*x*) to spread awareness and provide financing schemes for energy conservation.

List of energy intensive industries and other establishments specified as designated consumers are given below—

(*i*) Aluminium.

(*ii*) Fertiliser.

(*iii*) Cement.

(*iv*) Pulp and paper.

(*v*) Chlor-alkali.

(*vi*) Sugar.

(*vii*) Textile.

(*viii*) Chemicals.

(*ix*) Railways.

(*x*) Port trust.

(*xi*) Transport sector.

(*xii*) Petrochemicals, refineries and gas crackers.

(*xiii*) Thermal power stations, hydel power stations, electricity transmission and distribution companies.

(*xiv*) Commercial buildings or establishments.

16.13. ENERGY MANAGEMENT

Purpose of energy management is to utilise energy judiciously and effectively for maximization of profit and enhancement of competitive edge. The objective is to achieve optimum energy procurement and utilization in an organization with minimum energy cost and environmental impact.

Principle of energy management involves following—

(*i*) procurement of optimum energy at lowest cost.

(*ii*) consuming energy at highest efficiency.

(*iii*) reusing and recycling energy.

(*iv*) reducing energy wastages.

Energy management strategy involves following—

(*i*) setting up of energy generation and consumption monitory system.

(*ii*) conducting regular energy audit.

(*iii*) implementing detailed project plan.

Energy management system in an organisation requires technical and managerial expertise, For this purpose, an energy manager is recruited who looks after energy management activities in the organisation and is accountable to top management. The energy manager sets up energy monitoring and reporting system so as to collect and analyse data related to energy cost and consumption. Periodic energy audit is necessary to identify scope for energy savings. The entire staff is trained in energy management aspects for wider participation and success.

16.14. ENERGY STORAGE SYSTEMS

Energy storage is a method of storing energy so that when supply exceeds demand, this stored energy can be used. This ensures continuous supply of energy. This variation in energy demand may be due to daily and seasonal variation or due to intermittent nature of energy supply source, such as solar and wind energy systems etc.

16.14.1. Methods of Energy Storage

Methods of energy storage systems are classified as per following—

1. Mechanical energy storage.

   (*i*) Pumped hydro electric storage.

   (*ii*) Compressed air storage.

   (*iii*) Fly wheel.

2. Electrochemical Energy storage.

   (*i*) Batteries—lead acid, Ni–cd, Ni–Fe, Sodium Sulphur, Zinc–chloride.

3. Chemical energy storage
   (*i*) Fossil fuels—gas, oil and coal.
   (*ii*) Hydrogen.
4. Electromagnetic energy storage
   (*i*) Super conducting magnetic energy storage (SMES).
5. Electrostatic energy storage
   (*i*) Super capacitors.
6. Thermal energy storage
   (*i*) Sensible heat and latent heat (water, salt).
7. Biomass energy storage.
   (*i*) Dry wood, agricultural waste, agro-industrial waste etc.

The energy storage system is integrated with energy generation and distribution system. This ensures higher efficiency, safety and reliability of the energy delivery system.

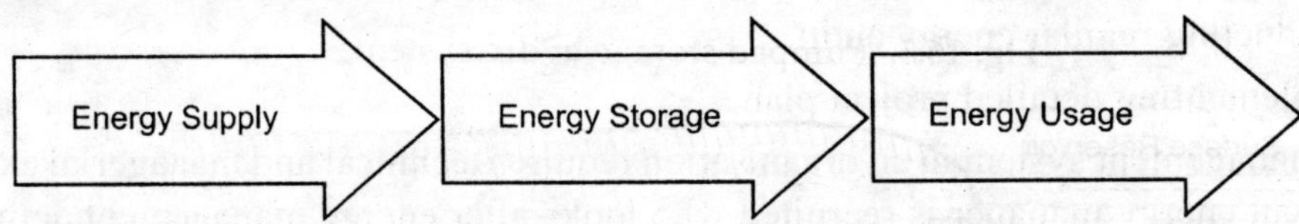

Fig. 16.4. Energy supply and usage network

Applications of energy storage are following—

(*i*) for remote use.
(*ii*) to meet peak demand.
(*iii*) for renewable energy supply system.
(*iv*) for data storage and computing.
(*v*) for emergency communication.
(*vi*) for power quality improvement (e.g. smoothening of fluctuations).
(*vii*) support during transient changes (e.g. load change, load switching etc).

Energy storage system is designed for long time (hours/days), short time (for few hours) and very short time (minutes/seconds).

1. **(*i*) Pumped hydro electric storage:**

   This is widely used energy storage technology used for meeting peak demand of the system. It consists of a hydro electric power plant with a reversible turbine generator system. In the pumping mode, generator becomes a motor and draws electricity from grid during off-peak hours when sufficient power is available. This motor drives the turbine which operates as pump. This pump-motor system lifts the water from tail race to head race at higher elevation .The head ranges from 30 to 300 m. Usually Francis turbine is used but for low head, propellor type turbine is used. The water, thus, stored at higher elevation can be used to generate power at the time of need.

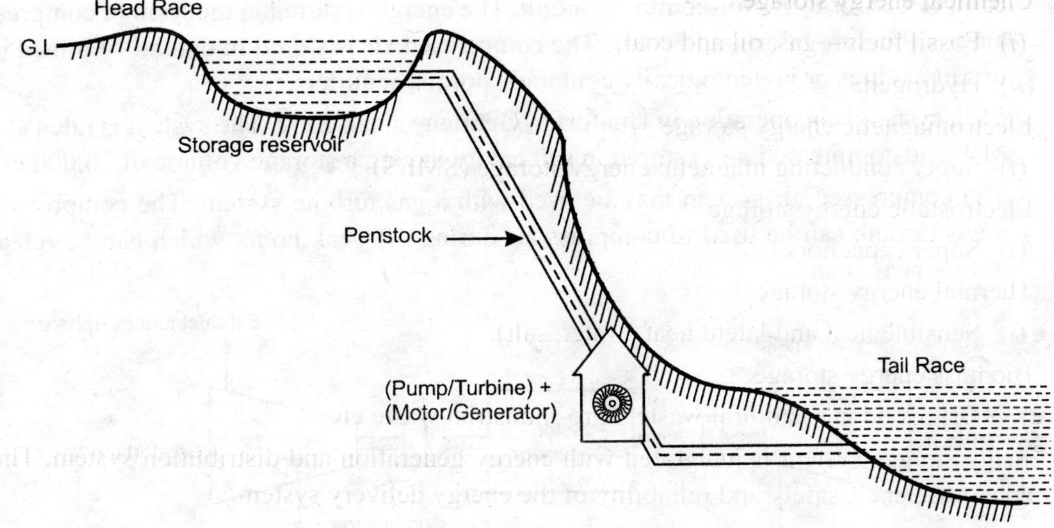

Fig. 16.5. Pumped storage hydro system

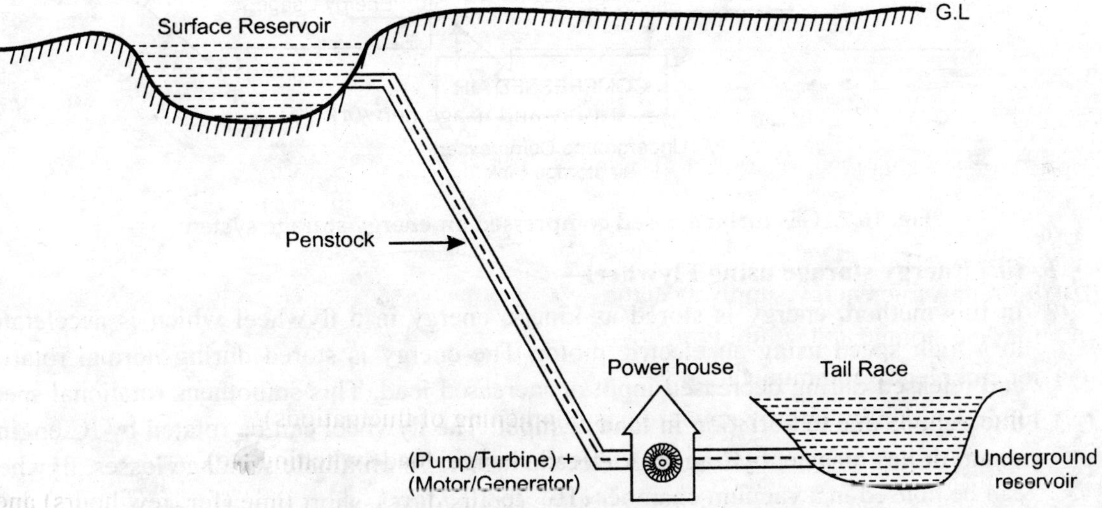

Fig. 16.6. Underground pumped storage hydro system

Pumped storage hydro plant has following advantages—

(*i*) it is a rugged and reliable energy storage system.

(*ii*) can be operated in remote control mode.

(*iii*) it causes no environmental pollution.

(*iv*) power required for pumping is available at cheap rate (during off-peak hour).

(*v*) power is available at short notice.

(*vi*) it can be used for load frequency control.

(*vii*) it has low capital cost compared to other peaking units.

1. (*ii*) Compressed Air storage—

In this system, excess electrical energy during off-peak hours is used to convert into compressed air by motor-compressor unit. The energy is stored in the form of compressed air at a pressure of around 50 bar. The compressed air is stored in natural or mined rock or salt cavities or in geologically contained porous acquifers.

Such system is in operation in Huntorf in Germany since 2002. The system is rated at 290 MW and compressed air is stored in salt cavity having a storage volume of 30,000 m^3.

The compressed air system may be used with a gas turbine system. The compressor of a gas turbine can be used to compress air during off-peak hours which can be released during peak hours.

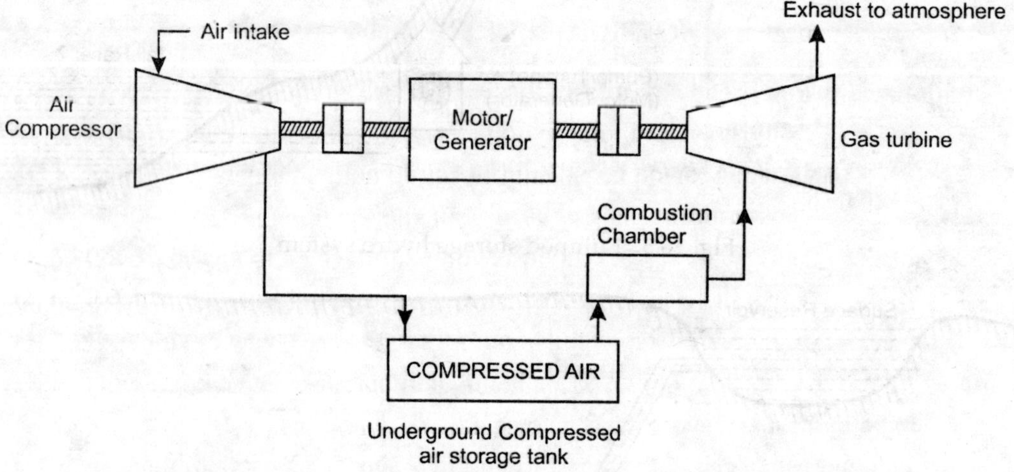

Fig. 16.7. Gas turbine based compressed air energy storage system

1. (*iii*) Energy storage using Flywheel—

In this method, energy is stored as kinetic energy in a flywheel which is accelerated to a high speed using an electric motor. The energy is stored during normal rotation and released during decreased input or increased load. This smoothens rotational speed fluctuations due to variation in load or input. The flywheel can be rotated by IC engine, steam or gas turbine, hydraulic or electric motor. To eliminate windage losses, flywheel can be housed in a vacuum chamber (10^{-3} to 10^{-5} torr).

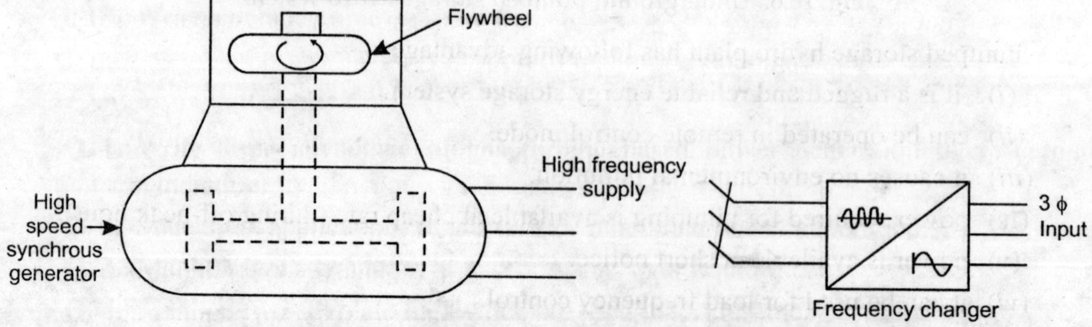

Fig. 16.8. Fly wheel energy storage system

This system is used to supply high peak demand, improve stability of electrical power system and damp sub-synchronous resonance (SSR) in electrical power system.

2. (*i*) Electrochemical Energy Storage System

In this system, electrical energy is stored as chemical energy in a battery. During discharge, the chemical energy is converted into electrical energy and is supplied to the load.

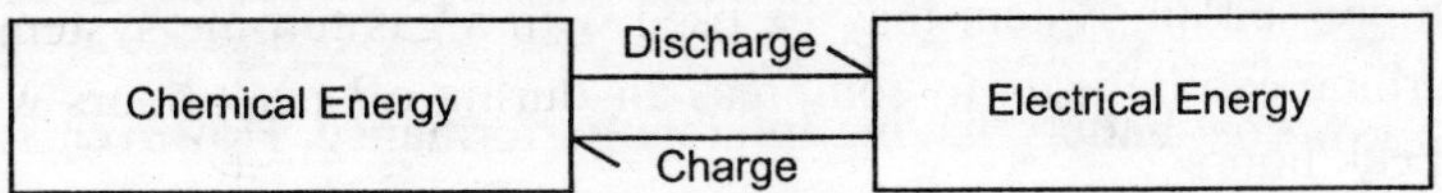

Fig. 16.9. Battery energy storage system

A battery storage system capable of delivering 10 MW for 4 hours continuously was installed in southern California, USA in 1991. The system consisted of 8000 battery modules.

Primary batteries are not rechargeable and are discarded after use. Secondary batteries are rechargeable and after useful life, these are discharged.

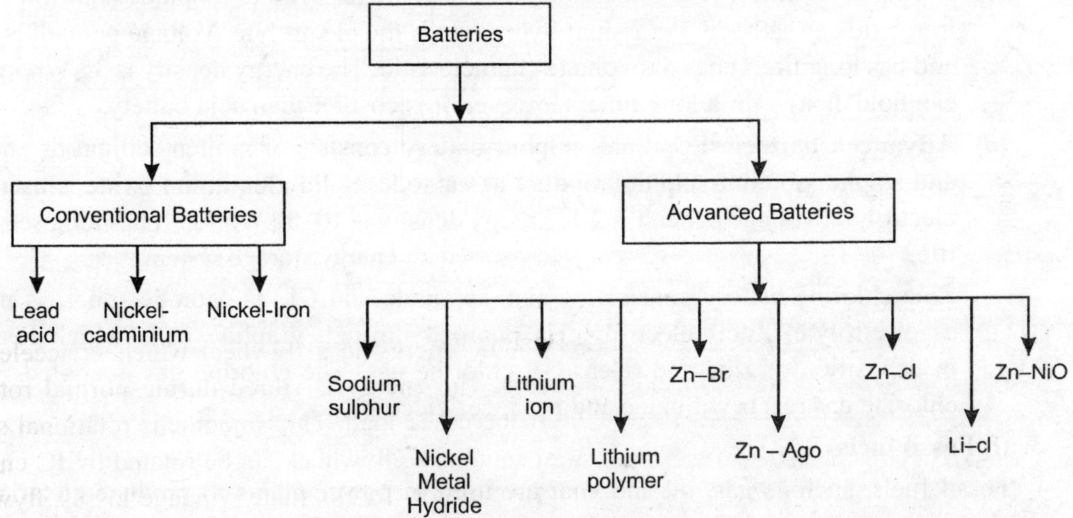

Fig. 16.10. Types of batteries

Selection of type of battery required is based on energy density (KWh/kg), performance characteristics (cell voltage/time), life in terms of number of charge/discharge cycles, ambient temperature, desired discharge rate (kWh/min), charging rate (kWh/hr), maintenance requirement, cost and type of application—mobile or stationary.

A battery energy storage system consists of several battery units connected in series or in parallel to get desired voltage or current.

(*a*) **Lead Acid battery:** It is well established technology used widely for variety of applications. It consists of lead oxide as anode and spongy load as cathode. Sulphuric acid is the electrolyte .A number of individual cell are connected in series. Anode and cathode are separated by microporous separator made of rubber/glass fibre/plastic. The container is made of rubber or plastic. Specific gravity of electrolyte when fully charged is 1.28 V/cell and when fully discharged 2.1 V/cell. The energy stored per unit of battery is 22 to 55 Wh/kg. The energy efficiency is 65 to 80%. Operating life is 2000 cycles, 10 years.

The chemical reaction during charging and discharge are given by—

$$Pb + PbO_2 + H_2SO_4 \underset{\text{Charge}}{\overset{\text{Discharge}}{\rightleftharpoons}} 2PbSO_4 + 2H_2O \quad (16.1)$$

It is a low cost battery having reliable performance. However, it is not suitable for large energy storage.

(*b*) **Nickel–Cadmium battery:** It is an alkaline battery unlike lead acid battery. It consists of cadmium as anode, nickel hydroxide as cathode and potassium hydroxide as electrolyte (specific gravity 1.2 at 16°C). Nominal voltage per cell is 1.3 V. Voltage/cell is 1.35 to 1.78 V during charging and 1.35 to 1.17 V during discharging. Energy density is 40 Wh/kg. The efficiency is 70 to 80%. It has low mass, long life and flat voltage characteristics. However, it is very expensive.

(*c*) **Nickel-Iron battery:** It consists of steel with nickel hydrate as anode and iron with iron oxide as cathode. Potassium hydroxide is the electrolyte. Voltage per cell is 1.2 and has long life. It has flat voltage characteristic. The energy density is 35 Wh/kg. It can hold charge for a long time. However, it is costlier than acid battery.

(*d*) **Advanced batteries:** Sodium–sulphur battery consists of molten sodium as anode and sulphur-sodium-sulphite mixture as cathode. Solid aluminium oxide is used as electrolyte. Voltage per cell is 2.1. Energy density is 40–50 Wh/kg. It has long service life.

Zinc-chloride battery consists of zinc as anode and Cl_2 as cathode. $Zncl_2$ is used as electrolyte. $Zncl_2$ electrolyte is pumped through graphite cells which results in deposition of zinc and release of chlorine gas. The chlorine gas is cooled. The chlorine gas reacts with zinc and produces electricity.

3. (*i*) Fossil fuels

Fossil fuels, such as gas, oil and coal are used in power plants to produce electricity. Hydrogen is used in fuel cell to produce electricity. The fuels can be stored and can be used, when required.

4. (*i*) Super Conducting Magnetic Energy Storage (SMES)

It is based on the principle that energy can be stored in magnetic field of a coil. If the coil is made of super conducting material and temperature is maintained below critical limit, then once the coil is charged, the energy will be stored in magnetic field indefinitely. The stored energy is released when the coil is discharged. Due to presence of super conducting state, the losses in the coil due to resistance of the coil is zero. However, the cost of such system is very high due to operation and maintenance of system in cryogenic state and large structural mass required.

5. Thermal energy storage

Energy can be stored as heat either sensible heat or latent heat. When heat energy is stored by increasing temperature of material, it is called sensible heat storage. When heat energy is stored by change of phase i.e. from solid to liquid or from liquid to vapour, it is called latent heat storage. It is possible to store sensible and latent heat.

Thermal energy storage is used for domestic water and space heating applications, process industries etc. The material used may be water, rock storage system, scrap aluminium, scrap iron, sodium bricks etc. A heat transfer fluid may be used to transfer heat from source and deliver it to thermal storage material. The disadvantage is that the temperature of working material varies during energy delivery process.

In thermal power plants, pressurised water sensible heat storage system is used. During off peak hours, thermal energy storage system receives excess steam from steam turbine at high pressure. This steam mixes with pressurised water and energy is stored. At peak hours, thermal storage system releases this steam which is used to drive a steam turbine unit to meet peak load.

6. **Bio mass energy storage**

The solar energy is stored in the plants through photosynthesis process. This energy is released during combustion of biomass. Some bio-fuels are liquids and gases which can be used in internal combustion engines to generate energy.

Following table 16.2 provides comparison of various energy storage systems—

Table 16.2: Comparision of Energy Storage Systems.

Sr. No.	*Type of energy storage*	*Storage capacity*	*Back-up time*	*Response time*	*Efficiency*	*Life*
1.	Pumped hydro	200 MW – 2GW	hours	about 12 minutes	about 75 %	about 50 years
2.	Compressed air	25 MW – 2.7 GW	hours	about 12 minutes	about 70%	less than 50 years
3.	Battery	upto 50 MW	hours	seconds	about 80%	less than 10 years
4.	Flywheel	5 kW – 3 MW	minutes	about 12 minute	less than 95%	about 20 years
5.	Super Conducting Magnet Energy Storage	10 kW – 3 MW	seconds	milli seconds	about 95%	about 30 years
6.	Super capacitors	upto 150 MW	seconds	milli seconds	less than 95%	more than 10 years

7. **Super Capacitors and Hybrid Capacitors**

Super capacitors use advanced materials which increases surface area of electrodes per unit mass thereby allowing higher energy storage. Power density of 3000 to 10,000 W/kg can be achieved. The advantages and disadvantages of super capacitors are following—

Advantages—

(*i*) high power density.

(*ii*) wide thermal operating range.

(*iii*) low cost.

(*iv*) long cycle life.

Disadvantages—

(*i*) low energy density than batteries.

First super capacitors for military applications was developed by Pinnacle Research Institute and later by Maxwell Technologies for power applications.

Super capacitors consists of two electrodes of highly porous material which are immersed in an electrolyte solution and separated by a separator. Electrolyte provides a conducting medium while separator prevents internal short circuit between electrodes. Voltage rating and internal resistance of super capacitors are determined by electrolytes. Electrolyte of any storage device are basically of two types viz. aqueous electrolyte and non-aqueous electrolyte. Aqueous electrolytes are–potassium sulphate, potassium hydroxide which are highly conductive, non toxic and possess efficient charge transfer mechanism. On the other hand, non-aqueous electrolytes are acenonitrile which are flammable, toxic in nature and costly. Based on electrolyte design, super capacitors are categorised into three types—

(*i*) Electric double layer.

(*ii*) Hybrid capacitor and

(*iii*) Pseudocapacitor.

Electric double layer and pseudo capacitor have same electrode material. In hybrid capacitor, one electrode is made up of carbon material and other of composite materials consisting of carbon and other metal oxide. Carbon with high specific surface area, low impurity and high porosity is suitable for electrodes of super capacitor. Carbon materials used are activated carbon, carbon nanotubes, graphene, carbon aerogels etc.

A hybrid capacitor uses conductive polymers to form entire electrolyte or in conjunction with a liquid electrolyte in a design known as hybrid capacitor. Recently, hybrid capacitors have combined an electrostatic carbon electrode with a lithium ion electro-chemical electrode.

Hybrid capacitors have large energy density, high power density and stable performance. A hybrid capacitor consists of two electrodes–electrolyte and a separator. The electrode materials used for hybrid capacitor should have characteristics, such as high porosity, high conductivity, high surface area and resistance to oxidation. The electrodes are separated by an insulating medium called separator. The purpose of separator is to provide physical separation between electrodes in order to prevent short circuit. It is very thin and porous material which has low internal resistance. Also, it is chemically inert to maintain conductivity and stability of electrolyte. Polyethylene is used as a separator due to low cost and high porosity. The difference between super capacitor and hybrid capacitor lies in construction of electrodes. Hybrides capacitors are asymmetric while super capacitors are symmetric in nature. Thus, correct polarity must be observed before applying voltage to a hybrid capacitor. The asymmetric nature of hybrid capacitor provides higher energy density compared to an equivalent electrolytic capacitor. Depending upon the voltage limit, two types of electrolytes are used in a hybrid capacitor viz aqueous and organic. Aqueous electrolytes are– dilute sulphuric acid, potassium hydroxide, sodium per chlorate, potassium sulphate, potassium chloride etc. These electrolytes have high conductivity, low operating temperature range and voltage withstand limit of 2 to 2.2 V per cell. While organic electrolytes are acetonitrile, propylene carbonate, diethyl carbonate etc. These are more expensive than aqueous electrolyte. These electrolytes have higher operating range and higher voltage withstand limit of 3 to 4 volt per cell. However, these electrolytes suffer from lower electrical conductivity and lower power density. These are other type of electrolytes such as ionic electrolytes which are non-volatile and stable at high temperature. These are composed of organic anions. The voltage withstand limit is 6 volt per cell. However, these are expensive.

Table 16.3: Comparison of Super Capacitor and Hybrid Capacitor

Sr. No.	*Parameter*	*Super Capacitor*	*Hybrid Capacitor*
1.	Capacitance	0.1 to 470 F	300 to 3300 F
2.	Charge/discharge cycles	105 to 106	104 to 105
3.	Temperature	–20 to +70°C	–20 to +70°C
4.	Energy density	1.5 to 3.9 Wh/kg	10 to 15 Wh/kg
5.	Power density	2 to 10 kW/kg	3 to 14 kW/kg
6.	Self discharge time	Weeks	Month
7.	Life time	5 to 10 years	5 to 10 years
8.	Efficiency	95 %	90 %

Advantages—

1. flexible structure is possible with hybrid capacitor.
2. high power density than conventional capacitors.
3. can be charged and discharged quickly which is faster than batteries.
4. do not release any heat and are free from any hazardous materials like batteries.
5. no danger of over charging and reversing of polarity does not cause fire or explosion.

Limitations of hybrid capacitors—

1. low cell voltage.
2. self discharge rate is higher than a battery.
3. high cost due to electrode material.

Solved Examples

Example 16.1.

A motor of 25 HP capacity operates at 85% efficiency. If this motor is to be replaced with a similar capacity motor of 90% efficiency, determine saving in annual cost of operation, if the moor operates 8000 hours per year. Assume, tariff rate of ₹ 6/kWh.

Solution:

$$\text{Power, Input at 85\% efficiency} = \frac{25 \times 0.746}{0.85} \qquad (\because 1\text{HP} = 746 \text{ W})$$

$$= 21.94 \text{ kW}$$

$$\text{Power input at 90\% efficiency} = \frac{25 \times 0.746}{0.9}$$

$$= 20.72 \text{ kW}$$

$$\text{Difference in power input} = 21.94 - 20.72 = 1.22 \text{ kW}$$

Annual cost saving for 8000 hours of operation @ Rs 6/kWh

$$= 1.22 \times 8000 \times 6$$

= ₹ **58,560/year** **Ans.**

Example 16.2.

A factory exterior is illuminated by twenty, 1000 W halogen lamps. The lamps operate 12 hours per day for 365 days in a year. In order to redcue the energy bill, it is decided to replace halogen lamps with more energy efficient HPSV (High Pressure Sodium Vapour Lamp). Determine the saving in annual energy bill by switching over to a more efficient light source. The data for both type of lamps is given below—

Types of lamps	*Lumens (lm)*	*Luminous Efficacy (lm/w)*
1000 W Halogen lamp	22,700	22.70
250 W HPSV lamp	24,600	98.40

Assume electricity tariff of ₹ 6.00/kWh.

Solution:

A 250 W HPSV lamp has higher lumens or light output and very high luminous efficacy compared to halogen lamp.

Annual energy consumed by twenty 1000 W halogen lamps—

$$= \frac{20 \times 1000 \times 12 \text{ hours/day} \times 365 \text{ days/year}}{1000}$$

$$= 87{,}600 \text{ kWh}$$

Annual energy consumed by twenty 250 W HPSV lamps—

$$= \frac{20 \times 250 \times 12 \text{ hours/day} \times 365 \text{ days/years}}{1000}$$

$$= 21{,}900 \text{ kWh}$$

$$\text{Saving in energy bill} = (87{,}600 - 21{,}900) \times 6$$

$$= 65{,}700 \text{ kWh} \times ₹\ 6 \text{ kWh}$$

$$= ₹\ \mathbf{3{,}94{,}200}$$ **Ans.**

Example 16.3.

An industrial unit uses electrical furnace for process heating. It is decided to convert electrical furnace into oil fired unit. The operating electrical load on furnace is 50 kW. Calculate the saving in operating cost due to changeover to oil fired furnace.

Given—

Efficiency of electrical furnace = 70%

Electricity tariff = ₹ 6/kWh

Efficiency of oil fired furnace = 55%

Calorific value of furnace oil = 9200 kcal/kg

Density of furnace oil at 15°C = 0.9 kg/litre

Cost of furnace oil = ₹ 60/litre

Operating hours = 6000 hours/year

Solution:

Useful heat at 50 kW load and 70% efficiency $= 50 \times 860 \times 0.7$

$$= 18{,}060 \text{ kcal} \qquad (\because 1 \text{ kWh} = 860 \text{ kcal})$$

$$\text{Furnance oil required to meet useful heat} = \frac{18060}{9200}\ \frac{\text{kcal}}{\text{kcal/kg}}$$

$$= 1.96 \text{ kg}$$

$$\text{Furnace oil required at 55\% efficiency of furnace} = \frac{1.96}{0.55} = 3.56 \text{ kg}$$

$$\text{Quantity of furnace oil required} = \frac{3.56}{0.9} = 3.95 \text{ litres}$$

$$\text{Cost of using electricity 6000 hours} = ₹\ 6/\text{kWh} \times 50 \text{ kW} \times 6000 \text{ hours}$$

$$= ₹\ 18 \times 10^5$$

$$\text{Cost of using furnace oil for 6000 hours} = ₹\ 60/\text{litre} \times 3.95 \text{ litres} \times 6000$$

$$= ₹\ 14.22 \times 10^5$$

$$\text{Annual saving} = 18 \times 105 - 14.22 \times 105$$

$$= ₹\ \mathbf{3{,}78{,}000}$$ **Ans.**

CHAPTER SUMMARY

Energy consumption is an indicator of economic progress of a country. Developed economies have higher per capita electricity consumption. In order to drive culture of energy conservation, govt of India has enacted Energy Conservation Act, 2001 making it mandatory for certain classes of industries to conduct energy audit by Bureare of Energy Efficiency (Under Ministry of Power, Govt. of India) certified energy auditors. These industries are required to improve energy efficiency. An energy manager (BEE certified) has to co-ordinate all energy audit and its implementation in these industries.

Electrical system provides a vast scope for energy conservation activities. Major savings accrue from energy efficient electrical devices such as energy efficient lighting, energy efficient motors, energy efficient transformers, variable speed drives etc. Energy conservation can also be done through efficient operation such as stoppage of energy wastages, voltage optimization, power factor improvement, controlling peak demand, optimum loading of motors and transformers etc. Even new buildings are constructed using efficient energy usage principles in construction and operation. These buildings are rated according to energy saved as per the set criteria. These buildings are sometimes called Green Buildings. In order to save energy in operation of large building complexes, building management system is used which saves energy in variety of services such as air conditioning, lighting, normal and emergency power supply, system security, voice and data communication etc. Solar energy is being extensively used not only in industry but also in residential complexes to augment convention electricity supply system.

The basic principle of energy conservation is reuse and recycle.

REVIEW QUESTIONS

Q. 1. Explain the meaning of energy conservation.

Q. 2. Discuss the need and importance of energy conservation.

Q. 3. Differentiate between energy conservation and energy efficiency.

Q. 4. Discuss various energy conservation opportunities in electrical system.

Q. 5. Write a brief note on (*i*) energy efficient motors (*ii*) energy efficient lighting.

Q. 6. Discuss the meaning, scope and advantages of green building.

Q. 7. Explain the meaning of building management system (BMS).

Q. 8. Discuss various types of variable speed drives available.

Q. 9. What is energy audit? Why is it needed?

Q. 10. Enumerate advantages and steps involved in energy audit.

Q. 11. Write a brief note on Energy Conservation Act, 2001.

Q. 12. What is energy storage system? Why is it needed?

Q. 13. Discuss various methods employed for energy storage.

Q. 14. What are other methods of energy conservation in mechanical and thermal systems?

Q. 15. Illustrate with practical examples, how energy conservation leads to environment protection?

Q. 16. Discuss how economic growth and energy demands are interrelated?

Q. 17. Explain the meaning of energy to GDP ratio.

Numerical Questions

Q. 1. It is decided to replace an aging motor of 50 HP capacity having an efficiency of 80% by another high efficiency motor of 50 HP having an efficiency of 92%. Calculate saving in energy cost if the motor is operated for 8000 hours in a year. Take electricity tariff of ₹ 6.50/kWh. [Ans: ₹ 316239 year]

Q. 2. Exterior of a garment export unit is illuminated by thirty five, 1000 W halogen lamps. The lamps operate 10 hours per day for 365 days in a year. In order to lower electricity bill, it is decided to replace existing halogen bulbs with high pressure sodium vapour lamps (HPSV). Calculate the saving in energy bill by switching over to more energy efficient light source. The data pertaining these two types of lamp is given below—

Types of lamps	*Lumens (lm)*	*Luminous efficacy (lm/w)*
1000 W Halogen lamps	22,700	22.70
250 W HPSV lamps	24,600	98.40

Assume electricity tariff rate of Rs 6.50/kWh. **[Ans:** ₹ 6,22,781.25]

SHORT ANSWER TYPE QUESTIONS

Q. 1. What are different energy efficient light sources?

Q. 2. Name the energy efficient material used for fabrication of transformer core.

Q. 3. Define energy audit.

Q. 4. Name five energy storage systems.

Q. 5. What are different types of audits?

Q. 6. What is the advantage of using star rated appliances?

Q. 7. List five benefits of energy efficient buildings.

Q. 8. Explain 'peak clipping' and 'valley filling'.

Multiple Choice Questions

Q. 1. Energy conservation means—

(*a*) reduction of energy consumption (*b*) improvement in energy efficiency

(*c*) both (*a*) and (*b*) (*d*) none of these

Q. 2. Efficiency of energy efficient motor is more than standard efficiency motor by

(*a*) more than 3–4% (*b*) less than 3–4%

(*c*) more than 6–8% (*d*) none of these

Q. 3. Amorphous metal cored transformer reduces no load losses compared to CRGO silicon steel by

(*a*) 50% (*b*) 60%

(*c*) 70% (*d*) 80%

Q. 4. Thermal energy storage system stores

(*a*) sensible heat only (*b*) latent heat only

(*c*) both sensible and latent heat (*d*) either sensible or latent heat

Q. 5. The least efficient energy storage system is

(*a*) pumped hydro (*b*) compressed air

(*c*) battery (*d*) flywheel

(*e*) super capacitor

Q. 6. Super capacitor stores energy in

(*a*) electromagnetic field (*b*) electrostatic field

(*c*) both electrostatic and electromagnetic (*d*) electro-mechanically

Q. 7. Waste heat recovery is an example of

(*a*) improved energy efficiency (*b*) energy conservation

(*c*) both (*a*) and (*b*) (*d*) none of these.

Answer to MCQ

1. (*c*) **2.** (*a*) **3.** (*c*) **4.** (*d*) **5.** (*b*)

6. (*b*) **7.** (*c*)

Chapter

SUBSTATION

Learning Objectives

After reading this chapter, reader will be able to

- Understand function, classification and various components of a substation.
- Understand factors governing choice of its location, and relative merits and demerits of indoor and outdoor substations.
- Differentiate between air insulated (AIS) and gas insulation substation (GIS) over construction, size, insulating medium and application area.
- Understand the meaning, need and types of earthing systems including different methods of equipment earthing and measurement of earth resistance.

"Being ignorant is not so much a shame, as being unwilling to learn."

— Benzamin Franklin

17.1. INTRODUCTION

A substation is defined as an assembly of apparatus meant to control, regulate, protect and change characteristics of power being fed into it. The substation may or may not perform all the functions mentioned above. For example, it may be a rectifier substation converting ac to dc or it may be a switching substation or a traction substation performing one or more of the functions mentioned above.

A substation is an intermediate port connecting power generating stations to consumers. It is interconnected with various generating power stations and loads forming an electricity grid.

17.2. CLASSIFICATIONS OF SUBSTATIONS

Substations are classified according to following basis—

(*i*) **According to design—**

(*a*) **Indoor substation**—An indoor substation houses all apparatus inside a building. These substations are used for voltage levels of 66 kV and below.

(*b*) **Outdoor substation**—An outdoor substation is erected in the open on foundations or on poles. Only panels (HT and LT), battery charger and battery banks etc. are housed inside the building. These substations are used for voltage levels of 132 kV and above.

(*c*) **Underground substation**—An underground substation may be located below ground level due to scarcity of levelled ground or terrain topology. These may be located near end user and reduce sub transmission voltage to lower level for use by end users.

(*ii*) **According to usage—**

(*a*) **Transmission substation**—It is used to step up the incoming voltage for feeding to transmission lines. It contains reactive power control equipment, such as capacitors, reactors, SVC etc. A phase shifting transformer is also used to control power flow between two adjacent transmission lines.

(*b*) **Distribution substation**—It transfers power from transmission network to distribution network at reduced voltage from 3.3 kV to 33 kV. Purpose is to isolate faults in transmission or distribution network.

(*c*) **Switching substation**—It is an intermediate substation meant for switching of capacitors and reactors. It does not contain transformer and hence, operates at single voltage level.

(*d*) **Traction substation**—It is used to feed power to railways for traction purpose (25 kV, single phase).

(*e*) **Converter substation**—It is used to either convert ac to dc or dc to ac in high voltage direct current (HVDC) transmission system.

(*f*) **Industrial substation**—It is a dedicated step down substation meant for feeding an industry (fertilizer, petrochemical, cement, refinery etc.).

(*iii*) **According to dielectric medium used—**

(*a*) **Air insulated substation (AIS)**—Air as insulating medium is used in busbars, circuit breakers, disconnecting switches etc.

(*b*) **Gas insulated substation (GIS)**—Sulphur hexa fluoride (SF_6) gas is used as insulating medium in busbars, circuit breakers, disconnecting switches etc.

(*c*) **Hybrid substation**—It is combination of both conventional and GIS. Some bays are GIS type while others are AIS type. Design consideration is based on cost, area available and local conditions.

(*iv*) **According to voltage level—**

(*a*) **High voltage substation (HV)**—Voltage is 11 kV to 66 kV.

(*b*) **Extra high voltage substation (EHV)**—Voltage level is 132 kV to 765 kV.

(*c*) **Ultra high voltage substation (UHV)**—Voltage level is 1000 kV and above.

17.3. SUBSTATION APPARATUS

All substation apparatus can be broadly classified into two categories viz. major apparatus and auxiliaries.

(*i*) Major apparatus—

(*a*) **Transformer**—Purpose of transformer is to step up or step down voltage. Generally, it is a three phase oil immersed power transformer installed outdoors having two or three windings. The voltage ratings are 765 kV, 400 kV, 220 kV and 132 kV.

11 kV and 33 kV transformers are dry type with epoxy cast insulation. It uses fans to maintain temperature. Advantages of dry type transformer over oil filled transformer are following—

- Very low risk of fire or explosion.
- Can be installed anywhere (over ground or underground).
- Well suited for densely populated area.
- No risk of ground pollution due to oil leakage.
- High reliability.

Transformer is costliest equipment in a substation

(*b*) **Circuit breaker**—It is used to make or break a circuit during normal and abnormal conditions. During abnormal condition, circuit breaker automatically switches off circuit. Different types of circuit breakers are air blast, SF_6 type, vacuum type, minimum oil type 'and air circuit breaker. For high voltage line, sF_6 or air blast circuit breaker is used. Operating mechanism of circuit breaker is spring operated, pneumatic or hydraulic.

(*c*) **Isolator**—It is used to isolate circuit under noload condition for the purpose of safety, maintenance and isolation. It consists of three poles which can be operated manually or by electric motor. Each pole has a rotating blade which swings in a horizontal plane. An isolator opens after circuit breaker has opened and closes before a circuit breaker is closed.

(*d*) **Busbars**—It is made of rectangular shaped aluminium flat and is used to carry current.

(*e*) **Earthing switch**—After opening circuit breaker and isolator, earthing switch is closed to discharge voltage to ground. This is done before maintenance is to be carried out on lines.

(*f*) **Current transformer (CT)**—It is used to reduce current magnitude for the purpose of measurement, control and protection. It has a round core of magnetic material which passes through a busbar. Secondary winding is connected to meters (ammeter, wattmeter etc) and for control purpose. If secondary winding is left open, very high voltage develops which may damage the insulation of CT.

(*g*) **Potential transformer (PT)**—It is used to step down voltage for the purpose of measurement and protection.

(*h*) **Lightning arrestor**—It is used in the beginning of the incoming overhead transmission line to protect lines and equipments in a substation from lightning.

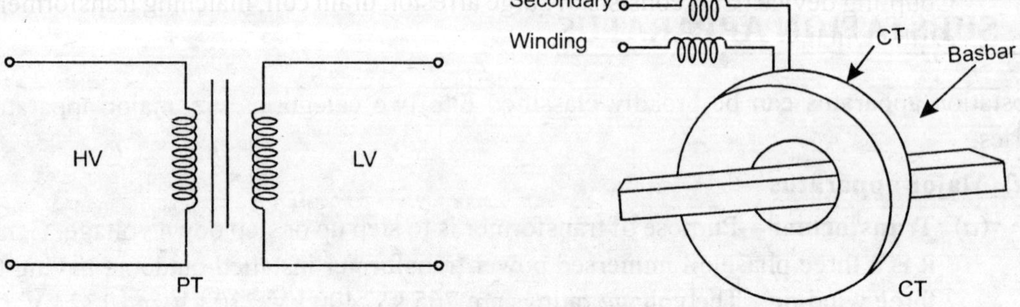

Fig. 17.1. CT and PT

It is a single pole unit connected between busbars and earth to transfer any surge due to switching or lightning to ground so that equipments are not damaged.

Different types of lighting arrestors are following—

- Rod gap arrestor.
- Horn gap arrestor.
- Expulsion type arrestor.
- Valve type arrestor.
- Multi gap arrestor.

Lightning stroke is visible discharge of static electricity accumulated in storm clouds occurring between clouds, between cloud and earthed structure. Cloud has negative charge which induces positive charge of equal magnitude on earthed objects underneath cloud. Current magnitude can reach several kilo ampers.

(*i*) **Protective relays**—Relays are used to protect substation equipments against faults, such as over current, earth fault, over voltage etc.

(*j*) **Series and shunt reactors**—These are used for line compensation. Series reactors are used to limit short circuit current.

(*k*) **Shunt capacitors**—These are used for voltage control by feeding reactive power into busbars.

(*l*) **Metering instruments**—These are ammeters, voltmeters, energy meters, frequency meters, wattmeters etc.

(*ii*) Substation auxiliaries—

(*a*) **Battery banks**—Battery banks provide reliable power supply to substation for control, protection and emergency lighting.

(*b*) **Communication system**—For communication amongst substations, power generating stations, load dispatch centres – power line carrier communication (PLCC), telephones etc. are used. PLCC transmits voice signal over power lines using carrier waves. Apart from voice communication, it can be used for telecontrol, teleprotection and data retrieval from RTU of SCADA (supervisory control and data acquisition) system.

Coupling device (CD) consists of surge arrestor, drain coil, matching transformer and earth switch.

Coupling device (CD) consists of surge arrestor, drain coil, matching transformer and earth switch.

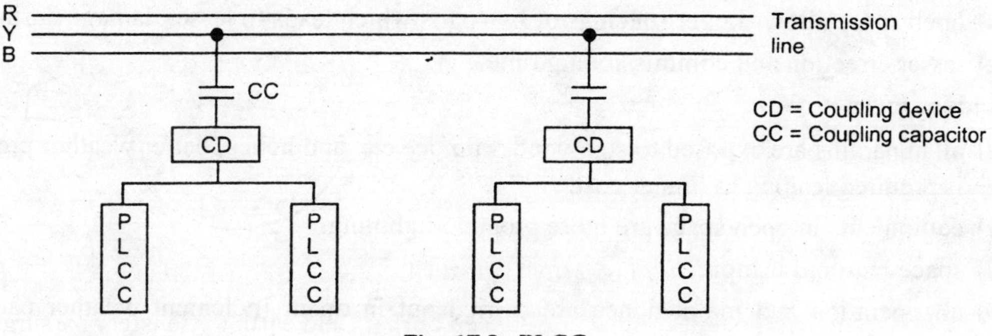

Fig. 17.2. PLCC

(c) **Station auxiliary transformer**—It supplies local power needs of substation.

(d) **Earthing system**—It provides earthing for safety and protection purpose. Equipment earthing connects body of equipment to earth for safety purpose. While the star point of power transformer is connected to earth to stabilize neutral to ground potential.

Permissible values of earth resistance for different types of installation are following—

- Large power station = 0.5 ohm
- EHV substation = 1.0 ohm
- 33 kV substation = 2.0 ohm
- Tower footing resistance = 10 ohm.

(e) **Fire protection system**—It consists of fire alarm and fire extinguishers (carbon dioxide type and dry chemical powder type).

(f) **Station lighting**—It consists of lights required for substation illumination. A part of lighting is on battered called emergency lighting which operate at the time of power failure.

17.4. FUNCTIONS OF A SUBSTATION

A substation may perform one or all of the following—

(*i*) control flow of power.

(*ii*) provide protection to transmission and distribution system.

(*iii*) help in loadshedding.

(*iv*) control voltage.

(*v*) transmit data for control and protection.

(*vi*) ensure steady state and transient stability of power network.

17.5. ADVANTAGES AND DISADVANTAGES OF OUTDOOR SUBSTATION OVER INDOOR SUBSTATION

Advantages—

(*i*) it is easy to carryout expansion and maintenance.

(*ii*) cost of substation is less as no building is required.

(*iii*) detection of fault is easier due to full visibility.

(*iv*) open space allows larger spacings of live parts which leads to lesser damage during fault.

(*v*) lesser errection and commissioning time.

Disadvantages—

(*i*) all apparatus are exposed to sun, wind, rain, ice etc. and hence, better weather protection is required leading to higher cost.

(*ii*) equipments in open space are more prone to lightning.

(*iii*) space required is more.

(*iv*) all operation and maintenance are carried out in open. Inclement weather can affect supervision and maintenance.

17.6. SELECTION OF SITE FOR SUBSTATION

Following factors govern the selection of site for substation—

(*i*) **Availability of sufficient land**—Sufficient land should be available with good quality of soil for installation of various substation apparatus at reasonable rate.

(*ii*) **Nearness to load centre**—The substation should be as near to load centre as possible.

(*iii*) **Availability of good transportation and communication facilities**—Good transportation and communication facilities are required for errection, commissioning and operation.

(*iv*) **Pollution free area**—The location should be free from atmospheric pollution which affects insulators and corrodes the metallic parts of substation apparatus and structure.

(*v*) **Nearness to basic amenities**—Basic amenities, such as hospitals, schools, housing, market etc. should be available.

(*vi*) **Free from water–logging**—The land should be free from water–logging during rainy season and fairly levelled.

(*vii*) **Low soil resistivity**—The soil should have low earth resistance.

(*viii*) **Availability of ROW**—Sufficient ROW (right of way) should be available for incoming and outgoing transmission lines.

17.7. AIR INSULATED AND GAS INSULATED SUBSTATION

There are two types of substation–air insulated substation (AIS) and gas insulated substation (GIS). In AIS, insulating medium is air at ambient temperature and pressure. While in GIS, the insulating medium is sulphur hexa flouride (SF_6). All the components of GIS are encapsulated in SF_6 gas. Due to excellent insulating properties of SF_6 over air, there is drastic reduction in size of substation. A GIS requires 5 – 6 acres of space compared to 30 – 40 acres for AIS.

17.7.1. Air Insulated Substation (AIS)

AIS are used for voltage levels upto 800 kV, especially where there is no space constraint. All the electrical and mechanical components of substation are site assembled. In outdoor design, all the apparatus are exposed to environmental effects. While in indoor design, all apparatus are housed inside substation building. AIS is suitable upto 8000 A and 80 kA short circuit current. The advantages of AIS are following—

(*i*) free accessibility to all equipments.

(*ii*) adequate protective clearances for installation and maintenance.

(*iii*) use of flame retardant and non-inflammable materials.

(*iv*) protection against surges and lightning strikes.

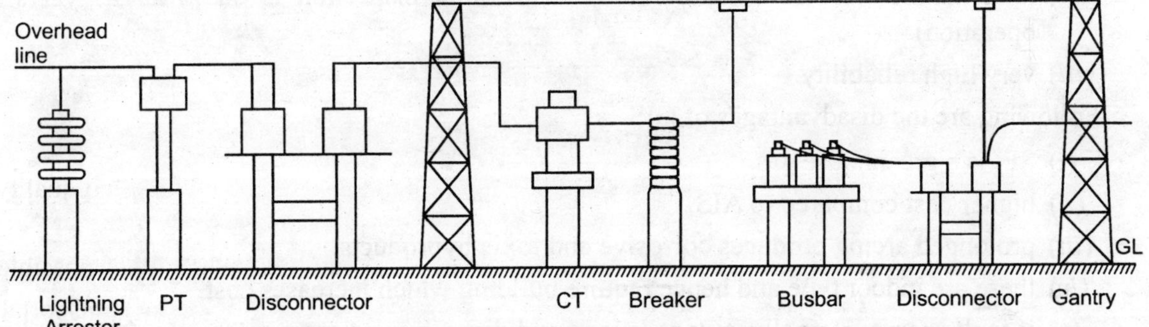

Fig. 17.3. Air insulated substation (AIS)

17.7.2. Gas Insulated Substation (GIS)

An air insulated substation uses air as dielectric medium between busbars. While transformers, CT, PT are oil immersed. Circuit breaker depending upon voltage rating is either oil circuit breaker, vacuum circuit breaker or air blast circuit breaker. In a gas insulated substation, all bus bars are enclosed in an air tight chamber containing sulphur hexa fluoride (SF_6) gas. SF_6 gas is an excellent dielectric medium used in SF_6 circuit breakers, gas insulated transformers and gas insulated transmission lines. GIS is useful where sufficient land is not available and atmosphere is highly polluted.

SF_6 gas is used for phase to phase and phase to ground insulation. Various components of a GIS are following—

(*i*) Power transformer.

(*ii*) Circuit breakers.

(*iii*) Disconnect and earth switches.

(*iv*) Density monitor.

(*v*) CT/PT.

(*vi*) Surge arrestor.

(*vii*) SF_6/air or SF_6/oil bushings.

(*viii*) Pressure relief device.

(*ix*) Protective relays.

(*x*) Power line carrier communication (PLCC).

(*xi*) Fire fighting and protection system.

All components such as busbars, CT/PT etc. are enclosed in a metal chamber filled with SF_6 gas.

Advantages of GIS are following—

(*i*) requires very less space compared to AIS (useful in urban area, industrial area, and mountainous regions).

(*ii*) protection of live parts against dust, moisture, sand storms, snow, rain, salt deposit etc.

(*iii*) these are very compact and hence can be installed indoor.

(*iv*) due to less area required, there is saving in land cost and heavy foundations.

(*v*) less time is required for errection of substation as all parts are factory assembled.

(*vi*) it is easy to transport substation elements due to small size.

(*vii*) long maintenance free life of components (first inspection is due after 25 years of operation).

(*viii*) very high reliability.

Following are the disadvantages of GIS—

(*i*) SF_6 is a greenhouse gas.

(*ii*) higher cost compared to AIS.

(*iii*) prolonged arcing produces corrosive and toxic byproducts.

(*iv*) these are indoor type and hence require building which increases cost.

(*v*) if fault occurs internally, outage is long and damage is severe.

(*vi*) presence of dust or moisture inside compartment can cause flashover.

(*vii*) switching operation produces very fast transient overvoltages.

(*viii*) non-uniform field reduces voltage withstand capacity.

17.7.2.1. Properties of SF_6 gas

SF_6 gas has excellent dielectric properties and electrical breakdown strength is 2 to 3 times more than air at atmospheric pressure. Properties of SF_6 are given below—

(*i*) it is a colourless, odourless, non-toxic and non-inflammable gas.

(*ii*) it is inert and non-corrosive.

(*iii*) it is thermally stable (does not decompose upto 500 °C).

(*iv*) its density is about 5 times that of air.

(*v*) dielectric strength is 2 to 3 times that of air at atmospheric pressure.

(*vi*) it has better arc quenching ability than air.

(*vii*) it dissipates heat better than air.

(*viii*) boiling point = – 63 °C

(*ix*) molecular weight = 146.06

(*x*) density of gas (at 1 bar and 20 °C) = 6.164 g/l

(*xi*) relative density w.r. to air = 5.10

(*xii*) specific heat = 7.09 cal/ml/°C at 25 °C

(*xiii*) thermal conductivity = 3.36 cal/sec/cm^2/°C/cm × 10^4

(*xiv*) vapour pressure = 150 psig

(*xv*) viscosity = 1.61 × 10^4 poise at 25 °C

(*xvi*) critical temperature = 45.6 °C

(*xvii*) critical pressure = 36.557 bar

17.7.2.2. *Gas insulated transformer and transmission lines*

A gas insulated transformer contains SF_6 in place of oil. The advantages of gas insulated transformer are following—

(*i*) gas insulated transformers are non-flammable compared to oil immersed transformer.

(*ii*) size of transformer is drastically reduced. This enables direct coupling with gas insulated switchchgear thereby reducing substation space.

(*iii*) as oil filtration and dehydration is not required hence installation and operation is easy.

(*iv*) very low maintenance required.

These transformers can be installed in underground, coastal area, desert, mountainous region, hospitals, shopping malls, hotels, chemical plants, refineries, petrochemical plants etc.

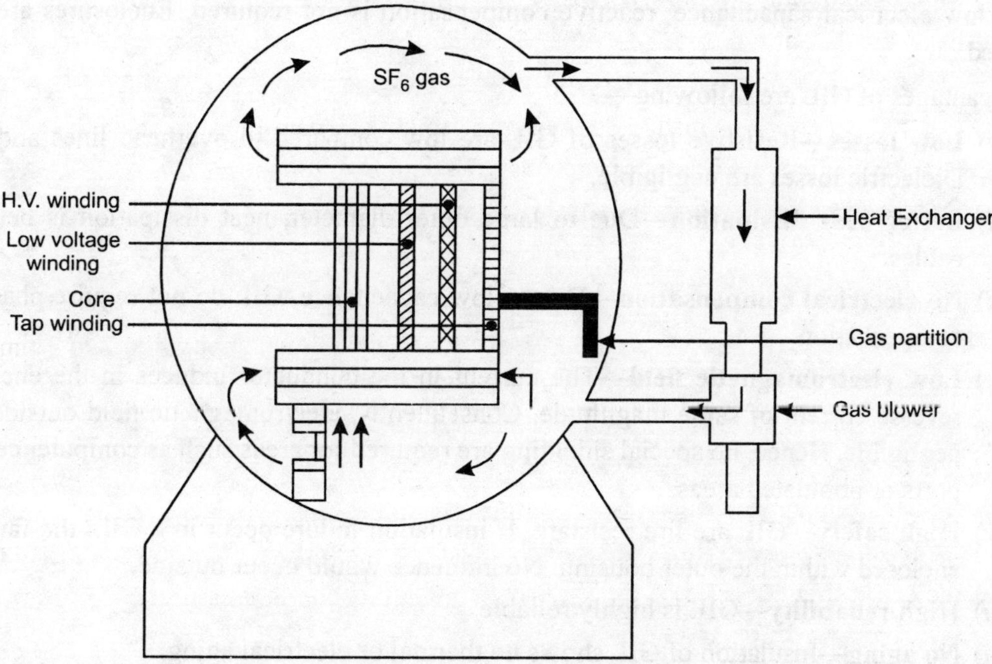

Fig. 17.4. Gas insulated transformer

Gas Insulated Transmission Line (GIL)—Gas insulated transmission line is a system for transmission of bulk power over long distances. In cases, where overhead lines are not possible, GIL can be laid underground without reduction of power transmission capacity.

The GIL consists of three single phase encapsulated aluminium tubes that can be directly buried in ground or laid in a tunnel. The outer aluminium enclosure is at ground potential. The interior annular space between conductor pipe and enclosure is filled with a mixture of 80% nitrogen and 20% SF_6.

The central aluminium conductor rests on cast resin insulators.

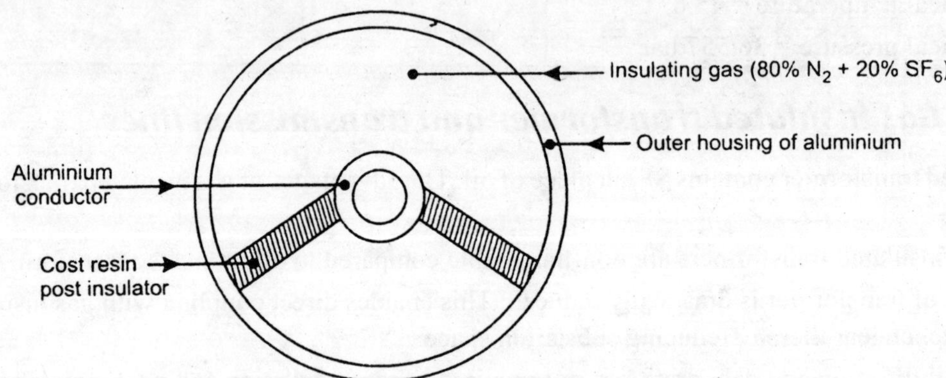

Fig. 17.5. Construction of gas insulated transmission line

Due to the modular design, the elements can be combined to a longer length. Typical GIL are used for transmission systems with 345 kV to 550 kV voltages and 2500 A to 5000 A currents. Due to low electrical capacitance, reactive compensation is not required. Enclosures are solidly grounded.

Advantages of GIL are following—

(*i*) **Low losses**—Resistive losses of GIL are low compared to overhead lines and cables. Dielectric losses are negligible.

(*ii*) **Better heat dissipation**—Due to large outer diameter, heat dissipation is better than cables.

(*iii*) **No electrical compensation**—Due to low capacitance, GIL do not require phase angle compensation.

(*iv*) **Low electromagnetic field**—The current in the conductor induces in the enclosure a reverse current of same magnitude. Consequently, electromagnetic field outside GIL is negligible. Hence, no special shielding are required for areas such as computer centre, air ports or populated areas.

(*v*) **High safety**—GIL are fire resistant. If insulation failure occur in a GIL, the fault arc is enclosed within the outer housing. No influence would occur outside.

(*vi*) **High reliability**—GIL is highly reliable.

(*vi*) **No aging**—Insulation of GIL shows no thermal or electrical aging.

(*vii*) **Maintenance free**—GIL are practically maintenance free.

(*viii*) **No corona**—GIL are free from corona losses.

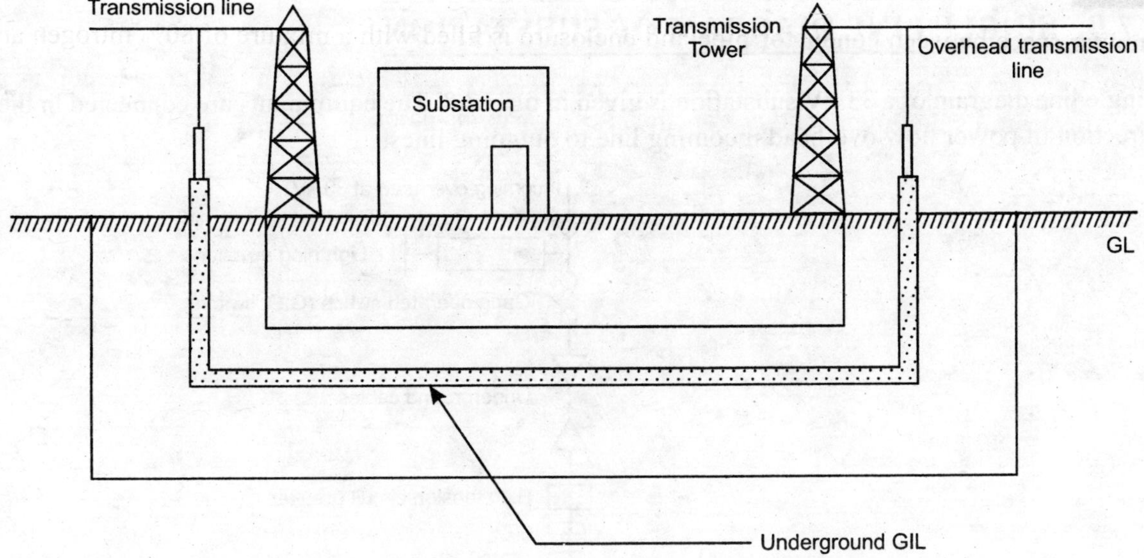

Fig. 17.6. Underground gas insulated transmission line

17.8. LAYOUT OF AIR INSULATED SUBSTATION (AIS)

Before erection of substation, a layout of diagram is prepared for installation of various substation equipments. Separate areas are earmarked for installation of transformer, switchyard, high tension panels, low tension panels, main control room, battery room, earthing area, cable route etc.

Land area required for AIS substation for different voltage levels is given below—

(*i*) 132 kV substation = 3.5 hectares.

(*ii*) 220 kV substation = 6.0 hectares

(*iii*) 400 kV substation = 20.0 hectares.

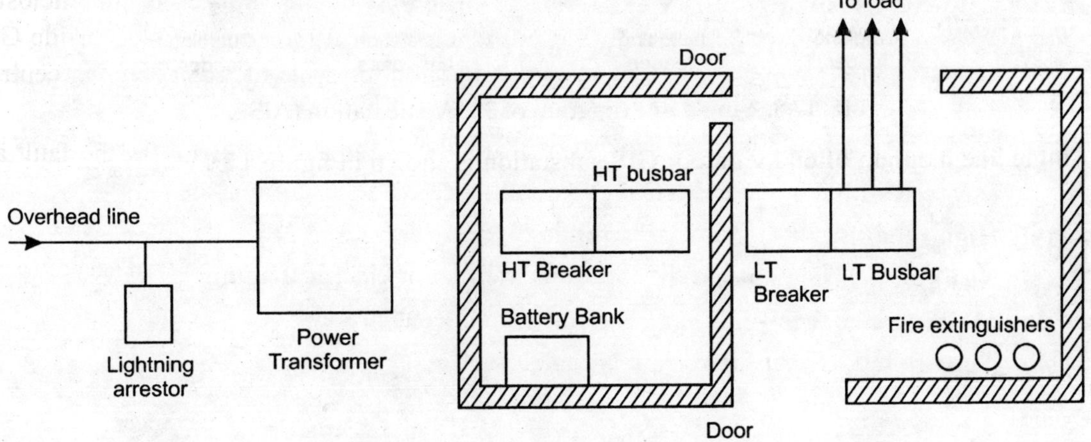

Fig. 17.7. Layout of indoor substation

17.9. SINGLE LINE DIAGRAM OF SUBSTATION

Single line diagram of a 33 kV substation is given in fig. 17.8. The equipments are connected in the direction of power flow overhead incoming line to outgoing lines.

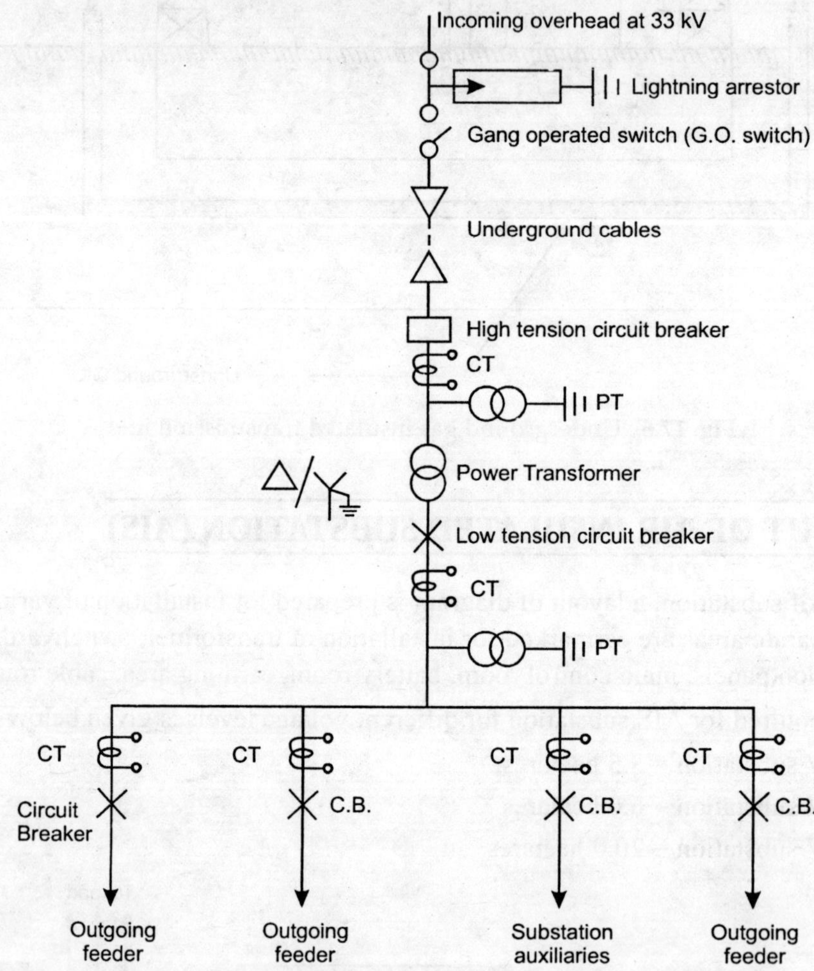

Fig. 17.8. Single line diagram of 33 kV substation (AIS)

Single line diagram of 66 kv indoor GIS substation is shown in figure 17.9

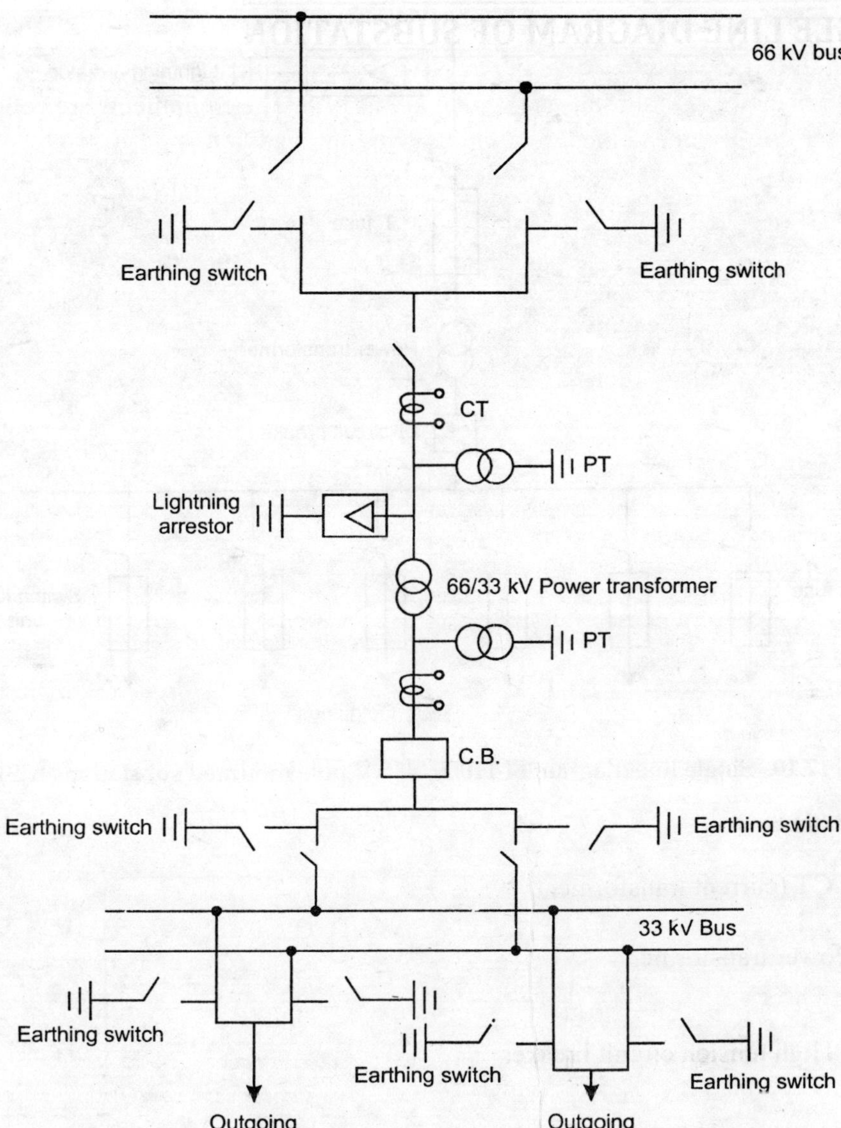

Fig. 17.9. Single line diagram of 66 kV Indoor GIS substation (2500 A)

Single line diagram of 11000/415 V pole mounted substation is shown in figure 17.10.

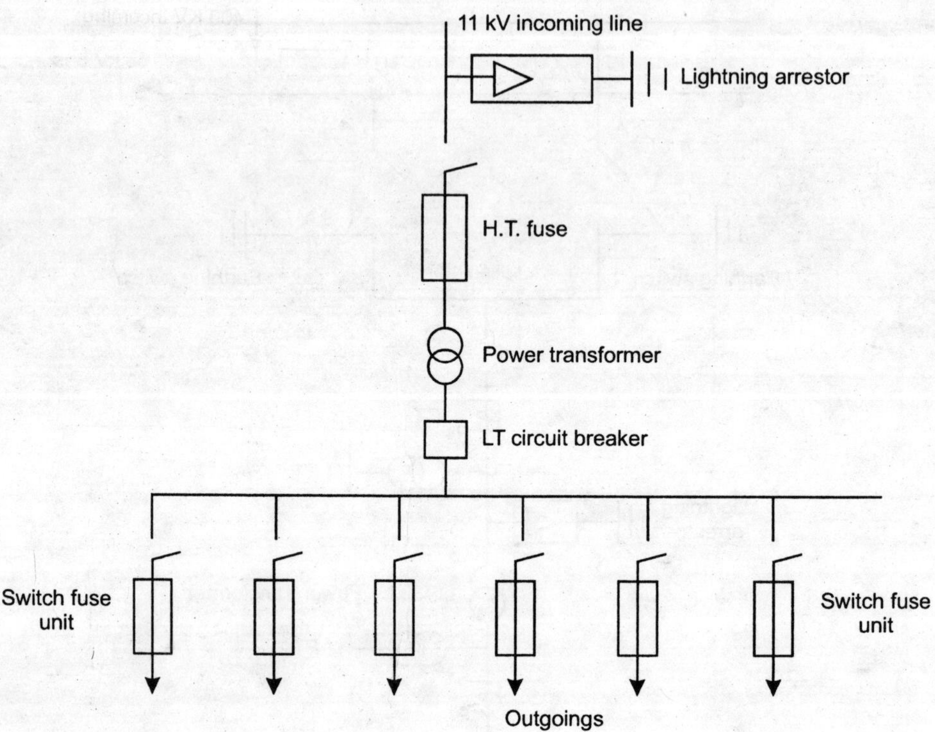

Fig. 17.10. Single line diagram of 11000/415 V pole mounted substation (AIS)

Legends used—

1. CT (current transformer)
2. Power transformer
3. High tension circuit breaker
4. Low tension circuit breaker
5. Lighting arrestor
6. PT (potential transformer)
7. Isolator

Key diagram of 400 kV substation is shown below (fig. 17.11)—

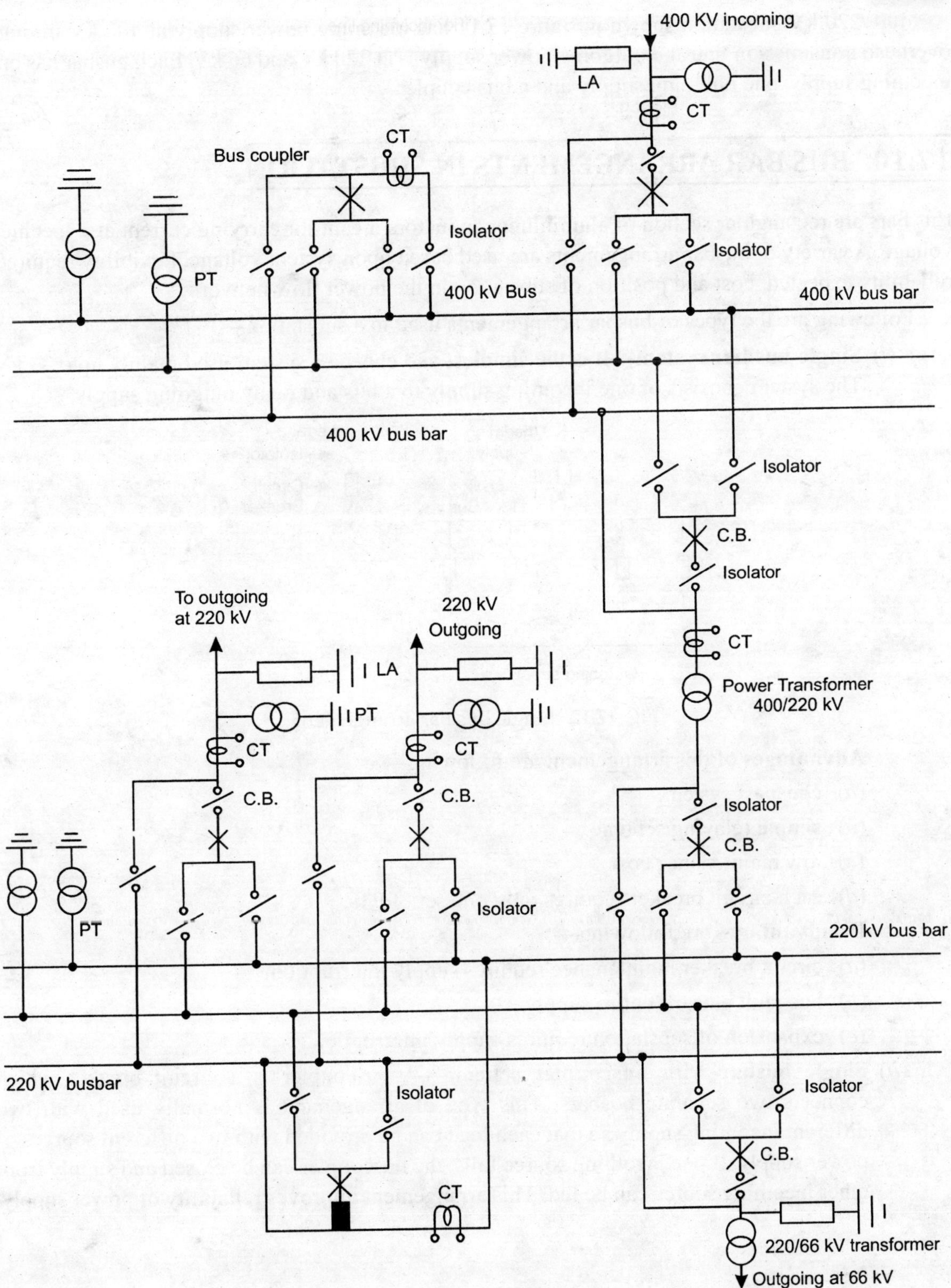

Fig. 17.11. Single line diagram of 400/220 kV substation (AIS)

400 /220 kV substation shown in figure 17.11 has incoming power supply at 400 kV through overhead transmission line and outgoing power supply is at 220 kV and 66 kV. Each busbar has one incoming supply, one outgoing supply and a bus coupler.

17.10. BUS BAR ARRANGEMENTS IN SUBSTATION

Bus bars are rectangular section of aluminium conductors meant for carrying current at a specified voltage. A variety of busbar arrangements are used based upon system voltage, flexibility required, reliability expected, cost and position of substation in the power flow network.

Following are the types of busbar arrangements used in a substation—

(*i*) **Single bus bar system**—It is the simplest and cheapest system used mainly upto 33 kV. The system consists of one incoming supply to a bus and many outgoing supply.

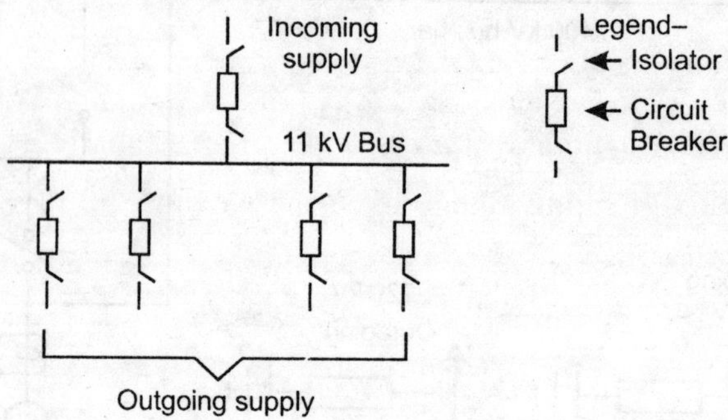

Fig. 17.12. Single bus bar arrangement

Advantages of this arrangement are following—

(*a*) cheapest system.

(*b*) simple relaying scheme.

(*c*) low maintenance cost.

(*d*) each circuit breaker requires only one set of PTs.

Disadvantages are following—

(*a*) circuit breaker maintenance requires supply interruption.

(*b*) bus fault cuts off entire supply.

(*c*) expansion of substation requires supply interruption.

(*ii*) **Single busbar with buscoupler scheme**—A buscoupler is a circuit breaker which connects two separate busbars. This type of arrangement is normally used with two different incoming supply so that each load can be provided with two different sources of power supply. If one incoming source fails, the buscoupler can be closed and supply from other incoming source can be fed. This arrangement improves reliability of power supply.

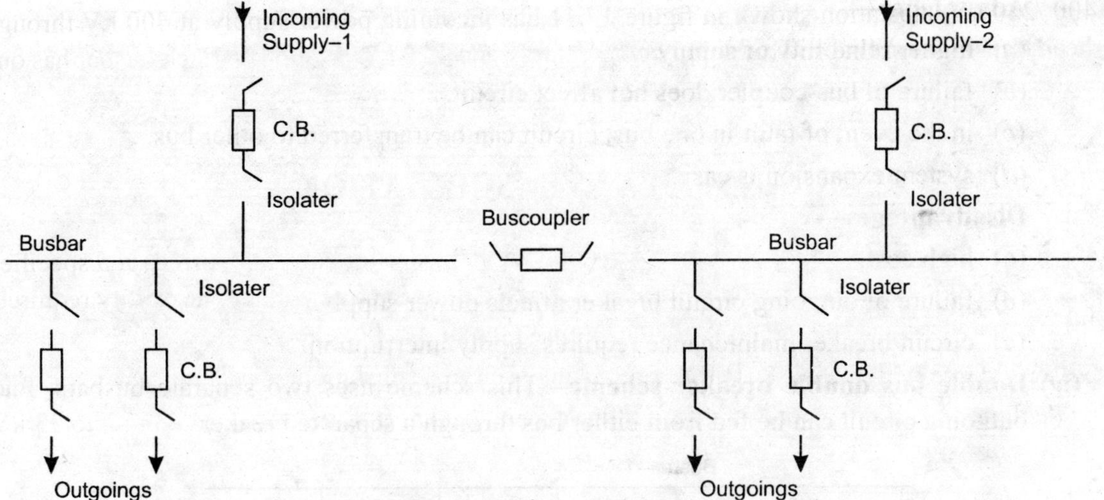

Fig. 17.13. Single busbar with buscoupler scheme

Advantages of this system are following—

(*a*) higher reliability of supply due to two separate power supplies.

(*b*) part of load can be shifted to other section of busbar.

(*c*) failure of one circuit breaker affects only one circuit.

(*d*) complete shutdown is not needed for maintenance. Half section can be switched off.

(*e*) system can be expanded easily.

Disadvantages—

(*a*) high cost

(*b*) large system size.

(*c*) buscoupler circuit breaker maintenance requires complete shutdown.

(*iii*) Double bus single breaker scheme—In this system, each circuit is fed from two buses. Outgoing of each circuit is controlled by one circuit breaker. If required, two separate buses can be coupled together with a circuit breaker.

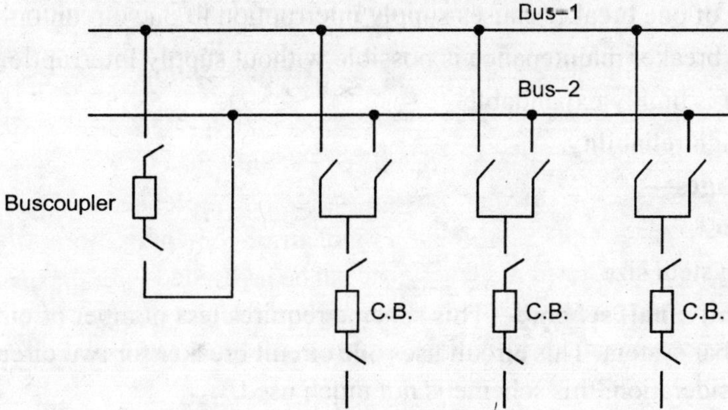

Fig. 17.14. Double bus single breaker system

Advantages—

(*a*) higher reliability of supply.

(*b*) failure of bus-coupler does not affect circuit.

(*c*) in the event of fault in one bus, circuit can be transferred to other bus.

(*d*) system expansion is easy.

Disadvantages—

(*a*) high cost.

(b) failure of outgoing circuit breaker affects power supply.

(c) circuit breaker maintenance requires supply interruption.

(*iv*) **Double bus double breaker scheme**—This scheme uses two separate busbars. Each outgoing circuit can be fed from either bus through a separate breaker

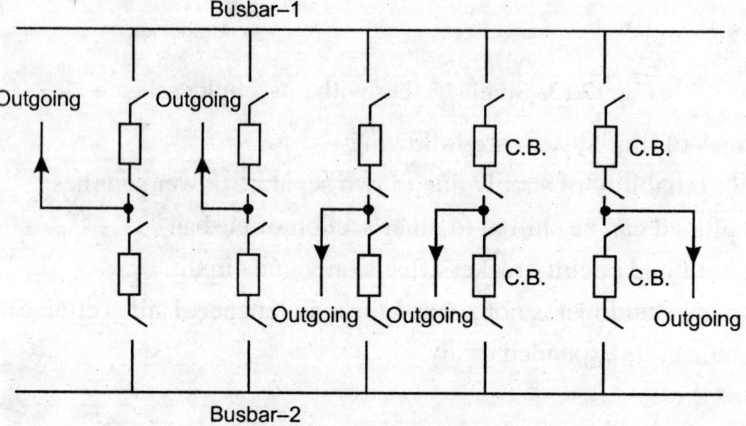

Fig. 17.15. Double bus double breaker scheme

Advantages—

(*a*) highly flexible arrangement.

(*b*) fault on one bus does not affect any circuit.

(*c*) failure of one breaker causes supply interruption to one circuit only.

(*d*) circuit breaker maintenance is possible without supply interruption

(*e*) system is highly expandable.

(*f*) very high reliability.

Disadvantages—

(*a*) high cost.

(*b*) large system size.

(*v*) **Breaker and a half scheme**—This scheme requires less number of circuit breakers than double busbar system. This circuit uses one circuit breaker for two circuits. However, due to cost consideration, this scheme is not much used.

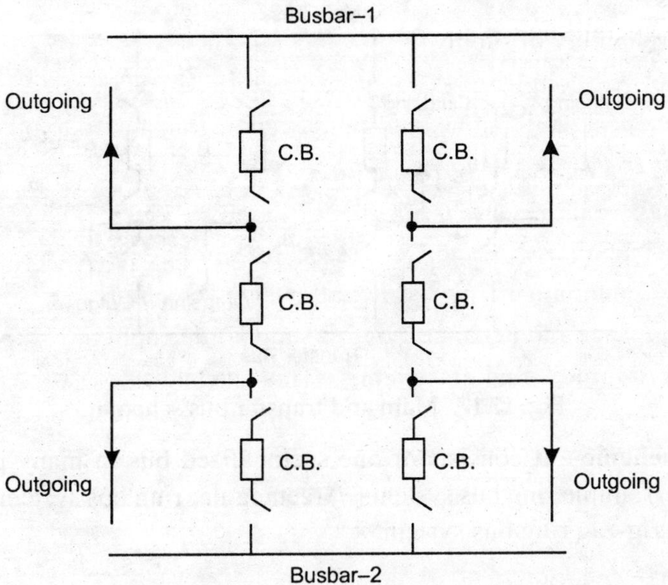

Fig. 17.16. Breaker and a half scheme

Advantages—

(*a*) cheaper than double bus double breaker scheme.

(*b*) fault in circuit breaker or bus does not affect power supply.

(*c*) highly expandable.

(*d*) failed circuit breaker causes loss of one circuit only.

(*e*) any bus can be taken up for maintenance.

Disadvantages—

(*a*) high cost.

(*b*) large system size.

(*c*) protection scheme more complicated.

(*d*) high maintenance cost.

(*vi*) Main and transfer busbar scheme—A double busbar scheme allows maintenance on other busbar but does not allow maintenance on circuit breakers. This scheme allows maintenance on circuit breakers but does not allow maintenance on busbars.

Advantages—

(*a*) circuit breaker maintenance is possible without shutdown.

(*b*) only one set of PT required.

Disadvantages—

(*a*) expensive system.

(*b*) normal operation is as single bus single breaker.

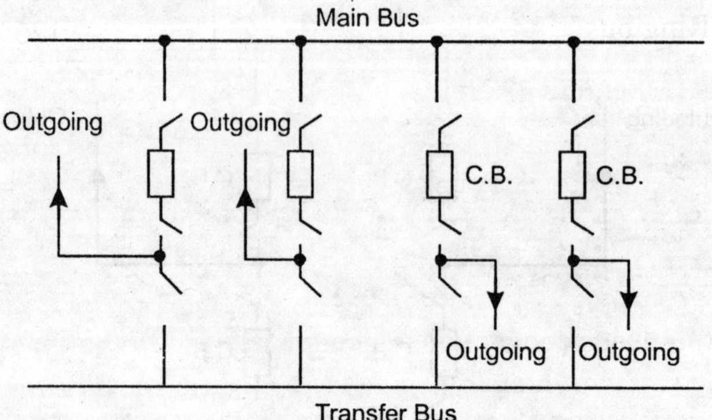

Fig. 17.17. Main and transfer bus scheme

(*vii*) Ring bus scheme—It consists of one sectonalized bus in many parts. Different types used are—(*i*) simple ring bus system (*ii*) rectangular ring bus system (*iii*) circular ring bus system (*iv*) zig-zag ring bus system.

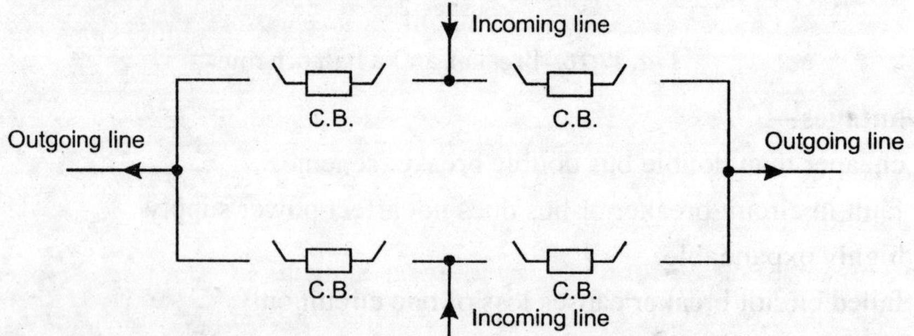

Fig. 17.18. Ring bus system

Advantages—

(*a*) circuit breaker maintenance is possible without shutdown.

(*b*) flexible operation.

(*c*) higher supply reliability.

(*d*) only one PT required.

Disadvantages—

(*a*) costly system.

(*b*) faulty line be isolated by tripping two breakers.

(*c*) system expansion is difficult.

Table 17.1: Cost comparison of different busbar schemes

Sr. No	***Busbar configuration***	***Relative cost***
1.	Single busbar	100%
2.	Single bus and bus coupler	120%

3.	Ring bus	125%
4.	Breaker and a half	145%
5.	Double bus double breaker	190%

17.11. EARTHING

Earthing in simplest term means connection to general mass of the earth. One of the major function of earthing is to provide safety to human beings from electric shock. All housedold appliances are properly connected to earth through a three pin plug. Out of three pins, earth pin is longer and has higher diameter than the rest of the pins. This is because as soon as the pin is inserted into socket, the earth pin being longer connects to earth before other pins are connected to phase and neutral. So, the appliance is earthed before it is energised. A higher diameter of pin allows lower resistance to earth & hence, easier flow of current to earth in the event of earth fault.

Apart from safety reason, the neutral point of generators and transformers are connected to earth to keep potential of neural point to zero. In addition, a discharge path is provided for lightning.

17.11.1. Need for Earthing

Earthing is needed due to following reasons—

(*i*) earthing protects human beings from electric shock.

(*ii*) it provides discharge path for lightning overvoltages.

(*iii*) it provides path to discharge stored energy in high voltage and extra high voltage systems before undertaking maintenance.

(*iv*) neutral earthing ensures longer insulation life for motors, generators, transformers etc. by suppressing transients and sustained over voltages associated with certain fault conditions.

(*v*) it improves protective relaying by providing fast and selective isolation of earth faults.

(*vi*) it protects large buildings from atmospheric lighting.

(*vii*) it minimizes over voltages due to restriking.

(*viii*) it minimizes persistent arcing grounds.

(*ix*) during fault, phase voltages on healthy lines are limited to phase to ground voltage level.

Table 17.2 Comparison of earthed and unearthed systems

Earthed system	*Unearthed system*
(*i*) Maximum voltage to earth is restricted to phase to neutral value at any time	(*i*) system is subjected to severe over voltages.
(*ii*) Earth fault in control wiring puts only 58% of line voltage to line to connected contactor coil. Hence, accidental starting of motor is not possible..	(*ii*) Earth fault in control wiring puts full voltage on contactor coil. Hence, accidental starting of motor is possible.

(*iii*) Earth faults are easily sensed and removed.	(*iii*) If first earth fault is not detected then second earth fault isolates two circuits.
(*iv*) Transient over voltages are minimized	(*iv*) Earth fault in ungrounded system are difficult to locate and subjects the insulation system to greater than normal voltage leading to severe over voltages and multiple insulation failures.

17.12. TYPES OF EARTHING

Earthing is basically of two types viz— (*a*) neutral earthing and (*b*) equipment earthing.

(*a*) **Neutral earthing**—In this type of earthing, neutral point of star point of transformer or alternator is connected to the earth. This ensures that neutral point remains at earth potential and all the phase voltages remain balanced.

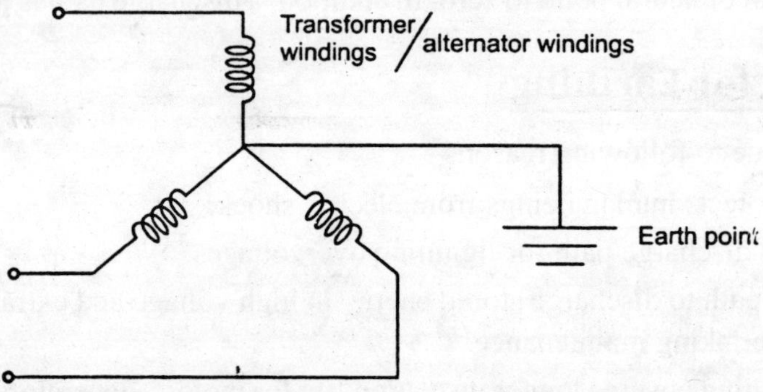

Fig. 17.19. Neutral earthing of transformer/alternator

(*b*) **Equipment earthing**—In this type of earthing, non-current carrying part of an electrical equipment is connected to general mass of the earth. This allows passage of any leakage current to earth by providing a low resistance path thereby protecting human being from electric shock.

Outer metallic body of all generators, transformers, motors, switchgers or any electric equipment are connected to earth at two points (double earthing).

17.12.1. Types of neutral earthing

Following are various systems used to earth the neutral of the power system—

(*i*) solid earthing.

(*ii*) resistance earthing.

(*iii*) reactance earthing.

(*iv*) resonant earthing or arc suppression coil earthing.

(*v*) voltage transformer earthing.

...ning—In this type of earthing, star point of generator or transformer is ...onnected to earth using earth electrodes and plates or pipes or rods of copper. These are inserted into earth to a sufficient depth such that the soil has sufficient moisture. Presence of high moisture provides low soil resistance and allows current to flow to earth. This method is used for system voltages upto 660 V and above 11000 V.

Advantages of solid earthing are following—

(*a*) it can control transient overvoltages.

(*b*) no multiple insulation failure takes place due to overvoltages.

(*c*) it is easy to detect earth fault.

(*d*) it permits use of discrimination in earth fault protection.

(*e*) earth fault on any phase reduces the voltage to zero but voltage of other healthy phases remain normal.

Disadvantage—

(*a*) due to solid earthing, there is heavy flow of current during earth fault which may cause burning of insulation of lamination of alternators.

(*ii*) **Resistance earthing**—With increase in system voltage, earth fault current also rises. This earth fault current may cause severe damage. In order to limit earth fault current, a resistance is introduced in the earth path to limit the current. A resistance made of mild steel or stainless steel is designed to carry rms value of symmetrical neutral current for a given time (10 seconds to maximum 60 seconds). This system of earthing is used in 3.3 kV to 11 kV voltage system.

Advantages of resistance earthing are following—

(*a*) presence of resistance limits earth fault current in alternators which prevents burning of iron core of stator of alternator.

(*b*) it reduces magnitude and duration of overvoltages in electrical machines thereby increasing life of insulation.

(*c*) hazards of arcing grounds are minimized.

Following are the **disadvantages**—

(*a*) this is expensive compared to solidly grounded system.

(*b*) at the time of earth fault, system neutral will be displaced from zero potential.

The value of earthing resistance for line to earth fault is given by following expression.

$$R_N = \frac{V_{ph}}{I} \qquad \text{...(17.1)}$$

where, V_{ph} = phase to neutral voltage of the system in volts.

I = full load current of largest alternator or transformer in amperes.

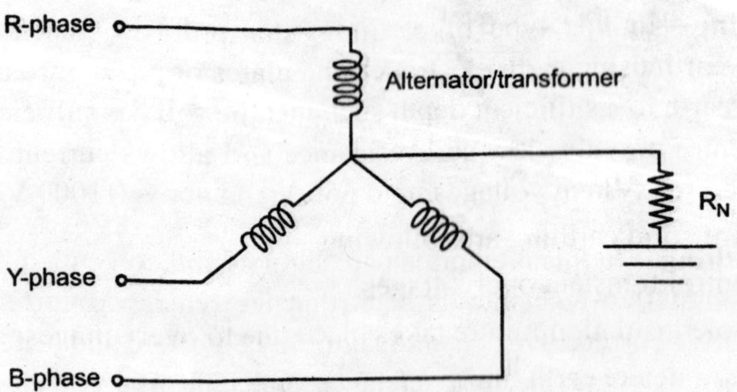

Fig. 17.20. Resistance earthing

(iii) **Reactance earthing**—In this method, a reactor is connected between neutral of equipment and earth. The only condition is that ratio of zero sequence reactance to positive sequence reactance should be greater than 3 i.e. $X_0/X_1 > 3$.

However, to minimize transient overvoltages, system earth fault current should not be less than 25% of three phase fault current.

Advantages of reactance earthing are following—

(*a*) size of reactor is small for same maximum line to earth fault current.

(*b*) reduced interference to neighbouring communication lines.

Only disadvantage is high transient over voltages.

This method of earthing is used where overhead lines are directly connected to low voltage rotating machines and are subjected to lightening exposure. The earth fault current is limited to maximum 100% of the value of a three phase fault current. This makes possible the selective operation of direct acting trip on low voltage circuit breakers.

$$\text{Earth fault current, } I_G = \frac{3V_{ph}}{X_1 + X_2 + X_0 + 3X_n} \quad \text{...(17.2)}$$

where, X_1 = positive sequence reactance of alternator.

X_2 = negative sequence reactance of alternator.

X_0 = zero sequence reactance of alternator.

X_n = reactance of neutral reactor.

V_{ph} = line to neutral voltage.

Now, three phase fault current,

$$I_{3\,ph} = \frac{V_{ph}}{X_1}$$

Assuming line to earth fault current = phase fault current

$$I_{LG} = I_{3\,ph}$$

$$\frac{3V_{ph}}{X_1 + X_2 + X_0 + 3X_n} = \frac{V_{ph}}{X_1}$$

Generally, $X_1 = X_2$

$$\frac{V_{ph}}{X_1} = \frac{3V_{ph}}{2X_1 + X_0 + 3X_n} \quad ...(17.3)$$

or $$2X_1 + X_0 + 3X_n - 3X_1 = 0 \quad ...(17.4)$$

or $$X_n = \frac{X_1 - X_0}{3} \quad ...(17.5)$$

(*iv*) **Resonant earthing**—In this method, an arc suppression coil called Peterson coil is used. The value of inductive reactance is such that the reactance current in coil neutralize network capacitive current. This resultant current being zero and hence unable to maintain the arc. In order to obtain perfect reactance matching, the coil may be provided with tapped connections.

This method of earthing is used in medium voltage overhead transmission lines which are connected to alternators through power transformers. However, on single line to earth fault, voltages on healthy phases can reach 3 times the normal value.

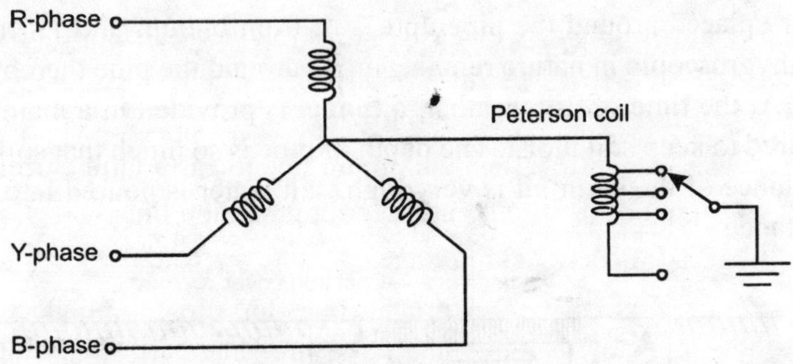

Fig. 17.21. Resonant earthing

(*v*) **Voltage transformer earthing**—This method uses a voltage transformer for earthing purpose. The primary side of this transformer is connected between earth and neutral point of equipment. The secondary side of this transformer contains a low resistance and a relay. Upon initiation of earth fault on primary side, the primary side will induce voltage in the relay thereby operating the protective device.

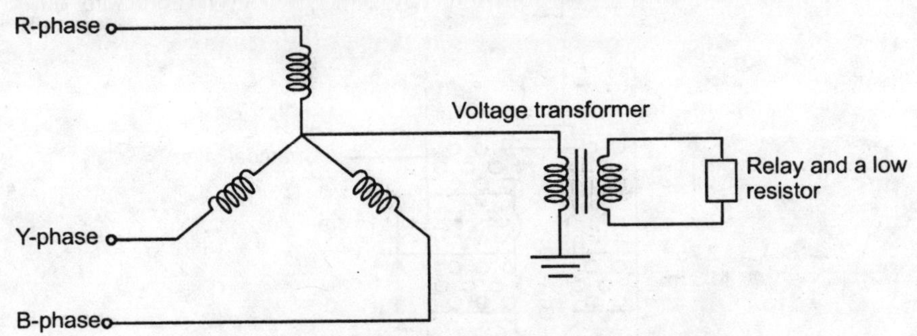

Fig. 17.22. Voltage transformer earthing

Following are the **advantages** of this method—

(*a*) transient overvoltages are reduced due to high reactance offered by the voltage transformer.

(*b*) arcing grounds are eliminated.

Only disadvantage is that travelling waves are reflected into the machine windings and hence, a surge diverter is required.

17.12.2. Equipment earthing

Aim of equipment earthing is to prevent electric shock and fire due to earth leakage current. External metallic body of electrical machines and appliances are connected to earth. All industrial equipments are doubly earthed.

Following are the various methods of equipment earthing—

(*i*) Pipe earthing (*ii*) Plate earthing

(*iii*) Rod earthing (*iv*) Strip earthing

(*i*) **Pipe earthing**—In this method, a galvanized iron pipe of minimum 40 mm diameter and minimum length of 2.75 m is inserted into the earth. Alternate layer of common salt and charcoal are placed around the pipe upto 2 m from bottom and 15 cm around the pipe. Salt being hygroscopic in nature remains moist around the pipe thereby minimizing earth resistance. At the time of dry weather, a funnel is provided in a main hole so that water can be poured to keep soil moist. The depth of pipe is so much that soil is very wet. When earth resistance of the earth pit is very high, salt water is poured into the pipe to reduce earth resistance.

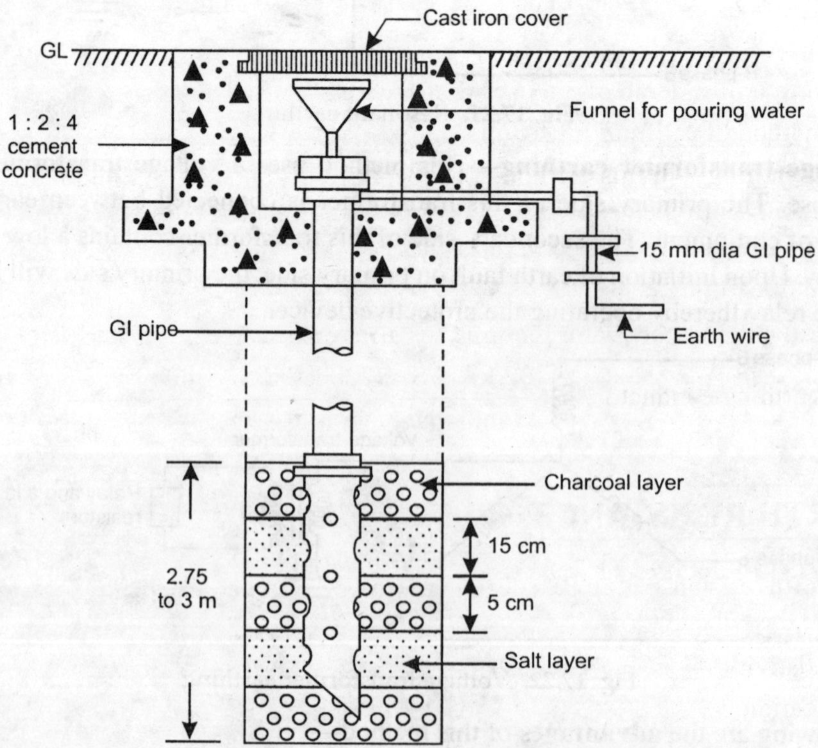

Fig. 17.23. Pipe earthing

(*ii*) **Plate earthing**—In this method of earthing, a galvanised iron (GI) plate measuring (600 × 600 × 6.36) cm or a copper plate measuring (600 × 600 × 3.18) cm is buried upto 3 to 4 m depth in soil. Space around the plate is filled with alternate layers of salt and charcoal. The plate is connected to GI pipe of 12.7 mm diameter for pouring water around the plate. An earth wire is either bolted or welded to the plate and taken out along with GI pipe.

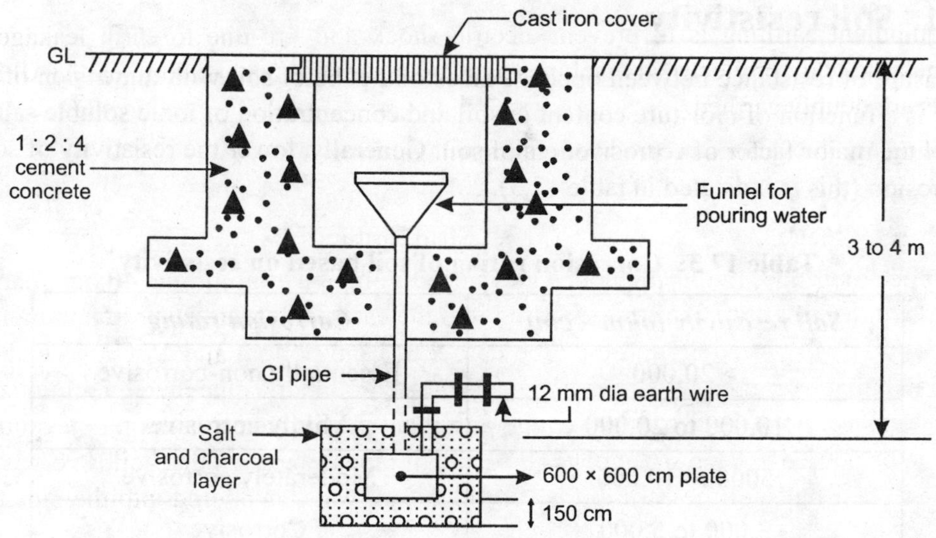

Fig. 17.24. Plate earthing

(*iii*) **Rod earthing**—A copper rod of 12.5 mm diameter or GI rod of 19 mm diameter is driven into earth upto a depth of 5 to 6 m. Earth wire is carried alongwith the rod.

This method of earthing is used in sandy soil.

(*iv*) **Strip earthing**—In this method, a copper strip of minimum 25 mm × 1.6 mm is buried horizontally in trenches of sufficient depth (minimum depth of 8 m or more). A grid of this strip is laid to reduce earth resistance.

This method of earthing is used in rocky soil.

Dimension of earthing conductor required for different voltage levels is given below—

	132 kV S/S	220 kV S/S	400 kV S/S
(*i*) Main earthing conductor—	25 mm dia MS rod	28 mm dia MS rod	40 mm dia MS rod

17.13. EARTH RESISTANCE

A low value of earth resistance is always desirable. However, its value depends upon several factors. These factors are described below—

(*i*) soil resistivity.

(*ii*) stratification.

(*iii*) size and type of electrodes used.

(*iv*) depth to which electrode is buried in the ground.

(*v*) moisture and chemical contents of soil.

Soil resistivity is a measure of how much the soil resists the flow of electricity. Its value is important as it is used to design earthing system in an electrical substation or for lightning conductors for high voltage direct current (HVDC) transmission system.

17.13.1. Soil resistivity

It is a measure of resistance between opposite sides of a cube of soil with dimension of 1 m. Soil resistivity is a function of moisture content in soil and concentration of ionic soluble salts. Hence, it is one of the major factor of corrosiveness of soil. Generally, lower the resistivity of soil, higher is the corrosion (this is indicated in table 17.3).

Table 17.3: Corrosion rating of soil based on resistivity

Soil resistivity (ohm – cm)	*Corrosion rating*
> 20,000	Essentially non-corrosive
10,000 to 20,000	Mildly corrosive
5000 to 10,000	Moderately corrosive
3,000 to 5,000	Corrosive
1,000 to 3,000	Highly corrosive
< 1,000	Extremely corrosive

Various factors affecting resistivity of soil are following—

(*i*) **Moisture content in soil**—Presence of moisture decreases resistivity of soil. This is shown in Table 17.4.

(*ii*) **Dissolved salts in water**—Higher the dissolved salt, lesser is the resistivity.

Table 17.4: Effect of moisture on soil resistivity

	Typical resistivity	
Moisture % by weight	*Clay mixed with sand (ohm – m)*	*Silica based sand (ohm – m)*
0	10^7	–
2.5	1500	3×10^6
5	430	50,000
10	185	2100
15	105	630
20	63	290
30	42	–

(*iii*) **Temperature of soil**—Increase in temperature of soil, decreases resistivity. When water in the soil freezes, resistivity increases appreciably as the ice has higher resistivity.

(*iv*) **Seasonal variations**—Seasonal variation affect the moisture content in air and temperature of soil.

(*v*) **Type of soil**—Resistivity is dependent upon type of soil. Sandy soils have higher resistivity than clay soils. This is shown in Table 17.5.

Table 17.5: Resistivity of different types of soils

Type of soil	*Typical resistivity (ohm –m)*
Clay	8 to 70
Clay and sand mixture	4 to 300
Shale, slates and sandstone	10 to 100
Peat, loom and mud	5 to 250
Sand	200 to 3000
Horain gravel	40 to 10,000
Ridge gravel	3,000 to 30,000
Solid granite	10,000 to 50,000
Ice	10,000 to 1,00,000

Variation of soil resistivity w.r. to moisture content, temperature of soil is shown in figure 17.25 and 17.26 respectively.

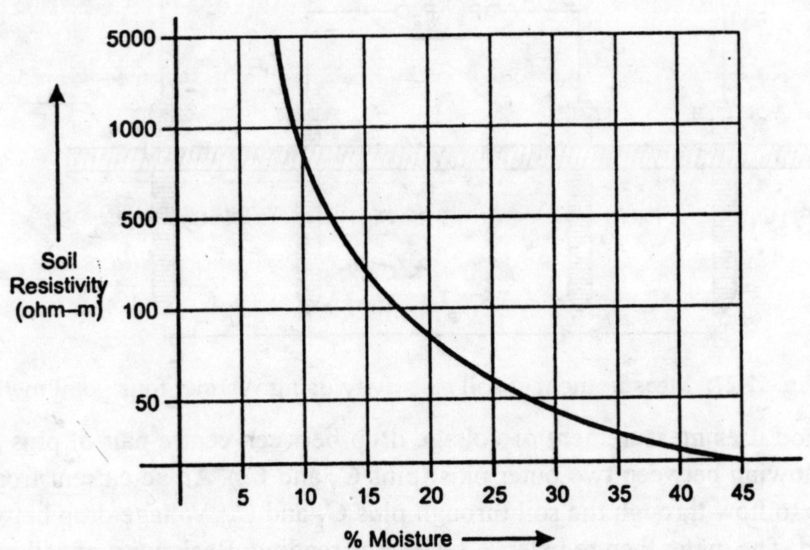

Fig. 17.25. Effect of variation of moisture on soil resistivity

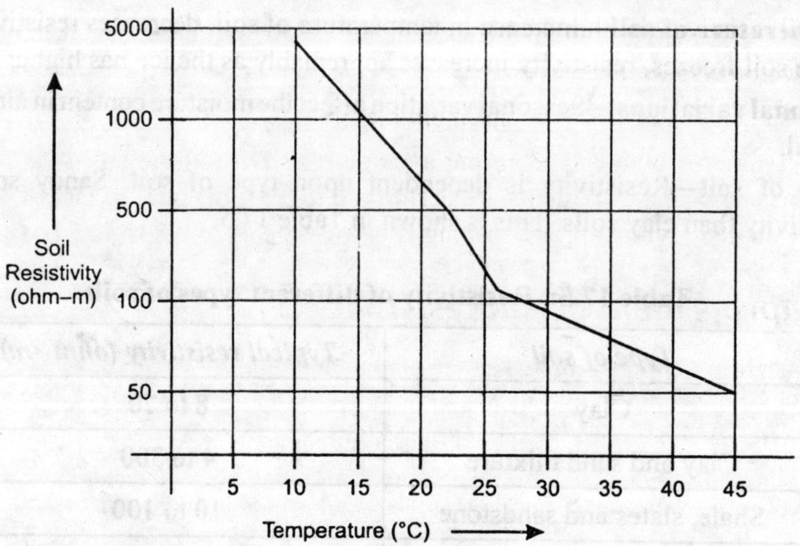

Fig. 17.26. Effect of variation of soil temperature on soil resistivity

17.13.1.1. Measurement of soil resistivity

Soil resistivity is measured by Wenner four pin method and a soil resistance meter. The Wenner method uses four metal electrodes driven into the ground along a straight line, equidistant from each other. This is shown in figure 17.27.

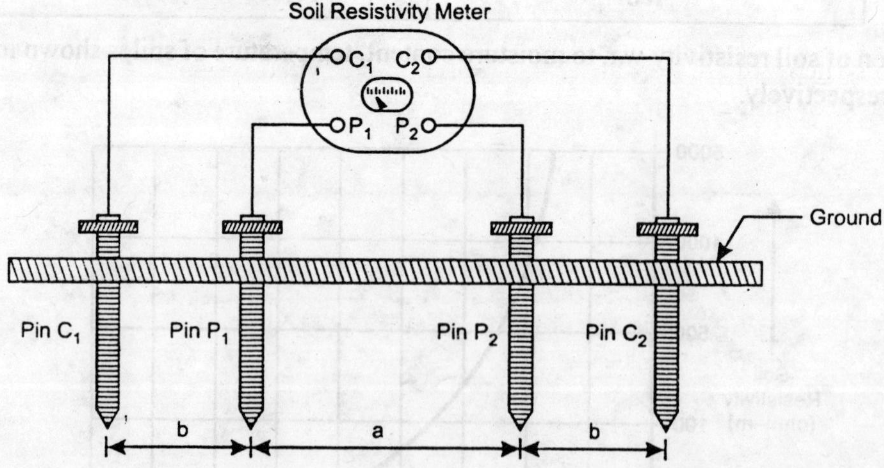

Fig. 17.27. Measurement of soil resistivity using Wenner four point method

This method uses measurement of voltage drop between centre pair of pins (pins P_1 and P_2) with current flowing between two outer pins (pins C_1 and C_2). An ac current from soil resistivity meter is made to flow through the soil through pins C_1 and C_2. Voltage drop between pins P_1 and P_2 is measured. The meter then registers a resistance reading. Resistivity of soil is calculated from meter reading according to the following formula.

Soil resistivity, $\rho = 2\pi AR$

where, ρ is soil resistivity in ohm – cm.

A is the distance between probes in cm.

R is the soil resistance indicated by instrument in ohms.

The resistivity value so obtained represent average resistivity of the soil to a depth equal to the pin spacing. Resistance measurements are performed to a depth equal to that of buried system (pipeline) being evaluated. Typical probe spacing is in increments of 0.8 m (2.5 ft).

17.13.1.2. Improvement of soil resistivity

Most electrical substation require earth resistance of one ohm or less. While for lightning protection, the earth resistance required is 10 ohm or less. Laying of copper grids, tapes and rods alone may not always provide the desired result. Seasonal fluctuations in soil moisture can cause variations in resistance. So, an application of earth enhancing compound may be used. Such compounds consist of chemical solutions of good electrical conductivity which, when mixed with water and poured into the earth pit makes surrounding soil a gelatinous mass thereby lowering earth resistance. Such compounds are 'Earth Gel', GEM' etc. (Erico make). In the absence of such compounds, pouring of salt water into earth pit will produce good result during summer seasons.

17.14. LIGHTNING PROTECTION IN SUBSTATION

In HV and EHV substation, protection against atmospheric lightning is provided through a shield wire or by lightning mast or combination of both.

(*i*) **Shield wire**—This system of protection against lightning is used where number of bays in the switchyard are less, area of substation is small and height of structures is normal. This system suffers from disadvantage that if the wire snaps, the system is unprotected.

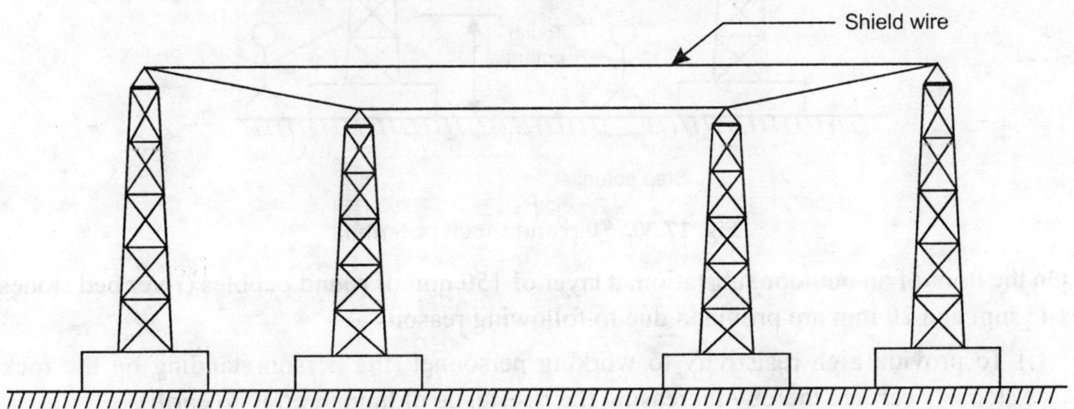

Fig. 17.28. Protection against lightning with shield wire

(*ii*) **Lightning mast**—It is used in large EHV substation where there are large number of bays. It can effect earth lightning strokes. Also, chances of back flashover in nearby equipments and structure is not possible.

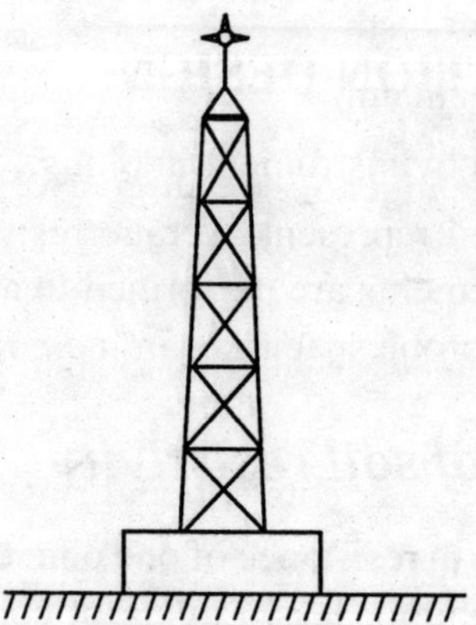

Fig. 17.29. Lightning mast

Apart from lightning protection, a substation is designed to achieve low step potential and touch potential.

Step potential is defined as the potential difference between feet of a person standing on the floor of substation with half meter spacing between two feet (i.e. one step). While touch potential is defined as the potential difference between fingers of raised hand touching the faulted structure and the feet of a person standing on the floor of a substation. The person should not get a shock even if the earth structure is carrying fault current.

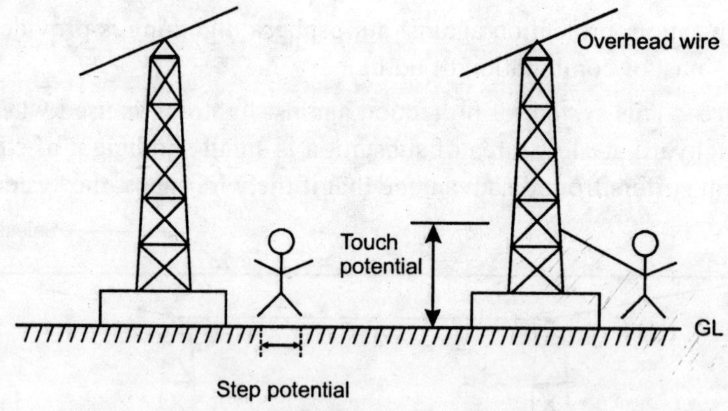

Fig. 17.30. Step and touch potential

On the floor of an outdoor substation, a layer of 150 mm of round pebbles (river bed stones) of sizes 15 mm and 20 mm are provided due to following reasons—

(*i*) To provide high resistivity to working personnel (the person standing on the rocks is loosely earthed thereby increasing the resistance of human body to earth).

(*ii*) To minimize hazards from reptiles (snakes etc.)

(*iii*) To minimize growth of weed.

(*iv*) To maintain lower resistivity of soil by retaining moisture on the ground (prevents direct exposure of sun leading to evaporation of moisture).

(*v*) To prevent water-logging, mud or oil spillage.

17.15. FUTURE SUBSTATION DESIGN

In order to reduce space requirement due to use of higher voltages, future substation design will use high temperature super conductor (HTS) technology. The design will use HTS transformer, HTS cable, HTS fault limiter etc.

HTS system will have cryogenic refrigeration system providing liquid helium to every HTS device in the substation.

Advantages of HTS substation over conventional substation are following—

(*i*) very high transmission and distribution efficiency.

(*ii*) high reliability.

(*iii*) high flexibility.

(*iv*) long life of equipments.

(*v*) very low maintenance need.

(*vi*) high safety.

(*vii*) very compact size (50 to 70% reduction in overall substation size).

Solved Examples

Example 17.1

A 66 kV, 50 Hz transmission network has capacitance to neutral value of 1.3 μF per phase. In order to avoid arcing ground, it is decided to use arc suppression coil. Determine the reactance of arc suppression coil.

Solution:

Given, phase to ground capacitance per phase = 1.3 μF

$$= 1.3 \times 10^{-6} \text{ F}$$

Reactance of arc suppression coil

$$\omega_L = \frac{1}{3\omega_C}$$

$$= \frac{1}{3 \times 2 \times \pi \times 50 \times 1.3 \times 10^{-6}} = 816.59 \text{ ohm}$$ **Ans.**

Example 17.2

A Peterson coil is to be used in a 220 kV, 3 phase, 50 Hz, 250 km long transmission line. The line to ground capacitance is 0.012 μF/ km/phase. Determine the inductance and kVA rating of Peterson coil.

Solution:

Given, phase to ground capacitance per phase = 0.012×10^{-6} F/km/phase

Capacitance of 250 km line = $250 \times 0.012 \times 10^{-6}$ F/phase

Inductance of Peterson coil

$$\omega_L = \frac{1}{3\omega_C}$$

$$L = \frac{1}{3\,\omega^2 C} = \frac{1}{3\times(2\pi\times 50)^2\times 250\times 0.012\times 10^{-6}}$$

$$L = 1.1269 \text{ H}$$ **Ans.**

Current passing through coil,

$$I_2 = \frac{V_{ph}}{\omega L} = \frac{220\times 10^3}{2\pi\times 50\times 1.1269}$$

(∵ transmission lines are 3 phase, 3 wire delta connected)

$$I_L = 621.74 \text{ A}$$

$$\text{kVA rating of coil} = \frac{V_{ph}\times I_L}{1000} = \frac{220\times 10^3\times 621.74}{1000}$$

$$= 136782.8 \text{ kVA}$$ **Ans.**

Example 17.3

It is required to neutralize the capacitive current of an overhead transmission lines having line to earth capacitance of such line as 0.015 μF. Calculate the value of reactance required at 50 Hz frequency.

Solution:

Inductive reactance required to neutralize capacitive current,

$$X_L = \frac{1}{X_C} = \frac{1}{\omega C}$$

$$\omega_L = \frac{1}{3\omega C} \Rightarrow L = \frac{1}{3\omega^2 C}$$

$$L = \frac{1}{3\times(2\pi\times 50)^2\times 0.015\times 10^{-6}} \Rightarrow \frac{10^6}{3\times(1000\pi)^2\times 0.015}$$

$$L = 225.39 \text{ H}$$ **Ans.**

Example 17.4

Determine the reactance of an earth fault neutralizer to neutralize the capacitance of a 50 Hz overhead line having phase to ground capacitance of 1.22 μF. The reactance should reutralize the capacitance of—

(*i*) 100% of transmission line (*ii*) 80% of transmission line.

Solution:

(*i*) Capacitance of 100% of transmission line = 1.22×10^{-6} F

$$\therefore \quad \omega_L = \frac{1}{3\omega C} \Rightarrow L = \frac{1}{3\omega^2 C} = \frac{1}{3\times(2\pi\times 50)^2\times 1.22\times 10^{-6}}$$

$$L = 2.7711 \text{ H}$$ **Ans.**

(*ii*) Capacitance of 80% of transmission line = $0.80\times 1.22\times 10^{-6}$ F

$$L = \frac{1}{3\omega^2 C} = \frac{1}{3\times(2\pi\times 50)^2\times 0.80\times 1.22\times 10^{-6}}$$

$$L = 3.4639 \text{ H}$$ **Ans.**

CHAPTER SUMMARY

A substation is an assembly of apparatus connected in particular sequence in order to control, regulate, protect characteristics of power being handled. It may be of different types depending upon specific application. It is an intermediate link between generating stations and loads. It could be either air insulated substation or gas insulated substation. Major equipment in a substation include transformer, circuit breaker, busbars, protective relays, reactors, capacitors etc. Substation auxiliaries consist of station batteries, communication systems, station auxiliary transformer, fire protection and station lighting.

Air insulated substations are used upto voltage level of upto 800 kV, 8000A. These substations are preferred where ample space is available. When there is space constraint, gas insulated substation is preferred. In a substation, different arrangements of busbars are used. All these arrangements of busbars have relative merits and demerits.

One of the vital point is substation earthing. It is of two types–neutral earthing and equipment earthing. Earthing in general refers to connection to general mass of the earth. In neutral earthing, neutral point of star connected transformer or generator is connected to earth. While in equipment earthing, non current carrying part of electrical apparatus is connected to earth for safety reasons. A grounded or earthed system is preferred over unearthed system.

Different methods of equipment earthing are pipe earthing, plate earthing, strip earthing and rod earthing. Each type of earthing is preferred for a specific type of soil.

In short, a substation is a one of the vital component of power supply system.

REVIEW QUESTIONS

Q. 1. Discuss classification of substation.

Q. 2. List and explain functions of various equipments in substation.

Q. 3. Describe functions of substation.

Q. 4. What are merits and demerits of outdoor substation over indoor substation.

Q. 5. What are the factors which govern the selection of site for a substation.

Q. 6. Describe in detail with a neat sketch, components of air insulated substation (AIS).

Q. 7. Write a brief note on gas insulated substation (GIS).

Q. 8. What are the merits and demerits of using SF_6 gas?

Q. 9. Draw a sketch of substation layout.

Q. 10. Draw a single line diagram of 11 kV substation.

Q. 11. What are various types of busbar arrangements in a substation.

Q. 12. Compare relative merits and demerits of single busbar system and double busbar system.

Q. 13. Compare ring bus scheme and main and transfer busbar scheme.

Q. 14. What do you mean by 'earthing'? Discuss the need for earthing.

Q. 15. Compare earthed and unearthed systems.

Q. 16. Discuss various types of earthing systems.

Q. 17. Explain with an example, difference between neutral earthing and equipment earthing.

Q. 18. Write a brief note on (*a*) resistance earthing (*b*) reactance earthing.

Q. 19. What are relative merits and demerits of resistance earthing over solid earthing?

Q. 20. What is the principle of resonant earthing?

Q. 21. Write a short note on (*a*) pipe earthing (*b*) plate earthing.

Q. 22. Write a brief note on (*a*) rod earthing (*b*) strip earthing.

Q. 23. Describe design features of a futuristic substation.

Q. 24. "Earthing is most important feature of any electrical system." Justify.

Numerical Questions

Q. 1. A transmission network of 66 kV, 50 Hz has line to neutral capacitance of 1.5μF per phase. Determine the reactance of an arc suppression coil to avoid arcing grounds.

[Ans: 707.7 ohm**]**

Q. 2. Determine the value of reactance required at 50 Hz to neutralize the capacitive current of an overhead transmission system having line to earth capacitance of 0.020 μF per phase.

[Ans: 169 H**]**

Q. 3. Calculate the reactance of an earth fault neutralizer to neutralize capacitance of 50Hz overhead transmission line having phase to ground capacitance of 1.25 μF. The reactance should neutralize the capacitance of (*i*) 90% of transmission line (*ii*) 70% of transmission line.

[Ans: (*i*) 3H (*ii*) 3.22 H**]**

SHORT ANSWER TYPES QUESTIONS

Q. 1. List three advantages of outdoor substation.

Q. 2. What is the voltage and frequency of traction substation in India?

Q. 3. Mention four advantages of gas insulated substation over air insulated substation.

Q. 4. What is the purpose of using CT and PT in substation?

Q. 5. Why lightning arrester is installed at the begining of a substation?

Q. 6. List three major functions of substation.

Q. 7. Why communication facilities are needed from one substation to another?

Q. 8. List five major components of a PLCC system.

Multiple Choice Questions

Q. 1. A substation performs function of

(*a*) change of voltage (*b*) switching

(*c*) reactive power compensation (*d*) all of these

Q. 2. An indoor substation (AIS) is used for voltage level of

(*a*) Above 132 kV (*b*) Above 220 kV

(*c*) Above 765 kV (*d*) Above 66 kV.

Q. 3. Gas insulated substation uses

(*a*) carbon dioxide (*b*) sulphur dioxide

(*c*) nitrogen dioxide (*d*) sulphur hexa fluoride

Q. 4. 1000 kV and above voltage is known as

(*a*) HV (*b*) EHV

(*c*) VHV (*d*) UHV

Q. 5. Dry type transformers are used for a maximum voltage level of

(*a*) 11 kV (*b*) 33 kV

(*c*) 66 kV (*d*) 132 kV

Q. 6. Isolator is

(*a*) full load break switch (*b*) partial load break switch

(*c*) no load break switch (*d*) none of these

Answer to MCQ

1. (*d*) **2.** (*d*) **3.** (*d*) **4.** (*d*) **5.** (*c*)

6. (*c*)

ANNEXURE–A

Table A.1 Installed Capacity of Conventional Power Stations in India

(As on 31.12.2015) (Source: Central Electricity Authority, GOI)

Region	***Ownership***	***Breakup***							***Grand Total***
		Thermal				***Nuclear***	***Hydro***	***RES***	
Northern Region		Coal	Gas	Diesel	Total				
	State	16538.00	2879.20	0.00	19417.20	0.00	7502.55	662.06	27581.81
	Private	13725.00	108.00	0.00	13833.00	0.00	2478.00	7187.08	23498.08
	Central	12000.50	2344.06	0.00	14344.56	1620.00	8266.22	0.00	24230.78
	Subtotal	42263.50	5331.26	0.00	47594.76	1620.00	18246.77	7849.14	75310.67
Western Region									
	State	21630.00	2993.82	0.00	24623.82	0.00	5480.50	311.19	30415.51
	Private	34271.00	4288.00	0.00	38559.00	0.00	447.00	13061.98	52067.98
	Central	12238.01	3533.59	0.00	15771.60	1840.00	1520.00	0.00	19131.60
	Subtotal	68139.01	10815.41	0.00	78954.42	1840.00	7447.50	13373.17	101615.09
Southern Region									
	State	14782.50	556.58	362.52	15701.60	0.00	11478.03	491.37	27671.00

	Private	6550.00	5557.50	554.96	12662.46	0.00	0.00	14968.59	27631.05
	Central	11890.00	359.58	0.00	12249.58	2320.00	0.00	0.00	14569.58
	Subtotal	33222.50	6473.66	917.48	40613.64	2320.00	11478.03	15459.96	69871.63
Eastern Region									
	State	7540.00	100.00	0.00	7640.00	0.00	3168.92	225.11	11034.03
	Private	8451.38	0.00	0.00	8541.38	0.00	195.00	234.43	8970.01
	Central	13001.49	90.00	0.00	13094.17	0.00	845.20	0.00	13936.69
	Subtotal	29082.87	190.00	0.00	29272.87	0.00	4209.12	459.54	33941.53
North Eastern Region									
	State	60.00	445.70	36.00	541.70	0.00	382.00	253.25	1176.95
	Private	0.00	24.50	0.00	24.50	0.00	0.00	9.37	33.87
	Central	250.00	1192.50	0.00	1442.50	0.00	860.00	0.00	2302.50
	Subtotal	310.00	1662.70	36.00	2008.70	0.00	1242.00	262.62	3513.32
All India	State	60550.50	6975.30	438.57	67964.37	0.00	28012.00	1948.23	97924.60
	Private	63.087.38	9978.00	554.96	73620.34	0.00	3120.00	35467.30	112207.64
	Central	49380.00	7519.73	0.00	56899.73	5780.00	11491.42	0.00	74171.15
	Subtotal	173017.88	24473.03	993.53	198484.44	5780.00	42623.42	37415.53	284303.30

Table A.2 Installed Capacity of Renewable Power Generation in India

(As on 31.12.2015) (Source: Central Electricity Authority, GOI)

Small Hydro (MW)	***Wind Power (MW)***	***Bio-Power (MW)***		***Solar Power (MW)***	***Total Capacity (MW)***
		Biomass Power/cogen	***Waste to energy***		
4146.82	24376.55	4418.55	127.08	4346.82	37415.53

Table A.3 Largest Operating Conventional Power Plants in the World (2015).

Sr. No.	*Type of Plant*	*Installed Capacity (MW)*	*Location*
1.	Thermal power plant	5,500	Taichung, Taiwan
2.	Hydro power plant	22,500	Three Gorges dam, China
3.	Nuclear power plant	7,965	Kashiwaza ki–kariwa, Japan
4.	Natural gas power plant	5,597	Surgut–2, Russia
5.	Fuel oil based power plant	5,600	Shoaiba, Saudi Arabia

Table A.4 Largest Operating Renewable Power Plants in the World (2015)

Sr. No.	*Type of Plant*	*Installed Capacity (MW)*	*Location*
1.	Solar-thermal power plant	377	Ivanpah, USA
2.	Solar–PV power plant	600	Charanka solar park, India
3.	Wind farm (on-shore)	5,160	Gansu, China
4.	Wind farm (off-shore)	630	London Array, UK
5.	Bio mass power plant	750	Tilbury-B, UK
6.	Geothermal power plant	1517	Geysers geothermal complex, California, USA
7.	Tidal power plant	254	Sihwa Lake, South Korea
8.	Fuel cell power plant	59	Gyeonggi greeen energy facility, Hwasung city, South Korea

Table A.5 Pumped Storage Hydro Power Plants in India (2015)

Sr. No.	*Location*	*State*	*Installed Capacity (MW)*	*Year of Commissioning*
1.	Nagarjunsagar	Andhra Pradesh	7 × 100	1980–85
2.	Srisailam	Andhra Pradesh	6 × 200	2001–03
3.	Ghatghar	Maharashtra	2 × 125	2008
4.	Bhira	Maharashtra	1 × 150	1995
5.	Paithan	Maharashtra	1 × 12	1984

6.	Sardar Sarovar	Gujarat	6 × 200	2006
7.	Kadana	Gujarat	4 × 60	1990–96, 1998
8.	Kadamparai	Tamil Nadu	1 × 400	1987–89
9.	Ujjain	Madhya Pradesh	1 × 12	1990
10.	Panchet (DVC)	Jharkhand	1 × 40	1990–91
11.	Purulia	West Bengal	4 × 225	2007–08
		Total	4804	

Table A.6 All India Annual Per Capita Electricity Consumption

Sr. No.	*Year*	*Per Capita Consumption (kWh)*
1.	2005–06	631.4
2.	2006–07	671.9
3.	2007–08	717.1
4.	2008–09	733.5
5.	2009–10	778.6
6.	2010–11	818.8
7.	2011–12	883.63
8.	2012–13	914.41
9.	2013–14	957
10.	2014–15	1010

Table A.7 Operational HVDC Power Projects in India (2015)

Sr. No.	*Name of Project*	*Connecting Region*	*Power rating (MW)*	*DC Voltage (kV)*	*AC Voltage (kV)*	*Length of line (km)*	*Commissioned on*
1.	Rihand–Dadri	ER--WR	1500	500	400	816	Dec. 1991
2.	Talcher–Kolar	ER–SR	2000	500	400	1369	June 2003
3.	Ballia–Bhiwadi	ER–NR	2500	500	400	780	March 2011
4.	Chandrapur–Padge	CR–WR	1500	500	400	752	1999

5.	Mundra-Mohindergarh	WR–NR	1500	500	400	986	2012
6.	Bishwanath–Agra	NER–NR	6000	80	400	1728	2015
7.	Vindhyachal (back to back)	WR–NR	2 × 250	70	400	—	April 1989
8.	Chandrapur (back to back)	WR–SR	2 × 500	205	400	—	Dec. 1997
9.	Sasaram (back to back)	ER–SR	500	205	400	—	Sept. 2002
10.	Gazuwaka (back to back)	ER–SR	2 × 500	Block–I = 205	400	—	Mar. 2005
				Block–II = 177	400		

Note: NR : Northern Region, WR: Western Region, SR : Southern Region, NER: North Eastern Region, ER: Eastern Region, CR: Central Region.

Table A.8 Cross Border Transmission Links (India and its Neighbours) 2015

Sr. No.	*Voltage (kV)*	*Transmission Link*	*Country*
1.	220, D/C	Birpara–Chukha–pling	India–Bhutan
2.	220, S/C	Birpara–Chukha–Malbase	India–Bhutan
3.	132, S/C	Salakati–Gelephu–Kurichhu	India–Bhutan
4.	132, S/C	Rangia–Kurichhu	India–Bhutan
5.	400, D/C	New Siliguri–Tala	India–Bhutan
6.	400, D/C	New Siliguri–Tala-Pagli	India–Bhutan
7.	132, S/C	Tanakpur–Mahendranagar	India–Nepal
8.	132, S/C	Ramnagar–Gandak	India–Nepal
9.	132, S/C	Kattaiya–Duhabi	India–Nepal
10.	400, D/C (back to back)	Behrampur–Bheramara	India–Bangladesh

Note: S/C = Single circuit, D/C = Double circuit

Table A.9 Power Intensity at Different Voltage Levels

Voltage (kV)	*132 AC*	*220 AC*	*400 AC*	*765 AC*	*1200 AC*	*± 500 DC*	*± 800 DC*
ROW (m)	27	35	46	64	90	52	70
Power capacity (MW)	Upto 70–80	Upto 160–170	Upto 600–700	Upto 2500–3000	Upto 6000–8000	Upto 2000–2500	Upto 6000–6400
Power intensity (MW/m)	3	5	15	45	90	48	90

Note: Row = Right of way

Table A.10 Line Parameters of 1200 kV/765 kV/400 kV Transmission System

Sr. No.	*Parameter*	*1200 kV*	*765 kV*	*400 kV*
1.	NominalVoltage (kV)	1150	765	400
2.	Highest Voltage (kV)	1200	800	420
3.	Resistance (pu/km)	4.338×10^{-7}	1.95×10^{-6}	1.862×10^{-5}
4.	Reactance (pu/km)	1.772×10^{-5}	4.475×10^{-5}	2.075×10^{-4}
5.	Susceptance (pu/km)	6.447×10^{-2}	2.40×10^{-2}	5.55×10^{-3}
6.	Surge Impedance Loading (MW)	6030	2315	515

Note: pu = per unit, Base MVA = 100, Base Voltage = 1200 kV, 765 kV, 400 kV

Some Facts

- First remotely controlled substation in India : 400 kV Bhiwadi-Ballabhgarh substation (remotely controlled from Ballabhgarh substation, Haryana)
- Longest transmission line in the world : 600 kV, HVDC, 2385 km, Rio Madeira transmission line, Brazil.

ANNEXURE–B

SAMPLE QUESTION PAPER—1

RENEWABLE ENERGY RESOURCES

Time : 3 Hours Maximum Marks : 100

NOTE: Question no. 1 is compulsory. Attempt all questions.

Q 1. (*a*) List five different types of renewable energy resources. (5 × 4 = 20)

(*b*) Mention limitations of wind power generation.

(*c*) Mention different schemes of power generation from geothermal energy.

(*d*) Explain the need for energy storage systems.

(*e*) Differentiate between a fuel cell and a battery.

Q 2. (*a*) Explain with a neat sketch the working of hot dry rock based geothermal power plant. (2 × 10 = 20)

(*b*) Derive the expression for voltage magnitude and power output of a MHD generator.

Q 3. (*a*) Compare advantages and limitations of phosphoric acid fuel cell with solid oxide fuel cell. (2 × 10 = 20)

(*b*) Analyse the performance of a thermionic converter.

Q 4. (*a*) What are the various factors which affect the performance of a flat plate collector? Compare flat plate collector with concentrating collector. (2 × 10 = 20)

(*b*) Explain the terms with respect to flat plate collector—

(*i*) Fin efficiency factor.

(*ii*) Collector efficiency factor.

(*iii*) Collector heat removal factor.

Q 5. (*a*) A bio gas digester consumes dung of 12 cows. Each cow consumes 2.5 kg of dry mass per day. If the retention time in digester is 30 days, calculate—

(*i*) volume of bio gas digester (*ii*) power output of digester.

Assume burner efficiency of 70%. (5 × 4 = 20)

(*b*) Compare fixed dome and float dome type bio digesters.

Sample Question Paper–2

RENEWABLE ENERGY RESOURCES

Time : 3 Hours | Maximum Marks : 100

NOTE: Question no. 1 is compulsory. Attempt all questions.

Q 1. Explain the following— (3 × 5 = 15)

(*a*) Write relative merit and demerits of flat plate and concentrating solar collectors.

(*b*) Differentiate between thermo chemical and bio chemical conversion of biomass.

(*c*) Discuss the limitations of wind energy.

(*d*) State and explain Peltier effect.

(*e*) What are various sources of bio energy?

(*f*) What is the difference between diurnal and long term storage?

(*g*) Explain the merits of thermionic converter.

(*h*) Mention limitations of thermo-electric energy conversion.

Q 2. (*a*) Explain the conversion process of biomass. (6)

(*b*) Derive the expression for power and efficiency of thermionic generator. (6.5)

Q 3. (*a*) Prove that in case of horizontal axis wind turbine, maximum power can be obtained when: $P_{max} = \frac{8}{27} \rho A v^3$ (6.5)

(*b*) Explain ocean thermal energy conversion process. (6)

Q 4. (*a*) Describe MHD open cycle system. What are the main advantages of MHD power generation? (6.5)

(*b*) Describe the working of a H_2–O_2 fuel cell. (6)

Or

Q 5. (*a*) A wind turbine is operating at a velocity of 10 m/s with a turbine blade diameter of 120 cm and 40 rpm speed at maximum efficiency. Calculate—

(*i*) power generated

(*ii*) maximum obtainable power density.

Assume $\eta = 40\%$. (6.5)

(*b*) Draw and explain the block diagram of solar photovoltaic system.

Q 6. (*a*) A photovoltaic system has following data—

Effective illumination area = 0.136 m^2, V_{mp} = 15.6 V, I_{mp} = 1.4 A.

(for standard test condition of 1000 W/m^2, 25°C, air mass = 1.5). Determine the efficiency of solar panel. (6.5)

(*b*) Discuss the advantages and limitations of geothermal energy. (6)

Or

Q 7. (*a*) An MHD generator has following data:

(*i*) Plate area = 0.20 m^2

(*ii*) distance between plates = 0.4 m

(*iii*) Flux density = 2 wb/m^2

(*iv*) average gas velocity = 1000 m/s

(*v*) conductivity of gas = 10 mho/m.

Determine open circuit voltage and maximum power output.

(*b*) Explain the principle and working of a typical solar pond with a neat sketch. (6)

Q 8. (*a*) Draw the diagram of equivalent circuit of photovoltaic solar cell. Derive the expression $I_O = I_{SC} \exp(-V_{OC}/a)$ for a photo cell. (6.5)

(*b*) What do you know about thermo-chemical conversion of biomass? (6)

Or

Q 9. (*a*) Explain with a diagram gassifier based biomass power plant. (6.5)

(*b*) Explain working principle of tidal power plant. What are the limitations? (6)

Sample Question Paper–3

POWER STATION PRACTICE

Time : 3 Hours Maximum Marks : 100

NOTE: Attempt all five questions.

Q 1. Comment with reasons, on following— (5 × 4 = 20)

(*a*) In order to have lower cost of electrical energy generation, the load factor and diversity factor should be low.

(*b*) For low head and high discharge, Kaplan turbine is used in hydro electric stations.

(*c*) The moderator used in fast breeder reactor is heavy water.

(*d*) The pH value of water used in boiler is 7.

(*e*) Circulating fluidised bed combustion boiler can burn coal with high ash content.

Q 2. (*a*) What is tariff? Compare various tariff structure used in practice. (2 × 10 = 20)

(*b*) Explain principle of operation and construction of

(*i*) economizer (*ii*) electrostatic precipitator

Or

Q 3. (*a*) Draw and explain layout of a thermal power plant. Also, explain working of

(*i*) Demineralised water plant (*ii*) Coal and ash handling system

(*b*) Explain with a neat sketch construction, principle and operation of gas turbine power plant. Discuss auxiliaries of gas turbine plant. (2 × 10 = 20)

Q 4. (*a*) Explain with diagrams how nuclear reactor is controlled for generation of electrical power?

(*b*) Draw and explain single line diagram of a 33 kV air insulated substation.

Or

Q 5. (*a*) Explain the various parts of a Diesel power plant.

(*b*) Draw a neat sketch of a hydrostation and explain function of—

(*i*) Forebay (*ii*) Surge tank.

(*iii*) Draft tube. (2 × 10 = 20)

Q 6. (*a*) What is a combined cycle power plant? Compare combined cycle power plant with open cycle gas turbine power plant.

(*b*) Why mini and micro hydro power plants are preferred over large hydro power plants?

Or

Q 7. (*a*) Compare air insulated and gas insulated substation.

(*b*) The fault level of a substation has increased substantially over a period of time. How do you propose to protect the substation against faults?

Q 8. (*a*) Describe in detail various busbar arrangements used in a substation. Compare merits and demerits.

(*b*) Discuss economic load dispatch.

Or

Q 9. (*a*) Derive expression for economic generator scheduling neglecting losses and generator limits.

(*b*) Derive expression for most economic power factor. Explain the assumptions.

Sample Question Paper–4

POWER STATION PRACTICE

Time : 3 Hours | Maximum Marks : 100

NOTE: Attempt all five questions.

Q 1. Comment with reasons, on following— (5 × 4 = 20)

(*a*) It is always preferable to use generators of same rating and make in a power plant.

(*b*) The total cost of power generation should also include cost of impact on environment.

(*c*) Pumped storage plant can be used with thermal power plant for peak load saving.

(*d*) Risk of nuclear hazards and radiation leakage far outweighs the need for power generation through nuclear fission.

(*e*) There is a need to find replacement of SF_6 gas due to ozone depletion potential.

Q 2. (*a*) Explain the purpose of—

(*i*) Spillways. (*ii*) Reservoir.

(*iii*) Trash screen. (*iv*) Desilting chamber.

(*b*) Why pulverised fuel firing is preferred over stoker firing?

Or

(*a*) Why superheated steam is used in steam turbine? What are super critical boilers?

(*b*) What are the functions of moderator and control rods in a nuclear power plant?

Q 3. (*a*) Why thermal neutrons are needed to sustain chain reaction? (2 × 10 = 20)

(*b*) Explain with neat sketch construction and working of PWHR.

Or

(*a*) Explain the term 'cavitation' as applicable to hydro power plant.

(*b*) Explain the operation of a combined cycle power plant.

Q 4. (*a*) Explain the term 'unit committment'. How does it affect the economic operation of power plant?

(*b*) Suggest the various applications of bottom ash in a thermal power plant.

Or

(*a*) What are the guiding factor which determine the framing of tariff structure?

(*b*) Explain the working of electrostatic precipitator (ESP).

Q 5. (*a*) Why thermal power plant are built with tall chimneys? How draft affect heat transfer in a boiler?

(*b*) Discuss factors affecting selection of site for a nuclear power plant.

Or

(*a*) Discuss radiation shielding in a nuclear power plant.

(*b*) Discuss nuclear waste disposal.

Sample Question Paper–5

ELECTRICAL POWER GENERATION

Time : 3 Hours Maximum Marks : 100

NOTE: Attempt five questions. All questions carry equal marks.

Q 1. (*a*) Explain the construction and working of water tube boiler.

(*b*) What are the factors that determine the height of chimney of a Diesel generator set?

Q 2. (*a*) What are the factors which govern the selection of site for a thermal power plant?

(*b*) Explain the working of a solar thermal system of power generation.

Q 3. (*a*) Discuss the advantages, limitations and future prospects of fuel cells.

(*b*) Explain the working of a run-off the river hydro-electric power plant with a diagram.

Q 4. (*a*) An ocean wave plant converts energy from 100 m area of ocean surface with a wave amtitude of 2m and a wave period of 5 sec. The efficiency of energy conversion is 30%. Determine the power rating. Assume density of water as 1025 kg/m^3.

(*b*) Discuss production of ethanol from biomass. What are various other applications?

Q 5. (*a*) Write brief note on any three—

(*i*) Energy from municipal waste.

(*ii*) Role of renewable energy in climate change mitigation.

(*iii*) Different types of biomass gassifiers.

(*iv*) Energy storage systems.

(*b*) A tidal power generation plant has tidal range of 10.8 m. The total area in estuary is 10 sq. km which can sustain power generation for 3 hours in each cycle. Assume efficiency of generations system to be 75% and available head at 10 m. Determine the total energy generated in a year. Assume density of sea water as 1025 kg/m^3.

Q 6. (*a*) Discuss different types of concentrating type collectors.

(*b*) What are the different methods of solar energy storage? Describe in detail thermal energy storage system.

Q 7. (*a*) Explain the purpose of draft tube in a hydro-electric power plant.

(*b*) Discuss applications of waste heat.

Q 8. (*a*) Discuss construction and working of PWR. Compare BWR and PWR as applicable to nuclear power plant.

(*b*) Explain why radioactive waste disposal is a big problem?

Sample Question Paper–6

Electrical Power Generation

Time : 3 Hours

Maximum Marks : 100

NOTE: Question no. 1 is compulsory. Attempt five questions in all.

Q 1. Attempt any ten questions— (10 × 2 = 20)

(*a*) What are three basic geothermal sources?

(*b*) List types of turbines used for hydro power generation.

(*c*) Describe the function of condenser in a thermal power plant.

(*d*) Why induction generator is used for wind power generation?

(*e*) What are the advantages of slow speed diesel engines?

(*f*) How the thermal efficiency of Brayton cycle can be improved?

(*g*) What are advantages of off-shore wind farms?

(*h*) What is the role of maximum power point tracker in solar PV generation?

(*i*) Describe the function of surge tank in a hydro power plant.

(*j*) What are the issues which restrict wide spread use of biomass power plants?

(*k*) Discuss Betz limit.

(*l*) Discuss yaw control of wind electric conversion system.

Q 2. (*a*) Draw single line diagram of a thermal power plant and explain water and flue gas circuit.

(*b*) What are the factors which govern the selection of site for a gas turbine power plant?

Q 3. (*a*) Explain the working of wind electric conversion system. What are the protections provided for wind turbine?

(*b*) Discuss pyrolysis based generation of power from biomass

Q 4. (*a*) Explain with a neat sketch the working of binary geothermal power plant.

(*b*) What are the various sources of pollution from geothermal power generation?

Q 5. (*a*) Why hybrid renewable energy generation system are preferred over single standalone renewable source?

(*b*) Discuss various ocean based power generation technologies in brief.

Q 6. (*a*) Discuss production of bio-diesel.

(*b*) Explain the advantages and disadvantages of horizontal and vertical axis wind turbines. What are the techniques employed to overcome intermittent power generation?

Q 7. (*a*) Describe thermo electric materials and various factors which govern selection.

(*b*) Discuss the reasons for low penetration of nuclear power in India.

Q 8. (*a*) With a block diagram explain working of closed cycle MHD generator.

(*b*) Explain various clean coal technologies available for power generation.

Q 9. (*a*) Discuss in detail various applications of solar energy.

(*b*) Discuss working of phosphoric acid fuel cell (PAFC).

Chapter

BIBLIOGRAPHY

1. Abbasi, S.A., Abbasi Naseema (2001), Renewable Energy Sources and their Environmental Impact, PHI.
2. Anna, Mani (2002), Wind Energy Resources Survey in India-III, Allied Publishers.
3. Annual report (2005), Ministry of Non-conventional Energy Source, GOI.
4. Bandopadhayay, S., Solar Energy, Universal Publisher.
5. Boyle, Godfrey (Edit), (1996), Renewable Energy Power for Sustainable Future, Oxford University Press.
6. BEE (2005), General Aspects of Energy Management and Energy Audit, a guide book for national certification examination for energy auditor, New Delhi GOI.
7. Bansal, N., Mathur, J. (2002), Wind energy utilization, Ananya Publishers, New Delhi.
8. Barbier, Enrico, Geothermal Energy Technology and Current Status: An Overview, Enewable and Sustainable Energy Review, vol. 6, pp. 3–65.
9. Black and Veatch, (1998), Power Plant Engineering, Chapman and Hall, N.Y., Indian edition, CBS Publishers and Distributers, New Delhi.
10. Chakraborty, S. et al (1999), Viability of National HVDC Transmission in India, cigre symposium, Kuala Lumpur, Malaysia.
11. Culp, A.W. (2000), Principle of Energy Conversion, Tata Mcgraw Hill Publisher, New Delhi.
12. Deb, Tanmoy (2012), Biomass based distributed power generation—current status and future challenges, conference proceedings, Northern India Engineering College, 13 Oct. 2012, pp. 20–26.
13. Deb, Tanmoy et al (2012), Renewable Energy issues, Technological Aspects and Policies, International Journal of Electronic and Electrical Engineering, vol. 5, no. 6, pp. 525–528.
14. Deb, Tanmoy et al (2012), Hybrid Renewable Energy Systems, International Journal of Electronic and Electrical Engineering, vol. 5, no. 6, pp. 529–532.

15. Deb, Tanmoy et al (2012), Economic and Technical Viability of Green Energy Technology, International Journal of Environmental Engineering and Management, vol. 3, no. 3, pp. 141–148.
16. Deb, Tanmoy (2008), Strategies for Optimizing Energy Efficiency in Industries, Conference Proceedings, APJ College of Engineering, Gurgaon 27th Sept., 2008.
17. Deb, Tanmoy (2006), Micro and Mini Hydel Based Distributed Power Generation, Conference Proceedings, Indian Institute of Plant Engineers, 16–18 March, 2006, Chandigarh.
18. Deb, Tanmoy (2003), Plant Energy Management, Conference Proceedings, ISHRAE, New Delhi, 10–12 Sept, 2003, pp. 141–148.
19. Deb, Tanmoy (2002), A Case Study of Small Frame Gas Turbine Commissioning, Operation and Debottlenecking, Journal of Plant Engineering, Oct–Dec, 2002, pp. 24–25.
20. Deb, Tanmoy (2002), A Case Study of Abnormal Vibration of 13.5 MW Alternator, Journal of Plant Engineering, Jan–Mar, 2002, pp. 15–16.
21. Dubey, S.K., Bhargava, S.K. (2012), Non-conventional Energy Sources, Dhanpat Rai, New Delhi.
22. Duffe, Bechman, Solar Energy Process, John Wiley.
23. Fritz, Jack, J. (1984), Small and Mini Hydro Power Systems, Mcgraw Hill.
24. Garg, R.P., Prakash, Jai, Solar Energy: Fundamental and Applications, Tata Mcgraw Hill.
25. Glassley, William, E. (2010), Geothermal Energy, Renewable Energy and Environment, CRC Press, U.K.
26. Gupta, B.R., Electric Power Generation, S.Chand and Co., New Delhi.
27. Ghoshal, M.K., Tiwari, G.N. (2007), Fundamentals of Renewable Energy Sources, Narosa Publishers, New Delhi.
28. http//mnes.nic.in
29. Gipe, P. (1995), Wind Energy Comes of Age, Wiley, New York.
30. Hall, D.O., Rao, K.K. (1987), Photosynthesis, Edward Arnold, London.
31. Iqbal, Mohammad (1983), An Introduction Solar Radiation, Academic Press.
32. Jenkins, N., Wind Energy Technology, John Wiley and Sons.
33. Kothari, D.P., Renewable Energy Sources and Emerging Technologies, PHI Learning, New Delhi.
34. Katti, P.K., Khedekar, M.K. (2005), Photovoltaic and Wind Energy, Electrical India, vol. 42, no. 14, pp. 20–22.
35. Khandelwal, K.C., Mahdi, S.S. (1986), Biogas Technology: A Practical Handbook, Tata Mcgraw Hill, New Delhi.
36. Manni, A. (1980), Handbook of Solar Radiation Data for India, Allied Publishers, New Delhi.

37. Mathew, S. (2006), Wind Energy: Fundamentals, Resource Analysis and Economics, Springer–Verlag, Berlin, Heidelberg.

38. Maniel, Maniel, Applied Solar Energy, Addision Wesley.

39. Mcneils, Desai, Frenkel, Solar and Wind energy Technology, Wiley Eastern.

40. Mittal, K.M. (1996), Biogas Systems: Principles and Applications, New Age International, New Delhi.

41. Ministry of Statistics and Program Implementation (2014), Energy Statistics, GOI, New Delhi.

42. Mittal, Non-conventional Energy Systems, Wheeler.

43. Nayar, P.M. (2003), Photovoltaic Development and Uses in India, Electrical India, vol. 43, no. 7, pp. 44–50.

44. Naidu, B.S.K. (1977), Scenario of Small Hydro in India, Conference Proceedings, 3–7 Feb. 1977, Hyderabad.

45. Overview of Power Sector in India (2005), Indiacore.com

46. Patel, Mukund (2006), Wind and Solar Systems: Design Analysis and Operation, CRC Press, U.K.

47. Palit, Debajit (2003), Renewable Energy in North-east India: Issues and Prospects, Conference Proceedings, Oct. 8–10, 2003, pp. 85–82.

48. Parulekar, B.B., Rao, S. (1999), Energy Technology, Khanna Publishers.

49. Pillai, G.M. (2005), The New Energy Economy, World Institute of Sustainable Energy, Pune.

50. Pippo, R. (2005), Geothermal Power Plants: Principles, Applications and Case Studies, Elsevier, UK.

51. Rathore, N.S., Panwar, N.L. (2007), Renewable Energy and Sustainable Development, New India Publishing Agency.

52. Rai, G.D. (2000), Non-conventional Sources of Energy, Khanna Publisher, Delhi.

53. Rai, G.D. (2000), Solar Energy Utilization, Khanna Publisher, Delhi.

54. Ramesh, R., Renewable Energy Technologies, Narosa Publisher, New Delhi.

55. Rasor, N.S. (1983), Thermionic Energy Converter: Fundamental Handbook of Electrical and Computer Engineering, vol. II, Wiley, New York.

56. Rabl, A. (1976), Comparision of Solar Concentrators, Solar Energy, vol. 18, pp. 93.

57. Reddy, Sudhakar, B. (1994), Biomass Energy of India: An Overview, Energy Conversion and Management, vol. 3, pp. 345–361.

58. Sutton, George, Direct Energy Conversion, Mcgraw Hill.

59. Singhal, R.K., Non-conventional Energy Sources, Dhanpat Rai, Delhi.

60. Singhal, D.K., Fundamentals of Nuclear Power Energy, Khanna Publisher, Delhi.

61. Sano, Seijiro, Mizukami, Hiroyuki, Kaibe, Hiromasa (2003), Development of High

Efficiency Thermo Electric Power Generation System, Komatsu Technical Report, vol. 49, no. 152.

62. Shaw, Ronald (1982), Wave Energy, John Wiley and Sons, New York.

63. Sharma, Kadambini (2002), Renewable energy: The Way to Sustainable Development, Electrical India, vol. 42, no. 14, pp. 20–21.

64. Sayed, P.M. (2005), Indian Power Sector–shaping Indian Economy. Electrical India, vol. 45, no. 11, pp. 157–164.

65. Soni, Gupta, Bhatnagar, A Course in Electrical Power, Dhanpat Rai, Delhi.

66. Singh, S.N., Electric Power Generation, Transmission and Distribution, PHI Learning, New Delhi.

67. Singhal, D.K., Fundamentals of Nuclear Power Energy, Khanna Publisher, Delhi.

68. Sukhatme, S.P. (1984), Solar Energy, Tata Mcgraw Hill, New Delhi.

69. Solanki, C.S. (2009), Solar Photo Voltaic, PHI Learning, New Delhi.

70. Sukhatme, S.P., Solar energy—Principles of Solar Energy Collection and Storage, Tata Mcgraw Hill, New Delhi.

71. TERI (2000), TERI Energy Data Directory and Year Book, The Energy and Research Institute, New Delhi.

72. Uppal, S.L., Electric Power, Khanna Publisher, Delhi.

73. Wahl, E.F. (1977), Geothermal Energy Utilization, John Wiley and Sons, New York.

74. Walker, J.F., Jenkins, Nikolas (1977), Wind Energy Technology, John Wiley and Sons, New York.

INDEX

U

V

W

Y

Z